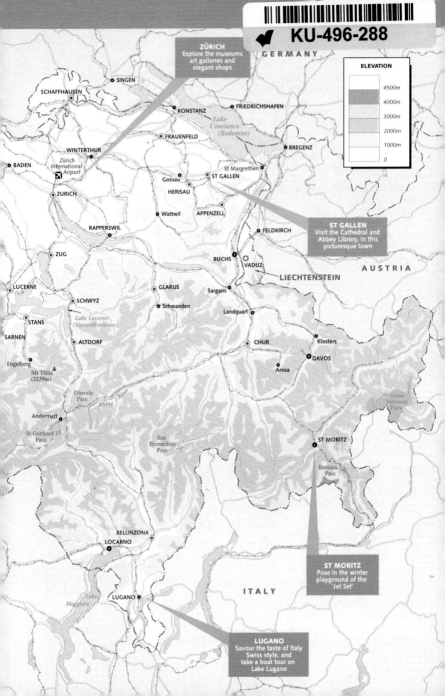

KU-496-288

ELEVATION

4500m
4000m
3000m
2000m
1000m
0

ZÜRICH
Explore the museums
art galleries and
elegant shops

ST GALLEN
Visit the Cathedral and
Abbey Library, in this
picturesque town

ST MORITZ
Pose in the winter
playground of the
'Jet Set'

LUGANO
Savour the taste of Italy
Swiss style, and
take a boat tour on
Lake Lugano

GERMANY

AUSTRIA

LIECHTENSTEIN

ITALY

SINGEN
SCHAFFHAUSEN
KONSTANZ
FRIEDRICHSHAFEN
Lake Constance (Bodensee)
FRAUENFELD
BREGENZ
WINTERTHUR
St Margrethen
BADEN
Zürich International Airport
Gossau
ST GALLEN
ZURICH
HERISAU
Wattwil
APPENZELL
RAPPERSWIL
FELDKIRCH
ZUG
BUCHS
VADUZ
LUCERNE
GLARUS
Sargans
SCHWYZ
Schwanden
STANS
Lake Lucerne (Vierwaldstättersee)
Landquart
SARNEN
ALTDORF
CHUR
Klosters
Engelberg
DAVOS
Mt Titlis (3239m)
Arosa
Oberalp Pass
Rhine River
Andermatt
St Gotthard Pass
San Bernardino Pass
ST MORITZ
Swiss National Park
Bernina Pass
BELLINZONA
LOCARNO
Lake Maggiore
LUGANO

Switzerland
3rd edition – July 2000
First published – January 1994

Published by
Lonely Planet Publications Pty Ltd A.C.N. 005 607 983
192 Burwood Rd, Hawthorn, Victoria 3122, Australia

Lonely Planet Offices
Australia PO Box 617, Hawthorn, Victoria 3122
USA 150 Linden St, Oakland, CA 94607
UK 10a Spring Place, London NW5 3BH
France 1 rue du Dahomey, 75011 Paris

Photographs
Many of the images in this guide are available for licensing from
Lonely Planet Images.
email: lpi@lonelyplanet.com.au

Front cover photograph
Souvenir cowbells, Grindelwald (Chris Mellor)

ISBN 0 86442 723 9

text & maps © Lonely Planet 2000
photos © photographers as indicated 2000

Printed by SNP Printing Pte Ltd, Singapore

Although the authors and Lonely Planet try to make the information as accurate as possible, we accept no responsibility for any loss, injury or inconvenience sustained by anyone using this book.

Switzerland

Mark Honan

LONELY PLANET PUBLICATIONS
Melbourne • Oakland • London • Paris

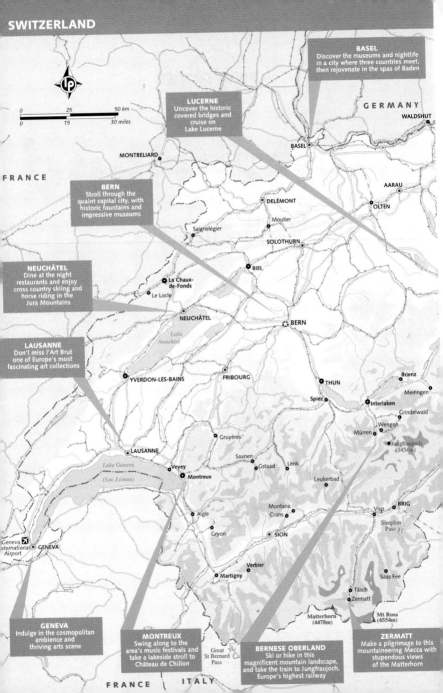

SWITZERLAND

BASEL
Discover the museums and nightlife in a city where three countries meet, then rejuvenate in the spas of Baden

LUCERNE
Uncover the historic covered bridges and cruise on Lake Lucerne

GERMANY

WALDSHUT

MONTBELIARD

FRANCE

DELÉMONT

Moutier

AARAU

OLTEN

BERN
Stroll through the quaint capital city, with historic fountains and impressive museums

Saignelégier

SOLOTHURN

NEUCHÂTEL
Dine at the night restaurants and enjoy cross country skiing and horse riding in the Jura Mountains

La Chaux-de-Fonds

BIEL

Le Locle

NEUCHÂTEL

Lake Neuchtel

BERN

LAUSANNE
Don't miss l'Art Brut one of Europe's most fascinating art collections

YVERDON-LES-BAINS

FRIBOURG

THUN

Brienz

Meiringen

Spiez

Interlaken

Grindelwald

Wengen

Mürren

LAUSANNE

Gruyères

Lake Geneva
(Lac Léman)

Veyey

Saanen

Gstaad

Lenk

Jungfraujoch
(3454m)

Montreux

Leukerbad

BRIG

Aïgle

Montana
Crans

Visp

Simplon
Pass

Gryon

SION

Geneva
International
Airport

GENEVA

Verbier

Martigny

Saas Fee

Täsch

Zermatt

Matterhorn
(4478m)

Mt Rosa
(4554m)

GENEVA
Indulge in the cosmopolitan ambience and thriving arts scene

MONTREUX
Swing along to the area's music festivals and take a lakeside stroll to Château de Chillon

Great
St Bernard
Pass

BERNESE OBERLAND
Ski or hike in this magnificent mountain landscape, and take the train to Jungfraujoch, Europe's highest railway

ZERMATT
Make a pilgrimage to this mountaineering Mecca with stupendous views of the Matterhorn

FRANCE   ITALY

0   25   50 km
0   15   30 miles

Contents – Text

THE AUTHOR   **5**

THIS BOOK   **7**

FOREWORD   **8**

FACTS ABOUT SWITZERLAND   15

History 15
Geography 20
Climate 21
Ecology & Environment 22
Flora & Fauna 22

Government & Politics 24
Economy 25
Population & People 26
Education 27
Science & Philosophy 28

Arts 29
Society & Conduct 30
Religion 31
Language 31

FACTS FOR THE VISITOR   33

Highlights 33
Suggested Itineraries 33
Planning 33
Responsible Tourism 35
Tourist Offices 35
Visas & Documents 36
Embassies & Consulates 37
Customs 38
Money 38
Post & Communications 42
Books 44
Newspapers & Magazines 46
Radio & TV 46
Video Systems 46

Photography & Video 46
Time 46
Electricity 47
Weights & Measures 47
Laundry 47
Toilets 47
Health 47
Women Travellers 50
Gay & Lesbian Travellers 51
Disabled Travellers 51
Senior Travellers 51
Travel with Children 52
Dangers & Annoyances 52
Legal Matters 53

Business Hours 53
Public Holidays &
Special Events 54
Courses 55
Work 55
Accommodation 56
Activities 58
Food 70
Drinks 72
Entertainment 72
Spectator Sports 72
Shopping 73

GETTING THERE & AWAY   74

Air 74
Land 78

Boat 84
Organised Tours 84

GETTING AROUND   85

Swiss Travel Passes 85
Air 86
Bus 86
Train 87

Car & Motorcycle 90
Bicycle 93
Hitching 93
Walking 93

Boat 94
Mountain Transport 94
Local Transport 94
Organised Tours 94

SWISS MITTELLAND   95

Bern **96**
Biel (Bienne) **106**

Around Biel 108
Emmental Region **109**

Solothurn **110**
Around Solothurn 112

BERNESE OBERLAND   113

Interlaken 113
Jungfrau Region **120**
Grindelwald 122
Lauterbrunnen 126

Gimmelwald 127
Mürren 128
Schilthorn 128
Wengen 129

Männlichen 129
Kleine Scheidegg 130
Jungfraujoch 130
The Lakes **131**

Thun 132
Spiez 134
Around Lake Thun 134
Giessbach Falls 135
Brienz 136

Freilichtmuseum
Ballenberg 137
East Bernese Oberland 137
Meiringen 137
Alpine Pass Tours 139

West Bernese Oberland 140
Stockhorn 140
Niesen 140
Kandersteg 140
Gstaad 141

CENTRAL SWITZERLAND 143

Lucerne 145
Lake Lucerne 152
Engelberg 159

Schwyz Canton 162
Schwyz 162
Einsiedeln 164

Zug 166
Andermatt 167

BASEL & AARGAU 187

Basel 187
Around Basel 195
Augusta Raurica 195

Goetheanum 195
Black Forest 195
Aargau Canton 197

Baden 197
Zofingen 198

ZÜRICH CANTON 169

Zürich 169

Around Zürich 183

Winterthur 184

FRIBOURG, NEUCHÂTEL & JURA 199

Fribourg Canton 201
Fribourg 201
Estavayer-le-Lac 205
Murten 206
Around Murten 208

Gruyères 208
Bulle 211
Broc 211
Neuchâtel Canton 211
Neuchâtel 211

Around Neuchâtel 215
La Chaux-de-Fonds 216
Neuchâtel Montagnes 219
Jura Canton 220
Franches Montagnes 220

GENEVA 222

LAKE GENEVA REGION 239

Lausanne 241
Around Lausanne 247
Swiss Riviera 247
Vevey 248
Around Vevey 249
Montreux 249

Around Montreux 253
North-West Vaud 253
Yverdon-Les-Bains 253
Grandson 256
Sainte Croix 256
Vallorbe 257

Vaud Alps 258
Château d'Oex 259
Leysin 259
Les Diablerets 260
Villars 260
Bex 261

VALAIS 262

Lower Valais 264
Sion 264
Around Sion 267
Martigny 268
Around Martigny 271
Mont Blanc 272
Verbier 274

Mauvoisin Dam 276
Sierre 276
Anniviers Valley 277
Crans Montana 277
Upper Valais 278
Leukerbad 278
Brig 279

Brigerbad 281
Visp 281
Zermatt 282
Saas Fee 286
Aletsch Glacier 288

TICINO 291

Bellinzona 293
Lugano 296
Around Lugano 301
Lake Lugano 301
Gandria 301

Campione d'Italia 302
Monte Generoso 303
Ceresio 303
Mendrisio 304
Meride 304

Locarno 304
Around Locarno 308
Northern Valleys 309

GRAUBÜNDEN

Chur 314
Around Chur 317
Lenzerheide & Valbella 317
Flims 317
Arosa 318
Davos 320
Klosters 324
Engadine Valley 325
Maloja 327

Sils 327
Silvaplana 328
St Moritz 328
Celerina 333
Zuoz 333
Zernez 334
Müstair 335
Guarda 335
Scuol 335

Bernina Pass Road 336
Pontresina 337
Chünetta 338
Diavolezza 338
Piz Lagalb 338
Alp Grüm 338
Bregaglia Valley 338
Soglio 338

NORTH-EAST SWITZERLAND

St Gallen Canton 342
St Gallen 342
Rapperswil 346
Walensee 346
Appenzellerland 346
Appenzell 347
Stein 348
Säntis 349

Schaffhausen Canton 349
Schaffhausen 349
The Rhine Falls (Rheinfall) ..351
Stein Am Rhein 352
Lake Constance 353
Constance (Konstanz) 356
Kreuzlingen 357
Romanshorn 357

Arbon 358
Rorschach 358
Bregenz 359
Lindau 359
Friedrichshafen 360
Meersburg 360

LIECHTENSTEIN

Facts about Liechtenstein ..361
Facts for the Visitor 363
Getting There & Away 363

Getting Around 364
Vaduz 364
Around Vaduz 366

Malbun 367

APPENDIX I – ALTERNATIVE PLACE NAMES

APPENDIX II – ACRONYMS

LANGUAGE

Swiss German 371
High German 371

French 374
Italian 377

Romansch 380

INDEX

Text 391

Boxed Text.........................395

MAP LEGEND

METRIC CONVERSION

Contents – Maps

INTRODUCTION

Switzerland 13

FACTS ABOUT SWITZERLAND

Cantons 17   Language Areas 32

FACTS FOR THE VISITOR

Activities 59

GETTING AROUND

Major Swiss Rail Routes 86   Distance Chart 91

SWISS MITTELLAND

Swiss Mittelland 96   Bern (Berne)..........................99   Biel (Bienne).......................107

BERNESE OBERLAND

Bernese Oberland 114   Jungfrau Region..................121   Meiringen 138
Interlaken...........................117   Thun 132

CENTRAL SWITZERLAND

Central Switzerland 144   Lake Lucerne   Engelberg............................160
Lucerne (Luzern) 146   (Vierwaldstättersee) 153

ZÜRICH CANTON

Zürich 170   Central Zürich 174   Winterthur..........................184

BASEL & AARGAU

Basel & Aargau 188   Basel (Bâle) 190   Black Forest Region 196

FRIBOURG, NEUCHÂTEL & JURA

Fribourg, Neuchâtel & Jura..200   Neuchâtel 212
Fribourg (Freiburg) 202   La Chaux-de-Fonds 217

GENEVA

Geneva (Genève) 224   Geneva (Old Town) 228   Geneva Station Area 231

LAKE GENEVA REGION   **239**

Lake Geneva Region   Lausanne 242   Yverdon-les-Bains 254
(Vaud) 240   Montreux............................250

VALAIS

Valais 263   Martigny 269
Sion 265   Zermatt 283

TICINO

Ticino....................................292
Bellinzona 294
Lugano 297
Lake Lugano 302
Locarno 305

GRAUBÜNDEN

Graubünden.......................312
Chur 315
Davos 321
St Moritz 329

NORTH-EAST SWITZERLAND

North-East Switzerland........341
St Gallen 343
Lake Constance
(Bodensee)..........................354

LIECHTENSTEIN

Liechtenstein 362
Vaduz 365

SWITZERLAND MAP INDEX

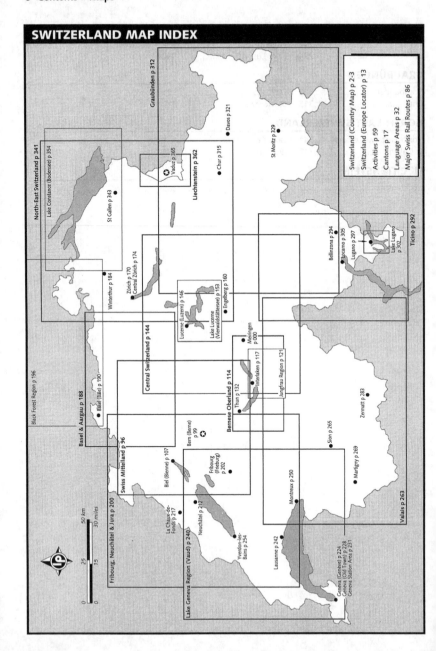

Switzerland (Country Map) p 2-3
Switzerland (Europe Locator) p 13
Activities p 59
Cantons p 17
Language Areas p 32
Major Swiss Rail Routes p 86

Graubünden p 312
Davos p 321
St Moritz p 329
Chur p 315
North-East Switzerland p 341
Lake Constance (Bodensee) p 354
St Gallen p 343
Vaduz p 365
Liechtenstein p 362
Ticino p 292
Bellinzona p 294
Locarno p 305
Lake Lugano p 302
Lugano p 297
Winterthur p 184
Zürich p 170
Central Zürich p 174
Lucerne (Luzern) p 146
Lake Lucerne (Vierwaldstättersee) p 153
Engelberg p 160
Meiringen p 000
Interlaken p 117
Jungfrau Region p 121
Central Switzerland p 144
Black Forest Region p 196
Basel (Bâle) p 190
Basel & Aargau p 188
Bernese Oberland p 114
Thun p 132
Zermatt p 283
Bern (Berne) p 99
Swiss Mittelland p 96
Sion p 265
Biel (Bienne) p 107
Fribourg (Freiburg) p 202
Martigny p 269
Montreux p 250
Valais p 263
La Chaux-de-Fonds p 217
Neuchâtel p 212
Fribourg, Neuchâtel & Jura p 200
Yverdon-les-Bains p 254
Lausanne p 242
Lake Geneva Region (Vaud) p 240
Geneva (Genève) p 224
Geneva (Old Town) p 228
Geneva Station Area p 231

50 km
30 miles
0   25   15
0   25

The Author

Mark Honan

After a university degree in philosophy opened up a glittering career as an office clerk, Mark decided that there was more to life than form-filling and data entry. He set off on a two year trip round the world, armed with a backpack and a vague intent to sell travel pictures and stories upon his return to England. Astonishingly, this barely-formed plan succeeded and his work subsequently appeared in a range of publications. He has been writing regularly for Lonely Planet since 1991, when he worked on the 1st edition of *Western Europe*.

Mark has written Lonely Planet guidebooks to *Switzerland*, *Austria* and *Vienna*, and worked on updated editions to *Central America*, *Mexico*, the *Solomon Islands* and *India* – the latter yielding the painful experience that he related in the *Lonely Planet Unpacked* collection of travel disaster stories. Mark's days of office clerkship are now behind him, but he regrets to report that life as a travel writer still entails a great deal of form-filling and data entry.

From the Author

Thanks to everyone who helped with my research, particularly Heidi, Evelyn and Russell at Switzerland Tourism in London, Sue Mallen in Geneva, the Donikian family in Zofingen, and the numerous staff at various tourist offices throughout Switzerland who patiently answered my detailed and obscure enquiries. Readers' letters provided some useful tips, updates and suggestions for this edition – please keep them coming!

This Book

The 1st and 2nd editions of *Switzerland* were researched and written by Mark Honan.

From the Publisher

The production of this edition of Switzerland was coordinated by Susannah Farfor (editorial) and Yvonne Bischofberger (mapping and design). Kate Kiely, Susie Ashworth, Yvonne Byron and Craig MacKenzie assisted with editing and proofing; Anna Judd, Tim Germanchis, Brett Moore and Jacqui Saunders assisted with map production. Adrian Persoglia produced the colour country map and Csanád Csutoros designed the climate charts. Thanks to Chris Lee Ack and Paul Piaia for technical support and Paul Dawson and Lisa Borg for assistance in QuarkXPress. Quentin Frayne prepared the Language section and the cover was designed by Andrew Weatherill. All images were supplied by LPI.

THANKS
Many thanks to the travellers who used the last edition and wrote to us with helpful hints, advice and interesting anecdotes. Your names appear in the back of this book.

Foreword

ABOUT LONELY PLANET GUIDEBOOKS

The story begins with a classic travel adventure: Tony and Maureen Wheeler's 1972 journey across Europe and Asia to Australia. Useful information about the overland trail did not exist at that time, so Tony and Maureen published the first Lonely Planet guidebook to meet a growing need.

From a kitchen table, then from a tiny office in Melbourne (Australia), Lonely Planet has become the largest independent travel publisher in the world, an international company with offices in Melbourne, Oakland (USA), London (UK) and Paris (France).

Today Lonely Planet guidebooks cover the globe. There is an ever-growing list of books and there's information in a variety of forms and media. Some things haven't changed. The main aim is still to help make it possible for adventurous travellers to get out there – to explore and better understand the world.

At Lonely Planet we believe travellers can make a positive contribution to the countries they visit – if they respect their host communities and spend their money wisely. Since 1986 a percentage of the income from each book has been donated to aid projects and human rights campaigns.

Updates Lonely Planet thoroughly updates each guidebook as often as possible. This usually means there are around two years between editions, although for more unusual or more stable destinations the gap can be longer. Check the imprint page (following the colour map at the beginning of the book) for publication dates.

Between editions up-to-date information is available in two free newsletters – the paper *Planet Talk* and email *Comet* (to subscribe, contact any Lonely Planet office) – and on our Web site at www.lonelyplanet.com. The *Upgrades* section of the Web site covers a number of important and volatile destinations and is regularly updated by Lonely Planet authors. *Scoop* covers news and current affairs relevant to travellers. And, lastly, the *Thorn Tree* bulletin board and *Postcards* section of the site carry unverified, but fascinating, reports from travellers.

Correspondence The process of creating new editions begins with the letters, postcards and emails received from travellers. This correspondence often includes suggestions, criticisms and comments about the current editions. Interesting excerpts are immediately passed on via newsletters and the Web site, and everything goes to our authors to be verified when they're researching on the road. We're keen to get more feedback from organisations or individuals who represent communities visited by travellers.

Lonely Planet gathers information for everyone who's curious about the planet – and especially for those who explore it first-hand. Through guidebooks, phrasebooks, activity guides, maps, literature, newsletters, image library, TV series and Web site we act as an information exchange for a worldwide community of travellers.

Research Authors aim to gather sufficient practical information to enable travellers to make informed choices and to make the mechanics of a journey run smoothly. They also research historical and cultural background to help enrich the travel experience and allow travellers to understand and respond appropriately to cultural and environmental issues.

Authors don't stay in every hotel because that would mean spending a couple of months in each medium-sized city and, no, they don't eat at every restaurant because that would mean stretching belts beyond capacity. They do visit hotels and restaurants to check standards and prices, but feedback based on readers' direct experiences can be very helpful.

Many of our authors work undercover, others aren't so secretive. None of them accept freebies in exchange for positive write-ups. And none of our guidebooks contain any advertising.

Production Authors submit their raw manuscripts and maps to offices in Australia, USA, UK or France. Editors and cartographers – all experienced travellers themselves – then begin the process of assembling the pieces. When the book finally hits the shops, some things are already out of date, we start getting feedback from readers and the process begins again ...

WARNING & REQUEST

Things change – prices go up, schedules change, good places go bad and bad places go bankrupt – nothing stays the same. So, if you find things better or worse, recently opened or long since closed, please tell us and help make the next edition even more accurate and useful. We genuinely value all the feedback we receive. Julie Young coordinates a well travelled team that reads and acknowledges every letter, postcard and email and ensures that every morsel of information finds its way to the appropriate authors, editors and cartographers for verification.

Everyone who writes to us will find their name in the next edition of the appropriate guidebook. They will also receive the latest issue of *Planet Talk*, our quarterly printed newsletter, or *Comet*, our monthly email newsletter. Subscriptions to both newsletters are free. The very best contributions will be rewarded with a free guidebook.

Excerpts from your correspondence may appear in new editions of Lonely Planet guidebooks, the Lonely Planet Web site, *Planet Talk* or *Comet*, so please let us know if you *don't* want your letter published or your name acknowledged.

Send all correspondence to the Lonely Planet office closest to you:

Australia: PO Box 617, Hawthorn, Victoria 3122
USA: 150 Linden St, Oakland, CA 94607
UK: 10A Spring Place, London NW5 3BH
France: 1 rue du Dahomey, 75011 Paris

Or email us at: talk2us@lonelyplanet.com.au

For news, views and updates see our Web site: www.lonelyplanet.com

HOW TO USE A LONELY PLANET GUIDEBOOK

The best way to use a Lonely Planet guidebook is any way you choose. At Lonely Planet we believe the most memorable travel experiences are often those that are unexpected, and the finest discoveries are those you make yourself. Guidebooks are not intended to be used as if they provide a detailed set of infallible instructions!

Contents All Lonely Planet guidebooks follow roughly the same format. The Facts about the Destination chapters or sections give background information ranging from history to weather. Facts for the Visitor gives practical information on issues like visas and health. Getting There & Away gives a brief starting point for re-searching travel to and from the destination. Getting Around gives an overview of the transport options when you arrive.

The peculiar demands of each destination determine how subsequent chapters are broken up, but some things remain constant. We always start with background, then proceed to sights, places to stay, places to eat, entertainment, getting there and away, and getting around information – in that order.

Heading Hierarchy Lonely Planet headings are used in a strict hierarchical structure that can be visualised as a set of Russian dolls. Each heading (and its following text) is encompassed by any preceding heading that is higher on the hierarchical ladder.

Entry Points We do not assume guidebooks will be read from beginning to end, but that people will dip into them. The trad-itional entry points are the list of contents and the index. In addition, however, some books have a complete list of maps and an index map illustrating map coverage.

There may also be a colour map that shows highlights. These highlights are dealt with in greater detail in the Facts for the Visitor chapter, along with planning questions and suggested itin-eraries. Each chapter covering a geographical region usually begins with a locator map and another list of highlights. Once you find something of interest in a list of highlights, turn to the index.

Maps Maps play a crucial role in Lonely Planet guidebooks and include a huge amount of information. A legend is printed on the back page. We seek to have complete consistency between maps and text, and to have every important place in the text captured on a map. Map key numbers usually start in the top left corner.

Although inclusion in a guidebook usually implies a recommen-dation we cannot list every good place. Exclusion does not necessarily imply criticism. In fact there are a number of reasons why we might exclude a place – sometimes it is simply inappropriate to encourage an influx of travellers.

Introduction

Switzerland is unique, multifaceted, enigmatic. First-time visitors often end up having their preconceptions about the country both confirmed and contradicted.

Consider these conundrums for a start. How is it possible that 700 years ago a band of woodsmen, a bunch of parochial William Tells, were able to repel the might of the all-conquering Habsburgs and thereby make possible the formation of the Swiss Confederation? How is it that the ultimately respectable banker's town, Zürich, spawned Dadaism, one of the most innovative and rebellious of modern art movements? How is it that such a militarily efficient nation as Switzerland could have avoided international warfare for so long? Why is it that (according to Orson Welles/Harry Lime in the film *The Third Man*) 500 years of Swiss democracy and peace has produced nothing more than the cuckoo clock?

Actually Orson Welles' character was wrong on more than one count. For one thing, the Swiss didn't invent the cuckoo clock – that came from the German Black Forest. But the Swiss are a brainy lot, and per capita have produced more Nobel Prize winners and registered more patents than any other country. Milk chocolate, DDT, life insurance, the pump-turbine – all are Swiss inventions. They also came up with the Alp horn, an instrument several metres long and about as portable as a posse of elephants – hardly ideal for carrying up and down the sides of mountains.

But the Swiss have a way of making the unexpected work. Like successfully knitting together people from four language groups into one small nation. When travelling around the country, the visitor gets a flavour of Germany, France and Italy, but it's always seasoned with a unique Swissness. The Swiss political system is one of the most complicated in the world, yet citizens dutifully inform themselves of the issues and vote regularly in a whole host of referenda. Every adult male has an army rifle at home but nobody goes around blowing people's

heads off. Trains throughout the world are late if they encounter the slightest obstacle, yet Swiss trains go over, around and through the Alps, and still generally arrive in minute-perfect time. Things work in Switzerland – and work well.

And the Alps! They are sufficient reason alone for visiting Switzerland. The countryside is visually stunning. Breathtaking views inspire peace and tranquillity and provide many sporting possibilities for the more adventurous. Skiers and hikers find paradise in the Alps. But you don't have to be a sportsperson to enjoy yourself; dreamers find their niche, and have done for centuries. The Romantics such as Byron and Shelley were drawn to the mountains for inspiration, as were many other writers, artists and musicians before and since.

Beyond the Alps and the chalet-style mountain resorts there are the towns and cities. Sober, responsible, business-oriented towns like Zürich, Geneva and Lugano are nevertheless attractively situated and packed with interesting sights and fine museums. There's the picturesque capital, Bern, that looks more like a museum piece than a seat of power. And there are many places, such as Lucerne, Murten and Stein am Rhein, that have old town centres so apparently unchanged by time that they could have been preserved under glass, like parts of a watch (yes, they make watches in Switzerland, too).

So here we have the fundamental dichotomy of things Swiss – the untamed, majestic, adventuresome Alpine landscape, set against the tidy, just-so, watch-precision towns and cities. Goethe summed it up succinctly in his description of Switzerland as a combination of 'the colossal and the well-ordered'. It's two different sides of a highly valued coin. Spend it at your leisure.

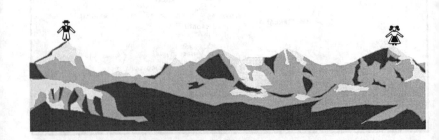

Facts about Switzerland

HISTORY

Switzerland is seen as the ultimate neutral state, a paragon of virtue, too pure and too clever to sully its hands in the base conflicts that plague the rest of the world. Yet in 1845 the Austrian Chancellor Metternich wrote:

The (Swiss) Confederation staggers from evils into upheavals and represents for itself and for its neighbours an inexhaustible spring of unrest and disturbance.

Maybe that was true. Or maybe Metternich was simply still smarting from the way the Austrians had been booted out of Switzerland centuries before.

Pre-Confederation

The first inhabitants of the region were Celtic tribes. The most important of these were the Helvetii, who lived in the Jura and the Mittelland plain, and the Rhaetians, located in the Alpine region that became Graubünden. The Romans appeared on the scene in 107 BC by way of the Great St Bernard Pass, but their attempted conquest was indecisive owing to the difficulty of the terrain. Nevertheless, under Julius Caesar they defeated the Gauls in 58 BC, thereby gaining control of Gaul and present-day Switzerland. Two centuries of prosperity followed, in which Aventicum (now the site of Avenches) was established as the capital of Roman Switzerland.

In 260 AD the Germanic Alemanni tribe began the first of many incursions southwards, and by around 400, succeeded in driving the Romans from the northern side of the Alps altogether. The Alemanni settled in eastern Switzerland, and were joined by another Germanic tribe, the Burgundians, who settled in the west. The latter adopted Christianity and the Latin language, thereby starting the division between what became French-speaking and German-speaking Switzerland. The Franks conquered both tribes in the 6th century, but the two areas were torn asunder when Charlemagne's empire was partitioned in 870.

The territory was united under the Holy Roman Empire in 1032 but central control was never very tight, allowing neighbouring nobles to contest each other for local influence. One of the most successful of these was the Zähringen family, which founded and fortified towns as a means of securing its scattered possessions. In the 1300s it founded Fribourg, Bern and Murten, and built a castle at Thun. It was not alone in this policy; the Savoy family established a ring of castles around Lake Geneva, most notably the Château de Chillon.

The internal fighting of the nobles was all changed by the Germanic Habsburg family, which gradually extended its power throughout Central Europe. Habsburg expansion was spearheaded by Rudolph I, who became the Holy Roman Emperor in 1273. He installed heavy-handed bailiffs to take care of the local administration of Swiss territories, and in this way gradually brought the squabbling nobles to heel. Ironically, though the Habsburgs were foreign invaders, they hailed from Aargau (within present-day Switzerland).

Swiss Confederation

Habsburg domination was deeply resented, and upon the death of Rudolph I in 1291, local leaders saw a chance to gain independence. The forest communities of Uri, Schwyz and Nidwalden formed an alliance on 1 August 1291. Central to the agreement was the assertion that they would not recognise any external judge or law. Their pact of mutual assistance is seen as the origin of the Swiss Confederation and the inaugural document is still preserved in the canton of Schwyz. The Latin name for the confederation, Confederatio Helvetica, survives in the 'CH' abbreviation for Switzerland (used on car number plates).

The efforts of the founding cantons to free themselves from the yoke of the Habsburgs is personified in the tale of William Tell, who in all probability never actually existed. According to the legend, it was the Habsburg bailiff, Gessler, who compelled Tell to shoot the apple off his son's head, in what must be the most famous episode in Swiss history. Apparently, Tell got his revenge by later murdering Gessler at Küssnacht, by Lake Lucerne. See the boxed text 'Tell: a Tale from the Dawn of the Confederation' in the Central Switzerland chapter.

Duke Leopold responded to the Swiss shenanigans by dispatching a powerful Austrian army in 1315. The duke must have anticipated a straightforward victory against such ill-equipped forest folk, but his army was thoroughly defeated by the Swiss at Morgarten. The effective action of the union soon prompted other communities to join. Lucerne (1332) was followed by Zürich (1351), Glarus and Zug (1352), and Bern (1353). Further defeats of the Habsburgs followed at Sempach (1386) and Näfels (1388).

Encouraged by these successes, the Swiss gradually acquired a taste for territorial expansion themselves. Further land was seized from the Habsburgs. They took on Charles the Bold (the Duke of Burgundy) and defeated him at Grandson and Murten. Fribourg, Solothurn, Basel, Schaffhausen and Appenzell joined the Confederation, and the Swiss gained independence from Holy Roman Emperor Maximilian I after their victory at Dornach in 1499.

In 1513 the Confederation was at the peak of its territorial influence, and even had Milan under its protection, but finally the Swiss overreached themselves. They squared up against a superior combined force of French and Venetians at Marignano in 1515 and lost. The Swiss army in the battle had been compiled without the support of several cantons, most noticeably the all-powerful Bern. This first defeat gave the Swiss cause for thought. In order to ensure that future armies would be full-strength, it would be necessary to curtail the autonomy of the cantons, something they were not prepared to do. Another consideration was that weaponry had advanced. Soldiers had

to be equipped with the new weapons – firearms – which was a very expensive proposition, as the Swiss fighting reputation had been previously built on the use of the halberd, a combination pickaxe, spear and pike on the end of a long staff.

The Swiss, therefore, decided to withdraw from the international scene by renouncing expansionist policies and declaring their neutrality. Not being a nation to waste useful skills, Swiss mercenaries continued to serve in other armies for centuries to come, and earned an unrivalled reputation for their skill and courage. (Even today the pope is protected by the Swiss Guard.) The mercenary policy (effectively, exporting war) actually helped to preserve Swiss neutrality in at least two ways. It provided an outlet for aggression without ever involving the country in international disputes under its own colours, and it showed the Swiss the economic sense of keeping war beyond its own borders – to feed off war rather than suffer from it. The policy only ceased when Swiss soldiers increasingly found themselves fighting on opposing sides, such as during the War of the Spanish Succession in 1709.

Reformation

The Reformation in the 16th century caused upheaval throughout Europe. Ulrich Zwingli, from eastern Switzerland, started teaching the Protestant word in Zürich in 1519. The new faith spread rapidly, but central Switzerland remained Catholic. The result was conflict, and Zwingli was killed in fighting between the factions in 1531. But Zwingli's death did not halt the spread of the Reformation in the Confederation, and in the meantime, John Calvin and William Farel were thumping the Protestant pulpit in Geneva and Neuchâtel.

The Catholic Church responded with the Counter Reformation, and while the rest of Europe was fighting it out in the Thirty Years' War, the Swiss closed ranks and kept out of trouble. They even prospered during the conflict, trading in food and materials that the fighting nations were unable to provide for themselves. At the end of the war in 1648 Switzerland was recognised in the Treaty of Westphalia as a neutral state.

Peasant unrest, fuelled by the burgeoning powers of the urban upper class over the rural areas, was quashed in 1653. However, religious disputes dragged on in Switzerland, in the Villmergen Wars of 1656 and 1712. At this time the Catholic cantons were sucked into a dangerous alliance with France that could have split the Confederation beyond repair had matters really come to a head. But the Catholic factions reluctantly agreed to religious freedom and the country was able to get on with the serious business of making money. Switzerland gradually prospered as a financial and intellectual centre, the economic aspect driven to a great extent by the textile industry in the north-east.

The French invaded Switzerland in 1798 and established the Helvetic Republic. The new regime was liberal in many ways – sovereignty was invested in the people and

cantonal frontiers were abolished – but the Swiss did not take too kindly to such centralised control. Internal fighting prompted Napoleon (who had now assumed power in France) to restore the former Confederation of cantons in 1803 (the Act of Mediation), but with France retaining overall jurisdiction. Further cantons also joined the Confederation at this time: Aargau, St Gallen, Graubünden, Ticino, Thurgau and Vaud. Napoleon was finally sent packing following his defeat by the British and Prussians at Waterloo. In 1815 the Congress of Vienna guaranteed Switzerland's independence and permanent neutrality, as well as adding the cantons of Valais, Geneva and Neuchâtel. But politically the country had moved backwards, with the aristocrats regaining most of their old powers in the Confederation.

Towards a Modern Constitution

The July Revolution in Paris in 1830 sparked off similar forces in several cantons so that

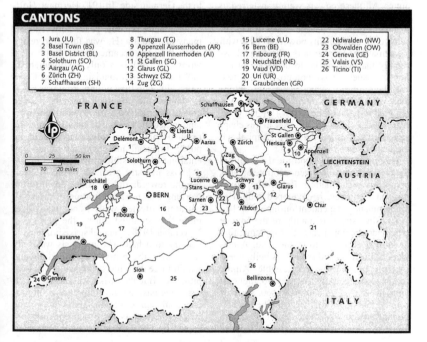

CANTONS

1 Jura (JU)	8 Thurgau (TG)	15 Lucerne (LU)	22 Nidwalden (NW)
2 Basel Town (BS)	9 Appenzell Ausserrhoden (AR)	16 Bern (BE)	23 Obwalden (OW)
3 Basel District (BL)	10 Appenzell Innerrhoden (AI)	17 Fribourg (FR)	24 Geneva (GE)
4 Solothurn (SO)	11 St Gallen (SG)	18 Neuchâtel (NE)	25 Valais (VS)
5 Aargau (AG)	12 Glarus (GL)	19 Vaud (VD)	26 Ticino (TI)
6 Zürich (ZH)	13 Schwyz (SZ)	20 Uri (UR)	
7 Schaffhausen (SH)	14 Zug (ZG)	21 Graubünden (GR)	

the liberals came to power. Lucerne was particularly volatile; coup was followed by counter-coup, and the liberals were appalled when the Jesuits were invited to take over cantonal education. Civil war broke out in 1847 when the Protestant army, led by General Dufour, quickly crushed the Catholic cantons (including Lucerne) who had formed a separatist league, the Sonderbund. Victory by liberal forces was quickly underlined with the creation of a new federal constitution in 1848, which is largely still in place today. Various civil liberties were granted, such as equality before the law, freedom of association and freedom of place of residence.

The constitution was a neat compromise between advocates of central control and conservative forces wanting cantonal authority to be retained. Throughout the gradual move towards one nation, each canton remained fiercely independent, even to the extent of controlling its own currency and postal services and levying its own custom duties. All these powers were transferred to federal authority, but cantons nevertheless retained legislative (Grand Council) and executive (State Council) powers to deal with local matters. Furthermore, the federal assembly that was set up to take care of national issues was composed of two chambers, one of which gave the cantons their voice. The consent of both houses was required to pass a federal law (see the Government & Politics section later in this chapter). Bern was established as the capital and the seat of power.

Having achieved political stability, Switzerland was able to concentrate on economic and social matters. Relatively poor in mineral resources, it developed industries predominantly dependent on highly skilled labour. Industry was mainly of the cottage type, based upon peasants supplementing dwindling earnings from the land. A network of railways and roads was built, opening up previously inaccessible Alpine regions and helping the development of tourism. Between 1850 and 1860, six new commercial banks were set up. The International Red Cross was founded in Geneva in 1863 by Henri Dunant (see the Geneva chapter for more on this movement), and compulsory free education was introduced.

Many of the new political leaders had fingers in various economic pies, and patronage and nepotism became the standard way to conduct government. Movements towards greater democracy soon gathered momentum in the cantons, particularly in Zürich, and made it inevitable that there would be some change at the national level. In 1874 the constitution was revised to enable citizens to partake in direct democracy. In the years that followed, political battle lines gradually moved from struggles between liberals and Catholics to one between workers and the bourgeoisie.

20th Century

During WWI, Switzerland came quite close to violating its much vaunted neutrality. German-speaking Switzerland (but not the French or Italian parts) was pro-Germany, and secret military information was passed to the German side. In 1917 Hermann Hoffmann, a federal councillor, even tried to bring about a separate peace between Germany and Russia. He was forced to resign when the plan became public. In physical terms, Switzerland's only involvement in WWI lay in the organising of Red Cross units, although the civilian army was ready to defend the country's borders if need arose. After peace was restored, Switzerland joined the League of Nations under the proviso that its involvement would be purely financial and economic rather than entailing any possible military sanctions.

Swiss industry profited during the war, but the rewards did not filter down to the working classes. Mobilisation of the civilian army affected wages, and food prices more than doubled during the period. In November 1918 a general strike brought the country to a halt. The paralysis was only temporary; the army was called in and within three days the strike leaders had capitulated. But the strike was not futile. It eased the passage of a referendum on proportional representation, and some of the strikers' demands were subsequently accepted by the Federal Council. A 48-hour week was introduced, collective contract-bargaining between workers and employers was developed, and the social security system was extended.

The conciliatory mood spread and in 1937 the Swiss Metalworkers and Watchmakers' Union created the Arbeitsfrieden with the Federation of Metal and Machine Industry Employers, under which all future disputes would be solved by agreement. One side would abandon strikes, and the other would no longer use such tactics as 'lockouts' and 'scab' labour. This contract has been periodically renewed, and subsequently imitated by other Swiss industries, giving the country an envied industrial relations record ever since.

Switzerland was left largely unscathed by WWII. Again the civilian army was mobilised; Henri Guisan was elected as the general. Surrounded by Axis powers, Switzerland was in a very vulnerable position in 1940. In July of that year, Guisan, in a symbolic but effective move, called all top military personnel to the Rütli meadow (the site of the 1291 Oath of Allegiance), and instilled in those present and the world at large the Swiss determination to defend its soil at all costs. Swiss neutrality remained unbreached (barring some accidental bombing in 1940, 1944 and 1945 – for more on this, see the boxed text 'The Second World War' in the North-East Switzerland chapter), and its territory proved to be a safe haven for escaping Allied prisoners. However, Swiss banks were also revealed to be a major conduit for Nazi plunder during WWII, a cause for much international criticism in the 1990s (see the boxed text 'Banks & Bank Accounts' later in this chapter).

Defence

Despite the fact that Switzerland has managed to avoid international conflicts for over 400 years, every able-bodied male starts national service at age 20. After 15 weeks of training he is released, but remains attached to a unit and eligible for call-up until the age of 32. From 33 to 42 (52 for officers) he remains in the military reserves, and has to attend a three-week refresher course every two years. Throughout this period he keeps his rifle, ammunition and full kit (including gas mask) at home, and has to attend target practice sessions. The army is subject to Federal Council control, and a general is only appointed as commander-in-chief of the armed forces in times of national emergency. Within 48 hours more than 400,000 civilian soldiers can be mobilised. Switzerland's army previously numbered 600,000, but the number was diminished in 1995 by reducing the stint in the reserves.

In December 1989 a surprisingly large number of people (35.6%) voted in favour of abolishing the army, yet conscientious objectors were still getting sentenced to imprisonment by military courts. Civil service as an alternative to military service for objectors was rejected in an earlier referendum in 1984, but finally got through in 1991.

In the last 60 years, Switzerland has made comprehensive preparations against foreign aggression. Besides the civilian army, a whole infrastructure is in place to repel any invasion. After military service, men then have to undertake civil protection service until age 60, requiring more training courses and assignment of duties in the event of attack. Roads and bridges have built-in recesses at key points so that they can be primed for explosion without delay. All new buildings must have a substantial air-raid capacity, and underground car parks can be instantly converted to bunkers.

Pretty much *all* the population can now be sheltered underground. Fully equipped emergency hospitals, unused yet maintained, await underneath ordinary hospitals. Food and raw materials have been stockpiled. It's a sobering thought, as you explore the countryside, to realise that those apparently undisturbed mountains and lakes hide a network of military installations and storage depots. The tranquillity of rural areas is often disturbed by the sound of the army engaged in target practice. The message that comes across today is the same as that dealt out by the country's fearless mercenaries of centuries ago – don't mess with the Swiss.

Post WWII

While the rest of Europe underwent the painful process of rebuilding from the ravages of war, Switzerland was able to expand from an already powerful commercial, financial and industrial base. Zürich developed as an international banking and insurance centre. The World Health Organization, the World Council of Churches, and many other international organisations based their headquarters in Geneva. Social reforms were also introduced, such as old-age pensions in 1948.

Post-war prosperity was largely built on the backs of foreign workers, who mostly had menial jobs, while Swiss workers were often elevated to supervisory roles. In 1945 foreigners made up 5% of residents in Switzerland; by 1974 this figure had grown to 17%. Foreign workers had (and have) few political rights, and in theory, could have their residency status rescinded in times of economic hardship. Indeed, tens of thousands left (voluntarily) in the depression of 1974–75.

Afraid that its neutrality would be compromised, Switzerland declined to become a member of the United Nations, NATO or the EEC (European Economic Community as the European Union was then called). It did, however, join UNESCO (United Nations Educational, Scientific and Cultural Organization) and EFTA (European Free Trade Association).

In the face of other EFTA nations applying for EU (European Union) membership, Switzerland finally made its own application in 1992. This was a pre-emptive move by the parliament, because in the meantime, it was necessary to hold a referendum on membership of the EEA (European Economic Area). Composed of EFTA members, the EEA was seen as a sort of halfway house towards the EU under which there would be the free trade advantages of the EU without the political commitment. In order for EEA membership to be ratified, a majority of citizens and a majority of cantons had to vote in favour.

Despite the strong support of industry and political parties, Swiss citizens were unimpressed, and the motion failed on both counts in the vote in December 1992. Although in percentage terms the defeat was narrow (49.7% voted 'yes', 50.3% 'no'), only seven cantons were in favour when at least 12 were needed. Those in favour included all the French-speaking cantons (Geneva, Vaud, Neuchâtel, Jura, Fribourg and Valais) and only one German-speaking canton (Basel). Overall, French speakers were three to one in favour of joining, and there was bitter resentment towards German speakers for keeping Switzerland isolated.

All this rather upset plans to join the EU. As a consequence of the EEA vote, Switzerland's EU application has been put on ice, without actually being withdrawn. The pro-EEA and EU lobby has not given up hope, and is pressing for the reopening of membership negotiations. In the meantime the government conducted lengthy bilateral talks with the EU to create closer alignment. An agreement was finally reached in December 1998 covering free movement of people, transport access and other matters. This was ratified by the Swiss parliament in October 1999, and will come into effect in 2001, unless a public referendum is forced.

GEOGRAPHY

Above all, landlocked Switzerland is known as an Alpine country. The Alps and Pre-Alps make up 60% of Switzerland's 41,285 sq km. The Jura Mountains account for 10% and the Swiss Mittelland (also called the Central Plateau) comprises the remaining 30%. The land is 45% meadow and pasture, 24% forest and 6% arable. Farming of cultivated land is intensive and cows graze on the upper slopes in the summer as soon as the retreating snow line permits.

The Alps occupy the central and southern regions of the country. The Dufourspitze (4634m) of Monte Rosa is the highest point, although the Matterhorn (4478m) is better known. A series of high passes in the south provide overland access into Italy. Glaciers account for an area of 2000 sq km; most notable is the Aletschgletscher, which at 169 sq km is the largest valley glacier in Europe.

The St Gotthard Massif in the centre of Switzerland is the source of many lakes and rivers, such as the Rhine and the Rhône. The Jura Mountains straddle the northern border with France. These mountains peak at around 1700m and are less steep and less severely eroded than the Alps.

The Swiss Mittelland is between the two mountain systems, running in a band from Lake Geneva (Lac Léman) in the south-west to Lake Constance (Bodensee) in the north-east. It is a region of hills crisscrossed by rivers, ravines and winding valleys. This area has spawned the most populous cities and is where much of the agricultural activity takes place. The one canton entirely south of the Alps is Ticino, home to the northern part of Lago Maggiore; at 193m the lake is the lowest point in the country.

Lakes are dotted throughout the country, except in the Jura where the substrata rock is mostly too brittle and porous. The majority of lakes, including all those in the Swiss Mittelland, were created from the depressions and basins left by glacial ice or moraines (the debris from melting glaciers) after the ice age.

CLIMATE

The mountains are mainly responsible for the variety of local and regional microclimates enjoyed (or suffered) by Switzerland. Air currents waft in from the four points of the compass, each bringing a different type of weather. Ticino in the south has a hot, Mediterranean climate. Most of the rest of the country has a Central European climate, with temperatures typically around 20° to 25°C in summer and 2° to 6°C in winter, with spring and autumn hovering around the 7° to 14°C mark. Valais in the south-west is noted for being dry. Staldenried in Valais gets just 53cm of precipitation per year, as opposed to 257cm at Rochers de Naye, Vaud, under 75km away as the cloud flies. The coldest area is the Jura, and in particular the Brevine Valley, which is a natural trap for cold air.

Summer tends to bring a lot of sunshine, but also the most rain. You will need to be prepared for a range of temperatures dependent on altitude. Look out for the *Föhn*, a hot, dry wind that sweeps down into the valleys and can be oppressively uncomfortable (though some find its warming effect refreshing). It can strike at any time of the year, but especially in spring and autumn. Daily weather reports covering 25 resorts are displayed in major train stations.

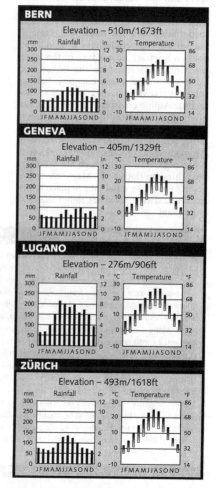

Statistics can be used to back up all sorts of meteorological claims. The sun obviously gets about a bit: La Chaux-de-Fonds, Sierre, Andermatt, Locarno, St Moritz and Crans-Montana are all said to enjoy the sunniest climate in Switzerland.

ECOLOGY & ENVIRONMENT

Since the 1950s, the federal government has introduced measures to protect forests, lakes and marshland from environmental damage. Mountain areas have fragile ecosystems and are extremely vulnerable to pollution and environmental damage. Global warming could have a serious impact on Switzerland because of the effect on Alpine glaciers (see the boxed text 'Glaciers' in the Valais chapter). Various pressure groups in Switzerland try to protect the Alpine environment, which annually receives 120 million visitors. One is the Alpine Initiative (☎ 027-924 22 26) in Brig, which is mainly concerned with Alpine transport routes, and has links with other organisations through its Web site www.alpeninitiative.ch. Many mountain resorts now have a policies in place to upgrading existing facilities rather than expand them.

Switzerland, along with its Alpine neighbours, signed the Alpine Convention in 1991, which seeks to reduce damage caused by motor traffic and tourism. Air pollution caused by vehicle emissions remains a major issue in Switzerland, and the country is determined to try to switch freight carriage from road to rail, which is less harmful to the environment. See the boxed text 'Alpine Tunnels' in the Getting Around chapter for more on this.

The country also has an efficient recycling industry; households dutifully separate their waste into different categories prior to collection (see the boxed text 'Switzerland Goes Green').

FLORA & FAUNA

Climatic variation means that vegetation ranges from palm trees in Ticino to nordic flora in the Alps. At higher elevations, flowers start to bloom from April to July, depending on the species. The famous Edelweiss, with star-shaped flowers, grows at up to 3500m. Alpine rhododendrons, known locally as Alpenroses, are numerous at 2500m. Spring gentians are small, violet-blue flowers. White crocuses are early bloomers (from March) at lower

Switzerland Goes Green

Switzerland produces 400kg of waste per annum per person, half the figure for the US. A Federal Office for the Environment slogan advocates 'Reduction, Recovery and Recycling' with some success – the Swiss are among the most diligent recyclers in the world.

Paper is collected regularly from households, provided it is tied in neat bundles (it invariably is!). Colour-coded recycling bins are common, accepting glass, aluminium, PET plastic, and used oil. One-litre beer bottles are invariably deposit-refundable, as are bottles for many of the cheaper cap-topped wines. Many supermarkets have automatic bottle-return machines *(Flaschen Rüchnahmne)* that will give you a credit note against your shopping. A returnable bottle may be re-used 50 times. The use of phosphate-containing detergents is banned in Switzerland, and since 1986 battery retailers have had to provide containers for the collection of used batteries. A law designed to reduce excess packaging entitles customers to unwrap unnecessary packaging on site (and many do) and leave it for the shop to dispose of.

Swiss diligence with recycling is encouraged by financial considerations. Cantons have introduced specially marked bags that must be used for all rubbish that is not recycled. These bags are extremely expensive (Sfr2 to Sfr6 each!) so they are used only when necessary (and as much is crammed in as possible). The high price covers incineration costs, and has been effective in reducing the quantity of refuse thrown away.

The Alpendohle is often seen hunting for food scraps at mountain-top restaurants.

The Red Spruce is especially abundant throughout northern Switzerland. Once favoured by farmers for its usefulness, it has now become susceptible to acid rain and the bark beetle.

The Edelweiss is the national floral emblem of Switzerland.

elevations. Alpine flowers are usually protected and should not be picked.

In the Swiss Mittelland, trees are a mixture of deciduous and conifers. At an altitude of 800m, conifers become more numerous. The red spruce is common at lower levels, while the arolla pine (*Arve* or *Zirbe* in German) and larch mostly take over higher up. At around 2000m, tall trees are replaced by bushes and scrub which finally yield to Alpine meadows (these can be rich in flora, despite the altitude). As in most of the continent, forests are being depleted by pollution and acid rain, increasing the risk of avalanches and landslides.

Despite strong environmental legislation, animal life is on the retreat in Switzerland. But there have been some success stories – species that were once extinct in the wild have been reintroduced and are thriving, not least in the protected environs of the Swiss National Park (see the Graubünden chapter). Eighty-one species of bird are currently threatened with extinction.

A bird often seen fluttering around on mountain tops is the *Alpendohle*, a relative of the crow; it has jet-black feathers and a yellow beak. Rather larger Alpine birds, with wingspans reaching 2.5m or more, are the golden eagle and the bearded vulture.

The most distinctive Alpine animal is the ibex, a mountain goat which has huge, curved and ridged horns. There are about 12,000 left in Switzerland, and they can migrate up to 3000m. The chamois (a horned antelope) is more timid but equally at home on the peaks – it can leap 4m vertically. Roe deer or the larger red deer can also be seen in forested regions and Alpine pastures. Marmots (chunky rodents related to the squirrel) are other famous residents. These hibernating, monogamous creatures live in colonies within complex labyrinthine burrows that can take generations to build. They mark their territory and recognise co-colonists by smell. A sentry, which raises itself on its hind legs to scan the horizon, is often posted to repel alien marmots and warn of predators.

GOVERNMENT & POLITICS

The modern Swiss Confederation is made up of 23 cantons; three are subdivided, bringing the total to 26. Each has its own constitution and legislative body for dealing with local issues, and has a great deal of autonomy. The Jura achieved full cantonal status as late as 1979, after a protracted struggle with its former ruler, Bern.

National legislative power is in the hands of the Federal Assembly, which consists of two chambers. The lower chamber, the National Council (Nationalrat), has 200 members. Seats are allocated to cantons in proportion to population size, though each canton gets at least one. The upper chamber, the States Council (Ständerat), is composed of 46 members, two per canton (one per half-canton).

The Federal Assembly elects seven members to form the Federal Council, which holds executive power. All elections are for a four-year term except for the posts of president and vice-president of the Confederation, which are rotated annually. The holder of these posts has no special authority over the rest of the Federal Council. The vice-president always succeeds the president. In this way the governing body is not dominated by any one individual. In fact, some Swiss would be hard-pressed to name their president, though a high-profile appointment was that of Ruth Dreifuss, Switzerland's first female president and first Jewish president. During her tenure in 1999, a second woman (Ruth Metzler) joined the cabinet – an unprecedented situation in Swiss politics.

Elected members of parliament are usually part-timers, and receive payment only for expenses. The cost of running the parliament is extremely low, though this will no doubt change if Switzerland joins the bureaucratic EU. At the last general election, in October 1999, the four main parties were the left-wing Social Democrats (51 national seats), the right-wing Swiss People's Party (44 national seats), the Radical Democrats (43 national seats) and the Christian Democrats (35 national seats). The most significant result of the election was the surge ahead of the anti-immigration, anti-EU People's Party (formerly in fourth place), which is led by Christoph Blocher, who is notorious for his scepticism that the Holocaust ever took place. Since 1959 the composition of the Federal Council has adhered to a 'magic formula' of two members each from the Radical, Christian and Social Democrats and one from the Swiss People's Party. Following its strong showing in the 1999 election, the People's Party is pressing for a second seat.

Laws can be influenced directly by the Swiss people, provided enough signatures can be collected from active citizens: 50,000 to force a full referendum on proposed laws, and 100,000 to initiate legislation. In any case, important federal decisions are generally subject to a referendum. The system is known as direct democracy, and is one that tends to lead to a government based on compromise. Surprisingly for such a democratic people, women only won the right to vote in federal elections in 1971. In Appenzell the right to a cantonal vote was granted as recently as 1990! Appenzell is also the last remaining canton that still conducts votes by a show of hands in an open-air parliament (Landsgemeinde).

As if these two tiers of government weren't enough, each Swiss citizen is also the member of a commune (Gemeinde), the smallest political unit. There are around 3000 in the whole country. Even communes have significant autonomy to act independently. Citizens regularly have to turn out to vote on issues at all three levels: federal, cantonal and communal. The commune has its own councillors with responsibility for finances, fire services, taxes, welfare, schools and civil defence. Most adults get involved in community service in one way or another.

The Swiss political system works from the bottom upwards, and it is actually membership of a commune that invests constituents with Swiss citizenship, rather than vice versa. The electorate (ie, private individuals) is viewed as holding ultimate authority, and is often referred to as the 'sovereign', as in 'the sovereign has decided' when a referendum has been accepted or rejected. Subsidiarity (Subsidiarität) is a principle that has guided Swiss politics for centuries. It states that the lowest level of authority that can effectively perform a task should be left alone to do so.

A new constitution for Switzerland was drafted in 1998; it was accepted by the people in a referendum in April 1999 but will still take a year or two to come into effect. It makes no substantial changes to the existing constitution – most alterations are of a formal

nature, eg, rewording existing provisions using contemporary, gender-neutral terms.

ECONOMY

Switzerland has a mixed economy with the emphasis on private ownership. The small public sector (eg, the post and the bulk of the railway network) was diminished with the partial privatisation in 1998 of Swisscom, the state-owned telecommunications operator. A good proportion of the wealth

Banks & Bank Accounts

Voltaire once said: 'If you see a Swiss banker jump out of a window, follow him. There is surely money to be made.' There's certainly no shortage of bankers to follow in Switzerland. At one time, the country had as many as 630 domestic banks and more than 200 foreign banks. Mergers (such as that between two of the world's biggest – Union Bank of Switzerland and Swiss Bank Corporation) and other factors have since reduced the number of domestic banks to 400. Yet the sector still employs 150,000 people, and contributes 9% of Switzerland's GDP (Gross Domestic Product). The Swiss are also great savers, storing away an unusually high level of their income. Banks have a long tradition, but really took off after WWII, thanks to their reputation for discretion and secrecy.

Numbered bank accounts are a well-known Swiss institution. These accounts are identified purely by a number, rather than being linked to a name, so anonymity is assured. The anonymity brings the risk of attracting funds of dubious origin, or money that is simply trying to avoid the attention of the tax inspectors.

Numbered accounts were introduced in WWII, allegedly to provide cover for funds escaping from Nazi control. In 1995 Swiss banks started receiving bad press for not doing enough to trace the owners of numerous deposit boxes and secret accounts, dormant since WWII. The banks owned up to finding US$34 million and had been quite happy to hang on to these assets all these years. But Israeli sources claimed that up to US$6.7 billion worth of cash and valuables could be involved, seized from Holocaust victims and deposited by Nazis. As investigations wore on, it emerged that the latter figure was nearer the truth – at least US$400 million (US$3.8 billion in today's values) was deposited, including gold bars allegedly smelted from dental fillings taken from concentration camps.

The issue remained in the headlines until 1998, with the Swiss banks dragging their heels in dealing with the issue. Upon facing a class action in the US from Holocaust survivors, UBS and Credit Suisse finally put a realistic offer on the table. They agreed to pay US$1.25 billion and the rehabilitation of Swiss banks could begin.

In 1990 a law against money laundering was introduced. There is now an obligation for the banks to identify the true owner of the monies deposited with them in the event of an investigation, and they can be prosecuted if they hinder the identification of suspected 'dirty money' (proceeds from drug or arms trafficking etc). The legislation was inspired by the arrest in Switzerland in 1988 of two drug traffickers who deposited Sfr1.5 billion in a Zürich bank (the deposit drew attention as it was marginally higher than the average Swiss salary cheque).

In practice, anybody can still open a Swiss bank account, numbered or otherwise. All you have to do is sign a form declaring that the money is rightfully yours. Responding to such a question with an untruth would hardly cause great pangs of conscience in the average underworld boss. The secrecy laws of the Swiss banks are unlikely to remain unscathed if Switzerland does eventually join the EU.

generated by the strong economy is channelled back into the community via social welfare programs. The overall result is very efficient and strikes are rare. But even Switzerland is not immune from economic downturns. Like much of the rest of the world, the Swiss economy went into recession in the early 1990s. In 1997, unemployment went over 5% (a record for Switzerland), partially caused by Swiss firms relocating abroad to seek lower costs. It has since dropped back to below 4%. Inflation was a mere 0.1% in 1998, and was expected to stay below 1% into the next decade.

Agriculture and forestry occupies about 4% of the working population, and Swiss farmers enjoy one of the highest levels of protection in the world, keeping prices high. Cartel agreements in other sectors of the economy also contribute to general high prices and restrict competition. About 67% of workers are employed in service areas compared to around 29% in industry. In the absence of other raw materials, hydro-electric power is now the main source of energy (57%). Switzerland's five nuclear power stations provide 43% of energy production. A 10-year moratorium on constructing new nuclear power stations runs out in 2000. Around 77% of Switzerland's industrial output is exported, and 40% of exports come from the mechanical and engineering industries. Exports include chemicals, machine tools, watches and clocks. Silks and embroidery, also important, are produced to a high quality.

The country usually has a negative visible trade balance, which is more than offset by earnings from investment income and the current account (Switzerland has the biggest balance of payments surplus of any industrialised nation). The GDP (Gross Domestic Product) per capita is one of the highest in the world, estimated to be over US$42,000 for 2000. Switzerland's most important trading partner is Germany, responsible for 32% of imports and 23% of exports. EU countries as a whole account for 79% of imports and 61% of exports.

SMH (Société Suisse de Microélectronique et d'Horlogerie) unleashed the Swatch onto the world. This innovative product revitalised the Swiss watch-making industry, which had been taking a battering at the hands of cheap Japanese models. At the top end of the watch market (where watches cost thousands in any currency you care to name) Swiss domination was never broken, and it has a 90% worldwide share. Swiss breakthroughs in science and industry include vitamins, DDT, gas turbines and milk chocolate. They also, for their sins, developed the modern formula for life insurance.

Swiss banks are a magnet for foreign funds, attracted by political and monetary stability. The biggest bank is UBS, known by these initials following the recent merger of the Union Bank of Switzerland and the Swiss Bank Corporation. The country is the fourth most important financial centre in the world, after New York, London and Tokyo. In most cantons there are more banks than dentists, and Switzerland is one of the world leaders for private banking.

Tourism is important to the economy – it earns about Sfr11.5 billion, comprising 5.6% of the country's GDP. This figure has declined 11% from the 1990 peak, due to poor snowfalls, a strong franc and under-investment in the sector. Yet Switzerland is still an easy place for the tourist to get to grips with (it's certainly easy to spend too much money!). Based on the number of overnight stays, Graubünden is the most popular holiday region, followed by Valais, Central Switzerland and the Bernese Oberland. Summer brings nearly 50% more foreign tourists than winter.

POPULATION & PEOPLE

With a population of 7,100,000 (1998 estimate), Switzerland averages 172 inhabitants per sq km. The Alpine districts are sparsely populated, meaning that the Mittelland is densely settled, especially around the shores of the larger lakes. Zürich is the largest city, with 354,000 inhabitants; next comes Basel (177,000), Geneva (175,000) and Bern (132,000). Most people are of Germanic origin, as indicated by the breakdown of languages spoken in Switzerland. German speakers account for 64% of the

The Swiss National Character

Some people believe that the magnificent, untamed Swiss landscape is wasted on the native dwellers. There's an old joke that imagines that heaven and hell are run by a number of European nations. In heaven, the Swiss are the organisers (and the French are the lovers). In hell, the Swiss are the lovers (and the Italians are the organisers). This joke illustrates the oft-expressed view that the people are a dull, serious, colourless, undemonstrative lot, somewhat petty, yet extremely efficient.

Like many generalisations, this picture of the Swiss character is an inadequate one. The Swiss people are as varied as the languages they speak. To make a few more generalisations: the French Swiss make a habit of kissing each other on both cheeks upon meeting (three kisses, alternating cheeks – but this doesn't happen man-to-man!); the Italian Swiss have a Mediterranean complexion and outlook in a canton where *dolce vita* competes with the *Arbeit* ethos; and in the valleys of south-east Switzerland, many villagers still speak Romansch, a language with its roots in ancient Latin that reflects their enduring, rural lifestyle.

But what about the majority, the German Swiss? They are what we mean by the typical Swiss – efficient and honest yet conventional, pedantic and sticklers for the rules. It's true they do exist – the German term *Bünzli* describes them, but every society has such people. Ask any German Swiss about the German Swiss national character and they'll probably tell you in great detail how the people in their town, their street, their house, are different to all other Swiss. I know somebody who goes to university in Zürich; she complains the Zürichers are cold and money-oriented, not like the people of Basel who are much more friendly and open.

The people of Appenzellerland have a reputation among other Swiss for being simple folk with intellects that could blunt the sharpest knife. The Bernese are considered slow and parochial. You may encounter many other regional differences if you travel with an open mind. Of course, you may also find that your preconceptions about the Swiss are confirmed, but travel is always more enjoyable if you allow yourself the possibility of being surprised by the people you meet.

population, French 19%, Italian 8% and Romansch under 1%.

Around 19% of people living in the country (over 1.34 million) are residents but not Swiss citizens. This figure does *not* include the many seasonal workers, temporary residents and international civil servants and administrators. Most of the permanent residents arrived after WWII, initially from Italy and Spain, and subsequently from the rest of southern Europe. Switzerland took in record numbers of asylum seekers in 1998 (41,000) and 1999 (45,000), particularly from Albania and Kosovo.

The other side of the equation is the Swiss community living abroad, which numbers about 528,000. Historically, Swiss left the country because of domestic food shortages (thousands died of hunger in 1817) and through mercenary service (halted in 1859). Nowadays, emigration is due more to the expansion of Swiss firms abroad.

EDUCATION

Control of education is at the cantonal level, with the consequence that there are 26 different systems in operation. They all adhere to a greater or lesser extent to a national standard, but there are variations in types of schools, curricula, and teaching methods. It wasn't even until the referendum in 1985 that it was agreed to universally start the school year at the end of summer.

Most children attend nursery school from age four. Compulsory schooling starts at age six or seven and continues for eight or (usually) nine years. Towards the end of this period students are eased into different streams: apprenticeship, vocational, or academic. The latter two streams usually continue with two to three years of post-compulsory education, leading to entry into a vocational college (medicine, teaching etc) or a general university or institute. There are nine cantonal universities. The country's literacy rate is 99%.

I Didn't Know They Were Swiss

Switzerland has always attracted celebrities in droves – famous 20th-century non-Swiss residents and former residents include Charlie Chaplin, Yehudi Menuhin, Audrey Hepburn, Richard Burton, Peter Ustinov, Roger Moore, Tina Turner, Phil Collins, the Aga Khan and Michael Schumacher. Yet plenty of native Swiss have made their mark on the world stage too. Some people you may not have known were Swiss include:

- Louis Chevrolet, founder of the Chevrolet Manufacturing Company in 1911, producer of archetypal 'American' automobiles
- César Ritz (1850–1918), 13th child of a poor Upper Valais family, and founder of the Ritz luxury hotels
- Ursula Andress (1936–), actress, famous for her bikini-clad appearance in Dr No
- Erich von Däniken, expounder of far-fetched early-history theories in the 1970s bestseller, Chariots of the Gods?
- Le Corbusier (1887–1965), architectural innovator, often believed to be French
- Jean-Luc Godard (1930–), more-Swiss-than-French avant-garde film-maker
- Albert Hofmann, the first person to synthesise and experiment with lysergic acid diethylamide (LSD)

Apprenticeships are given in private companies, and at the same time the trainee usually attends part-time courses in a college. There remains a shortage of skilled labour in the country, forcing some Swiss firms to expand abroad. Switzerland is one of the highest spenders on research and development in the world (2.7% of GDP).

SCIENCE & PHILOSOPHY

Perhaps it's something to do with the beneficial effect of pure mountain air, but Switzerland has an unusually high number of Nobel Prize winners, and leads the world in terms of the number of patents registered per person. The Swiss Federal Institute of Technology in Zurich attracts world-famous scientists to its faculty.

Though he was born in Germany, Albert Einstein came up with his theories of relativity while working in Bern (see the boxed text 'Doing Time in the Bern Patent Office' in the Swiss Mittelland chapter). Otherwise, the most widely recognised name is probably Carl Gustav Jung, who founded the analytical school of psychology. He was born on 26 July 1875 in Kesswil, Thurgau, and graduated in medicine in 1902 from Basel and Zürich universities. Initially an ally of Freud, he soon rejected the Viennese psychoanalyst's purely sexual interpretation of subconscious drives. Jung identified the distinct personalities, extrovert and introvert, in *Psychological Types*, published in 1921. He later proposed the existence of the collective unconscious (inherited feelings, thoughts and memories shared by all humanity), which individuals have to integrate with their own personal unconscious in order to achieve wholeness of self. Jung died in Küsnacht, Zürich, on 6 June 1961.

Paul Müller won the Nobel Prize for medicine in 1948 for his work in harnessing the insecticidal properties of DDT. Within 10 years of its introduction DDT had saved an estimated five million lives, though it has since been banned in many countries due to its persistence in the soil and its ability to creep up the food chain.

Other Nobel Prize winners in the field of Physiology & Medicine have been Emil Theodor Kocker (1909), Walter Hess (1949), Tadeus Reichstein (1950), Daniel Bovet (1957), Werner Arber (1978), and Rolf Zinkernagel (1996). Chemists who have received the Nobel Prize include Alfred Werner (1913) for his formulation of the coordination theory of valency, Paul Karrer (1937), who first isolated the vitamins A and K, Leopold Ruzicka (1939), Vladimir Prelog (1975) and Richard Ernst (1991). Physicists include Wolfgang Pauli for his work on atomic structure (1945), and more recently, Heinrich Rohrer (1986) and Alexander Müller (1987). Perhaps the unluckiest Swiss physicist was Ernst Stueckelberg. Over the years, his pioneering work in various aspects of theoretical physics paved the way for the winning of four Nobel Prizes. Unfortunately, all four were awarded to other physicists. He died in 1984 without a Nobel to his name.

Other Swiss notables include child psychologist Jean Piaget (1896-1980) who identified key stages in the mental growth of children, Werner Arber who has recently made important contributions to experimental research into genes, and biologist Adolf Portmann. In 1995, two Swiss astronomers (Michel Mayor and Didier Queloz) were the first to prove the existence of a planet outside our solar system.

ARTS

Switzerland does not have a very strong tradition in the arts, even though many foreign writers and artists (such as Voltaire, Byron, Shelley and Turner) have visited and settled, attracted by the beauty and tranquillity of the mountains and lakes. Madame de Staël, after fleeing the French Revolution, set up an international salon in Coppet, on Lake Geneva, which became a centre of European literary life during the 18th century. Influential artists settled in Zürich in the early 20th century and created the Dada movement.

In contrast, many creative Swiss left the country to make their name abroad, such as the film director Jean-Luc Godard, the artist Paul Klee and the architect Le Corbusier.

Writers & Artists

Few Swiss writers have gained international attention. Hermann Hesse is by far the best known novelist, though he was German born and naturalised Swiss. The linguistic diversity in the country makes it very hard to have a literary tradition. Carl Spitteler (1845-1924) won the Nobel Prize in 1919 for his writings in German. Max Frisch, writing a generation later, has been translated into English and often dwells on the restrictions of Swiss society.

Jean-Jacques Rousseau (1712-78) was born in Geneva but spent most of his life in France. His writings, such as *The Social Contract* (1762), played an important part in the development of democracy, though

he also wrote works on subjects as diverse as education (influencing, among others, Swiss educational reformer Johann Heinrich Pestalozzi) and botany, and even penned operas and novels.

Paul Klee was born in Bern yet he never actually acquired Swiss citizenship and did most of his work in Germany. Klee (1879-1940) created abstract works which used colour, line and form to evoke a variety of sensations. His work can be seen in the Kunstmuseum in Bern.

Alberto Giacometti (1901-66), a sculptor from Graubünden who settled in Paris, dabbled in cubism and surrealism before developing his distinctive stick-like figures (expressive, apparently, of individual isolation). His father, Giovanni, and his uncle, Augusto, are also well-known artists. You can see much of their work in the art museums in Chur and Zürich.

The most 'Swiss' artist in lineage, residence and the subject matter of his work is Ferdinand Hodler (see the boxed text 'Ferdinand Hodler' in the Swiss Mittelland chapter). The motorised sculptures of Jean Tinguely, mostly cobbled together from discards, can be seen especially in Basel and Fribourg.

Music & Theatre

Until the 17th century, folk music and religious music were the only genres that developed in Switzerland. The country still lacks truly famous exponents. Composers Ernest Bloch (1880-1959), who explored Hebraic elements in his music, and Frank Martin (1890-1974), whose output was stylistically diverse, were both born in Geneva. Arthur Honegger (1892-1955), another progressive composer of note, was born in France but had Swiss parents and considered himself Swiss. He settled in Paris and co-founded the avant-garde 'Les Six'.

Despite this dearth, music is strongly emphasised; there is a full-sized symphony orchestra in every main city. Music festivals are held throughout the year: two of the most famous, with a worldwide reputation, are the Lucerne International Music Festival and the Montreux Jazz Festival.

The theatre scene flourishes, even in English in Geneva and Zürich. Go to Bern to visit small-scale, atmospheric cellar *(Keller)* theatres, where plays are often performed in dialect.

Architecture

Some evidence of Roman architecture remains in Switzerland, particularly at Avenches (see the Fribourg, Neuchâtel & Jura chapter). Gothic (popular in the 13th to 15th centuries) and Renaissance (16th century) architecture are evident in urban areas, especially Bern. Lausanne's cathedral is perhaps the best example of the Gothic style in Switzerland, though Bern's cathedral comes close. Other cathedrals combine Gothic and Renaissance features, such as those in Basel and Chur. Baroque and its extreme version, rococo, in vogue in the 17th and 18th centuries, had little impact in Switzerland, though paintings and stucco work in this style can be seen in the cathedral and adjoining library in St Gallen.

Rural Swiss houses vary according to region, but the typical chalet style is generally characterised by steep, ridged roofs with wide, overhanging eaves, and balconies and verandahs which are usually enlivened by colourful floral displays, particularly of geraniums. Anybody interested in regional architecture should visit the Ballenberg Museum outside Brienz (see the Freilichtmuseum Ballenberg section in the Bernese Oberland chapter). The region of Ticino offers an architectural itinerary exploring more modern styles.

Le Corbusier is the country's best known architectural export – he had a lasting impact on 20th century architecture (see the boxed text 'Le Corbusier – Man of Concrete' in the Fribourg, Neuchâtel & Jura chapter).

SOCIETY & CONDUCT
Traditional Culture

In a few mountain regions such as Valais, people still wear traditional rural costumes, but dressing up is usually reserved for festivals. Every spring, hardy herders climb to Alpine pastures with their cattle and live in summer huts while tending their herds. They gradually descend back to village level as the grassland is grazed. Both the departure and the return is a cause for celebrations and processions through the village. Cows are decorated with garlands of flowers for the processions to and from the pastures, and they each have a bell hung around their necks, with a distinct ring which helps them to be found.

Yodelling and playing the Alp horn are also part of the Alpine tradition. Swiss wrestling is another event that is featured in frequent festivals.

Festivals and carnivals crop up in urban as well as rural areas. Sometimes ancient traditions and customs are inherent in the celebrations.

Dos & Don'ts

In general the Swiss are law-abiding; even minor transgressions such as littering can cause offence. Always shake hands when being introduced to a Swiss, and again when leaving. This is standard behaviour, even with young and casual people. Formal titles should also be used, except among youngsters – *Herr* for men and *Frau* for women. It is also customary to greet the proprietor when entering a shop, bar or cafe, and to say goodbye when leaving. Public displays of affection are fine, but are more common in French Switzerland than in the slightly more formal German-speaking parts. Exchanging kisses (three times, alternating cheeks) upon meeting is a common ritual in French Switzerland.

The Swiss are punctual, and will expect you to be too. At the dinner table, everybody waits for the host to make a toast prior to drinking, and before your impatient lips stretch for that soothing libation, you must chink glasses with all present while looking them in the eye. Before tucking into the food, the cry of *en Guete* or *bon appétit* is heard. Most Swiss go to bed early so don't overstay your welcome if you're invited to somebody's home (and if you do get invited, take a gift), and don't telephone anybody after about 9 pm.

On the beach, nude bathing is usually limited to restricted areas, but topless bathing is common in many parts.

Dress codes are pretty relaxed in Switzerland. It's not unusual to see office workers and bank clerks wearing casual clothes like jeans. But men would be advised to wear a jacket and tie when dining in some of the top restaurants mentioned in this book.

RELIGION

The country is split pretty evenly between Protestantism (in decline since WWII, now down to 40%) and Roman Catholicism (46%). Most of the rest of the population are 'unaffiliated'. The predominant faith varies between cantons. Bern is a Protestant stronghold, as are Vaud, Zürich, Thurgau, Neuchâtel and Glarus. Strong Catholic areas are Valais, Ticino, Uri, Unterwalden and Schwyz, as well as Fribourg, Lucerne, Zug and the Jura. Curiously, the two half-cantons of Appenzell are at odds: Ausserrhoden is strongly Protestant while nine out of 10 people in Innerrhoden are Catholic. Some churches are supported entirely by donations from the public while others receive state subsidies.

LANGUAGE

Located in the corner of Europe where the German, French and Italian language areas meet, the linguistic melting pot that is Switzerland (Schweiz, Suisse, Svizzera) has three official federal languages: German (spoken by about 64% of the population), French (19%) and Italian (8%). A fourth language, Rhaeto-Romanic, or Romansch, is spoken by under 1% of the population, mainly in the canton of Graubünden. Derived from Latin, it's a linguistic relic which, along with Friulian and Ladin across the border in Italy, has survived in the isolation of mountain valleys. In 1938, Romansch was recognised as an official national language by referendum. In 1996, a further referendum gave Romansch partial status as an official federal language, together with guarantees for its preservation and promotion.

Nein Merci

Some of the uneasiness between French and German speakers in Switzerland is because of difficulties with Schwyzertütsch, though there are other factors (eg, the geographical line separating French and German speakers has been coined the *Röstigraben*, or Rösti ditch, to reflect the culinary difference). French Swiss learn High German at school, and are completely at a loss when their German-speaking compatriots lapse into Schwyzertütsch. The German speakers don't have that difficulty when French is spoken, but they do have a different problem. They are happier and more fluent in Schwyzertütsch than in High German, and feel acutely disadvantaged when encountering articulate Germans. This is one factor behind the Swiss Germans' reluctance to become part of a German-dominated EU, much to the dismay of the pro-EU French Swiss.

Being Understood in English

The English language is not a compulsory subject in Swiss schools. That's surprising, as generally the Swiss speak English very well, especially in German Switzerland. Ask a German-speaking Swiss if they speak English and you normally get one of two answers: 'a little' means they speak it fluently, but a philosophical discussion on etymology and epistemology in English would probably be beyond their grasp; a simple 'yes' means that your ego is about to get a battering – they speak English better than you do, and no doubt know what those obscure 'ology' words mean into the bargain. Most people working in 'service' areas (tourist office staff, telephone operators, hotel and office receptionists, restaurant staff, shopkeepers) speak some English.

Nevertheless, don't automatically assume that everyone you meet does speak English, especially in smaller, less-touristy towns where English has less penetration. It is simple courtesy to greet people in German-speaking areas with *Grüezi* (hello) and to inquire *Sprechen Sie Englisch?* (Do you speak English?) before launching into English. And don't feel discouraged if your clumsy attempts at speaking German immediately elicit a response in English – your efforts will still be appreciated.

In French Switzerland you shouldn't have too many problems being understood either, though the locals' grasp of English is likely to be less complete than that of German speakers. Italian Switzerland is where you will have the greatest difficulty. Most locals speak some French and/or German in addition to Italian, but English has a lower priority. Even so, you will find that the majority of restaurants and hotels have at least one English-speaking staff member.

In the Romansch-speaking parts of Graubünden, those involved in the tourist industry usually speak English, but ordinary country folk probably won't. Instead, they

LANGUAGE AREAS

- Romansch
- German
- French
- Italian

Basel, Zürich, Bern, Lucerne, Chur, Lausanne, St Moritz, Bellinzona, Geneva

may offer you one of the other three national languages, usually German.

For more information on the languages of Switzerland, including pronunciation guidelines and a list of useful words and phrases, turn to the Language chapter at the end of this book.

Facts for the Visitor

HIGHLIGHTS
Despite its small size, Switzerland offers many magnificent options for sightseeing and activities. It boasts three World Heritage sites: Bern's historic city centre, St Gallen's abbey church and library, and the church of St John in Müstair.

Castles & Churches
There are many interesting castles scattered through the country. The Château de Chillon is one of the most famous (see the Montreux section in the Lake Geneva chapter). Also try and take a day tour of the castles around Lake Thun. Basel and Bern both have fine cathedrals. The most impressive abbey churches in the country, quite breathtaking in their scale, are those in Einsiedeln and St Gallen.

Museums & Galleries
Basel and Zürich each have an excellent art museum, the Kunstmuseum and the Kunsthaus. Getting away from the mainstream, my personal favourite is the bizarre l'Art Brut collection in Lausanne. Zürich's national museum (Schweizerisches Landesmuseum) gives the most complete rundown of Swiss life and times, making all but redundant equivalent regional museums. The sprawling Art and History Museum in Geneva covers a bit of everything. The best clock and watch museum is the Museum of Horology in La Chaux-de-Fonds. For food fans there are various show cheese dairies (eg, at Gruyères and Stein), or visit the Lindt & Sprüngli chocolate factory in Zürich.

Picturesque Town Centres
Rathausplatz in Stein am Rhein is harmonious and perfectly preserved; the main street in Gruyères is almost as photogenic. Lucerne is worthy of its fame as a tourist centre. Schaffhausen and St Gallen sport historic centres bristling with oriel windows. Bern is unbelievably quaint for a capital city. Murten, and to a lesser extent, Estavayer-le-lac, proudly display ancient centres ringed by fortifications, virtually unchanged by time.

Scenery & Ski Resorts
In a country so blessed with beautiful vistas it is difficult to select favourites. You can't get much better than the view from Schilthorn, or from its neighbour across the valley, Jungfrau. The three or four-pass tour (see the Bernese Oberland chapter) is unforgettable on a fine day. The combination of mountains and lakes, seen from one of the summits round Lake Lucerne (Mt Pilatus, Mt Rigi, Mt Stanserhorn), is as seductive as views from higher peaks. The ski resorts invariably provide great panoramas to go with the pistes. Zermatt has excellent skiing and inspiring views of the Matterhorn. Davos and Verbier offer some of the best skiing in the world.

SUGGESTED ITINERARIES
Depending on the length of your stay, you might want to see and do the following things:

One week
Visit Geneva and Château de Chillon near Montreux. Take the Panoramic Express to Interlaken and explore the Jungfrau Region. Finish up at Lucerne.

Two weeks
As above, but spend longer in the mountains. Visit the Gruyères cheese dairy after Montreux. Detour to Bern and Basel and visit Zürich.

One month
As above, but after Zürich, explore St Gallen and eastern Switzerland before looping down to take in Graubünden, Ticino and Valais.

Two months
As above, but take your time. Visit Neuchâtel and the Jura from Bern.

PLANNING
When to Go
You can visit Switzerland at any time of the year. Summer lasts roughly from June to September, and offers the most pleasant

climate for outdoor pursuits. Unfortunately, you won't be the only tourist during summer – prices can be high, accommodation fully booked, and the sights packed. You'll find much better deals, and less crowds, in the shoulder seasons either side of summer: in April and May or September and October. In Ticino, flowers are in bloom as early as March and hints of summer warmth are already seeping through.

On the other hand, if you're keen on winter sports, resorts in the Alps begin operating in early December and move into full swing around Christmas, closing down again when the snows begin to melt around April. The summer season for Alpine resorts is from late June to late October, with peak time being July and August. Between the summer and winter seasons, Alpine resorts all but close down (except in resorts where year-round glacier skiing is on offer).

At any time of year, as you travel around the country you'll hit many different climatic conditions. The continental climate in the Alps tends to show the greatest extremes between summer and winter. Mid-August to late October generally has fairly settled weather, and is a good period for hiking trips. See Climate in the Facts about the Country chapter for weather considerations.

Maps

There are several good map publishers based in Switzerland. Hallwag produces clear country maps, including a ring-bound map book designed for drivers. Kümmerly + Frey (K+F) is another major Swiss map publisher; its Swiss Atlas is also a good buy for drivers – it contains a country map and 35 town plans. K+F publishes a comprehensive series of maps for hikers, mostly on a 1:60,000 scale. Swiss Hiking Federation maps (1:50,000 scale, with orange covers) are an even better buy. The Swiss Travel System brochure, free from Switzerland Tourism, contains a clear A3 map of bus and rail routes, though for more detail buy the SBB (Swiss Federal Railway) rail map from a Swiss train station.

Once you're in Switzerland, it usually pays to go directly to the local tourist information office to stock up on its free maps and brochures. Another excellent source of free maps is the larger branches of the UBS and Credit Suisse banks – just ask at the counters.

What to Bring

Pack as lightly as you can. Anything you forget to bring you can easily buy in Switzerland, though prices are high. Allow for colder weather in winter and at high altitudes (several layers of thin clothing keep you warmer than one thick one). Even if you prefer to dress informally, consider packing proper shoes (not trainers or running shoes), smart trousers/dress/skirt (not jeans) and men should pack a tie for formal outings, such as to top restaurants, though dress codes are usually pretty relaxed at places like nightclubs. Being able to present a smart appearance helps when dealing with officialdom (like at border controls).

Whether to take suitcases or a backpack is a matter of personal choice. If you're travelling by car it doesn't really matter what you take, but a backpack is better if you plan to do much walking. Unfortunately, it doesn't offer too much protection for your valuables; the straps tend to get caught on things and some airlines may refuse to take responsibility if the pack is damaged or broken into. Travel packs are a nifty combination of backpack and shoulder bag, where the backpack straps zip away inside the pack. During city sightseeing, a small daypack is better than a shoulder bag for deterring bag snatchers.

A padlock and chain are useful to lock your bag to a train or bus luggage rack, and may also be needed to secure a youth hostel locker. Swiss Army knives are the most versatile pocket knives available; get one with at least a bottle opener and corkscrew (yes, you can buy them in Switzerland and they're not too expensive).

Other items that might be useful include a compass, a torch (flashlight), an alarm clock or watch alarm, an adapter plug for electrical appliances, a universal bath/sink plug, sunglasses, clothes pegs and string (impromptu clothesline), and a film canister. Unprocessed film should be OK through the x-ray machines but, as always, carry it in your hand luggage. A few hostels charge extra for sheets in dormitories so you may save money if you have your own. If you take a water bottle you won't have to keep buying expensive drinks when sightseeing. Consider also acquiring a cup water heater to make your own hot beverages, as hotel rooms rarely have such facilities. A supply of passport photos is useful for visas for onward travel, rail/bus passes etc. Tampons and condoms are widely available in Switzerland.

Compile a packing list before you leave home, and don't forget wet-weather gear. Pack a few plastic carry bags; they can help keep your clothes separate, clean and dry. Tag your luggage both inside and out with your name and address.

RESPONSIBLE TOURISM

Your main concern as a responsible tourist in Switzerland, apart from being law-abiding and observing social etiquette, is to leave the rural environment as you found it.

When hiking, stick to the marked paths. Short cuts straight down a slope (bypassing a switchback, for example) could turn into a watercourse during the next heavy rainfall and cause soil erosion. Don't pick Alpine wild flowers – they really do look lovelier on the mountainsides. Farm gates should be left as you found them. Animal watchers should approach wildlife with discretion; moving too close will unnerve wild animals, distracting them from their vital summer activity of putting on fat for the long Alpine winter. Don't light fires, except in established fire places. Everything you take into the mountains with you, you should take out again – don't discard rubbish or used packaging. That includes your cigarette butts and used tampons. If you really can't avoid leaving some memento of your visit behind, such as faeces, bury it in the ground at least 100m away from any watercourse.

TOURIST OFFICES

Switzerland Tourism abroad and local tourist offices in Switzerland are extremely helpful and have plenty of literature in English to give out. They usually also have specialised information for travellers with special requirements. Some brochures are mere glossy sales-pitches, but others will contain good practical information too.

Local Tourist Offices

For specific and detailed resort information, you're better off contacting the local tourist office direct. Information is nearly always free, including maps, and somebody invariably speaks English. Local offices can be found everywhere tourists are likely to go, and will often book hotel rooms. It's always worth asking about this if you haven't pre-booked somewhere – many offices don't charge to telephone around for personal callers. Some offices even book hotels in other towns too, though there's usually a commission for this (Sfr10). Tours and excursions are also often arranged, as are all-in packages for stays of a few days including accommodation and sightseeing. In German-speaking Switzerland offices are called *Verkehrsbüro*, or *Kurverein* in some resorts. In French they are *office du tourisme* and in Italian, *ufficio turistico*.

As if the combination of national and local tourist offices weren't already enough to meet the needs of visitors, the Swiss have made doubly sure that every angle is covered by dividing the country up into 12 tourist regions, each with its own regional or sub-regional tourist office. Each chapter in this book covers one tourist region, and the address of the regional office is given in the chapter introduction.

AngloPhone (☎ 157 50 14) is a privately-run, premium-rate (Sfr2.13 a minute) English-language service providing 'information on living in Switzerland'.

Tourist Offices Abroad

The Switzerland Tourism headquarters is in Zürich (see the Zürich chapter for details). Swiss tourist offices abroad include:

Canada
(☎ 416-695 2090, fax 695 2774,
✉ sttoronto@switzerlandtourism.com)
926 The East Mall, Etobicoke, Toronto, Ontario M9B 6K1

France
(☎ 01-44 51 65 51, fax 47 42 43 88,
📧 stparis@suissevacances.ch)
Porte de la Suisse, 11 bis, rue Scribe,
F-75009 Paris

Japan
(☎ 03-3589 5588, fax 3224 0888,
📧 tourist@switzerlandtourism.or.jp)
CS Tower, 2nd floor, 1-11-30 Akasaka,
Minato-ku, Tokyo 107

UK
(☎ 020-8734 1921, fax 437 4577,
📧 stlondon@switzerlandvacation.ch)
Swiss Centre, Swiss Court, London W1V 8EE

USA
(☎ 212-757 59 44, fax 262 61 16,
📧 stnewyork@switzerlandtourism.com)
Swiss Center, 608 Fifth Ave, New York,
NY 10020

Switzerland Tourism has no office in Australia, but you can get information from Swissair in Sydney (☎ 02-9231 3744, fax 02-9251 6531, 📧 swissair@tiasnet.com.au). There are offices in many Western Europe countries, and in several German cities.

VISAS & DOCUMENTS

As a precaution against loss or theft, keep a separate record of document numbers, or a photocopy of key pages. Ensure your passport is valid until well after you plan to end your trip – six months is usually considered a safe minimum; if it's due to expire in that time, renew it before you depart. Once you start travelling, carry your passport at all times and guard it carefully. Swiss citizens are required to carry personal identification, so you also will need to be able to identify yourself. Citizens of many European countries don't need a valid passport to travel to Switzerland; a national identity card or expired passport may be sufficient (this doesn't apply to British citizens). Be sure to check with your travel agent or the Swiss Embassy well before departure.

Visas

Visas are not required for passport holders of the UK, Ireland, the USA, Canada, Australia, New Zealand or South Africa, whether visiting as a tourist or on business. A maximum three-month stay applies although passports

are rarely stamped. The few people (mostly Old World and Arab nationals) who require visas should have a passport valid for at least three or six months after their intended stay.

Inquire at a Swiss Embassy before departure if you're going to Switzerland to take up an employment offer, as you will need to acquire an 'Assurance of a Residence Permit'. Visa requirements can change, and regardless of the purpose of your trip, you should always check with the embassy or a reputable travel agent before travelling.

Being able to show a return ticket and 'sufficient means of support' are not an entry requirement, but if a border guard has cause to question the purpose of your trip you may have problems if you can't show either or both.

Travel Insurance

Good travel insurance is essential. You should inquire about claims procedures, especially in the event that medical treatment is required. A few insurers require notification *before* treatment is received – tricky in an emergency situation. Other things to look for are whether the policy covers activities such as adventure sports, skiing and mountaineering, and whether ambulances, helicopter rescue or emergency repatriation are included. An annual travel policy is probably the best deal for frequent travellers.

Student & Youth Cards

An International Student Identity Card (ISIC) can get the holder all sorts of discounts on admission prices, air and international train tickets, even some ski passes. If you're under 26 but not a student, you can apply for a Federation of International Youth Travel Organisations (FIYTO) card; this is not so useful, but may work for reductions in lieu of an ISIC. Both cards should be issued by both student unions and by youth-oriented travel agents in your home country.

SSR-Reisen in German Switzerland (☎ 01-297 11 11) or Voyages-SSR in French Switzerland (☎ 021-614 60 30) is a budget travel agency specialising in student and budget fares. SSR (@ info@ssr.ch) is linked to STA and can make changes to STA-issued tickets for a US$25 fee (about Sfr40). SSR also sells activity packages for Switzerland. There are branches in Zürich, Geneva, Bern, Basel, Lausanne, Biel, St Gallen, Winterthur, Chur, Fribourg, Lucerne and Neuchâtel; these are listed in the appropriate chapters. ISIC cards (Sfr15) can be issued by SSR, or by Globetrotter in Zürich and other towns.

Other Documents

Other useful documents are mentioned in the appropriate sections, eg, driving-related documents are discussed under Car & Motorcycle in the Getting There & Away chapter.

Photocopies

All important documents (passport data page and visa page, credit cards, travel insurance policy, air/bus/train tickets, driving licence etc) should be photocopied before you leave home. Leave one copy with someone at home and keep another with you, separate from the originals.

It's also a good idea to store details of your vital travel documents in Lonely Planet's free online Travel Vault in case you lose the photocopies or can't be bothered with them. Your password-protected Travel Vault is accessible online anywhere in the world – you can create it at www.ekno.lonelyplanet.com.

EMBASSIES & CONSULATES
Swiss Embassies

Swiss embassies abroad include:

Australia (☎ 02-6273 3977, fax 6273 3428, @ swissembcan@dynamite.com.au) 7 Melbourne Ave, Forrest, Canberra, ACT 2603
Canada (☎ 613-235 1837, fax 563 1394, @ swissemott@compuserve.com) 5 Marlborough Ave, Ottawa, Ontario K1N 8E6
Ireland (☎ 01-218 6382, fax 218 6383, @ swiemdub@iol.ie) 6 Ailesbury Rd, Ballsbridge, Dublin 4
New Zealand (☎ 04-472 1593, fax 472 1593) 22 Panama St, Wellington
South Africa (☎ 012-436 707, fax 436 771, @ swiempre@cis.co.za)

818 George Ave, Arcadia 0083, PO Box 2289, 0001 Pretoria
UK (☎ 020-7616 6000, fax 7724 7001, @ vertretung@lon.rep.admin.ch) 16-18 Montague Place, London W1H 2BQ
USA (☎ 202-745 7900, fax 387 2564, @ vertretung@was.rep.admin.ch) 2900 Cathedral Ave NW, Washington, DC 20008-3499

Foreign Embassies & Consulates in Switzerland

All embassies are located in Bern. Consulates can be found in several other cities, particularly in Zürich and Geneva. Australia and New Zealand don't have an embassy in Switzerland, but each has a consulate in Geneva. Most of Bern's embassies can be found south-east of the Kirchenfeldbrücke.

Australia
Consulate: (☎ 022-799 91 00) 2 Chemin des Fins, Geneva
Austria
Consulate: (☎ 01-283 27 00) Seestrasse 161, Zürich
Canada
Embassy: (☎ 031-357 32 00) Kirchenfeldstrasse 88, Bern
Consulate: (☎ 022-919 92 00) 5 Ave de l'Ariana, Geneva
Ireland
Embassy: (☎ 031-352 14 42) Kirchenfeldstrasse 68, Bern
France
Embassy: (☎ 031-359 21 11) Schosshaldenstrasse 46, Bern
Consulate: (☎ 061-272 63 18), Elisabethenstrasse 33, Basel
Consulate: (☎ 01-268 85 85) Mühlebachstrasse 7, Zürich
Consulate: (☎ 022-311 34 41) 11 Rue J Imbert Galloix, Geneva
Germany
Embassy: (☎ 031-359 41 11) Willadingweg 83, Bern
Consulate: (☎ 061-693 33 03), Schwarzwaldallee 200, Basel
Consulate: (☎ 01-265 65 65) Kirchgasse 48, Zürich
Italy
Embassy: (☎ 031-352 41 51) Elfenstrasse 14, Bern
Consulate: (☎ 031-381 19 11) Belpstrasse 11, Bern
Consulate: (☎ 091-922 05 13), Via Ferruccio Pelli 16, Lugano

Consulate: (☎ 01-286 61 11) Tödistrasse 67, Zürich
Consulate: (☎ 022-839 67 44) 14 Rue Charles Galland, Geneva
South Africa
  Embassy: (☎ 031-350 13 13) Alpenstrasse 29, Bern
Netherlands
  Consulate: (☎ 031-352 70 63/64/65) Kollerweg 11, Bern
New Zealand
  Consulate: (☎ 022-734 95 30) 28A Chemin du Petit-Saconnex, Geneva
UK
  Embassy: (☎ 031-359 77 00) Thunstrasse 50, Bern
  Consulate: (☎ 091-950 06 06), Via Motta 19, Lugano
  Consulate: (☎ 01-383 65 80) Minervastrasse 117, Zürich
  Consulate: (☎022-918 24 00) 37-39 Rue de Vermont, Geneva
USA
  Embassy: (☎ 031-357 70 11) Jubiläumsstrasse 93, Bern
  Consulate: (☎ 01-422 25 66) Dufourstrasse 101, Zürich
  Consulate: (☎ 022-798 16 05) 29 Route de Pré-Bois, Geneva

CUSTOMS

Duty-free limits are as follows: visitors from Europe may import 200 cigarettes, 50 cigars or 250g of pipe tobacco. Visitors from non-European countries may import twice as much. The allowance for alcoholic beverages is the same for everyone: 1L above 15% and 2L below 15%. Tobacco and alcohol may only be brought in by people aged 17 or over. Gifts up to the value of Sfr100 may also be imported, and food provisions for one day.

MONEY
Currency

Swiss francs are divided into 100 centimes (known as *Rappen* in German-speaking Switzerland). There are notes for 10, 20, 50, 100, 500 and 1000 francs, and coins for five, 10, 20 and 50 centimes, as well as for one, two and five francs.

If you're driving to Switzerland and intend to use the motorways, you'll have to pay a one-year motorway tax of Sfr40. Have this money ready, since there may not always be an exchange facility at the border.

Exchange Rates

Some exchange rates for the Swiss franc are:

country	unit		Swiss franc
Australia	A$1	=	Sfr1.06
Austria	AS10	=	Sfr1.17
Canada	C$1	=	Sfr0.10
euro	€1	=	Sfr1.62
France	FF10	=	Sfr2.46
Germany	DM1	=	Sfr0.83
Italy	IL1000	=	Sfr0.83
Japan	¥100	=	Sfr1.51
New Zealand	NZ$1	=	Sfr0.83
UK	UK£1	=	Sfr2.60
USA	US$1	=	Sfr1.60

Your Own Embassy

It's important to realise what your own embassy – the embassy of the country of which you are a citizen – can and can't do to help you if you get into trouble. Generally speaking, it won't be much help in emergencies if the trouble you're in is remotely your own fault. Remember that you are bound by the laws of the country you are in. Your embassy will not be sympathetic if you end up in jail after committing a crime locally, even if such actions are legal in your own country.

In genuine emergencies you might get some assistance, but only if other channels have been exhausted. For example, if you need to get home urgently, a free ticket home is exceedingly unlikely – the embassy would expect you to have insurance. If you have all your money and documents stolen, it might assist with getting a new passport, but a loan for onward travel is out of the question.

Some embassies used to keep letters for travellers or have a small reading room with home newspapers, but these days the mail holding service has usually been stopped and even newspapers tend to be out of date.

Eurozone Finances

On 1 January 1999 the long-awaited and long-debated Economic and Monetary Union (EMU) came into effect within 11 of the 15 EU countries. These 11 countries are Austria, Belgium, Finland, France, Germany, Ireland, Italy, Luxembourg, Netherlands, Portugal and Spain. Their currencies are now irrevocably fixed against the new single currency, the euro, even though euro notes and coins won't be introduced until January 2002. You can already buy travellers cheques in euros. The 11 local currencies will remain in circulation till June 2002, after which the euro will be the sole legal tender in those countries.

The Swiss franc is not fixed against the euro, though it does tend to shadow its movements on the international exchanges. Approximately, Sfr1 = €0.63, €1 = Sfr1.62. However, if the euro proves to be a horrible mistake and goes into free-fall, the Swiss franc will probably be seen as a safe-haven currency and will rise in value against it.

Exchanging Money

The Swiss make it as easy as they can for you to spend your money. Bank opening times vary depending on the bank, place and branch, but typical hours are 8.30 am to 4.30 pm Monday to Friday, except on public holidays. You can also change money at airports and nearly every train station every day until sometime in the evening. Rates for travellers cheques are sometimes about 1% better than those for cash. Ask about commission charges before exchanging, as some banks now charge for changing cash (as yet, travellers cheque transactions are commission-free). Exchange rates are pretty similar everywhere, though some private money-exchange bureaux do slightly undercut the banks. Big hotels change money too, though at poor rates. All fully convertible currencies are equally acceptable, and as there's often no commission, Switzerland is a good place to get rid of small sums of unneeded currencies.

Cash Avoid carrying large amounts of cash, but taking some will allow more flexibility in exchanging upon arrival and departure. Secreting an emergency stash of cash (say around US$50) away from your main money and documents, is a good idea. Towards the end of your trip, you don't want to change more than you think you'll need as you will lose out if you have to reconvert the excess. Banks rarely accept coins in currencies other than their own, so spend your last coins before departure.

Travellers Cheques All major travellers cheques are equally acceptable, though you may want to stick to those from American Express, Visa or Thomas Cook because of their 'instant replacement' policies.

Keeping a record of the cheque numbers and the initial purchase details is vital when it comes to replacing lost cheques. Without this, you may well find that 'instant' is a very long time indeed. You should also keep a record of which cheques you have cashed. Keep these details separate from the cheques themselves. American Express (AmEx) has offices in Basel, Geneva, Lausanne, Lucerne and Zürich; addresses are listed in the appropriate city sections. Buy cheques in your home currency (as long as it's freely convertible and stable), for if you buy too many in Swiss francs you'll lose on the 'spread' of the exchange rate when cashing in the excess back home.

Guaranteed Cheques Eurocheques are the most popular form of guaranteed personal cheque. Each cheque is guaranteed for up to Sfr300, and you get a Eurocheque card which is valid at banks for cash withdrawals and advances. But first you need a European bank account, and it can be an expensive system to use – there's a fee per annum and a fee per cheque cashed. Many hotels, restaurants and shops accept Eurocheques.

Credit Cards & ATMs Using a credit card can limit or even remove the need to carry travellers cheques. Not only can you pay for many goods and services by card (eg, Swiss train tickets worth more than Sfr20), but you can also use it to get cash advances at most banks. Not all shops, hotels or restaurants will accept credit cards, however, and their use is less widespread than in the UK or USA. EuroCard, MasterCard and Visa are the most popular cards. Charge cards like AmEx and Diners Club are generally less widely acceptable than ordinary credit cards.

Automated teller machines (ATMs), known as Bancomats in banks and Postomats in post offices, are reasonably common and are accessible 24 hours a day. They are linked up internationally and have English instructions. Your credit card company will usually charge a 1% to 2% fee on the total withdrawal, and there may also be a small charge at the ATM end. You can avoid the monthly interest charged on your credit card account (due from the day of withdrawal) by leaving your account in credit at the start of your holiday. Beware – Visa cards are *not* accepted in all ATMs, though they are at UBS EC-Bancomat machines, and at post office Postomats.

International Transfers If you need to get money sent from home, nominate a large bank in a major city to receive the funds, instead of some out-of-the-way branch. There are always charges made by the sending bank, and there may be charges at the receiving bank too. An electronic transfer can take anything from two to 10 days (quicker means higher charges). Note that the receiving bank may not agree to this unless the recipient is an account-holder of their's, and Swiss banks won't let non-residents open a bank account unless they have a huge amount of money to deposit. Other possibilities are sending a money order or international banker's draft, but again the recipient will have to pay it into a bank account rather than receiving cash.

You can also transfer money through AmEx, Thomas Cook or Western Union, which should be a better option provided there are convenient sending/receiving offices. Charges are on a sliding scale, depending on the amount sent, and the money is received in local currency within a few minutes and with no charges at the receiving end. In Switzerland, Western Union has a receiving agent in most towns; call ☎ 0512-22 33 58 for information. A 'moneygram' sent via AmEx is a service usually reserved for its cardholders.

The easiest option if you have a credit card is to get a cash advance, as already discussed – get a friendly benefactor at home to feed the account.

Post Office Accounts

Opening a postcheque account *(Postcheck-konto, compte de cheque postal)* is an efficient way to organise your money in Switzerland, especially if you plan a long or repeat trip to the country. There is no charge to open an account or make withdrawals (you even earn a small amount of interest), and post offices are open longer hours than banks. You can open one on arrival (the drawback is that you have to make your initial deposit in cash). You could also arrange it before departure through your national post office postgiro system (if there is one; it's mostly a European network), which can also transfer funds for you. Don't ask for the paying bills facility as you would then have to lodge a large deposit as a guarantee. Inquire of your national system, as it may enable you to make cash withdrawals directly at Swiss post offices.

Costs

Switzerland, as you will quickly discover, is expensive. Nevertheless, prices aren't quite as horrendous as they were in the mid-1990s, when the Swiss franc was the Rambo of the monetary markets. The consequent dip in tourism and exports prompted a fiscal re-alignment, and nowadays Switzerland is about as expensive as Scandinavia, with prices around 10% higher than in Britain and about 25% higher than in the USA or Australia.

Despite the 'depressing' prices, you needn't emerge from your trip as a pauper. The secret to low costs is cheap accommodation. Camping and staying at hostels are the cheapest option and are often great places to meet people. A student card can cut the cost of entrance fees (see the Student & Youth

Cards section earlier in this chapter) and travel passes almost invariably save money (see the Getting Around chapter). Don't forget to apply for the consumer tax rebate on large purchases (see the Taxes & Refunds section later in this chapter). Hitching, preparing your own meals and avoiding alcohol are other good ways of saving money.

Your budget depends on how you live and travel. If you're moving around fast, going to lots of places, spending time in the big cities, then your day-to-day living costs are going to be quite high; if you stay in one place and get to know your way around, they're likely to come down.

Daily Costs & Budgets Hotel prices are the biggest variable; expect to pay more than the average in Zürich, Geneva, Lucerne, Bern and plush ski resorts. Average costs are:

Hostel	Sfr20 to Sfr34
Cheap hotel	Sfr45
Set lunch	Sfr14 to Sfr18
Two-course dinner (without drinks)	Sfr22 to Sfr35
Loaf of bread	Sfr3.20
Glass of draught beer	Sfr3.60 (0.3L)
Big Mac	Sfr5.90
Petrol	Sfr1.25 per litre (super)
100km by train	Sfr33
City bus ride	Sfr1.50 to Sfr2.80
Local telephone call	Sfr0.60
Time magazine	Sfr5.90

The minimum budget travellers can expect to scrape by on is about Sfr50 (US$35) per day, and that's if they stick to camping/hostelling, self-service restaurants or self-catering, hitching (or have previously purchased a rail pass), hiking instead of using cable cars, visiting only inexpensive sights, and confining alcohol consumption to bottles purchased in supermarkets. Add at least Sfr20 (US$14) a day if you want to stay in a budget pension instead, and a further Sfr30 if you want to enjoy a wider choice of restaurants and sightseeing options. You still have to be very careful with your money at this level; see the boxed text 'Tourist Spending'. If you have a larger budget available, you will have no

trouble spending it! Add an allowance for rail passes or petrol, souvenirs, telephone calls home and postage. Always allow some extra cash for emergencies.

Admission prices are usually Sfr5 to Sfr12 or can even be free (some museums). An occasional expense that can blow any budget is trips in cable cars; these are rarely covered by travel passes (at best you can expect a 25% to 50% reduction). A short to medium ascent can cost Sfr10 to Sfr25. Return trips up Mt Titlis and Schilthorn exceed Sfr70. If you have the time and energy, walk up instead.

Tipping & Bargaining
Tipping is not normally necessary as hotels, restaurants and bars are required by law to include a 15% service charge in bills. Even taxis have a charge included in some towns. If you've been very happy with a meal or service you could round up the bill (locals often do); hotel and railway porters will expect a franc or two per bag. Bargaining is virtually nonexistent, though you could certainly try haggling on hotel prices in the low season.

Taxes & Refunds
VAT (*MWST* in German, *TVA* in French) is levied on goods and services at a rate of 7.5%, except with hotel bills it's only 3.5%. Nonresidents (including Europeans) can claim the tax back on purchases over Sfr500. This doesn't apply to services or

hotel/restaurant bills. Before making a purchase, ensure the shop has the required paperwork. Refunds are given at main border crossings and at Geneva and Zürich airports, or you can claim later by post. Note that you'll be able to buy most things cheaper in neighbouring countries, where you'll also be able to claim tax back (unless you're from the EU), and at a higher rate.

If you're driving to Switzerland, see the Getting There & Away chapter for important information about paying the motorway tax.

POST & COMMUNICATIONS

As you might expect, the mail and telephone systems are very efficient, and with equally predictably high prices. Post office opening times vary but typically are 8 am to noon and 2 to 6.30 pm Monday to Friday, and 8 to 11 am on Saturday. The larger post offices offer services at an emergency counter *(Dringlichkeitsschalter)* outside normal hours (eg, lunchtime, evening, Saturday afternoon, Sunday morning), but transactions are subject to a Sfr1 to Sfr2 surcharge. Many post offices have a Postomat ATM, which allows cash advances with Visa, MasterCard and other cards.

Postal Rates

Within Switzerland, deliveries are either by A-Post (98% delivered next working day) or B-Post (takes two to three days). Letters and postcards by A-Post cost Sfr0.90, or Sfr1.60 if over 250g. By B-Post they cost Sfr0.70 or Sfr1.30.

For international deliveries, the categories are Priority/Prioritaire and Economy/Economique. Priority deliveries to Europe take two to five days, and to elsewhere, four to 10 days. Economy service to Europe takes four to 10 days and to other destinations takes six to 30 days.

Priority rates are:

weight (not over)	Europe (Sfr)	elsewhere (Sfr)
20g	1.10	1.80
50g	1.80	3.00
100g	2.80	4.30
150g	5.00	7.50

Economy rates are:

weight (not over)	Europe (Sfr)	elsewhere (Sfr)
20g	0.90	1.10
50g	1.20	1.40
100g	1.50	2.00
150g	2.20	3.00

Prices for countries bordering the Mediterranean are the same as for Europe. For sending parcels, you can buy special cardboard boxes in various sizes from the post office. Paketpost rates are cheaper for heavier items than Briefpost (letter post).

Receiving Mail

Mail can be sent to any town with a post office and is held for 30 days. Unless specified otherwise, it will go to the town's main post office and you need to show your passport to collect. There's no charge for this service. The international term for this system, *poste restante*, is widely understood although you might prefer to use the German term, *Postlagernde Briefe*. Ask people writing to you to print and/or underline your surname; if an expected letter isn't there, ask staff to check under your first name. The four digit postal code or other means of identifying a particular post office are given in this book for major destinations. If you use these in conjunction with the appropriate term for the post office, namely *Postamt* in German (or if it's the main post office, you can write *Hauptpost* instead), *PTT* in French, *Posta* in Italian, then a letter will get there even if you don't quote a street name. An example of a correctly addressed letter is:

William TELL
Poste Restante
Hauptpost
Luzern 1
CH-6000
Switzerland

AmEx also holds mail (but not parcels) for one month for people who use its cheques or cards.

Telephone

The main telephone provider is Swisscom (☎ 0800-800 114), which evolved from the former state-run monopoly when the telecommunications market was deregulated in 1998. Its public telephone boxes are numerous, and there are invariably some outside post offices and in train stations. The minimum charge is a massive 60c, which then increases by 10c increments. Coin-operated call boxes have mostly been replaced by boxes which take only telephone cards; the *Taxcard* comes in values of Sfr5, Sfr10 and Sfr20, and can be purchased from post offices and other outlets. A few telephones take credit cards. Swisscom's Web site is at www.swisscom.com.

Swisscom has two zones for domestic phone calls – local (German: *Nahbereich*, French: *locale*), for calls within 10km, or national *(Fernbereich, interurbaine)*, for anywhere else. Either way, the normal tariff rate applies from 8 am to 5 pm Monday to Friday; rates are quarter-price from 10 pm to 6 am every night of the week, and half-price at all other times.

To find a telephone number in Switzerland check the telephone book or dial ☎ 111 (minimum charge Sfr1.10/1.80 cheap/normal rate). For Germany dial ☎ 1152, France ☎ 1153, Austria ☎ 1151, and for anywhere else, ☎ 1159. All these inquiry numbers incur premium charges. There's no surcharge for calling the international operator (☎ 1141).

Hotels can charge as much as they like for telephone calls, so avoid using their telephones to make calls (even if they are direct dial). Telephone numbers with the code 0800 are toll-free, those with 0848 are local rate. Numbers beginning with 156 or 157 (without an area code) are always premium rate. Numbers with the code 079 are mobile phones (known as a 'handy' locally), and dialling one is also more expensive.

Since the deregulation of the telecommunications market, alternative providers have sprung up (such as Sunrise, DiAx, Orange) that undercut Swisscom's rates significantly, for both national and international calls. You can access their services via Swisscom public phones. Inquire at telephone discount centres or newsagents. Global One (☎ 0800-199 199) has very cheap rates via its prepaid cards.

International Dialling The country code for Switzerland is ☎ 41. When telephoning Switzerland from abroad you miss out the initial zero from the area code, hence to call Bern you dial ☎ 41 31 (preceded by the overseas access code of the country you're dialling from).

The international access code from Switzerland is ☎ 00. So to call Britain (country code 44), you would start dialling with ☎ 00 44. Other country codes are: Australia ☎ 61, Canada ☎ 1, Hong Kong ☎ 852, India ☎ 91, Ireland ☎ 353, Japan ☎ 81, New Zealand ☎ 64, Singapore ☎ 65, South Africa ☎ 27 and USA ☎ 1.

Swisscom's international cheap rate applies all weekend and Monday to Friday from 7 pm to 8 am to Europe or Africa, 7 pm to 10 am to North and South America, 6 pm to 8 am to the Middle East, and 1 pm to 7 am to the Far East and Australasia. You can direct dial to just about anywhere worldwide. The normal/cheap tariff for one minute is: Sfr0.75/0.60 to Britain, USA and Canada, Sfr1.60/1.20 to Australia, and Sfr1.92/1.44 to New Zealand. Reverse-charge (collect) calls are not possible to every country, so check with the operator.

You can usually save money on the normal international tariff by buying prepaid cards – Swisscom has them to the value of Sfr10, Sfr20, Sfr50 and Sfr100. But other providers are significantly cheaper. Global One's 24-hour rate per minute is Sfr0.20 to the USA, Sfr0.25 to the UK, Sfr0.30 to Australia and Sfr0.75 to New Zealand.

WARNING

From 12 April 2001 there will no longer be regional codes in Switzerland. Instead, the existing regional code, minus the initial '0', will become part of a nine-digit subscriber number. For example, the Lucerne tourist office number will change from ☎ 041-410 71 71 to ☎ 41 410 71 71.

Phonecards There's a wide range of local and international phonecards. Lonely Planet's eKno Communication Card is aimed specifically at independent travellers and provides budget international calls, a range of messaging services, free email and travel information – for local calls, you're usually better off with a local card. You can join on-line at www.ekno.lonelyplanet.com, or by phone from Switzerland by dialling ☎ 0800-111 345. Once you have joined, to use eKno from Switzerland, dial ☎ 0800-897 306.

Check the eKno Web site for joining and access numbers from other countries and updates on super budget local access numbers and new features.

Fax
Larger post offices have an expensive fax service. To send to Switzerland/Europe/elsewhere costs Sfr4/8/9 for the first page plus Sfr0.50/4/5 per following page. To receive a fax costs Sfr4 for the first page and Sfr0.50 for subsequent pages. You'll probably be able to do it cheaper at your hotel.

Email & Internet Access
As you'd expect in such a technologically developed country, email is in common use and cybercafes have opened up in most towns. Surfing costs are generally high (around Sfr15 per hour), though occasionally you might be able to find places with free terminals (eg, in some of the larger libraries). Some hotels have upgraded their phone systems to allow easy modem plug-in in hotel rooms. It is not possible to plug your own modem/laptop into Swisscom public phone boxes, but nearly all of these phone boxes now have an electronic phonebook, which allows you to send short emails worldwide for just Sfr1.50 each.

Switzerland Tourism has an internet Web site: www.switzerlandtourism.ch. It has links to a whole host of other useful Web sites, covering accommodation, sports, travel (eg, with SBB and Swissair timetables), and various other useful related organisations, such as the Swiss Embassy. Just about every Swiss business you can think of has its own Web site (including hotels,

Internet Resources

The World Wide Web is a rich resource for travellers. You can research your trip, hunt down bargain air fares, book hotels, check on weather conditions or chat with locals and other travellers about the best places to visit (or avoid!).

There's no better place to start your Web explorations than the Lonely Planet Web site (www.lonelyplanet.com). Here you'll find succinct summaries on travelling to most places on earth, postcards from other travellers and the Thorn Tree bulletin board, where you can ask questions before you go or dispense advice when you get back. You can also find travel news and updates to many of our most popular guidebooks, and the subWWWay section links you to the most useful travel resources elsewhere on the Web.

restaurants, pubs, festivals etc); your Internet search engine should have no trouble tracking these down. Web addresses are often similar to the email address.

BOOKS
Most books are published in different editions by different publishers in different countries. As a result, a book might be a hardcover rarity in one country while it's readily available in paperback in another. Fortunately, bookshops and libraries search by title or author, so your local bookshop or library is best placed to advise you on the availability of the following recommendations.

English-language books are readily available in Switzerland, though for imported titles you always pay around Sfr2 to Sfr10 more than a straight conversion of the cover price. English-language books can be picked up cheaply second-hand in many cities.

Lonely Planet
Walking in Switzerland by Clem Lindenmayer is detailed, easy to follow and has lots of maps. There's hardly any overlap with this book. Switzerland is also covered in the *Western Europe*, *Central Europe* and *Europe* guides; each has a companion phrasebook.

Guidebooks

Switzerland Tourism sells camping and hiking guides and other books and maps on Switzerland in English. The TCS (Swiss Touring Club) and the SCCV (Swiss Camping & Caravanning Federation) both publish comprehensive guides to Swiss camp sites. The TCS guide has more detail, but annoyingly for backpackers it's printed on very heavy paper. *Off the Beaten Track – Switzerland* (various authors) concentrates, as the name suggests, on lesser known destinations, while missing out places like Geneva altogether.

Switzerland: A Phaidon Cultural Guide, edited by Niklaus Flüeler, gives a vast amount of detail on art and architecture. *Baedeker's Switzerland* has very extensive information on sightseeing in an A-Z format, but barely deals with accommodation, restaurants or transport details. Michelin's green *Tourist Guide to Switzerland* is similar.

Living and Working in Switzerland by David Hampshire is self-explanatory. This excellent practical guide covers every angle thoroughly, and is updated every two years. *Culture Shock! Switzerland* by Shirley Eu-Wong is a less comprehensive, more personal guide for foreign residents and visitors.

Nonfiction

The best book for people wanting to understand the historical, social and political side of Switzerland is *Why Switzerland?* by Jonathan Steinberg. His enthusiasm for Switzerland leaps off the page. *Switzerland – People, State, Economy, Culture* by Kümmerly + Frey (the map publishers) is a compact but very informative book that's updated annually.

The Xenophobe's Guide to the Swiss by Paul Bilton is an informative and sometimes amusing small volume. Bilton covers similar ground but from a personal point of view in his diary-style *The Perpetual Tourist*. The latter is published by Bergli Books (☎ 061-373 27 77, ✆ info@bergli.ch), Eptingerstrasse 5, Basel, CH-4502, a Swiss publisher which offers a number of books that illuminate aspects of Switzerland.

These include *Ticking Along With the Swiss* and *Ticking Along Too*, both edited by Dianne Dicks, which are crammed full of anecdotes and stories about the Swiss. Although there is a common perception to the contrary, the Swiss do have a sense of humour, as the book *Tell me a Swiss Joke* by René Hildbrand indicates.

Two entertaining anecdotal travel books about Europe, where the author spent a fair amount of time in Switzerland, are Mark Twain's *A Tramp Abroad* and Bill Bryson's *Neither Here Nor There*. What's the best way to make a Swiss roll? Take him to a mountain top and give him a push (Bryson's joke, not mine). The Swiss chapter in Mark Lawson's *The Battle for Room Service* is also very amusing.

The Arts Council of Switzerland is called Pro Helvetia (☎ 01-267 71 71, fax 267 71 06, ✆ phmail@pro-helvetia.ch) and it's at Hirschengraben 22, CH-8024, Zürich. Pro Helvetia promotes cultural activities and publishes a range of books covering specific interests such as music, dance, ballet, and languages. It can send books abroad.

Fiction

Graham Greene's *Dr Fischer of Geneva or The Bomb Party* is a short but entertaining novel about the doctor, a misanthropic control-freak, and his son-in-law. Anita Brookner won the Booker Prize in 1984 for *Hotel du Lac*, a novel set around Lake Geneva, which homes in on out-of-season hotel guests. Patricia Highsmith's *Small g: a summer Idyll* is a rather lightweight story about some gay people living in Zürich. Thomas Mann's *The Magic Mountain* is a weighty, reflective novel set in the Alps. The mountains also influenced the work of John Ruskin and Leslie Stephen. Mary Shelley wrote *Frankenstein* in Switzerland and set much of the action around Lake Geneva. This was when she was a neighbour of Lord Byron, who wrote the poem *The Prisoner of Chillon* about the unfortunate but true fate of Bonivard, chained to a pillar in the dank dungeon below the water level in Château de Chillon. Sherlock Holmes met his death in Switzerland, in a struggle with Moriarty at Reichenbach Falls. This episode is recounted by Sexton Blake in the short story *The Adventure of the Final Problem*.

Heidi, the famous story for children by Johanna Spyri, is set in the Maienfeld region, just north of the Graubünden capital of Chur. The *Chalet School* series by Elinor Brent-Dyer is very popular with young girls, and many of the books are set in Switzerland.

NEWSPAPERS & MAGAZINES

English-language newspapers are widely available on the evening of the same day or a day late (depending on where you are) and cost around Sfr3.50 or more. All the main British and American titles are available; the *Guardian*, *Financial Times*, *Herald Tribune* and *USA Today* tend to hit the news stands the earliest. If you don't want to buy a newspaper, consider having a coffee in a plush hotel and reading the newspapers there. English-language newspapers are held in the larger libraries in main cities.

In the news-magazine category, *Time*, *Newsweek* and the *Economist* are widely available. A local English-language magazine worth looking at is *Swiss News* (Sfr7.50 monthly). It's fairly sober and dwells rather a lot on business news, but it still has good cultural features and illuminating news snippets, as well as a comprehensive *What's on in Switzerland* section.

RADIO & TV

The BBC World Service (Web site: www.bbc.co.uk/worldservice/schedules) broadcasts on short wave at 3955, 6195, 9410, 12095 and 15575kHz (but not all at the same time) and on medium wave on 648kHz. The American Forces Network is on the FM band (101.8MHz) and The Voice of America (VOA) can usually be found on 1197kHz.

Swiss Radio International (SRI; Web site: www.swissinfo.org) broadcasts in English. Pick it up on 3985, 6165 and 9535kHz. It also has a 24-hour telephone news service in English (☎ 157 300 30); calls cost

Sfr1.50 per minute. World Radio Geneva (FM 88.4) is a 24-hour, English-language station broadcasting music and news that can be picked up throughout the Lake Geneva area.

TVs in hotel rooms almost invariably offer cable or satellite viewing, usually with a couple of English-language channels such as CNN (the American Cable News Network), BBC Prime or the news-based BBC World, as well as music channels, Eurosport and a host of other options. Often radio stations will be linked in too, including SRI and BBC World Service broadcasts.

The Swiss complain that their national TV is boring. It's highly information-oriented, designed to clue-in the populace on current affairs. The Swiss tune in to the networks of neighbouring countries for their entertainment.

VIDEO SYSTEMS

If you want to record or buy video tapes to play back home, you won't get a picture if the image registration systems are different. Switzerland uses PAL (as do Britain and Australia), which is incompatible with the North American and Japanese NTSC system.

PHOTOGRAPHY & VIDEO

Inter Discount has low prices for film in Switzerland. For a 36-exposure roll it charges Sfr7.50 for Kodak Gold and Sfr17.90 for Kodachrome. Some department stores have decent prices too, especially for two or three-pack deals. Buy plenty – as soon as you hit the mountains you'll reel off a roll in no time. Photography in snow can be tricky. The whiteness of snow can dominate a picture and cause the subject to be underexposed (dark and dull on the photograph). Some cameras will allow you to compensate for this. If you buy slide film (*Diafilm* in German), check whether processing *(Entwicklung)* is included, and whether it has to be done in Switzerland.

TIME

Swiss time is GMT/UTC plus one hour. If it's noon in Bern it is 11 am in London,

6 am in New York and Toronto, 3 am in San Francisco, 9 pm in Sydney and 11 pm in Auckland. Daylight-saving time comes into effect at midnight on the last Saturday in March, when the clocks are moved forward one hour; they go back again on the last Saturday in October. The Swiss use the 24-hour clock when writing times, instead of dividing the day up into am and pm.

Note that in German *halb* is used to indicate the half-hour before the hour, hence *halb acht* means 7.30, not 8.30.

ELECTRICITY
Voltages & Cycles
The electric current in Switzerland is 220V, 50Hz. Most appliances that are set up for 240V will handle 220V quite happily without modifications (and vice versa), but anything set up for 110/125V would require a transformer if it doesn't already have built-in voltage adjustment. Appliances set for 60Hz (eg, as sold in North America) will run slower on Switzerland's 50Hz, so electric clocks and tape recorders will be useless, but things like electric razors, hair dryers, irons and radios will still be fine.

Plugs & Sockets
In a country where most things are well organised, plugs are a pain. Plugs and sockets vary, even sometimes inside the same building. Pins are round – three is usual, but two is not uncommon. The standard continental type, with two round pins, can be used in a three-pin socket, but it depends on the shape. Many are recessed, either circular, or more commonly, a squashed hexagonal (six-sided) shape. Continental plugs are no good for these. Basically this means that you may be able to get by with the standard continental plug, but it's probably easier to buy the hexagonal shape once in Switzerland as this also fits into the three-pin round socket. To wire it up, getting the earth wire in the centre pin is crucial. It doesn't matter which way around the other wires go.

Using an adapter is an alternative to rewiring. Most hotels of the tourist class and above have adapters you can use, but they may not fit plugs from your home country.

You can try and buy an adapter before you leave home, but then it may not fit the Swiss sockets (many so-called 'universal' adapters don't). There's generally no problem in finding a spare power point, even in hostels or camp grounds.

WEIGHTS & MEASURES
The metric system is used. Note that cheese and other foods may be priced per 100g rather than per kg (a futile attempt to cushion the shock of the high prices?). Like other continental Europeans, the Swiss indicate decimals with commas and thousands with points.

LAUNDRY
There is no shortage of coin-operated or service laundrettes *(Waschanstalt, laverie, lavanderia)* in cities – some are listed in this book. Expect to pay Sfr10 or more to wash and dry a 5kg load. Many youth hostels also have washing machines, and prices are usually slightly cheaper. Tourist class hotels always have a laundry service, but prices are high, and are charged per item.

TOILETS
Public toilets are invariably spick-and-span. Usually you'll find urinals are free but cubicles may have a pay slot of between Sfr0.20 and Sfr1. The most expensive cubicles in the country are probably those in Zürich Hauptbahnhof, costing a bladder-busting Sfr2. Toilet cubicles in self-service restaurants are generally free; they're supposed to be for customers only, but who will know?

HEALTH
No vaccinations are necessary for travel to Switzerland. However, if you're coming from an area where cholera and yellow fever are prevalent, such as Africa or South America, you'll need an International Health Certificate.

Some routine vaccinations are recommended for all travellers. They include polio, tetanus and diphtheria, and sometimes measles, mumps and rubella. These vaccinations are usually administered in childhood, but some require booster shots.

There is no state health service in Switzerland and all treatment must be paid for. No reciprocal agreements exist for free treatment with any other country. Medication and consultations are expensive; charges vary, but you can expect the briefest consultation to cost about Sfr120. The local tourist office can tell you where to get treatment if no contact is given in this book.

Predeparture Planning
Health Insurance Make sure that you have adequate health insurance. See Travel Insurance under Visas & Documents in this chapter for details.

Other Preparations If you require a particular medication take an adequate supply, as it may not be available locally. Take part of the packaging showing the generic name rather than the brand, which will make getting replacements easier. It's a good idea to have a legible prescription or letter from your doctor to show that you legally use the medication. It's always a good idea to carry a small medical kit, even in a place like Switzerland where first-aid items are readily available.

Basic Rules
Switzerland is a healthy place, but it still pays to take care in what you eat and drink.

Tap water is safe to drink but always beware of natural water, even crystal clear Alpine streams. Take a water bottle with you if you're going on long walking trips. Drinking fountains are found along many well-transited hiking paths and are safe to drink from. In the unlikely event you need to resort to natural water, it should be boiled vigorously for five minutes; remember that at high altitude water boils at a lower temperature, so germs are less likely to be killed. Iodine is very effective in purifying water and is available in tablet form (such as Potable Aqua), but follow the directions carefully and remember that too much iodine can be harmful. Occasionally you will come across a tap or fountain labelled *Kein Trinkwasser* or *eau non potable* – that means it's *not* drinking quality.

Food should not really cause any health problem – salads, fruit and dairy products are all fine but try to vary your diet. Be careful with food that has been cooked and left to go cold, which might happen in some self-service places.

Medical Kit Check List

Following is a list of items you should consider including in your medical kit – consult your pharmacist for brands available in your country.

☐ **Aspirin or paracetamol (acetaminophen in the USA)** – for pain or fever

☐ **Antihistamine** – for allergies, eg, hay fever; to ease the itch from insect bites or stings; and to prevent motion sickness

☐ **Cold and flu tablets, throat lozenges and nasal decongestant**

☐ **Multivitamins** – consider for long trips, when dietary vitamin intake may be inadequate

☐ **Antibiotics** – consider including these if you're travelling well off the beaten track; see your doctor, as they must be prescribed, and carry the prescription with you

☐ **Loperamide or diphenoxylate** – 'blockers' for diarrhoea

☐ **Prochlorperazine or metaclopramide** – for nausea and vomiting

☐ **Rehydration mixture** – to prevent dehydration, which may occur, for example, during bouts of diarrhoea; particularly important when travelling with children

☐ **Insect repellent, sunscreen, lip balm and eye drops**

☐ **Calamine lotion, sting relief spray or aloe vera** – to ease irritation from sunburn and insect bites or stings

☐ **Antifungal cream or powder** – for fungal skin infections and thrush

☐ **Antiseptic (such as povidone-iodine)** – for cuts and grazes

☐ **Bandages, Band-Aids (plasters) and other wound dressings**

☐ **Water purification tablets or iodine**

☐ **Scissors, tweezers and a thermometer** – note that mercury thermometers are prohibited by airlines

Environmental Hazards

Altitude Sickness Lack of oxygen at high altitudes (over 2500m) affects most people to some extent. The effect may be mild or severe and occurs because less oxygen reaches the muscles and the brain at high altitude, requiring the heart and lungs to compensate by working harder. Symptoms of Acute Mountain Sickness (AMS) usually develop during the first 24 hours at altitude but may be delayed up to three weeks. Mild symptoms include headache, lethargy, dizziness, difficulty sleeping and loss of appetite. AMS may become more severe without warning and can be fatal. Severe symptoms include breathlessness, a dry, irritative cough (which may progress to the production of pink, frothy sputum), severe headache, lack of coordination and balance, confusion, irrational behaviour, vomiting, drowsiness and unconsciousness. There is no hard-and-fast rule as to what is too high: AMS has been fatal at 3000m, although 3500m to 4500m is the usual range.

Treat mild symptoms by resting at the same altitude until recovery, usually a day or two. Paracetamol or aspirin can be taken for headaches. If symptoms persist or become worse, however, *immediate descent is necessary*; even 500m can help. Drug treatments should never be used to avoid descent or to enable further ascent.

Hypothermia Hypothermia occurs when the body loses heat faster than it can produce it and the core temperature of the body falls. It is surprisingly easy to progress from very cold to dangerously cold due to a combination of wind, wet clothing, fatigue and hunger, even if the air temperature is above freezing. It is best to dress in layers; silk, wool and some of the new artificial fibres are all good insulating materials. A hat is important, as a lot of heat is lost through the head. A strong, waterproof outer layer (and a 'space' blanket for emergencies) is essential. Carry basic supplies, including food containing simple sugars to generate heat quickly and fluid to drink.

Symptoms of hypothermia are exhaustion, numb skin (particularly toes and fingers), shivering, slurred speech, irrational or violent behaviour, lethargy, stumbling, dizzy spells, muscle cramps and violent bursts of energy. Irrationality may take the form of sufferers claiming they are warm and trying to take off their clothes.

To treat mild hypothermia, first get the person out of the wind and/or rain, remove their clothing if it's wet and replace it with dry, warm clothing. Give them hot liquids – not alcohol – and some high-kilojoule, easily digestible food. Do not rub victims; allow them to slowly warm themselves instead. This should be enough to treat the early stages of hypothermia. The early recognition and treatment of mild hypothermia is the only way to prevent severe hypothermia, which is a critical condition.

Motion Sickness Eating lightly before and during a trip will reduce the chances of motion sickness. If you are prone to motion sickness try to find a place that minimises movement – near the wing on aircraft, close to midships on boats, near the centre on buses. Fresh air usually helps; reading and cigarette smoke don't. Commercial motion-sickness preparations, which can cause drowsiness, have to be taken before the trip commences. Ginger (available in capsule form) and peppermint (including mint-flavoured sweets) are natural preventatives.

Sunburn You can get sunburnt surprisingly quickly, even through cloud. Use a sunscreen, a hat, and a barrier cream for your nose and lips. Calamine lotion or a commercial after-sun preparation are good for mild sunburn. Protect your eyes with good quality sunglasses, particularly if you will be near water or snow.

Infectious Diseases

Diarrhoea Simple things like a change of water, food or climate can all cause a mild bout of diarrhoea, but a few rushed toilet trips with no other symptoms is not indicative of a major problem.

Dehydration is the main danger with any diarrhoea, particularly in children or the elderly as dehydration can occur quite quickly. Under all circumstances *fluid replacement* (at least equal to the volume being lost) is the most important thing to remember. Weak black tea with a little sugar, soda water, or soft drinks allowed to go flat and diluted 50% with clean water are all good. Keep drinking small amounts often. Stick to a bland diet as you recover.

HIV & AIDS Infection with the human immunodeficiency virus (HIV) may lead to acquired immune deficiency syndrome (AIDS), which is a fatal disease. Any exposure to blood, blood products or body fluids may put the individual at risk. The disease is often transmitted through sexual contact or dirty needles – vaccinations, acupuncture, tattooing and body piercing can be potentially as dangerous as intravenous drug use. HIV/AIDS can also be spread through infected blood transfusions; some developing countries cannot afford to screen blood used for transfusions.

Cuts, Bites & Stings

Ticks Ticks are found throughout Switzerland up to an altitude of 1200m, and typically live in underbrush at the forest edge or beside walking tracks. A very small proportion are carriers of bacterial and viral encephalitis diseases, which may become serious if not detected early. Both types of encephalitis initially appear with influenza-like symptoms, and can affect the skin, nervous system, muscles or the heart, often causing headaches and sore joints. Treatment is usually with antibiotics, but inoculations are available for those particularly at risk. In rare instances, encephalitis can be fatal.

The tick embeds its head in the host's skin in order to suck its blood. While a good insect repellent will often stop ticks from biting, Swiss medical authorities now strongly discourage using oil, alcohol or the heat of a flame to persuade ticks to let go, as this may actually release encephalitis pathogens into the bloodstream. The recommended removal method is to grab the insect's head with a pair of tweezers (or ideally a special tick-removal instrument sold cheaply in local pharmacies) then pull the tick out slowly without 'levering' or twisting the hand.

Snakes Snakes tend to keep a very low profile, but to minimise your chances of being bitten, always wear boots, socks and long trousers when walking through undergrowth where snakes may be present. Tramp heavily and they'll usually slither away before you come near. Don't put your hands into holes and crevices, and be careful when collecting firewood.

Switzerland is home to several types of snakes, a couple of which can deliver a nasty although not fatal bite. They are more prevalent in the mountains. If the worst happens, keep the victim calm and still, wrap the bitten limb tightly, as you would for a sprained ankle, and then attach a splint to immobilise it. Then seek medical help. Tourniquets and sucking out the poison are now comprehensively discredited.

Rabies Though rare in Europe, rabies sometimes crops up. Many animals can be infected (such as dogs, cats and foxes) and it is their saliva which is infectious. Any bite, scratch or even lick from an animal should be cleaned immediately and thoroughly. Scrub with soap and running water, and then apply alcohol or iodine solution. Medical help should be sought promptly to receive a course of injections to prevent the onset of symptoms and death.

WOMEN TRAVELLERS

Women travellers should experience no special problems. Some older Swiss men believe that a woman's place is in the home – under Swiss marriage laws, wives weren't granted equal rights until 1988! – but the independence of female travellers is respected. Sexual harassment (catcalls and the like) is much less common than in most other countries, though Ticino males tend to suffer from the same machismo leanings as their Italian counterparts. If it happens, it's best to ignore the perpetrator(s). Common sense is the best guide to dealing with potentially dangerous situations like hitching, walking alone at night etc.

Some women experience irregular periods when travelling, due to the upset in routine. Don't forget to take time zones into account if you're on the pill; if you run into intestinal problems, the pill may not be absorbed. Ask your physician about these matters.

Organisations

INFRA is a nationwide network of information centres for women, which can advise on a range of topics. Offices include those in Bern (☎ 031-311 17 95), Bollwerk 39, and Basel (☎ 061-693 05 55), Genzacherstrasse 34. Somebody usually speaks English.

GAY & LESBIAN TRAVELLERS

Gays and lesbians should get in touch with their national organisation at home for more comprehensive information than space permits here. The *Spartacus International Gay Guide*, published by Bruno Gmünder (Berlin), is a good international directory of gay entertainment venues worldwide (mainly for men). The same publisher also puts out *Stuttgart & Zürich Von Hinten*, covering those cities and most of Switzerland. Lesbians can turn to *Places of Interest for Women* (Ferrari Publications).

Public attitudes to homosexuality in Switzerland are reasonably tolerant. The revision of the criminal code on sexual offences, granting equality of treatment under the law for homosexuals, was approved by referendum in May 1992. That means, among other things, that the age of consent for gay sex is the same as for heterosexuals – 16.

The Swiss gay scene, according to the Spartacus guide, is 'renowned for its high standards of service, cleanliness and friendliness'. There are a number of gay bars and saunas in all the main cities. Some bars are listed in this book, as well as contact addresses for gay and lesbian organisations in Basel, Bern, Geneva and Zürich. The *Cruiser* magazine (☎ 01-261 82 00, @ info@cruiser), Postfach, CH-8025, Zürich, has extensive listings of gay and lesbian organisations, places and events in Switzerland (Sfr4.50). Pink Cross (Web site: www.pinkcross.ch) is

a very brief guide to the Swiss gay scene in French and German. There are pride parades in Geneva (early July) and Zürich (mid-July).

DISABLED TRAVELLERS

If you have a physical disability, get in touch with your national support organisation at home (preferably the travel officer if there is one). They often have complete libraries devoted to travel, and can put you in touch with travel agents who specialise in tours for the disabled, or provide useful advice on independent travel.

Within Switzerland, many hotels have disabled access (though budget pensions tend not to have lifts), and most train stations have a mobile lift for train-boarding. Switzerland Tourism and local tourist offices should be able to offer travel tips for the disabled. The Swiss Invalid Association (☎ 062-206 88 88, fax 206 88 89), or Schweizerischer Invalidenverband, is at Froburgstrasse 4, CH-4600 Olten. It has some information in English, and a travel agency; details are on the Web site (www.siv.ch) in German, French and Italian.

The British-based Royal Association for Disability and Rehabilitation (RADAR; ☎ 020-7250 3222) has some information about travel abroad, but perhaps a better organisation is the Holiday Care Service (☎ 01293-77 45 35), 2nd floor, Imperial Buildings, Victoria Rd, Horley Surrey, RH6 6PZ. This charity has information sheets on several countries, including Switzerland; send a stamped addressed envelope for details.

SENIOR TRAVELLERS

Senior citizens are entitled to many discounts in Europe on public transport (no longer on Swiss railways, but sometimes on cable cars), museum admission fees, ski passes and so on. Proof of age must be shown. The minimum qualifying age for Swiss men is 65; for Swiss women, the age is 62, rising to 63 in 2001, and eventually to 65. Tourists will *probably* be held to the same age limits within Switzerland. The abbreviation for senior citizens is *AHV* in German and *AVS* in French.

In your home country, a lower age may already entitle you to all sorts of interesting travel packages and discounts (on car hire, for instance) through organisations and travel agents that cater for senior travellers. Start hunting at your local senior citizens advice bureau.

TRAVEL WITH CHILDREN

Successful travel with young children can require some special effort. Don't try to overdo things; even for adults, packing too much into the time available can cause problems. And make sure the activities include the kids as well – balance that day seeing Lugano's churches with a day in the miniature fun park (Swissminiatur) at nearby Melide. Include children in the trip planning; if they have helped to work out where you will be going, they will be much more interested when they get there. See Lonely Planet's *Travel with Children* by Maureen Wheeler for much more information.

Places that might interest kids include Klagenfurt's Europa Park, the Swiss Museum of Games in Vevey, the frogs in Estaveyer's Regional Museum, the mirror maze in Lucerne's Glacier Garden, and the Knie Children's Zoo in Rapperswil. Look out also for the Knie travelling circus in summer.

Hotels that offer special facilities for families (eg supervised play rooms) are listed on the Switzerland Tourism Web site at www.switzerlandtourism.ch. Families should acquire the Family Card, good for free travel for children (see Swiss Travel Passes in the Getting Around chapter).

DANGERS & ANNOYANCES

The average Swiss person's idea of living-on-the-edge law-breaking is to drop a sweet-wrapper on the pavement, or maybe if they're feeling really anarchic, a bit of jaywalking (for which a fine is theoretically possible, but unlikely). That's not to knock the Swiss – rather that than the situation in places in the USA, where trading gunshots is a polite way to say hello. The Swiss are very rule-oriented, and some will have no qualms about pointing out to you any transgression

you might make. Crime may be relatively uncommon but it's not unknown, so don't become too casual about security. Based on the conviction rate, nearly half of all crimes are committed by foreigners.

Emergency telephone numbers you can call are police ☎ 117, fire brigade ☎ 118, motoring assistance ☎ 140, and ambulance ☎ 144 (most areas). In call boxes you need to insert 60c, though it comes back at the end. (Too bad if you have an emergency and have no change!) For helicopter rescue by REGA, the airborne emergency service, call ☎ 1414.

Theft

Even in 'safe' Switzerland, you should always be security-conscious – you're never more vulnerable to theft than when travelling. Be wary of leaving valuables in hotel rooms. Staff will look after expensive items if you ask them, even in hostels. Don't even leave valuables in cars – especially not overnight. Beware of pickpockets (who thrive in crowds) and snatch-thieves (a daypack is more secure than a shoulder bag). Carry your own padlock for hostel lockers. Use a moneybelt and keep some emergency money hidden away from your main stash.

Generally, keep your wits about you, and be suspicious of anything out of the ordinary, even unlikely offers of help. Sadly, other travellers are sometimes the people you most have to guard against.

In the event of theft or loss, get a police report – this will be necessary for you to claim on travel insurance. Your consulate should be able to help if you're left in a desperate situation.

Drugs

Always treat drugs with a great deal of caution. Don't ever think about trying to carry drugs across the border. There is a fair bit of dope available, and some young Swiss in places like Geneva aren't particularly shy about smoking it in public parks. It's illegal of course, but the police tend not to do much about it. If you're unlucky and get caught with a small amount of dope clearly for personal use, you might just get a small fine, say around Sfr100 to Sfr400. Possession of over about 30g may mean being looked upon as a dealer, and possibly liable for a large fine and jail or deportation. The police spend more time trying to solve the heroin problem – Switzerland has a surprisingly large number of young heroin addicts, and possession of this drug can get you in real trouble.

LEGAL MATTERS

Switzerland is notorious for its draconian laws covering imprisonment on remand (*Untersuchungshaft* in German, *prévention* in French). Anybody can be imprisoned for months without charge or trial, purely on suspicion of having committed a crime. Minor transgressions are subject to a fine, which is often referred to as an 'administrative measure'.

Large cities and some towns offer free or inexpensive legal advice, including in English – the local tourist office should be able to help you find a suitable legal office *(Notariat)*. Alternatively, many consulates keep lists of suitable lawyers. In Geneva, for example, free legal advice is dispensed at Permanence de l'Ordre des Avocats (☎ 022-310 24 11), 13 rue Verdaine, from 10 am to 7 pm weekdays, though you have to pay Sfr60 tax for the consultation. For Zürich,

the city Web site (www.stadt-zuerich.ch) gives contact details (in German) for all sorts of legal, cultural and social resources.

Local Laws

There are 26 different cantons, and each has its own cantonal laws. Generally the rules and regulations are the same, but there may be some variation in specifics. In Zürich, for example, women are not allowed to use or carry a pepper spray *(Pfefferspray)* to deter attackers, whereas in neighbouring Aargau they are. Similarly, busking (playing music in the streets) may be allowed in some places and not in others, or only between certain times. Very confusing for a visitor, but all you can do is ask the local police or tourist office if you're unsure about anything. Prostitution is legal, but not in residential areas.

BUSINESS HOURS

Most shops are open 8 am to 6.30 pm Monday to Friday, with a 90-minute or two-hour break for lunch at noon. A few close on Monday morning. In towns there's often a late shopping day till 9 pm, typically on Thursday or Friday. Closing times on Saturday are usually 4 or 5 pm. In some places souvenir shops can open on Sunday, though

Rules for Life

Switzerland is a very regulated society and rules are everywhere – some may seem laughably petty to outsiders, but the Swiss learn to live with them. Restrictions against working on Sunday, the day of rest, even extend to prohibiting gardening or washing the car. As you might expect, there are strict regulations against making noise during anti-social hours, but the following are also genuine rules for some (or most) apartment dwellers:

• No bathing or flushing the toilet is allowed between 10 pm and 7 am (if using the toilet between these hours, men must sit!)
• Airing of bedding from windows is allowed only during specified times of the day
• Use of the communal washing machine and laundry room is prohibited between certain hours
• No footwear is to be left outside the door
• Net curtains at windows are compulsory

But controls and civil restrictions occur on a more serious level too. In 1990, there was public outrage when news broke that the federal police had kept 900,000 secret files on Swiss citizens and foreigners – that's over 13% of the population!

it's unusual for other shops to be open that day – exceptions are Zürich's Shop Ville and supermarkets at some train stations.

Offices are typically open 8 am to noon and 1.30 or 2 pm to 5 or 6 pm Monday to Friday; they're rarely open on Saturday. Banks are open 8.30 am to 4.30 pm Monday to Friday, with local variations.

PUBLIC HOLIDAYS & SPECIAL EVENTS

National holidays are:

New Year's Day 1 January
Easter March/April – Good Friday, Easter Sunday and Monday
Ascension Day 40th day after Easter
Whit Sunday and Monday 7th week after Easter
National Day 1 August
Christmas Day 25 December
St Stephen's Day 26 December

Some cantons observe their own special holidays and extra religious days, eg, 2 January,

1 May (Labour Day), Corpus Christi, 15 August (Assumption) and 1 November (All Saints' Day). Ticino and Lucerne are the luckiest (laziest?) cantons, enjoying an extra eight/seven public holidays respectively. The third Sunday in September is a federal fast day, and some cantons (eg, Vaud and Neuchâtel) take the following Monday as a holiday.

Numerous events take place at a local level throughout the year, so it's worth checking with the local tourist office. Most dates vary from year to year. Following is a brief selection of the main events; more information and further special events are mentioned in the relevant sections. Switzerland Tourism annually brings out a booklet giving an exhaustive list of local events, including cultural, social and sporting occasions.

January

Costumed sleigh-rides in the Engadine, and the Lauberhorn ski race at Wengen. International Hot Air Balloon Week in Château d'Oex and the Vogel Gryff festival in Basel.

EXPO.02 – Switzerland Welcomes the World

In 2002 Switzerland hosts Expo.02, which is expected to pull in nearly 11 million visitors over 180 days. It will be based at five locations in western Switzerland from 3 May to 29 October.

Each expo site will explore a different theme. Advance publicity suggests that the displays will be ambitious, imaginative, and not a little pretentious. Expo.02, it is intended, will 'illustrate the potential of a nation' and 'will not merely reproduce what has already been experienced, it will redefine what we know and present the ordinary in extraordinary ways.'

Neuchâtel explores nature and artificiality ('code word: need. In a phrase: red tomatoes roll'. That's their phrase – don't ask me what it means!). Displays include simulations of violent weather and some sort of art event involving a toilet. Murten's subject is the moment and eternity ('in a phrase: I drink the dew of rose leaves'); there'll be a photographic project and a genuine wedding chapel catering for importunate couples. Biel's task is to explore power and freedom ('watering flowers in the rain'). Yverdon-les-Bains deals with the Universe and I, including sexuality ('you kiss mighty good') and featuring performances staged within an oversized blood corpuscle. The fifth site is a mobile one that will roam around Jura canton. It concentrates on notions of limits ('the foal frolicks'), and will begin its frolicking in 2000, before the expo officially begins.

Expect the region's infrastructure to be given a facelift prior to the expo (also expect other regions to try to cash in on the extra visitors by staging related events). To supplement existing hotels, 'modular hotels' are being constructed, by which modules (ie rooms) can be added on like Lego to achieve any shape or size of building. There will also be tent villages established.

For more information contact Expo.02 (☎ 032-726 20 01, fax 726 20 05), Place de la Gare, 2001 Neuchâtel. Admission to the sites is expected to cost Sfr48 for one day, Sfr120 for three days or Sfr240 for the season. Check out the Web site at www.expo-01.ch.

February

Carnival time *(Fasnacht)* in many towns, particularly in Catholic cantons, with parades, costumes and musicians. Basel's Fasnacht is best known, but it's also lively in Zürich, Lucerne and Fribourg.

March

Engadine Skiing Marathon, Graubünden. Cow fighting (yes, the cows fight each other!) starts at the end of the month in lower Valais and continues for most of the summer.

April

Meeting of the Landsgemeinde in Appenzell.

May

May Day celebrations, especially in St Gallen and Vaud.

June

The annual performance of *William Tell* starts in Interlaken, and continues until early September. Open-air music festivals in Ticino (late June to August).

July

Montreux Jazz Festival, Nyon Rock Festival.

August

National Day (1 August) celebrations and fireworks, and Swiss wrestling in the Emmental. The middle of the month sees the start of the Geneva Festival and the International Festival of Music in Lucerne.

September

Shooting contest *(Knabenschiessen)* in Zürich, and a religious festival in Einsiedeln.

October

Vintage festivals in wine-growing regions such as Morges, Neuchâtel and Lugano.

November

Open-air festivals on the fourth Monday in November including the onion market *(Zibelmärit)* in Bern.

December

St Nicholas Day celebrations on 6 December and the Escalade festival in Geneva.

COURSES

Apart from learning new physical skills, you can enrich your mind in a variety of structured ways. Probably the best organisation for adult education courses in Switzerland is the Migros Klubschule *(école-club, scuola club)*. It has schools in all the large towns and cities, and offers a huge number of courses, including mainstream and marginal subjects such as astrology, astronomy, bonsai, cooking, dance, karate, photography, politics and music. It

also has comprehensive coverage of languages, including Swiss-German.

Courses start at different times of the year and durations vary. Language courses range in intensity, frequency and focus (eg, conversational, examination-oriented); expect to pay between Sfr12 to Sfr18 per hour for group lessons. Write in advance for information to the schools mentioned in the sections on Bern, Zürich, Geneva and Lugano. The language school, Inlingua, also has many outlets in Switzerland.

WORK

It's not impossible to find legal work, especially if you're an EU citizen. Obviously your chances are vastly improved if you're fluent in at least one of the local languages. The trick is to start writing or asking around early. If you do find a temporary job, the pay is likely to be less than that offered to locals, but the rates will still be good. For the full story on regulations and possibilities concerning employment, turn to *Living and Working in Switzerland*, mentioned earlier under Books.

Work Permits

In December 1998 Switzerland and the EU signed a bilateral agreement concerning the free movement of persons. This gives a timetable for the abolishment of employment/wage quotas and other discriminatory controls between the EU and Switzerland. However, the earliest it can come into force will be 1 January 2001. Even then it will take a dozen years before EU citizens will have full residence and employment rights within Switzerland (the first easing of controls occurs after two years).

At the time of writing, the official line was that only foreigners with special skills could work legally, and the job offer and paperwork should be sorted out before departure. Getting a work permit in this way can be tough, but in practice people manage to find work upon arrival just by asking around. Although it's beyond their brief, tourist offices can often be helpful. Employers sometimes have unallocated work permits that they can assign to you, or there's always the possibility of undeclared cash-in-hand work. If you get caught working illegally you can be fined and deported.

The seasonal 'A' permit *(Permis A, Saisonbewilligung)* is valid for up to nine months, and the elusive and much sought-after 'B' permit *(Permis B, Aufenthaltsbewilligung)* is renewable and valid for a year.

Types of Work

Language skills are particularly crucial for any type of work in service industries. Wages are among the highest in Europe, even for casual workers. Generally, the ski resorts are the most likely places to find something. *Working in Ski Resorts – Europe* (paperback) by Victoria Pybus and Charles James provides specific information and case histories. Potentially all sorts of jobs are available during the season, ranging from snow clearing to washing dishes. Workers in a ski resort would normally get a ski pass thrown in, though they may not get too many spare hours to use it. Your best chance of finding work is to start writing or asking around early – in summer for winter work and in winter for summer work. Try to get it all organised before places close for the off season (November to mid-December, mid-April to late June).

Hotel work has the advantage of including meals and accommodation. Within Switzerland, check the ads for hotel and restaurant positions in the weekly newspaper, *hotel + touristik revue* (Sfr4.10), which is mostly in German. Its online version is at www.htr.ch; other useful Web sites for job hunting include www.hoteljob.ch and www.gastronet.ch.

In October, work is available in vineyards in Vaud and Valais. Rates are good and the quality of accommodation and food offered to grape-pickers is usually better than in other countries. WWOOF (Willing Workers on Organic Farms; ✆ wwoof@dataway.ch) will find volunteer work on small organic farms throughout Switzerland. You can travel about, working on a succession of farms, but you usually only get board and lodging, not wages. For information, send two international reply coupons to WWOOF Switzerland, Postfach 59, CH-8124, Maur.

Work Your Way Around the World by Susan Griffith gives good, practical advice on a wide range of issues. The same publisher, Vacation Work, has a book entitled *The Au Pair and Nanny's Guide to Working Abroad* by Susan Griffith & Sharon Legg, which may also help. Busking (playing music in the street) is fairly common nowadays in Swiss towns and may make you a few francs if you have the required skills. Check with the local police if you plan to do this, as there are usually regulations on where and for how long you can play.

ACCOMMODATION

Accommodation is efficiently classified and graded according to the type of establishment and level of comfort provided. Tourist offices invariably have extensive brochures listing prices and facilities of local accommodation. Often the office will find and book hotels and pensions for little or no commission; this service could save you a lot of time and effort, especially in somewhere like Zürich where finding a place to stay can be a problem. However, they may only try places affiliated to the national hotel network – cheaper places sometimes aren't affiliated, and such places may also be overlooked in tourist office brochures. It's wise to book ahead where possible; sometimes a deposit is required, sometimes a telephone call is sufficient. Special deals are often available with advance bookings. If you plan to stay in two star to four star hotels, ask Switzerland Tourism about the Hotel Pass; it costs Sfr120 or Sfr220 annually, and saves 50% on normal room rates.

Hotels, pensions and hostels almost always include breakfast as standard – places mentioned in this book *do*, unless stated otherwise. In budget places, breakfast is basic, maybe only a beverage, bread rolls, butter, cheese spread and jam. As you pay more, breakfast gets better – usually it's a buffet (including cold meats and cereals) in places with two or three stars.

(continued on page 67)

ACTIVITIES

Among the Swiss the number one activity is hiking, with 40% of the population regularly taking walks in the countryside. Skiing is of course very popular, and Swiss competitors usually win a good haul of medals at international winter sports events (though not so many of late). Swimming, mountaineering, cycling, fishing and football are also favourite pastimes.

Shooting and gymnastic clubs are popular with male adults. The interest in shooting is a spillover from the need to maintain a minimum standard with service weapons while in the reserves. There are 3600 shooting clubs in Switzerland. Look out for a strange running race, unique to Switzerland, called the *Waffenlaufen*, where runners complete a course of between 18 and 42km, dressed in military uniform, complete with rucksack and rifle.

For tourists, the outdoor life in Switzerland is a bigger draw than the cities. The mountains and lakes make more than just a pretty picture; they're a natural playground for active people. If instead you prefer rest and recuperation, visit one of the Swiss health spas. The Swiss Spa Association (☎ 041-726 52 16, fax 726 52 17) is in Zug.

Skiing

There are dozens of ski resorts throughout the Alps, the Pre-Alps and the Jura. The resorts favoured by the package-holiday companies do not necessarily have better skiing facilities, but they do tend to have more diversions off the slopes, in terms of sightseeing and nightlife. Make sure your travel insurance covers you for winter sports. Airlifts can be costly.

The skiing season generally lasts from early December to late March, though at higher altitudes, skiing is possible until way into the summer, or even year-round on some glaciers. Snow conditions can vary greatly from one year to another, so telephone ahead to the local tourist office to ask about the state of the runs. January can get cold on the slopes. Christmas and February tend to be the best (and busiest!) months, and most resorts are fairly dead in May and November, and for a week or two either side.

Prices for ski passes are usually quoted in this book for one day (and sometimes one week to give an idea of the relative cost) but you can invariably specify the exact number of days you want, or even buy segments of one day. Expect to pay around Sfr35 to Sfr60 for a one-day pass, depending on the size of the area. Price per day reduces over longer periods. Free use of ski buses is usually included. Beginners might consider buying ski coupons (where available) as a cheaper alternative if they only want to try a couple of experimental runs.

Equipment can always be hired at resorts; for one day you'll pay about Sfr43 for downhill skis, poles and boots or Sfr20 for cross-country gear. You can buy new equipment at reasonable prices, or inquire about buying ex-rental stock – affluent Swiss spurn such equipment so you might pick up real bargains.

Previous page: Skiing in the Alps. (Photo by Richard Nebeský)

ACTIVITIES

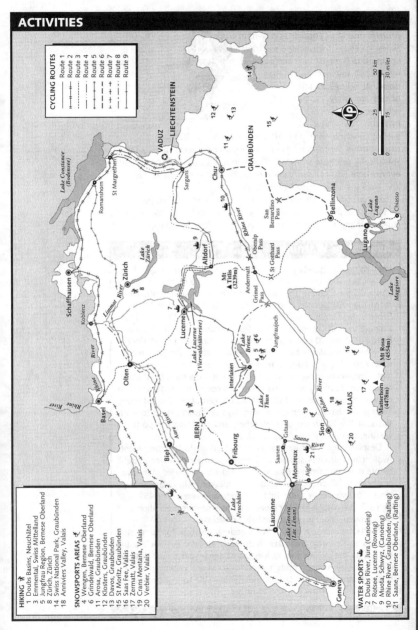

CYCLING ROUTES
- Route 1
- Route 2
- Route 3
- Route 4
- Route 5
- Route 6
- Route 7
- Route 8
- Route 9

HIKING
1. Doubs Basins, Neuchâtel
2. Emmental, Swiss Mittelland
3. Jungfrau Region, Bernese Oberland
8. Zürich, Zürich
14. Swiss National Park, Graubünden
18. Anniviers Valley, Valais

SNOWSPORTS AREAS
4. Wengen, Bernese Oberland
6. Grindelwald, Bernese Oberland
11. Arosa, Graubünden
13. Klosters, Graubünden
13. Davos, Graubünden
15. St Moritz, Graubünden
16. Saas Fee, Valais
17. Zermatt, Valais
19. Crans Montana, Valais
20. Verbier, Valais

WATER SPORTS
2. Doubs River, Jura (Canoeing)
7. Rotsee, Lucerne (Rowing)
7. Muota, Schwyz, (Canoeing)
9. Rhine River, Graubünden, (Rafting)
21. Saane, Bernese Oberland, (Rafting)

LIECHTENSTEIN

VADUZ

GRAUBÜNDEN

VALAIS

BERN

Schaffhausen
Koblenz
Basel
Biel
Olten
Lausanne
Geneva
Fribourg
Montreux
Aigle
Gstaad
Saanen
Sion
Zürich
Lucerne
Interlaken
Altdorf
Andermatt
Chur
Sargans
St Margrethen
Romanshorn
Bellinzona
Lugano
Chiasso

Lake Constance
(Bodensee)
Lake Zürich
Lake Lucerne
(Vierwaldstättersee)
Lake Brienz
Lake Thun
Lake Neuchâtel
Lake Geneva
(Lac Léman)
Lake Maggiore
Lake Lugano

Rhine River
Limmat River
Aare River
Rhône River
Saane River

Mt Titlis
(3239m)
Mt Rosa
(4554m)
Matterhorn
(4478m)

Oberalp Pass
Grimsel Pass
St Gotthard Pass
San Bernardino Pass
Jungfraujoch

0   25   50 km
0   15   30 miles

Cross-country skiing (Langlauf, ski de fond) is nearly as popular as downhill skiing, and Switzerland's trails compare to the best in Scandinavia. It works out much cheaper than downhill skiing, as lift tickets are rarely required. Snowboarding, the snow-surfing phenomenon favoured by the young, has caught on in Switzerland as elsewhere. Some places, such as Davos, specifically promote snowboarding, though it's possible pretty much everywhere you can ski. Variations on normal skis, such as 'Big Foot' and caving skis, are also to be found.

MARTIN HARRIS

Switzerland has some of the best downhill skiing in Europe, but it's no surprise to discover that it is also about the most expensive. If you're contemplating nipping across the border to look for cheaper skiing,

Avalanche Warning

Though modern safety precautions have reduced the dangers from avalanches, they are still a major hazard in Alpine regions. This was brought home during the heavy snowfalls of March 1999, when more than 80 people died in a matter of days (worst hit were Evolène, Switzerland and especially Galtür, Austria). Yet even in an average year 200 people are killed by avalanches in the Alps, and there are about 10,000 avalanches annually in Switzerland alone.

Problems usually originate on slopes high above the prepared ski runs. Accordingly, mountain resorts now have a series of crisscross metal barriers built high on peaks to prevent snow slips. In addition, helicopters routinely drop explosive devices in the mountains to cause controlled slides and prevent the dangerous build-up of snow. Resorts also have a system involving flags or flashing lights to warn skiers of the likelihood of avalanches, and up-to-date reports on weather conditions are always available.

Despite these measures, skiers cannot afford to be complacent. Avalanche warnings should be heeded, and local advice sought before detouring from prepared runs. If skiers are buried in an avalanche snowfall, chances of rescue are improved if they carry an avalanche transceiver, a radio that transmits and receives a 457 kHz signal. These cost US$200 or more. A more expensive precaution (but of unproven value) is an ABS air balloon rucksack.

The latest research by the Swiss Federal Institute for Snow and Avalanche Research indicates that nearly all fatal avalanches are caused by the victims themselves. Most are set off by off-piste or cross-country skiers, though around 20% are down to snowboarders and hikers. Locations most vulnerable to avalanches are narrow valleys below or close to ridges.

France is almost as expensive, Austria and Germany a bit cheaper, and Italy perhaps cheaper still. But price isn't everything. There are not many places that can compare with Swiss resorts such as Zermatt and Verbier for the combination of great skiing, great scenery and great nightlife.

There are also many schools where you can learn to ski or snowboard in Switzerland. All the ski resorts listed in this book have at least one ski school (there are more than 200 in total), and you can join a group class (fees around Sfr35 to Sfr45 for half a day) or pay for individual tuition on a per lesson basis. It shouldn't be necessary to arrange these in advance, but if you want to, contact the Swiss Ski School Federation, SSSV (☎ 081-854 07 77, fax 854 00 53), Cinuos-chel, CH-7526, Graubünden. Its Web site is at www.swiss-ski-school.ch.

If you want to stick to one resort for your skiing, ask hotels about weekly package deals – they often include a ski pass in the rate.

Nowhere is particularly highlighted for budget skiing, though you can cut costs even in expensive resorts by staying in youth hostels or dormitories (eg, in Zermatt and St Moritz) and by limiting your skiing to specific areas in the resort; for example in Davos (which has dormitory accommodation) the general ski pass is Sfr116 for two days, but the Schatzalp/Strela area is only Sfr26 for one day. Note that young adults and senior citizens often get discounts on ski pass prices. See under Student & Youth Cards and Senior Travellers in the Facts for the Visitor chapter.

Among the top resorts in Switzerland are:

Arosa, Graubünden
This family resort has 70km of easy to medium ski runs. Ski passes cost Sfr50 for one day and the resort is reached via a scenic train or car ride from Chur.

Crans-Montana, Valais
These spread-out twin resorts above the Rhône Valley enjoy a sunny, dry climate. Skiing (160km of runs) is suitable for all skill levels. A day pass costs Sfr47, or Sfr56 to include the Plaine-Morte Glacier which can also be skied in summer.

Davos, Graubünden
Davos is a sporty ski town with 315km of varied ski runs, including some long and demanding slopes; it's linked with Klosters under the general REGA pass costing Sfr116 for a minimum of two days.

Grindelwald, Bernese Oberland
This chalet village lies under the north face of the Eiger. Skiing is suitable for all abilities, and there are good off-piste possibilities. It is part of the Jungfrau Top Ski Region. Passes cost Sfr105 for two days, good for 45 ski lifts and 205km of runs, though you can also buy more specific passes for Sfr52 per day.

Klosters, Graubünden
Klosters shares the same ski slopes as Davos (see entry earlier) but this traditional chalet ski village provides a quieter base.

Saas Fee, Valais

This car-free chalet village is surrounded by glaciers and 4000m peaks. There is something to suit all levels in the 100km of runs accessible with the Sfr58 day pass. There's also 20km of summer glacier skiing.

St Moritz, Graubünden

This is an exclusive and expensive resort, with varied ski runs and plenty of nightlife. It's also famous for tobogganing and cross-country skiing. The general Engadin ski pass covers 350km of downhill runs and costs Sfr58 for one day.

Verbier, Valais

Verbier is a modern, sophisticated chalet resort within reach of Geneva and with good après ski options. It gives access to a vast skiing area, mostly unsuitable for beginners, with challenging off-piste skiing. The Sfr56 one-day general pass is good for 400km of runs and 100 ski lifts.

Wengen, Bernese Oberland

A favourite with the British, this car-free family resort has mostly easy and medium runs as well as off-piste skiing. Linked with Grindelwald (see entry earlier) under the Jungfrau Top Ski Region, it is also home of the international Lauberhorn downhill ski race.

Zermatt, Valais

This car-free chalet village has knock-out views of the Matterhorn. A pricey and trendy resort, its runs are mostly medium and difficult, with challenging off-piste opportunities. The expensive one-day pass for Sfr62 gives access to 245km of runs. Zermatt also has the most extensive summer glacier skiing in Switzerland, as well as the chance to ski Cervinia in Italy.

Hiking

There are 50,000km of designated footpaths (German: *Wanderweg*, French: *sentier*) with regular refreshment stops en route. Bright yellow direction signs along the trail make it difficult to get lost; each usually gives an average walking time to the next destination. Yellow markers are often painted on trees alongside the path. Such paths are considered suitable for everybody. At higher altitudes, signs and markers for mountain paths *(Bergweg, sentier de montagne)* are painted white-red-white. These paths are deemed to be more suitable for experienced mountain walkers, though really anybody with reasonable fitness and agility should be OK. But be sure you have sturdy, non-slip footwear. High Alpine routes are white-blue-white. Not surprisingly, the best trails are away from the towns and in the hills. If you can afford it, take a cable car to get you started. Always wear proper hiking boots and take rain gear and a water bottle.

The 'planetary paths' were conceived as a scale version of the solar system with information boards and mini planets along the route. The one in the Anniviers Valley in Valais has the best models of the planets and higher mountain peaks at which to gaze. See also Emmental, Doubs Basins and Zürich. A popular area for hikes – either long or short, easy or demanding – is the Jungfrau Region (see the Bernese

Oberland chapter). Here you will find a great all-day hike, from Grindelwald-First to Schynige Platte (or vice versa), and the much shorter, easy walk from Männlichen to Kleine Scheidegg. Alternatively, if you want to get away from the crowds and encounter plenty of wildlife, head for the Swiss National Park (see under Zernez in the Graubünden chapter). For lots of walking suggestions and detailed route descriptions, refer to Lonely Planet's *Walking in Switzerland*.

The Swiss Hiking Federation, SAW (☎ 061-606 93 40, fax 606 93 45), Im Hirshalm 49, CH-4125 Riehen, organises guided walking tours and produces good hiking maps. The Swiss Alpine Club, or Schweizer Alpenclub (SAC; ☎ 031-370 1818, fax 370 18 00), Monbijoustrasse 61, Bern, maintains huts for overnight stays at altitude – SAC members get a substantial discount. Its Web site is at www.sac.cas.ch. See under Accommodation in the Facts for the Visitor chapter.

Mountaineering

Mountaineering is not for the uninitiated and you should never climb on your own, or without being properly equipped/attired. There are well-established mountaineering schools in Pontresina and Meiringen, and in many other locations. Zermatt is perhaps the most famous destination for experienced mountaineers, and has a Mountain Guides Office to help organise climbs in the region. Ski mountaineering is also popular along the Haute Route in Valais. See Verbier, Zermatt and Saas Fee in the Valais chapter for more information. The Swiss Mountain Guide Federation, or Schweizerischer Bergführerverband (☎ 01-291 49 33, fax 291 49 78) is at Kansleistrasse 127, CH-8004, Zürich. Check out its Web site at www.bergtourismus.ch. The Swiss Association of Mountaineering Schools, or Schweizer Verband der Bergsteigerschulen (☎ 041-872 09 00, fax 872 09 50) is at Postfach 141 CH-6490, Andermatt. Its Web site is at www.bergschule-uri.ch. See also the Swiss Alpine Club (under Hiking earlier).

Cycling

Cycling in Switzerland is about as good as it gets in Europe – there are good cycling paths (most are not too hilly as they follow the courses of lakes or rivers), unbeatable views, lots of places to rent bikes, and no hassle about putting your bike on a train and enjoying a rest. Within the last five years, nine national cycle routes have been constructed:

Route 1
Rhône route from Geneva to Andermatt via Lausanne, Montreux and Sion
Route 2
Rhine route from Basel to Andermatt via Schaffhausen, Lake Constance and Chur

Route 3

North-south route from Basel to Chiasso via Lucerne, Andermatt and Lugano

Route 4

Alpen Panoramic route from St Margrethen on the Austrian border to Aigle near Lake Geneva, via Altdorf, Lake Lucerne and Fribourg

Route 5

Mittelland route from Lake Geneva (Lausanne) to Lake Constance (Romanshorn) via Biel, Olten and close to Zürich Airport

Route 6

Graubünden route from Bellinzona to Chur

Route 7

Jura route from Basel to Geneva running close to the north-west border of the country

---

Cycling in Switzerland

Cycling in Switzerland is a real pleasure. Not only is there a good network of well-signposted national cycle routes, but even on normal roads dangers are diminished as Swiss drivers are among the most courteous in Europe. At weekends one sees families out on bikes together, from grandparents down to young children. It seems to be the accepted way to get around.

I led a two-week tour of CTC members (ages 26 to 56) in the summer of 1999. We cycled for 10 days, plus four optional cycling days, and covered about 800km in total. Of the cycle routes we used, most were paved, but even when we were on tracks the surface was suitable for our road bikes. Along the routes some cafes had the Cycle Route flag or sign outside welcoming passing cyclists. We stayed overnight in hostels as they are cheap and they seem to understand the needs of cyclists better than hotels.

From Zürich airport we joined Route 5 to Brugg, the old Roman crossing point of the river Aare. Following the route was no problem with the distinctive red and blue signs to point the way. We then joined Route 2 along the rivers Aare and Rhine to Lake Constance. Much of this route was flat, frequently through woods and with glimpses of the river not far away.

We continued south through Liechtenstein and then west on Route 9 along the banks of the charming Walensee. Drawing closer to Lake Lucerne the scenery became more mountainous and there were some long steady climbs to be made.

Ten days from Zürich we reached Grindelwald and the ever impressive Eiger, Mönch and Jungfrau. After a last view of the snow-capped Alps and stops at Bern and Solothurn, Routes 8 and 5 returned us to our starting point at Zürich.

Roger Nash
CTC Tour Leader

(Information on CTC is in the Getting There & Away chapter)

Jungfrau's shimmering peak, Bernese Oberland

Cycle through Appenzell, on Routes 4 and 9

Phantom cable car

The simple beauty of an Alpine wild flower

A serene spot, Bettmeralp, Valais

Magical views of the Matterhorn, Valais

CHRIS MELLOR

CHRIS MELLOR

Staubbach Falls, Bernese Alps

DALE BUCKTON

Riederhorn, Valais

MARK HONAN

ROTHORN

Grindelwald-First Region

More Hiking! Brienz, Berner Oberland

CHRIS MELLOR

Jungfraujoch, the start of the Aletsch Glacier, Bernese Oberland

Route 8
Aare route from the Grimsel Pass to Koblenz via Interlaken, Bern and Olten
Route 9
Lakes route from Lake Geneva (Montreux) to the south-eastern end of Lake Constance near St Margrethen, via Gstaad, Lucerne and Sargans

The routes are described in German in the *Veloland Schweiz* series, each describing three routes and costing Sfr37.80 each. There's also a 1:500,000 overview map (Sfr24), available in four languages including English. Buy them from bookshops in Switzerland or from Switzerland Tourism.

For information on getting your bike to Switzerland, see under Bicycle in the Getting There & Away chapter; for bike rental and bicycle train passes, turn to the Getting Around chapter.

Aerial Sports

Mountains are made for paragliding and hang-gliding. Both are popular, especially paragliding (called Delta gliding or *para-penting* locally), for which the equipment is more portable. Many resorts have places where you can hire the gear, get tuition, or simply go as a passenger on a flight. Ballooning is also taking off (sorry!), despite the high costs. Château d'Oex is one of the best-known locations.

Water Sports

The lakes are equally as developed for sports as the mountains. Water-skiing and particularly sailing and windsurfing are common on most lakes. Courses are usually available, especially in Graubünden and central Switzerland.

There are more than 350 beaches in the country, most of which are private and require an entrance fee (around Sfr5 per day). Anglers should contact the local tourist office for a fishing permit valid for lakes and rivers.

The Rotsee, near Lucerne, is a favourite place for rowing regattas. Rafting is possible on many Alpine rivers including the Rhine (see Flims and Scuol in the Graubünden chapter) and the Saane (see the Bernese Oberland chapter). Canoeing is mainly centred on the Muota River in Schwyz canton and on the Doubs River in the Jura. Paddleboats *(Pedalos)* are usually waiting for hire in lakeside resorts.

Adventure Sports

So-called 'adventure sports' became a growth area in the 1990s, heralded by the popularity of bungy jumping a decade earlier. Several Swiss companies offer a range of high-adrenalin, 'white knuckle' experiences for thrill seekers. These include bungy jumping, abseiling, white-water rafting, caving and tailor-made adventure courses. What is claimed to be the world's highest fixed-point bungy jump can be experienced in the Jungfrau Region (see the Bernese Oberland chapter). Canyoning is a relatively recent craze, involving abseiling down waterfalls, rock climbing and swimming through gorges.

As you would expect, the Swiss operations are strong on the safety aspects, but accidents do happen. Nothing is risk free. This was especially brought home with the death of 21 canyoners in the Saxetschlucht (which feeds into the Brienzersee) in 1999. They had been caught in a flash flood which caused water levels to rise by over 1m in a matter of seconds. In response to the tragedy a common standard for canyoning operations and training amongst all adventure-sport companies has been instigated in Switzerland; canyoning was already banned in parts of the USA.

Most people head to Interlaken and the Jungfrau Region to indulge in their adrenalin hit (see the Bernese Oberland chapter for names of companies), but there are also good possibilities in Central Switzerland (see listings under Lucerne and Engelberg). Check out the Web site of Swissraft (www.swissraft.ch) which offers a range of adventure sports and has offices in Graubünden, Ticino and elsewhere.

(continued from page 56)

Except in some towns and cities, it is normal to have a low, middle and high season. The date of the changeover from low to high season prices varies not only from resort to resort but sometimes even from hotel to hotel in the same resort. This factor, together with possible special offers in slack times, makes it always worth phoning around to compare prices before you select somewhere. It also doesn't hurt to ask for a discount for cash – for longer stays, in low season, or (in business-class hotels) during weekends.

Prices in budget hotels tend not to change very much between seasons, but the price difference in higher rated hotels can be quite marked, especially in mountain resorts. In this book, prices are usually quoted as 'starting from...', meaning the price for the cheapest rooms during the *main* season. Off season prices may be 10% (towns) to 40% (Alpine resorts) lower, but you may have to pay more during specific events or festivals, such as at Christmas. Another consideration when budgeting is that the cheapest rooms may not always be available – some hotels offer a range of prices for rooms, depending on size, facilities and fittings. If you're a family, or a group of backpackers travelling together, ask about family rooms, which work out cheaper per person. These are commonly available, and usually have a double bed and one or two singles.

In many resorts (rarely cities) there's a visitor's card, sometimes called a Guest Card *(Gästekarte)* or Resort Card *(Kurkarte)*, which provides various useful benefits such as reduced prices for museums, swimming pools or cable cars. The aim is to entice tourists to stay in the locality instead of just breezing in on a day trip. Cards are issued by your accommodation (even hostels and camp sites) though if you're in a holiday apartment you'll need to get one from the tourist office. They're well worth having, so ask if such a scheme exists if your hotel doesn't supply one spontaneously.

Camping

There are about 450 camp sites, which are classified from one to five stars depending upon their amenities and convenience of location. They are often scenically situated in an out-of-the-way place by a river or lake. Fine if you're exploring the countryside, but a bit of a pain if you want to sightsee in a town. For this reason, and because you have so much extra gear to carry, camping is more viable if you have your own transport. Hostels, especially for solo travellers, don't work out much more expensive. Charges per night are around Sfr7 per person plus Sfr5 to Sfr10 for a tent, and from Sfr3 for a car. Telephone ahead as in high season camps might be full; at the beginning or end of the season camps may close down if demand is low or the weather poor. Camping Gaz replacement canisters are widely available.

Many sites offer a slight discount if you have an International Camping Card (formerly Camping Carnet). This is basically a camping ground ID, obtainable from your local automobile association or camping federation. They incorporate third-party insurance for damage you may cause. The Swiss Camping & Caravanning Federation (☎ 041-210 48 22, fax 210 00 02), or Schweizerischer Camping und Caravanning-Verband (SCCV), is at Postfach 24, Habsburgerstrasse 35, CH-6004 Lucerne. The Swiss Camping Association (☎ 033-823 35 23, fax 823 29 91), or Verband Schweizer Campings, is at Seestrasse 119, CH-3800 Interlaken.

Free camping *(Wildes camping)* is not strictly allowed and should be discreet, but it is perfectly viable in the wide open mountain spaces, and is fairly common in places like Ticino. If the police come across you, they may not do anything (especially if you've been responsible with your rubbish) or they may move you on. A fine is theoretically possible. Farmers might let you pitch on their land – but ask first.

Youth Hostels

Official youth hostels are no longer specifically aimed at youths, though most people who stay in them are young, and noisy school groups can sometimes disrupt the peace of such places. Facilities in hostels are improving: four to six-bed dorms with private shower/WC are common, and some places even have double rooms (with bunk beds) or family rooms. Having to do chores is a thing of the past, but the annoying habit of locking the doors during the day (usually from 9 am to 5 pm) still persists in many places. Only rarely can you check in before 5 pm. Some places have a night-time curfew, though often you can get a key or a door code number to avoid this. Despite the hassles, they're one of the cheapest ways to get a roof over your head.

Youth hostel is *Jugendherberge* in German, *auberge de jeunesse* in French, and *alloggio per giovanni* in Italian. The national hostel organisation is the Swiss Youth Hostel Association (SYHA), which is affiliated with Hostelling International (HI). The SYHA runs 62 hostels, and membership cards must be shown by guests. Nonmembers pay a Sfr5 'guest fee', but that's not as bad as it sounds, as six guest fees add up to a full international membership card. Alternatively, you can make a one-off payment of Sfr30, though you'll find it cheaper and more convenient to become a member in your own country before you depart. Swiss membership costs Sfr33/22 for Swiss nationals over/under 18 years.

More than half the Swiss hostels have a kitchen, and most have TV and games rooms. Evening meals are often available; they're usually three-course and cost about Sfr11.50. Bed prices are mostly in the range of Sfr20 to Sfr34. Many hostels charge Sfr2.50 less per night during low season, though when low season falls depends on the place. It is the full *high season price* that is quoted in this book. In busy times a three-day maximum stay may apply. Sheets are provided in SYHA hostels, unlike in independent hostels where you can sometimes save money by having your own.

Some hostels have brochures or noticeboards with good recommendations for restaurants and nightspots. Nearly all hostels should be able to provide you with an excellent free map of Switzerland giving full details of all hostels on the reverse. Switzerland Tourism can usually supply this map too.

The SYHA or Schweizer Jugendherbergen office (☎ 01-360 14 14, fax 360 14 60, ✉ bookingoffice@youthhostel.ch) is located at Schaffhauserstrasse 14, Postfach, CH-8042, Zürich. Hostels do get full; telephone reservations are not accepted but there are various alternatives. Bookings for all Swiss youth hostels can be made through the Web site (www.youthhostel.ch) or directly at the hostels themselves (their email addresses all follow the same format, beginning with the town name, eg, zuerich@youthhostel.ch, geneve@youthhostel.ch). There's also a 'voucher' system, under which Swiss hostels will reserve ahead to the next hostel for you but you must give specific dates and claim your bed by a set time. You pay Sfr10, but as you get a Sfr9 reduction at the next hostel the effective cost is only Sfr1. Some hostels are also part of the international booking network (IBN; reservation fee Sfr7.50).

Other Hostels & Dormitories

Private hostels of the 'backpacker' type, extremely rare a few years back, have begun to appear – there are about 30 such places in Switzerland now. Some were formerly SYHA hostels. They tend to be more flexible in regulations, reception times and opening hours than SYHA hostels, and are generally pleasantly free of school groups. Membership is not required. Some of these are loosely affiliated within an organisation called Swiss Backpackers (Web site: www.backpacker.ch/hostels). Look out for its excellent occasional free magazine, *Swiss Backpacker News* – hostels and some tourist offices stock it.

Dormitory accommodation in ski resorts has been well established for years. Take care in studying accommodation lists, as the dormitory (*Touristenlager* or *Massenlager* in German, *dortoir* in French) may only take groups. It's not unusual for mattresses to be crammed side by side in massive bunks in these places; to compensate, there are usually no curfew restrictions or the hassle of the doors being locked during the day. They are usually run by an adjoining hotel or a restaurant. Some camp sites offer simple dorm beds too.

Alpine huts tend to be dormitory-style and prices are comparable to youth hostels. These are maintained by the Swiss Alpine Club, and there are around 150 of them at higher altitudes. Some are only accessible to experienced climbers. They're rarely full, or at worst you'll probably be offered a place on the floor rather than being turned away. If there's no warden about, payment depends on an honesty system, and there will be a book for signing in. Look out also for Naturfreundehaus (Friends of Nature) hostels.

Hotels & Pensions

Swiss levels of service are renowned throughout the world. Accommodation is geared towards value for money rather than low cost, so even bottom-of-the-range rooms are fairly comfortable (and pricey), and often have a sink *(lavabo)*. Hotels and pensions are star rated according to an efficient and standardised system, and almost invariably you get the level of comfort you're prepared to pay for. Prices start at around Sfr40/70 for a basic single/double room in a small town or village, or Sfr55/100 in top resorts. In these places, the showers and toilets will be down the corridor. Count on at least Sfr10 more per person for a room with a private shower. The shorthand used in this book to indicate this difference is 'with/without shower'. In low-budget accommodation, the private shower may be merely a shower cubicle rather than a proper en suite bathroom.

Pensions tend to be smaller than hotels, and usually provide a more personal service and less standardised fixtures and fittings. They often offer a better size and quality of room for the price than hotels. Where they usually can't compete is in back-up services (eg, room service, laundry service) and on-site facilities (eg, private car parking, bar and/or restaurant). If none of that matters to you, stick with the pensions. Mid-price places generally have a room telephone (direct-dial, but at inflated call rates), cable TV and mini-bar. With very few exceptions TVs can pick up a range of channels in different languages, usually even one or two English-language channels.

A pension that has only breakfast available is a *Frühstückspension*; the hotel equivalent is *Hotel-Garni*. Other hotels and pensions will offer the option of paying for half or even full board. Small pensions with a restaurant often have a 'rest day', when check-in may not be possible, unless by prior arrangement (so telephone ahead).

The top hotels in Switzerland are among the top hotels in the world. Apart from meticulous service, in these places you can expect pristine fixtures and fittings, all the comforts of home, and facilities on site such as a swimming pool, sauna, fitness room (gym), nightclub, bars, elegant boutiques and a gourmet restaurant.

For further information contact the Swiss Hotel Association (☎ 031-370 41 11, fax 370 44 44, ✉ shv@swisshotels.ch), or Schweizer Hotelier-Verein (SHV), at Monbijoustrasse 130, CH-3001 Bern.

Other Accommodation

Private houses in rural areas sometimes offer inexpensive rooms; look out for signs saying *Zimmer frei*, (*Chambres libres*, *Camere libere*: 'room(s) vacant'). Some farms also take paying guests. Student rooms in university towns may be offered during holidays (such as in Geneva), which can be very good value.

Self-catering accommodation is available in holiday chalets, apartments or bungalows. These are often booked out well in advance – for peak times, reserve six to 12 months ahead of time. In low season, you can sometimes get apartments on demand. A minimum stay of one week (Saturday to Saturday) is common. Local tourist offices will send lists if requested. REKA (☎ 031-329 66 33, fax 329 66 01), Schweizer Reisekasse, Neuengasse 15, CH-3001 Bern, has '14 days for the price of 10' deals on some apartments in low season. Its Web site is at www.reka.ch. Interhome has an office in the USA (☎ 201-882 6864), Australia (☎ 02-9976 2155) and England

(☎ 020-8891 1294), and gives one-third off bookings made in the week preceding the rental period. The head office (☎ 01-786 12 22, fax 497 27 23) is at Buckhauserstrasse 26, CH-8048, Zürich.

Another possible way to beat high Swiss prices is house swapping, where people agree to 'loan' each other their home for the duration of a holiday. There's usually an upfront fee of US$40 to US$60 to register with a home exchange agency. You can find such organisations on the Internet.

FOOD

The Swiss emphasis on quality extends to meals. Basic restaurants provide simple but well cooked food, and prices are generally high. Many budget travellers rely on picnic provisions from supermarkets, but even here prices can be a shock, with cheese costing over Sfr20 a kg! The main supermarket chains are Migros and Coop. Aperto supermarkets are in some train stations; they're a little more expensive but are open from around 6 am to 9 or 10 pm daily.

In the larger Migros and Coop outlets, and in many department stores (especially the EPA chain) there are inexpensive self-service restaurants. Migros is generally not licensed for alcohol, Coop and EPA often are. These places are great value and the food is always fairly palatable, sometimes downright tasty. They are usually open to around 6.30 pm on weekdays (sometimes with late opening on Thursday or Friday) and until 4 or 5 pm on Saturday. In most towns they are the cheapest place for a hot meal, with dishes starting at around Sfr9.

University restaurants (Mensas) are also a bargain, even if the food tends to be fairly bland. Mensas mentioned are freely open to everyone. Other Mensas may be restricted to ISIC-carrying students or local students, but controls are rarely tight and you can usually get away with it if you're determined.

Buffet-style restaurant chains, like Manora and Inova, offer good, cheap food. Despite the low prices they are comfortable inside, the food is freshly cooked in front of you, and you can sometimes select the ingredients yourself. Draught beer in these

places is only around Sfr2.90 for 3dL (300 mL). Some wine bars (Weinstübli) and beer taverns (Bierstübli) serve meals.

The best value is a fixed-menu dish of the day (Tagesteller, plat du jour, or piatto del giorno), frequently available at midday only. Fast food is available, particularly at train stations. Kiosks often sell cheap snacks that, like sausage and bread in St Gallen, are as much a regional speciality as the fancy dishes. McDonald's has long since moved into Switzerland. Its hamburgers are distressingly expensive but still cheaper than many alternatives.

Main meals in Switzerland are eaten at noon. Cheaper restaurants tend to be fairly rigid about when they serve; lunch is noon to around 1.30 pm and dinner about 6.30 to 9 or 9.30 pm. Don't be fooled if some of the closing times given in this book are much later; the place may stay open several hours after the kitchen closes, catering for drinkers. Go to a hotel or more upmarket restaurant for more flexible, later eating. Pizzerias are an inexpensive yet flexible option; it's not unusual for the ovens to be kept glowing straight through from around 11 am to 11 pm. The self-service places are often flexible during the day, too.

If you have dietary restrictions, tourist offices should be able to help with lists of suitable restaurants. Dedicated vegetarian restaurants can be hard to come by, but it's common nowadays for restaurants to offer one or two nonmeat choices. Information on vegetarian places is given in this book for all major towns. Fitness Tellers for the calorie counters are a growing phenomenon, especially in ski resorts. The Jewish Travel Guide published by Vallentine Mitchell details kosher restaurants, synagogues, and relevant institutions. There are seven pages on Switzerland in its worldwide listings. The Coop, Migros, EPA, Manora and Inova restaurants have nonsmoking sections, but other restaurants rarely do.

The classier restaurants tend to have pretensions towards nouvelle cuisine, with beautifully presented but fairly insubstantial courses. Carbohydrates are anathema in these places, as if they're trying to distance themselves from the filling meat-and-potatoes fare of earthier joints.

Monday and Tuesday are the quietest nights in restaurants, and some places take the opportunity to have a rest day *(Ruhetag)*. These rest days may expand in off season and be eliminated in high season. Weekends are the busiest times, yet some of the very top restaurants close on Saturday and/or Sunday, probably because they get a lot of their trade from expense-account business people.

There are currently only two restaurants in Switzerland with three Michelin stars: *Pont de Brent* (☎ 021-964 52 30), Brent, near Montreux, and *Restaurant l'Hôtel de Ville* (☎ 021-634 05 05), 1 Rue d'Yverdon, Crissier, near Lausanne. Both are closed on Sunday and Monday.

Swiss Cuisine

Switzerland hasn't got a great indigenous gastronomic tradition – instead, Swiss dishes borrow from the best of German, French and (in Ticino) Italian cuisine. In addition, Zürich and particularly Geneva have loads of restaurants of all sorts of nationalities. You don't have to spend a fortune to enjoy a meal; a picnic lunch on a mountain top or by a lake can be one of the recurring highlights of any trip.

The typical breakfast is of the continental variety. *Müsli* (muesli) was invented in Switzerland at the end of the 19th century but few people seem to eat it here – *Bircher-müsli* is the most common variety. Soups are popular and often very filling, and sometimes contain small dumplings *(Knöpfli)*.

Cheeses form an important part of the Swiss diet. Emmental and Gruyère are combined with white wine to create *fondue*, which is served up in a vast pot and eaten with bread cubes. According to tradition, if your cube leaps off your fork and disappears in the pot, you have to buy a round of drinks. *Raclette* is another melted cheese dish, usually served with potatoes and small onions.

Rösti (crispy, fried, shredded potatoes), sometimes spelled *Röschti*, is German Switzerland's national dish. A wide variety of *Wurst* (sausage) is available. Veal is

highly rated throughout Switzerland. In Zürich it is thinly sliced and served in a cream sauce *(Geschnetzeltes Kalbsfleisch)*. *Bündnerfleisch* is air-dried beef, smoked and thinly sliced. Fresh fish from the numerous lakes frequently crop up on menus, especially perch and trout. Swiss chocolate, excellent by itself, is often used in desserts and cakes. Regional specialities are usually mentioned in the appropriate chapter. Be sure to visit a cheese dairy or chocolate factory during your visit – there are various locations in Switzerland.

Food Glossary

These are some food terms you may come across in German (G), French (F) and Italian (I):

soup
　Suppe (G), *potage or consommé* (F), *brodo* (I)
shrimp cocktail
　Krevetten Cocktail (G), *cocktail de crevettes* (F), *cocktail di gamberi* (I)
butter-fried trout
　Forelle Müllerinart (G), *truite à la meunière* (F), *trota fritata al burro* (I)
whitefish fillets (with almonds)
　Felchenfilets (mit Mandeln) (G), *filets de féra (aux amandes)* (F), *filetti di coregone (alla mandorle)* (I)
grilled salmon
　Grillierter Salm (G), *saumon grillé* (F), *trota salmonata alla griglia* (I)
veal
　Kalb (G), *veau* (F), *vitello* (I)
fillet of beef
　Rindsfilet (G), *filet de boeuf* (F), *filetto di manzo* (I)
sirloin steak
　Zwischenrippenstück (G), *entrecôte* (F), *costata di manzo* (I)
pork
　Schwein (G), *porc* (F), *maiale* (I)
lamb cutlets
　Lammkoteletten (G), *côte d'agneau* (F), *entrecôte d'agnello* (I)
boiled potatoes
　Salzkartoffeln (G), *pommes nature* (F), *patate bollite* (I)
rice
　Reis (G), *riz* (F), *riso bianco* (I)
vegetables
　Gemüse (G), *légumes* (F), *vedura* (I)
pasta
　Teigwaren (G), *pâtes* (F), *paste or pasta* (I)

flat pasta/noodles
Nudeln (G), *nouilles* (F), *tagliatelle* (I)
ice cream
Rahmeis (G), *glace* (F), *gelato* (I)
fruit salad
Fruchsalat (G), *macédoine de fruits* (F), *macedonia di frutta* (I)

DRINKS
Nonalcoholic Drinks

Mineral water is readily available but tap water is fine to drink. Coffee is more popular than tea – the latter will come without milk unless you ask especially for it. Hot chocolate is also popular. Note that milk from Alpine cows contains a high level of fat.

Alcoholic Drinks

In bars, lager beer comes in 0.3L or 0.5L bottles, or on draught *(Bier vom Fass, bière à la pression, birra alla pressione)* with measures ranging from 0.2L to 0.5L. There isn't the tradition of beer drinking as there is in neighbouring Germany, but the many small breweries dotted round the country testify to the popularity of the beverage. Beer and wine in basic beer halls or cafes aren't too pricey (comparatively speaking), but chic bars can be very expensive. Spirits are expensive everywhere. Happily, beer and wine prices in supermarkets are fairly low.

Wine is considered an important part of the meal even though it is rather expensive. For the cheapest options, ask for decanted 'open' wines, sold by the decilitre (100mL). Local wines are generally good but you may not have heard of them before; output can not even meet domestic demand so they are rarely exported. The main growing region is the French-speaking part of the country, particularly in Valais and by lakes Neuchâtel and Geneva. Both red and white wines are produced, and each region has its own speciality. Ticino is known for Merlot. See the boxed text at the start of the Valais and Ticino chapters for more information.

There is also a choice of locally produced fruit brandies, often served with or in coffee. Kirsch is made from the juice of compressed cherry pits. Appenzeller Alpenbitter (Alpine Bitters) is a liquor made from the essences of 67 different flowers and roots.

ENTERTAINMENT

The Swiss read more newspapers and watch less TV than any other European nationals. Jass is the national card game, played with 36 cards; it's so complicated that only native Swiss understand it. Listening to music is popular throughout the country, meaning that classical, folk, jazz and rock concerts can be found in many towns and cities. Two of Switzerland's best known orchestras are the Tonhalle in Zürich and the Suisse Romande in Geneva. Most headline rock bands eventually find their way to Switzerland. Bern has several good jazz venues.

In German Switzerland, cinemas nearly always show films in the original language. To confirm this, check the advertisements for the upper-case letter – E/f/g means that the film is in English with French and German subtitles. In French Switzerland, look for *VO*, which signifies 'original version'. Prices are lower on Monday.

Nightlife is not all it could be in the cities, and where it does exist, it is expensive. Geneva is the best place for late nightclubs *(boîtes)*, but Zürich is also lively. Alternative arts flourish in many towns, usually centred in one main venue or locality. Two of the best places are l'Usine in Geneva and Rote Fabrik in Zürich – music, art, theatre, dance and cinema are featured. Zürich and Geneva are also the best places to catch up on English-language theatre.

Swiss folklore shows are standard tourist fare. If you want to investigate this strange phenomenon of alphorns, yodelling and flag throwing, there are places in Bern, Interlaken, Geneva and elsewhere.

Ski resorts have an atmosphere all of their own. 'Après ski' entertainment seems to consist of drinking large amounts in bars, then adjourning to expensive nightclubs to dance, talk loudly and fall over.

SPECTATOR SPORTS

Football is a popular spectator sport, with most towns having their own professional team. Tennis is also popular, especially since Martina Hingis (Czech-born but naturalised Swiss) became one of the top female professionals. Tennis events include the Swiss Open in Gstaad in July and an indoor tournament in Basel in October. Winter sports are also highlighted, with most ski resorts hosting something special. Look out for the World Alpine Ski Championships in St Moritz in 2003.

Alpine festivals are common in the summer in rural villages, and may include some unique Swiss sports such as *Schwingen* (Swiss wrestling), *Hornussen* (bat and ball game, played with strange curved bats), and *Unspunnenstein* (rock throwing). A listing of local events is invariably available from tourist offices.

SHOPPING

Watches, penknives, textiles and embroidery are all popular buys. Swiss knives range from simple blades (Sfr10) to mini tool boxes (Sfr100 or more). A grotesquely tacky cuckoo clock with a girl bouncing on a spring will set you back at least Sfr25, a musical box will cost anything upwards of Sfr35. Should you want a cowbell to warn people of your arrival, one with a decorative band will cost from Sfr8 to a fortune, depending on the size.

Most of these goods are available in numerous souvenir shops in all tourist centres. Heimat or Heimatwerk shops tend to sell handmade goods which can be pricey but are generally good quality. Department stores often sell similar products (eg, Swiss knives) at more competitive prices. Video and cassette tapes, records and CDs, photographic film and tape recorders are all reasonably priced by European standards. A cheap outlet (especially for film) is Inter Discount, with branches all over Switzerland. EPA is an inexpensive department store.

Getting There & Away

Air travel is the quickest, easiest, and sometimes cheapest means of transcontinental travel. If you're visiting Switzerland from outside Europe, it may be cheaper to fly to a European 'gateway' city and travel on from there. Basel, for example, is only three hours and Sfr96 from Frankfurt by rail. Paris is Sfr98 and less than four hours from Geneva by the *train à grande vitesse* (TGV). There are some great fares available on certain routes thanks to severe competition between the airlines. Students, people aged under 26 and senior citizens often qualify for excellent deals.

Don't forget to arrange travel insurance. Paying for your ticket with a credit card often in itself provides limited travel accident insurance. For additional protection, limit your business dealings to travel agents who are bonded in some way (eg, to ABTA in the UK), so you'll get reimbursed in the event of bankruptcy.

Travel within most of the EU, whether by air, rail or car, has been made easier following the Schengen Agreement, first signed in 1997, which abolished border controls between participating states (ie, all EU countries except Britain and Ireland).

AIR

The main entry points for international flights are Zürich and Geneva. There are direct services to all main European destinations and to most major transport hubs worldwide. Both airports are linked directly to the Swiss rail network. EuroAirport, serving Basel, Mulhouse (France) and Freiburg (Germany), is another busy centre for European flights. Bern and Lugano airports also have some international flights. See the respective city sections.

Swissair is the national carrier and has the most extensive services to/from Switzerland. Its Web address is www.swissair.com. Crossair, its subsidiary, also has international flights. Swissair has partnerships and code-sharing arrangements with a number of other airlines, the most important being Austrian Airlines, Sabena and Delta. There are Swissair luggage check-in facilities at many Swiss train stations and there are Swissair offices in all Swiss cities. For reservations in Switzerland, dial the local-rate numbers: ☎ 0848-852 000 for Crossair, ☎ 0848-800 700 for Swissair economy class, ☎ 0848-800 600 for Swissair business class and ☎ 0848-800 500 for Swissair 1st class.

Remember that most airlines require you to reconfirm your onward or return flight – usually 72 hours before departure on international flights.

Buying Tickets

A plane ticket is a major expense, and it pays to spend some time researching the current state of the market. Start early: some of the cheapest tickets have to be bought months in advance (such as Apex tickets), and some popular flights sell out early. Alternatively, if your plans are flexible enough, you might risk waiting for last-minute bargains. Look for special offers that crop up from time to time.

Airlines release discounted tickets through selected travel agents, and they are often the cheapest deals going. Some airlines now also sell discounted tickets direct, and it's worth contacting airlines anyway for information on routes and timetables. Return tickets usually work out much cheaper than two one-way tickets, unless you travel on one of the new 'no frills' airlines. Open Jaw returns allow you to fly into one city and out of another.

Round-the-World (RTW) tickets are another possibility, and are comparable in price to an ordinary long-haul return ticket. RTW tickets start at about UK£850, A$1800 or US$1300 depending on the season, and may be valid for up to a year. Special conditions might be attached to such tickets (eg, you can't backtrack on a route). Also beware of cancellation penalties for these and other tickets.

Air Travel Glossary

Cancellation Penalties If you have to cancel or change a discounted ticket, there are often heavy penalties involved; insurance can sometimes be taken out against these penalties. Some airlines impose penalties on regular tickets as well, particularly against 'no-show' passengers.

Courier Fares Businesses often need to send urgent documents or freight securely and quickly. Courier companies hire people to accompany the package through customs and, in return, offer a discount ticket which is sometimes a phenomenal bargain. However, you may have to surrender all your baggage allowance and take only carry-on luggage.

Full Fares Airlines traditionally offer 1st class (coded F), business class (coded J) and economy class (coded Y) tickets. These days there are so many promotional and discounted fares available that few passengers pay full economy fare.

Lost Tickets If you lose your airline ticket an airline will usually treat it like a travellers cheque and, after inquiries, issue you with another one. Legally, however, an airline is entitled to treat it like cash and if you lose it then it's gone forever. Take good care of your tickets.

Onward Tickets An entry requirement for many countries is that you have a ticket out of the country. If you're unsure of your next move, the easiest solution is to buy the cheapest onward ticket to a neighbouring country or a ticket from a reliable airline which can later be refunded if you do not use it.

Open-Jaw Tickets These are return tickets where you fly out to one place but return from another. If available, this can save you backtracking to your arrival point.

Overbooking Since every flight has some passengers who fail to show up, airlines often book more passengers than they have seats. Usually excess passengers make up for the no-shows, but occasionally somebody gets 'bumped' onto the next available flight. Guess who it is most likely to be? The passengers who check in late.

Promotional Fares These are officially discounted fares, available from travel agencies or direct from the airline.

Reconfirmation If you don't reconfirm your flight at least 72 hours prior to departure, the airline may delete your name from the passenger list. Ring to find out if your airline requires reconfirmation.

Restrictions Discounted tickets often have various restrictions on them – such as needing to be paid for in advance and incurring a penalty to be altered. Others are restrictions on the minimum and maximum period you must be away.

Round-the-World Tickets RTW tickets give you a limited period (usually a year) in which to circumnavigate the globe. You can go anywhere the carrying airlines go, as long as you don't backtrack. The number of stopovers or total number of separate flights is decided before you set off and they usually cost a bit more than a basic return flight.

Transferred Tickets Airline tickets cannot be transferred from one person to another. Travellers sometimes try to sell the return half of their ticket, but officials can ask you to prove that you are the person named on the ticket. On an international flight tickets are compared with passports.

Travel Periods Ticket prices vary with the time of year. There is a low (off-peak) season and a high (peak) season, and often a low-shoulder season and a high-shoulder season as well. Usually the fare depends on your outward flight – if you depart in the high season and return in the low season, you pay the high-season fare.

Courier fares, where you get cheap passage in return for accompanying an urgent package through customs, offer low prices but there are usually special restrictions attached, and demand for couriers is decreasing in this electronic age.

If you are travelling from the USA, UK or South-East Asia, you will probably find that the cheapest flights are being advertised by obscure agencies. Most of these firms are honest and solvent, but there are some rogue fly-by-night outfits around. If you feel suspicious about a firm, it's best to steer clear, or only pay a deposit before you get your ticket, then ring the airline to confirm that you are actually booked onto the flight before you pay the balance.

Established outfits, such as those mentioned in this book, offer more safety and are almost as competitive as you can get. The cheapest deals are only available at certain times of the year, or on weekdays, and fares are particularly subject to change. Always ask about the route: the cheapest tickets may involve an inconvenient stopover. Don't take schedules for granted, either: airlines usually change their schedules twice a year, in late March and late October.

Airlines can often make arrangements for travellers with special needs if they're warned early enough (eg, arrangements for wheelchairs, vegetarian or kosher meals). Children aged under two travel for 10% of the standard fare (or free on some airlines) as long as they don't occupy a seat. They don't get a baggage allowance. 'Skycots', baby food and nappies should be provided by the airline if requested in advance. Children aged between two and 12 can usually occupy a seat for half to two-thirds of the full fare, and do get a baggage allowance.

Departure Taxes

There is no departure tax to pay at the airport when flying out of Switzerland, as taxes must be paid when buying your ticket. Airport taxes at the Swiss end are about Sfr16, depending on the airport – ask if this is included in the initial price quoted by the travel agent. Travel agents may also quote prices which exclude the departure tax levied by the country at the origination of the flight, even if (as in the UK) this sum must be included in the final ticket price. The departure tax from the UK to Zürich or Basel is UK£20, yet it's only UK£10 to Geneva.

Fly-Rail Baggage Service

Most world airlines (except American carriers for outward flights from Switzerland) are part of this program. It allows you to wave goodbye to your luggage when you check in at your departure airport and pick it up again at your choice of any one of 116 Swiss train stations. This saves you having to wait for your luggage at the arrival airport or accompany it through customs. Similarly, upon departure you can check in your luggage at any of these train stations up to 24 hours before your flight and pick it up at your destination airport. The charge is Sfr20 per item of luggage. Note that 'bulky' items such as bicycles and surfboards are excluded.

The following Swiss train stations provide a complete check-in service for Swissair, including issuing boarding passes: Aarau, Arosa, Basel SBB, Bern, Biel/Bienne, Davos Platz and Dorf, Fribourg, Geneva, Interlaken Ost and West, Lausanne, Locarno, Lugano, Lucerne, Montreux, Neuchâtel, St Gallen, St Moritz, Solothurn, Thun, Zug and Zürich.

The UK

London is one of the world's major centres for buying discounted air tickets. You should be able to find a scheduled return flight including taxes from about UK£80 to UK£160, which compares favourably with the train fare (London to Zürich return is £127). For stays under 31 days, a charter flight may be cheaper than a scheduled fare. Try the Charter Flight Centre (☎ 020-7931 0504).

Check the cheap fares advertised in *Time Out*, the *Evening Standard* and *TNT* (a free magazine dispensed at tube stations). The Sunday national papers are also a good source of ads for cheap fares.

EasyJet (☎ 0870-6000 000), a 'no-frills' airline selling direct to the customer, has opened up Switzerland to cheap flights. It flies daily to Geneva from Liverpool, Luton, Gatwick and London-Stansted, and to Zürich from Luton. Single fares are about UK£39. The Web site address is www.easyJet.com.

In 1999 Swissair launched Swissair Express, flying twice daily from London-Stansted to Zürich. The London office of Swissair and Crossair (☎ 020-7434 7300) is at Swiss Court, W1. British Airways (☎ 0345-222 111) has cheap fares called 'World Offers', but you're probably better off trying Go (☎ 0845-605 4321), its low-cost subsidiary, which flies once daily Stansted–Zürich from UK£80 return. The Web site is www.go-fly.com.

STA Travel (☎ 020-7361 6161) is an agency for budget and student tickets, and has offices in London (eg, at 85 Shaftesbury Ave, W1 and 40 Bernard St, WC1) and other British cities, such as Manchester (☎ 0161-834 0668). The Web address is www.statravel.co.uk.

Trailfinders has decent fares. There are branches in London (☎ 020-7937 5400), Manchester (☎ 0161-839 6969), Glasgow (☎ 0141-353 2224) and other big cities. USIT Campus (☎ 020-7730 3402), 52 Grosvenor Gardens, London SW1, has good deals (especially for students and those under 26) and cheap travel insurance. Then there's Council Travel (☎ 020-7437 7767), 28A Poland St, London W1, the USA's largest student and budget travel agency.

Continental Europe

Depending on your starting point, taking the train may be cheaper and just as convenient. Across Europe many travel agents have ties with STA Travel, where budget tickets can be purchased and STA-issued tickets can usually be altered for US$25, including at SSR branches in Switzerland (SSR addresses are listed in the regional chapters). Outlets in major European cities include: Voyages Wasteels (☎ 08 03 88 70 04 from within France only, fax 01 43 25 46 25), 11 rue Dupuytren, 756006 Paris; STA Travel (☎ 030-311 0950, fax 313 0948), Goethestrasse 73, 10625 Berlin; Passaggi (☎ 06-474 0923, fax 482 7436), Stazione Termini FS, Gelleria Di Tesla, Rome; and ISYTS

(☎ 01-322 1267, fax 323 3767), 11 Nikis St, Upper Floor, Syntagma Square, Athens.

In Continental Europe, Athens is a recognised centre for cheap flights. Check the many travel agents in the backstreets between Syntagma and Omonia squares. As well as ISYTS, try Magic Bus (☎ 01 323 7471, fax 322 0219).

Amsterdam also has a good reputation for cheap fares: try the national student travel agency, NBBS Reizen (☎ 020-624 09 89), at Rokin 66 and elsewhere, or Malibu Travel (☎ 020-626 32 30) at Prinsengracht 230.

The USA

Consolidators (budget travel agents) can be found through the *Yellow Pages* or the major daily newspapers. The *New York Times*, the *Los Angeles Times*, the *Chicago Tribune*, the *San Francisco Chronicle* and the *San Francisco Examiner* all produce weekly travel sections in which you'll find numerous travel agency ads.

Fares start at around US$400 for return flights into Switzerland or a gateway city. Swissair, for example, has low-season fares from US$399 for its daily Boston–Zürich flight. It also flies daily from Los Angeles to Zürich, and nonstop flights from New York's JFK airport operate daily to both Zürich and Geneva. American Airlines and Delta also fly direct into Switzerland.

Council Travel (☎ 800-226 8624 toll free) and STA Travel (☎ 800-777 0112 toll free) sell discounted tickets from numerous outlets across the USA. The STA's Web address is www.statravel.com. One-way fares can be very cheap on a stand-by basis. Airhitch (☎ 800-326 2009, ❷ airhitch@netcom) specialises in this sort of thing, and can get you from the east/west coast to Europe one-way for US$159/239. Try the Web site at www.airhitch.org. For courier flights, try Now Voyager (☎ 212-431 16 16) in New York.

Canada

Check ads for consolidators in the *Globe & Mail*, the *Toronto Star*, the *Montreal Gazette* and the *Vancouver Sun*. Travel CUTS

(☎ 800-667-2887) is Canada's national student travel agency and has offices in all major cities. Its Web address is www.travecuts.com.

Fares average around 10% higher than from the USA. Swissair flies from Montreal to Zürich daily, with return fares starting at C$644 in low season.

Australia and New Zealand

STA Travel and Flight Centres International are major dealers in cheap airfares. Check the travel agency ads in the Telecom Yellow Pages, and newspaper travel sections, particularly the *Sydney Morning Herald*, Melbourne's *Age*, and the *New Zealand Herald*. STA has many offices, including ones at 224 Faraday St, Carlton, Vic 3053 (☎ 03-9347 2411); 24-30 Springfield Ave, Sydney (☎ 02-9368 1111); and 10 High St, Auckland (☎ 09-309 0458). The Web site is www.statravel.com.au.

Flight Centre (☎ 131 600 Australia wide) also has many offices, including those at 82 Elizabeth St, Sydney, and in Auckland's National Bank Towers (☎ 09-309 6171) on the corner of Queen and Darby Sts, Auckland. The Web site is www.flightcentre.com.au.

None of the airlines fly direct into Switzerland from Australia or New Zealand – connections are usually via Singapore or Bangkok. Expect to pay around A$2500/2000 or NZ$2700/2400 return fare in high/low season. Round-the-World (RTW) tickets may not be more expensive than normal returns and are well worth considering.

Africa

Nairobi and Johannesburg are probably the best places in East and South Africa to buy tickets to Europe. A nonstop Nairobi–Zürich flight (Tuesday, Thursday and Sunday) on Swissair will start at around US$870 for a one-month return, though you could probably find lower fares through budget agencies like Flight Centre (☎ 02-210024) in Lakhamshi House, Biashara St, Nairobi. Swissair flies direct to Zürich from Johannesburg every day. STA Travel (☎ 011-447 5551) has an office in Johannesburg on Tyrwhitt Ave in Rosebank.

Several West African countries such as Burkina Faso, Gambia and especially Morocco offer cheap charter flights to France. From Cairo, the best option might be taking a flight to Athens, then a budget bus or train from there.

Asia

Hong Kong, Singapore and Bangkok are the best places to pick up cheap tickets, but beware of unreliable, fly-by-night agencies who aren't even around long enough to make it into the telephone book. Ask the advice of other travellers before buying a ticket. STA has branches in Hong Kong, Tokyo, Manila, Singapore, Bangkok and Kuala Lumpur.

Mumbai (Bombay) is a major air transport hub of Asia, with many transit options to/from South-East Asia, but tickets are slightly cheaper in Delhi. Try STIC Travels (☎ 011-332 5559) in the Imperial Hotel, Janpath, Delhi.

Swissair flies between Zürich and Karachi, Bombay, Delhi, Bangkok, Singapore, Hong Kong, Beijing, Seoul, Tokyo and Manila, with connecting flights to/from Geneva.

LAND
Bus

Buses are generally slower, cheaper and less comfortable than trains. Europe's biggest network of international buses is provided by a group of bus companies operating under the name Eurolines.

Addresses for Eurolines include:

Blaguss Reisen (☎ 01-712 04 53) in Vienna's international Autobusbahnhof (bus station)
Deutsche Touring (☎ 069-790 32 40) Am Romerhof 17, Frankfurt
Eurolines (☎ 1-43 54 11 99) 55 Rue Saint Jacques, Paris
Eurolines Italy (☎ 06-44 04 00 9 or 055-215 155) Ciconvallazione Nonentana 574, Lato Stazione Tiburtina, Rome
Eurolines Nederland (☎ 020-560 87 87) Rokin 10, Amsterdam
Eurolines UK (☎ 0990-143 219) 52 Grosvenor Gardens, Victoria, London SW1. Web site: www.eurolines.co.uk

On most return trips, youth/senior fares are around 10% less than the ordinary full fare, eg, a London–Zürich return ticket (via Basel; valid six months) costs £94 for adults or £84 for youths under 26 and seniors over 60. Some prices are higher in summer, or if you book at least two weeks in advance you can sometimes get much cheaper tickets, eg, £69 return for London–Basel/Zürich/Geneva. The journey time from London to Zürich or Geneva is 20 hours, with two departures (four in summer) per week to Zürich and four (daily in summer) to Geneva. Geneva also has international bus routes heading to Rome, the south of France, and along the eastern coast of Spain (see the Geneva chapter). Eurolines' representative in Zürich is Marti Travel (☎ 01-215 70 70), Usteristrasse 10.

If you want to visit several countries by bus, investigate the UK-based Busabout (☎ 020-7950 1661, ✉ info@ busabout.co.uk). It has buses completing set routes across Europe, and you can jump on and off as many times as you like within the given time. There are various time spans available, the minimum being the 15-day pass costing UK£155/139 for adults/ students. There are also several Flexi Passes, such as 10 days' travel within two months for £235/210. The Web site is www.busabout.com.

Eurolines UK also has European passes – its routes are more flexible but also more expensive (from UK£199/159 per adult/youth for 30 days).

Train

Trains are a popular, pollution-free and convenient way to travel. They are also good meeting places, comfortable and reasonably frequent.

Stories about train passengers being gassed or drugged and then robbed occasionally surface, though bag-snatching is more of a worry. Sensible security measures include not letting your bags out of your sight (or at least chaining them to the luggage rack) and locking compartment doors overnight.

The *Thomas Cook European Timetable* is the trainophile's bible, giving a complete listing of train schedules, supplements and reservations information. It is updated monthly and is available from Thomas Cook outlets. In the USA, call ☎ 800-367 7984.

The UK & Continental Europe Paris, Amsterdam, Munich, Milan and Vienna are all important hubs for international train connections. Switzerland, located at the heart of Europe, has excellent services to/from these hubs and the rest of the continent. Zürich is the busiest international terminus. It has two day trains (takes nine hours) and one night train to Vienna, and has four daily trains (takes four hours) to Munich. From either city there are extensive onward connections to/from eastern Europe.

There are several trains a day to both Geneva and Lausanne from Paris, and the journey time is three to four hours by the super-fast TGV. Paris to Bern takes 4½ hours by TGV. Most connections from Germany pass through Zürich or Basel. Nearly all connections from Italy pass through Milan before branching off to Zürich, Lucerne, Bern or Lausanne. From the UK, the quickest route is London–Paris via Eurostar, where you can transfer to a train to Basel or Geneva. Allow about 14 hours for the trip.

Travellers aged under 26 can pick up Billet International de Jeunesse (BIJ) tickets, which cut fares on international journeys by up to 50%. Unfortunately, you can't always bank on a substantial reduction, eg, the youth return from London to Zürich costs UK£108, saving just £19 on the normal fare. Various agents issue BIJ tickets in Europe, such as Wasteels (☎ 020-7834 7066) in London's Victoria Railway Station and Voyages Wasteels (☎ 1-43 43 46 10) at 2 Rue Michel Chasles, Paris. Rail Europe (☎ 0990-848 848) sells BIJ tickets and railpasses; it has London offices at 179 Piccadilly and in Victoria Railway Station.

Express trains can be identified by the symbols EuroCity (EC, serving international routes) or InterCity (IC, serving national routes). The French TGV and the German Intercity Express (ICE) trains are even faster. Supplements can apply on fast trains, and it is a good idea (sometimes obligatory) to make seat reservations at

European Railpasses

European railpasses make train travel affordable, but unless you want to explore other countries in Europe as well, it will probably work out cheaper to pay the normal fare to Switzerland then use one of the Swiss railpasses to explore the country (see the Getting Around chapter). This is because within Switzerland, Swiss railpasses are valid on more private rail lines than the European passes, and you can get discounts on mountain transport that the European passes tend not to include.

Reservation costs (and most supplements) are not covered by any railpasses, and pass holders must always carry their passport on the train for identification purposes. Rail Europe (☎ 800-438 7245) in the USA sells railpasses. See the Web site www.raileurope.com. Buying a circular ticket might be a viable alternative to a full railpass, such as the 'Explorer' tickets sold under the name Eurotrain.

Treat railpasses as if they were cash, as replacement can be difficult or expensive, and always study the terms and conditions. European senior citizens can buy a Rail Europe Senior Card, entitling the holder to reductions on European train fares.

Eurail Pass This pass can only be bought by residents of non-European countries. Eurail passes are valid for unlimited travel on national railways and some private lines in Austria, Belgium, Denmark, Finland, France (including Monaco), Germany, Greece, Hungary, Italy, Luxembourg, the Netherlands, Norway, Portugal, Ireland, Spain, Sweden and Switzerland (including Liechtenstein). The UK is not covered. The pass is also valid for free or discounted travel on various international ferries and national lake/river steamers.

A standard Youthpass for travellers under 26 is valid for unlimited 2nd-class travel within the given time period, ranging from 15 days (US$388) up to three months (US$1089). The Youth Flexipass, also for 2nd class, is valid for freely chosen days within a two-month period: 10 days for US$458 or 15 days for US$599.

The corresponding passes for those aged over 26 are available in 1st-class only. The standard Eurail pass costs from US$554 for 15 days up to US$1558 for three months. The Flexipass costs US$654 for 10 days or US$862 for 15 days. Two people travelling together can save around 15% each by buying 'saver' versions of these passes (child fares available).

Europass This gives from five to 15 freely chosen days' unlimited travel within two months in France, Germany, Italy, Spain and Switzerland. The youth/adult fare is US$233/348 for five days, and US$513/728 for 15. A few extra 'associate' countries (such as Austria) can be added for a price. This pass is only available to non-Europeans.

Inter-Rail Pass This pass is available in Europe to people who have been resident there for at least six months. The standard Inter-Rail pass is for travellers aged under 26, though older people can get the Inter-Rail 26+ version. The pass divides Europe into eight zones (A to H); Switzerland is in zone C, along with Denmark, Germany and Austria. The standard/26+ fare for any one zone is UK£159/229, valid for 22 days. To purchase two/three/all zones (valid one month) costs UK£209/229/259, or UK£279/309/349 for the 26+ version.

All-zone (global) pass This pass will take you everywhere covered by Eurail, plus Poland, Czech Republic, Slovakia, Slovenia, Romania, Croatia, Yugoslavia, Bulgaria, Macedonia and Turkey. As with Eurail, the pass gives discounts or free travel on some ferry, ship and steamer routes.

Euro-Domino Pass There is a Euro-Domino pass for each of the countries covered in the Inter-Rail pass, except for some eastern countries. Adults (travelling 1st or 2nd class) and youths (under 26) can opt for three to eight chosen days within a month. The Domino pass for Switzerland is a viable alternative to buying one of Switzerland's national railpasses. For three/eight days in 2nd class it costs UK£79/109 for adults and UK£59/89 for youths.

Switzerland Flexipass This is similar to the Switzerland Domino Pass. It may be marketed simply as a Swiss Railpass, and is only available to non-Europeans. It's valid for one month, giving free travel on any number of days between three (US$156, or US$234 in 1st class) and nine (US$303 or US$456).

peak times and on certain lines. Overnight trips usually offer a choice of couchette (around US$28) or a more expensive sleeper. Long-distance trains have a dining car or snacks available. Supplements sometimes apply on international trains. Reservations made in Switzerland are subject to a surcharge of Sfr5 to Sfr30 or more, depending upon the day and/or the service.

Asia It takes 48 hours by train from Basel to Moscow (via Frankfurt and Cologne) and costs Sfr336, plus a compulsory sleeper (from Sfr39). From there you can take four different trains for onwards eastern travel. Three of them (the trans-Siberian, trans-Mongolian and trans-Manchurian) follow the same route to/from Moscow across Siberia but have different eastern railheads. The fourth, the trans-Kazakstan, runs between Moscow and Ürümqi (north-western China) across central Asia. Prices can vary enormously, depending on where you buy the ticket and what is included, but you won't save money compared to flying. If you have time (between six and nine days minimum) they are an interesting option, but only really worthwhile if you want to stop off and explore China and Russia on the way through. They could become more popular as tourism expands in the region.

Car & Motorcycle

Getting to Switzerland by road is simple, as there are fast, well-maintained motorways (freeways) through all surrounding countries. German motorways *(Autobahnen)* have no tolls and in some sections have no speed limits, whereas Austrian, French *(autoroute)* and Italian *(autostrada)* motorways have both. Austria has tunnel tolls and a motorway tax (from AS70/US$7). The Czech Republic and Slovakia also impose a motorway charge. To avoid a long drive to Switzerland, consider putting your car on a motorail service, which are run by the national railways. Many of them head south from Calais and Paris.

The Alps present a natural hazard to entering Switzerland, but main highways tend to blast straight through such immovable objects. An important tunnel if approaching

from the south is the Grand St Bernard between Aosta (Italy) and Bourg St Pierre (toll from Sfr30 for cars and motorbikes). The minor roads are more fun and scenically more interesting but they can be time-consuming, and special care is needed when negotiating mountain passes. Some, such as the N5 (E21) route from Champagnole (in France) to Geneva, are not recommended if you have not had previous experience of driving in the mountains.

Petrol is at least 10% cheaper in Switzerland than in all neighbouring countries, so aim to arrive with a nearly empty tank and leave with a full one.

Paperwork & Preparations Proof of ownership of a private vehicle should always be carried (Vehicle Registration Document for British-registered cars) when touring Europe. An EU driving licence is acceptable for driving throughout Europe. If you have any other type of licence it is advisable or necessary to obtain an International Driving Permit (IDP) from an automobile association. If you're a member of one of these associations, ask about free reciprocal benefits offered by affiliated organisations in Europe.

Third-party motor insurance is a minimum requirement in Europe: get proof of this in the form of a Green Card, issued by your insurers. Also ask for a 'European Accident Statement' form. Taking out a European breakdown assistance policy, such as the AA Five Star Service or the RAC Eurocover Motoring Assistance, is a good investment.

Every vehicle travelling across an international border should display a nationality plate of its country of registration. A warning triangle, to be used in the event of breakdown, is compulsory almost everywhere in Europe, including Switzerland. Recommended accessories are a first-aid kit (compulsory in Austria, Slovenia, Croatia, Yugoslavia and Greece), a spare bulb kit, and a fire extinguisher. In the UK, contact the RAC (☎ 0800-550 055) or the AA (☎ 0990-500 600) for more information.

Driving is on the right hand side of the road throughout Continental Europe, and priority is usually given to traffic approaching from the right. The RAC annually brings out its *European Motoring Guide*, which gives an excellent summary of regulations in each country, including parking rules. Motoring organisations in other countries have similar publications. Road signs are generally standard throughout Europe.

One thing to be aware of when driving through the continent is that Europeans are particularly strict on drink-driving laws. The blood-alcohol concentration (BAC) limit when driving is usually 0.05% or 0.08%, but in some areas (Gibraltar, Eastern Europe, Scandinavia) it is *zero* per cent.

Within Switzerland, you can drive a vehicle registered abroad for up to 12 months, and foreign driving licences are also valid for a period of one year. For more on Swiss motoring regulations, see the Getting Around chapter.

If you're from outside Europe and want to buy a vehicle to tour around, you'll find that buying a vehicle is problematic or illegal in most European countries. Britain is one of the cheapest and easiest places to buy secondhand cars, however, vehicles are left-hand drive (ie, the driver's seat will be on the 'wrong' side for driving on the right), and the headlights would need to be adjusted. A good alternative to purchasing is to lease. Renault has its Eurodrive Scheme by which non-EU residents can take out leases of 17 to 170 days. Peugeot and Citroën have similar deals.

Camper Van Travelling in a camper van can be a surprisingly economical option for budget travellers, as it can take care of eating, sleeping and travelling in one convenient package. In London you would expect to pay at least £2000 (US$3200) for something decent, though prices are lower in autumn and higher in spring. VW campers are popular, and VW spare parts are widely available in Europe. Discreet free camping is rarely a problem, and is certainly permitted in autobahn rest areas in Austria, Germany and Switzerland.

Motorcycle Touring Europe and Switzerland are ideal for motorcycle touring, with winding roads of good quality, stunning scenery to stimulate the senses, and an active motorcycling scene. The wearing of crash helmets for rider and passenger is compulsory everywhere in Europe nowadays. Austria, Belgium, France, Germany, Luxembourg and Spain require that motorcyclists use headlights during the day; in Switzerland it is recommended.

Motorway Tax Upon entering Switzerland you will need to decide whether you wish to use the motorways and semi-motorways (identified by green signs). There is a one-off charge of Sfr40 if you do. Organise this money beforehand, since you might not always be able to change money at the border – or try to buy it in advance from a Switzerland Tourism office or a motoring organisation such as the AA. The tax is payable if using either the St Gotthard tunnel or the San Bernardino tunnel. Officials at some major crossings may insist you pay the charge even if you declare you only want to use minor roads, in which case backtrack and re-approach via a smaller road, where you should have no trouble getting in.

The sticker (called a *vignette*) you receive upon paying the motorway tax must be displayed on the windscreen. It is valid for a calendar year with a month's leeway either side (ie, if you visit on 1 December you can buy the following year's tax, or up to 31 January you can visit on the previous year's tax). If you're caught on the motorways without the vignette you pay a fine of Sfr100 plus the tax. A separate vignette is required for trailers and caravans, and motorcyclists are also charged the Sfr40.

Bicycle

This is one of the best ways to travel in terms of your bank balance, your health, and the environment. But it does require a high level of commitment to see it through.

Starting from Britain, consider joining the Cyclists' Touring Club (CTC; ☎ 01483-417 217, ✉ cycling@ctc.org.uk), Cotterell House, 69 Meadrow, Godalming, Surrey GU7 3HS. It can supply information to members on cycling conditions in Europe as well as detailed routes, itineraries and cheap insurance. Membership costs UK£25 per year, or £15 for senior citizens and people aged 26 or under.

Good routes into the country from the north are through the German Black Forest or around Lake Constance. Access from the south is difficult because of the Alps. Coming from the west you need to negotiate the Jura Mountains chain to get into French Switzerland. The approach from Austria in the east is also mountainous, but scenically rewarding.

If coming from farther afield, bikes can be carried by aeroplane, but check with the carrier in advance, preferably before buying your ticket. To take it as a normal piece of luggage, you may need to remove the pedals or turn the handlebars sideways, but beware of possible excess baggage costs.

A primary consideration on long cycling trips is to travel light, but you should take a few tools and spare parts including a puncture repair kit and a spare inner tube. Panniers are essential to balance your possessions on either side of the bike frame. A bike helmet is also a very good idea, as is a good bike lock. Seasoned cyclists can average 80km a day but there's no point overdoing it. The slower you travel, the more locals you're likely to meet.

Bicycles are not allowed on European motorways – not that you would want to use those tedious bits of concrete anyway. Stick to small roads or dedicated bike tracks where possible. If you get weary of pedalling or simply want to skip a boring section, you can put your feet up on the train. On slower trains, bikes can usually be taken on board as luggage, subject to a small supplementary fee. As fast trains (IC, EC etc) can rarely accommodate bikes, they may need to be sent as registered luggage and may end up on a different train from the one you take. (One solution is to semi-dismantle your bike, shove it in a bag or sack and take it on a train as hand-luggage.) British trains are outside the European luggage registration scheme, except for Eurostar. In Switzerland, it costs Sfr24 to send a bike as international luggage.

Hitching

Hitching is never entirely safe in any country in the world, and we don't recommend it. Travellers who decide to hitch should understand they are taking a small but potentially serious risk. People who do choose to hitch will be safer if they travel in pairs and let someone know where they are going.

Throughout Europe, hitching is illegal on motorways – stand on the slip roads, or approach drivers at petrol stations, border posts and truck stops. You can increase your chances of getting a lift by looking presentable and cheerful and making a cardboard sign indicating your intended destination in the local language. Showing a flag or some other indication of your country of origin can also help. Never hitch where drivers can't stop in good time or without causing an obstruction. Once you find a good spot, stay put and hope for the best. When it starts getting dark – forget it!

Ferry tickets for a vehicle usually cover all passengers, so hitchers may be able to secure a free passage by hitching before cars board the boat. This also applies to Le Shuttle through the Channel Tunnel.

A safer way to hitch is to arrange a lift through an organisation, such as Allostop-Provoya in France and Mitfahrzentrale in Germany, or to scan university noticeboards.

Skiing & Hiking

The most dramatic way to arrive or leave Switzerland is over the Alps. This is straightforward by car, but there are more exciting ways to do it. By skis is one, on the Ventina route to Italy (see the Zermatt section in the Valais chapter for details). Ski mountaineers cross the Valais Alps on the Haute Route to Chamonix in France.

There are also various hiking trails. A famous route is over the Great St Bernard Pass, via the historic hospice, towards Mont Blanc (see Bourg St Pierre in the Valais chapter). One route around Mont Blanc, taking in three countries, is described in the Mont Blanc boxed text, also in the Valais chapter.

BOAT

Getting to Europe by boat is still possible, even in these days of long-haul air travel. Luxury cruise ships traverse the Atlantic, or a more adventurous option is to travel as a paying passenger on a freighter. Either way, consult the *OAG Cruise & Ferry Guide* published by the UK-based Reed Travel Group (☎ 01582-60 01 11), Church St, Dunstable, Bedfordshire, LU5 4HB.

Once in Europe, you can use the river network to get about; it's slower, more expensive, but probably more enjoyable than getting about by land. It is possible to take a cruise down the Rhine all the way from Basel to Amsterdam but you'll need a boatload of money to do so. The German Köln–Düsseldorfer (KD) Line (☎ 0221-20 88 288), 15 Frankenwerft, 50667 Cologne, Germany, is a major Rhine operator, and its agent in Britain is Travel Renaissance (☎ 01372-742 033), 28 South St, Epsom, Surrey. KD's eight-day Amsterdam–Basel trip costs upwards of UK£895 per person (higher rates in summer), and there are also Basel–Düsseldorf cruises. Services operate from late April to mid-October. Scylla Tours (☎ 061-264 94 84, fax 264 94 80, @ info@scylla-tours.com), Blumenrain 2, Basel, also offers several Basel–Amsterdam cruises, starting from Sfr1290 for seven days. In the USA, Uniworld (☎ 800-733 7820) is a specialist in European river cruises.

Switzerland can also be reached by steamer from several lakes: from Germany via Lake Constance (Bodensee in German); from Italy via Lake Maggiore; and from France via Lake Geneva. (See the regional chapters for more information.)

ORGANISED TOURS

All-in skiing holidays are the most popular way to visit Switzerland using a tour operator. All the large companies, such as Kuoni (well it is a Swiss company!) and Thomson include Swiss ski resorts in their brochures. Inquire at travel agents or look in the national press for details of these and other special interest holidays. You're sure to find plenty of outdoors-based tours. In the UK, for example, Sherpa Expeditions (☎ 020-8577 2717), whose Web address is at www.sherpa-walking-holidays.co.uk, and Ramblers Holidays (☎ 01707-331133) both offer hiking holidays.

There are also bus tours based on hotel or camping accommodation, geared mainly towards young people wanting a lively time. Prices start around US$45 to US$50 per day for Europe-wide tours that include Switzerland. Contiki is a major operator in this field, and has outlets worldwide (they're listed on the Web site www.contiki.com). Top Deck is similar, and sells through Flight Centres and STA, or there's Tracks with international bookings through the internet. Tracks' Web address is www.tracks-europe.com.

For people aged over 50, Saga Holidays (☎ 0800-300 500), Saga Building, Middelburg Square, Folkestone, Kent CT20 1AZ, Britain, offers good-value all-in holidays, including a coach/train tour of Switzerland. The Web address is www.saga.co.uk.

Saga Holidays also operates in the USA (☎ 0800-343 0273), at 222 Berkeley St, Boston, MA 02116, (see its Web address www.sagaholidays.com) and in Australia (☎ 02-9957 4266), at 10-17 Paul St, Milson's Point, Sydney.

WARNING

The information in this chapter is particularly vulnerable to change: prices for international travel are volatile, routes are introduced and cancelled, schedules change, special deals come and go, and rules and visa requirements are amended. Airlines and governments seem to take a perverse pleasure in making price structures and regulations as complicated as possible. You should check directly with the airline or a travel agent to make sure you understand how a fare (and any ticket you buy) works. In addition, the travel industry is highly competitive and there are many lurks and perks.

The upshot of this is that you should get opinions, quotes and advice from as many airlines and travel agents as possible before you part with your hard-earned cash. The details given in this chapter should be regarded as pointers and are not a substitute for your own careful, up-to-date research.

Getting Around

Swiss public transport is a fully integrated and comprehensive system incorporating trains, buses, boats, funiculars and cable cars. It can claim to be one of the most efficient transport networks in the world and it is a rare luxury to travel on a system that works so well. The Swiss think nothing of coordinating schedules where there may be only a few minutes leeway between arrivals and departures. Missing a connection through a late arrival is rare. Various special tickets are available to tourists to make the system even more attractive.

Information is readily available as and when you need it, but if you like to plan things down to the very last detail, pick up the complete timetable of trains, boats, buses and mountain transport that covers the whole country (Sfr16, in two volumes), which is sold at most Swiss train stations. Timetables often refer to *Werktags* (work days), which means Monday to Saturday, unless there is the qualification *'ausser Samstag'* (except Saturday).

European railpasses, such as Inter-Rail and Eurail, entitle you to free travel on the federal network, which will get you most places you might want to go. Nevertheless, European passes cover fewer routes than the Swiss travel passes mentioned below, and have no validity on bus routes. Inter-Rail is valid for a wider range of boats and private railways than Eurail, but usually only for a 50% discount whereas Eurail, if valid, is normally good for free travel. Railpasses of any sort are rarely valid for free travel on cable cars – the best you can hope for is a discount.

SWISS TRAVEL PASSES

The best deal for people planning to travel extensively is the Swiss Pass, entitling the holder to unlimited travel on almost every train, boat and bus service in the country, and on trams and buses in 35 towns. Reductions of 25% apply on funiculars and cable cars. Passes are valid for four days (Sfr216), eight days (Sfr270), 15 days (Sfr314), and one month (Sfr430). Note that these prices are for 2nd-class tickets – 1st class is about 50% higher.

The Swiss Card allows a free return journey from your arrival point to any destination in Switzerland, 50% off rail, boat and bus excursions, and 25% to 50% reductions on mountain railways. The cost is Sfr144 (2nd class) or Sfr175 (1st class) and it is valid for a month. The Half-Fare Card is a similar deal, minus the free return trip. The cost is Sfr90 for one month, Sfr150 for one year or Sfr222 for two years. If you plan to use many cable cars, it may pay to get the Half-Fare Card rather than the Swiss Pass, as the reduction is greater (50% as against 25%). This pass would certainly be worth considering for car drivers – it would pay for itself after only three or four mountain trips. The Swiss Flexi Pass allows free, unlimited trips for three days out of 15. The cost for 2nd class is Sfr216.

These cards are best purchased before arrival in Switzerland from Switzerland Tourism or travel agents, as they are only available from a few major transport centres once within the country (eg, at Zürich's Hauptbahnhof). The exception is the Half-Fare Card, which is readily available in Switzerland but rarely available abroad. You may find additional passes are available only in your home country. An example is the 21-day version of the Swiss Pass in the USA (US$305 for two people travelling together).

The Family Card can save families a lot of money. It's good for free travel (on trains, buses and boats – even on some cable cars) for children aged under 16 accompanied by at least one of their parents. Most vendors of the various Swiss travel passes will supply a Family Card free to pass purchasers; if not, they can be bought from major Swiss train stations for Sfr20. Holders of the Half-Fare Card can buy a Flexi Card at Swiss stations for Sfr52 per day; it's good for free travel within Switzerland.

Regional passes are available for free travel on certain days and for half-price travel on other days within a seven or 15-day period, but they are only valid within that particular region. Details are given at the beginning of the relevant chapters. Buy these passes in the region or at some major stations before you get there.

Another option worth considering is a Euro-Domino Pass (see the boxed text 'European Railpasses' in the Getting There & Away chapter). The pass for Switzerland is sold by European national railways *outside* Switzerland and can be bought by non-Swiss Europeans. Compared to the Swiss Pass, it's slightly cheaper per day and you can nominate your travel days within a one-month period. However, it's not valid on postbuses, city transport and some private lines (eg, the Zermatt route), and it gives no discounts on cable cars.

AIR

Internal flights are not of great interest to most visitors, owing to Switzerland's excellent ground transport. Swissair has flights between Zürich and Geneva, but it is Crossair, a subsidiary of Swissair, that is the major carrier. It has several flights daily between Zürich, Geneva, Basel, Bern and Lugano. The full one-way fare from Zürich to Geneva is Sfr225, though the return fare can be as low as Sfr190, depending on special deals. Swissair is a sales agent for Crossair. See the Getting There & Away chapter for information on the Fly-Rail program.

Some mountain resorts have helicopter operators which offer hugely enjoyable but highly expensive cruises around the Alps.

BUS

Yellow postbuses are a supplement to the rail network, following postal routes and linking towns to the more inaccessible regions in the mountains. In all, routes cover some 8000km of terrain. They are extremely regular, and departures tie in with train arrivals. Postbus stations are almost invariably next to train stations. Tickets are usually purchased from the driver, although on some routes over the Alps (for example, the Lugano-St Moritz service) it is necessary to reserve a place in advance. A few tourist-oriented Alpine routes levy a surcharge (Sfr3 to Sfr10) that's not covered by the Swiss Pass. Details are given in the relevant chapters. For a flat fee

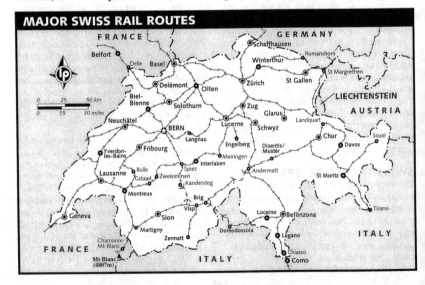

MAJOR SWISS RAIL ROUTES

of Sfr10/12 (Sfr40/48 if you don't have a bus ticket) unaccompanied luggage/bikes can be sent ahead to a post office and picked up later – an especially useful service for hikers relying on the postbus network.

TRAIN

The Swiss rail network covers 5000km and is a combination of state-run and private lines. The train is a great way to see the country and classic scenic rail routes abound – see the boxed text 'Alpine Tunnels' in this chapter.

The Swiss Federal Railway is abbreviated to SBB in German, CFF in French and FFS in Italian. Its Web address is www.rail.ch. All major stations are connected to each other by hourly departures, and the normal operating time is between 6 am and midnight. Trains are clean, reliable, frequent and as fast as the

terrain will allow. A rack and pinion (cogwheel) system is utilised on railtracks with severe gradients. An example is the line to Zermatt. Carriages are always divided into smoking and nonsmoking sections and long-distance trains usually have a dining car. In fact, in 1992 Switzerland earned the dubious distinction of becoming the first country in the world to have a McDonald's restaurant on board (since withdrawn).

Information & Tickets

Larger stations have separate information offices that can help you plan your route and give you a computerised print-out of your itinerary. Even small stations can usually give advice in English and itineraries. Free timetable booklets are invariably available. A Switzerland-wide number for train

Alpine Tunnels

The issue of transport routes across the Alps has been a very contentious one in Switzerland during the 1990s. The debate between road and rail was a major sticking point in the country's lengthy bilateral talks with the EU. The Swiss, determined to reduce pollution and environmental damage in the Alps, banned 40-tonne trucks from transiting the country, despite opposition from the EU. As a result some one million trucks annually are now diverted around Switzerland – many ending up in Austria's congested Brenner Pass. To compensate, Switzerland agreed to build two new rail tunnels through the Alps, in an effort to improve the efficiency of transporting goods on the nation's rail system (on which the percentage carried had fallen from 53% to 37% between 1970 and 1998).

Work on the new Alpine railway crossing (Neue Eisenbahn-Alpen Transversale, abbreviated as Neat) got underway in 1999. The current 15km Gotthard tunnel, built in 1880 with the loss of 307 lives, will be replaced by the world's longest rail tunnel, longer even than the Channel Tunnel (connecting Britain and France) at 57km. The new Lötschberg tunnel will also be no minnow, clocking in at 33km. The new tunnels (which will have a maximum gradient of 12.5%, compared to 27% for the present tunnels) are longer as they will be burrowing through the mountains at a much lower altitude. Complex engineering challenges will be created by unstable geological formations and the intense heat caused by the pressing down on the tunnels of up to 3km of solid rock. The tunnels will be able to support longer, heavier and faster trains than at present. The rail capacity of the Gotthard, for instance, will double.

The Lötschberg tunnel should be finished in about 2005 and the Gotthard tunnel in about 2011. The tunnels are only the main elements of a massive Sfr30.5 billion modernisation of the rail system. When completed, the Alpine routes will be linked in with Europe's high speed rail network, and passenger trains will be able to speed along at up to 250 kmph. Travel time from Zürich to Milan should fall to 2½ hours and from Basel to Milan to 3½ hours. The Neat project will be partially funded by a new weight and distance toll levied on heavy goods vehicles.

The tunnels should greatly ease pollution and congestion in the Alps. Yet part of the 1998 agreement with the EU committed Switzerland to lift its ban on 40-tonne trucks by 2005. Hopefully the rail network will be ready to meet the new challenge from road haulage by then.

Transports of Delight

That old cliché about travel – getting there is half the fun – is actually true in Switzerland. The country is crammed full of majestic vistas. Travel by train and you can recline in the comfort of your seat, sipping a drink from the buffet trolley, and simply let the views unwind before your eyes. Those views get even more spectacular when you venture onto funiculars and cable cars. The boat trips aren't bad either. Additionally, the practical aspects of organising your trip present no problem; information on schedules and services is readily available. And what's more, schedules are not the stuff of fantasy as they are in some other countries - transport actually runs on time.

It would be impossible to give an exhaustive summary of all the best journeys Switzerland has to offer here – there are simply so many of them. Basically, any trip in or around the Alps will yield something memorable. This fact is by no means lost on those selling Switzerland and its transport network. The virtues of several train routes are packaged as the ultimate travel experience. The Glacier Express (Zermatt to St Moritz or Chur) is perhaps the most famous of these and hard on its heels is the Golden Pass route from Lucerne to Montreux. Others include the Bernina Express (a train/bus combination from Chur to Lugano) and the William Tell Express (a boat/train package from Lucerne to Lugano or Locarno).

While these much-trumpeted trips are undeniably special, in my view they are not much better than numerous other journeys that are not marketed as ends in themselves. They are certainly a great way to get from A to B, but unless you actually want to be in A or B, I wouldn't worry about experiencing them over-much, as you'll encounter plenty of great journeys in the course of your normal travel around the country. In any case, 'normal' trains ply exactly the same routes, and without requiring special reservations or the payment of surcharges.

The Glacier Express takes 7½ hours, crosses 291 bridges and reaches 2033m when it hits Oberalp Passhöhe. But you don't have to do the whole thing – the Brig-Zermatt leg is pretty special all by itself, and there are no surcharges for this section. Also, the passage from Chur to Disentis/Mustér is not as good as the leg from Disentis/Mustér to Andermatt. The Golden Pass route is a six hour stint requiring at least three changes, and can also be experienced in smaller sections. The Lucerne-Interlaken leg is best around the Brünig Pass, and the Panoramic Express part (Montreux-Zweisimmen) is best from Montreux to Château d'Oex, especially the climb from Lake Geneva. There are around four Panoramic Express trains per day, though trains ply this route hourly, and some

information is ☎ 157 22 22; calls are charged at Sfr1.19 per minute.

Single train tickets for journeys over 80km are valid for two days and it is possible to break the journey on the same ticket, but tell the conductor of your intentions before your ticket is punched. Train schedules are revised yearly at the end of May, so you should double-check all fares and frequencies quoted. Ordinary fares are expensive, meaning that one of the special passes mentioned will almost certainly save you money.

If you have a specific itinerary and don't require flexibility, then a *Rundfahrt* (*Billet Circulaire* in French) ticket might do the job instead. This is a return ticket that allows you to take a circuitous route, with stops along the way. Like all return tickets over 160km (ie, over 80km each way), it is valid for one month. Unfortunately, these tickets are now priced according to a different system, and aren't the bargain they once were.

All fares quoted are for 2nd-class unless stated otherwise, and fares for 1st-class average about 65% higher. Return fares are cheaper than two singles only on longer trips. Look out for special deals offered by SBB, such as cheap day passes in low season, off-peak tickets or special promotions.

Some rural, smaller rail lines have a 'self-control' ticketing system – look out for the yellow eye pictogram. On these services, be sure to buy a ticket before boarding, or you'll risk a fine.

Transports of Delight

non-surcharge express trains (eg, the Regional Panoramic) even have the Panoramic Express-type extended-height windows for better appreciation of the views.

Train journeys are less interesting in the Swiss Plateau, on the main express route between Zürich and Bern, and in the northern densely populated region around Basel and Aarau. In Valais, the Rhône Valley is rather broad, and views along here aren't as spectacular as they are in the valleys branching off either side. Generally, the scenery is less dramatic in the north-east than in the south, but there are still some fun journeys to be had here, such as the Rhine-Bodensee route, or the green, rolling hills along the St Gallen-Appenzell route. Almost any train journey in and around the Jungfrau Region will leave you gasping for more.

Boat trips are popular in Switzerland, and you can easily plan these to be part of your onward travel rather than just using them as round-trip excursions. The lake that attracts the most visitors is Lake Lucerne (Vierwaldstättersee), and its irregular coastline provides constantly unfolding views. Other lakes that pull in the visitors are the lakes of Geneva, Zürich and Thun.

Some mountain passes that offer breathtaking scenery are accessible only by car or postbus. These include the series of passes near Andermatt – the Susten Pass, the Nufenen Pass, the Furka Pass and the Grimsel Pass. You can visit all of these on a round-trip. Another great postbus route is the Palm Express from Lugano to St Moritz, that skirts lakes Lugano and Como (in Italy) before rising into the mountains via the Maloja Pass. An equally good alternative is to take the postbus from Lugano to Tirano in Italy, then the Bernina Express train to St Moritz, which soars to 2253m at Ospizio Bernina. The whole trip can be done on the Swiss Pass.

Cable cars are a great way to experience fabulous views quickly and with minimal effort. Inevitably they are expensive, with return trips to important sites costing around Sfr60, Sfr70 or much more, though sometimes you can get cheaper deals for ascents late in the day. An excellent but relatively unheralded viewpoint, which costs less to reach than more famous ones, is Stanserhorn (1898m), on the southern side of Lake Lucerne. Various viewpoints in Ticino are also better value than in most other places, such as Monte Brè or Monte San Salvatore above Lugano and Cimetta above Locarno. On the other hand, if money is no object, be sure to experience the panoramic delights from Schilthorn, Jungfraujoch and Mt Titlis. The latter features the world's first revolving cable car.

Luggage

Train stations invariably offer luggage storage, either at a special counter (usually Sfr5 per piece) or in 24-hour lockers (Sfr2 to Sfr4 small, Sfr3 to Sfr5 large). Nearly every station allows train ticket-holders the option to send their luggage ahead by train where they can pick it up at their destination station in the evening. This is especially useful if you're on a tight schedule and are visiting several different locations in the course of the day before your overnight stop. The charge is Sfr10 per piece (Sfr12 for bikes).

Platforms & Trains

Station announcements state on which track (*Gleis* in German, *voie* in French, *binario* in Italian) the train is due. Station platforms are long and are divided into sections, A to D. Take care – a small rural train may already be waiting at one end while you're vainly waiting for it to arrive at the other end.

In SBB trains, 1st-class seats are comfortable and spacious, usually a single and a pair across the width of the carriage. A few private lines are less generous with space, or may not have 1st-class at all. It is rare for 1st-class to be full and it's often virtually empty. The main irritation of 1st-class travel is that you constantly have to listen to business-people babbling into their mobile phones. The placement of 1st-class sections is usually announced over the loudspeaker in stations, or shown in a diagram on the platform.

As the train approaches, look for the easy-to-see horizontal yellow stripe along the carriage.

Second-class, however, is perfectly comfortable, with two seats either side of the aisle. These carriages are sometimes fairly full, especially when the army is on the move, but it is rare that you'll have to stand.

CAR & MOTORCYCLE

Driving is an enjoyable experience in Switzerland. Roads are well maintained, well signposted and generally not too congested. You may find it frustrating to have to concentrate on the road while magnificent scenery unfolds all around, but at least you can stop at frequent parking bays to take it all in.

Travelling in your own vehicle gives you the most flexibility, and compared to many other countries, it is not necessary to spend very long on the road between places of interest. Unfortunately, the independence you enjoy does tend to isolate you to some extent from the local people. You should also consider the effect your exhaust emissions have on the Alpine environment. Cars are usually inconvenient in city centres, where it's probably worth ditching your trusty chariot and relying on public transport.

You generally have a choice when driving in mountainous areas. Principal routes are as direct as the terrain will allow, often ploughing through mountains via long tunnels. Smaller roads go over the mountains. They take much longer to negotiate and add miles to your journey, but are scenically much more rewarding. Some of these minor passes are closed from November to May (see the Alpine Passes section later in this chapter) and you should stay in low gear on steep stretches. Carrying snow chains is recommended in winter.

The Swiss Touring Club (☎ 022-417 27 27), or Touring Club der Schweiz (TCS), is at 4 Chemin de Blandonnet, Case postale 820, CH-1214, Geneva. It is the largest motoring organisation in Switzerland, is affiliated with the AA in Britain, and has reciprocal agreements with other motoring organisations worldwide. Its Web address is www.tcs.ch. The Swiss Automobile Club (☎ 031-328 31 11, fax 312 25 83), or Automobil-Club der Schweiz (ACS), at Wasserwerkgasse 39, CH-3000 Bern 13, also has worldwide links. Its Web address is www.acs.ch.

TCS operates the national 24-hour emergency breakdown service (☎ 140). It can be used free by members of the Swiss motoring clubs or their affiliates; anybody else has to pay (charges are Sfr95 to Sfr350). The TCS or the ACS can provide detailed information about motoring in Switzerland. Call ☎ 163 for traffic conditions (recorded information).

Petrol prices per litre are around Sfr1.28 for leaded (Super) and Sfr1.18 for unleaded (Bleifrei, sans plomb) or diesel.

Road Rules & Signs

A handbook on Swiss traffic regulations (in English) is available for Sfr12 from cantonal registration offices and at some customs posts. The minimum driving age for car and motorcycles is 18, for mopeds it's 14.

The Swiss drive on the right, and if in doubt, always give priority to traffic approaching from the right. Vehicles on roundabouts have priority over those about to enter it. On mountain roads, the ascending vehicle has priority, unless a postbus is involved, which always has right of way. Postbus drivers let rip a multi-tone bugle that sounds like a call to a cavalry charge when approaching blind corners. In towns, allow trams plenty of respect, and give way to disembarking passengers.

Many driving infringements incur an on-the-spot fine, and you should always ask for a receipt. Speed limits are 50km/h in towns (though certain stretches may be as low as 30km/h in some towns), 120km/h on motorways, 100km/h on semi-motorways and 80km/h on other roads. Car occupants are required to wear a seat belt (even in the back seat, if they're fitted), and vehicles must carry a breakdown warning triangle which must be readily accessible (ie, not in the boot). Dipped headlights must be used in all tunnels, and are recommended for motorcyclists during the day. Motorcyclists must not overtake a line of vehicles. Both motorcyclists and their passengers must wear crash helmets.

Switzerland is tough on drink-driving, so don't risk it. The blood alcohol content (BAC) limit is 0.05%, and if caught exceeding this limit, you may face a heavy fine, a ban from driving in Switzerland for a year, or even imprisonment. If you're involved in a car accident, the police must be called if anyone receives more than superficial injuries.

Road signs are straightforward, easy to follow, and adopt internationally recognised conventions. Triangular signs with a red border warn of dangers and circular signs with a red border illustrate prohibitions. Signs you may not have come across before are: a crisscrossed white tyre on a blue circular background means snow chains are compulsory, and a yellow bugle on a square blue background means it is a mountain postal road and you must obey indications given by postbus drivers.

As in most other European countries, motorways and principal routes are designated by two different numbering systems: the national one (N) and the pan-European one (E). Both versions are usually listed in the text. A motorway is identified by the sign showing a white dual carriageway on a rectangular green background, and a semi-motorway by one showing a white car on a rectangular green background. This is important if you don't want to stray onto a motorway without a vignette (see the Motorway Tax section in the Getting There & Away chapter).

Urban Parking It is difficult to park in many city centres (especially Zürich). Street parking in suburban white zones is unrestricted, but in the centre (assuming traffic isn't banned altogether, as it often is), street parking is controlled by parking meters during working hours (8 am to 7 pm Monday to Saturday). These cost around

DISTANCE CHART (km)

	Basel (Bâle)	Bellinzona	Bern (Berne)	Biel (Bienne)	Brig	Chur	Fribourg	Geneva (Genève)	Interlaken	Lausanne	Lugano	Lucerne (Luzern)	Neuchâtel	St Gallen	St Moritz	Schaffhausen	Sion	Zürich
Basel (Bâle)	---																	
Bellinzona	241	---																
Bern (Berne)	97	253	---															
Biel (Bienne)	93	247	41	---														
Brig	190	161	91	129	---													
Chur	228	115	242	237	174	---												
Fribourg	132	285	34	71	179	274	---											
Geneva (Genève)	267	420	171	209	214	409	138	---										
Interlaken	153	195	57	92	73	209	92	230	---									
Lausanne	203	359	107	146	151	346	72	62	167	---								
Lugano	267	28	279	273	187	141	331	446	221	383	---							
Lucerne (Luzern)	103	140	115	107	149	140	147	280	71	218	166	---						
Neuchâtel	141	294	46	31	141	283	43	123	104	73	320	156	---					
St Gallen	191	217	204	197	288	102	236	371	225	307	243	138	244	---				
St Moritz	313	150	327	321	241	85	359	494	294	430	176	225	368	178	---			
Schaffhausen	161	246	173	167	259	182	205	340	228	276	272	108	214	80	266	---		
Sion	252	214	160	195	53	399	128	161	86	98	240	271	166	356	294	329	---	
Zürich	113	195	125	119	208	118	157	292	177	229	221	57	166	81	203	51	281	---

Sfr1 to Sfr1.50 per hour with a maximum of one or two hours. Central streets outside metered areas are usually marked as blue zones, allowing 1½ hours stay during working hours, or as (increasingly rare) red zones, with a 15-hour maximum. In either case parking is free but you need to display a parking disc in your window, indicating the time you first parked. Discs are obtainable free from offices of the Swiss motoring organisations (TCS and ACS), and sometimes from tourist offices or banks.

Alpine Passes

Some minor Alpine passes are closed from November to the end of May. Most of the major ones are negotiable year-round, depending on the weather. Exceptions are the Grand St Bernard, St Gotthard and San Bernardino, but these have a tunnel you can take instead. Passes that are open year-round are Bernina, Brünig, Flüela, Forclaz, Il Fuorn (Ofen), Julier, Maloja, Mosses, Pillon and Simplon. Passes that are open only from June to October are Albula, Furka, Grand St Bernard, Grimsel, Klausen, Oberalp, San Bernardino, Susten and Umbrail. Other passes are Lukmanier (open May to November), Nufenen (June to September), Splügen and St Gotthard (May to October).

More information on important passes is given throughout the book. A motoring organisation should be able to supply greater detail (gradients, altitudes etc), and a decent road map will also have that information. The local tourist office can tell you if passes are open, or signs on approach roads will state if passes are open and if snow chains are required.

You can also take your car on some trains, such as through the Lötschberg tunnel south of Kandersteg.

Car Rental

For the lowest prices, organise car rental before departure. Holiday Autos has good rates for Europe. Its office in Britain (☎ 0870-400 0011) charges UK£139 all-inclusive per week for the lowest-category car in Switzerland. Holiday Autos has branches across Europe, and its office in the USA is Kemwel Holiday Autos (☎ 914-825 3100), which also has leasing deals (leasing is a good option for longer stays). The UK-based Autos Abroad (☎ 020-7409 1900) claims to undercut everyone else; its weekly rate for Switzerland is UK£135.

EU residents should note that they are currently prohibited from driving non-EU hire cars (eg, those with Swiss number plates) into EU countries. The car rental industry is lobbying to get this inconvenient regulation changed.

Prices are much higher for on-the-spot rates in Switzerland. Local firms are the cheapest operators, though with the multinationals you usually get the option of one-way drop-off (normally no charge within Switzerland). National reservation numbers (local rate) and Web addresses are: Avis ☎ 0848-81 18 18, www.avis.ch; Europcar ☎ 0848-80 80 99, www.europcar.ch; and Hertz ☎ 0848-81 10 10, www.hertz.com. Budget's central reservations number is ☎ 01-838 58 88 or fax 838 58 68. Working out the best deal can sometimes be confusing (eg, there's the 'Hotel Tariff' or the 'Leisure Tariff') though all these operators charge about Sfr130 for one day's rental (unlimited kilometres), with reductions beyond three days.

Look out for special deals over the weekend, usually lasting from 9 am Friday to 9 am Monday – Europcar charges Sfr259 including 1500km. Cheaper operators include Sixt (☎ 0848-88 44 44), with branches at the main airports and in big cities. Its unlimited kilometres cheapest rates are Sfr88 for one day and Sfr133 over the weekend.

No matter where you rent, make sure you understand what is included in the price (unlimited kilometres, tax, insurance, collision damage waiver etc) and what your liabilities are. Rental terms are not always comparable between operators, eg, CDW (collision damage waiver) is an optional extra with Sixt (from Sfr26.20 per day) whereas with the multinationals it's automatically included.

The minimum rental age varies from 20 to 25 depending upon the company and category of vehicle, and you'll probably need a credit card (life will certainly be easier with one). Be wary of signing anything in a language you can't read and if you're dealing with a local, cut-price operator it might be worth looking over the car before you agree to the terms.

Motorcycle and moped rental is not very common in Switzerland, but there are a few places that do this (see the Geneva and Zürich chapters).

Car Purchase

The price of new and used cars in Switzerland is not bad compared to the rest of Europe. The TCS publishes the *Eurotax* monthly guide to used car prices. Car registration plates are issued to the owner, so whether you buy new or secondhand the vehicle will come without plates (though the vending garage can apply for the plates on your behalf). Likewise, if you sell a vehicle, you remove the plates and return them to the cantonal motor registration office (or transfer them to your new car, unless you move canton).

The problem for visitors is that normal plates are only issued to Swiss residents. However, in some circumstances non-residents can buy a duty-free car in Switzerland and run it on special 'Z' plates – inquire at a cantonal motor registration office. All Swiss-registered cars must undergo an emission test every two years (annually for older cars) and a serviceability control test every three years.

Importing a vehicle into Switzerland is no longer as problematic as it once was, but it would need to conform to current Swiss regulations. All newly registered cars, for example, must be fitted with a catalytic converter. The Swiss embassy should be able to inform you of documentation required. You can drive for one year in a vehicle registered abroad.

BICYCLE

Despite the hilly countryside, cycling is popular in Switzerland. Cycles can be hired from most train stations and returned to any other station with a rental counter, though there is a Sfr6 surcharge if you don't return it to the same station (declare your intentions at the outset). The rental charge for ordinary bikes (seven-speed) is Sfr20 for half a day, Sfr26 for a full day or Sfr100 per week. Counters are open daily, usually from the crack of dawn until some time in the evening. The larger stations also rent mountain bikes (Sfr25/32 for a half/full day, Sfr128 for one week). All prices are reduced around 20% if you have one of the Swiss travel passes (excluding regional passes). In Basel, Bern, Geneva and Zürich there are places where you can borrow bikes *free of charge* – see the city sections for details. Many local and regional tourist offices have free cycling maps to give out.

Bikes can be taken with you (in the luggage carriage) on slower trains and sometimes even on IC or EC trains. The charge is Sfr15 (Sfr10 if you have a Swiss travel pass, excluding regional passes) which is a per day fee and you can make more than one journey. On other trains your bike needs to go as unaccompanied luggage (Sfr12), and may end up on a different train to the one you take.

HITCHING

Although illegal on motorways, hitching is allowed on other roads. Sometimes it can be fairly easy, at other times it's slow and frustrating. Indigenous Swiss are not all that sympathetic towards hitchers, and you'll find that most of your lifts will come from foreigners. A sign is helpful. Make sure you stand in a place where vehicles can stop. This in itself can be a problem, as rural roads may not be wide enough to allow stopping (except for passing bays), and there's often no pedestrian walkway beside the road. In other words, you can't really walk between lifts so find a good spot and stay there. To get a ride on a truck, ask around the customs post at border towns (also see the Hitching section in the Getting There & Away chapter).

WALKING

Many city centres are compact enough to enable major tourist sights to be seen on a walking tour, but walking really comes into its own in rural areas. Hikes are an excellent way to leave behind the wail of car horns and the opaque logic of train schedules.

(For more information, see the Activities chapter, as well as the individual regional chapters.) Lonely Planet's *Walking in Switzerland* is a detailed and extensively mapped guidebook. Local tourist offices can often supply free or cheap hiking maps.

BOAT

All the larger lakes are serviced by steamers operated by Swiss Federal Railway (SBB), or allied private companies for which national travel passes are valid. Lakes covered include Geneva, Constance, Lucerne, Lugano, Neuchâtel, Biel, Murten, Thun, Brienz and Zug, but not Lake Maggiore. Railpasses are not valid for cruises offered by smaller companies on these lakes. A Swiss Navigation Boat Pass costs Sfr35 and entitles the bearer to 50% off fares of all services operated by SBB and major lake carriers (like CGN on Lake Geneva). It is valid for a calendar year, but only a few services operate in winter. The pass is well worth buying for those who aren't covered by a railpass (eg, car drivers).

MOUNTAIN TRANSPORT

There are five main modes of transport used in steep Alpine regions. A funicular *(Standseilbahn, funiculaire, funicolare)* is a pair of counter-balancing cars drawn by cables along an inclined track.

A cable car *(Luftseilbahn, téléphérique, funivia)* is a cabin dramatically suspended from a cable high over a valley, also with a twin that goes down when it goes up. A gondola *(Gondelbahn, télécabine, cabinovia)* is a smaller version of a cable car except that the gondola is hitched onto a continuously running cable once the passengers are inside. Nowadays people use the term 'cable car' to describe a gondola as well, so I haven't worried too much about the distinction in the text. A cable chair or chair lift *(Sesselbahn, télésiège, seggiovia)* is likewise hitched onto a cable but is unenclosed. A ski lift *(Schlepplift, téléski, sciovia)* is a T-bar hanging from a cable, which pulls skiers uphill while their ski-clad feet slide along

the snow. T-bars aren't as safe as modern cable cars (as they are vulnerable to skiers letting go or occasionally falling off) and are being gradually phased out.

LOCAL TRANSPORT
Public Transport

All local city transport is linked together on the same ticketing system, so you can change lines on the same ticket. Usually you have to buy tickets before boarding from ticket dispensers at stops (though occasionally, such as in Montreux/Vevey, you can also buy from machines on board). In some towns, single tickets may give a time limit (eg, one hour) for travel within a particular zone, so you can break the journey within that time. Multi-strip tickets may be available at a discount (validate it in the on-board machine at the outset of the journey), or one-day passes are even better value. There are regular checks for people travelling without tickets. Those found wanting pay an on-the-spot fine of Sfr40 to Sfr60.

Taxi

Good bus, rail and underground railway networks make the taking of taxis all but unnecessary, but if you need one in a hurry they can usually be found idling like a gang of street urchins by train stations, or you can telephone for one. They are always metered and work on the basis of a starting flat fee plus a charge per km. Prices are high.

ORGANISED TOURS

Tours are booked through local tourist offices. The country is so compact that excursions to the major national attractions are offered from most towns. A trip up to Jungfraujoch, for example, is available from Zürich, Geneva, Bern, Lucerne and Interlaken. Most tours represent reasonable value. They tend to be more expensive than going it alone, but can be the best option if you are pressed for time. A short city tour will give you a quick overview of the place and can be a good way to begin your visit.

Swiss Mittelland

The Swiss (Schweizer) Mittelland comprises the canton of Solothurn and the flattish, northern part of canton Bern (often known as Berner Mittelland or Le Plateau Bernois). The main focus of the area is the Swiss capital, Bern, an enticing city with a provincial feel that belies its status. The Berner Mittelland is also known as the home of the famous cheese, Emmental.

History

In the 12th century the Dukes of Zähringen were the most powerful family in the locality, and in 1191 founded the fortified town of Bern. Shortly after it became established, Bern independently concluded alliances with lesser nobles and gradually extended its own sovereignty in the region. In 1218 it managed to win the status of an imperial city under the direct responsibility of the Habsburgs (see History in the Facts About Switzerland chapter). Meanwhile, it continued with its territorial ambitions and entered into a series of alliances known as the Burgundian Confederation.

Bern joined the Swiss Confederation in 1353, as it was concerned with protecting itself in the east while it expanded in other directions. In 1415 Bern gained control of Aargau in the north, and in the 16th century, most of the territory around Lake Geneva fell under Bernese rule, largely at the expense of the House of Savoy. At this stage, Bern had reached the peak of its power and influence, a situation that continued until 1798. Solothurn was not absorbed by Bern and its relations with its more powerful neighbour were not always cordial (see the Solothurn section).

In 1798 the French invaded Switzerland and completely destroyed Bern's power base. Under the ensuing Helvetic Republic, Bern was chopped down to size and lost control of the Oberland. In 1803 Bern was reunited with the Oberland but, in the

- Discover the Gothic cathedral, clocktower and colourful fountains in Bern's historic centre.
- Join the free tours of the Swiss Federal Assembly.
- View the world's largest Paul Klee collection in Bern's Museum of Fine Arts.
- Indulge the senses at the Emmental cheese demonstration dairy in Affoltern.
- Explore the churches, fountains and weaponry in Solothurn.

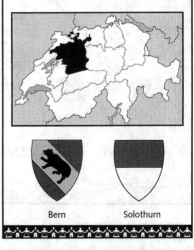

Bern   Solothurn

new Switzerland that emerged from the Congress of Vienna (1814–15), it was stripped of Aargau and Vaud, which became separate cantons. Although it was chosen as the capital of Switzerland in 1848, more land was lost when the canton of Jura was created in 1979.

Orientation & Information

The Swiss Mittelland is a fertile plain wedged between the Alps and the Jura. The

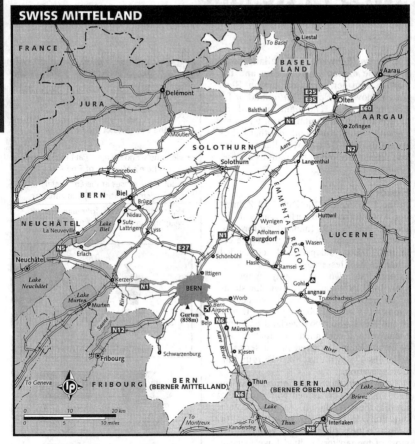

SWISS MITTELLAND

countryside is characterised by small villages and rolling, green hills. German is the principal language spoken, except for a small area around Biel where French is on an equal footing.

The regional tourist office is Schweizer Mittelland Tourismus (☎ 328 12 28, fax 311 12 22, ℮ info@swit.ch), Postfach, CH-3001 Bern. Its Web site is at www.smit.ch. The Bern tourist office dispenses region-wide information to personal callers.

Bern canton has a public holiday on 2 January (Berchtoldstag).

Bern

☎ 031 • pop 132,000 • elevation 540m

Founded in 1191 by Berthold V, Bern (Berne in French, and, usually, English) is Switzerland's capital and fourth-largest city. Its name, so the story goes, is in honour of the bear (*Bär* in German, and *Bärn* in local dialect) that was Berthold's first kill when hunting in the area. Even today the bear remains the heraldic mascot of the city.

In 1405 the predominantly wood-built town was all but destroyed by a devastating

Church Tower, Thun, Bernese Oberland

Gourmet fare in a delicatessen window, Bern

Zeitglockenturm, Bern, Swiss Mittelland

One of Bern's ornate, colourful fountains

Schynige Platte Railway, Jungfrau Region

MARTIN MOOS

Kappellbrücke, Lucerne

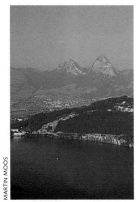

MARTIN MOOS

Lake Lucerne

MARTIN MOOS

Blooming - Lake Lucerne area

MARTIN MOOS

The ornately frescoed guildhall, Lucerne

MARK HONAN

Everyone in Lucerne gets dressed up, or down, for the Fasnacht festival.

fire. It was rebuilt using sandstone, and although most of the houses were replaced in the 16th and 17th centuries, the structure of the centre remains largely unaltered from that period. Bern was elected as the seat of federal authority upon the adoption of the new Swiss Constitution in 1848. The other main candidate at the time was Zürich, but French-speakers swayed the vote in Bern's favour as they considered Zürich too Germanic.

Despite playing host to the nation's politicians, Bern retains a relaxed, small-town charm. However, in the train station during rush hour, you will feel like a cork bobbing in a sea of surging humanity; mere flotsam in a tide of purposeful commuters. Its picturesque Old Town contains 6km of covered arcades and 11 historic fountains, as well as the descendants of the city's first casualty (the bear) who perform tricks for tourists.

Orientation

The compact centre of town is contained within a sharp U-bend of the Aare River, and access to some of the main streets is restricted to pedestrians and public transport. The main train station is in the mouth of this 'U' and is within easy reach of all the main sights. The station has luggage lockers (Sfr4), bicycle rental (from 6.10 am to 11.45 pm daily), Swissair check-in, and an Aperto supermarket (open till 10 pm daily).

Information

Tourist Offices Bern Tourismus (☎ 328 12 12, fax 312 12 33, ✆ info-res@ bernetourism.ch), in the train station, is open 9 am to 8.30 pm daily. From 1 October to 31 May it shuts two hours earlier and Sunday hours are reduced to 10 am to 5 pm. Services include hotel reservations (Sfr3 commission, so use the free phone outside instead) and excursions. Its free booklet, *Bern aktuell*, contains much practical and recreational information in three languages. The train information office is opposite the tourist office, open 8 am to 7 pm Monday to Friday and 8 am to 5 pm Saturday.

Another tourist office is by the bear pits, open 9 am to 5 pm daily in summer, 10 am to 4 pm in March, April, May and October.

Money Exchange facilities, including cash advances with Visa, Eurocard and Diners Card, are in the SBB office in the lower level of the train station. It is open 6.15 am to 9.45 pm daily (8.45 pm from mid-October to May).

Business Hours Some shops are shut on Monday morning, and most have extended hours until 9 pm on Thursday evening.

Post & Communications The main post office (Schanzenpost 3001) is at Schanzenstrasse. It is open 7.30 am to 6.30 pm Monday to Friday and 7.30 to 11 am on Saturday. There's an out-of-hours emergency counter open daily (surcharge payable).

Email & Internet Access The LOEB department store on Spitalgasse has internet terminals in the 2nd-level basement (✆ edvbern@jaeggibu.ch). Two are free (20 minute limit), and two cost Sfr5 for 30 minutes (these are pre-bookable). The Stauffacher bookshop (see below) also has internet terminals, but it's more expensive.

Travel Agencies The Swiss budget and student travel agency SSR (☎ 302 03 12) has two branches: Falkenplatz 9 (10 am to 6.30 pm weekdays) and Rathausgasse 64 (9.30 am to 6 pm weekdays). Both have late opening to 8 pm on Thursday and are open 10 am to 3 pm Saturday.

Bookshops Stauffacher (☎ 311 24 11), at Neuengasse 25, has many books in English and French, both fiction and nonfiction. Atlas (☎ 311 90 44), at Schauplatzgasse 21, specialises in travel books and backpacking accessories. Check Postgasse, Rathausgasse or Kramgasse for places selling second-hand books.

Library The Municipal and University Library, Münstergasse 61, has a reading room with English-language newspapers, and is open 8 am to 9 pm weekdays and to noon Saturday. The book collection is open 10 am to 6 pm weekdays and 10 am to noon Saturday.

Laundry Jet Wash (☎ 330 26 38), Dammweg 43, is self-service and north-east of the train station. It's open 7 am to 9 pm Monday to Saturday and 9 am to 6 pm Sunday.

Medical & Emergency Services There is a police station (☎ 321 21 21) and a chemist in the train station. For a doctor, dentist or chemist out-of-hours, call ☎ 311 22 11. The national emergency numbers can also be used:

Police ☎ 117
Fire brigade ☎ 118
Ambulance ☎ 144
Car breakdown service ☎ 140

The university hospital (☎ 632 21 11), with a casualty department, is on Fribourgstrasse.

Gay & Lesbian Information HAB (☎ 311 63 53), Mühleplatz 11, 5th floor, is a gay counselling and information centre. There's a bar most evenings (not Monday).

Walking Tour

The city map from the tourist office details a picturesque walk through the Old Town. The core of the walk is Marktgasse and Kramgasse with their covered arcades and colourful fountains. The fountains appear every 150m and were constructed in approximately 1545. The **Ogre Fountain** on Kornhausplatz, dividing the two streets, depicts an ogre enjoying a light snack – with one child mid-mouth, and a few more waiting their turn!

Nearby is the **Zeitglockenturm**, a clock tower on which revolving figures herald the chiming hour. Congregate at Kramgasse (on the tower's east side) at least four minutes before the hour to see them twirl. Originally a city gate, the clock was installed in 1530. The next fountain along shows a bear holding a shield bearing the Zähringen coat of arms – this appears on many a postcard.

Just over the Aare River to the east are the **bear pits** *(Bärengraben)*, open 8 am to 6 pm daily (9 am to 4 pm October to March). Bears have been at this site since 1857, although records show that as far back as 1441 the city council bought acorns

to feed the ancestors of these overgrown pets. Up the hill is the **Rose Garden**, which has 200 varieties of roses and an excellent view of the city. Another good place to wander is the **Botanical Gardens** (free entry), on the north side of the Lorrainebrücke.

Cathedral

The unmistakably Gothic, 15th-century cathedral *(Münster)* stands tall with the highest spire (100m) in Switzerland. The tower gives a fine view extending to the Bernese Alps, with the reddish rooftops of Bern itself scattered below. The best feature of the church is the **main portal**, with an elaborate tympanum depicting the Last Judgement – notice one pope ascending to heaven and another being cast into the fires of hell. The cathedral was Catholic until the Reformation, at which point many of the statues were thrown out (hence the empty recesses in the chancel), but the Catholic saints on the ceiling remain as they were too high to get at.

Other features to notice are the stained-glass windows (mostly built between 1421 and 1450) and the carved choir stalls (1523). The cathedral is open 10 am (11.30 am Sunday) to 5 pm daily except Monday most of the year. From November to Easter Sunday, however, hours are 10 am to noon and 2 to 4 pm (5 pm Saturday; Sunday hours are 11.30 am to 2 pm). The tower always closes half an hour earlier than the rest of the cathedral, and costs Sfr3 or Sfr1 for children.

LISA BORG

The brown bear has been both the mascot and symbol of Bern for over 500 years.

BERN (BERNE)

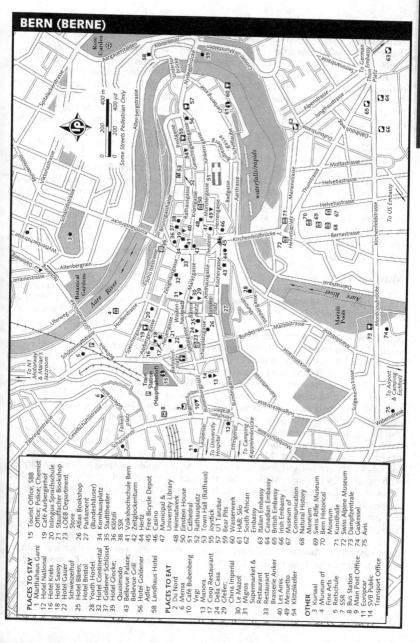

PLACES TO STAY
1 Marthahaus Garni
12 Hotel National
16 Hotel Krebs
18 Hotel Savoy
22 Hotel Gauer
25 Schweizerhof
  Hotel Bären;
  Hotel Bristol
28 Youth Hostel
32 Hotel Continental
37 Goldener Schlüssel
39 Hotel Glocke;
  Quasimodo
43 Bellevue Palace;
  Bellevue Grill
56 Hotel Goldener
  Adler
58 Landhaus Hotel

PLACES TO EAT
2 Du Nord
6 Mensa
10 Café Bubenberg
13 Vegi
17 Manora
24 Coop Restaurant
29 Della Casa
  Cfeiler;
30 China Imperial
31 Le Mazot
  Migros
33 Supermarket &
  Restaurant
40 Brasserie Anker
49 Les Amis
54 Klötzlikeller

OTHER
3 Kursaal
4 Museum of
  Fine Arts
5 Reitschule
7 SSR
8 Bus Station
9 Main Post Office
11 Europcar
14 SVB Public
  Transport Office

15 Tourist Office; SBB
  Office; Police; Chemist
19 Café Aarbergerhof
20 Inlingua Sprachschule
21 Stauffacher Bookshop
23 LOEB Department
  Store
26 Atlas Bookshop
27 Parliament
  (Bundeshäuser)
34 Kornhausplatz
35 Stadttheater
36 Klötzli
38 SSR
41 Volkshochschule Bern
42 Zeitglockenturm
44 Hertz
45 Free Bicycle Depot
46 Casino
47 Municipal &
  University Library
48 Heimatwerk
50 Einstein House
51 Cathedral
52 Rathausplatz
53 Town Hall (Rathaus)
55 Joystick
57 U1 Tanzbar
59 Wasserwerk
60 Bear Pits
61 HAB: Silo
62 South African
  Embassy
63 Italian Embassy
64 Canadian Embassy
65 British Embassy
66 Irish Embassy
67 Museum of
  Communication
68 Natural History
  Museum
69 Swiss Rifle Museum
70 Bern Historical
  Museum
71 Kunsthalle
72 Swiss Alpine Museum
73 Dampfzentrale
74 Gaskessel
75 Avis

Parliament

Well worth a visit is the Bundeshäuser, on Bundesplatz, home of the Swiss Federal Assembly. There are free daily tours (45 minutes) when the parliament is not in session. Arrive early and reserve a place for later in the day. A multilingual guide takes you through the impressive chambers. This grand, domed building was built in 1902, and on the glass of the dome are displayed the coats of arms of 22 cantons (the canton of Jura wasn't yet inaugurated). Inside are other plaques, pictures and statues that reflect important events in Swiss history. There are two main chambers, the National Council and the Council of States; the latter having a huge chandelier, a tangled mess of wrought iron weighing 1½ tonnes and sprouting 214 bulbs. During parliamentary sessions you can watch from the public gallery.

Museums

There is no shortage of museums. Many are grouped together on the south side of the Kirchenfeldbrücke.

Museum of Fine Arts The Kunstmuseum, Hodlerstrasse 8-12, holds the world's largest Paul Klee collection, a total of over 2000 works (mostly drawings), although it is not possible to show all of them at once. The museum also displays canvasses by Italian masters from the 14th, 15th and 16th centuries, such as Fra Angelico *(Madonna and Child)* and Duccio. Swiss artists since the 15th century are well represented, particularly Ferdinand Hodler. More modern schools of art are not overlooked, either, with paintings by Cézanne, Matisse and Picasso, and works by contemporary artists. It is open 10 am to 9 pm Tuesday, and 10 am to 5 pm Wednesday to Sunday. Entry costs Sfr6 (students Sfr4, children free).

Bern Historical Museum This interesting museum (Bernisches Historisches Museum) is on Helvetiaplatz, and is open 10 am to 5 pm Tuesday to Sunday (admission Sfr5, or Sfr3 for students and senior citizens). Highlights include the original sculptures from the Münster doorway depicting the Last Judgement, Niklaus Manuel's macabre *Dance of Death* panels, and the ridiculous codpiece on the William Tell statue upstairs. Elsewhere, the museum contains Habsburg Church treasures (from the Königsfelden Abbey), and tapestries captured from the Burgundian troops of Charles the Bold. Various rooms show how life was lived in the canton of Bern in the last two centuries, and, somewhat tangentially, there is also an Islamic collection of Henri Moser-Charlottenfels.

Natural History Museum This museum (Naturhistorisches Museum) on Bernastrasse, has eye-catching and extensive displays of animals depicted in realistic dioramas. Near the entrance are the stuffed remains of Barry, the most famous of the 40 St Bernard dogs who between them rescued an estimated 2000 travellers stranded in the Alps since the 11th century. Such moth-eaten preservation is a dubious reward for sterling service. It is open 9 am to 5 pm weekdays (except it opens 2 pm Monday and closes 8 pm Wednesday), and 10 am to 5 pm weekends. Entry is Sfr5, or Sfr3 for students and seniors.

Other Museums Situated on Kramgasse 49, **Einstein House** is where the physicist developed his special theory of relativity in 1905, but there's relatively little here to excite the visitor (Sfr3; closed Sunday and Monday in December and January). The **Swiss Alpine Museum**, Helvetiaplatz 4, will whet your appetite for the mountains if you haven't yet headed into the Alps (closed Monday morning). It details the history of Alpine mountaineering and cartography and has an impressively comprehensive collection of relief maps (Sfr5, concessions Sfr3). Across the square is the **Kunsthalle**, an exhibition space for contemporary artists (Sfr6, concessions Sfr3; closed Monday, with late opening on Tuesday).

Philatelists will stamp their feet with joy at the **Museum of Communication**, Helvetiastrasse 16, where countless postage stamps are displayed on endless panels (Sfr5, concessions Sfr3), and interactive displays enliven the history of post and telecommunications. Afterwards, shoot over to the **Swiss Rifle Museum** (Schweizerisches Schützenmuseum), Bernastrasse 5, for a collection of firearms made since 1817 (free). Both are closed on Monday.

Markets

There is an open-air vegetable, fruit and flower market at Bärenplatz on Tuesday and Saturday (daily in summer). Waisenhausplatz has a general market on Tuesday and Saturday. On the first Saturday of the month there's a craft market in front of the cathedral.

Activities

Near the town is the hilltop, **Gurten**, where you can hike and enjoy the fine views. Take tram No 9 to Gurtenbahn then the funicular. Tickets cost Sfr4/7 one way/return or alternatively you can do the whole trip on the Sfr7.50 version of the city pass.

Something the Bernese enjoy on a sunny summer's day is floating down the **Aare River**. They take the plunge in the Sandrain district and float downstream in the swift current to where they left their possessions at the open-air swimming pools at Marzili or Lorraine (both pools are free and open May to September).

Courses

Inlingua Sprachschule (☎ 311 24 13) is at Waisenhausplatz 28. See its Web site www.inlingua.com/bern.htm. Volkshochschule Bern (☎ 311 41 92), at Kornhausplatz 7, is a non-profit organisation which has adult education courses (usually of eight weeks minimum) for all sorts of disciplines ranging from languages to gymnastics. Migros Klubschule (☎ 310 36 36), on the 2nd floor at Marktgasse 46, also offers a wide variety.

Organised Tours

There is a two-hour tour of the city by coach, which costs Sfr23 and departs at 2 pm daily (Saturday only in winter) from outside the tourist office. The multilingual commentary is informative. The guided walking tour of the centre costs Sfr12 and leaves at 11.15 am daily from May to October. There are also tours departing daily to all the main attractions in the Bernese Oberland, central Switzerland and to some other lesser-known local destinations. Prices are from Sfr23 to Sfr173. The tours are worth considering if you're on a lightning visit.

Doing Time in the Bern Patent Office

There is hope for all daydreaming clerks. Albert Einstein, gazing into space instead of attending to his tedious job at the patent office, had in 1907 what he later described as 'the happiest thought of my life.' It was the realisation that a person in freefall would not feel his own weight. This apparently trivial insight impelled him to a new theory of gravitation, the General Theory of Relativity. Einstein postulated that gravity was caused by the curvature of space-time, a hypothesis subsequently confirmed by scientific tests.

Einstein worked at the patent office from 1902 to 1907. During that time he also came up with his Special Theory of Relativity (1905). This explained the puzzling fact that the speed of light is always the same, irrespective of the relative motion of observers, by stating that time itself must be relative.

Einstein was born of Jewish ancestry in Germany in 1879. He did not excel at school, but was admitted to Zürich Polytechnic on the strength of his mathematics test alone. Upon graduating, his failure to find a teaching post led him to the patent office in Bern and a place in history. He won the Nobel Prize for Physics in 1932, and later emigrated to the USA where he died in 1955.

Special Events
On the 4th Monday in November, Bern hosts its famous **onion market** (*Zibelemärit*), where traders take over the whole of the centre of town. According to tradition, the origin of the market dates back to 1405 and the great fire. The farmers of the canton of Fribourg helped the Bernese to recover from the resulting devastation and were allowed to sell their produce in Bern as a reward. But it's more than just a market – people walk around throwing confetti and hitting each other on the head with plastic hammers, and many street performers (particularly South American bands) add to the carnival atmosphere.

Bern also has an important **jazz festival** in early May. Prices for evening events are between Sfr10 and Sfr50. Also look out for the **Gurten Rock Festival** in mid-July. Tickets for both events are available from the Ticket Corner (☎ 0848-800 800) in branches of the UBS Bank. The **Altstadtsommer** comprises concerts and other events (some are free) in the Old Town centre during July and August.

Places to Stay – Budget
Camping Near the river but to the south of town is *Camping Eichholz* (☎ 961 26 02, *Strandweg 49*). Take tram No 9 from the station to Wabern. The site is open from 1 May to 30 September, and charges Sfr6.90 per person, from Sfr5 for a tent and Sfr2 for parking. It also has bungalows for Sfr15 plus Sfr6.90 per adult (students Sfr5.50). Prices are about the same at *Camping Kappelenbrücke* (☎ 901 10 07), except during July and August when they rise to Sfr8.35 per adult, Sfr6.50 for a tent and Sfr3 for a car. It's open year-round except for the last three weeks in January. Reception is shut from 1 to 4 pm but you can still select a site at this time. Take the Hinterkappelen postbus to Eymatt.

Hostel The SYHA *hostel* (☎ 311 63 16, fax 312 52 40, *Weihergasse 4*) is in a good location below Parliament (the paths down are signposted). It is often full in summer, and a three-day maximum stay usually applies. Reception is shut from 10 am to 3 pm (summer) or to 5 pm (winter), but bags can be left in the common room during the day.

Dorm beds are Sfr20.25, breakfast is Sfr and lunch/dinner are Sfr12/11 respectively. There are lockers, and washing machines a Sfr4 to wash and Sfr3 to dry.

Hotels There's a limited choice of budget rooms in Bern, though ask the tourist offic for its list of B&Bs. *Bahnhof-Sü (☎ 992 51 11, fax 991 95 91, Bümplizstrass 189)*, to the west of town beyond the auto bahn, has singles/doubles using hall showe for Sfr50/85. Doubles with shower ar Sfr100. Phone ahead. To get there, take bu No 13 from the city centre.

Take bus No 20 from Bahnhofplatz fo *Marthahaus Garni* (☎ 332 41 35, fax 333 3. 86, *e* pension.marthahaus@ bluewin.ch *Wyttenbachstrasse 22A*). It's a friendly plac with comfortable rooms, TV lounges and kitchen. Singles/doubles are Sfr60/95 an triples/quads are Sfr120/150. Prices fo singles/doubles/triples with private showe toilet and TV are Sfr90/120/150.

Conveniently close to the train station i *Hotel National* (☎ 381 19 88, fax 381 68 78 *e* info@nationalbern.ch, *Hirschengrabe 24*). It has good-for-the-price singles doubles from Sfr60/100, or Sfr85/120 wit private shower and toilet. Family rooms (u to five people) are Sfr170 to Sfr260.

Near the bear pits and recently renovate is *Landhaus Hotel* (☎ 331 41 66, fax 33 69 04, *e* landhaus@ spectraweb.ch, *Alten bergstrasse 4*). Dorms (Sfr30) are split int two-person cubicles; modern, minimalis doubles cost from Sfr140 with shower o Sfr110 without (Sfr100/75 single occu pancy). Bedding (Sfr5) and breakfast (Sfr7 cost extra in dorms only, and there's fre jazz on Thursday in the restaurant, excep during summer.

Goldener Schlüssel (☎ 311 02 16, fa 331 02 16, *e* info@goldener-schluessel.ch *Rathausgasse 72*) has rooms with TV, radi and telephone. Singles/doubles are Sfr99/14. with shower/WC or Sfr75/110 without. Als ideally situated is *Hotel Glocke* (☎ 311 37 71 fax 311 10 08, *Rathausgasse 75*). Singles doubles are Sfr70/116 using hall shower an doubles/triples are Sfr136/150 with privat shower/WC.

Places to Stay – Mid-Range

Hotel Goldener Adler (☎ *311 17 25, fax 311 37 61, Gerechtigkeitsgasse 7*) offers comfortable rooms with TV in a traditional house for Sfr120/160 with private shower/WC or Sfr80/130 without.

Another good choice for mid-price accommodation is *Hotel Krebs* (☎ *320 15 15, fax 311 10 35,* ✉ *hotel-krebs@thenet.ch, Genfergasse 8*), near the train station. Singles with shower, toilet and TV are expensive at Sfr128; the corresponding doubles are a much better deal at Sfr160, while the family room for four costs Sfr245. There are a few singles/doubles with showers in the hall for Sfr90/130, and guests get free tea and coffee in the cafe.

Hotel Continental (☎ *329 21 21, fax 329 21 99, Zeughausgasse 27*) has new fittings and lower rates Friday to Sunday: Sfr100/140 instead of Sfr125/170.

Places to Stay – Top End

Hotel Bären (☎ *311 33 67, fax 311 69 83,* ✉ *reception@baerenbern.ch, Schauplatzgasse 4*) and the adjoining *Hotel Bristol* are effectively the same hotel. They're part of the Best Western chain and have comfortable if uninspiring rooms from Sfr170/230. The best place to stay without jumping to the luxury class is the *Hotel Savoy* (☎ *311 44 05 or 0800-88 61 61 toll-free, fax 312 19 78, Neuengasse 26*). Prices start at Sfr167/219, or Sfr142/184 at weekends. The rooms are bigger, better furnished, and overall have a more welcoming feel than those of its rivals.

There are two five-star hotels in town, and both are suitably sumptuous: the *Bellevue Palace* (☎ *320 45 45, fax 311 47 43,* ✉ *t.zimmermann@bellevue-palace.ch, Kochergasse 3-5*) and the *Hotel Gauer Schweizerhof* (☎ *326 80 80, fax 326 80 90,* ✉ *info@schweizerhof-bern.ch, Bahnhofplatz 11*). The latter is slightly cheaper, starting about Sfr260/360.

Places to Eat

Self-Catering There are several snack and take-away places in the lower level of the train station. *Migros* supermarket at Marktgasse 46 has a cheap self-service restaurant on the 1st floor. *Coop* restaurant is in the Ryfflihof department store on Neuengasse and Aarbergergasse. Both are open normal shop hours, with late opening to 9 pm on Thursday.

Also good value is the university *Mensa* (*Gesellschaftsstrasse 2*), on the 1st floor. Menus cost around Sfr10 to Sfr14, and there's a Sfr2.30 reduction for students. It is open 11.30 am to 1.45 pm and 5.45 to 7.30 pm Monday to Friday (closed Friday evening). The cafe downstairs has drinks and snacks from 7.30 am to 6 pm on weekdays (5 pm on Friday). Both parts close from mid-July to early August.

Manora (*Bubenbergplatz 5a*) is a busy and sometimes hectic restaurant, but usually has the tastiest food of the self-service bunch. Meals are Sfr9 to Sfr16, and the pile-it-on-yourself salad is Sfr4.20 to Sfr8.90 per plate. It is open 7 am to 10.30 pm daily (from 9 am Sunday and holidays).

Budget Restaurants *Café Bubenberg Vegi* (☎ *311 75 76, Bubenbergplatz 8*), has terrace seating and good vegetarian food for Sfr12 to Sfr20. During the evening Indian food is a speciality (from Sfr23.80) and it is open 7.30 am to 10.30 pm daily (11.30 am to 9 pm on Sunday). *Menuetto* (☎ *311 14 48, Münstergasse 47*) is generally slightly more expensive for vegetarian food, though it does have a daily special for Sfr13. It is closed on Sunday.

Several pleasant restaurants with outside seating line Bärenplatz, though there's little to choose between them. *Gfeller* has a reasonable range of inexpensive food. On the 1st floor above is *China Imperial*, offering an extensive and expensive buffet of Chinese food. The Tellerservice is the best deal: for Sfr17.80 you can select a plateful, and take a bowl of rice with sauces. It's available daily, lunchtime and after 10 pm. Go to *Le Mazot* at No 5, open daily, to try Swiss specialities such as Rösti (Sfr14) and fondue (Sfr20.50).

Restaurant Brasserie Anker (*Kornhausplatz 16*) has standard Swiss food for a similar price, and the meals really do resemble the colour pictures on display. It's also popular with drinkers – beer is only

Sfr4 for half a litre – and is open until 11.30 pm except on Sunday when it shuts at 6 pm.

Mid-Range & Top End Restaurants

Klötzlikeller (☎ 311 74 56, Gerechtigkeits-gasse 62) is an atmospheric wine cellar with occasional live music. Menus (cheapish to mid-price) change periodically and feature food and wine from different regions. It's open from 4 pm, Tuesday to Saturday.

Du Nord (☎ 332 23 38, Lorrainestrasse 2) is a newish bar-restaurant which is very popular with a youngish clientele. Swiss and Italian food costs Sfr13 to Sfr30 (closed Wednesday). On Sunday night the only option is an Indian two-course meal (Sfr20.50/25.50 for vegetarian/meat). Look out for Jazz brunches or other events. At *Les Amis (☎ 311 51 87, Rathausgasse 63)*, main courses (around Sfr30) have a French-Italian influence. It's tucked away below a trendy bar and is open 7 pm to midnight Tuesday to Saturday.

The dingy exterior of *Della Casa (☎ 311 21 42, Schauplatzgasse 16)* hides a good-quality restaurant within. The local special-ity, Bernerplatte (a selection of meats with sauerkraut, potatoes and beans) costs Sfr40, but occasionally you can find it on the ex-cellent three-course daily menu for Sfr23. The menu is available on the ground floor only, from 11.30 am to 2 pm and 6 to 9 pm. The upstairs section has a smarter ambience. Della Casa is open 8 am to 11.30 pm Mon-day to Friday and 8 am to 3 pm Saturday.

Bellevue-Grill in the Bellevue Palace Hotel (see Places to Stay) is considered the best restaurant in Bern. Reserve ahead as, despite the high prices, it is often full. Main courses start at Sfr40 but most people go for the creative menu for Sfr119. The food is presented with a flourish here: the servers troop out in file, each bearing a main course for a particular table. When all the plates are carefully placed before the appropriate diner, they simultaneously whip off the metal cover to reveal the feast beneath. They then stand reverently in a circle, covers held aloft, as the head server recites a short spiel describing each dish. It's almost a religious ceremony and has to be seen to be believed.

Entertainment

Bärenplatz is a great place to linger on a sunny day. There's always something hap-pening, whether it be street music, giant chess games, or demonstrations outside the parliament building. There are a couple of cinemas on Laupenstrasse. On Mondays, tickets cost Sfr10 instead of the usual Sfr15.

Bars, Clubs & Arts Venues There are some expensive discos in the Old Town, but young people with fewer francs go to places like *Wasserwerk (☎ 312 12 31, Wasser-werkgasse 5)*. Its Web site is at www.wasserwerk.ch. There's a not too expensive bar with pool tables (open 8 pm) and a disco (entry up to Sfr15; open from 10 pm) and about 10 times a month there's live music (Sfr18 to Sfr35). It's in a graffiti-covered building with no signs and there's an alter-native cinema next door. *Silo*, a nearby bar on the 1st floor of Mühleplatz 11, is open from 9 pm. Entry is free and there's pool tables, traditional jazz on Tuesday, and dancing and DJs on Friday and Saturday.

For food and drink there's the bright bar/cafe, *Café Aarbergerhof (Aarberger-gasse 40)*. *Joystick (☎ 312 22 01, Gerechtigkeitsgasse 50)* is a cellar bar de-signed for (according to its sign) 'bi and happy people' and, strangely, 'shopping people'. *U1 Tanzbar (Junkerngasse 1)*, has a different mood depending on the night, from the 'chill out bar' on Monday (free entry) to techno DJs on Friday and Saturday (entry Sfr10 or Sfr15). People tend to dress up for an outing to the trendy *Quasimodo* bar (in Hotel Glocke), where there are also DJs on Friday and Saturday (free entry).

Reitschule (☎ 302 63 17, Schützen-mattstrasse), a former riding school, is a fas-cinating place to spend time. It's a semi-legal centre for alternative arts housed in several graffiti-splattered, derelict-looking buildings under the railway line. On site there is a music venue, theatre, library, cafe and cheap restaurant (open from 5 pm; closed Sunday). There's also a women's-only disco on the first Friday of the month. Entry fees for events are reasonable. The place looks a bit seedy, and there have been safety problems in the past, but nowadays it is pretty safe and almost respectable, though there's still something of a drug culture in the bar.

Gaskessel (☎ *372 49 00, Sandrainstrasse 25)*, in two domed buildings in Marzili, has concerts, theatre, cinema, live music and discos. Near to the Marzili pools is *Dampfzentrale* (☎ *311 63 37, Marzilistrasse 47)*, a venue for jazz, soul, funk, avant-garde and art exhibitions, either in the main hall or the Musikkeller bar. Jazz is also on the agenda at *Marian's Jazzroom* (☎ *309 61 11, Engestrasse 54)*, a slightly more expensive and exclusive venue north of the city centre.

Theatre & Concerts The *Stadttheater* has productions almost every day and tickets are available from the Theaterkasse (☎ 311 07 77), at Kornhausplatz 18. There is also a number of small theatre groups (including a puppet theatre) which perform in the cellars along Kramgasse and Gerechtigkeitsgasse; plays are in local dialect or High German. Bern has a symphony orchestra, and there's always something going on in the classical music field. Concerts are often held in the large hall of the *Casino* (☎ *311 42 42, Herrengasse 25)*. Check the free Information booklet, *Bern aktuell*, for events listings.

Spectator Sports

North of the centre is the Wankdorf football and athletics stadium. Nearby is a famous ice-hockey stadium (Allmend Eisstadion). It's one of the biggest in Europe and Bern has one of the best teams in the country.

Shopping

Bern's covered arcades make shopping a weather-proof experience. There's no better place to buy Toblerone chocolate, as it's made in Bern. The Swiss Craft Centre (Heimatwerk) on Kramgasse 61 offers handmade but expensive souvenirs, such as wood-carvings, jewellery and Bernese pottery. There are many other souvenir shops on Kramgasse and Gerechtigkeitsgasse. Klötzli, at Rathausgasse 84, boasts a huge selection of Swiss army knives.

Getting There & Away

Air Air Engiadina (☎ 960 12 00) flies daily to London and Amsterdam, and daily except Saturday to Munich. Crossair (☎ 960 21 21) has daily direct flights to/from Paris and Brussels, and provides connections to many other international destinations. The Swissair check-in counter in the train station will take your luggage and get it on your flight from Zürich or Geneva. See the Getting There & Away chapter for details.

Bus Postbuses depart from the west side of the train station, although the train service should meet the needs of most visitors.

Train Bern has excellent train connections. There are departures at least hourly to most destinations, including Geneva (Sfr50, takes 1¾ hours), Basel (Sfr37, 70 minutes), Interlaken (Sfr25, 50 minutes) and Zürich (Sfr48, 1½ hours).

Car & Motorcycle There are three motorways which intersect at the northern part of the city. The N1 (E25) is the route from Neuchâtel in the west and Basel and Zürich in the north-east. The N6 connects Bern with Thun and the Interlaken region in the south-east. The N12 (E27) is the route from Geneva and Lausanne in the south-west.

There are several underground parking spots in the city centre, including one at the train station (Sfr2.50 per hour). The tourist office map lists locations. 'Park & Ride' parking is free at Guisanplatz, Wankdorf in the north, Neufeld in the north-west and Gangloff, Bümpliz in the south-west.

Car Rental Hertz (☎ 318 21 60) is in the Old Town at Kasinoplatz, and Avis (☎ 378 15 15) is at Wabernstrasse 41. Both have an office at the airport. Europcar (☎ 318 75 55) is at Laupenstrasse 22.

Getting Around

To/From the Airport The small Bern-Belp airport is 9km south-east of the city centre. A small white shuttle bus links the airport to the train station (Sfr14). It takes 20 minutes and is coordinated with flight arrivals and departures. There's no easy cheaper alternative – the train to Belp (Sfr6.20) leaves you 30 minutes' walk from the airport.

Bus & Tram Getting around on foot is easy enough if you're staying in the city centre. Bus and tram tickets cost Sfr1.50 (maximum six stops) or Sfr2.40. A day pass for the city and regional network is Sfr7.50. A 24/48/72-hour pass for only the city costs Sfr6/9/12. Buy tickets from dispensers at stops; day passes can also be bought from the tourist office or the public transport office (☎ 321 86 31) at Bubenbergplatz 5. Special night buses depart Friday and Saturday nights from Bahnhofplatz at 12.45 am and 2 am; fares start at Sfr5 and passes are not valid.

Taxi Many taxis wait by the station. The cost is around Sfr6.50 plus Sfr2.70 (Sfr3 on Sunday and at night) per km.

Bicycle There's *free* daily loans of city bikes at Casinoplatz and by the LOEB department store. ID and a Sfr20 deposit are required. The rental huts are open 7.30 am to 9.30 pm from May to October.

Biel (Bienne)

☎ 032 • pop 49,000 • elevation 429m

Biel (in German) or Bienne (in French) is one of those Swiss towns nonchalantly spanning the linguistic divide. The town has expanded greatly since the end of the 19th century, thanks in part to cashing in on the burgeoning watch and clock-making industry. This expansion has recently reversed (the town has relatively high unemployment), but still some of the biggest names, such as Omega and Rolex, are based in Biel. Its lake and Old Town centre are the main attractions.

Orientation & Information

Biel is at the northern end of Lake Biel (Bielersee, Lac de Bienne). It's a bilingual city and all street names are shown in both languages. The Biel-Bienne train station is between the lake and the Old Town and has bike-rental

and money-exchange counters open daily. The tourist office (☎ 322 75 75, fax 323 77 57, ✉ tbs@bielstar.ch) and bus information are in the car and bicycle park in front of the station. Opening hours are 8 am to 12.30 pm and 1.30 to 6 pm weekdays, and (May to October) from 9 am to 3 pm Saturday. Another tourist office is in the Congress Centre, Zentralstrasse 60. The main post office (2500 Biel 1) is by the train station. The Old Town is a partially pedestrian-only knot of streets around Burggasse and the Ring, 12 minutes' walk north of the station (or take bus No 1).

SSR (☎ 328 11 11), the budget travel agency, is at Unterer Quai 23.

Things to See & Do

The Old Town has as its centrepiece the **Ring**, a very picturesque square with a 16th-century fountain. The name harks back to bygone days when justice was dispensed in the square. The community big-wigs would sit in an intimidatory semicircle to pass judgement upon the unfortunate miscreants brought before them.

Adjoining the Ring on Obergasse (Rue Haute) is another 16th-century fountain, depicting an angel with a leering devil at her shoulder. Leading from the opposite side of the Ring is Burggasse (Rue de Bourg), where there's the step-gabled town hall and theatre, the Fountain of Justice (1744), and attractive shuttered houses. The centre doesn't take long to explore. If you have some time to kill, drop into a cafe and indulge in some eavesdropping, but only to admire the ability of the locals to switch between French and German with barely a break in the rhythm of their conversations.

The **Schwab Museum**, Seevorstadt 50 (Faubourg du Lac 50), is a museum of prehistory and archaeology, named after the 19th-century colonel who was instrumental in unearthing the secrets of the ancient lake-dwellers of the region. Many of the more interesting finds from around the lakes of Biel, Murten and Neuchâtel are on display. The 6000-year-old settlements were revealed when the level of the lakes fell by some 2m following measures introduced to control the water flow in the Jura. The museum is open 10 am to noon and 2 to 5 pm Tuesday to Saturday, and 11 am to 5 pm Sunday; entry costs Sfr5.

The **Omega Museum** (☎ 344 92 11), Stämpflistrasse 96, gives a free glimpse of the company's watch-making activities, past and present (open on request). There's also **Museum Neuhaus**, Schüsspromenade 26, covering art and history (Sfr7, closed Monday).

Special Events

The town puts on a weekend carnival starting the Friday after Ash Wednesday. Bieler Braderie, on the last weekend in June, is one of the biggest markets in Switzerland. Biel is also a venue for Expo.01 (see the boxed text in the Facts for the Visitor chapter).

Places to Stay

Camping There are four camp sites clustered round the southern end of Lake Biel. Much nearer Biel and also by the lake is *Sutz-Lattrigen* (☎ 397 13 45). The train to Sutz runs every 30 minutes (Sfr3.60) and brings you to within 1km of the site. It's open from Easter to late October and costs Sfr8 per person and from Sfr5.50 per tent.

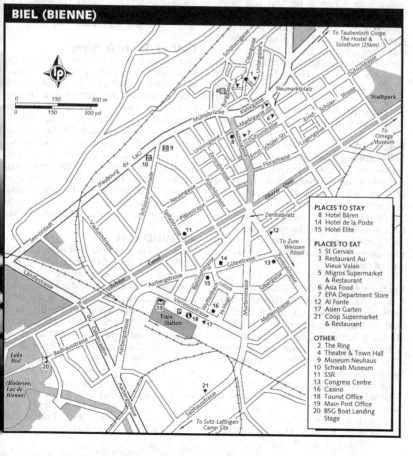

BIEL (BIENNE)

0   150   300 m
0   150   300 yd

To Taubenloch Gorge,
The Hostel &
Solothurn (25km)

Neumarktplatz

Stadtpark

To
Omega
Museum

Zentralplatz

To Zum
Weissen
Rössli

PLACES TO STAY
8 Hotel Bären
14 Hotel de la Poste
15 Hotel Elite

PLACES TO EAT
1 St Gervais
3 Restaurant Au
   Vieux Valais
5 Migros Supermarket
   & Restaurant
6 Asia Food
7 EPA Department Store
12 Al Fonte
17 Asien Garten
21 Coop Supermarket
   & Restaurant

OTHER
2 The Ring
4 Theatre & Town Hall
9 Museum Neuhaus
10 Schwab Museum
11 SSR
13 Congress Centre
16 Casino
18 Tourist Office
19 Main Post Office
20 BSG Boat Landing
   Stage

Lake
Biel

(Bielersee,
Lac de
Bienne)

Train
Station

To Sutz-Lattrigen
Camp Site

Hostel *The Hostel* (*☎/fax 341 29 65,* **@** *hostelbiel@access.ch, Solothurnstrasse 137)* is an independent hostel with beds for Sfr23 to Sfr30. There are kitchen facilities and reception is open all day until 10 pm, but it's inconveniently located (take bus No 1 or the preferable but less frequent 3N).

Hotels & Pensions *Hotel de la Poste* (*☎ 322 25 44, Güter-strasse 3)* has basic, old-fashioned singles/doubles using hall showers for Sfr60/100. There's an affordable restaurant which is closed on Sunday.

Hotel Bären (*☎ 322 45 73, fax 322 91 57, Nidaugasse 22)*, near the Old Town, has singles/doubles for Sfr98/145, all with shower or bath, toilet, TV, radio and telephone. The rooms are a bit plain but reasonably large, and there's a lift. Reception is at a small counter in the busy pizza restaurant.

At the four star *Hotel Elite* (*☎ 328 77 77, fax 328 77 70,* **@** *hotelelite@ swissonline.ch, Bahnhofstrasse 14)* the normal rate is Sfr195/285, but if you stay Friday or Saturday night you'll pay Sfr150/190.

Places to Eat

Self-Catering There's a large *Coop* supermarket and restaurant around the back of the station on Salzhausstrasse, with late opening till 9 pm on Friday. More convenient for the centre is *EPA* on Nidaugasse, or the *Migros* on Neumarktplatz, which are both open till 9 pm on Thursday. *Asia Food*, on Neumarktstrasse, has some very cheap Chinese and Thai takeaway dishes. It's open normal shop hours.

Restaurants For sit-down Chinese and Thai food, go to *Asien Garten (Verresuisstrasse 2)*, by the train station. The food is tasty, and weekday lunch deals start at Sfr10.50 (closed Monday). There are plenty of inexpensive pizzerias around; *Al Fonte (Zentralstrasse 57)* is one of the better choices (open daily, but closed till 5 pm on weekends).

For authentic ambience, explore the places in the old centre. Look for the *Restaurant Au Vieux Valais* (*☎ 322 34 55)*, off the Ring at Untergässli 9, which has lunches with soup from Sfr15, fondue for Sfr18 and other Swiss

meals (closed Monday). Nearby is *St Gervais (Untergasse 21)*, a cooperative dishing up good meals from Sfr10.50, including many vegetarian options. There are outside tables adjoining the quiet, cobbled street. It's closed till 5 pm on Sunday.

The *Hotel Elite* (see Places to Stay) has a quality restaurant which is closed on Sunday.

Entertainment

The *Congress Centre (Kongresshaus; ☎ 323 33 11)*, on Zentralstrasse, hosts concerts and cultural events. Biel has its own orchestra and municipal theatre with productions usually in German. There are a few bars on and around Zentralstrasse, and a new casino near the station.

Getting There & Away

Biel is less than 30 minutes from Bern by train (Sfr11.80). Solothurn (Sfr8.60, 20 minutes), Neuchâtel (Sfr10, 20 minutes), and Murten (Sfr11.80, 50 minutes) are also close by train, but a more enjoyable way to get to these towns is by boat. To Murten (Sfr27 one-way or Sfr46 return, 3½ hours) and Neuchâtel (Sfr23 one-way or Sfr40 return, 2½ hours), boats depart daily in summer. Solothurn can be reached by BSG boat along the Aare River. There are five departures a day (except on Monday) and it takes around 2½ hours (Sfr26 one-way, Sfr45 return). Also see the following Around Biel section.

AROUND BIEL

Flora and fauna abound in **St Peter's Island** (St Peterinsel, Île de St Pierre), at the southwest end of Lake Biel, particularly birdlife. The whole island is a nature reserve. Political theorist Rousseau spent, in his own words, the happiest time of his life here. The carefully preserved 11th-century monastery where he stayed can be visited.

The island became connected to the shore when the level of the lake dropped, exposing a natural causeway. It's a relaxing 1½-hour stroll to the island along this causeway from the town of Erlach on the shore. From Biel, a train runs to La Neuveville and an infrequent bus continues to Erlach. But the easiest way to get to the island is by boat from Biel (Sfr8.60, 50 minutes), which calls at several lakeside villages en route.

The shore of **Lake Biel** offers many swimming spots; those at Erlach, Sutz-Lattrigen and La Neuveville are enjoyable and free. The northern shore is noted for a string of wine-growing villages. The tourist office has a leaflet (in German or French) showing a walking path connecting these villages, including information on several wine cellars *(caveaux)* where produce can be sampled and purchased.

The neighbouring lakes of Neuchâtel and Murten are connected to Lake Biel by canal, and day-long tours of all three lakes are offered in summer. Boats are run by two boat companies: BSG (☎ 322 33 22), based in Biel, and LNM (☎ 032-725 40 12), based in Neuchâtel. BSG's tour departs Biel daily at 9.50 am (Sfr56). LNM's tour departs Murten daily except Monday at 11.40 am (Sfr38.80 inclusive). Other services between and around the lakes are regular only in summer, though there are special cruises (eg, fondue evenings) during other seasons. Both companies share the same prices on scheduled services that overlap, though only LNM has a day pass for Sfr42.

Roughly 30 minutes' walk along the road to Solothurn (or take bus No 1) is the **Taubenloch Gorge**. A path runs along its 2.5km length (no entry charge, but there's a donation box).

Emmental Region

Emmental is the region to the east of a line drawn between the towns of Langenthal, Bern and Thun. The core of the area is the valley of the Emme River, from which the name is derived (valley in German is *Tal)*. A tour along the banks of the river yields picturesque towns and villages, and many buildings display architecture typical of the area. The angled roof is the most distinctive feature; it hangs very low over the sides of the house and usually has a section over the front facade, forming a triangular covering. Below this triangle there is often a semicircular trim framing the upper windows.

Things to See & Do
The local tourist offices promote hiking (among other things), and an interesting path is the **Plantenenweg** from Burgdorf to Wynigen, on which tiny models of the planets allow you to pretend you're marching through the universe on a scale of one to 1000 million. It takes about three hours to walk from the sun to Pluto. Afterwards, you can get the train back to **Burgdorf** which has a castle bearing a large representation of the emblem of the canton. There is a historical museum inside the castle, open daily from 1 April to 1 November, Sunday only in winter (Sfr5).

The town of **Langnau** is known for its ornamental crockery; the production process may be viewed at a pottery demonstration *(Schautöpferei)* in a couple of places in town, or in nearby **Trubschachen**, reached by rail or bus. For more details contact the tourist office for the Emmental (☎ 034-402 42 52, ✉ info@emmental.ch), Schlossstrasse 3, in Langnau. Ask the office about dates of local markets *(Märit)* and traditional fairs *(Chilbi)*. The office also arranges various excursions, eg, to see alphorns being made.

The best known product of the area is **Emmental cheese**. The Emmentaler Schaukäserei (Emmental Show Dairy) gives you the chance to see the stuff being made into huge wheels (60 to 130 kg – a bit bulky to take on a picnic). It is at **Affoltern**, 6km east of Burgdorf. From Burgdorf, take the train to Hasle, then catch the postbus. The dairy is open 8.30 am to 6.30 pm daily, but it's better to get there between 9 and 11 am or 2 and 4 pm when the various production stages are being instigated (free entry). **Kiesen**, on the rail route running south-east of Bern (Sfr7.40), has a museum of dairy products (Milchwirtschaftliches Museum) that can provide more background information. It's open 2 to 5 pm daily, between 1 April and 31 October, and entry is free.

Places to Stay
There are only a few camp sites in the area. There's a TCS (Touring Club Schweiz) site, *Waldegg (☎ 034-422 79 43)*, by the river in Burgdorf, (open 1 April to 1 October) and

another site, **Mettlen** (☎ 034-402 36 58), at Gohl, near Langnau (open year-round).

Langnau has an SYHA **hostel** (☎ 034-402 45 26, Mooseggstrasse 32), 10 minutes' walk from the station. Beds cost just Sfr14 without breakfast and the hostel is closed for a few weeks in early February and late September.

Tourist offices can help you find somewhere to stay locally, though contact the Emmental office for region-wide reservations. Accommodation is mostly in small-scale country inns and pensions which are very reasonably priced, starting at Sfr35 per person.

Getting There & Away
Every hour from Bern to Burgdorf there's a fast train (takes 15 minutes) and a local train, and the fare is Sfr8. Langnau can be reached by direct train from Bern (Sfr12.60) or Burgdorf.

Solothurn

☎ 032 • pop 15,900 • elevation 440m

Solothurn, originally a Celtic settlement, grew in importance when the Romans built a fort here in 370 AD. In 1481 it was the 11th canton to join the Swiss Confederation. The people of Solothurn took this number to their hearts: the town features 11 towers, 11 churches and chapels, 11 guilds and 11 historic fountains. Despite this evident strong allegiance to the Confederation, Solothurn maintained close links with France, and sent many mercenaries to fight for French kings. It rejected the Reformation, choosing to remain Catholic, thereby placing itself in opposition to nearby Bern and Basel and strengthening the affinity with France. The town was the residence of French ambassadors from 1530 to 1792.

Orientation & Information
Solothurn is a cantonal capital. The train station is south of the Aare River and has an information office, money-exchange counters and bike rental, all open daily. There's also left luggage and 24-hour lockers. The

main post office (4501 Solothurn 1) is just to the left of the station as you exit.

Across the river lies the Old Town, less than 10 minutes' walk away. The core of the centre is Kronenplatz, dominated by the cathedral. The tourist office (☎ 626 46 46, fax 626 46 47, @ info@stadt-solothurn.ch) is on this square, open 8.30 am to noon and 1.30 to 6 pm Monday to Friday, and 9 am to noon Saturday. Staff will phone for hotel rooms without charging. They also conduct informative guided walking tours of the centre at 2.30 pm Saturday from May to September (lasting one to two hours; Sfr5 per person).

Things to See & Do
Despite the French influences in its history, the centre of town is dominated by an Italianate church, the 18th century **Cathedral of St Ursus**. It was designed and overseen by the Ticino architect, Gaetano Matteo Pisoni, with help from his nephew. The cathedral is dedicated to the two patron saints of Solothurn, Ursus and Victor, who were beheaded in the town during Roman times for refusing to worship the Roman gods. Inside it features a fine pink marble pulpit.

A stone's throw down Hauptgasse is the **Jesuit Church**. It's unprepossessing on the outside yet inside it displays magnificent baroque embellishments and stucco work. The coats of arms of the families who funded the building can be seen at the back of the church. Incidentally, all the 'marble' in here is fake: just spruced up wood and plaster. It's a common deception in baroque churches.

A little further down Hauptgasse you reach the **Zeitglockenturm**, a 12th-century astronomical clock where the figures do a little turn on the hour. Don't be confused by the clock hands – the smaller one shows the minutes. It was added centuries later than the large hour hand, and only became necessary when modern life dictated that people become yoked to the tyranny of timetables.

The rest of the old centre merits exploration. There are a couple of city gates to see and several old fountains. Especially note the **Justice Fountain** (1561) in Hauptgasse.

It shows a blindfolded representation of Justice, holding aloft a pair of scales, and at her feet are the four most important figures in Europe at that time. The Holy Roman Emperor, in red and white robes, is by Justice's right foot, then proceeding anticlockwise: the Pope, the Turkish Sultan, and…the mayor of Solothurn!

Museums The **Old Arsenal** is essential viewing in Solothurn. It efficiently illustrates the town's past status as a centre for mercenaries, and contains armour for 400 men, plus canons, guns and uniforms. The only exhibit you can touch is the small suit of armour near the entrance: lift up the visor to receive a special greeting (it's not a typical Solothurn welcome). The Arsenal is open 10 am to noon and 2 to 5 pm Tuesday to Sunday. From November to April it's closed on weekday mornings (adults Sfr6, families Sfr10, students and seniors Sfr4).

For a provincial museum, the **Museum of Fine Arts** (Kunstmuseum), Werkhofstrasse 30, holds some impressive works. The *Madonna of Solothurn* (1522) by Holbein the Younger is the most striking, along with *Virgin in the Strawberries* (1425) by the Master of the Garden of Paradise. Swiss artists are strongly represented, especially Ferdinand Hodler, whose famous portrait of William Tell is here. It is open 10 am to noon and 2 to 5 pm Tuesday to Saturday and 10 am to 5 pm Sunday. Entry is free, though a donation is expected.

Places to Stay & Eat

The SYHA *hostel* (☎ 623 17 06, fax 623 16 39, Landhausquai 23) is in the town centre by the river. A range of beds and prices are available, starting at Sfr26.50 for the largest dorms. Reception is open all day and the place shuts from late November to mid-January.

Hotel Kreuz (☎ 622 20 20, fax 621 52 32, Kreuzgasse 4) is near the hostel. Uncluttered and spacious singles/doubles/triples with hall showers are Sfr48/87/113 (deduct Sfr5 if staying more than one night). It is a cooperative and has a restaurant with inexpensive organic food. Ring the bell for reception when the restaurant is shut.

Ferdinand Hodler

Ferdinand Hodler was the most important Swiss painter of his generation. He was born in Bern in 1853 and was influenced early on by the landscape works of Sommer and Calame. He produced many landscapes of his own, right up to the end of his life, with Lake Thun and Alpine scenes cropping up frequently. Hodler embraced the art nouveau style and particularly explored the use of allegory and symbolism. He spent most of his working life in Geneva, despite the fact that its climate of Calvinistic rectitude was often hostile towards him. He died in Geneva in 1918.

Historical themes were also important in Hodler's paintings. Some of his works hark back to the early days of the Swiss Confederation, when ill-equipped rural villages pitted themselves against the might of the Habsburgs. His famous picture of William Tell is in the Museum of Fine Arts in Solothurn. Hodler re-worked the scene of the show-of-hand vote several times (eg, the *Einmütigkeit* in Zürich's Fine Arts Museum), where villagers stand in a cohesive group listening to an orator. All are rugged he-man types with physiques carved out of granite – the sort who cut their razors when shaving. The lack of three dimensional perspective makes them seem like a solid wall. All the men are about the same height and all have a hand raised in seamless unison. The line of heads and the line of hands create two intimidating tiers of defiance that make it seem plausible that such men could take on the Habsburgs – and win.

Nelson (☎ 622 04 22, fax 623 60 21, Rossmarktplatz 2), by the north side of the Wengibrücke, is a British pub, closed until 4 pm (2 pm on weekends). Reasonably-sized singles/doubles are Sfr70/120 with shower and toilet or Sfr50/100 without, and there's no breakfast. It's just off Berntorstrasse, where there's a wide choice of restaurants.

Schlüssel Bar (☎ 622 22 82, Kreuzgasse 3) has a few large rooms with shower/WC from Sfr80/100, without breakfast.

Baseltor (☎ 622 34 22, fax 622 18 79, ℮ baseltor@solnet.ch, Hauptgasse 79), near the tourist office, has modern rooms with private shower, toilet, TV and telephone for Sfr90/150. The restaurant is a great (and busy) choice for excellent food at affordable prices. Meals start at Sfr17, service is friendly and it's closed Sunday lunchtime and holidays (the hotel is open daily). *Hotel Astoria (☎ 622 75 71, fax 623 68 57, Wengistrasse 13)* has modern, well-equipped rooms from Sfr105/165, and a good mid-price restaurant. *Hotel Krone (☎ 622 44 12, fax 622 37 24, Hauptgasse 64)*, opposite the tourist office, has an older, baroque feel. Prices start at Sfr140/170 and there's a restaurant.

The impecunious can find fodder at the *Coop* supermarket and restaurant, Dornacherplatz, 200m left of the station and opposite a large car park. Self-service restaurants in the Old Town, with late opening till 9 pm on Thursday, are in the *Migros* supermarket on Wengistrasse and the *Manor* department store on Gurzelngasse. *Rebstock (Kronengasse 9)* is a simple cafe with cheap food; it's open daily.

Getting There & Away
Solothurn has two trains an hour to Bern on the private RBS line (Sfr13, 40 minutes, railpasses valid). Regular trains also run to Basel (Sfr25, takes one hour or more, change required), and Biel (Sfr8.60, 20 minutes). A more enjoyable way to get to and from Biel is to take the boat along the Aare River (see Biel for details). By road, the Weissenstein mountain impedes access directly north, but the N1/E25 motorway is nearby to the east of town, providing a fast route to Bern, Basel and Zürich. Take highway 5 for Biel.

AROUND SOLOTHURN
The grand **Schloss Waldegg**, a few kilometres north of town, was built in the 17th century and displays period furniture and paintings. The design betrays French and Italian influences. It is open daily except Monday and Friday from mid-April to 31 October, and on weekends only from November to mid-December (entry fee as for Solothurn Arsenal). Take bus No 4 from the station to St Niklaus. The nearby **Weissenstein** (1284m) to the north, is a hiking and cross-country skiing centre (see Jura Canton in the Fribourg, Neuchâtel and Jura chapter for information on scenic driving routes). A few kilometres north-west of Solothurn is **Lommiswil**, where dinosaur footprints have recently been discovered in the forest. A viewing platform has been built (free access).

Bernese Oberland

The Bernese Oberland (Berner Oberland) is where the scenic wonders of Switzerland come into their own. People often end up staying longer than they planned, such are the toe-twitching hikes and eye-spinning sights on offer. Good weather is essential to fully enjoy the stunning landscape, so if the sun shines, flee the cities and head for here. From Bern, a train will get you to Interlaken in less than an hour.

Orientation & Information

The Bernese Oberland tourist region covers the southern part of the canton of Bern, stretching from Gstaad in the west to the Susten Pass (2224m) in the east. The regional tourist office for the whole area is the Berner Oberland Tourismus (☎ 033-823 03 03, fax 823 03 30, @ info@berneroberland.com), 1st floor, Jungfraustrasse 38, CH-3800, Interlaken. There's just a small plaque by the door, and the opening hours are 7.30 am to noon and 1 to 5.30 pm Monday to Friday. Pick up the detailed *Summer* or *Winter* brochures covering sights and sports in the whole region. There are also *Budget* and *Hotels* accommodation brochures. Its Web site is at www.berneroberland.ch. See the Swiss Mittelland chapter for information on the history of the canton.

Getting Around

The Berner Oberland Regional travel pass is one of the most useful regional passes available. It is also one of the most expensive, costing Sfr205 for 15 days or Sfr165 for one week, with reductions for holders of Swiss travel passes (around 20% off). It gives free travel on five days (three days with the Sfr165 pass) on certain routes, such as cruises on Lake Brienz and Lake Thun, the cogwheel train up Rothorn, the funicular up Neisen, and trains as far as Gstaad, Kleine Scheidegg, Thun and Meiringen. On the other days there is a 50% reduction. Many other routes (including to Bern, Zermatt, Jungfraujoch, Schilthorn and Mt Titlis), and the three-pass

Highlights

- Discover Lucerne's medieval centre and covered bridges.
- Explore Switzerland's best technology museum, the Transport Museum in Lucerne.
- Take boat trips on Lake Lucerne.
- Enjoy the splendid vistas from mountain viewpoints, like Pilatus, Rigi, Stanserhorn and Titlis.
- Visit Einsiedeln, Switzerland's prime pilgrimage site.

Bern

bus tour, are 50% off on all days, and a few other mountain-top routes (Axalp, Riechenbach Falls etc) are 25% off. The pass is available from 1 May to 31 October.

Interlaken

☎ 033 • pop 15,000 • elevation 570m
Interlaken, flanked by two lakes and within striking distance of the mighty peaks of the

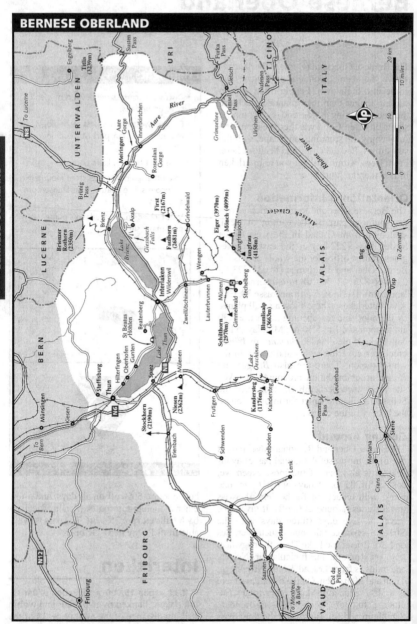

BERNESE OBERLAND

Jungfrau, Mönch and Eiger, is an ideal centre from which to explore the surrounding delights. But if time allows, an overnight stay farther inside the Jungfrau Region is even more rewarding.

Orientation & Information

Most of Interlaken is coupled between its two train stations: Interlaken West and Interlaken Ost. Each station offers bike rental and daily money changing facilities (including credit card cash advances), and behind each is a boat landing for boat services on lakes Thun and Brienz. The main shopping street, Höheweg, runs between the two stations. You can walk from one to the other in less than 20 minutes.

The tourist office (☎ 822 21 21, fax 822 52 21, ✉ mail@InterlakenTourism.ch, Höheweg 37), is nearer to Interlaken West train station and is open 8 am to noon and 1.30 to 6 pm Monday to Friday, and 8 am to noon Saturday. During July and August it closes at 6.30 pm weekdays, 5 pm Saturday and is also open from at least 5 to 7 pm Sunday. The staff will book rooms (no commission), or you can use the hotel board and free phone outside and at both railway stations. Jungfrau Region railway information is in the same office.

The main post office (Interlaken 3800, Postplatz) is near the Interlaken West station. It is open for postal services from 7.45 am to noon and 1.30 to 6.15 pm Monday to Friday, and 8.30 to 11 am Saturday. There are telephones and stamp machines outside.

The Wave (✉ admin@fintan.com, Rosenstrasse 13), has many Internet terminals. Charges are Sfr4 (Sfr3 for students/seniors) per 15 minutes; it's open from 11 am daily (from 4 pm Sunday) and closes from 2.30 to 5.30 pm in winter). You can also log-on at Buddy's Pub (see the Entertainment section) and Backpackers Villa (see the Places to Stay section).

The hospital (☎ 826 26 26) is at Weissenaustrasse 27.

Things to See & Do

Most of the points of interest are around Interlaken rather than in the town itself. All the attractions in the Jungfrau Region and around Lakes Thun and Lake Brienz can be reached on a day trip from Interlaken.

A good circular walk is to wander down Höheweg, glancing at the souvenir shops and grand hotels, and at either station, cut back to the tree-lined footpaths along the Aare River. The prettiest area of Interlaken is around the **Stadthaus** dating from 1471, on the northern side of the Aare in Unterseen. There's a large cobbled square bordered by attractive old buildings, with a church tower at two opposite corners. One of the old buildings is the **Tourist Museum**, Obere Gasse 26. It gives a rundown of the development of tourism and transport in the region, displaying models, old posters and photos, skis and chair lifts. Explanations are in German but you can pick up a summary in English, and it's worth spending up to an hour in here. Entry costs Sfr5 (Sfr3 with Guest Card), and it's open 2 to 5 pm Tuesday to Sunday from May to mid-October.

If you're a train enthusiast, or travelling with children, the **Model Railway Exhibition** (Modelleisenbahn-Treff) by Interlaken West train station on Rugenparkstrasse could take up another hour of your time. There are model trains whizzing all over the place on perimeter tracks (you can even get a train to serve you coffee) and elaborate representations of famous railway routes. Not to suggest that they're biased or anything, but it's funny that, while the trains chug along freely, most of the cars shown are either held up by road works or passing cows, or being towed out of a ditch. It's open 10 am to noon and 1.30 to 6 pm daily from 30 April to mid-October. Entry costs Sfr7 or Sfr3 for children.

The 15-minute model railway show at **Heimwehfluh** costs Sfr6 (children Sfr5) and gives you less for your money. Heimwehfluh does at least have a play area outside that's quite fun (free, or Sfr5 for the Bob-Run) and a good view of the town and lakes from the tower by the pricey restaurant. The **funicular** (Sfr10 return, children Sfr7) only saves 20 minutes climb via the signposted path, or even less if you take the more direct, steeper route up (unsignposted) that starts 10m to the right of the base funicular station as you face it.

The village of Wilderswil can be reached in eight minutes by bus No 5 from Interlaken West (see the Jungfrau Region map). It's a good deal quieter than Interlaken, and many of the wooden houses look exactly how you would expect Swiss chalets to look. Wilderswil is also the starting point for a cog-wheel train (Sfr32, closed late October to late May) that runs up **Schynige Platte** to 2001m. The views are terrific from here and there is also an Alpine garden (Sfr3) with 500 types of flora. At this altitude, many flowers are just beginning to bloom in June or July. There is a great all-day hike from here to Grindelwald-First (see the Grindelwald section for more information), or you can complete a shorter loop overlooking Brienzersee (2½ hours).

Numerous hiking trails dot the area surrounding Interlaken, all with signposts giving average hiking times. The funicular up to **Harder Kulm** (Sfr12.80 up, Sfr20 return, closed late October to late April) yields a memorable panorama and further prepared paths. While you're waiting for the funicular, wander around the enclosures containing ibexes and marmots (free). The restaurant with the pointed roof at Harder Kulm appears regularly in tourist brochures. To walk up from Interlaken takes about 2¼ hours. Below and to the right of the pointed roof, when viewed from the town, is an illusory moustached face in the tree-free section of the cliffs, known as the **Harder Mann**.

For adventure activities, see the Jungfrau Region section.

Places to Stay

Interlaken has lots of budget options. All types of accommodation issue the useful Guest Card (refer to Accommodation in the Facts for the Visitor chapter). Except in some hostels, winter prices are generally slightly lower. Call ahead in the off season, as some places close.

Places to Stay – Budget

Camping There are five camp sites close together north-west of Interlaken West; the cheapest is **Alpenblick** (☎ 822 77 57), on Seestrasse by the Lombach River, which charges Sfr7 per adult, from Sfr9 per tent and Sfr4 for a car. It's open year-round. Behind Interlaken Ost train station is **Sackgut** (☎ 822 44 34), on Brienzstrasse, which costs Sfr7 per adult and from Sfr6.50 for a tent. It's open from May to mid-October.

Hostels The SYHA **hostel** (☎ 822 43 53, fax 823 20 58, Aareweg 21, am See, Bönigen), is a 20-minute walk around the lake from Interlaken Ost, or take bus No 1. It has an excellent lakeside location, with swimming facilities and a kitchen. Beds in large dorms are Sfr26.40, doubles (bunk beds) are Sfr77.80, and dinner is Sfr11.50. Check-in is from 4 pm, but the communal areas stay open during the day. The hostel is closed mid-November to late January, except over Christmas/New Year.

Balmer's Herberge (☎ 822 19 61, fax 823 32 61, ✉ balmers@tcnet.ch, Hauptstrasse 23) is a 15-minute walk (signposted) from either station. Excellent communal facilities include a kitchen, leisure rooms, videos every night, cellar bar, store and book-exchange. Balmer's also organises excursions, rents bikes and gets discounts on adventure activity packages. It's a sociable place but at peak times the noise, American summer-camp atmosphere and queuing for showers and breakfast can get a bit too much. Beds cost Sfr22 in dorms; singles/doubles are Sfr40/64 and triples/quads are Sfr84/112. Showers are Sfr1 and evening meals are Sfr5 to Sfr10. Sign for a bed during the day (facilities are open) and check in at 5 pm (or before noon in summer). If it's full, get a mattress on the floor for Sfr13. It is open all year, and in summer they also open **Balmer's Tent**, 800m south (reception in the Herberge).

Nearer Höheweg, overlooking the park, is **Backpackers Villa Sonnenhof** (☎ 826 71 71, fax 826 71 72, ✉ backpackers@villa.ch, Alpenstrasse 16). This well-run, renovated villa has a kitchen, new showers, lockers and dorms/doubles for Sfr29/37 per person. Reception is open 7.30 to 11 am and 4 to 9 pm (10 pm in summer).

BERNESE OBERLAND

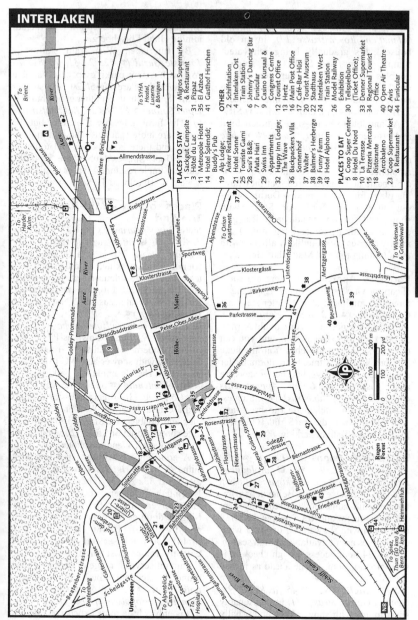

INTERLAKEN

PLACES TO STAY
1 Sackgut Campsite
3 Hôtel du Lac
11 Metropole Hotel
14 Hotel Splendid;
  Buddy's Pub
19 Alp Lodge;
  Anker Restaurant
21 Hotel Sonne
25 Touriste Garni
28 Susi's B&B;
  Mata Hari
29 Swiss Inn
32 Happy Inn Lodge;
  The Wave
36 Backpackers Villa
  Sonnenhof
37 Walter
38 Balmer's Herberge
39 Funny Farm
43 Hotel Alphorn

PLACES TO EAT
5 Coop Super Center
8 Hotel Du Nord
10 La Terrasse
15 Pizzeria Mercato
18 Ristorante
  Arcobaleno
23 Coop Supermarket
  & Restaurant

27 Migros Supermarket
  & Restaurant
31 Pizpaz
35 El Azteca
41 Gasthof Hirschen

OTHER
2 Schiffstation
4 Interlaken Ost
  Train Station
6 Johnny's Dancing Bar
7 Funicular
9 Casino Kursaal &
  Congress Centre
12 Tourist Office
13 Hertz
16 Main Post Office
17 Café-Bar Hüsi
20 Tourist Museum
22 Stadthaus
24 Interlaken West
  Train Station
26 Model Railway
  Exhibition
30 Tellspielbüro
  (Ticket Office);
33 Denner Supermarket
34 Regional Tourist
  Office
40 Open Air Theatre
42 Avis
44 Funicular

Also convenient is **Happy Inn Lodge** (☎ 822 32 25, fax 822 32 68, 🅔 happyinn @tcnet.ch, Rosenstrasse 17), in an old house that's gradually being renovated. Simple dorms are Sfr19 and singles/doubles are Sfr35/70. There's a restaurant/bar with affordable food and free live music on Thursday (not in summer). Check-in is from 3 or 4 pm, and breakfast is Sfr7.

An antidote to Swiss-style regimentation and efficiency is **Funny Farm** (☎ mobile 079-652 61 27, 🅔 James@funny-farm.ch) on Hauptstrasse, which has an Australasian ambience. This new, free-and-easy place is a bit basic and unstructured, but they have big plans for improvements. Dorms (without sheets) are Sfr25 or Sfr35 with shower/WC. Good outside facilities (garden, swimming-pool and bar/music) are mostly courtesy of an unlikely alliance with the adjoining top-end Mattenhof Hotel.

Rooms & Apartments There are some cheap private rooms, many requiring a three-day minimum stay. Shorter stays are OK at **Walter** (☎ 822 76 88, Oelestrasse 35). This friendly host has four doubles (hall shower) for Sfr23 per person, and you can make lunchtime sandwiches from the huge Sfr7 breakfast. Apartments are normally for a minimum seven days, but shorter stays are also possible at **Orion Appartments** (☎/fax 822 92 25, Bühlstrasse 40). Singles/doubles with a kitchenette (no breakfast) and fold-down beds are Sfr60/100. Both places have off-street parking.

Hotels & Pensions **Alp Lodge** (☎ 822 47 48, fax 822 92 50, 🅔 alplodge@ InterlakenTourism.ch, Marktgasse 59) is a low-budget annexe of the Bellevue, a comfortable mid-range hotel. Creatively decorated rooms for one to six people are Sfr39 per person with shower/WC or Sfr29 without. Singles aren't available in high season. There's 24-hour access though check-in is from around 3 pm. Phone ahead as it may close down.

Susi's B&B (☎ 822 25 45, fax 822 25 79, General Guisan Strasse 31) has reasonably sized rooms with shower/WC, and usually a kitchen. Singles/doubles are Sfr90/110, or Sfr60/95 in winter. Reception is in the adjoining Hotel Lötschberg.

By Interlaken West train station is **Touriste Garni** (☎ 822 28 31, fax 822 28 28), with a few parking spaces. Variable singles/doubles are Sfr55/120 with shower or Sfr48/95 without. Another good choice is **Hotel Sonne** (☎ 822 88 35, Bahnhofstrasse 9). The furnishings are a bit old, but the rooms are more spacious than in a modern place, and there is a shower and toilet on every floor. Singles/doubles are Sfr48/92, and the simple restaurant serves meals from around Sfr10 (closed Tuesday in winter).

Places to Stay – Mid-Range & Top End

Swiss Inn Appartments (☎ 822 36 26, fax 823 23 03, 🅔 info@swiss-inn.ch, General Guisan Strasse 23), is small, central and friendly, with parking, a garden and free tea/coffee. Singles/doubles with shower/WC and TV are Sfr100/130, and apartments are Sfr120/190. Breakfast is Sfr12. Not far away, **Hotel Alphorn** (☎ 822 30 51, fax 823 30 69, 🅔 accommodation@Hotel-Alphorn.ch, Rugenaustrasse 8), also known as Pilgerruhe, offers modern or old-style rooms for Sfr95/140 with shower and WC (Sfr70/110 in winter). There's ample free parking.

Hotel Splendid (☎ 822 76 12, fax 822 76 79, Höheweg 33), offers three-star comfort and a central location. Well-presented singles and doubles are Sfr120/190 with private shower/toilet or Sfr90/120 without; all rooms have a TV and telephone.

A good choice without spending vast sums of money is **Hôtel du Lac** (☎ 822 29 22, fax 822 29 15, Höheweg 225), overlooking the Brienzersee boat-landing stage and convenient for the Jungfrau train. Singles/doubles with private bath/toilet and TV are Sfr110/180 (low season) to Sfr145/250 (high season). Riverside and balcony rooms cost slightly more. The restaurant serves a range of meals; the set dinner is excellent. The high-rise **Metropole Hotel** (☎ 828 66 66, fax 828 66 33, 🅔 mail@metropole-interlaken.ch, Höheweg 37) is only a little more expensive, and has good views, free Internet access and an indoor swimming pool.

Places to Eat

The *Migros* supermarket opposite Interlaken West has a self-service restaurant, with late opening till 9 pm on Friday. Meals are around Sfr10. Similarly priced is the *Coop* supermarket, which is also open late on Friday, yet the restaurant is also open 9 am to 5 pm Sunday. It's at two locations: Bahnhofstrasse 33 and opposite Interlaken Ost. There are a number of *Denner* supermarkets around town, providing picnic fare and alcohol.

Anker Restaurant (Marktgasse 57), has a varied menu with dishes costing from Sfr12 to Sfr38, and substantial portions. There is a games area at the back, but the restaurant section is fairly civilised. There's occasional live music, except in summer (entry from Sfr10). It's closed on Thursday. Opposite is *Ristorante Arcobaleno*, good for Italian food (closed Tuesday). It doesn't serve pizzas, but there are several decent pizzerias dotted around, where smallish pizzas start at about Sfr11. Try *Pizzeria Mercato (Postgasse)* or *Pizpaz (Centralstrasse)*; both open daily.

For Mexican food and free live music (Friday/Saturday nights), go to *El Azteca (Jungfraustrasse 30)*. Meals start at Sfr15; it's closed on Wednesday in the off season. *Mata Hari (General Guisan Strasse 31)* is popular locally for Indonesian and Asian cuisine. Most prices start at Sfr17; it's closed on Tuesday and till 5.30 pm Wednesday.

The restaurant at *Hotel Splendid* (see Places to Stay section earlier) is a good place for fondue from about Sfr19; it's open from 6 pm nightly (11 am on Sunday), but only Friday to Sunday in winter.

A good place for traditional food in rustic yet comfortable surroundings is *Gasthof Hirschen*, on the corner of Hauptstrasse and Parkstrasse. There's a range of main courses from Sfr12.50 to Sfr40 and a pleasant garden. It's closed till 5 pm Monday and Wednesday, and all day Tuesday.

Il Bellini, in the Metropole Hotel (see Places to Stay section earlier), has quality Italian fare. It's a fairly expensive place but has a cheaper lunch menu from Monday to Saturday. The *Panoramic Bar/Café* is on the 15th floor of the hotel. It's worth going up for a beer or a coffee to admire the view and to walk around the balcony. It also has affordable lunches.

The restaurant in the *Hotel Du Nord* (☎ 822 26 31, Höheweg) offers Swiss food (Sfr20 to Sfr40) in a rustic setting or on the terrace. There are also multi-course menus from Sfr41.50; it's open daily. For splendid surroundings and attentive service you can't beat *La Terrasse* in the Victoria-Jungfrau Hotel (☎ 828 28 28, Höheweg 41). Soothing piano music in the evening helps you digest excellent French cuisine from around Sfr50, with full menus starting at Sfr80. Lunchtime dining is slightly less expensive (open daily).

Entertainment

For a traditional Swiss folklore show, go to the *Casino Kursaal*, where the Spycher restaurant serves up Swiss food to complement the entertainment. Three-course menus including the show start at around Sfr40, or it's Sfr16 for the show only. Shows are mostly in the summer; check with the tourist office for schedules, or phone ☎ 827 61 00.

Balmer's Bar (see Places to Stay section earlier) is open from 9 pm. Another place popular with young English speakers is *Buddy's Pub* in the Hotel Splendid, Höheweg 33, or look out for parties and live music at *Funny Farm* (see Places to Stay section earlier). There's also *Johnny's Dancing Bar* in the Hotel Carlton, Höheweg 92 (open from 9.30 pm, closed Monday). Local youths hang out in *Café-Bar Hüsi (Postgasse 3)*, open from 4 pm Tuesday to Sunday.

Between late June and mid-September there are twice-weekly performances of Schiller's *Wilhelm Tell* in the *open-air theatre* in the Rugen forest. The first performance was in 1912 and it's now an annual event. More than 200 amateur actors take part in the production, not to mention the many horses, cows and goats that wander around and add sound effects as appropriate. It is staged in German but an English synopsis is available. Tickets (Sfr14 to Sfr34) are available from Tellspielbüro (☎ 822 37 22, fax 822 57 33, Bahnhofstrasse 5). Its Web site is at www.tellspiele.ch.

The biggest local event, with more than 2500 participants, is the Alpine shepherds' Unspunnen Festival. Unfortunately it's only every 12 years, and the next one isn't until 2005.

Shopping
There are plenty of souvenir shops along Höheweg, many with a good selection of Swiss army knives. If you're interested in wood carvings, it's better to buy directly in Brienz.

Getting There & Away
Trains to Lucerne depart hourly from Interlaken Ost train station. Trains to Brig (via Spiez and Lötschberg) and to Montreux (via Bern or Zweisimmen) depart from Interlaken West or Ost. Main roads head east to Lucerne and west to Bern, but the only way south for vehicles without a big detour round the mountains is to take the car-carrying train from Kandersteg, south of Spiez.

Car Rental Reasonably central are both Avis (☎ 822 19 39), Waldeggstrasse 34a, near a 24-hour petrol station, and Hertz (☎ 822 61 72), Harderstrasse 25.

Getting Around
Interlaken taxis cost Sfr5 plus Sfr2.80 to Sfr4.40 per kilometre, depending upon the number of passengers. Taxis usually wait by the railway stations, or call ☎ 822 80 80. Bus fares start at Sfr3 (Swiss Pass valid).

Jungfrau Region

☎ 033

Some of the best scenery in the whole of Switzerland can be found in the Jungfrau Region. Magnificent views and hikes compete for attention from various vantage points, usually accessible by railway or cable car. Attention is wrested by the towering triplets: the Jungfrau (4158m), Mönch (4099m) and Eiger (3970m), which head a series of mountains exceeding 3000m that undulate to the south. But the shimmering peaks of these snow-topped giants are only half the story; the white and grey of their rugged flanks are made all the more beautiful by the green, gold and brown of the nearer hills and valleys. It's a hard place to leave.

Orientation & Information
There are two valleys branching southward from Interlaken. The valley that curves to the east is dominated by Grindelwald, a well-established skiing and hiking centre. The valley that runs more directly south leads first to Lauterbrunnen, a leaping-off point for the car-free resorts clinging to the hills above. Above Lauterbrunnen (via funicular) on the western ridge is Grütschalp. Walking or taking the train along the ridge yields tremendous views across the valley to the Jungfrau, Mönch and Eiger peaks, and brings you to the ski resort of Mürren (fare from Lauterbrunnen Sfr9.40). A 40-minute walk down the hill from Mürren is tiny Gimmelwald, relatively undisturbed by tourists. Gimmelwald and Mürren can also be reached from the valley floor by the Stechelberg cable car, which runs all the way up to Schilthorn at 2970m (Sfr87 return). Wengen perches on the eastern ridge of the Lauterbrunnen Valley.

Save mountain-top excursions for clear days. There are revolving cameras on Jungfraujoch, Schilthorn, Kleine Scheidegg, Männlichen and Grindelwald-First, and live pictures are shown on the local cable TV information channel. However, weather conditions are volatile in mountain areas, and the outlook might have changed by the time you get up there.

Staying in resorts earns a Guest Card (Gästekarte), which is good for a number of discounts throughout the Jungfrau Region. Benefits are listed in the informative (free) Jungfrau *Top Magazine*, or tourist offices and hotels can provide details. Grindelwald and Mürren even have two types of Guest Card – the superior version (called 'A' or 'Sports Center Pass' respectively) gives extra benefits at the local sports centre (eg, free swimming).

Holiday chalets or apartments are ubiquitous in this area. They sleep from one to eight people or more and can work out as little as Sfr25 per day per person. In the off season these may be available on demand, but for peak season contact the local tourist office around six months in advance. Chalets are generally available for one week minimum, Saturday to Saturday.

Activities

Skiing is a major activity in the winter months, with a good variety of intermediate runs and a demanding run down from the Schilthorn. In all there are 205km of prepared runs and 45 ski lifts. A one-day ski pass for either Grindelwald-First, Kleine Scheidegg-Männlichen or Mürren-Schilthorn costs Sfr52 (Sfr26 for children, Sfr42 for ages 16 to 20, Sfr47 for those over 62). Ski passes for the whole Jungfrau Top Ski Region cost Sfr105/53/84/95 for a minimum two days, or Sfr780/390/575/700 for

the whole season, though switching between ski areas by train can be slow and crowded.

The Jungfrau Region is a major centre for adventure sports with many daredevil-type activities on offer, such as river rafting, rock climbing and canyoning. You can even bungy jump off the Stechelberg-Mürren cable car – the 100m jump is Sfr100 and the 180m jump, claimed to be the world's highest fixed-point jump, is Sfr220 (May to October only). Local operators include Alpin Raft (☎ 823 41 00, fax 823 41 01, ℮ mail@alpinraft.ch), based in Interlaken. Its Web site is at www.alpinraft.ch. Adventure World (☎ 826 77 11, fax 826 77 15, ℮ info@adventureworld.ch), near Wilderswil Bahnhof, has a Web site at www.adventureworld.ch. There's also Alpin Center (☎ 823 55 23), Web site: www.alpincenter.ch; Swiss Alpine Guides (☎ 822 60 00), Web site www.swissalpineguides.ch; and Paragliding Interlaken (☎ 823 8233).

BERNESE OBERLAND

JUNGFRAU REGION

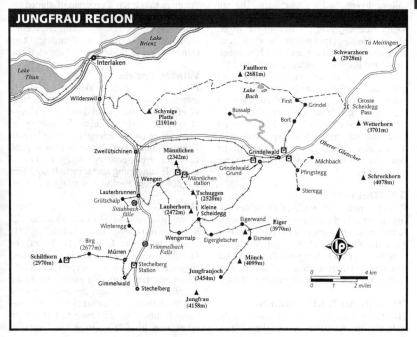

Scenic helicopter flights of the Jungfrau Region are conducted by Bohag (☎ 822 90 00). The usual departure point is Gsteigwiler, near Interlaken, though it's also possible from Männlichen (in winter) or Jungfraujoch (summer in fine weather). Prices for a short, eight-minute trip start at Sfr60 per person (minimum three people) but the views are incredible, and it's worth doing if your budget can handle it. They even do tandem parachute jumps.

If you just want to watch others being active, there's the **Jungfrau Marathon** in early September. Around 3000 masochistic competitors run from Interlaken to Kleine Scheidegg, via Wengen – an ascent of 1525m!

Getting There & Around

One or two trains depart for the region per hour from Interlaken Ost train station; sit in the front half of the train for Lauterbrunnen or the back half for Grindelwald. The two sections of the train split up where the two valleys diverge at Zweilütschinen. The rail tracks loop around and meet up again at Kleine Scheidegg, at the foot of the Eiger. Many cable cars close briefly for servicing at the end of April and at the end of November. Eurail and Europass holders usually get 25% off transport in the region, but Inter-Rail no longer gets a reduction on Jungfrau Railways. Worth considering is the Jungfrau Railways Pass, offering five days of unlimited travel for Sfr133 (Sfr85 with Swiss Pass or Swiss Card), though you still have to pay half-price from Kleine Scheidegg to Jungfraujoch. Its Web site (www.jungfraubahn.ch) has more information.

GRINDELWALD

☎ 033 • pop 3850 • elevation 1090m
Grindelwald is the largest ski village in the Jungfrau, and occupies an enviable position under the north face of the Eiger. It is also a great base for hiking, especially in the First region where there are 90km of paths above 1200m. Of these, 48km stay open in winter.

Orientation & Information

The main village is to the east of the train station. At either end of the village,

Terrassenweg loops north off the main street and takes a scenic, elevated east-west course. Below and south of the main street is the Schwarze Lütschine River. The tourist office (☎ 854 12 12, fax 854 12 10, @ touristcenter@ grindelwald.ch) is in the centre at the Sportzentrum; it's open 8 am to noon and 2 to 6 pm weekdays and till noon on Saturday. In high season it also opens Saturday afternoon and for a few hours on Sunday.

Postbuses and local buses depart from near the train station, and a post office (3818) is close by. Local buses are free with the Guest Card in winter. There are several open-air car parks scattered around. Many sports shops along the main street rent ski equipment, and a couple of banks have ATMs (including for Visa cards).

The gondola from Grindelwald to First (Sfr28 up/Sfr45 return, 25 minutes) takes you to the main skiing and hiking area. The Bergsteigerzentrum (☎ 853 52 00, fax 853 12 22, @ bergsteigerzentrum@grindelwald.ch), on the main street, has a program of guided activities in summer and winter. Options include ski touring, mountaineering and hiking. It doubles as the ski and snowboarding school (same ☎/fax, @ skischule@grindelwald.ch).

Winter Sports

First offers a variety of **skiing** runs (mostly intermediate or difficult) stretching from Oberjoch at 2486m, right down to the village at 1050m. From Kleine Scheidegg or Männlichen there are long, easy runs back to Grindelwald. Grindelwald is also a good base for cross-country skiing (33km of trails). **Tobogganing** routes include the 12km run down from Faulhorn, starting at 2543m.

Hiking

From First, you can hike to Schwarzhorn (2 hours 50 minutes), Grosse Scheidegg (1½ hours) the Upper Glacier (1½ hours), or Grindelwald (2½ hours). The westward ridge, to Lake Bach and beyond, treats hikers to excellent unfolding panoramas of the Jungfrau massif, though the best views (of the Wetterhorn and Schreckhorn) are initially behind you. The hike to Lake Bach takes one hour. Continue 1½ hours to

Thomas Cook: the First Conducted Tour of Switzerland

Thomas Cook, the excursionist who spawned the worldwide travel company, was instrumental in opening up Switzerland to mass tourism in the 19th century. He embarked on his first conducted tour of Switzerland in 1863. Previously Mr Cook had concentrated on Scotland for excursions into lake and highland scenery but, frustrated by the refusal of the English and Scottish Railway to renew a cheap excursion ticket to that country, he decided to look further afield. Switzerland seemed the ideal substitute. Various notices subsequently appeared about his plans in the regular newsletter written and produced by Mr Cook, *Cook's Excursionist and Advertiser*.

Public interest was immediate and extensive. Cook initially wanted a party of 25, but ultimately in excess of 130 people set off from London on 26 June 1863. They travelled by ferry to Dieppe and then took the train to Paris. The original party was whittled down to 62 who were scheduled to continue the whole way to Switzerland, and included in that number were many independently minded Victorian ladies. One of these, Miss Jemima Morrell, wrote a book about their experiences (*Miss Jemima's Swiss Journal* – now out of print but still available in some libraries). Various locations in Switzerland were included in the tour, with the main focus of the trip being the Jungfrau Region. This was in the days before the mountains had been tamed by funiculars and cable cars, yet these hardy ladies were undaunted as they negotiated steep mountain passes. Some trails, Miss Jemima wrote, were 'a mere groove cut in the face of (a) huge cliff, just wide enough for a mule to pass'.

The trip proved to be a great success, even though not everything about foreign countries appealed to the tourists (French tea, Miss Jemima considered, was 'truly peculiar'). It's worth noting, in our current climate of supposedly free movement between European nations, that these Victorian British travellers did not need a passport to enter France and Switzerland. Mr Cook followed up his success with regular subsequent trips, but not everybody appreciated the influx of masses; the English gentry, who had previously made the Swiss Alps their private playground, were particularly miffed.

In those days, Switzerland was relatively cheap. The exchange rate was around £1 = Sfr24. Mr Cook's personal bill for tea, bed and attendance in the Hotel Clerc, Martigny, where the treatment was 'kind and liberal' was Sfr4.50. Costs for mules and guides over the mountain passes were less than Sfr8 per person. Mr Cook reckoned that with careful spending, all-in costs for a 14-day jaunt to Switzerland could be as little as £10 to £12, or £20 for a month. Nevertheless, £20 was still a substantial amount of money for the average Victorian. But not, apparently, for Mr Cook, because he wrote in his *Excursionist* (21 July 1863) that £20 was 'a sum often spent at home, in fashion and folly, in a single night, leaving little for the disbursement but aching heads, wearied limbs and restless ennui'. Mr Cook himself was teetotal, but it seems, was in the habit of indulging in wild nights out in the company of dissolute spendthrifts!

JENNY JONES

Faulhorn (2681m), where there's a restaurant and a 360° panorama. Then on to Schynige Platte (another three hours), and return by train. Alternatively, take the steepish descent from Faulhorn to Bussalp (1800m, 1½ hours), and return by bus to Grindelwald (Sfr15.40).

The **Upper Glacier** (Oberer Gletscher) is well worth a visit. It's a 1½ hour hike from the village, or catch a postbus to the

Hotel-Restaurant Wetterhorn, from where it's just 15 minutes. Entry costs Sfr5 (with Guest Card Sfr4, children Sfr2.50) to see the ice grottoes, open mid-May to 31 October. The sculptures themselves are pretty pathetic, but notice the air bubbles and stones trapped in the ice that create kaleidoscopic patterns.

From here it's a few minutes' walk up to the Restaurant Milchbach where a further track, incorporating wooden ladders, climbs up alongside the ice. It's a good route but it's annoying to have to pay to use it (Sfr4, allow around 1½ hours return). There's a viewpoint up there looking over the sea of ice (Eismeer), but if you carry on along a less defined path to where there's a 'skull and crossbones' glacier avalanche warning, there's an even better perspective looking up to the top.

A cable car glides up to **Pfingstegg** (Sfr9.20, or Sfr14 return) from May to October. Apart from enjoying the view, you can take short hiking trails to Stieregg, near the Unterer Gletscher, or to the Restaurant Milchbach. Along the latter route you pass the **Breitlouwina**, a sloping terrace of rock billed as a geologist's paradise. You can see potholes, scratches on the rock caused by stones inside moving ice, and places where two different types of rock (40 million years and 120 million years old) have fused together.

The **Glacier Gorge** (Gletscherschlucht) is a 35-minute walk from the village centre. It's not a bad spectacle, but you can get a good idea of what it looks like from the entrance and it doesn't get much better further in (entry Sfr6, open May to October).

Special Events

The World Snow Festival in mid-January sees international teams create inventive sculptures from blocks of ice (free to spectate). In July or August, Grindelwald also hosts a yodelling festival and shortly after there's Swiss wrestling at nearby Grosse Scheidegg.

Places to Stay

There are hundreds of holiday chalets, especially on Terrassenweg and near the Glacier Gorge. The tourist office has prices and availability logged on its computer, and some are listed in the hotel information hut (free telephone) at the bus station.

There are also various hotels (many with dorms) outside the village, such as *Wetterhorn* (☎ 853 12 18) at the bottom of the Upper Glacier, *Glecksteinhütte SAC* (☎ 853 11 40) high up on the mountain overlooking the glacier (for experienced climbers only), *Berggasthaus First* (☎ 853 12 84) by the First top station, and *Berghaus Bort* (☎ 853 36 51), halfway up by the Bort station.

Camping Grindelwald has several camp sites. The most convenient is *Gletscherdorf* (☎ 853 14 29), near the Pfingstegg cable car, open May to late October for tents or year-round for caravans. *Aspen* (☎ 853 11 24), on the lower slopes of the Männlichen, is open year-round.

Hostels The SYHA *hostel* (☎ 853 10 09, fax 853 50 29, Terrassenweg) is a 20-minute climb from the train station, taking the road that follows the tracks on the north side. If you're walking, don't miss the small sign on the brown and white house indicating the steep short-cut footpath up to the right. Beds in six-bed dorms (including local tax) are Sfr30.60. These (and reception) are in the typical wood chalet which must have accounted for a couple of forests' worth of wood all by itself. The view is fantastic and there is an open fire and musical instruments. The house is always open (no curfew) but reception and check-in is from 3 pm (5 pm on Sunday). The newer wood building next door houses doubles or four-bed rooms (bunk beds) with sink for Sfr35.60 per person, and doubles (twin beds) with shower/WC for Sfr46.10 per person. The hostel is closed between seasons.

A 10-minute walk from the youth hostel along Terrassenweg is the *Naturfreundehaus* (☎ 853 13 33, fax 853 43 33) which has two to six-bed rooms for Sfr30 (Sfr27 with a HI membership). Add Sfr5 for breakfast and Sfr18 for dinner (compulsory during peak times), though there is a kitchen.

Child rates are lower, and it closes in the off season.

If you don't fancy the walk to these hostels, bus No 4 departs from the bus station every 30 minutes and completes a circuit of Terrassenweg.

Mountain Hostel (☎ 853 39 00, fax 853 47 30), by the Grund cable car, has a vivid blue exterior and dorm beds from Sfr32 (Sfr37 if you need sheets; reductions for children). There's 24-hour access and a TV and games room. Take bus No 1 or 3.

Hotels & Pensions *Lehmann's Herberge* (☎ 853 31 41) has simple but good-value rooms for one to six people, usually with shower. The price is Sfr40 or Sfr45 per person in this family-run place. It's in the centre of the village just off the main road (signposted). At the same turning on the main street, with private parking, is *Hotel Tschuggen* (☎ 853 17 81, fax 853 26 90). Attractive singles/doubles are Sfr90/144 with private shower/WC and TV. There are also some rooms for Sfr65/118 with hall shower and a radio instead of TV.

Hotel Alpen-blick (☎ 853 11 05, fax 853 44 84, ✉ alpenblick@grindelwald.net), at the eastern end of the village, is also worth a try. Prices are Sfr35 to Sfr48 for cramped dorms or Sfr58/96 to Sfr75/140 for singles/doubles with hall shower – the best rates are in low season and mid-week. There's an American-style bar with a pool table. *Gydisorf* (☎ 853 13 03, fax 853 13 11) by the bottom First cable station, is a small, staid place with a nice flower garden. It's often booked ahead by regulars: singles/doubles with own shower/WC are Sfr70/140.

Moving upmarket a bit, try *Fiescherblick* (☎ 853 44 53, fax 853 44 57, ✉ hotel@fiescherblick.ch), in a flower-strewn chalet towards the east of the village on the main street. Rooms start at Sfr180, or Sfr110 for single occupancy. *Sunstar-Hotel* (☎ 854 77 77, fax 854 77 70), charges from Sfr135/270 for four-star rooms and has good facilities including a swimming pool, sauna and tennis court. Its Web site is at www.sunstar.ch.

Places to Eat

There's a *Coop* supermarket opposite the tourist office.

Generally, eating is pricey, which makes *Onkel Tom's Hütte*, on the eastern side of the village, even better! Pizzas start at only Sfr8.50 for the smallest (but still adequate) size. The main problem is getting a table in this small place, which is closed on Monday and till 6 pm on Tuesday.

Hotel Derby, by the train station, has a range of Swiss meals from Sfr13 (open daily). On the main street, in the centre, is *Restaurant Rendez-vous*, with a panoramic terrace. Meals also start from around Sfr13, including simple vegetarian food. Fondue costs Sfr42 for two (closed Tuesday).

Across the road is *Hirschen Restaurant*, on the main street, which also has a few cheap dishes, though most are above Sfr20. The lunch and evening *menu du jour* is around Sfr37 for four courses (closed Thursday in low season).

Fiescherblick and *Sunstar* (see Places to Stay section earlier) have two restaurants apiece, which are usually open daily. Fiescherblick's main restaurant is gourmet quality, with main dishes from Sfr39; its Swiss Bistro has typical Swiss food from Sfr15. Sunstar's bargain is the Älpli, a family restaurant with a terrace. Spaghetti starts at Sfr9.50, or Sfr18.50 gets you a main course, dessert and drinks.

Entertainment

A popular watering hole is the small *Espresso Bar* in the Spinne Hotel, just one of several places in the centre. The hotel also has a disco with a DJ and occasional live music, open Monday to Saturday in winter, Thursday to Saturday in summer (free entry but pricey drinks). There's usually live music in the Hotel Derby's *Cava Bar*, open Thursday to Sunday in winter only.

Getting There & Away

Grindelwald is only 40 minutes by train from Interlaken Ost (Sfr9.40 each way). It can also be reached by a good road from Interlaken. A smaller road continues from the village over the Grosse Scheidegg Pass (1960m).

This is a great way to get to Meiringen – the hillside is very desolate looking with many rocks half overgrown with grass and shrubs, and the views are excellent. Take the postbus (from early July to early October only; Sfr40, two hours). The army performs manoeuvres here twice a year, though apparently this has no relevance to the fact that private traffic is banned from using the road.

LAUTERBRUNNEN
☎ 033 • pop 1000 • elevation 806m
This village can be reached by car or rail. It's a suitable base for a number of excursions, although many people simply use it as a car park before visiting the nearby car-free resorts. There is a multistorey car park by the station with space for 900 cars; summer rates are Sfr9 for a day and Sfr59 for a week. Winter rates are slightly higher. There is also an open-air car park by the Stechelberg cable-car station, costing Sfr5 for a day.

The tourist office (☎ 855 19 55, fax 855 10 32, @ info@lauterbrunnen.tourismus.ch) is on the main street above the train station. Its opening hours are 8 am to noon and 2 to 6 pm Monday to Friday. In summer it is also open on Saturday depending upon demand, and even on Sunday in July and August. The post office, bank and nearly all the shops and hotels are along this same street. Crystal Sport (☎ 855 20 80) rents bikes, ski equipment and mountaineering gear. The valley floor is good for cross-country skiing in the winter.

Spare a glance for the **Staubbach Falls** just outside the village, where wispy threads of spray cascade down the sheer face of the western ridge. It's just one of many waterfalls in the valley. Lauterbrunnen has the small **Tal Museum**, or Heimat Museum, featuring historical exhibits and mountain-related stuff. It's open 2 to 5.30 pm, on Tuesday, Thursday, Saturday and Sunday, and costs Sfr3 (Sfr2 with Guest Card, Sfr1 for children).

Trümmelbach Falls
A short bus ride (Sfr3) or a 50-minute walk down the valley is the Trümmelbachfälle, which drains the detritus from 24 sq km of Alpine glaciers and snow deposits. It's

viewed mainly from inside the mountain (illuminated), and as you get quite damp anyway, it's something to do if the weather is poor. The water generates incredible power – up to 20,000L of water is propelled down per second, and the noise is unceasing. The fissures of rock have been sculptured into dramatic shapes by the swirling waters over the 10 stages of the falls. It's well worth seeing, though Sfr10 (Sfr4 for children) is a lot to charge to view a natural phenomenon, even if they did build a few staircases and install a lift. An hour is ample time to see the whole thing. The falls are open between 9 am and 5 pm daily (8 am to 6 pm June to September) from April to November.

Places to Stay
Lauterbrunnen is well fixed for self-catering dormitory accommodation. *Camping Schützenbach* (☎ 855 12 68) and *Camping Jungfrau* (☎ 856 20 10) both offer kitchen facilities, year-round camping, and rooms and dorms from around Sfr20/14 per person respectively. The sites are on either side of the river a few minutes' walk to the south of the village.

A basic but good budget place to bed down, amid a street of quaint wooden chalets, is *Matratzenlager Stocki* (☎ 855 17 54). To get there from the station, follow the white signs that take you around the right side of the multistorey car park and over the river. It's about 200m down the road on the right; see Frau Graf in the next house along for check-in by 6 pm. She's a trusting soul and runs free-and-easy lodgings for Sfr13 a night (closed November). Mattresses in the dorms are side-by-side and there's only one shower, but there are free kitchen facilities and the open communal area generates a sociable atmosphere.

Valley Hostel (☎/fax 855 20 08, @ valleyhostel@bluewin.ch), in the village centre, charges Sfr20/25 per person in dorms/doubles in a newly built place with balconies, kitchen, washing machine and a garden. This friendly place is open all day year-round, reception is open until 10 pm.

Chalet im Rohr (☎ 855 21 82, fax 855 21 82) by the church, has variable one to four-bed rooms for Sfr26 per person in a creaky, old but attractive, wood chalet. There's a kitchen (Sfr0.50 per day) and hall showers. Nearby *Hotel Horner* (☎ *855 16 73, fax 855 46 07,* ✆ *hotelhorner@ tcnet.ch)*, another wood chalet, has singles/ doubles sharing a hall shower from Sfr32/64, and doubles with TV and a shower cubicle from Sfr86. It has a pub with Internet access (Sfr12 per hour), and a dance bar open till late.

None of the above places supply breakfast, though you do get it at the following hotels. At *Hotel Staubbach* (☎ *855 54 54, fax 855 54 84,* ✆ *hotel@staubbach.ch)*, near the church, a Swiss/American couple offer old-fashioned rooms, some with good views and balconies, for Sfr65/110 with shower/WC or Sfr55/80 without. *Hotel Crystal* (☎ *856 90 90, fax 856 90 99,* ✆ *info@crystal-lauterbrunnen.ch)*, opposite the tourist office, has huge, modern doubles with shower/WC and TV for Sfr140. *Hotel Jungfrau* (☎ *855 34 34, fax 855 25 23,* ✆ *hotel-jungfrau@tcnet.ch)* charges up to Sfr105/180, reducing for longer stays and in low season. There's shower/WC and sometimes TV, and children up to 14 stay free in their parents' room. The hotel has a swimming pool and a solarium on the premises.

Places to Eat

There is less choice when it comes to cheap eating in Lauterbrunnen, though there are a couple of supermarkets. The *Metzg-hus* meat store, between the Coop and the tourist office, offers hot sausage snacks, and usually has spit-roasted chickens cooking outside (Sfr9, or Sfr4.50 for a half). It closes on Wednesday afternoon in winter.

Hotel Crystal (see Places to Stay section earlier), has a sun terrace and serves Swiss meals from Sfr12. The kitchen stops around 8 pm and it closes lunchtime and Wednesdays in low season. Nearby, the restaurant in *Hotel Oberland* has good food and reasonable prices. *Hotel Silberhorn*, behind the Grütschalpbahn, is another good choice for food. It's generally a little more expensive, but has senior and child plates, and

serves fondue for Sfr16.50. *Hotel Jungfrau* (see Places to Stay section earlier) has a variety of meals, including vegetarian dishes, starting at Sfr14.50.

GIMMELWALD
☎ 033 • pop 140 • elevation 1370m

There's nothing to do in car-free Gimmelwald except relax, enjoy the view and keep away from the crowds. Various hiking trails lead up and around the mountains from the village. In winter, it's perfectly viable to enjoy the ski runs around Mürren and to retreat back down here for the night. It's cheaper to stay here than in Mürren, and you still get the normal Jungfrau Guest Card.

The steep hike down from Gimmelwald to Stechelberg takes around 1¼ hours; take the trail which is to the right of the cable car as you face the valley.

Places to Stay & Eat

The *Mountain Hostel* (☎ *855 17 04, fax 855 26 88,* ✆ *mountainhostel@tcnet.ch)*, close to the cable-car station and with a great view, has dorms without breakfast for Sfr16, and kitchen facilities. There's no curfew and check-in is from 5.30 pm to 10.30 pm. Phone ahead, especially in winter. Bring your own food as there's no village supermarket, though the hostel does sell a few provisions.

Next door is *Restaurant-Pension Gimmelwald* (☎/*fax 855 17 30)*, with simple singles/doubles for Sfr45/90, but avoid the terrible loft beds for Sfr28. Most meals in the restaurant cost Sfr15 or more. Close by is *Esther's Guest House* (☎ *855 54 88, fax 855 54 92,* ✆ *evallmen@bluewin.ch)*, with a few rooms for about Sfr35 per person, without breakfast, but there is a kitchen.

Five minutes up the hill, along a tarmac then cinder path, is *Mittaghorn* (☎ *855 16 58)*, sometimes known as Walter's. Ageing singles/doubles are Sfr55/60, triples/quads are Sfr85/105, and dormitory beds in the loft are Sfr25. A couple of doubles for Sfr70 have a shower, but there's only one communal shower. Beds are available from May to mid-November only, as it's pre-booked in winter. Beer in

BERNESE OBERLAND

the small cafe costs Sfr4 for 0.5L, but the tasty meals are only for guests who must pre-order.

MÜRREN

☎ 033 • pop 320 • elevation 1650m

This car-free resort hosted the first ever Alpine ski race in 1922, and has had a long association with British skiers. The tourist office (☎ 856 86 86, fax 855 86 96, *e* info@muerren.ch) is in the sports centre, open 9 am to noon and 2 to 5 pm Monday to Friday in the off season. Hours lengthen with demand, and in the high season it's open Saturday and Sunday afternoons. The bank has a non-Visa ATM.

Hiking and skiing are the main seasonal pursuits, or you could simply enjoy the views of the mountains and the numerous quaint chalets. There are 50km of prepared ski-runs in the vicinity, mostly suited to intermediates. The ski school (☎ 855 12 47) charges Sfr30 for half a day. Other activities on offer include swimming, ice-skating and curling. There's a yodelling festival every year in late July at Allmendhubel, above Mürren. Other annual events include the Alphorn Week (mid-June) and two weeks of hot-air ballooning (mid-August).

Places to Stay & Eat

Mürren is more expensive than either Lauterbrunnen or Gimmelwald, but it does have a couple of budget options. *Chalet Fontana* (*☎ 855 26 86, fax 856 86 96*), a small wooden house opposite the Coop supermarket, has a few singles/doubles for Sfr40/70 (phone ahead). It's usually pre-booked in winter, when prices rise. *Eiger Guesthouse* (*☎ 855 35 35, fax 855 35 31, e eigerguesthouse@muerren.ch*), opposite the train station, has dorms from Sfr39 and singles/doubles with shower and toilet from Sfr85/130, or Sfr60/100 without. It also has an affordable restaurant, and Internet access for guests.

Hotel Edelweiss (*☎ 855 13 12, fax 855 42 02, e edelweiss@muerren.ch*) is a three-star place charging Sfr90/190 for renovated rooms with shower/WC, TV and balcony. The restaurant has good views from the terrace, and food from about Sfr12 (open daily, but closes at 6 pm in summer).

The small *Stägerstübli*, a few paces from the Coop supermarket, has filling meals from Sfr12.50, including fondue for Sfr18.20. It's open daily.

SCHILTHORN

This 2970m peak provides a perfect viewing platform from which to gaze at the mountains across the valley. It's easily (if expensively) reached from the Stechelberg cable car, via Gimmelwald and Mürren. From the top there's a fantastic 360° panorama, and the film clips in the **Touristorama** will remind you that James Bond performed several stunts here in *On Her Majesty's Secret Service*. The view is more spectacular than that from Jungfraujoch in some ways, as you see a broader expanse of peaks, and you get a real sense of the height of the mountains across the valley. The view from Birg (2677m), the station after Mürren, is well worth stopping off for; the 'big three' are closer here than from the summit and you get a great perspective of the dark ridge of the Männlichen.

The high cost of the trip by cable car can sometimes be reduced by special offers. There are usually lower prices in the spring and autumn, or for the first/last ascent of the day – Sfr66 return instead of Sfr87, or Sfr44 if starting from Mürren. At the top, refreshment is provided by the *Piz Gloria* revolving restaurant, with meals from Sfr19, except for the *Wochen-Hit* (weekly special) for Sfr12.90.

The hike up is a strength-sapping four hours from Mürren, often very steep and rocky. You're likely to encounter snow above Birg. The walk down is more manageable, facing the mountains across the valley, rather than climbing with your back to them. About halfway between Mürren and Birg there's a grassy knoll to the valley side of the path which is an ideal place to break for a picnic.

Since 1928, Schilthorn has welcomed amateur skiers eager to take on the difficult course down to Mürren, known as the **inferno run**. It takes place in mid-January and attracts around 1800 participants, making it the largest event of its kind in the world.

WENGEN
☎ 033 • pop 1050 • elevation 1350m

Also car-free, this chalet-style ski resort is slightly more developed than Mürren, across the valley, and is popular with British skiers. As with most places in this region, the views are breathtaking.

From the train station, take a left at Hotel Silberhorn and walk 100m to get to the tourist office (☎ 855 14 14, fax 855 30 60, ✉ information@wengen.com). Opening hours in the low season are 8 am to noon and 2 to 6 pm Monday to Friday, and 8.30 am to 11.30 pm Saturday. In the high season it is also open 4 to 6 pm on both Saturday and Sunday. Next door is the post office (3823).

The high point in Wengen's calendar is when it hosts the international **Lauberhorn downhill ski race** in late January; it costs Sfr20 to watch the race or Sfr10 to watch just the training. Expect price hikes and accommodation shortages at this time. Wengen's ski school (☎ 855 20 22) has half-day classes costing Sfr44 each or Sfr210 for six. The ski runs are reached by gondola to Männlichen, or by railway to Allmend, Wengernalp or Kleine Scheidegg. The same areas are also excellent for hiking in the summer, and 20km of paths stay open in winter too. The hike down to Lauterbrunnen takes about an hour, or the frequent train does it in 15 minutes (Sfr5.60). Other attractions include a natural and an artificial ice rink, tennis courts and a cinema, with a pool hall next door.

Places to Stay & Eat
The Hot Chili Peppers (☎/fax 855 50 20, ✉ Chilis@wengen.com), is a young hangout near the tourist office, with six or eight-bed dorms for Sfr26 in summer (no breakfast), or Sfr45 in winter (compulsory breakfast). Single/double rooms with breakfast and hall showers are around Sfr50 per person. There's a kitchen, a popular bar with limited Tex-Mex food, and a downstairs disco bar (winter only). Check in from 2 pm.

Another good option is the *Bergheim YMCA* (☎ 855 27 55, fax 855 27 26, ✉ jungfraublick@wengen.com) where a place in the mixed six-bed dorm costs Sfr22 in summer and Sfr28 in winter, without breakfast. To get there, follow the sign posts. It's run by the plush Hotel Jungfraublick, five minutes away, where you check in. Singles/doubles in the comfortable main *Bergheim* are around Sfr100/170 (with shower and breakfast) but dorm users can use the TV room there, or even the library in the Jungfraublick.

En route to Jungfraublick from Chili Peppers, you pass *Bernerhof* (☎ 855 27 21, fax 855 33 58) where dorm beds for Sfr23 are in a large room, partitioned into unappealing two-person boxes. The hotel also has quite acceptable rooms for Sfr60/110, or Sfr85/170 including shower/WC and TV. All prices are without breakfast, and there are lower rates in summer. The best thing about its restaurant is the salad bar, which costs Sfr6.50, Sfr9.80, or Sfr14.50 for a plate the size of a wok. The restaurant also has a wide choice of Swiss dishes from Sfr14.

Half-board rates at *Hotel Bären* (☎ 855 14 19, fax 855 15 25) are Sfr55 for dorms, Sfr100/190 for singles/doubles with shower/WC and TV. Around the back of this place, *Hotel Edelweiss* (☎ 855 23 88, fax 855 42 88) is family-oriented and has reasonable rooms and the best prices for stays of three days or more. Singles/doubles with shower/WC cost from Sfr60/120 and Sfr50/80 without. Add Sfr20 for half-board. To get to both these hotels, take the road passing under the train tracks and look for the signs.

The large *Coop* across from the station provides budget provisions. *Da Sina*, by the cinema, is comfortable and has good pizza/pasta from Sfr13.50 (open daily in season). Part of the same building is *Sina's Pub*, which usually has a disco or live music for après-ski and on summer evenings (free entry).

MÄNNLICHEN
Männlichen (2230m) is up on the ridge dividing the two valleys. Take the gondola

(Sfr20 up, Sfr33 return) from Wengen or make the pleasant three-hour hike up through the trees.

From the top station, walk 10 minutes up to the crown of the hill for a magnificent panorama. At the southern end of the ridge are the dark conical shapes of Tschuggen (2520m) and Lauberhorn (2472m), with the snow-capped giants looming impressively in the background. These are flanked by the two valleys, and their different characteristics are particularly evident from here; the broad expanse of the Grindelwald Valley to the left, and the glacier-formed Lauterbrunnen Valley to the right with its severe square sides. This valley is the deepest hanging or 'u' valley in the world. To the north you can see gentler green hills and a stretch of Thunersee. The hike from here to Kleine Scheidegg is an extremely rewarding gradual descent on the Grindelwald side, and takes a little over an hour. By foot, Grindelwald itself can be reached in three hours, or you can take the 30-minute cable car to Grindelwald-Grund (Sfr28 one way, Sfr45 return). It is the longest gondola cableway in Europe, traversing 6.2km.

KLEINE SCHEIDEGG

This small place is little more than a few buildings grouped around the train station, yet it occupies such an enviable position at the base of the Eiger that it's surprising that it is not more developed. It looks like a toy village against the backdrop of soaring peaks. Most people only linger a few minutes while changing trains for Jungfraujoch (see the Jungfrau Region section earlier), but Kleine Scheidegg (2061m) is a good base for a longer exploration of this scenic area. There are short (one hour apiece), undemanding hiking trails to Eigergletscher, down to Wengernalp, and up the Lauberhorn (green in summer, red-brown in autumn) behind the village. These areas become intermediate ski runs from early December to April.

The train station has local information and money changing facilities. The small post office is also in the train station, as is the *Röstizzeria Bahnhof Restaurant (☎ 855*

11 51, fax 855 11 52). This offers simple dorm beds for Sfr38, and a few singles/doubles for Sfr53/106; add Sfr17 for half-board. *Restaurant Grindelwaldblick (☎ 853 13 74, fax 855 42 05)*, eight minutes' walk towards Grindelwald, has slightly cheaper dorms and reasonable food, but it closes in the off season. There's only one hotel in Kleine Scheidegg, *Bellevue – Des Alpes (☎ 855 12 12, fax 855 12 94)*. It's in two buildings by the station, and has an old-fashioned aura. Singles/doubles including dinner are a little pricey, starting at Sfr160/250 with shower/WC or Sfr100/200 without.

JUNGFRAUJOCH

The trip to Jungfraujoch by railway (the highest railway in Europe) is excellent. Unfortunately, the price is as steep as the track and is hardly worth it unless you have good weather – call ☎ 855 10 22 for forecasts in German, French and English. From Interlaken Ost, trains go via Grindelwald or Lauterbrunnen to Kleine Scheidegg. From here, the line is less than 10km but took 16 years to build. Opened in 1912, the track powers through both the Eiger and the Mönch with majestic views from windows cut into the mountain side, before terminating at 3454m at Jungfraujoch.

On the summit there are several things to do and see. The **ice palace** is a gallery cut in the glacier featuring various ice sculptures such as an Eskimo, igloo and sumo wrestler. The terrace of the Sphinx Research Institute (a weather station) reveals an unforgettable panorama of peaks, including the Aletsch Glacier to the south, and mountains as distant as the Jura and the Black Forest in Germany. Entry to the above places is free. Climatic and environmental issues that impact on the work of the weather station is covered in an informative free booklet available from various dispensers. By the terrace lifts are places to send free emails.

You can walk across the glacier behind the Mönch on a marked path, but remember to keep a leisurely pace because of the high altitude (compared to sea level there's one third less oxygen in the air at Jungfrau). The views keep getting better. On the glacier there's a very tame ski lift; skis or snowboard are provided in the Sfr30 charge. A sled ride courtesy of a team of husky dogs is another attraction (Sfr6), or there are plastic disks on which you can take a free slide on the snow. The more adventurous can contemplate guided glacier treks or abseiling.

Take warm clothing any time of the year, and sunglasses if you're going to walk on the glacier. Bringing your own food will help to cut costs, although the self-service restaurant in the complex has meals from Sfr15. There is another, more expensive, restaurant upstairs. If you walk the full way across the glacier along the prepared path (50 minutes) you reach the *Möchsjochhutte* (☎ 971 34 72) at 3650m. This mountain hut offers dorms, refreshments and a great view across the mountains fringing the glacier. It closes between seasons.

Getting There & Away

Despite the high cost, nearly half a million people do this trip annually. From Interlaken Ost, journey time is 2½ hours each way and the return fare is Sfr159 (Eurail Sfr119.60, Swiss Pass Sfr109). Allow at least three hours at the site. The last train back is 6.10 pm in the summer and 4 pm in the winter. There's a cheaper 'good morning ticket' of Sfr120 (Eurail Sfr104.60, Swiss Pass Sfr90) if you take the first train (6.35 am from Interlaken) and leave the summit by noon. From 1 November to 30 April the reduction is valid for the 6.35 am and 7.35 am trains, and the noon restriction doesn't apply.

Getting these early trains is not such an effort if you start from farther down the track. If you stay overnight at Kleine Scheidegg, you can pick up the excursion-fare train at 7.02 am in the summer and at 8.02 am or 9.02 am in the winter. From here, the full return is Sfr97 (Sfr48.50 with the Jungfrau Railways Pass) and the 'good morning' return is Sfr58. Ordinary return fares are valid for one month. The farthest you can walk is up to Eigergletscher (2320m), which only saves you Sfr6.40/10.60 one way/return from Kleine Scheidegg (strange how the final section where you have no option but to take the train is by far the most expensive).

The Lakes

A boat tour of Lake Thun (Thunersee) or Lake Brienz (Brienzersee) is a popular and enjoyable excursion. Lake Thun has the greater number of resorts and villages clustered around it, and has more facilities to offer water sports enthusiasts. Lake Brienz, in contrast, has a more rugged shoreline and fewer diversions. It is said to be the cleanest lake in Switzerland, ideal for angling. No fishing permit is needed for the shore of the lakes; if you fish from a boat or in a river you need to get a permit from the tourist office (Sfr50 for one day or Sfr150 for one week, valid for the whole canton). At one time the lakes were one great waterway, but deposits from the Lütschine in the south and the Lombach in the north gradually formed a plain (the Bödeli, upon which Interlaken now stands) that divided it in two. The lakes are still linked by the Aare River, but boats can't navigate this stretch.

Steamers are most frequent from the end of May to late September. Both lakes also have services in spring and autumn, and Lake Thun even has occasional special cruises through most of the winter. For more information contact BLS (☎ 334 52 11), or visit their Web site at www.bls.ch. A day pass valid for both lakes costs Sfr34 (Sfr52 in 1st class) or Sfr46 (Sfr66) in July and August. Children travel half price and people with a Half-Fare Card pay Sfr23 (Sfr33 in 1st class) any time of the year. Passes are also available for seven and 15 days, or even longer. Eurail passes, the Regional Pass and the Swiss Pass are valid on all boats and Inter-Rail and the Swiss Half-Fare Card are good for 50% off the fare of individual rides. See the Swiss Travel Passes section in the Getting Around chapter for further details.

The most famous ferry on Lake Thun is the *Blümlisalp*, a paddlesteamer built in 1906. It started operating again in 1992 after plans to scrap it were overturned in a public referendum. It sails daily in the summer months.

THUN

☎ 033 • pop 38,700 • elevation 563m

Evidence of habitation in Thun dates back to 2500 BC. Its name is derived from the Latin, *Dunum* (meaning fortified hill), and its castle remains its most dominant feature today. The town was acquired by the canton of Bern in 1384.

Orientation & Information

Thun (pronounced toohn) is the largest town on the lake. The Aare River separates the train station (which has bike rental and money-exchange counters) from the medieval centre around the castle. The river itself is split by a sliver of land which has Bälliz, a partly pedestrian-only street, running along its length. This island is laced to the mainland by several roads and footpaths. The central area can easily be covered on foot.

The tourist office (☎ 222 23 40, fax 222 83 23, ✆ thun@thunersee.ch) is in the train station. It's open 9 am to noon and 1 to 6 pm Monday to Friday, and 9 am to noon Saturday. Hours are extended in July and August. If it's shut, the train information counter usually has a hotel list. The main post office on Bälliz is open 7.30 am to 6 pm Monday to Friday, and 7.30 to 11 am Saturday.

Internet access is available at Skipper Club, Bälliz 25, from 1.30 pm (closed Monday), or the more expensive Space Gate, Mönchstrasse 2b (closed Sunday).

Things to See & Do

Roaming around the river and the, enjoying the views, is an attraction in itself. **Obere Hauptgasse**, leading off the harmonious Rathausplatz, is a two-tier street, where the roofs of the shops on the lower level provide the walkways for the upper level. Wherever you are in the town, attention is drawn to the 12th-century hill-top castle, **Schloss Thun** which contains the **Historical Museum** (entry Sfr5, students Sfr2,

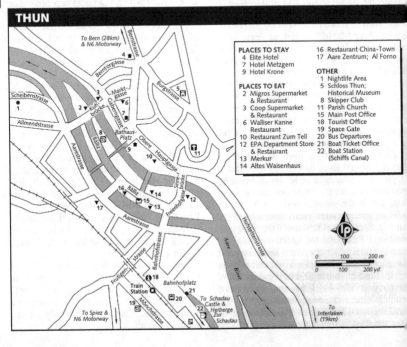

THUN

PLACES TO STAY
4 Elite Hotel
7 Hotel Metzgern
9 Hotel Krone

PLACES TO EAT
2 Migros Supermarket & Restaurant
3 Coop Supermarket & Restaurant
6 Walliser Kanne Restaurant
10 Restaurant Zum Tell
12 EPA Department Store & Restaurant
13 Merkur
14 Altes Waisenhaus

16 Restaurant China-Town
17 Aare Zentrum; Al Forno

OTHER
1 Nightlife Area
5 Schloss Thun; Historical Museum
8 Skipper Club
11 Parish Church
15 Main Post Office
18 Tourist Office
19 Space Gate
20 Bus Departures
21 Boat Ticket Office
22 Boat Station (Schiffs Canal)

hildren Sfr1). It's open 10 am to 5 pm daily
'om April to October (9 am to 6 pm from
June to 31 August), and 1 to 4 pm from
ebruary and March. The museum contains
everal interesting exhibits, encompassing
veapons, toys, ancient coins and pottery-
naking. It also provides access to the Ro-
nanesque tower with its four corner turrets,
ielding fine views. The parish church,
vhich shares the skyline with the castle, is
airly nondescript inside.

On Thursday in July and August there
re free folklore performances (yodelling
tc) in Rathausplatz. For nightlife, explore
ne former industrial quarter round
cheibenstrasse, where several lively bars,
lubs and concert venues have spawned.

In July, every odd-numbered year, Thun
as its International Barrel Organ Festival.

Places to Stay
he new *Herberge Zur Schadau* (☎ 222
2 22, **@** info@herberge.ch, Seestrasse 22)
; eight minutes' walk from the station, and
harges Sfr35 (Sfr32 in winter) per bed in
orms of four beds or more. There's a
itchen, TV room and garden area, and re-
eption is open from 8 am to 10 pm (8 pm
i winter). It's a bit pricey, especially in the
ery cramped attic dorms, but there are no
ther convenient budget places.

Rathausplatz is an attractive cobbled
quare in the medieval part of town, below
ie castle. At one side of it is *Hotel Met-
zern* (☎ 222 21 41, fax 222 21 82), with
mple singles/doubles for Sfr55/110. It's
osed Monday. On the other side of the
quare, with its own pointed tower, is
Iotel Krone (☎ 227 88 88, fax 227 88 90,
@ krone-thun@bluewin.ch), with spacious
ut not-particularly-plush-for-the-price
ooms with TV, telephone, minibar and
rivate shower/toilet. Singles/doubles start
: Sfr125/195. It has a couple of restau-
ants, catering for a range of preferences
nd budgets.

Elite Hotel (☎ 223 28 23, fax 223 18 57,
@ elite-hotel-thun@swissonline.ch, Bern-
rasse 1), is not so comely as the Krone
om the outside, but has similar-standard
ooms and lower rates.

Places to Eat
Thun is a great place to eat well and
cheaply. There are dozens of restaurants
clustered around the Old Town, offering all
types of cuisine. Pizzerias are particularly
numerous, with pizzas starting at Sfr12.

Self-Service The usual stand-bys are here,
offering daily specials from around Sfr9. A
Migros restaurant and supermarket is on the
island by Kuhbrücke. Across the river is a
Coop supermarket and restaurant. On the
other side of the island by Sinnebrücke is an
EPA department store and restaurant.
They're all open normal shop hours, with
late closing on Thursday.

The Aare Zentrum shopping centre on
Aarestrasse has a take-away pizza place, *Al
Forno*. It's an excellent bargain during the
day – big pizzas start at Sfr8. However, if you
buy outside shopping hours from the window, prices rise by about Sfr6 (open daily).

Restaurants A small place with friendly
service and inexpensive Swiss food is
*Restaurant Zum Tell (Obere Hauptgasse
28)*. It's closed Monday. Another small and
cosy restaurant is *Walliser Kanne (Marktgasse 3)*, with a good selection of Röstis
and fondues from Sfr16. This rustic-style
place is closed Sunday until the evening (all
day in summer) and on Monday.

Merkur Restaurant (Bälliz 62) has affordable food, including various vegetarian
choices, but it closes at 7 pm weekdays (10
pm Thursday) and 6 pm weekends. Nearby
at No 54 is *Restaurant China-Town*, open
Monday to Saturday, and where two-course
lunches are only Sfr12.50. Other meals, including Thai food, are around Sfr20 (open
daily).

For mid-priced Italian dining, especially
Tuscan dishes, try *Altes Waisenhaus
(☎ 223 31 33, Bälliz 61)*. It's open daily and
has a popular bar.

Getting There & Away
Thun is on the main north-south rail route
from Frankfurt to Milan and beyond. From
Interlaken West, Thun is Sfr16.60 each way
by steamer, Sfr13.60 by train.

SPIEZ

☎ 033 • pop 11,000 • elevation 628m

Spiez (pronounced 'Schpee-its') is a pretty little town hunched around a horseshoe-shaped bay. Its medieval castle and lakeside views are the main attractions.

Orientation & Information

The tourist office (☎ 654 20 20, fax 654 21 90, ☻ spiez@thunersee.ch), outside the train station, is open 8 am to noon and 2 to 6 pm Monday to Friday. In the summer season it's open on Saturday and weekday hours are extended. It has an Internet terminal (Sf1 for five minutes). Seestrasse, the main street, is down to the left, and ultimately leads to the castle (12 minutes).

Things to See & Do

The castle, **Schloss Spiez**, was the home of the influential von Bubenburg and von Erlach families. Many of the portraits hang on the walls. It's amusing to note how the children have no childlike quality at all; they all look like midget adults, especially the dour grandchildren of Franz Ludwig von Erlach (painted in 1645). The castle tower was constructed in the 16th to 17th centuries and provides a fetching view of the town and the bay. Elsewhere, the castle contains weapons, period furniture, impressive wooden doorway surrounds and stucco ceilings. The Romanesque church by the castle dates from the 10th century. Schloss Spiez is open 10 am to 5 pm (2 to 5 pm on Monday) daily from Easter to mid-October; entry costs Sfr4 (Sfr1 for children).

Near the castle is the small **Heimat und Rebbaumuseum** with exhibits on wine cultivation; it's free and open 2 to 5 pm Wednesday, Saturday and Sunday from May to October.

On the last Sunday in September there's a Vintage Wine Festival, the Läsetsunntig, with a fair, parades and music.

Places to Stay & Eat

The tourist office has information about cheap private rooms. Otherwise, the only convenient budget option is **Krone** (☎ 654 41 31), a hotel and restaurant near the station on Seestrasse. Singles/doubles go for Sfr50/9 with access to a hall shower, and it's close on Sunday (noon onwards) and Monday.

Nearby is **Bellevue** (☎ 654 84 64, fax 65 84 48, ☻ hotel@bellevue-spiez.ch, Seestrass 36) charging Sfr65/120 with shower/WC an TV. Its restaurant has a good selection o meals starting at Sfr16. Next door, **Des Alpe** (☎ 654 33 54, fax 654 88 50, Seestrasse 34) has comparable but bigger rooms fror Sfr75/134. The restaurant is not bad eithe (menus from Sfr14), though prices ar slightly higher in the terrace section with har bour views.

A couple of pizzerias await by the lake near the boat landing stage. Prices are OI but pizzas are small. Most supermarkets ar on and near Seestrasse, but the **Migros** b the train station has a self-service restauran with cheap food, decent views and late clos ing on Friday.

A good view is also gained from the four star **Strandhotel Belvédère** (☎ 654 33 3 fax 654 66 33, ☻ hotelbelvedere.spie @bluewin.ch), on Schbachenstrasse, whic is open from 1 March to 30 Novembe: Well-equipped rooms start from Sfr135/25C and there's a large garden. The renowne restaurant boasts a sumptuous dining are where French-style main courses are aroun Sfr30 to Sfr50.

Getting There & Away

From Interlaken West, Spiez is Sfr11.4 each way by steamer, Sfr8.60 by trair Spiez is also the rail junction for the car carrying train to Brig (see Brig in the Vala chapter for more details) and the MOB lin south-west to the Vaud Alps and Montreux

AROUND LAKE THUN

There are sailing schools at Spiez, Hilterfir gen and Interlaken-Neuhaus; contac Segelschule Thunersee (☎ 243 08 8C fax 243 08 81, ☻ info@swiss-sail.ch) a Hilterfingen for details.

The **St Beatus Caves** (St Beatus Höhler feature some impressive stalagmite and sta lactite formations, a small museum and laughably feeble 'realistic reconstruction of prehistoric settlement'. Combined entry i expensive at Sfr14, or Sfr12 for students and seniors, and the guided cave tour lasts 50 minutes. The caves are open 10.30 am to 5 pm daily from Palm Sunday to late October, and can be reached from Interlaken by bus, a 90-minute walk or a short Sfr6.20 boat ride.

The loudest sound in quiet **Faulensee** is the wind rustling in the sails of the windsurfers. Get on board by calling Maluco Sportferien (☎ 654 54 68, fax 654 00 68, @ info@ maluco.ch), which rents various sports equipment and organises outings. It also provides cheap dormitory accommodation.

Därligen, towards Interlaken, is a water sports centre; inquire at its tourist office (☎ 823 27 37, @ daerligen@thunersee.ch). **Gunten**, on the north shore, is similar; it has a water-skiing school, a diving centre and a tourist office (☎ 251 11 46, @ gunten@ thunersee.ch). On the hill above Gunten is **Sigriswil**, where there are two folklore-related festivals in July.

Castles

One of the best castles around the lake is **Schloss Oberhofen**. It looms over Oberhofen boat-landing stage and dates from the 13th century. It was held by the Habsburgs for a while before Bernese troops wrested control after the Battle of Sempach (1386). The castle contains a good collection of grand furniture, portraits, weapons, children's toys, and even a Turkish smoking room. It's open 10 am to noon and 2 to 5 pm daily except Monday morning, mid-May to mid-October; entry costs Sfr5 (Sfr1 children). The gardens were landscaped in the 19th century and are a fine place for a stroll (free; open 15 March to 15 November). About 300m east of the castle is the **Museum für Uhren und mechanische Musikinstrumente**, with numerous clocks, music boxes, organs and the like. Many are activated on the guided tour which is in English (Sfr6, concessions Sfr5). It's closed Monday and, except for Sunday and holiday afternoons, from November to April.

In Oberhofen, compile a picnic at the **Coop** on the main street (closed Wednesday afternoon), or chomp cheap meals in the **Berger Tea-Room** (open till 6.30 pm; closed Thursday). *Hotel Restaurant Kreuz (☎ 243 16 76, fax 243 52 76)* has fair-sized rooms with shower and WC from about Sfr65/100. Oberhofen is a 14-minute bus ride from Thun train station (every 15 minutes).

Another interesting castle is **Schloss Hünegg**, one boat stop down the lake at Hilterfingen. The interior illustrates the comfortable lifestyle of the 19th-century elite. Particularly evocative is the main bedroom with adjoining Lady's Dressing Room, Master's Dressing Room, and split-level bathroom complete with a gleaming nickel-plated bathtub and complicated taps. It was built in the 1860s and renovated in 1900, and provides a fascinating mix of Neo-Renaissance and Art Nouveau (Jugendstil) styles. It's open 2 to 5 pm daily, plus 10 am to noon Sunday morning from early May to mid-October. Entry costs Sfr8 (children Sfr1.50). Hilterfingen also has a free concrete-and-grass 'beach'.

There's time enough to fit in a rushed visit to all the castles at Spiez, Thun, Oberhofen and Hilterfingen in a single day trip by boat. They're all worth seeing, but that's probably a bit of overkill, especially as the first three collections cover similar ground. Keep your sanity by skipping an interior, probably Spiez or Thun, as they contain fewer and less diverse exhibits. On the other hand, if your appetite is insatiable, you can also digest the **Swiss Museum of Gastronomy**. It's in the castle at Schadau, on the outskirts of Thun, where the Aare River meets the lake. On display are 5000 cookery books dating from the 16th century, plus crockery and pottery. It is open on request; call ☎ 223 14 32. All the castles offer a discount with the Guest Card.

GIESSBACH FALLS

These falls by Lake Brienz are a popular excursion, one hour from Interlaken Ost by boat (Sfr10.60 each way). The water spills down over several stages and makes an attractive rather than a spectacular sight. A funicular runs up from the boat station (Sfr4.50/6 one way/return) but the walk doesn't take long. The sun is at a better angle for photography in the afternoon. Various footpaths traverse

BERNESE OBERLAND

the surrounding hillside. It takes a little over an hour to walk around the lake to Brienz; unfortunately the route is along the road rather than on a separate footpath.

BRIENZ
☎ 033 • pop 3200 • elevation 566m
Brienz is the centre of the Swiss woodcarving industry and the main town on the shores of Brienzersee. It is a convenient base for visiting the Ballenberg museum.

Orientation & Information
Orientation in Brienz is easy. The train station, boat station, Rothorn Bahn lower terminal, post office (3855) and a Coop supermarket are all within a stone's throw of each other in the town centre. The tourist office (☎ 952 80 80, fax 952 80 88, @ tourismus@ brienz.ch) is also here; opening hours are 8 am to noon and 2 to 6 pm Monday to Friday, and also 8 am to noon Saturday from April to June. In July and August, hours are extended to 8 am to 6.30 pm Monday to Friday and 8 am to noon and 4 to 6 pm Saturday. Brienz is linked with Meiringen (see following section) under the Alpenregion; check the Web site www.alpenregion.ch. The local Guest Card gives excellent benefits, including free water-skiing (Monday at 5.30 pm) and reduced entry to Brienz beach.

Things to See & Do
There are many touristy shops and boutiques along Hauptstrasse, selling locally carved statues and mementoes. Linden is a popular wood to use for sculpting as it is so soft. Some shops have factories attached where you can take a quick tour and see the craftspeople at work. **Jobin** (Hauptstrasse 111) has been in business since 1835, and weekday tours cost Sfr5; if you have a spare Sfr34,400 you can buy its top-of-the-range music box. **Walter Stähli** at No 41 gives free workshop tours from 8 am to 7 pm daily.

The **Woodcarving School** (Schnitzlerschule) is open for free visits on weekday mornings during term time (check dates with the tourist office), and has an exhibition room packed with finished work. The

Violin-making school opposite also displays work. Inquire at the tourist office about carving courses.

The **Rothorn Bahn** is the only cog-wheel steam train still operating in Switzerland. It hauls passengers up to 2350m for excellent views and hikes. Departures are hourly; check with the station as a standard diesel train is sometimes used (often the first ascent/descent of the day). The fare is Sfr42 single or Sfr66 return (25% discount with Swiss Pass); getting a discount with Eurail or Inter-Rail is as likely as stopping a runaway train with a pocket magnet). As always, there's a hotel and restaurant at the summit. Walking to the top from Brienz takes around five hours.

Brienz gives access to Axalp, where skiing is neither extensive nor expensive: a one-day pass costs Sfr36 (Sfr22 for children).

Places to Stay & Eat
Camping Aaregg (☎ 951 18 43) is by the lake, 15 minutes' walk east of the centre, and is open from April to October. The SYHA *hostel* (☎ 951 11 52, fax 951 22 60, Strandweg 10) is nearby, in a brown and white house by the rail tracks. Prices per person are: dorms Sfr25.50, family rooms Sfr27.50 and doubles Sfr30.50. It has a kitchen for guest use. The reception is closed from 10 am to 5 pm, but the doors stay open. It is closed from mid-October to around Easter.

The cheapest hotel is *Sternen am See* (☎ 951 35 45, fax 951 35 88, Hauptstrasse 92), costing from Sfr50/80 for singles/doubles or Sfr80/110 with shower/WC. A few minutes east of the station on Hauptstrasse is *Schültzen am See* (☎ 951 16 91), an oldish house with double rooms for Sfr60 per person – single occupancy is possible outside high season. *Schönegg Garni* (☎ 951 11 13, fax 951 38 13, Talstrasse 8), by the Rothorn tracks, is based in several attractive wood chalets and charges Sfr95/170 with shower/WC or Sfr60/120 without.

All the restaurants are ranged along Hauptstrasse, and many have seating overlooking the lake. One of these is *Tea-Room Hotel Walz* (☎ 951 14 59, Hauptstrasse

102). It has a two-course Tagesmenu for Sfr14.50, pizza/pasta from Sfr12.50, and double rooms with shower/WC for about Sfr120. It's open 8 am to 10.30 pm daily till 6.30 pm and closed Wednesday in winter). *Seerestaurant Löwen (Hauptstrasse 8)* also overlooks the water, and has mid-price fish specialities (closed Monday in winter).

Restaurant Steinbock (☎ 951 40 55, Hauptstrasse 123) has meticulously arranged pink tablecloths, ruffled napkins and a good local reputation. Similar care is devoted to the food. Dishes cost from Sfr12.50 to Sfr42.50, and include fish, steaks, regional specialities and vegetarian choices (closed Tuesday in winter).

A youngish environment for a drink is *Helvetia Pub (Hauptstrasse 59)*, which also serves pizzas (from Sfr10) and fast food. It's open 8 am to 12.30 am daily. *Quinzi's Bistro*, above the Coop, is also a good drinking venue, and has Internet access, pizzas from Sfr8.50. Its open 9 am to 11 pm Tuesday to Saturday.

Getting There & Away
From Interlaken, Brienz is Sfr13.20 by steamer or Sfr6.20 by train. The scenic Brünig Pass (1008m) is the road route to Lucerne.

FREILICHTMUSEUM BALLEN-BERG
This open-air park east of Brienz displays traditional Swiss crafts and houses from all over the country. The wide diversity of architectural styles between different regions is clearly shown. It's too big to absorb the whole thing in one visit so don't even try. Instead, pick up a plan at the entrance (Sfr2), check the times of special demonstrations on the board, and work out an itinerary. According to the plan, the park is 4km across; this may be slightly exaggerated, but it still takes a lot of walking to get round. It's set in parkland and there are often big gaps between groups of buildings.

Most of the properties were slated for demolition before they were moved piece-by-piece to the park. The Geneva Farmhouse (No 551) contains an exhibition outlining its own history; it took eight months and

Sfr1,880,000 to move it in 1984. Entry costs Sfr14 (students Sfr12, children Sfr6). The park is open 10 am to 5 pm (exit until 6 pm) daily, from 15 April to 31 October. There are restaurants on site or you can buy sausages and cheese and make use of the barbecue areas (free firewood).

Getting There & Away
From Brienz, take the hourly bus (Sfr2.80) or walk for one hour. There are car parks (free) at each of the two entrances; take the east entrance if coming from Lucerne or Meiringen. The nearest train station is Brienzwiler, east of Brienz.

East Bernese Oberland

East of the Jungfrau Region is the Hasli Valley (Haslital), with its main town of Meiringen.

MEIRINGEN
☎ 033 • pop 4660 • elevation 595m
Meiringen is a suitable base for exploration of the Hasli Valley. Ask about the Haslipass, which offers various discounts, if you're staying several days in the region.

Orientation & Information
The town is on the northern bank of the Aare River. The train station (where bike rental is available) is in the centre, with the main post office and postbus departures opposite. Three minutes' walk away is the tourist office (☎ 972 50 50, fax 972 50 55, ✉ info@meiringenhasliberg.ch) on the main thoroughfare, Bahnhofstrasse. It's open 8 am to noon and 2 to 6 pm Monday to Friday, 8 am to noon Saturday and (in July and August) from 4 to 6 pm.

Things to See & Do
Reichenbach Falls achieved notoriety when Arthur Conan Doyle allowed his famous hero, Sherlock Holmes, to tumble down from them to his death in a struggle with the evil Moriarty. Eccentric fans of

the fictional detective still make an annual pilgrimage to the site in the summer (his 'death' was on 4 May). A funicular makes the journey up from Willigen, south of the Aare River, from mid-May to early October, and the fare is Sfr5/7 one way/return (children Sfr2.50/4). It takes nearly an hour to walk back down to Meiringen from the top.

Reichenbach Valley, the route to Grindelwald, is certainly worthy of exploration. The views of the mountains (particularly the Welhorn and the Wetterhorn) and the glacier are tremendous. A path leads to the Rosenlaui Glacier Gorge (Gletscherschlucht), which is open from around May to October (Sfr6, Sfr5 seniors, Sfr4 students). Buses somehow negotiate the dramatically winding road along the valley from the end of May to mid-October. The walk back to Meiringen takes two hours or more.

Less than 2km from the town in the direction of Innertkirchen is the **Aare Gorge** (Aareschlucht). The sides are precipitous, narrow (as little as 1m apart in places) and worn smooth by thousands of years of erosion. The gorge is open from April to October; and buses make the trip regularly in summer (takes 12 minutes). Entry to the gorge costs Sfr6 (students Sfr4).

Meiringen really milks its tenuous Sherlock Holmes connection; a statue of the detective reclines in Conan Doyle Place, and the Sherlock Pub is in 'Baker St' (the real Baker St in London was never like this!). There's also the **Sherlock Holmes Museum**, featuring a replica of the study at 221b Baker St. It's nicely done but they need to extend the theme somehow to make it worthwhile – a visit doesn't take more than 10 or 15 minutes. It's open 1.30 to 6 pm Tuesday to Sunday between 1 May and 30 September, and 3 to 6 pm Wednesday to Sunday the rest of the year. Entry costs Sfr3.80 or Sfr2.80 for children.

Meiringen has a large mountaineering school, the Castor Bergsteigerschule Haslital (☎ 971 43 18, fax 971 60 40, ✉ pollux.sport@swissonline.ch), CH-3860 Meiringen.

Places to Stay & Eat
The most central of several camp sites is *Balmweid* (☎ 971 51 15, Balmweidstrasse 22), about 2km west of the station, across the Aare River. It's open year-round.

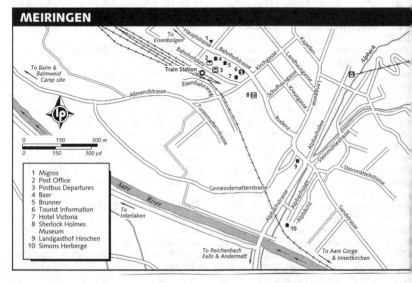

MEIRINGEN

1 Migros
2 Post Office
3 Postbus Departures
4 Baer
5 Brunner
6 Tourist Information
7 Hotel Victoria
8 Sherlock Holmes Museum
9 Landgasthof Hirschen
10 Simons Herberge

Simons Herberge (☎ 971 17 15, fax 971 9 19, Alpbachstrasse 17) is a signposted 0-minute walk east of the station near the racks. Variable-sized dorms cost Sfr28/26 first/subsequent nights, and the hostel closes between seasons. Reception is closed from 0 am to 5 pm although guests have daytime access.

Landgasthof Hirschen (☎ 971 18 12, fax 971 47 12) is the cheapest convenient hotel. It's a creaky old house that needs exterior renovations, but the rooms are fine; singles/doubles using hall showers are Sfr40/80. The restaurant has average prices for Swiss food and opens daily.

Brunner (☎ 971 14 23, fax 971 31 98, Bahnhofstrasse 8) is a bakery and cafe with non-standardised rooms with shower for Sfr70/120. The cafe serves full meals or cakes – meringue, said to have been invented in Meiringen, is a speciality.

The three-star *Baer* (☎ 971 46 46, fax 971 46 98) has modern, comfortable rooms bang in the centre of town. Singles/doubles with own shower/WC and TV cost around Sfr75/130. It has a good, informal restaurant with meals starting at only Sfr10 (closed Sunday evening in low season).

Hotel Victoria (☎ 971 10 40, fax 972 10 45, ✉ info@victoria-meiringen.ch, Bahnhofplatz) is a good place to stay, despite the strange wooden phallic shapes in the garden. It has modern, nicely presented rooms from Sfr130/180 with shower/WC and TV. It also has one of the best restaurants in town. Pasta, vegetarian and meat dishes start at Sfr18, and lunch menus start from Sfr14 (open daily).

A 50m walk from the front of the station is a *Migros* supermarket and restaurant. It has standard prices and opening times, and outside tables.

Getting There & Away
Meiringen has frequent trains to Lucerne (Sfr17.20, 80 minutes; with a scenic ride over the Brünig Pass) and Interlaken Ost (Sfr10; 30 minutes, via Brienz). In summer, buses and cars can take the pass road southeast (Andermatt) but the road south-west over Grosse Scheidegg (to Grindelwald) is closed to private vehicles.

ALPINE PASS TOURS
The Three Alpine Pass Tour is a wonderful all-day excursion if the weather is clear. Starting from Meiringen, you can make a circular trip crossing the Susten, Furka and Grimsel passes before returning to Meiringen in the late afternoon. The views are excellent all the way round, with the mountain ranges showing huge variations in colour and profile. From the Susten Pass there's a great view over the Stein Glacier and lake. The Furka Pass has the Rhône Glacier, which looks stupendous between rocky shoulders of brown and green. There's an ice grotto (entrance fee Sfr5 adults, Sfr3 students), and if you take the Panoramaweg and cut down over the rocks you'll enter the closed-off area without realising you were supposed to pay. On the south-west side of the pass the landscape looks browner and more parched, and the road twists away into the distance like lengths of unfurled ribbon.

At the Grimsel Pass, to the south you can see tufts of snowy peaks above the lake. To the north there are two more lakes, dammed by the power station that barely disturbs the view of the valley beyond. The pass marks the cantonal border between Bern and Valais.

By making a larger loop south, you can take in the Gotthard Pass and the Nurfenen Pass at the cost of missing the Furka Pass (or if you have your own car you can detour and double-back at Gletsch to include that as well). If you don't have a car, or simply want your eyes free to take in the views, the three or four-pass tour can be taken by postbus, costing Sfr102.80 and Sfr129.80 respectively (Swiss Pass valid, but you have to pay a Sfr10 'Alpine Ticket' supplement). As the road constantly winds back on itself, it doesn't really matter which side of the bus you sit, except for the stretch between Susten and Furka, where the left side is better. On the three-pass tour, there's a break at Andermatt (see the Central Switzerland chapter) for lunch. The tours only operate from early July to early October as the passes are closed for most of the rest of the year.

A cheaper alternative is to use the private Postcar bus, for which you must reserve a

BERNESE OBERLAND

seat the day before, at Meiringen bus station or by telephoning ☎ 971 00 85. The three-pass tour costs Sfr49 and departs on Tuesday and Friday, and the four-pass tour (Grosse Scheidegg, Grimsel, Furka and Susten; Sfr79 including lunch) departs on Wednesday. You can commence these tours in Interlaken and elsewhere. Swiss Passes are not valid.

West Bernese Oberland

At the western side of the Jungfrau are Simmental and Frutigland, dominated by two river valleys, the Simme and the Kander. In the extreme west of the Bernese Oberland is Saanenland, known mainly for the ski resort of Gstaad.

STOCKHORN

This summit (2190m) offers a heart-pumping view of mountains and lakes. Mont Blanc is visible on a clear day, and you can watch the hang-gliders leaping off into space. There are 70km of mountain and hiking trails; you can walk to/from the summit but the path is fairly steep. The cable car costs Sfr24/38 one way/return and usually closes between seasons. The lower station is 15 minutes' walk from Erlenbach train station, easily reached from Spiez (Sfr6.20, 15 minutes).

Erlenbach is the starting point for **white-water rafting** on the Simme River. There are several companies that arrange this – see the listings in the Bernese Oberland summer brochure.

NIESEN

This ascent is from the Mülenen train station in the Kander Valley. Niesen (2362m) offers views nearly as good as those from better known peaks. The funicular up this conical peak runs from early May to the end of autumn and costs Sfr40 return. There's a guesthouse (☎ 033-676 11 13) at the top, charging Sfr40 per person without breakfast.

KANDERSTEG

☎ 033 • pop 960 • elevation 1176m

Kandersteg is a good base for **hiking** excursions. The trip to the **Blue Lake** (Blausee) and the **Klus Gorge** are well worth considering. Contact the tourist office (☎ 675 80 80, fax 675 80 81, @ info@kandersteg.ch) for advice. Its office is in the village centre, straight ahead from the train station then left on the main street. Opening times are 8 am to noon and 2 to 6 pm Monday to Friday; in high season it's open 8 am to noon and 1.30 to 4.30 pm Saturday.

The Blausee is part of a nature park and entry costs Sfr4.50 (child/family reductions are available). The best outing is to the **Lake Oeschinen** (Oeschinensee). This lake is superbly situated with sturdy mountains crowding its shores. In summer, its waters are sparkling blue; in winter, it's an iced-over cross-country ski trail. The ancient ('nostalgic' according to the marketing spin) chair lift costs Sfr13, or Sfr18 return, and it leaves you about a 20-minute walk away from the lake. Once at the lake, it only takes an hour to walk directly back to Kandersteg.

In winter there are 75km of cross-country skiing trails, and 55km of hiking tracks stay open. The limited downhill skiing is suited to beginners and day passes cost Sfr33.

Places to Stay & Eat

Rendez-vous Camp Site (☎ 675 15 34), by the chair lift, is open year-round. It costs Sfr7 per adult, Sfr3 for a car and from Sfr6 for a tent. Next door is the unrelated **Restaurant Rendez-vous** (☎ 675 13 54). It has Swiss food from Sfr14 and closes on Tuesday during low season. It also offers dorms for Sfr22; showers are Sfr1 and breakfast, if required, is Sfr10. Like many other places in the resort, it closes between seasons. **National** (☎ 675 10 85, fax 675 22 85) has dorms for Sfr30, plus Sfr8 if you need sheets. Singles/doubles are Sfr55/100, and it's open all day. To get there from the station, take a right once you're on the main street and walk 10 minutes. About 10 minutes farther south is the **Pfadfinderzentrum** (☎ 675 11 39, fax 675 82 89, @ kandersteg@world.scout.org), or International Scout Centre, providing camping (Sfr8 or Sfr10) and dorms (Sfr15, with kitchen, without breakfast) for scouts and non-scouts alike.

In the centre, *Hotel zur Post* (☎ 675 12 58, fax 675 22 58, @ hotel-zur-post@ datacom.ch) offers compact rooms for Sfr44 per person using hall showers, or Sfr54 with private shower. Swiss food in the restaurant costs Sfr12 to Sfr30 (closed Monday and Tuesday). Nearby is *Chalet-Hotel Adler* (☎ 675 80 10, fax 675 80 11, @ chaletadler@bluewin.ch), where good rooms with shower and TV are Sfr105/180. Guests have free use of the new swimming pool and sauna. The pleasant restaurant is cheapish to mid-price (open daily) and there's a fast-food kiosk outside.

The *Bahnhof* has a restaurant, and between there and the main street is a *Coop* supermarket.

Getting There & Away

Kandersteg is at the northern end of the Lötschberg tunnel, through which car-carrying trains trundle south to Brig (see Brig in the Valais chapter for details). The traditional way to head south is to hike; it takes a little over five hours to get to the Gemmi Pass and a further one hour and 40 minutes to reach Leukerbad.

GSTAAD

☎ 033 • pop 2500 • elevation 1100m

This resort exudes an aura of affluence. Compared to St Moritz, it's smaller and not quite so elitist, but still attracts many fur-lined celebrities who come to pose on the slopes and in the chic bars. The pronunciation of the name is tricky to get right, and sounds halfway between spitting and stifling a sneeze; try saying *Hchstaadt*.

Orientation & Information

The train station is in the centre, on a parallel street to the main street, Hauptstrasse. It has bike rental, luggage storage and money-exchange counters; the post office is next door. Turn right on Hauptstrasse and walk 200m along the pedestrian-only section to the tourist office (☎ 748 81 10, fax 748 81 33, @ gst@gstaad.ch). Opening hours are 8 am to noon and 1.30 to 6 pm Monday to Friday, and 8.30 am to noon Saturday. In the high season it closes at 6 pm on Saturday.

Activities

There's reasonable **skiing** for intermediates but little for experts, and the fact that the lifts around the village only go up to around 2000m is also limiting. To enjoy more varied skiing you need to take the train or bus to neighbouring resorts such as Saanen, Saanenmöser, Zweisimmen and St Stephan. These are only some of the places that are included in the Region Ski Gstaad, totalling 250km of ski runs. In all, 69 lifts are covered, some as far afield as Château d'Oex and the Diablerets Glacier (see the Lake Geneva Region chapter). The regional pass is available for a minimum two days (Sfr90); for single days, buy specific sectors (Sfr24 to Sfr49). There are reductions for youths under 20 and seniors, and ski coupons are available.

Four main valleys radiate out from Gstaad, offering a good variety of **hikes**. The tourist office sells hiking maps. Take the cable car up to Wispile (Sfr17 up, Sfr23 return) and walk down to the valley on either side. From Lauenen or Feutersoey a bus runs back to Gstaad. A long but undemanding excursion is to walk to Turbach, over the Reulisenpass, and down to St Stephan or Lenk in the adjoining Simmen Valley (around 4½ hours total). From either resort, a train runs back to Gstaad (change at Zweisimmen).

Various other sports are on offer, such as swimming, tennis (Sfr28 per hour), skating and horse riding. **River rafting** on the Saane River happens between the end of April and August, and is offered by several companies (inquire at the tourist office). Expect to pay about Sfr85 for a half-day excursion.

Every year at the beginning of July, Gstaad hosts the **Swiss Open** tennis tournament. Nearby Saanen is a pretty little village which is the location for a **Yehudi Menuhin Festival** of classical music in August. It's held in Saanen's 15th-century Mauritius church and in a marquee in Gstaad.

BERNESE OBERLAND

Places to Stay & Eat

There is year-round camping in the west of the village at **Bellerive** (☎ 744 63 30), by the river. The SYHA **hostel** (☎ 744 13 43, fax 744 55 42) is at Chalet Rüblihorn in nearby Saanen, just four minutes away by train. It is closed in the off season and costs Sfr25.60.

Gstaad itself is bristling with hotels sporting three or more stars. On Hauptstrasse by the station is **Sporthotel Victoria** (☎ 748 44 22, fax 748 44 20, ✉ sporthotel.victoria@ bluewin.ch). Rooms with rustic wooden furniture and private shower/WC start at Sfr120/220 (Sfr80/150 in low season). The restaurant has pizzas from Sfr13 and other meat and fish dishes above Sfr16 (open daily). There's also a disco, open winter only.

Right outside the station stands **Bernerhof** (☎ 748 88 44, fax 748 88 40, ✉ bernerhof@gstaad.ch). Good rooms are Sfr121/202 to Sfr145/360, depending on the season, the hotel swimming pool and sauna are free for guests. The busy restaurant has affordable, standard Swiss fare, though there's a Chinese food section (closed Monday), which is quite expensive unless you choose vegetarian options.

The turrets on the hill belong to the palatial **Gstaad Palace** (☎ 748 50 00, fax 748 50 01, ✉ palace@gstaad.ch), where rooms cost at least Sfr350/600. Of comparable quality for dining is **Chesery** (☎ 744 24 51), near the tourist office on Lauenenstrasse. Expect to pay above Sfr50 for a main course or Sfr125 for a multi-course menu. It's closed Monday and (in the off season) Tuesday. Downstairs there's a piano bar and a casino.

The cheapest eating is at the **Coop**, where menus are about Sfr10. It is on Hauptstrasse to the left of the station, and has late opening till 8 pm on Friday. The restaurant (but not the supermarket) also opens until 5 pm on Sunday.

Getting There & Away

Gstaad is on the Panoramic Express rail link between Montreux (Sfr24, 1½ hours) and Spiez (Sfr25, one hour 20 minutes; change at Zweisimmen). There is also a postbus to Les Diablerets (Sfr11.80, 50 minutes), that runs about five times daily. Highway 11 is the principal road connecting Aigle and Spiez, which passes close to Gstaad at Saanen.

Central Switzerland

This region sums up what many visitors believe to be the 'true' Switzerland. Not only is it rich in typical Swiss features – mountains, lakes, tinkling cowbells and Alpine villages – but it is also where Switzerland began as a nation 700 years ago, with the signing of a pact in 1291 by the communities of Uri, Schwyz and Nidwalden. The focus for tourism in the region is Lucerne, which annually receives five million visitors, and the convoluted contours of its namesake lake that links the founding cantons.

Orientation & Information

The tourist region of Central Switzerland has at its heart Lake Lucerne, known as Vierwaldstättersee in German (lake of the four forest cantons). The four cantons in descending order of size are Lucerne, Uri, Schwyz and Unterwalden. Unterwalden is sub-divided into two half-cantons, Nidwalden and Obwalden. Also included in this region is Zug: at just 239 sq km it's the smallest rural canton in Switzerland.

In the north and west, Central Switzerland is fairly flat, but a southern tongue of territory reaches deep into the Alps, as far as the St Gotthard Pass. Lake Lucerne is ringed by other large lakes, notably Lake Zug (Zugersee) to the north. There are also several mountains thrusting up from its irregular shoreline, providing good hiking and excellent views.

The regional tourist office is Zentralschweiz Tourismus (☎ 041-418 40 80, fax 418 40 81, @ Information@Central Switzerland.ch) Alpenstrasse 1, CH-6002 Lucerne. It sends out useful brochures covering accommodation, hiking and cycling, but isn't set up to deal with inquiries in person. For hotel reservations throughout Central Switzerland, contact ☎ 041-318 41 41, fax 318 41 40, @ LTI@LTI.ch; no commission is charged.

The half-canton of Obwalden (including Engelberg) has a religious holiday on 25

Highlights

- Discover Lucerne's medieval centre and covered bridges.
- Explore Switzerland's best technology museum, the Transport Museum in Lucerne.
- Cruise Lake Lucerne.
- Enjoy the splendid vistas from the mountain viewpoints of Pilatus, Rigi, Stanserhorn and Titlis.
- Visit Einsiedeln, Switzerland's prime pilgrimage site.

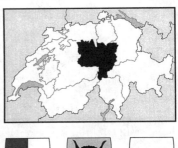

Lucerne　　Uri　　Zug

Obwalden　　Schwyz　　Nidwalden

September, while Lucerne has several public holidays in addition to the national ones: Corpus Christi, Assumption, St Leodegar's Day (2 October), All Saint's Day (1 November), Immaculate Conception (8 December), New Year's Eve and 2 January.

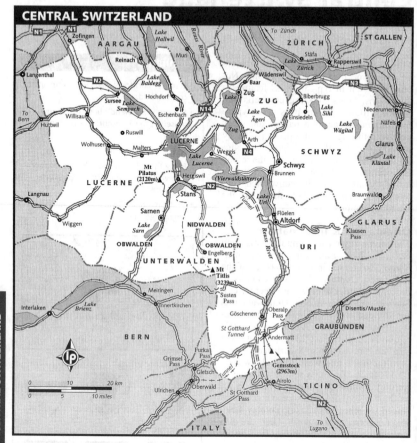

CENTRAL SWITZERLAND

Getting There & Away

The nearest airport is at Zürich. Road and rail connections are excellent in all directions. An interesting way to leave the region is by the William Tell Express, which runs from mid-May to late October. Departing from Lucerne, it includes 1st-class passage on a paddlesteamer to Flüelen, with multilingual commentary and a gourmet meal along the way, then a train ride through the St Gotthard Tunnel to either Lugano or Locarno. The fare is Sfr134, or Sfr89.50 with the Swiss Half-Fare Card. Reservations are advised; contact the Lake Lucerne Navigation Company SGV,

Werftestrasse 5, PO Box 4265, CH-6002, Lucerne (☎ 041-367 67 67, fax 367 68 68, ℮ info@lakelucerne.ch). For timetables and other information, see the Web site, www.lakelucerne.ch.

Getting Around

The Central Switzerland Regional Pass is a good buy if you want to spend a lot of time exploring Lake Lucerne (unless you have a Eurailpass or a Swiss Pass, both of which give free boat rides). It is valid for seven or 15 days, and gives half-price fares on public transport for the whole period as well as unlimited free travel for two or five days on selected routes, including Lake Lucerne steamers, the different routes up Mts Pilatus and Rigi, and most of the way up Mt Titlis. The seven-day pass costs Sfr131, and the 15-day pass costs Sfr179 (Sfr105 and Sfl44 with Swiss travel passes). Prices are slightly higher if you want 1st-class boat travel, and it is available from 1 April to 31 October. Get free travel for children with a Family Card (see the Getting Around chapter).

Lucerne

☎ 041 • pop 61,000 • elevation 435m

Lucerne (Luzern in German), once a small fishing village, increased in size and importance when the St Gotthard Pass became a trade route around 1220. As late as the 19th century, merchandise had to be sent to Lucerne before being transported by barge to Flüelen, and then over the pass. In 1332, Lucerne was the first town to join forces with the original three forest cantons, and was one of the few Swiss cities to remain Catholic during the Reformation. Ideally situated in the historic and scenic heart of Switzerland, it is an excellent base for a variety of excursions, yet also has a great deal of charm in its own right, particularly the medieval town centre. Indeed, it is one of the main tourist destinations in the whole of Switzerland, which is reflected by its myriad souvenir shops.

Orientation

Lucerne is on the western edge of Lake Lucerne, on both sides of the Reuss River. The train station is on the south bank within walking distance of the medieval town centre. Extensive station facilities below the ground level include a self-service restaurant, ticket and information counters, bike rental (6 am to 9 pm), money-exchange (open to 7.30 pm or later daily), and a pricey supermarket (open to 8 or 9 pm daily).

City buses leave from outside the train station at Bahnhofplatz. Boats for excursions on Lake Lucerne depart from the quays around Bahnhofplatz. The old part of town and the city towers and ramparts are on the north bank.

Information

Tourist Offices Take the left (west) exit of the train station for the tourist office (☎ 227 1717, fax 227 17 18, ✉ luzern@luzern.org) at Zentralstrasse 5, in the train station. From 1 November to 31 March it's open 8.30 am to 6 pm Monday to Friday, 9 am to 6 pm Saturday and 9 am to 1 pm Sunday. Summer hours are: 8.30 am to 7.30 pm Monday to Friday, 9 am to 7.30 pm Saturday and Sunday. From 16 June to 15 September hours are 8.30 am to 8.30 pm Monday to Friday and 9 am to 8.30 pm Saturday and Sunday. Telephone inquiries are only dealt with from 8 am to 12 noon and 2 to 5.30 pm Monday to Friday, year round. Pick up a copy of the useful *Official Guide*. The office also has a free room-booking service. Staff sell mountain excursions, such as guided tours to Mt Titlis or Mt Pilatus for Sfr85; off-season discounts may make such trips cheaper than going independently. Two-hour guided tours of the Old Town cost Sfr15 (drink included). Many other excursions are available, all detailed in the tourist office brochure.

Post & Communications The main post office (Hauptpost, Luzern 1, 6000), by the station, is open 7.30 am to 6.30 pm Monday to Friday and 8 to 11 am on Saturday. There is another post office on Löwengraben in the Old Town.

Email & Internet Access Café-Bar Parterre (✉ parterre@parterre.ch), Mythenstrasse 7, has computers and a relaxed environment (Sfr4 per 15 minutes). It's open 7 am (9 am Sunday and holidays) to 12.30 am daily. Hotel Löwengraben (see Places to Stay) also has one internet terminal in the bar.

Travel Agencies On the north side of the river is American Express (☎ 410 00 77), Schweizerhofquai 4, open 8.30 am to 6 pm, Monday to Friday (5 pm for financial services), and 8.30 am to noon on Saturday. SSR (☎ 410 86 56), in the Old Town at Grabenstrasse 8, is open 10 am to 6 pm on

CENTRAL SWITZERLAND

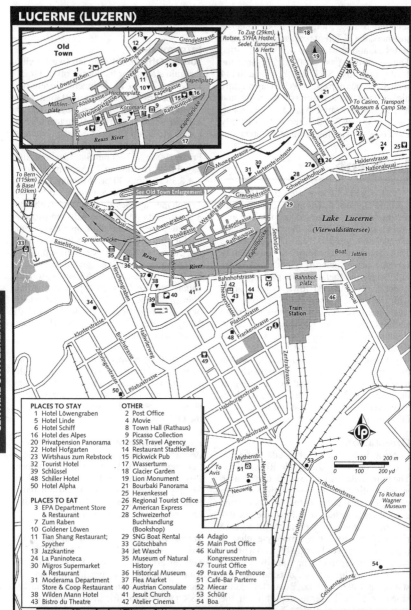

LUCERNE (LUZERN)

PLACES TO STAY
1 Hotel Löwengraben
5 Hotel Linde
6 Hotel Schiff
16 Hotel des Alpes
20 Privatpension Panorama
22 Hotel Hofgarten
23 Wirtshaus zum Rebstock
32 Tourist Hotel
39 Schlüssel
48 Schiller Hotel
50 Hotel Alpha

PLACES TO EAT
3 EPA Department Store
  & Restaurant
7 Zum Raben
10 Goldener Löwen
11 Tian Shang Restaurant;
  Spycher
13 Jazzkantine
24 La Paninoteca
30 Migros Supermarket
  & Restaurant
31 Moderama Department
  Store & Coop Restaurant
38 Wilden Mann Hotel
43 Bistro du Theatre

OTHER
2 Post Office
4 Movie
8 Town Hall (Rathaus)
9 Picasso Collection
12 SSR Travel Agency
14 Restaurant Stadtkeller
15 Pickwick Pub
17 Wasserturm
18 Glacier Garden
19 Lion Monument
21 Bourbaki Panorama
25 Hexenkessel
26 Regional Tourist Office
27 American Express
28 Schweizerhof
  Buchhandlung
  (Bookshop)
29 SNG Boat Rental
33 Gütschbahn
34 Jet Wasch
35 Museum of Natural
  History
36 Historical Museum
37 Flea Market
40 Austrian Consulate
41 Jesuit Church
42 Atelier Cinema
44 Adagio
45 Main Post Office
46 Kultur und
  Kongresszentrum
47 Tourist Office
49 Pravda & Penthouse
51 Café-Bar Parterre
52 Miecar
53 Schüür
54 Boa

weekdays (8 pm on Thursday) and 10 am to 4 pm on Saturday.

Bookshops Schweizerhof Buchhandlung, Schweizerhofquai 2, sells English-language books, as do branches of Raeber in the Old Town.

Laundry Jet Wasch (☎ 240 0151), Bruchstrasse 28, has service washes for Sfr16 per load, and closes at 6.30 pm weekdays, and 1 pm Saturday.

Medical & Emergency Services For an out-of-hours pharmacy or doctor, dial ☎ 111. The cantonal hospital (☎ 205 11 11) is on Spitalstrasse, north of the Old Town. Call the police on ☎ 117.

Things to See & Do

The tourist office sells *A short city guide* detailing several walking tours of the centre. The picturesque Old Town centre certainly merits a leisurely stroll. There are many 15th-century buildings with painted facades, particularly in the vicinity of Weinmarkt and Kornmarkt. The **town hall** *(Rathaus)* is Renaissance in style and was built in the early 17th century. Overlooking the centre are the **city towers**, some of which can be climbed in the summer for extensive views.

North-east of the city walls is the poignant **Lion Monument**, on Denkmalstrasse, carved out of natural rock in 1820. It is dedicated to the Swiss soldiers who died in the French Revolution in 1792. They were slaughtered on the steps of the Tuileries Palace while defending Louis XVI and the French royal family. Next to the monument is the unique **Glacier Garden** (Gletschergarten), where giant glacial potholes prove that Lucerne was a subtropical palm beach 20 million years ago. The potholes can be perused daily (except Monday from mid-November to the end of February), and admission costs Sfr8, or Sfr6 for students. It includes a mirror maze that is incredibly disorientating.

Also worth a look is the nearby and newly restored **Bourbaki Panorama**, Löwenstrasse 18, an 1100-sq metre circular painting of the Franco-Prussian war. The scene is brought to life with recorded commentary (in English). It's open 9 am to 6 pm daily; entrance costs Sfr6, Sfr5 students/seniors, Sfr4 children.

Be sure to walk along the two covered bridges over the River Reuss. **Kapellbrücke**, built in 1333, is the most famous, and together with its octagonal water tower appears in just about every photograph of Lucerne. The sides and gabled roof of the bridge were burnt away when a tethered boat caught fire in 1993. Under the replacement roof are scenes from national and local history in the form of photo reproductions of the originals (by Heinrich Wägmann in 1614). The **Spreuerbrücke** dates from 1408 and likewise features pictorial scenes, completed from 1625 to 1635. The artist, Caspar Meglinger, chose a rather more macabre theme, *The Dance of Death*.

Between the bridges on the south bank is the **Jesuit Church**, the oldest baroque church in Switzerland, consecrated in 1677. The interior is characteristically ornate. There's a fine **view** of the town and lake from the Gütsch Hotel; walk uphill for 15 minutes or take the Gütschbahn (Sfr2 each way).

Museums All the following museums are covered by the Museum Pass, valid for one month and costing Sfr25. The biggest and best museum in Lucerne is the **Transport Museum** (Verkehrshaus), Lidostrasse 5, which receives more visitors than any other Swiss museum – half a million a year. Bus No 6, 8 or 24 from Bahnhofplatz drops you right outside, as does the boat. It has large halls filled with old trains, cars, aeroplanes and boats, plus a planetarium and a gallery devoted to the artist, Hans Erni.

There are several hourly shows, the best of which is the Swissorama, a 20-minute, 360° film which whizzes you around the sights of Switzerland as if you were travelling by air, sea, road and foot. You get a real sense of motion as your 'aircraft' banks between the mountains. Also great fun, especially for kids, is the communications section, with lots of toys and interactive machines. Explanations are in English. It's open 9 am to 6 pm daily (10 am to 5 pm from 1 November to 31 March). Entry costs Sfr18, Sfr16 for students, Sfr12 for railpass-holders and Sfr10 for children. On site is IMAX, a giant-screen cinema showing nature or transport-related films on the hour, from 11 am to 9 pm (Sfr14; combination ticket available).

The **Picasso Collection** in the Ann Rhyn House, Furrengasse 21, demands an hour of your time. There are some paintings and graphics by the man himself, but the best part is nearly 200 photographs taken by David Douglas Duncan. They show Picasso at work and at play in the clutter of his house, 'La Californie', in Cannes, over the last 17 years of his life. Admission costs Sfr6 (Sfr3 for students and senior citizens), and it is open 10 am to 6 pm daily from April to October, and 11 am to 1 pm and 2 to 4 pm daily from November to March.

The **Historical Museum**, with its exhibits and short film (in English), successfully places the city and region in their historical context. Next door, natural history and archaeology are combined in the **Museum of Natural History** (Naturmuseum). Interesting for music lovers is the **Richard Wagner Museum**, Wagnerweg 27, in Tribschen, on the southern shore of the lake. All three museums are closed on Monday and each costs Sfr5 (Sfr4 for students).

Alphornbau Stocker (☎ 340 88 86), south of Lucerne in Schweighof (take bus No 1 to Kriens, then bus No 16), is an Alphorn workshop (free entry). Visitors get a brief tour of the workshop, a short video showing, and (of course) the chance to buy. It's open 8 am to noon and 2 to 6 pm on weekdays and Saturday morning.

Markets Fruit and vegetable stalls spring forth along the river quays on Tuesday and Saturday mornings. There's a flea market at Unter Burgerstrasse/Reusssteg every Saturday from May to October.

Activities

Water pursuits are important in summer, when international rowing regattas take place on the Rotsee. SNG (☎ 368 08 00), at the north side of Seebrücke, rents out rowing boats (Sfr22 for three people), motorboats

(Sfr44 for up to five people) and pedalboats (Sfr21 for three people); these rates are for one hour. SNG also offers an hour-long lake cruise for Sfr13.

There is swimming in the confines of the Lidostrandbad (☎ 370 38 06) near Camp Lido (see Places to Stay); entry costs Sfr5 (kids Sfr2.50). You can save money by swimming for free on the other bank of the lake by Seepark, off Alpenquai.

For a range of high-adrenalin activities, such as tandem paragliding off Pilatus, bungy-jumping, caving and canyoning, contact Outventure (☎ 611 14 41, fax 611 14 42, @ info@outventure.ch), Hansmatt 5, CH-6370 Stans.

Special Events

Six days of **Fasnacht** celebrations begin on the Thursday before Ash Wednesday. There's music and folklore in the **city festival** (Altstadtfest) on the 4th Saturday in June. Lucerne also hosts the **International Festival of Music** from mid-August to mid-September, one of the most important annual classical music events in Switzerland. Details are available from the Internationale Musikfestwochen (☎ 226 44 00, fax 226 44 60), Hirschmattstrasse 13, CH-6002 Luzern. You can also check out the Web site, www.lucernemusic.ch/. Telephone bookings are accepted from early May (☎ 226 44 80, fax 226 44 85, @ ticketbox@ lucernemusic.ch). Concerts take place in the renovated Kultur und Kongresszentrum, which has exceptionally good acoustics.

Places to Stay

Ask the staff where you're staying to stamp your *Official Guide*; this entitles you to discounts on entry fees to most attractions.

Places to Stay – Budget

Camping *Camp Lido* (☎ 370 21 46, Lidostrasse 8), is on the north shore of the lake and east of the town. It is open from 15 March to 31 October and charges Sfr7.70 per person, from Sfr3 per tent and Sfr5 per car. It also has six-bed wooden cabins for Sfr13 per person (no breakfast, sleeping bag required), plus a kitchen, shop and cheap

washing machines. To get there from Bahnhofplatz, take the bus (No 6, 8 or 24; two
zones) or boat to the Transport Museum
(Verkehrshaus).

Hostels The modern SYHA *hostel (☎ 420
88 00, fax 420 56 16, Sedelstrasse 12)* is north
of the centre, 15 minutes by footpath or 25
minutes walking by road. Bus No 18 from the
train station gets you closest (stop: Goplis-
moos), but after 7.40 pm you'll have to take
bus No 1 (stop: Schlossberg). Dorm beds
with lockers are Sfr30.50; doubles are Sfr87
with shower/WC or Sfr75 without. Dinners
are Sfr11.50. Reception is shut 10 am to 2 pm
in summer, and 9.30 am to 4 pm in winter.

*Backpackers Lucerne (☎ 360 04 20, fax
360 04 42, Alpenquai 42)* is a friendly, independent hostel, a 12-minute walk south-
east of the station. It charges Sfr21.50 per
person in dorms or Sfr26.50 in doubles,
without breakfast and excluding sheets.
There's a lift, balconies and two kitchens.
Reception is closed 10 am to 4 pm.

Hotel Löwengraben (see the following
Pensions & Hotels) also has dorms.

Pensions & Hotels *Hotel Löwengraben
(☎ 417 12 12, fax 417 12 11, ✉ hotel@
loewengraben.ch, Löwengraben 18)* is a
new hotel, bar, restaurant and entertainment
venue, all housed in an ex-prison. The description of 'cell-like' rooms is particularly
apt, as they all retain the original bare walls,
barred windows and heavy doors. Though
it's a novelty for a night, the rooms are
bleak and cramped for longer stays, and the
dorms have no lockers. Mixed dorms with
toilet (shower in hall) are Sfr20/31/35 with
eight/four/three beds. Doubles are Sfr90
with WC, and singles/doubles with
shower/WC are Sfr75/111. Except for the
eight-bed dorms, prices drop slightly in
winter. Check-in is from 3 pm. Optional
buffet breakfast (prisoner rations – only one
cup of coffee!) is Sfr7.

The small *Hotel Linde (☎/fax 410 31 93,
Metzgerrainle 3)*, off Weinmarkt, has fairly
spartan singles/doubles without breakfast
for Sfr40/80 with use of shared hall
showers. The walls are paper-thin and the

streets outside can be noisy, but it has an excellent central location. Rooms are available from 1 April to 31 October. Check-in
is done through the restaurant, which is
closed on Sundays.

*Tourist Hotel (☎ 410 24 74, fax 410 84 14,
✉ info@touristhotel.ch, St Karli Quai 12)* has
dorms for Sfr28 or Sfr31, and doubles for
Sfr134 with private shower and toilet (Sfr108
without or Sfr88 with bunk beds). If there's
space, single occupancy is possible for Sfr81,
Sfr69 and Sfr54 respectively. Students get a
10% discount, and triples and quads are also
available. There's a good breakfast buffet,
plus bike rental, internet access, washing machine and plans to install kitchens.

*Privatpension Panorama (☎ 420 67 30,
fax 420 67 30, ✉ panorama@swissonline.ch,
Kapuzinerweg 9)* is a good deal. It's in a residential area uphill from the Glacier Garden,
and charges from Sfr45/70 for singles/
doubles (using hall showers) up to Sfr100
(two-person apartment with TV, kitchen and
bathroom) or Sfr140 (family room for four).
There's internet access and a kitchen.

*Hotel Alpha (☎ 240 42 80, fax 240 91 31,
Zähringerstrasse 24)* is fairly nondescript
but reasonably priced, charging Sfr60/92
for rooms with hall shower, or from Sfr110
for doubles with private shower.

*Schlüssel (☎ 210 10 61, fax 210 10 21,
Franziskanerplatz 12)* is central and small-
scale. It has rooms from Sfr95/135 with
shower or Sfr75/100 without. Phone ahead,
as it's often full.

Places to Stay – Mid-Range & Top End
Overlooking the river is the comfortable
*Hotel des Alpes (☎ 410 58 25, fax 410 74
51, Rathausquai 5)*. It has decent-sized
rooms, all with shower, toilet and a TV, and
includes a buffet breakfast. Singles/doubles
start at Sfr110/175, reducing by about 20%
in winter. *Hotel Schiff (☎ 418 52 52, fax 418
52 55, ✉ contact@hotel-schiff-luzern.ch,
Unter der Egg 8)* is similar in situation and
standard. Rooms start from Sfr130/180, or
Sfr80/130 using hall showers.

*Wirtshaus zum Rebstock (☎ 410 35 81,
fax 410 39 17, ✉ rebstock@hereweare.ch,*

St Leodegar-Strasse 3) has rooms from Sfr140/240 decorated with flair and more than a touch of modern art. Adjacent to it is the linked *Hotel Hofgarten* (☎ 410 88 88, fax 410 83 33, Stadthofstrasse 14), which is similarly stylish and marginally more expensive.

Schiller Hotel (☎ 226 87 87, fax 210 34 04, Pilatusstrasse 15) starts at Sfr170/190 (Sfr130/160 in winter) and has comparable facilities. The cheaper rooms have modern fittings and stucco work around the ceilings. Pay a bit more and you'll get a larger room with elaborate stylised decor, ranging from Thai to nautical.

Places to Eat

Lucerne is bursting with restaurants of all types. Eating can get pricey but there are still plenty of places with a *Tagesmenu* from Sfr15. The local speciality is the *Kügelipastetli*, a vol-au-vent stuffed with meat and (usually) mushrooms, and served with a rich sauce.

For the cheapest chomping, look to the self-service places, which have late opening till 9 pm on Thursday and Friday. *Migros* supermarket and restaurant is at Hertensteinstrasse 44. Next door is the Moderama department store with a *Coop* restaurant on the first floor. The *EPA* department store on Mühlenplatz has an excellent self-service restaurant with unbeatable prices for Switzerland: meals from Sfr8.80, soup from Sfr2, salad buffet at Sfr1.90 per 100g, and tea or coffee for Sfr2.

La Paninoteca (Haldenstrasse 9) is a pizzeria mostly of interest to late-nighters. The price of its pizzas are slashed to Sfr6 or Sfr7 after 10 pm. It's closed till 5 pm on Sunday; last orders are at midnight.

A mainly young hang-out is *Jazzkantine* (Grabengasse 8), a new bar-restaurant with a Tagesteller for Sfr12.50 and various vegetarian meals. There are free jazz concerts on Wednesday and Thursday night, except during school holidays (closed Sunday lunch).

Bistro du Theatre (Theaterstrasse 5) is a French-style bar and restaurant which manages to be both elegant and informal. Midday menus with soup are Sfr14 and Sfr16; evening dining is mostly above Sfr17, though the chicken wings *(Knusperli)* for Sfr12.50 are popular. It's open daily, but closed till 3 pm on weekends.

Goldener Löwen (Eisengasse 1) has a typical local ambience, despite the touristtat signs outside. Swiss specialities start at around Sfr14 in this small restaurant; try the chocolate fondue (you dip fruit in the mix) at Sfr29 for two.

At Eisengasse 15 is a curious hybrid – *Tian Shang Restaurant* on the ground floor, with Chinese weekday lunches for Sfr12.50, and *Spycher* on the first floor, serving Swiss and cheese specialities, including raclette and fondue (Sfr23).

Wirtshaus zum Rebstock (see Places to Stay) has several eating areas open daily, including a garden and bar-cafe. Meals cost Sfr18 to Sfr38, and there are always vegetarian dishes, especially in the linked *Hofgarten* vegetarian restaurant beyond the garden.

The restaurant in the *Hotel Schiff* (see Places to Stay) has lunch specials with soup from Sfr15, and it's also a good place to shed some francs and gain some pounds on quality evening dining (starting from Sfr17). Cuisine from different nationalities is featured in winter festivals. A giant version of the local speciality, called *Aechti Lozärner Chögelipastete* here, costs Sfr26. There's also a riverside bistro section (lunches are without soup down here) that's open March to October. The nearby *Zum Raben* (☎ 410 01 77, Kornmarkt 5) is also good, and has mostly French-style meals for Sfr17 to Sfr40.

The *Wilden Mann Hotel* (☎ 210 16 66, Bahnhofstrasse 30) serves quality dishes from Sfr30 in the French-style Wilden Mann Stube. Its Burgerstube has more of a Swiss atmosphere and some cheaper choices. Both are open daily. There's also a terrace, which is open during fine weather.

Entertainment

Restaurant Stadtkeller (☎ 410 47 33, Sternenplatz 3) has two folklore shows a day to allow you to yodel with your mouth full. Meals cost from Sfr25 (eg, the three-course lunch) up to Sfr50, plus it's Sfr8/10 for the midday/evening show (there's a bar – you don't have to eat). Reservations are usually necessary for meals. The show is professionally done, and most guests eagerly participate in the party mood. Although lunch is cheaper, there tends to be less atmosphere. From November to mid-March, the show is replaced by live music (evening only).

Sedel (☎ 420 63 10), near the SYHA hostel, behind Rotsee at Emmenbrücke, is a former women's prison which holds rock concerts and/or discos at the weekend. Local bands practise in the cells during the week, so it can be fun to just walk around the corridors, absorbing the clashing sounds and the vivid colours of the graffiti-covered walls. Other good, slightly alternative venues are *Schüür* (☎ 368 10 30, Tribschenstrasse 1) for live music and *Boa* (☎ 360 45 88, Geissensteinring 41) for music, theatre and dance (closed mid-June to mid-August).

There are several decent bars in the centre and most close around midnight or just afterwards. The Schiller Hotel (see Places to Stay) shelters the small *Casablanca* bar, the *Grand Café* with its huge Greek-style statues, and *Cucaracha*, a Mexican bar and restaurant. Along the road, the Hotel Astoria has the *Pravda* nightclub (closed Sunday to Tuesday; cover Sfr10 or more) and *Penthouse* rooftop bar (free entry).

Hexenkessel (Haldenstrasse 21) is a large and busy bar with loud music, games and dancing. The decor is halfway between a beach hut and a junk shop. It's open 8 pm to 3 am. There's no entry charge as such – you pay for your first drink (from Sfr6) as you go in.

Adagio on Seidenhofstrasse attracts a wider age range, with its mixed music and medieval-castle ambience. Entry is Sfr10 on Friday and Saturday, or free on other nights (open from 9 pm). Dress standards are casual but not scruffy.

On the north side of the river is the *Pickwick Pub* near the Kapellbrücke, a pseudo-English bar where the punters overflow onto the quayside. On Weinmarkt is *Movie*, a bar with film star pics and movie promos on the walls. If you go through to the section around the side where they serve food,

the premises open out into a terrace overlooking the river. The *Casino* (☎ 418 56 56, Haldenstrasse 6) caters for gamblers and dancers, and has a summer folklore show.

There are many cinemas in town, with reduced prices on Monday. *Atelier* (☎ 210 12 30) on Theaterstrasse has some interesting non-mainstream offerings (Sfr14, students Sfr10).

Shopping

A few shops are shut on Monday morning but most stay open until 9 pm on Thursday and Friday. Gift stalls at the boat quays and some other souvenir shops even open on Sunday. The *Official Guide* will remind you of the real purpose of tourism (spending money) by detailing many shopping outlets. You can buy anything you could possibly want (and lots of things you couldn't), such as Swiss knives, cuckoo clocks, beer tankards and pug-faced dolls. More practical goods can be bought in the many department stores.

Getting There & Away

Hourly trains connect Lucerne to Interlaken (Sfr26, two hours, via the scenic Brünig Pass), Bern (Sfr32, 1¼ hours), Lugano (Sfr58, 2¾ hours) and Geneva (Sfr70, 3¼ hours, via Olten or Langnau). Zürich-bound trains are every 30 minutes (Sfr2, one hour). The N2 (E9) motorway connecting Basel and Lugano passes by Lucerne, and the N14 provides the road link to Zürich.

Car Rental Europcar (☎ 444 44 28), AMAG, Luzernerstrasse 17, and Hertz (☎ 420 02 77), Maihofstrasse 101, are north of Lucerne in Ebikon. Avis (☎ 310 16 16) is to the south-west at Luzernerstrasse 56, Kriens. Local firm Miecar (☎ 210 00 44), at Neuweg 4, has daily rates from Sfr65/78 including 100/300km, or weekend rates from Sfr140/156 (two/three days including 600/1000km).

Boat For information on boat transport, see the following Lake Lucerne section. The main departure points are the quays around Bahnhofplatz.

Getting Around

Walking is the best way to explore the centre where many of the streets are pedestrian-only anyway. Bus tickets cost Sfr1.70 for one zone, Sfr2.20 for two and Sfr2.70 for three. Ticket dispensers state the number of zones for each destination. The expensive 24-hour pass (Sfr10) covers all zones, though with a stamped *Official Guide* you can get a three-day bus ticket for just Sfr8. There's an underground car park at the train station.

Lake Lucerne

You could spend several days exploring the historic locations and scenic mountains around Lake Lucerne (Vierwaldstättersee). The views are constantly changing around its twisting coastline and there are many typical villages and attractive resorts to enjoy along the way.

The Vierwaldstättersee guest card is definitely worth having, so ask for it if

Mountain Myths & Legends

On a dark evening, when the brooding shapes of giant peaks blot out half the night's stars, it's easy to believe the ancient legends associated with the mountains. One tall tale tells of a cooper who fell down a mountain crevice and into a cave. He survived the fall as he landed on the backs of two peaceful dragons. Although the dragons left him alone, there was no escape and he lived through the winter by licking the salty water seeping from the cave walls. In the spring the dragons ventured out, and one gave the cooper a ride to safety on his tail.

A rather less amiable dragon lived in a cave above Oedwil. It preyed on the local villagers and livestock and was finally slain by the knight Struthan von Winkelried. The knight tossed his sword in the air in triumph, but three specks of the wicked beast's blood fell from the sword onto his head, and he died instantly. In 1420 a farmer saw a dragon fly between Mt Pilatus and Mt Rigi, and simultaneously stumbled across what has become known as the 'dragon stone' (on display in Lucerne's Natural History Museum).

The souls of evil tyrants are said to haunt the Enziloch on the Napf massif. Pontius Pilate rises out of the lake on Mt Pilatus every Good Friday (the day he condemned Jesus Christ) to wash the blood from his hands. Apparently, anybody who witnesses this event will die within the year.

Tiny 'wild folk' called Chlyni Lüüt once inhabited Mt Rigi. Their children always had their spleen removed at birth, giving them the ability to leap around mountain slopes with the agility of the chamois. They had other powers, but disappeared from view in the face of constant mockery by humans.

A foolhardy shepherd boy once baptised a favoured lamb, which instantly changed into a fearsome monster. It was given the name 'Griess' and it preyed on the populace. A special bull was reared to take on the monster. It was led by a white-clad maiden to the Alpine meadow where the Griess lived. Her hair ribbons were tied to the bull's nose ring. Although the monster was defeated, the bull also died. The maiden was never seen or heard of again, but the bull is remembered in the Uri coat of arms.

Suitably desperate bachelors may be tempted to seek the enchanted virgin who inhabits the Schibenloch cave on the Schrattenfluh. After rejecting an honest but poor suitor the virgin had been buried alive with her money. Every year, on the Thursday before Easter, she appears at the cave entrance to count her cash. Only at this time can a young man enter the cave to seek her hand. To be successful, he must meet three challenges. First, he must pass under a huge millstone held only by a thread. If the man already has a girlfriend, the thread will break. Next he must overcome a monstrous giant cat which dwells in the deeper recesses of the cave. Finally, upon reaching the virgin, he must answer three riddles to free her. If he fails to solve all the riddles he will be lost in the cave forever. The virgin still awaits – no one has yet completed these three challenges.

your accommodation doesn't offer it spontaneously. Benefits include various discounts on sporting facilities, 10% to 50% off certain cable cars, and reductions on some admission prices in Lucerne and elsewhere.

If contemplating an ascent of Mt Pilatus or Rigi, inquire about weather conditions at the Lucerne tourist office. In winter, also ask about special low-season prices.

The telephone code of all places around the lake is ☎ 041.

Getting Around

Old-fashioned paddlesteamers operate at certain times of the day, more frequently in summer, although any of the boats provide a fun day out. Boats operated by the Lake Lucerne Navigation Company (www.lakelucerne.ch) sail daily year-round, though for the Lake Uri section the winter service past Rütli is only on Sunday and national holidays. Longer trips are relatively much cheaper than short ones, and you can alight from the boat as often as you want. Swiss Pass and Eurail are valid on all scheduled boat trips and Inter-Rail gets you half price. All passes are valid or will get you discounts on selected mountain railways and cable cars.

From Lucerne, destinations include Alpnachstad (Sfr17.40, 40 minutes), Weggis (Sfr12.60, 45 minutes), Vitznau (Sfr17.40, 55 minutes), Brunnen (Sfr25, 110 minutes) and Flüelen (Sfr29, 160 minutes). Return fares are about 60% more than singles, and 1st-class prices (less crowded, but otherwise not particularly more comfortable) are about 50% more than 2nd-class prices. There are also special dinner/dancing cruises. Lake Lucerne attracts more boat passengers than any other lake in Switzerland – around two million per year.

Driving around the lake is perfectly viable. Roads run close to the shoreline all the way around, with the exception of the stretch from Flüelen to Stansstad. Here there is a motorway (N2) that ploughs a fairly straight line, sometimes underground, usually away from the water.

Bissig Automobil (☎ 820 11 51, fax 820 44 05), Föhneneichstrasse 29, Brunnen, sells good-value bus tours to regional attractions during summer, and can pick up in Lucerne, Weggis, Vitznau and Schwyz.

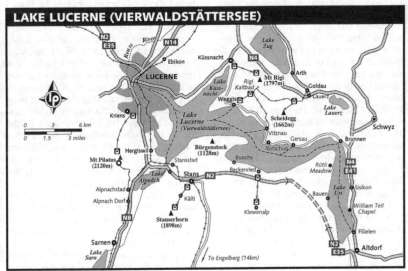

LAKE LUCERNE (VIERWALDSTÄTTERSEE)

Mt Pilatus

The rugged contours of Mt Pilatus (2120m) overlook Lucerne from the south. According to tradition it was named after Pontius Pilate, who apparently haunted its heights; any climber with the temerity to approach the summit would cause his spirit to unleash storms onto the populace below. Foolhardy tourists ignore this ancient wisdom and regularly ascend for panoramic views of the lake and the Alpine range. The inspiring vistas make it worth risking Pilate's wrath. However, there is a more prosaic and probably more accurate derivation of the name – *pileatus* in Latin means covered in clouds.

A popular route from Lucerne is to take the lake-steamer to Alpnachstad, the cog railway up Mt Pilatus, the cable car down to Kriens and bus No 1 back to Lucerne. The total cost for this jaunt is Sfr77.60. Kriens-Pilatus return or Alpnachstad-Pilatus return is Sfr58. Reductions are: Swiss Pass 25%, Eurail 35%, and Inter Rail 50%. Children (six to 16) go half-price. Inquire about discounts for late ascents during the summer.

This cog railway is the steepest of its kind in the world, reaching a gradient of 48%. It's closed from 1 December to early May. The cable car is closed for maintenance from around 2 to 12 November.

The cog railway is an all-or-nothing trip but the cable car is in several stages, allowing you to ride some of the way and walk the rest. The last stage to the summit is the steepest. Walking up from Alpnachstad takes around four hours and from Kriens about five hours. From the summit, it's three hours down to Alpnachstad, 3½ hours to Kriens or three hours down to Hergiswil boat station. The cable station of Fräkmüntegg is about halfway up in walking terms, so you could ride Alpnachstad-Mt Pilatus-Fräkmüntegg for Sfr40 and take the easy walk down from there. Fräkmüntegg has Switzerland's longest toboggan ride (Rondelbahn). It's 1350m long and rides cost Sfr7 (children Sfr6).

At the top of Mt Pilatus are two hotels, *Pilatus Kulm* and *Hotel Bellevue*. They share the same reception (☎ 670 12 55, fax 670 26 35, ✉ hotel.pilatus.kulm-bellevue@ bluewin.ch) in the circular building.

Singles/doubles cost Sfr108/192 with private shower/WC and TV or Sfr62/124 without. At the top there's also a new arrivals hall and self-service restaurant.

If you want to stay in Alpnachstad, look for the private *B&B* run by Frau Schnider (☎ 670 19 32, Brünigstrasse 23), which has rooms for Sfr45/75. There is a better selection of restaurants a couple of kilometres down the road in Alpnach Dorf than in Alpnachstad itself.

Mt Rigi

From the top of Mt Rigi (1797m), there is a great view of tiers of mountain peaks to the south and east. On a clear day Mt Titlis and the Jungfrau Region giants are visible. The view to the north and west is also good, with an aeroplane-eye view of Arth-Goldau below, and the Lake Zug (Zugersee) curving around until it almost joins Küssnacht and an arm of Lake Lucerne. The green slopes of Mt Rigi itself, the swathes of conifers and the constantly tinkling cowbells all add to the scene. Seeing the sunrise from the summit is a popular activity with a long precedent.

The mountain can be ascended in a number of ways. Of course, hiking is the cheapest, but it's at least a four-hour slog from Weggis. Walking can be made more manageable by taking the cable car from Küssnacht up to Seeboldenalp (Sfr11 one way, Sfr18 return). There are two paths from there: the shortest takes a little over two hours, and the last section is quite steep. The less athletic can take the rack railway to within 200m of the summit in 40 minutes. Two rival tracks were built in the 1870s: one from Arth-Goldau and the other from Vitznau. Either route costs Sfr28 one way or Sfr56 return. The Arth-Goldau service closes for two weeks in late May but Vitznau operates year-round.

The Vitznau track gives the further option of diverting at Rigi Kaltbad and taking the cable car to/from Weggis instead. The whole thing can be done from Lucerne for Sfr84 (reductions with railpasses).

Being at the top for the sunrise is made easier by the presence of the *Rigi Kulm*

Mt Rigi & 19th-Century Tourism

Everything works so well in Switzerland. The people are affluent, well-dressed, courteous, unflappable ... and above all, in command. As a tourist it's not hard to get the feeling that you're the poor relation from an underdeveloped country visiting a successful cousin. The balance of power is definitely with the Swiss.

But it wasn't always like that. The picture that emerges from 19th-century texts is that tourists were like visiting royalty, with the Swiss scurrying around attending to their needs and desperately hoping to make a few coins to eke out a meagre living. Many locals – men and boys bearing mules and eager grins – would offer their services as guides for tourists walking in the hills. Always there would be people determinedly trying to sell snacks and trinkets. In his travel reminiscences, Mark Twain reported being plagued by Alp horn players at Mt Rigi. He paid them generously to get rid of them, only to find their number had doubled at the next village, hoping for a similar pay-off. Such stories ring bells with any traveller to the Third World.

Jemima Morrell, writing in 1863 *(Miss Jemima's Swiss Journal)*, describes being surrounded by dozens of would-be guides at Weggis: 'We were literally infested by, dogged and danced around by these importunates. Our efforts to evade them were numerous and varied.' As they walked (unguided) up Mt Rigi they were continually confronted by would-be vendors who 'dangled branches of cherries in our faces with the cry "Vingt centimes, vingt centimes!" These cherry vendors regarded us as their legitimate prey.'

The cherry danglers may have been unlucky with Miss Morrell's party, but they had plenty of other tourists to pester instead. Morrell reported that there were as many as 150 early risers congregated at the summit of Mt Rigi the next morning, all there to enjoy the view at sunrise.

Hotel (☎ 855 03 03, fax 855 00 55, ✉ rigikulm@bluewin.ch), just a five minute walk from the summit (closed mid-November to mid-December). South-facing singles/doubles with private shower/WC cost Sfr90/160, and with a bath, Sfr100/180. North-facing rooms cost Sfr60/100 with use of a hall shower, and rooms in the annexe cost Sfr45/70. Dorms are Sfr25 per person. The restaurant is fairly expensive, though the self-service side is more affordable. A snack kiosk is open during the day on the terrace.

Halfway between Vitznau and the summit is *Berghaus Unterstetten (☎ 855 01 27)*, an hour's walk from Rigi Kaltbad. It's an ideal place if you want to get away from it all. There's a restaurant, dorms for Sfr17 and rooms for Sfr35/70.

Weggis
☎ 041 • pop 3000 • elevation 440m
This south-facing lakeside resort enjoys plenty of sunshine, meaning that the quayside parades a palette of colours from its flowerbeds, magnolias, palm trees and fig trees. Musicians play in the Kurplatz on summer mornings (except Monday), and there are a couple of churches worth peeking into. There's also a monument to Mark Twain, who stayed here. It's also the base for the cable car up to Rigi Kaltbad (Sfr36 return). There's swimming in the lake and in an indoor pool at Lido-Hallenbad (Sfr6, free with Weggis guest card) to the west of the centre, and bikes can be hired through the tourist office. Don't expect much nightlife – it's a quiet resort favoured mainly by older visitors.

The helpful tourist office (☎ 390 11 55, fax 391 00 91, ✉ info@weggis.ch) is next to the boat station. It's open 8 am to 5 pm Monday to Friday in winter, 8 am to 5.30 or 6 pm Monday to Friday in summer and 9 am to 2.30 pm Saturday and Sunday. Ask about its guided walks (Sfr5 per person).

Places to Stay & Eat
Budget-Hotel Weggis (☎ 390 11 31, fax 390 14 80, ✉ info@budgethotel.ch, Parkstrasse 29) has simple rooms with TV, and sometimes a balcony. Rooms (one to three people) are

Sfr79.50 with shower/WC or Sfr64.50 without; doubles (bunk beds) are Sfr59. Reception is only open from 3.30 to 7.30 pm and breakfast (Sfr5) must be pre-ordered.

Hotel-Restaurant Viktoria (☎ *390 11 28, fax 390 01 90*) overlooks the lake promenade (closed mid-December to mid-January). Reasonably spacious rooms, some with balconies, are Sfr45 per person, with use of a hall shower. The restaurant (closed Wednesday in winter) has a shady garden and meals for around Sfr14 to Sfr30. There are supermarkets close by.

Just 100m to the east along the promenade is *Hotel Gotthard am See* (☎ *390 21 14, fax 390 09 14*). Newly renovated rooms with private shower/toilet are about Sfr100 per person (closed mid-October to mid-December). The restaurant serves affordable Swiss and Italian food and has an open-air section right by the lake. Another good option for Italian food is *Versilia*, by the lake, a 15-minute walk west.

Hotel Albana (☎ *390 21 41, fax 390 29 59,* **@** *albanaweggis@access.ch*), on Luzernerstrasse, is a comfortable four-star place with lake views, a bar and restaurant. Prices start at Sfr100/200.

Stans

The capital of Nidwalden, Stans is the starting point for the excellent excursion up the **Stanserhorn** mountain (1898m). It is not as popular as the trip up Mt Rigi, which faces it across the lake, but it provides a view just as good. The big ranges to the south (including Mt Titlis and the Jungfrau massif) are closer and seem to surround you more, yet you still have the panorama of the lakes and hills to the north, including a wide expanse of Lakes Lucerne, Zug, and also Lake Sarnen, squeezed between the mountains in the south-west. There are plenty of viewing boards at the top to help you identify the different mountains and lakes. From the cable station it's just a 10-minute hike to the summit, and you can return by a different route. As always, a restaurant awaits by the top cable station; this one has outside seating.

The journey up – by 'old-timer' funicular to Kälti, then a cable car – costs Sfr24 one way or Sfr44 return, and the base station is a five-minute walk (signposted) from the train station. It operates from mid-April to mid-November. The hike up the grassy slopes from Stans takes around 4½ hours, or if you have a car you can save almost an hour by driving up to Kälti and parking there.

In the main town, the central Dorfplatz is worth a stroll. It has a fountain and attractive 18th-century buildings, as well as essentials such as hotels (around Sfr60 per person), supermarkets, restaurants and a pharmacy. Its centrepiece is the early baroque **Parish Church**, tastefully decorated inside in white and black, rather than the usual overdose of gilding. Adjoining the church is a Romanesque belltower with a 16th-century spire. In the centre is a tourist office, Tourismus Vierwaldstättersee (☎ 610 88 33, fax 610 88 66, **@** lakelucerne@bluewin.ch), Bahnhofplatz 4.

Stans is on the Lucerne-Engelberg railway, or it can be reached by hourly bus from Buochs boat station.

Beckenried

Beckenried, on the southern shore, is a bus ride from Stans. Just a few minutes' walk from the boat station is a cable car which makes the 10-minute ascent to **Klewenalp** (Sfr17 one way or Sfr27 return). The views across the lake are good, and there are a number of hiking trails heading into the hills and valleys beyond. A map at the top outlines the options.

Gersau

Remarkably, this tiny place (population 1700) was an independent republic, the world's smallest, between 1390 and 1817 before joining the canton of Schwyz. There is an SYHA *hostel* (☎ *828 12 77, fax 828 12 63*) between Vitznau and Gersau at Rotschuo (some boats stop here). It's open from 1 March to 30 November and charges Sfr21.50. The reception is closed from 10 am to 4.30 pm, and there's a kitchen.

Brunnen

☎ 041 • pop 7000 • elevation 443m

This resort is at the dog-leg where Lake Uri (Urner See) and Lake Lucerne meet. It's worth visiting if only for the view, with the two stretches of lake shimmering on either side of the spit of land on the opposite shore. The green patch to the left of that promontory is the famous Rütli Meadow where the 1291 pact was signed. Brunnen is one of the livelier resorts on the lake (which, to be honest, isn't saying very much), and it's a good base for exploring in either direction, or for visiting Schwyz. It offers sailing, water-skiing and windsurfing, and there are schools for each of these activities. There's also swimming in the lake (at the Lido) or in the adjoining heated indoor pool *(Hallenbad)*; a day ticket for the whole complex is Sfr5.50. The Swiss Holiday Park (☎ 825 50 50) offers a range of sporting or bathing options, such as thermal pools. See the Web site at www.swissholidaypark.ch. Touch and Go (☎ 820 54 31), Parkstrasse 14, arranges paragliding tandem flights (Sfr150) and other activities, such as canyoning. For more information, see the Web site www.paragliding.ch.

The tourist office (☎ 825 00 46, fax 825 00 49, @ info@brunnentourismus.ch), Bahnhofstrasse 32, is open 8.30 am to noon and 1.30 to 6 pm Monday to Friday, and variable hours on Saturday. Don't forget to ask about the guest card; discounts are listed in the *Gäste Information* booklet.

Places to Stay & Eat There are two camp sites overlooking the lake in west Brunnen: *Camping Urmiberg* (☎ 820 33 27) and *Camping Hopfreben* (☎ 820 18 73). Both have similar facilities and are open for the summer season. Urmiberg is the cheaper of the two and costs Sfr6.90 per person, Sfr3 to Sfr5 per tent and Sfr2.50 per car.

In Brunnen you must pay at least Sfr60 per person for any hotel overlooking the water. *National* (☎ 820 18 78, Bahnhofstrasse 47) is more affordable, starting at Sfr48/90 for singles/doubles using hall facilities, or Sfr55/100 with private

shower/WC. It has a moderately-priced restaurant with outside seating, is family-friendly, and has adequate parking. The restaurant is shut on Sunday. National is conveniently located near the train station, which has money-exchange counters and bike rental available daily.

Nearer the lakefront is *Brunnerhof* (☎ 820 17 57, fax 820 48 81, Kapellplatz), with rooms starting at Sfr70/90. Some slightly more expensive rooms have TV and/or balcony. Brunnerhof has a decent restaurant offering meals from Sfr16.50 and several non-meat choices. It is open daily in season but the restaurant closes for two days mid-week in winter. Not far away is the busy *Pizzeria Bacco* (Gersauerstrasse 21). Good pizzas start from Sfr13 and there's a wide range of more expensive fish and meat dishes (closed Tuesday). A *Migros* supermarket is opposite the train station, and a *Coop Center* is in Parkstrasse near the tourist office.

Entertainment *Dodo Bar* (Bahnhofstrasse 10) is one of the 'in' drinking places in town. *Hotel Eden*, on the waterfront, houses the casino, with gambling from 10 pm (casual dress OK; closed Sunday and Monday). There's also a piano bar, and the Weinkeller bar where there's often dancing (open from 8 pm every night).

Lake Uri

There are several historic sights on Lake Uri (Urner See). If you take the ferry from Brunnen towards Flüelen, the first sight you pass is a natural obelisk protruding from the water to a height of nearly 26m. Inscribed on it in gold lettering is a dedication to Schiller, the author of the play *Wilhelm Tell* (1859), who was so instrumental in creating the Tell legend.

Next stop is the **Rütli Meadow**, where the Oath of Eternal Alliance was signed by the three cantons of Uri, Schwyz and Nidwalden. You can see it well enough from the boat, but if you want to alight, all you will find is a flagpole, a grassy field, and (inevitably) a souvenir shop which doubles as a cafe and post office.

To commemorate the 700th anniversary of the 1291 pact, the **Swiss Path** was built, which runs all the way around Lake Uri from Rütli to Brunnen. It is in 26 sections, each representing one of the 26 cantons, starting with the first three to sign up and concluding with Jura (1979). Right at the end in Brunnen is a square dedicated to the Swiss living abroad, featuring a surprisingly ugly metal structure. The length of each section of the path is determined by the population of the canton, with every 5mm representing one person. Surprisingly, the Swiss haven't been so meticulous as to inscribe the name of every individual person along the path, but they have marked off each section with a stone plaque. It would require determination to walk the whole 36km, but one or two sections (for example, between boat stops) are easily manageable and worth undertaking. The hilliest stretches are from Rütli to Bauen and from Sisikon to Brunnen. Bauen to Flüelen (around 4½ hours in total) is almost flat and Flüelen to Sisikon (2½ hours) isn't too strenuous either.

One of the boat stops on the lake is the **William Tell Chapel** (Tellskapell). The walls are covered in murals depicting four episodes in the Tell legend, including the one that's supposed to have occurred on this spot, involving his escape from Gessler's boat (see the boxed text 'The William Tell Tale').

The last port of call on the lake is Flüelen, important because it's on the main road and rail route through the St Gotthard Pass, and historically it was a staging post for the mule trains making this crossing. Near the town is **Altdorf**, where William Tell is reputed to

The William Tell Tale

Hermann Gessler, the newly installed Austrian bailiff of Uri and Schwyz, placed his hat on a pole in Altdorf town square. Everyone was compelled to bow in respect to this symbol of Habsburg rule. But William Tell from Bürglen was unaware of the requirement, and was pulled up for his non-compliance when walking through the square.

Gessler, who knew of Tell's reputation as a crossbow marksman, decreed he would forfeit his life and that of his son, unless he shot an apple off his son's head. To Gessler's disappointment, Tell succeeded. Yet Gessler noticed that Tell had secreted a second arrow about his person. Tell was forced to admit that the second arrow was intended for Gessler himself, had his aim not been true and his son harmed. The affronted Gessler arrested Tell and took him on his boat, intending to imprison him for life in his fortress above Küssnacht.

As they crossed the lake, *Föhn* winds whipped up and threatened to capsize the boat. Tell, who was also a master helmsman, was untied in order to steer the boat to safety. Tell took the opportunity to steer close to the shore. He leapt off the boat and onto a rock (at the site of the Tellskapell), at the same time pushing the boat back into the stormy waves. Realising his family would never be safe from Gessler, Tell rushed over to Küssnacht to ambush the tyrant. He hid by the Hohle Gasse, a sunken lane. The bailiff and his entourage soon approached, and Tell's aim was true once more. Gessler died instantly from a single arrow into his heart.

JENNY JONES

have performed his apple-shooting stunt. A statue of the man himself stands in the main square, and Schiller's play is sometimes performed in Altdorf's Tellspielhaus.

Engelberg

☎ 041 • pop 3500 • elevation 1050m
This sunny resort at the foot of Mt Titlis is an ideal day trip from Lucerne, or a base for a longer stay. In summer, the hills above Engelberg sing with the melodic yet insistent sound of cowbells – it sounds like there's a never-ending procession of Hare Krishna devotees up there.

Orientation & Information
Engelberg, in the canton of Unterwalden, is visited in summer and winter. The main street is Dorfstrasse (partially pedestrian-only). Most of the shops and restaurants are on Dorfstrasse, or the intersecting Bahnhofstrasse.

The tourist office (☎ 637 37 37, fax 637 41 56, ❻ tourist.center@engelberg.ch) is a five-minute walk from the train station, in the Tourist Center at Klosterstrasse 3. Opening hours are 8 am to noon and 2 to 6.30 pm Monday to Friday, and 8 am to 6.30 pm on Saturday. During the summer and winter high season there's no lunch break and it also opens on Sunday. Hotel prices vary according to the season: peak times are late January to early March, and early July to mid-September. In May and November most of Engelberg closes down. The tourist office has a free room-booking service for hotels and has lists of holiday chalets, private rooms and cheap mountain lodgings.

The guest card is good for various discounts, including 20% off the Mt Titlis cable car in summer and 10% off winter ski passes exceeding four days. The benefits are off-set by the resort Kurtaxe (Sfr3.20 per night), which is *excluded* from the accommodation prices listed here. Ski buses are free for everyone in winter.

Banks are open till 5.30 pm on weekdays; several have a Bancomat. Internet access is at Hotel Bellevue (see Places to Stay).

Engelberg Monastery
This is one of only five such Benedictine monasteries in Switzerland. The original building dated from 1120 but was burnt down three times before finally being rebuilt in stone. There is a guided tour at 10 am and 4 pm from Tuesday to Saturday. It costs Sfr6 and lasts around 45 minutes. Visitors are taken around several rooms decorated with incredibly detailed wood inlays, all made by a monk who continued this task until he was well into his 70s. A typical panel measuring around 50 cm by 20 cm contains 300 pieces of wood, and he spent years on each room. The baroque monastery church is also impressive (free entry), with its numerous side-altars. It even has a one-handed clock above the main altar so parishioners can time the sermon.

Tal Museum
This small museum at Dorfstrasse 6 is merely of passing interest. One floor is a representation of a typical late-18th century dwelling. It is open most afternoons and costs Sfr6.

Mt Titlis
The trip to the top cable station at 3020m is the most spectacular excursion in Engelberg. First, there is the ascent to Gerschnialp (1300m), then there's a horizontal passage over cow pastures, before rising again to Trübsee (1800m). From here you transfer to a gondola which goes to Stand (2450m) and provides a sweeping view back down to the lake and the valley below. Finally you board the world's first revolving gondola (completed in December 1992) for the passage over the Titlis Glacier, a dazzling expanse of ice with ridges, hollows and hints of blue. From Mt Titlis station to the 3239m summit it's about a 45-minute hike (wear sturdy shoes) in the summer – it doesn't look far but at this altitude you need to take it slow. The station complex provides a sun terrace, restaurant, and the highest bar in Europe. There are also south-facing windows that can be reached through a tunnel in the

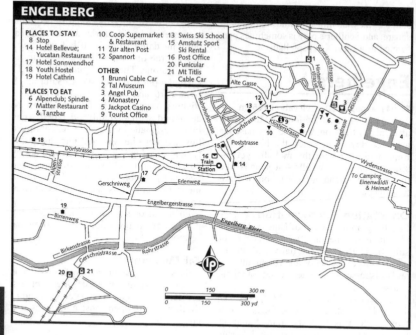

ENGELBERG

PLACES TO STAY
8 Stop
14 Hotel Bellevue;
   Yucatan Restaurant
17 Hotel Sonnwendhof
18 Youth Hostel
19 Hotel Cathrin

PLACES TO EAT
6 Alpenclub; Spindle
7 Matter Restaurant
   & Tanzbar

10 Coop Supermarket
   & Restaurant
11 Zur alten Post
12 Spannort

OTHER
1 Brunni Cable Car
2 Tal Museum
3 Angel Pub
4 Monastery
5 Jackpot Casino
9 Tourist Office

13 Swiss Ski School
15 Amstutz Sport
   Ski Rental
16 Post Office
20 Funicular
21 Mt Titlis
   Cable Car

ice, an ice grotto, and free 150m-long slides on a rubber tyre.

The whole journey is rather expensive and if you go up in cloud you've wasted your money. One-way/return prices from Engelberg are: Gerschnialp (Sfr6/8), Trübsee (Sfr17/24), Stand (Sfr34/48), and Titlis (Sfr52/73). Reductions are: Swiss Half-Fare Card and Regional Pass 50%, Swiss Pass 25%, Eurail and Inter-Rail 20%. From Engelberg to the Mt Titlis station takes around 45 minutes. The cableway closes for maintenance for a few days in late November. Ask about off-season reductions.

As ever, you can save on the cost and walk some sections. Between Stand and Trübsee the *panoramaweg* is open from July to September; it takes about 1¾ hours up and 1¼ hours down. From Trübsee up to Jochpass takes about 1½ hours (or there's a chairlift beyond the lake), and down to Engelberg takes around the same time.

Brunni

The Brunni cable car, on the opposite side of the valley, goes up 1600m and provides access to a number of hiking trails. A traveller complained to me that the 5½-hour Benediktusweg went up and down too many hills, but I suppose that's what happens when you go hiking in the mountains! The Brunni cable car costs Sfr12 or Sfr19 return (half-price for kids), or you can make the steep hike up in a little over an hour.

Skiing

Engelberg is well known as a skiing centre. Most of the runs are intermediate; the few easy ones are mainly around Brunni and the lifts branching from Gerschnialp. The main season is from mid-December to mid-April and a full one-day pass costs Sfr48 (Sfr55 on weekends and holidays) or Sfr29 for children. Specific day passes cost Sfr18 (kids Sfr14) for Gerschnialp and Sfr32 (Sfr18) for Brunni.

There are lots of places that hire out skiing equipment. One of the cheapest is Amstutz Sport (☎ 637 11 78), Dorfstrasse 39. Skis, poles and ski boots for Alpine skiing cost Sfr43 for one day, reducing per day over longer periods. Cross-country equipment is Sfr20 for one day. The Swiss ski school (☎ 637 10 74, fax 637 44 84) is at Dorfstrasse 34, or there is another school in the tourist office.

Other Activities

For a different perspective of the mountains, you can bounce around on the end of a bungy-rope in the company of Outventure (☎ 611 14 41, fax 611 14 42, @ info@ outventure.ch), Hansmatt 5, CH-6370 Stans. The jump, from a cable car on Mt Titlis, costs Sfr99 for 70m or Sfr149 for 130m, including transfers. The experience is brief but memorable. Outventure or Adventure Engelberg (☎ 637 20 30) in the Tourist Center can organise a range of other activities, such as kayaking, river-rafting, canyoning or cycling. Engelberg also boasts a sporting park and a complex of swimming pools.

Places to Stay

Camping Einenwäldli (☎ 637 19 49) is about a 25-minute walk from the train station, at the swimming pool complex. Head down Klosterstrasse until it becomes Wydenstrasse, then take the right fork. In the winter you can take the ski bus instead. It's open year-round and costs Sfr7 per person, Sfr8.50 for a small tent and Sfr5 for a car.

The SYHA *hostel (☎ 637 12 92, fax 637 49 88, Dorfstrasse 80)* is 10 minutes back down the railway line on the north side of the tracks. Dorm beds are Sfr26 and the dinners are a bargain at Sfr8.50. It is closed between seasons. The main doors are locked between 9 am and 5 pm (you can leave your bags in the ski room and check in later).

Hotel Bellevue (☎ 637 12 13, fax 637 44 49, @ bellevue.engelberg@telalpin.ch), on Bahnhofplatz overlooking the station, is the best deal. It has a surprisingly majestic lobby, with pseudo-marble pillars and a grand piano. Singles/doubles vary in size; most are renovated, and prices start from just Sfr25/50 (perhaps with bunk beds) using hall shower and without breakfast, or Sfr100/170 with private shower/WC and breakfast. Many English-speaking exchange students stay here (open year-round).

Stop (☎ 637 16 74, Klosterstrasse) has simple rooms with TV and hall showers for Sfr55 per person. The restaurant serves Swiss dishes and is popular with resort workers. *Heimat (☎ 637 13 32)*, on Schweizerhausstrasse, is more comfortable but it's a 10-minute walk east of the centre. This wooden chalet has just seven beds for Sfr60 per person with shower/WC, and there's a restaurant (closed Monday and Tuesday).

A good choice for personal service is *Hotel Cathrin (☎ 637 44 66, fax 637 43 28)*, on Birrenweg, near the Mt Titlis cable car. Singles/doubles with private shower are about Sfr92/164 and great four-course dinners are an extra Sfr27. Book ahead (closed in the off season). *Hotel Sonnwendhof (☎ 637 45 75, fax 637 42 38, Gerschniweg 1)* is convenient for both Mt Titlis and the centre. Pristine rooms (it was built in 1990) are neatly laid out with all required amenities, and cost Sfr130/200.

Places to Eat

Engelberg is not cheap for food, but if you study menus carefully down Dorfstrasse you may find Tagestellers from around Sfr15. The budget place to go is the *Coop* supermarket and restaurant on Klosterstrasse, which is open 8 am to 6.30 pm daily. There are also restaurants at all the cable car stations.

Yucatan, a Mexican-style bar and restaurant opposite the train station, is the most popular après-ski place in town. Another lively place is *Matter Restaurant & Tanzbar* on Dorfstrasse. The cafe-restaurant *Zur alten Post* on Dorfstrasse has Swiss dishes from Sfr13; it's open 8 am to 7 pm daily.

There are several places to eat at *Alpenclub* on Dorfstrasse. Downstairs is a pizzeria, open from 5 pm, with pizzas starting at Sfr14.50. Also open from the afternoon onwards are the ground floor restaurant serving Swiss food from Sfr30, and the 1st-floor section serving fondue for Sfr23.50. All are closed Tuesday and Wednesday in the low season. **Spannort** *(☎ 637 26 26, Dorfstrasse 28)* is a gourmet restaurant serving Swiss and French food (expect prices above Sfr30). It is closed on Monday.

Entertainment

By the monastery is the **Angel Pub**, an English-style venue with darts and pool. An un-English touch is the tree trunk in the corner of the bar. This is used in a German game where you try to hammer in a nail using the thin end of the hammer head. The last person to succeed buys the drinks. It is open 9 am to 12.30 am daily, and beer is Sfr4.80 per half-litre. The **Jackpot Casino** on Dorfstrasse has a bar (live music in winter) as well as gambling (noon to 3 am daily). Close by, **Spindle** has dancing from 10 pm to 3 am (closed Sunday to Tuesday).

Getting There & Away

By train, Engelberg is at the terminus of the line, an hour or less from Lucerne (Sfr14.80 one way; change usually required at Hergiswil). Seeing Engelberg and Mt Titlis in a day trip from Lucerne is easily viable; the first train leaves Lucerne at 6.30 am and the last one back leaves Engelberg at 10.25 pm. The Lucerne tourist office sells special excursion tickets. (See the Getting Around section at the beginning of this chapter for details.)

Hiking Unless travelling by road from Lucerne or Stans, the only other way to leave or reach Engelberg is by foot, but the passes are only accessible in the summer. The Surenen Pass (2291m) is the route to Attinghausen, and from there a bus can take you to Altdorf and the southern end of the Urner See. It takes around seven hours to get to Attinghausen; taking a cable car along the route can save two hours. From Jochpass a path goes to Meiringen via Engstenalp and Tannalp. The highest point you reach is 2245m. From Meiringen it is easy to get to Brienzersee. Acquire a decent map and check on snow conditions before you try one of these routes.

Schwyz Canton

The fame of Schwyz rests upon the fact that it gave Switzerland both its name and flag. Together with the communities of Uri and Nidwalden, it was signatory to the Oath of Eternal Alliance of 1291. This charter is considered to be the birth of the Swiss Confederation and can be viewed in Schwyz town. Some destinations in Schwyz canton are covered in the earlier Lake Lucerne section.

Cherries are grown locally, and different towns are grouped under an itinerary called the Kirschstrasse (Cherry Road). One destination along the way is the Fabio-Fassbind distillery (☎ 041-859 04 00, fax 855 51 10) in Oberarth, between Arth and Goldau. Reserve ahead for a guided tour of the distillery in English (Sfr8), including a tasting of the cherry spirit made there.

SCHWYZ

☎ 041 • pop 13,500 • elevation 517m

Schwyz (pronounced Schvits), the capital of its canton, cowers beneath the twin peaks of the Mythen (1898m and 1811m).

Orientation & Information

Schwyz train station is 2km away from the town centre in Seewen. To get to the centre take any bus outside the station marked Schwyz Post, and get off at Postplatz (Sfr2.40; Swiss Pass valid). The tourist office (☎ 811 27 10) is a counter inside the post office at Oberer Steisteg-Märcht, 100m down the hill. It is open 7.30 am to noon and 1.30 to 6.30 pm Monday to Friday and 8 to 11 am on Saturday. Pick up the *Gäste Information* booklet, which also covers Brunnen and Morschach, and ask about the guest card. Other than this, there's little information available, but staff will telephone free of charge for rooms.

Federal Archives

Historic charters and other agreements are collected in the Bundesbriefarchiv building on Bahnhofstrasse in the town centre. Entry is Sfr4 (students Sfr2.50) and it is open 9.30 to 11.30 am and 2 to 5 pm daily. Th inaugural 1291 charter displayed here is the only copy in existence. It is written in Latin and bears only the seals of Uri and Nidwalden – Schwyz's own seal has been lost. In the document, the partners agreed to work for mutual defence and security and formulated their own legal system. They successfully defended this pact in 1315 by defeating the Habsburg force at Morgarten. The second charter marks this victory by restating the original agreement (in German) and making provision for a common foreign policy.

The other charters mark the acceptance of further cantons to the Confederation, with a corresponding increase in the number of heavy seals attached to each document. The last charter proclaims the entry of Appenzell in 1513 and resolves not to admit any other members to its elite circle. The Confederates kept this resolution intact until the French marched onto the scene in 1798.

Also on display are charters relating to privileges won by Schwyz through the years, and flags and banners carried in important battles.

Other Things to See & Do

The **Forum of Swiss History**, in the old granary, enlivens its subject matter with interactive displays (Sfr5, children free). It's closed on Monday. In Hauptplatz there is the 17th-century **Rathaus**, complete with 19th-century murals depicting famous events in Swiss history, particularly the Battle of Morgarten. On the other side of the square is **St Martin's Church**, with baroque fixtures and a marble pulpit.

Schwyz was the home of many of the 16th- and 17th-century mercenaries who fought in foreign armies. Those who returned with body and fortune intact built some of the grand houses that can still be seen around the town today. The grandest,

The Swiss Flag

Soldiers from the canton of Schwyz went to the aid of the excommunicated Emperor Frederick II in 1240, during his campaign in Italy. As a reward Schwyz was granted freedom from sovereign overlords and the right to use a red flag, the blood banner of the Holy Roman Empire, complete with heraldic cross. But a subsequent Diet in Nuremberg declared Frederick's dispensation invalid, so Schwyz pitched in behind Rudolf I of Habsburg in a battle against the Burgundians in 1289, and were rewarded by having their privileges confirmed.

The different Swiss cantons all had their own flags, yet they soon accepted the use of the white cross as a common emblem for Swiss mercenary soldiers. When Napoleon created the Helvetic Republic in 1798 he gave the country its first official national flag, a green, red and yellow tricolour. This flag was ditched in 1803, but it wasn't until 1841 that the cantons agreed to accept the freestanding white cross on the red field as a federal flag. Tireless campaigning by General Henri Dufour was instrumental in getting the flag accepted.

But debate did not end there. People got very excited about whether the cross should consist of four equal squares arranged around a central square, or whether the bars of the cross should be one-sixth longer than their width. The federal constitutions of 1848 and 1874 neglected to settle this burning issue, and it wasn't until 1889 that the federal parliament voted for the latter cross. Even so, debate raged on this crucial matter for years to come.

The federal decision was vindicated when in 1906 the international community honoured the Swiss flag by choosing to reverse its colours (to make a red cross on white) as a universal emblem for army medical corps. Nowadays the Swiss seem to have forgotten the passions aroused by the extra one-sixth, and seem content in the knowledge that they have the only square national flag in the world.

CENTRAL SWITZERLAND

the **Ital Reding-Hofstatt**, is now a museum (Sfr4). It's closed on Monday and in winter.

At the rear of Schwyz train station is a building that looks like a block of cheese. This is the **Schaukäserie Schwyzerland** (☎ 811 61 61), where the different stages of cheese making are shown and explained. Entry is free and it's open 9 am to 6 pm Tuesday to Saturday.

Hiking and skiing are possible on the surrounding mountains, accessible by cable car or funicular. A newly restored route is the 20km Schwyzer Panorama Weg. For information on the Mythen or Hoch-Ybrig ski regions, ask the tourist office. There is also skiing at Stoos (1300m), a car-free resort. From Schwyz, take bus No 3 to Schlattli, then the funicular (Sfr11 one way, Sfr20 return). A cable car goes up from Stoos to Frontalpstock (1922m). A good, if steep, circular hike from Stoos around the Frontalpstock area takes three to four hours.

Schwyz is near both Lake Lauerz and Brunnen (see the Lake Lucerne section for details). From Brunnen, you can get to Stoos via bus No 4 to Morscharch, then a cable car (Sfr11 up, Sfr20 return).

Places to Stay & Eat

Hotel Engel (☎ 811 12 42, Schulgasse) is by St Martin's Church. Singles/doubles with a shower cubicle and sometimes a balcony are only Sfr35 per person, plus Sfr5.50 for breakfast. Around the corner is *Gasthaus Schwyzer Stubli (☎ 811 10 66, fax 811 80 67, Riedstrasse 3)*, with a few quaint, flower-dominated doubles from Sfr80 with shower. The old-style restaurant has a garden terrace and Swiss meals from Sfr13.50 (closed Monday and Tuesday).

Hirschen Garni (☎ 811 12 76, Hinterdorf Strasse 14) is typically Swiss, with comfortable singles/doubles starting at Sfr50/95 (less 10% if three nights or more). *Restaurant Löwen* is opposite and affordable (closed Wednesday).

For budget private rooms, ask the tourist office. Note that some pension receptions are closed on Monday.

The *supermarket* by the tourist office serves hot food and snacks. *Sternen (Zeughausstrasse 6)*, uphill behind the Postplatz bus stop, has good-value pizzas from Sfr10 to Sfr19 (closed Monday). A good restaurant for Swiss food is the recently-remodelled *Ratskeller (☎ 811 10 87, Strehlgasse 3)*. Main courses are above Sfr25, though there's a plainer area where you can eat for less than Sfr20 (closed Sunday evening).

Getting There & Away

Schwyz station is 30 minutes away from Zug on the main north-south rail route; Lucerne is 40 minutes away (Sfr12.60). The Schwyz centre is only a few kilometres detour off the N4 which passes through Brunnen. (See the Zug and Einsiedeln Getting There & Away sections for more information.)

EINSIEDELN
☎ 055 • pop 7000 • elevation 900m

Einsiedeln is the most important pilgrimage destination in Switzerland, and its church is worth visiting simply for its sumptuous interior. Einsiedeln's reputation stems from 964, when the Bishop of Constance attempted to consecrate the original monastery. He was halted in his tracks by a heavenly voice declaring 'Desist – God Himself has consecrated this building'. Presumably somebody checked the premises for ventriloquists, because a papal bull subsequently acknowledged the miracle as genuine.

Orientation & Information

Einsiedeln is south of Lake Zürich and by the western shore of Sihlsee. The train station and the post office (8840) are together in the centre of town. In front of them is Dorfplatz, from which leads the main street, Hauptstrasse. The church is at the end of this street, overlooking Klosterplatz (eight minutes walk from the station). The tourist office (☎ 418 44 88, fax 418 44 80, @ info@einsiedeln.ch), near the church at Hauptstrasse 85, is open 9 am to noon and 1.30 to 5 pm from Tuesday to Friday, and 10 am to 4 pm on Saturday and Sunday.

Things to See & Do

The main focus of activity in Einsiedeln is the **Abbey Church**, or Klosterkirche. This majestic baroque edifice was built from 1719 to 1735 by the architect Caspar Moosbrugger. Much of the interior of the church is the work of the Asam brothers from Bavaria. The frescoes and stucco embellishments are exceptional, though the overpowering hues (pink, purple, fluorescent green etc) fail to be a miracle of colour co-ordination. The church influenced the design of the similarly lavish St Gallen Cathedral; conversely, the original monastery here was based on the original monastery in St Gallen.

The main prize for pilgrims is the **Black Madonna**, housed in a chapel by the entrance to the church. Most prayers are directed to this small statue, which has somehow survived three fires. The chapel is built on the spot where St Meinrad was murdered in 861.

In front of the church is a large square (plenty of parking) where stalls sell kitsch religious souvenirs. Continuing the religious theme, there's a **diorama** of Bethlehem, featuring 450 figures, and a **panorama** painting of Calvary. Situated in Benzigerstrasse, entry for each costs Sfr3.50 (children Sfr1.50) and they are open daily from Easter to the end of October and on Sunday during December.

Every year on the 14 September there is the **Festival of the Miraculous Dedication** involving a torchlit procession. Every five to seven years is the formidable production of *The Great Theatre of the World*, a religious drama by Calderón de la Barca. More than 600 villagers act in the event. It runs from around mid-June to mid-September and there was one in 2000.

Activities in the surrounding area include winter cross-country skiing, hiking, and boating and bathing in nearby **Sihlsee**. Fishing permits for the lake cost Sfr15 per day and Sfr35 per week (sold by a few lakeside restaurants and hotels). There are suggestions for hikes in the free *Gäste Information* booklet from the tourist office. Walk beside the church through the monastery buildings (pausing to pat the horses in the paddock) and continue along the path for 15 minutes for a good view of the church, green hills, the lake and the adjoining mountains.

Places to Stay & Eat

There's *camping* (☎ 412 17 31) on the far shore of Sihlsee at Willerzell. *Hotel National* (☎ 412 26 16, fax 412 66 05, Hauptstrasse 18)*, near the station, has rooms with up to six beds (bunk beds) for Sfr35 per person without breakfast.

Hotel St Josef Garni (☎ 412 21 51, Ilgenweidstrasse 2)*, by the church, has tidy, sober singles/doubles from Sfr60/95 with shower or Sfr50/85 without. Close by is *Hotel-Restaurant Sonne* (☎ 412 28 21, fax 412 41 45, Klosterplatz)*, offering rooms with shower/WC, telephone and radio for Sfr57/94. The restaurant has pizzas and a terrace. *Storchen* (☎ 412 37 60, fax 412 61 04, Hauptstrasse 79)* has largish singles/doubles with shower/toilet and TV from Sfr85/130, and a good restaurant with meals for Sfr12 to Sfr32.

There's a *Coop* supermarket at Dorfplatz and a *Migros* supermarket and restaurant (late opening till 8 pm on Friday) 200m away by the railway line. *Restaurant Sihlsee (Hauptstrasse 28)* has lunch menus, or try the speciality of the house – half chicken in a basket for Sfr14 (closed Wednesday). *Landgasthof Heidenbühl (Zürichstrasse)*, on the opposite side of the rail tracks, has good meals from Sfr12 (closed Wednesday evening and Thursday).

Getting There & Away

Einsiedeln is in a rail cul-de-sac, so getting there usually involves changing at Biberbrugg, but this is rarely a problem as arrivals/departures coincide. It is also within range of the canton of Zürich's S-Bahn trains. Zürich itself (Sfr15.40) is less than one hour away (via Wädenswil). There are trains to Lucerne (Sfr22 one-way, Sfr38 return; takes one hour), sometimes requiring a change at Goldau (70 minutes). From Einsiedeln to Schwyz, you can take the scenic 'back route' in the summer: postbus to Oberiberg, then private bus (Swiss Pass not valid) from there.

By car, Einsiedeln is 5km off highway 8 between Schwyz and Rapperswil.

Zug

☎ 041 • pop 21,640 • elevation 426m

Many multinational companies are registered in affluent Zug, thanks to the canton's status as a tax haven. The canton is easily the richest in Switzerland, earning an incredible Sfr75,300 per inhabitant in 1996, over 70% higher than the national average. Tourists, however, will be attracted more by its delightful medieval town centre and the nearby lake. Maybe the lake is a little too nearby – parts of the town sank into it in 1435, 1594 and 1887.

Orientation & Information

Zug (pronounced Tzoogk) hugs the northeast shore of Lake Zug. The train station is 1km north of the Old Town centre, and has bike rental and money-exchange counters. The tourist office (☎ 711 00 78, fax 711 79 29, ✉ tourism@zug.ch), Alpenstrasse 14, by the south exit of the train station, is open 8.30 am to 6 pm Monday to Friday, 8.30 am to 3 pm Saturday and 9 am to 3 pm Sunday. For the Old Town *(Altstadt)*, continue south for another 700m. En route is Postplatz, where you'll find the main post office (6301).

Things to See & Do

The medieval town centre can easily be explored on foot. Start with the emblem of the town, the **clocktower** (Zytturm) in Kolinplatz. Its distinctive tiled roof is painted in the blue and white of the cantonal colours. The shields below the 1557 clockface are those of the first eight cantons to join the Confederation (Zug was the seventh in 1352). The fountain in Kolinplatz was built in honour of Wolfgang Kolin, the flag bearer of the Swiss army that was defeated in the Battle of Arbedo (1422) by a vastly superior force led by the Duke of Milan.

Leading off from Kolinplatz are the pedestrian-only medieval streets of Fischmarkt, Ober Altstadt and Unter Altstadt. The old step-gabled houses are notable for their overhanging balconies. Nearby, and next to the lake, is Landsgemeindeplatz,

where you can hire pedalos (Sfr11/19 per 30/60 minutes) and other boats.

Also off Kolinplatz is Kirchenstrasse, which leads to the 13th-century castle, now containing the **Museum in der Burg**. It shows temporary exhibitions of a historical or archaeological nature (entry Sfr5, kids Sfr1). Opening hours are 2 to 5 pm Tuesday to Friday and 10 am to noon on Saturday and Sunday. Almost opposite is **St Oswald's Church**, built in late-Gothic style from the 15th and 16th centuries. It has a number of interesting features including a trio of carved wooden altars.

There are various beaches: free ones are near the camp site (see Places to Stay) and just south of Landsgemeindeplatz. The funicular from Schönegg will take you up the Zugerberg (988m) for Sfr3.60 one way, where there are hiking trails and an unobstructed view.

A good excursion from Zug is to the **Höllgrotten** (Stalactite Grottoes) near Baar, about 8km to the north-east. These limestone caves are open 9 am to noon and 1 to 5.30 pm daily from 1 April to 31 October. Entry costs Sfr8 (Sfr7 for students and children); allow about an hour to get around. To get there by public transport, take the Menzingen bus (No 2) and get off at Tobelbrücke-Höllgrotten.

Places to Stay

There is *camping* (☎ 741 84 22) on the shore of the lake, 2km west of the centre, along Chamer Fussweg. Charges are Sfr6.40 per adult and Sfr6.50 per tent. The SYHA *hostel* (☎ 711 53 54, fax 710 51 21, Allmendstrasse 8) is a 10-minute walk west of the station along Gubel Strasse. Dorm beds cost Sfr28, and there are kitchen facilities and evening dinners. The hostel is closed from early January to early March.

The only budget place in town is *Pension Bahnhof* (☎ 711 00 89, Alpenstrasse 6), 200m south of the tourist office. Simple singles/doubles using hall shower are Sfr48/78, and reception is only open 8.30 to 11.30 am and 4.30 to 7 pm Monday to Friday. For other cheap choices you have to travel – the tourist office can advise.

Twenty minutes and 7km east of Zug by bus No 2, beyond Höllgrotten, is *Adler* (*☎ 755 33 93, Hauptstrasse 9, Menzingen*), where rooms with hall shower are Sfr40/80.

Hotels in Zug all have three stars or more. If you can afford it, *City-Hotel Ochsen* (*☎ 729 32 32, fax 729 32 22, ❷ ochsen.zug@bluewin.ch, Kolinplatz*) is a good choice. This quiet place has well-equipped singles/doubles from Sfr156/252. Dating from 1480, it's the oldest inn in Central Switzerland; Goethe once stayed here.

Places to Eat

Cherry trees are grown locally, so look out for the speciality, Zug cherry cake *(Zuger Kirschtorte)*. It's a diet-busting combination of pastry, biscuit, almond paste, and butter cream with cherry brandy.

Several self-service places in town provide budget eats. Across Baarstrasse from the train station there's a *Migros* supermarket and restaurant in the huge Metalli shopping mall. Just down the street there's a large *Coop* supermarket and restaurant in the arcade opposite Bundesplatz. On Bundesplatz itself there's an *EPA* department store restaurant. All have late opening till 9 pm on Thursday.

On Landsgemeindeplatz there's *Café Platzmühle*, with pizzas and other meals from Sfr15. *Suan Long (Neugasse 13)* has takeaway Chinese food. Both places are open daily.

By the clocktower in Ober Altstadt are two quality restaurants offering both Swiss and French cuisine. The *Rathauskeller* (*☎ 711 00 58*) has gourmet food (around Sfr60) on the 1st floor, and meals from Sfr21 downstairs. Both parts are closed Monday. *Aklin* (*☎ 711 18 66*) also has different sections; prices start at Sfr25 and it's closed Sunday and Monday.

Getting There & Away

Train connections are good. Zug is on the main north-south rail route from Zürich to Lugano, and it is also the station at which trains from Zürich branch off to Lucerne and the Bernese Oberland.

By road, the north-south N4 (E31) runs from Zürich, sweeps around the western shore of Lake Zug and joins the N2 (E35), which continues through the St Gotthard Pass and on to Lugano and Italy. Highway 25 peels off the N4 north of Zug at Sihlbrugg, completes the corset around the eastern shore of the lake, then rejoins the N4 at Goldau.

Boats depart from Zug's Schiffsstation train station and chug south to Arth in the summer, and to many other destinations around the lake. Swiss Pass holders get half-price travel.

Andermatt

☎ 041 • pop 1600 • elevation 1447m
Andermatt is a skiing resort at the crossroads of four major Alpine passes: Susten, Oberalp, St Gotthard and Grimsel. The views from the town itself are surprisingly unspectacular given the mountain ranges all around, but that changes as soon as you gain some altitude.

Orientation & Information

Andermatt is at the southern end of the canton of Uri, and was formerly an important staging-post on the north-south St Gotthard route. Nowadays the town has been bypassed by the St Gotthard tunnel, but it still remains an important transport junction. The train station is 400m north of the core of the village, and has hotel brochures. The tourist office (☎ 887 14 54, fax 887 01 85, ❷ verkehrsverein-andermatt@bluewin.ch), 200m to the left of the station, shares the same hut as the postbus ticket office. It's open 9 am to noon and 2 to 5.30 pm Monday to Friday and variable hours on Saturday in high season.

The post office (6490) is on the main street, Gotthardstrasse, the site of most of the hotels and restaurants. Andermatt has a useful Guest Card.

Things to See & Do

The **skiing** is between 1438 and 2963m, with runs mostly for experts and intermediates. A one-day general ski pass costs Sfr56 (Sfr38 for children). There is cross-country skiing along the broad, flat valley towards Realp. Realp also has a small ski lift where beginners can hone their skills (Sfr25 for one day, children Sfr14).

From Realp, steam trains run to Furka from Friday to Sunday between mid-June and early October (daily from mid-July to late August). The return fare for this 50-minute ride is Sfr36 for adults and Sfr12.60 for children.

The high passes on all four sides make for excellent driving tours. Buses also tour these passes, but you can't visit all four on the same day starting/ending in Andermatt unless you first take the train to Göschenen (see Alpine Pass Tours in the Bernese Oberland chapter for more on bus tours). It's also fun to watch the trains winding their way backwards and forwards over the mountains.

The **St Gotthard Museum** (☎ 091-869 15 25), on the St Gotthard Pass (2109m), is open 9 am to 6 pm daily (Sfr8, students and seniors Sfr5), but only between June and October when the pass itself is open. The museum uses reliefs, models, documents and weapons to tell the history of the pass, highlighting mule drivers, stagecoaches, and the St Gotthard tunnel (there's English text).

The tourist office has information on walking tours to/from the passes and other points of interest, taking one to six hours. From **Gemsstock** (2963m), there's a panorama of 600 Alpine peaks. The journey to the top by cable car from Andermatt costs Sfr18 up or Sfr36 return (children half-price, reductions with Swiss railpasses).

Places to Stay & Eat

Beware of places closing in off-season. *Löwen* (☎ 887 12 23, Gotthardstrasse 51) has singles/doubles using hall shower for only Sfr40/80, but prices may change once extensive renovations are completed. Swiss food starts from Sfr13 in the hotel restaurant. Under the same ownership is *Helvetia*

Sporthotel (☎ 887 07 87, Gotthardstrasse 60) with new-looking rooms for Sfr60/100 with bath and toilet.

Bergidyll (☎ 887 14 55, fax 887 05 55, Gotthardstrasse 39) offers pleasant, reasonably spacious rooms for Sfr85/150 with private shower or Sfr70/120 without. There's also a lounge with easy chairs and an open fire. *Hotel Monopol-Metropol* (☎ 887 15 75, fax 887 19 23, ✉ hotel-monopol@bluewin.ch, Gotthardstrasse 43) has a small swimming pool, and better-appointed rooms from Sfr95/190 with private shower/WC and TV.

Haus Bonetti (☎ 887 19 60, fax 887 00 40), near the gondola station, looks like business premises but has singles/doubles with shower from Sfr50/90 and four-bed rooms for Sfr140. In winter, prices for doubles/quads are Sfr60/55 per person, including dinner. The public self-service restaurant upstairs has affordable meals. It, and the reception, are open 7.30 am to noon and from 4 pm until customers leave.

For eating, check the hotel restaurants for daily specials, or try *Badus*, close to the station on Gotthardstrasse. It has meals from Sfr13, including many vegetarian dishes. There is also a *Coop* supermarket on Gotthardstrasse.

Getting There & Away

Andermatt is a stop on the Glacier Express from Zermatt to St Moritz. For north-south destinations, change at Göschenen, 15 minutes away. Andermatt train station (☎ 887 12 20) can supply details on the car-carrying trains over the Oberalp Pass (direction: Graubünden) and through the Furka tunnel (the route to Valais). Postbuses stop by the train station. The St Gotthard tunnel (N2/E35) is one of the busiest north-south routes across the Alps. The 17km tunnel opened in 1980, and extends from Göschenen to close to Airolo, bypassing Andermatt. It will soon be superseded by an even longer tunnel.

Zürich Canton

The canton of Zürich is the most populous in Switzerland with 1,178,000 inhabitants. It is also one of the most affluent – in Küsnacht (which has low taxes) millionaires are commonplace. The canton is a hub of industry and the financial centre of the country. Heavy industry (metals and machines) are particularly important for a number of towns; as a tourist centre it is not so preeminent. Zürich itself welcomes many visitors – tourists and business people – who can enjoy the old centre, museums and galleries, and lakeside setting. Otherwise, there's little in the canton to detain the visitor, except perhaps a visit to Winterthur, or a boat tour on Lake Zürich.

Information

The tourist office in Zürich city (see the Zürich section) handles inquiries for the whole Zürich tourist region. Though it's not set up for in-person visits, the headquarters of Switzerland Tourism (☎ 288 11 11, fax 288 12 05, **@** postoffice@switzerlandvacation.ch) is also in Zürich, at Tödistrasse 7.

Zürich

☎ 01 • pop 363,000 • elevation 409m

The city of Zürich started life as a Roman customs post with the name of Turicum. Expansion thereafter was slow, but merchants trading in textiles gradually increased the financial clout of the town, and in 1218 it graduated to the status of a free city under the Holy Roman Empire. In 1336 the increasingly powerful merchants and artisans formed guilds which took over the governing of the city.

Zürich's reputation as a cultural and intellectual centre began after it joined the Swiss Confederation in 1351. Zwingli helped things along with his teachings during the Reformation, from 1519, and became a key figure in the running of the city. Zürich's intellectual

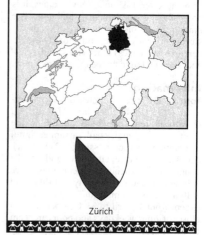

Highlights

- Explore the elegant shops and diverse museums in Zürich.
- Visit Switzerland's largest zoo.
- Take advantage of complimentary chocolate samples and free bike loans.
- Enjoy Zürich's varied cycle of festivals.
- View the art collections in Winterthur.

Zürich

and artistic tradition continued during WWI with the influx of luminaries such as Lenin, Trotsky, Tristan Tzara, Hans Arp and James Joyce (Joyce's grave can be seen in the Fluntern cemetery). The Dada art movement was born in Zürich in 1916. Around the same time, Carl Jung was honing his psychoanalytical theories in the city. Johann Heinrich Pestalozzi (1746-1827), seminal educationalist, was also a citizen of Zürich, and his statue stands on Bahnhofstrasse.

On the financial side, Zürich's international status as an industrial and business centre is thanks in no small part to the efforts of the energetic administrator and railway magnate Alfred Escher in the 19th century.

ZÜRICH

His statute is in front of the train station. Zürich's stock exchange was founded in 1877 and is the most important in the country.

Switzerland's most populous city offers an ambience of affluence and plenty of cultural diversions. In recent years, the Social Democrats have been at the helm of Zürich's administration, but the guilds retain a powerful, if behind-closed-doors, voice in the running of the city.

Orientation

Zürich is at the northern end of Lake Zürich (Zürichsee), with the city centre split by the Limmat River. Like many Swiss cities, it is compact and conveniently laid out. The main train station (Hauptbahnhof) is on the west or left bank of the river, close to the old centre. Note: Unless otherwise stated, references can be found on the main Zürich map.

Information

Tourist Offices The Zürich Tourist Service (☎ 215 40 00, fax 215 40 44, ✉ information@zurichtourism.ch) in the train station's main hall, arranges hotel reservations (no commission; ☎ 211 40 44), car rentals and excursions, and stocks country-wide brochures. Opening hours are 8.30 am to 8.30 pm Monday to Friday and 8.30 am to 6.30 pm Saturday and Sunday, except from 1 April to 31 October when it closes at 7 pm weekdays and hours are 9 am to 6.30 pm weekends. Staff charge for city maps but you can get them free from one of the larger city banks instead.

Money There's no shortage of choice in this banking city for exchanging money or seeking credit card cash advances. Unfortunately some banks have now introduced commission charges for cash exchanges (eg, Sfr5 in UBS, Sfr2.50 in Credit Suisse); this doesn't apply to cashing travellers cheques. Most banks are open 8.15 am to 4.30 pm Monday to Friday (6 pm Thursday), though a few branches keep later hours.

The exchange office in the main hall of the Hauptbahnhof is open 6.30 am to 10.45 pm daily (no commission charges). In the airport, don't change banknotes at the UBS bank

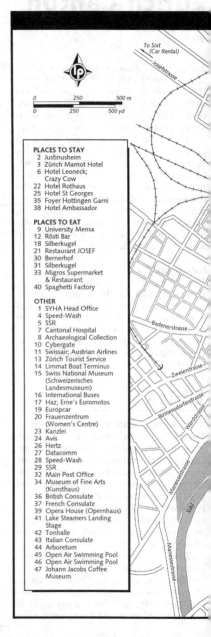

PLACES TO STAY
2   Justinusheim
3   Zürich Marriot Hotel
6   Hotel Leoneck;
     Crazy Cow
22 Hotel Rothaus
25 Hotel St Georges
35 Foyer Hottingen Garni
38 Hotel Ambassador

PLACES TO EAT
9   University Mensa
12 Rösti Bar
18 Silberkugel
21 Restaurant JOSEF
30 Bernerhof
31 Silberkugel
33 Migros Supermarket
     & Restaurant
40 Spaghetti Factory

OTHER
1   SYHA Head Office
4   Speed-Wash
5   SSR
7   Cantonal Hospital
8   Archaeological Collection
10 Cybergate
11 Swissair; Austrian Airlines
13 Zürich Tourist Service
14 Limmat Boat Terminus
15 Swiss National Museum
     (Schweizerisches
     Landesmuseum)
16 International Buses
17 Haz; Erne's Euromotos
19 Europcar
20 Frauenzentrum
     (Women's Centre)
23 Kanzlei
24 Avis
26 Hertz
27 Datacomm
28 Speed-Wash
29 SSR
32 Main Post Office
34 Museum of Fine Arts
     (Kunsthaus)
36 British Consulate
37 French Consulate
39 Opera House (Opernhaus)
41 Lake Steamers Landing
     Stage
42 Tonhalle
43 Italian Consulate
44 Arboretum
45 Open Air Swimming Pool
46 Open Air Swimming Pool
47 Johann Jacobs Coffee
     Museum

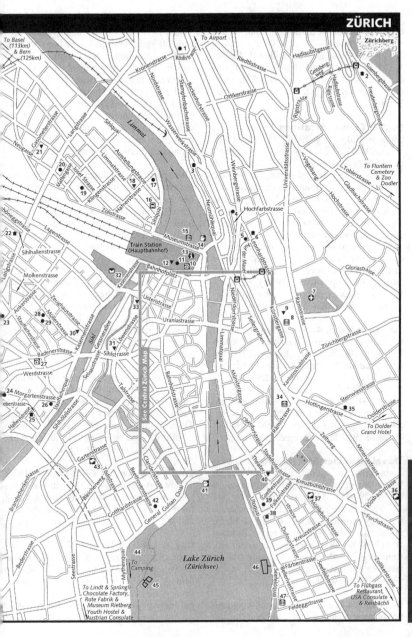

ZÜRICH

Zürichberg

To Basel
(113km)
& Bern
(125km)

To Airport

To Fluntern
Cemetery
& Zoo
Dodler

To Dolder
Grand Hotel

To Flühgass
Restaurant,
USA Consulate
& Reisbächli

Lake Zürich
(Zürichsee)

To Lindt & Sprüngli
Chocolate Factory,
Rote Fabrik &
Museum Rietberg
Youth Hostel &
Austrian Consulate

To
Camping

Train Station
(Hauptbahnhof)

See Central Zürich Map

ZÜRICH

(Sfr5 commission) – use the commission-free Credit Suisse, or the SBB counters in the airport train station.

The American Express office (CZ map; ☎ 228 77 77) at Uraniastrasse 14 has financial and travel services. It's open 8.30 am to 6 pm Monday to Friday and 9 am to noon Saturday.

Post & Communications The main post office is Sihlpost (☎ 296 21 11), Kasernenstrasse 95-97, 8021. It is open 7.30 am to 8 pm Monday to Friday, and 8 am to 4 pm Saturday. Like many other large Swiss post offices, there's a counter open daily (to 8 pm Saturday, 10.30 pm other days), but with a Sfr1 surcharge outside normal hours for many transactions (not payable when collecting poste restante).

The post office in the Hauptbahnhof is open normal hours. Swisscom has an office in the mid-lower level of the station main hall, which is open to 9 pm daily. There's a fax and telegram service, and many telephones – one with a modem connection.

Email & Internet Access In the main hall of the train station, part of the Stars bar/cafe, is Cybergate (@ info@stars.ch), open 11.30 am to 11 pm daily. It charges Sfr5 for 20 minutes, or Sfr10 per hour for children. Internet Café (CZ map;@ info@cafe.ch), Uraniastrasse 3, charges Sfr0.25 per minute. It's open 10 am to 11 pm daily (6 pm Monday). Datacomm (@ centerzuerich@ datacomm.ch), at Badenerstrasse 29, is less convenient but cheaper.

Travel Agencies SSR (@ info@ssr.ch) is a specialist in student, youth and budget fares. Branches are at Leonhardstrasse 10 (☎ 261 29 55) and Bäckerstrasse 40 (☎ 241 12 08). Both are open Monday afternoon to Saturday morning; or call ☎ 297 11 11 for telephone sales. Globetrotter (CZ map; ☎ 213 80 80, @ zuerich@globetrotter.ch), Rennweg 35, also has worldwide budget fares, and a travel noticeboard and magazine. It's open weekdays only.

Bookshops English and French-language books are available at Libraire Payot (see the Central Zürich map; ☎ 211 54 52), Bahnhofstrasse 9. It's closed till noon Monday and open till 8 pm Thursday. There is a very large general bookshop, Orell Füssli, at Füsslistrasse 4 (CZ map). Its English-language section is nearby at Bahnhofstrasse 70.

The Travel Book Shop (☎ 252 38 83; CZ map), Rindermarkt 20, has a huge selection of English-language travel books and can order anything you want. It also runs the map shop next door. It's closed till 1 pm Monday, otherwise hours are standard.

Libraries The Pestalozzi Library, Zäringerstrasse 17 (CZ map), has magazines and newspapers in English. The reading room is open 9 am to 8 pm weekdays and until 5 pm Saturday. The nearby Zentralbibliothek (Central Library) Zähringerplatz, has English books and computer terminals.

Laundry Speed-Wash (☎ 242 99 14), at Weinbergstrasse 37 and Müllerstrasse 55, is self-service. Machines cost from Sfr5.50 to wash and Sfr1.50 per 10 minutes for drying. They're open daily until 10.30 pm. The Waschsbär, Mühlegasse 11, is more central but charges Sfr17 to wash and dry (closed weekends).

Medical Services For emergency medical and dental help, ring ☎ 261 61 00. The Cantonal University Hospital (☎ 255 11 11), Ramistrasse 100, has a casualty department. There is a 24-hour chemist at Bellevue Apotheke (see the Central Zürich map; ☎ 252 56 00), Theaterstrasse 14.

Emergency The police (CZ map; ☎ 216 71 11) are at Bahnhofquai 3. The national emergency numbers are: ☎ 117 for police, ☎ 118 for the fire brigade, ☎ 144 for an ambulance and ☎ 140 for the car breakdown service.

Gay & Lesbian Haz (☎ 271 22 50), 3rd floor, Sihlquai 67, is a gay and lesbian centre, open 7.30 pm to 11 pm Tuesday to Friday, and noon to 2 pm Sunday. It has a library, cafe (open Friday), distributes the gay newspaper *Cruiser*, and has a list of Zürich's gay venues. Helplines are: gays

(☎ 271 70 11), open 8 to 10 pm Tuesday and Thursday; lesbians (☎ 272 73 71), open 6 to 8 pm Thursday. The Frauenzentrum (see next heading) organises lesbian events.

Women Travellers Frauenzentrum (☎ 272 85 03, ✉ frauenzentrum@ access.ch), Mattengasse 27, is a women's centre which has a health centre (☎ 272 77 50) and a bar on the premises.

Toilets Zürich Hauptbahnhof has expensive toilets (Sfr2) – they're cheaper in the adjoining Shop Ville.

Walking Tour

The pedestrian streets of the Old Town on either side of the Limmat River contain most of the major sights (CZ map). Features to notice are winding alleyways, 16th- and 17th-century houses and guildhalls, courtyards and fountains. Zürich has 1030 fountains and the locals insist the water is drinkable in them all. Don't be surprised if a waiter heads for the nearest fountain if you ask for tap water in a restaurant!

Lindenhof, a raised terrace on the west bank, has trees, gravel and giant chess games. This is the spot where the Romans

---

The Birth of Dada

Dada was a phenomenon that delighted in contradictions. It was an art movement that was anti-art. It had an intellectual dimension, yielding countless erudite polemics, yet was also fun, rebellious, and often plain strange. It used manufactured objects and re-defined them as art; it delighted in chance outcomes. Dada was short-lived but very influential, and paved the way for Surrealism.

The birth of the movement is accepted to be the creation of the Cabaret Voltaire in February 1916 by Hugo Ball. Raucous artistic events (including poetry, singing and dancing) were held at a room in a pub at Spiegelgasse 1, in the heart of the Old Town. The Alsatian artist, Hans Arp, and especially the Romanian poet, Tristan Tzara, were key figures in these early days.

---

founded their customs post in 15 BC. The elegant **Bahnhofstrasse** was built on the site of the city walls which were torn down 150 years ago. Underfoot are bank vaults crammed full of gold and silver. Zürich is one of the world's premier precious metals markets but the vaults (for some reason) aren't open to the public. The 13th-century tower of **St Peter's Church**, St Peterhofstatt, has the largest clock face in Europe (8.7m in diameter). The **Fraumünster Church** nearby is noted for the distinctive stained-glass windows in the choir, created by Marc Chagall in 1970, and completed when he was 83. The building itself dates from the 13th century (closed lunchtime). Augusto Giacometti also made a window here, as well as in the **Grossmünster Cathedral** across the river, where Zwingli preached his message of 'pray and work' in the 16th century. The figure glowering from the south tower of the Grossmünster is Charlemagne, who founded the church that was originally at this location. This part of Zürich was once an island, said to be the burial site of the town's patron saints, Felix and Regula, who, legend has it, carried their heads here after they were decapitated by the Romans.

Museums

Museum of Fine Arts This Museum of Fine Arts (☎ 251 67 65), Heimplatz 1, is one of the most important of Zürich's many museums. The large permanent collection ranges from 15th-century religious art to the various schools of modern art. Most big names, such as Dali, Arp, Man Ray, Hockney, Bacon, Cézanne, Renoir, Manet, Monet and Gauguin have works on display. There's a fair sprinkling of Picassos, a whole room devoted to Marc Chagall and the largest Edvard Munch collection outside Scandinavia. Franz Gertsch's *Franz und Luciano (1973)* is a remarkable image in the photorealism genre, capturing seventies fashion.

Swiss artists are well represented, too. Johan Heinrich Füssli (1741-1825) favours waif-like, pale figures against dark backgrounds. Ferdinand Hodler's *Einmutigkeit* depicts a show-of-hands vote and dominates

ZÜRICH

CENTRAL ZÜRICH

Train Station
(Hauptbahnhof)
Bahnhofplatz
Bahnhof Brücke
Central
3

Gessneralle
Löwenstrasse
Schützengasse
Waisenhausstrasse
Bahnhofquai
1
2
4
5
7
6

Usteristrasse
Linthescher gasse
Bahnhofstrasse
Beatengasse
Beatenplatz
Mühlesteg
Limmatquai
Niederdorfstrasse
Zähringerstrasse
Hirschengraben
Seilergraben

Löwenstrasse
Seidengasse
Werdmühlestrasse
Werd-
mühle-
platz
Amtshäuser
13
Rudolf Brun
Brücke
Limmat River
11 10
9
8
Mühlegasse
Zähringerplatz
To
Hospital

19
18 17
Uraniastrasse
16 15
14
12

Stein-
mühleplatz
Sihlstrasse
Bahnhofstrasse
Oetenbachgasse
Rennweg
Hirsch
Spitalgasse
31
32
33
Predigergasse

20
Sihlstrasse
Füsslistrasse
22
23
24
25
Fortunagasse
Kuttelgasse
Lindenhof
26
Schipfe
30
Rosengasse
Brunngasse
28
29
27
Neumarkt

21
St Annagasse
Pelikanstrasse
Wohllebgasse
Rindermarkt
34
35
36
Leuengasse
Untere Zäune

Bahnhofstrasse
Strehlgasse
Rathaus
Brücke
37
Marktgasse
38
Ankengasse
Schoffelgasse
39
40
41
Spiegelgasse
Obere Zäune

43
St Peterstrasse
42
Storchengasse
Limmat River
Limmat Quai
Kirchgasse
52

44
48
47
In Gassen
49
Münsterbrücke
50
51
Kirch gasse
Oberdorfstrasse
Trittligasse

45
46
Poststrasse
Kappelerstrasse
Fraumünsterstrasse
Stadthausquai
Limmat Quai
Geiger
Uto Quai
Kruggasse

Talacker
Bärengasse
Talstrasse
Schanzen Graben
Bleicherweg
58
57
Börsenstrasse
Bahnhofstrasse
Quai Brücke
56
Uto Quai
Bellevueplatz
53
55
54
Rämistrasse
Stadelhoferstrasse
Theaterstrasse

ZÜRICH

0   100   200 m
0   100   200 yd

LP

CENTRAL ZÜRICH

PLACES TO STAY
2   Hotel Limmathof
5   Hotel Leonhard
4   Du Théâtre
7   Hotel Martahaus
8   Hotel Scheuble
11   Alexander Guesthouse
21   Hotel Glockenhof
29   City Backpacker
30   Hotel Splendid
31   Goldenes Schwert Hotel
37   Zic-Zac Rock-Hotel

PLACES TO EAT
1   Coop Supermarket
3   Mensa Polyterrace
15   Brasserie Lipp
18   Manora
20   Hiltl Vegi
23   Coop Restaurant &
       Supermarket
26   EAM

27   Gran Café
28   Königstuhl
32   Café Zähringer
39   Café Schlauch
40   Bodega Española
41   Mère Catherine
43   Cafeteria zur Münz
47   Zeughauskeller
48   Restaurant Kropf
54   EPA Department Store
55   Kronenhalle

OTHER
6   Rheinfelder Bierhalle
9   Pestalozzi Library
11   Heimatwerk
13   Police Station
14   Internet Café
16   Orell Füssli (English Books)
17   Credit Suisse Bank
19   American Express
22   Orell Füssli (Bookshop)

24   Globetrotter Travel
       Agency
25   Zürich Toy Museum
31   Barfüsser
33   Central Library
34   The Travel Bookshop
35   Oliver Twist
38   Älplibar
42   St Peter's Church
44   Beyer Museum
45   UBS Bank
47   Sprüngli
49   Zunfthaus zur Meisen
       Guildhall
50   Fraumünster Church
51   Grossmünster Cathedral
52   German Consulate
53   Bellevue Apotheke
56   Bürkliplatz
57   Zürcher Kantonalbank &
       Billettzentrale
58   Libraire Payot

the stairway. On the 1st floor are many sculptures by Alberto Giacometti (pin-headed, lumpy, skinny figures with seven-league boots) and some of his paintings. The gallery is open 10 am to 9 pm Tuesday to Thursday, and 10 am to 5 pm Friday to Sunday. Entry costs Sfr6 (students and seniors Sfr4) except on Sunday when it's free. Temporary exhibitions always cost extra.

Swiss National Museum The Swiss National Museum (Schweizerisches Landesmuseum; Museumstrasse 2, is housed in a pseudo-castle built in 1898. It gives the ultimate rundown on Swiss life and times from the prehistoric to the present. It exhibits a good selection of church art, plus weapons, coins, room interiors, costumes and utensils. The fresco in the Hall of Arms, the *Retreat of the Swiss Confederates at Marignano* is by Ferdinand Hodler. In the basement there's an interesting section on book-inscribing in the Middle Ages (you'll discover that the colour purple was extracted from snails), including some fine facsimiles of 14th-century books to leaf through. Opening hours are 10.30 am to 5 pm Tuesday to Sunday and entry to the permanent collection is free. Some signs are in English.

Other Museums The tourist office has information on many other museums, covering a range of interests. The **Zunfthaus zur Meisen** guildhall (CZ map), Münsterhof 20, was built in the 18th century and houses a collection of ceramics. Admission is free and it's closed on Monday. Also free is the **Zürich Toy Museum** (Züricher Spielzeugmuseum; CZ map) at Fortunagasse 15 (closed mornings and Sunday). The measurement of time is the theme in the **Beyer Museum** at Bahnhofstrasse 31, open 2 to 6 pm Monday to Friday (free entry). In the university on Rämistrasse 73, is an **Archaeological Collection** (Archäologische Sammlung), mainly from southern Europe and the Middle East. It is open 1 to 6 pm Tuesday to Friday and 11 am to 5 pm weekends; entry is free. **Museum Rietberg**, Gablerstrasse 15 (off Zürich map), to the south (take tram No 7), has non-European art and artifacts. It's open 10 am to 5 pm Tuesday to Sunday (Sfr5, students Sfr3). Look out also for the numerous private art galleries around the city.

The **Lindt & Sprüngli chocolate factory** (☎ 716 22 33) is a few kilometres south of the centre at Seestrasse 204 (take bus No 165 from Bürkliplatz to Schooren, or

S-Bahn No 1 or 8 to Kilchberg). It has a free museum (ask for the extensive English notes) and a rather self-congratulatory film, but it's well worth visiting, not least for the very generous free gift of chocolate at the end. It's open 10 am to noon and 1 to 4 pm Wednesday to Friday. Coffee-lovers might want to make it to the free **Johann Jacobs Coffee Museum** (☎ 388 61 51), Seefeld-Quai 17, at 2 to 5 pm Friday and Saturday or 10 am to 5 pm Sunday.

Zoo
Zoo Dolder, Zürichbergstrasse 221, vies with the zoo in Basel for the status of being the most important in the country. Whereas Basel's zoo is in the city centre, this one is on the Zürichberg, allowing it to spread out more. It has 250 animal species from all around the world, in all about 2500 animals. It's open 8 am to 6 pm daily. Entry costs Sfr14 (students Sfr7) and you can get there by tram No 5 or 6 from the town centre. The zoo backs on to Zürichberg woods, ideal for walks away from the noise of the city.

Activities
Don't neglect a stroll around the shores of Lake Zürich. The concrete walkways give way to trees and lawns in the Arboretum on the west bank. Look out for the flower clockface at nearby Bürkliplatz. On the east bank, the Zürichhorn park has sculptures (eg, by Jean Tinguely), and a Chinese Garden that's apparently the most important one outside China (Sfr4, open daily), but there's not much to it.

Designated areas for outdoor swimming and sunbathing are open from May to September, and entry costs Sfr6. Well-known places are Utoquai, Uto-Quai 49, on the east shore of the lake and Mythenquai, Mythen-Quai 95, on the west shore. There are also various free swimming spots, such as just north of the confluence of the Sihl and Limmat rivers.

Many sports and activities are listed in *Zürich News*, or for more details ask for *Sport in Zürich*; both are free from the tourist office.

Courses
Numerous options are listed under *Bildung* in the *Züritipp* magazine, available in the tourist office. Perhaps the best organisation for education courses, including language courses, is the Migros Klubschule (☎ 277 27 44, fax 277 28 97), Limmatstrasse 152.

Organised Tours
Informative if expensive guided walks around the Old Town, organised by the tourist office from 1 May to 31 October, last around 2½ hours and cost Sfr18 (Sfr9 for students and children). The tourist office books tours ranging from a two-hour motorised tour of Zürich (Sfr29, in an antique-style 'classic trolley') to day trips to Mt Titlis (Sfr110) and Lucerne (Sfr45). These are available year-round.

Special Events
Most shops are shut in the afternoon on the third Monday in April when Zürich's spring festival, **Sechseläuten**, is held. Guild members parade down the streets in historical costume and later complete a tour of the guildhalls, playing music. A fireworks-filled 'snowman' (the *Böögg)*, is ignited at 6 pm to celebrate the end of winter. Another local holiday is **Knabenschiessen**, held during the second weekend of September. Events revolve around a shooting competition for 12 to 16-year-old youths. In November's **Expovina**, wines from around the world can be sampled on the boats on Bürkliplatz (there's an entry fee).

Fasnacht brings lively musicians and a large, costumed procession. The carnival commences with typical Swiss precision at 11.11 am on 11 November, but the big parades and the liveliest atmosphere is saved until late February. During the **Züri Fäscht** a huge fairground takes over central Zürich and there's a lavish fireworks display. It's only held once every three years, from Friday to Sunday at the start of July; the next is 6 to 8 July, 2001. The **Zürcher festspiele**, mid-June to mid-July, concentrates on music and the arts, and the **Züri Jazz Woche** takes place in early September.

Holy Cow! Don't Jump!

UBS Headquarters - magnet for foreign funds

Shop selling hemp products, Zürich

Chagall Window in the Fraumünster, Zürich

Streetscape, Zürich

"Schoggi" souvenir anyone?

And they're on the track...

View from the Limmatbrücke

Zürich's Paradeplatz and the tower of St Peter's Church

Places to Stay

Accommodation can be a problem, particularly from August to October, and cheaper hotels fill early. Book ahead if you can, or use the information board and free phone in the train station. The tourist office accommodation service can sometimes get lower rates than those published. Private rooms are virtually nonexistent. Central hotels, although more convenient, are noisier, and parking can be a problem.

Places to Stay – Budget

Camping *Camping Seebucht* (☎ 482 16 12, Seestrasse 559) is on the west shore of the lake, 4km from the city centre. It's well signposted, open from 1 May to 30 September, and can be reached by bus No 161 or 165 from Bürkliplatz. It has good facilities including a shop and cafe, but travellers report that staff have a bad attitude towards young backpackers. Prices are Sfr8.50 per adult, Sfr12 for a tent, Sfr3 for parking or Sfr16 for a camper van.

Hostels Note that some budget hotels mentioned later offer dorm beds.

The SYHA *hostel* (☎ 482 35 44, fax 480 17 27, Mutschellenstrasse 114, Wollishofen) has 24-hour service. To get there, take tram No 6 or 7 to Morgental, or the S-Bahn to Wollishofen. Four or six-bed dorms (with lockers; own padlock needed) are Sfr31, and doubles are Sfr90. There's a restaurant, laundry facilities (Sfr8 to wash and dry), TV room (with CNN) and games.

City Backpacker (CZ map; ☎ 251 90 15, fax 251 90 24, ✉ backpacker@ access.ch, Niederdorfstrasse 5), also known as Hotel Biber, is more convenient. Singles/doubles are Sfr65/88 and triples/quads are Sfr120/156, all with sheets. Dorms are Sfr29, though sheets are Sfr3 unless you have your own. Prices are without breakfast but there are kitchens, Internet access, a rooftop area and hall showers. Reception is closed noon to 3 pm.

Hotels *Hotel Martahaus* (CZ map; ☎ 251 45 50, fax 251 45 40, ✉ info@martahaus.ch, Zähringerstrasse 36) is well located in the Old Town. Singles/doubles/triples cost Sfr70/98/120, and Sfr35 gets you a place in a six-bed dorm which is separated into individual cubicles by partitions and curtains. There is a comfortable lounge and breakfast room, and a shower on each floor. Book ahead (telephone reservations OK), particularly for single rooms. Prices reduce slightly in winter, and there's also one apartment with shower/WC and TV (from Sfr150).

Foyer Hottingen Garni (☎ 256 19 19, fax 256 19 00, Hottingerstrasse 31) has a calm ambience and kitchen facilities. Singles/doubles with shower/WC are Sfr95/140 or Sfr65/100 without; triples/quads are Sfr180/200 with, Sfr130/160 without. Prices are slightly lower in winter. Dorms are for women only and cost Sfr30. Telephone reservations are accepted.

Justinusheim (☎ 361 38 06, fax 362 29 82, Freudenbergstrasse 146) is a student home. Most beds are available during student holidays (particularly from mid-July to mid-October), though it usually has a few vacancies in term time too. Singles/doubles are Sfr60/100 with shower or Sfr50/80 without. Triples are Sfr120/140 with/without. It's just a few paces away from the woods of Zürichberg, in an attractive old building with balconies, a terrace and good views of Zürich and the lake. Take tram No 10 from the Hauptbahnhof to Rigiplatz and then the Seilbahn to the top (it runs every few minutes and city network tickets are valid).

Hotel Splendid (CZ map; ☎ 252 58 50, fax 261 25 59, Rosengasse 5) is good value, and offers 43 beds in renovated rooms in the Old Town. Singles/doubles/triples for Sfr56/93/123 are with hall showers. The optional breakfast is Sfr9.50 and there's live piano music nightly in the bar downstairs (open till 2 am).

Zic-Zac Rock-Hotel (CZ map; ☎ 261 21 81, fax 261 21 75, ✉ rockhotel.ch@ bluewin.ch, Marktgasse 17) is nearby Hotel Splendid. This theme hotel has varying rooms with rock pics and gold discs. Singles/doubles are around Sfr80/150 with shower or Sfr60/110 without, and breakfast is Sfr4.50. There's the lively Rock-Garden cafe downstairs.

ZÜRICH

Hotel Rothaus (☎ 241 24 51, fax 291 09 95, Sihlhallenstrasse 1), is in a seedy part of town south-west of the station, but has reasonable rooms with shower/WC and TV. Prices start as low as Sfr60/98, depending on room size and length of stay.

Hotel St Georges (☎ 241 11 44, fax 241 11 42, Weberstrasse 11), on the west bank of the Sihl river, is quiet and comfortable and has a lift. Most singles/doubles are Sfr74/96, though there are also a few with private shower/WC for Sfr97/130.

Places to Stay – Mid-Range

In the city centre, *Hotel Limmathof* (CZ map, ☎ 261 42 20, fax 262 02 17, Limmatquai 142) has modern fittings but you may experience slight noise from the adjoining funicular and tram stops. Singles/doubles with bath or shower and WC are from Sfr100/132, and triples are Sfr198.

Close by and slightly better is the small-scale *Hotel Leonhard* (☎ 251 30 80, fax 252 38 70, ❷ leonhard@ access.ch, Limmatquai 136), charging up to Sfr140/180. A larger, similar-standard place is *Hotel Leoneck* (☎ 261 60 70, ❷ leoneckhotel@bluewin.ch, Leonhardstrasse 1), where rooms sport Swiss folklore murals. Prices (up to Sfr130/175) are flexible, depending on demand, and there's no breakfast.

Alexander Guesthouse (CZ map; ☎ 251 82 03, fax 252 74 25, ❷ info@ hotel-alexander.ch, Niederdorfstrasse 40), offers shower/WC and TV as standard. Rooms cost from Sfr95/140 in the nearby guesthouse, which gives the best value. They're Sfr145/200 in the main hotel, though here nearly all have air-conditioning.

Goldenes Schwert (☎ 266 18 18, fax 266 18 88, ❷ hotel@rainbow.ch, Marktgasse 14) has creatively-decorated rooms for Sfr130/160 with private bath and toilet. It's a gay-friendly hotel and one floor has elaborate gay-themed rooms. Breakfast (Sfr9.50) is via room service. There's a disco downstairs.

The following three-star places all have singles/doubles with shower/WC, cable TV and telephone. The *Hotel Scheuble* (☎ 251 87 95, fax 251 76 78, ❷ info@scheuble.ch, CZ map), is in the Old Town at Mühlegasse

17, and has sizeable, fairly cosy singles/doubles starting at Sfr120/150 in winter and Sfr150/170 in summer.

Also good is the *Du Théâtre* (☎ 252 60 62, fax 252 01 54, ❷ hotel-du-theatre@ swissonline.ch) nearby at Seilergraben 69, with rooms for Sfr120/170 in summer, Sfr90/130 in winter. Prices will increase slightly once renovations are completed.

Places to Stay – Top End

All rooms mentioned in this section have private shower or bath, toilet, TV and other luxuries. The four-star *Hotel Glockenhof* (☎ 211 56 50, fax 211 56 60, ❷ glockenhof@ access.ch, Sihlstrasse 31) has renovated singles/doubles from Sfr230/340, and a pleasant garden restaurant and terrace. The rooms are quiet and there is good disabled access.

Hotel Ambassador (☎ 261 76 00, fax 251 23 94, ❷ mail@ambassadorhotel.ch, Falkenstrasse 6), is near the lake but without lake views. Standard four-star rooms are Sfr260/360, with reductions at weekends and in January, February, July and August.

The top hotels in Zürich are very nearly the top hotels in the world. The pick of them all is perhaps the *Dolder Grand Hotel* (☎269 30 00, fax 269 30 01, ❷ reservations@dodlergrand.ch, Kurhausstrasse 65). This hotel has turrets and balconies and occupies a quiet and panoramic position on the edge of the Zürichberg. It has a whole heap of facilities including a nine-hole golf course, tennis courts, swimming pool, and ice rink (in winter), all of which are free to guests. Its restaurant is also highly rated, especially for its French cuisine. There is garage parking, or to get there by public transport take tram No 3, 8 or 15 to Römerhof and the Dolderbahn from there. Rooms cost upwards from Sfr400/550 for singles/doubles.

Slightly more affordable luxury comes from the modern high-rise *Zürich Marriot Hotel* (☎ 360 70 70, fax 360 77 77, Neumühlequai 42), overlooking the Limmat River. Facilities include an indoor swimming pool, a sauna and health club. Singles/doubles start at Sfr255/275, without breakfast.

Places to Eat

Zürich has hundreds of restaurants serving all types of regional and international cuisine. A local speciality is Geschnetzeltes Kalbsfleisch (thinly sliced veal in a cream sauce). The large *Coop* supermarket opposite the Hauptbahnhof (CZ map) has a snack section serving hot food. The *Migros* supermarket under the station in Bahnhofpassage is open till 8 pm daily. Beer halls (see the Entertainment section) are often good places for an inexpensive meal and there's also fast-food stands which offer Bratwurst and bread from around Sfr5.50. From the tourist office, *Zürich News* lists a variety of restaurants, or there's the more detailed *Gastro Züri-Guide*.

Places to Eat – Budget

Self-Catering *Mensa Polyterrace (Leonhardstrasse 34, CZ map)* is next to the Polybahn Seilbahn (funicular) exit, overlooking the city. It has good meals for Sfr10.50 (Sfr8.10 for ISIC holders) including vegetarian options. The self-service counters are open 11.15 am to 1.30 pm and 5.30 to 7.15 pm Monday to Friday, and 11.30 am to 1 pm every second Saturday. From early July to early October it's open for lunch only. There is a busy cafe upstairs which is open longer hours. Just along the road is another *Mensa* in the university building, Rämistrasse 71 (enter from Künstlergasse), open 7.30 am to 8 pm Monday to Friday, and alternate Saturdays to the Polyterrace.

The underground area by the station is called Shop Ville, and it's a good place to find cheap food. *Silberkugel* is a basic cafe and takeaway with very low prices, open until 10 pm daily (7.30 pm Sunday). At the western end is *Restaurant Marché Mövenpick*, where well-presented buffet-style food costs around Sfr10 to Sfr18. Salad or vegetable plates are Sfr4.10 to Sfr10.90, and it's open 6.30 am (7.30 am Sunday) to 11 pm daily. Other branches of Silberkugel are at Löwenstrasse and Limmatstrasse.

The *EPA* department store on Bellevueplatz (CZ map) has a very cheap self-service restaurant. The Manor department store on Bahnhofstrasse has a good *Manora* buffet-style restaurant (CZ map), and there

is a *Migros* restaurant in the Migros City shopping centre at Löwenstrasse 35. A *Coop* restaurant and supermarket is in the Annahof department store on Bahnhofstrasse (CZ map). All these places are open until 8 pm weekdays and 4 pm on Saturday.

East Bank In the centre, explore the smaller streets off the main thoroughfares for the best value. *Café Schlauch (CZ map; Münstergasse 20)* offers an unusual combination of pocket-less pool tables and food encompassing free-range meat and vegetarian dishes (from Sfr12). It's closed on Monday and Tuesday.

An 'alternative' cafe, run by a collective, is *Café Zähringer* on Spitalgasse (CZ map). It serves up mostly organic, vegetarian food (from Sfr15), and is a good place for a coffee and a game of chess. Most Wednesday nights there's live music (sometimes free; not in summer). It's open till midnight daily, though it's shut until 6 pm on Monday.

Gran Café (CZ map; Limmatquai 66) does look fairly grand, but usually has a bargain meal, such as all-you-can-eat spaghetti for Sfr9.50. There are also numerous types of coffee on offer (open daily).

The *Spaghetti Factory (Theater Strasse 10 and elsewhere)* has pizza and pasta for Sfr11 to Sfr21. They're of interest to late-night revellers as they keep late hours – this one is open 11 am to 2 am (to 4 am Saturday, to 7 am Sunday).

Crazy Cow (Leonhardstrasse 1) is a popular, quirky, fun place serving Swiss food from about Sfr16. Bread arrives in its own slipper (don't ask me why). It's open 6 am to midnight daily.

West Bank For a range of Rösti, try the inexpensive *Rösti Bar* in the main hall of the train station (open daily).

EAM (CZ map; Schipfe 16) is a busy little place with outside tables overlooking the Limmat River. Menus with soup start from just Sfr10.50 and it is open daytime, Monday to Friday.

Bernerhof (Zeughausstrasse 1) has satisfying, filling food in an unpretentious

ZÜRICH

environment. Several daily menus from Sfr12 (including soup) are available midday and evening. At night, locals come to drink and play cards and board games. Hot food stops around 9 pm. It closes at 6 pm Saturday and is closed all day Sunday.

Cafeteria zur Münz (CZ map, *Münzplatz 3*) features Jean Tinguely mobiles hanging from the ceiling. It is open 6.30 am to 7 pm Monday, Tuesday and Friday, till 8 pm Wednesday and Thursday, and 8 am to 5 pm Saturday.

Places to Eat – Mid-Range

Vegetarians will have a field day in the meat-free environment of *Hilti* (CZ map; ☎ 227 7000, *Sihlstrasse 28*), on two floors. Varied lunches cost from Sfr16 and the salad buffet is very extensive but quite expensive (100 grams for Sfr3.90, or Sfr2.90 takeaway). Every evening at 5 pm there's an Indian buffet which costs Sfr4.50 per 100 grams, or it's Sfr38 for all you can eat.

Splurge on French food amid the mirrors and gleaming metal of *Brasserie Lipp Restaurant* (CZ map; ☎ 211 11 55, *Urania-strasse 9*). The décor reflects the Parisien Belle Epoque period. A clientele of all ages is attracted by the wide choice of sumptuous dishes in the Sfr20 to Sfr40 range (open daily). Servings are generous and there are English menus.

Restaurant JOSEF (☎ 271 65 95, *Gasometerstrasse 24*) attracts mainly youngish, trendy diners with its changing daily specials for around Sfr25 to Sfr40. It's closed Saturday and Sunday lunchtime, and has a bar area. Reservations are advised.

To sample quality Spanish fare (Sfr17 to Sfr45) go to *Bodega Española* (CZ map; ☎ 251 23 10) on the 1st floor at Münstergasse 15. The paella (Sfr37 per person) is a popular choice here, and rightly so. There is a good selection of Spanish wines from Sfr33.50 a bottle. Reserve ahead (open daily). The cafe-bar downstairs also does food.

Mère Catherine (CZ map; ☎ 250 59 40, *Nägelhof 3*) near Schoffelgasse, is a popular French restaurant in a small courtyard. It's open 11 am to midnight daily. Main courses

are about Sfr19.50 to Sfr38, though weekday lunch menus are Sfr15.50 and Sfr17.50.

Housed in a former armoury, *Zeughaus-keller* (CZ map; *Bahnhofstrasse 28*), is an atmospheric, busy restaurant serving decent portions of Swiss food for around Sfr15 to Sfr30 (open daily). Close by and slightly pricier is *Restaurant Kropf* (CZ map; *In Gassen 16*), another historic place with murals and ornate pillars. It's closed on Sunday and holidays.

Places to Eat – Top End

As you might expect, there are plenty of these. *Königstuhl* (CZ map; ☎ 261 76 18) on the 1st floor of Stüssihofstatt 3, has vivid decor and cultured cuisine (main courses from Sfr32; closed Sunday and Monday). The bistro downstairs is cheaper (different menu, same kitchen), less formal and open daily.

Kronenhalle (CZ map; ☎ 251 66 69, *Rämistrasse 4*), is a long-established restaurant attracting the artistic elite. Many original artworks (especially by Chagall) hang on the walls. Swiss/French dishes are Sfr25 to Sfr58 and it's open daily.

Flühgass (☎ 381 12 15, *Zollikerstrasse 214*), 2km from the centre on the east bank, is the gourmet's choice for French food. *Riesbächli* (☎ 422 23 24) is another top restaurant – it's a little out of the way at Zollikerstrasse 157. Both places are closed on Saturday and Sunday.

Entertainment

Pick up free from the tourist office the events magazine, *Züritipp*. If you have the money and inclination to visit lots of bars and clubs, the Zürich Night Card (Sfr20, valid three nights) has useful benefits; inquire at the tourist office.

Tickets for most events in the city can be obtained from the *Billettzentrale* (CZ map; ☎ 221 22 83, *Bahnhofstrasse 9*). Prices are usually the same as buying direct from the venue concerned. It's open 10 am to 6.30 pm Monday to Friday, to 2 pm Saturday, except in July and August when activity in the arts die down. Zürich has a famous orchestra, the *Tonhalle*, which performs in the venue of the

ame name (☎ 206 34 34) at Claridenstrasse
7, as does the Zürich Chamber Orchestra.
Prices range from Sfr10 to Sfr125, depending
on the seat and the event. The *Opernhaus*
(Opera House; ☎ 268 66 66, Falkenstrasse 1)
also has a world-wide reputation.

The *Comedy Club* performs plays in
English. Venues vary, so check the events
magazines. Cinema prices are reduced to
Sfr11 or Sfr12 every Monday from their
normal price of around Sfr15. Films are
usually in the original language.

Many late-night pubs, clubs and discos are
in Niederdorfstrasse and adjoining streets in
the Old Town. This area is also a red-light
district. If you're making a night of it in
Niederdorfstrasse, kick off with a few cheap
beers (Sfr4.70 for half a litre) at *Rheinfelder*
Bierhalle at No 76 (CZ map). The food is
tasty and good value, with all-day menus including soup starting from Sfr13.50, and
other meals from Sfr10. Opening hours are 9
am to midnight daily. There are many other
beer halls in this part of town.

Oliver Twist (Rindermarkt 6) is a magnet
for English speakers, with draught Guinness and Irish and British sports on satellite
TV. Happy hour is 5 to 7 pm on weekdays
(open daily).

Älplibar (Ankengasse 5) is a rustic bar,
with Swiss folklore music (free) and fondue
for Sfr22. It's open from 6 pm nightly.

Rote Fabrik (☎ 481 91 21 for music,
☎ 482 42 12 for theatre, Seestrasse 395), is
a venue for alternative arts, though it's getting more mainstream nowadays. It has
concerts most nights ranging from rock and
jazz to avant-garde (Sfr15 to Sfr305), as
well as original-language films, theatre,
dance, and a bar and restaurant. It's generally closed on Monday. Take Bus No 161 or
165 from Bürkliplatz. Its Web site is at
www.rotefabrik.ch.

Kanzlei, (☎ 241 53 11, Kanzleistrasse
56), another fairly alternative venue, has a
cinema (the Xenix Filmclub: ☎ 242 04 11),
bar and disco (mostly funk, house, techno).
Its Web site is at www.kanzlei.ch.

Barfüsser (☎ 251 40 64, Spitalgasse 14)
is Switzerland's oldest gay bar, open 5 pm
to midnight daily.

Zürich is also known for its rave/techno
parties, and has Europe's largest techno parade every August.

Spectator Sports
Zürich has two football teams, which means
there's a match in the city every weekend
during the season. Ice hockey is played at
the Hallenstadion in the district of Oerlikon.
In early August, Zürich hosts an important
international athletics meeting at the Letzi-
grund stadium (take tram No 2).

Shopping
Many shops are now open till 8 pm on weekdays; in Shop Ville under the Hauptbahnhof
a great variety of shops stay open every day.

Bahnhofstrasse is a famous shopping
street, and has large department stores, such
as Manor, and specialist shops. Sprüngli
(CZ map) is the place to go for quality confectionery.

Heimatwerk sells hand-made Swiss souvenirs, and the good quality is reflected in
the prices. There's a large store on the west
side of the Rudolf Brun bridge, and
branches in the train station and airport.

At Rosenhof, in the Old Town on the east
bank, there's a crafts market on Thursday
and Saturday.

Getting There & Away
Air The major gateway of Kloten Airport is
10km north of the city centre and has several daily flights to/from all important destinations. Swissair and Austrian Airlines
share an office in the Hauptbahnhof which
is open 8 am to 6 pm Monday to Friday and
8.30 am to 1 pm Saturday. For Swissair
reservations till 10 pm daily, ring ☎ 0848-
800 700 (local rate). The airport has two
terminals, A and B: Swissair and Crossair
are among the airlines using terminal A.

Train The busy Hauptbahnhof has direct
trains to Stuttgart (Sfr62), Munich (Sfr85),
Innsbruck (Sfr69) and Milan (Sfr75) as well
as to many other international destinations.
There are also hourly departures to most
Swiss towns, eg, Lucerne (Sfr22, 50 minutes), Bern (Sfr48, 70 minutes) and Basel

ZÜRICH

(Sfr31, 65 minutes). Winterthur (Sfr10.60) is only 20 minutes away by train and there are four to five departures an hour.

Car & Motorcycle The N3 approaches Zürich from the south along the shore of Lake Zürich. The N1 is the fastest route from Bern and Basel and the main entry point from the west. The N1 also services routes to the north and east of Zürich.

Rental The agencies Europcar (☎ 271 56 56), Josef Strasse 53, Hertz (☎ 242 84 84), Mortgartenstrasse 5 and Avis (☎ 296 87 87), Gartenhofstrasse 17, also have airport branches. See the introductory Getting Around chapter for rates.

Of the local firms, Unirent (☎ 363 61 11), Nordstrasse 110, charges from Sfr57 per day including 300km or Sfr279 per week with unlimited kilometres. Weekend deals at Sixt (☎ 445 90 90), Pfingstweidstrasse 3, start at Sfr133.

Motorcycle rental is at Erne's Euromotos (☎ 272 77 72, fax 272 82 83), Sihlquai 67, starting from Sfr50 per day.

Getting Around

To/From the Airport You're unlikely to need a taxi (around Sfr40). On average, five trains an hour go to/from the Hauptbahnhof between around 6 am and midnight, and the journey takes 10 minutes. Buy your ticket before boarding (Sfr5.40).

Public Transport There is a comprehensive and unified bus, tram and S-Bahn service in the city, which includes boats on the Limmat River. Operating times are approximately 5.30 am to midnight, and tickets

Zürich's Transport System.

In the 1970s Zürich's citizens voted against constructing an underground system, thereby forcing a re-introduction of the old city trams. Environmental concerns were paramount in this decision. It was backed up by the introduction of a non-profit ticket in the late 1980s for use on the city's public transport network. Zürich was anxious to avoid the situation in cities like Los Angeles where an unbelievable 70% of ground space is devoted to the motor car – in the form of roads, car parks, driveways and petrol stations. In contrast, thanks to Zürich's forward-looking transport policy, car-parking spaces have been gradually converted over to pedestrian areas with seating and planted shrubs. Motorists have been enticed and persuaded to use public transport for commuting. The city's environmentally-sound transport policy even extends to providing free use of bicycles.

For the most part, ex-motorists are happy to use the tram network. The Swiss have studied the problem of how to make public transport an acceptable option, and they have concluded that what is psychologically crucial is not how long the journey takes, but how long one expects it to take. Reliability is therefore the key. The progress of trams in Zürich is monitored by a series of ultra-sound beacons at the roadside (those inconspicuous little boxes at junctions) which are triggered by passing trams but are unaffected by normal traffic. The signals are relayed back to transport headquarters which then passes instructions to the appropriate driver to either speed up or slow down. If a rogue tram route is shown to be consistently behind time, the schedule is adjusted accordingly. Zürich trams, therefore, should always be on time.

But reliability isn't the only criterion: waiting time is important too. Studies also showed that the average limit of acceptability for waiting is 10 minutes. Most Zürich trams run at six-minute intervals.

Many other large cities in Switzerland now pursue similar transport policies, but it is a pity that more cities worldwide don't follow Zürich's lead. Zürich's streets have always been clean, but now the air is cleaner too – trams are much more environmentally friendly than cars. Road junctions are safer as well – everybody knows who has the right of way as trams *always* have priority over cars. And the greening of the city is another positive effect – it's much more enjoyable spending time in a tree-lined pedestrian cul-de-sac than in a concrete car park.

ZÜRICH

must be bought in advance from dispensers at stops. Selecting your desired ticket is reasonably straightforward – there are basic instructions in English – though there's a wide range of options. Your ticket allows you to switch between modes of transport as you like. Depending on the ticket, it must be validated on the bus/tram, etc, at the commencement of travel.

Short, single-trip *Kurzstrecke* tickets, valid for about five stops (destinations are listed on the ticket machine) are Sfr2.10. Tickets covering all Zürich city cost Sfr3.60 and are valid for one hour. It's worth getting a 24-hour city pass for Sfr7.20, or a strip of six passes for Sfr36 (validate once per person per day). The range of this ticket is sufficient for most purposes, including very short trips on the lake. Getting to the airport involves travel in an extra zone (Sfr10.80 for a 24-hour pass, including Zürich city).

A 24-hour pass valid for unlimited travel within the whole canton of Zürich costs Sfr28.40, including access to virtually all the lake. The *9-Uhr-Pass* is a canton-wide daily ticket for Sfr20, valid after 9 am on weekdays and all day on weekends. Zürich's suburban trains (S-Bahn) reach Baden, Schaffhausen, Stein am Rhein, Zug and Einsiedeln, but these places are just beyond the validity area of the cantonal ticket.

Weekend nightbuses (around Sfr5, passes not valid) depart from Bellevue at 1, 1.30 and 2 am for suburban destinations.

Taxi Taxis in Zürich are expensive even by Swiss standards, at Sfr6 plus Sfr3.20 per km, though this does include a tip. Taxi numbers include ☎ 222 22 22 and ☎ 444 44 44.

Car & Motorcycle The tourist office has a list of car-parking garages in Zürich (eg, there's one opposite the main post office). Parking on the street in the centre is a bit of a problem; streets with meters usually have a one hour (Sfr2) or two hour (Sfr5) maximum. Parking garages cost anything from Sfr1 to Sfr3.50 per hour, with the lowest rates applying to suburban garages. For unrestricted parking in blue zones, buy a day pass for Sfr10 from a police station.

Bicycle There's daily bike rental in the Hauptbahnhof through the SBB – see the Getting Around chapter for rates.

City bikes may be borrowed *free of charge* from various locations in the city. In the Hauptbahnhof they're at Velogate, from 6.30 am to 10 pm daily year-round. Bikes are available from 7.30 am to 9.30 pm daily, from 2 May to 31 October, from the following locations: near the Globus department store, Bahnhofstrasse; Tessinerplatz by Enge station; Theaterplatz near Stadelhofen station; Marktplatz near Oerlikon station; and Altstetterplatz, at Altstetten. A passport or identity card and Sfr20 must be left as a deposit.

Boat Lake steamers leave from Bürkliplatz, departing every 30 to 60 minutes from early April to late October (Swiss Pass and Eurail valid, Inter-Rail 50% discount). For boat information, phone ☎ 487 13 33.

AROUND ZÜRICH
Uetliberg
One of the best short excursions out of Zürich starts off with the train (line S10) to Uetliberg at 813m (23 minutes, departures every 30 minutes). From here, there is a panoramic two-hour **Planetary Path** (Planetenweg) running along the mountain ridge overlooking the lake to Felsenegg. En route you pass models of the planets in the solar system: these and the distances between them are on a scale of one to 1000 million. At Felsenegg, a cable car descends every 10 minutes to Adliswill, from where frequent trains return to Zürich (line S4, takes 16 minutes). The round-trip costs Sfr14.40, including a city pass (the tourist office sells tickets).

Maur
The village of Maur is close to Greifensee where swimming, boating and hiking are possible.

A good possibility for accommodation is in the farming village of Maur, 10km south-east of the city. Reinhard Lüder (☎ 01-980 22 48, @ reini@dataway.ch, Kehlhofstrasse 518) offers bed and breakfast in his 200-year old country house. This health-conscious and

ZÜRICH

friendly place has a kitchen, bike rental for only Sfr1 per day, laundry for Sfr3 per load, and occasional communal meals. Singles/doubles/triples are Sfr34/56/75, and every seventh night is free (telephone ahead).

Get to Maur from Zürich by taking tram No 3, 8 or 15 to Klusplatz, then a 20-minute bus ride on No 747 to Maur Dorf. The whole journey can be undertaken on a Sfr7.20 ticket (Sfr14.40 for a 24-hour pass).

Winterthur

☎ 052 • pop 90,000 • elevation 447m

Although a mechanical engineering and textiles centre, Winterthur attracts visitors with its impressive museums and art galleries – 15 in all.

Orientation & Information

Winterthur is in the north-east of Zürich canton and has a compact Old Town centre. The tourist office (☎ 267 67 00, fax 267 68 58, ℮ tourist-service@win.ch), is in the train station, near Platform 1. Opening hours are 8.30 am to 6.30 pm Monday to Friday, and 8.30 am to 4 pm Saturday. Pick up its extensive and free *Winterthurer Freizeitführer*, covering sightseeing, restaurants, bars and much else.

Budget travel agency, SSR (☎ 213 81 25), is at Neustadtgasse 1a, open Monday afternoon to Saturday morning.

The main post office (8401) is opposite the train station.

DataComm, Graben 30, has dozens of machines for Internet surfing (Sfr3/5 for 30/60 minutes). It's open 9 am to 10 pm Monday to Saturday and 2 to 8 pm Sunday. Internet Treff, Rudolfstrasse, offers free surfing noon to 5 pm Saturday.

Things to See & Do

Simply walking round the elegant pedestrian centre, with its tall, shuttered buildings

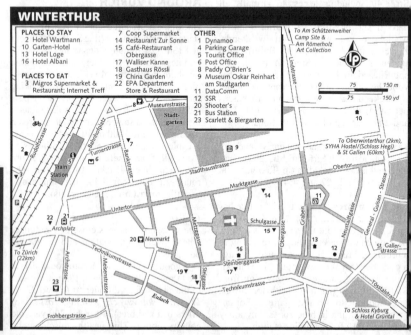

WINTERTHUR

PLACES TO STAY
2   Hotel Wartmann
10 Garten-Hotel
13 Hotel Loge
16 Hotel Albani

PLACES TO EAT
3   Migros Supermarket & Restaurant; Internet Treff

7   Coop Supermarket
14 Restaurant Zur Sonne
15 Café-Restaurant Obergasse
17 Walliser Kanne
18 Gasthaus Rössli
19 China Garden
22 EPA Department Store & Restaurant

OTHER
1   Dynamoo
4   Parking Garage
5   Tourist Office
6   Post Office
8   Paddy O'Brien's
9   Museum Oskar Reinhart am Stadtgarten
11 DataComm
12 SSR
20 Shooter's
21 Bus Station
23 Scarlett & Biergarten

To Am Schützenweiher
Camp Site &
Am Römerholz
Art Collection

To Oberwinterthur (2km),
SYHA Hostel/(Schloss Hegi)
& St Gallen (60km)

To Zürich
(22km)

To Schloss Kyburg
& Hotel Grüntal

and designer shops, is an enjoyable experience. If you're into museums, consider buying the museum pass for Sfr20/25/28, valid for one/two/three days. But note that some museums are free anyway.

Winterthur owes much of its eminence as a centre of art to Oskar Reinhart, who turned his back on the banking and insurance enterprises of his powerful family and collected art instead. Upon his death in 1965, the whole collection was bequeathed to the nation and entrusted to his home town. The **Sammlung Oskar Reinhart am Römerholz** is sited in his former home at Haldenstrasse 95, a 20-minute walk or short bus ride (No 3 to Spital) from the centre. The extensive impressionist section includes works by Van Gogh, Renoir, Manet, Monet and Cézanne, plus there are notable paintings by Rubens, Rembrandt, Greco and Goya.

Less well-known but conveniently central is the collection of Swiss, German and Austrian art at the **Museum Oskar Reinhart am Stadtgarten**, on Stadthausstrasse, which he established during his lifetime. Entry for each gallery costs Sfr8 (Sfr6 for students), or a combined ticket is Sfr12 (Sfr8) and they are open 10 am to 5 pm daily except Monday. The museum is on the border of the Stadtgarten, which is a relaxing park graced by several naked ladies (in statue form only).

The **Swiss Technorama**, Technoramastrasse 1 in Oberwinterthur, has hands-on exhibits and creative displays that demystify science and technology. It's open 10 am to 5 pm Tuesday to Sunday and costs Sfr15 (Sfr8 for children). To get there, take bus No 5 from the bus station to its terminus.

Winterthur also has four castles, including Schloss Hegi, which houses the SYHA hostel. The best is the **Schloss Kyburg**, 6km south of town over the Töss River. Dating from the 10th century, it was occupied by the Habsburgs for several centuries until possession was won by the city of Zürich in 1452. It has an interesting Romanesque chapel and makes a good starting place for a number of hikes. Admission costs Sfr4 (students and children Sfr2). Recently renovated, it's closed on Monday and in December.

Places to Stay

Finding accommodation can be difficult in spring and autumn when there are many trade conventions, but the tourist office can help with its free room-booking service for people who visit in person.

The camping site *Am Schützenweiher* (☎ 212 52 60, *Eichliwaldstrasse 4*), which is open year-round, is north-west of the centre by an area of woodland. Get there by taking bus No 3 to Seuzacherstrasse and walking five minutes north.

The SYHA *hostel* (☎ 242 38 40, *fax 242 58 30, Schloss Hegi, Hegifeldstrasse 125*) is in a 15th-century castle, and has large dorms where beds are just Sfr16, without breakfast. Reception is closed 10 am to 5 pm and the hostel is open from 1 March until 31 October. There's a kitchen. Take bus No 1 or the train to Oberwinterthur and then it's 10 to 15 minutes' walk to the castle.

Hotel prices are sky high in the centre. The cheapest place is *Albani* (☎ 212 69 96, *fax 212 69 86, Steinberggasse 16*), with singles/doubles/triples without breakfast for Sfr80/100/120. Rooms have TV, but the shower/WC is in the hall. It's only good value if you like music (see the following Entertainment section) – guests get free entry to see bands, though the bands themselves often occupy all the rooms.

Grüntal (☎ 232 25 52, *fax 232 25 33, Im Grüntal 1, Oberseen*) offers singles/doubles with private shower from Sfr75/120, and some showerless singles for Sfr65. It's south-east of town; take bus No 6. Light, sparsely-furnished rooms with shower/WC and cable TV are at *Hotel Loge* (☎ 213 91 21, *fax 212 09 59, ✉ hotelloge@ access.ch, Graben 6*) and cost Sfr145/175. There's a cinema and theatre downstairs, and a good restaurant.

Hotel Wartmann (☎ 212 84 21, *fax 213 30 97, ✉ wartmann@wartmann.ch, Rudolfstrasse 15*) has modern three-star rooms from Sfr115/168 with shower/WC and TV. It is convenient for the station and has a bar and two restaurants (one vegetarian).

ZÜRICH

The best hotel in Winterthur is the four-star *Garten-Hotel* (☎ *265 02 65, fax 265 02 75, Stadthausstrasse 4)*, with convenient parking and good facilities. Singles/doubles start at Sfr230/315.

Places to Eat

Clustered around the train station are *Coop*, *Migros* and *EPA*; each has a supermarket and cheap self-service restaurant, with late opening on Thursday. The salad buffet in EPA's restaurant is only Sfr1.90 per 100 grams. Look out also for the open-air markets in the centre on Tuesday and Friday morning.

China Garden (Steinberggasse 55) has good Chinese food and is open daily. On weekdays (except Friday night) it offers set meals from Sfr12.50, and there are always takeaway meals for just Sfr8. *Café-Restaurant Obergasse*, on the corner of Obergasse and Schulgasse, is a lively place with a young clientele. It serves good-sized plates of spaghetti and various salads, with most dishes in the range of Sfr12 to Sfr25. The beer is inexpensive (closed Monday and during the day at weekends).

Restaurant Zur Sonne (Marktgasse 15) offers many varieties of Rösti from Sfr14, and lunch and evening specials (with soup) start at Sfr16.50. There is a 1st floor terrace and it is open daily.

More staid but quite cosy is the *Walliser Kanne* (☎ *212 81 71, Steinberggasse 25)*, which specialises in fondues from Sfr22.50. Other dishes start at Sfr25, though there are also two-course lunch menus from Sfr13.50. It is closed on Saturday and Sunday in summer.

For quality Swiss food (from Sfr27) go to *Gasthaus Rössli* (☎ *213 66 44, Steiggasse 1)*. It's closed Monday and (usually) Sunday.

Entertainment

Winthurthur is a student town and offers plenty of bars – the tourist office can tell you the latest 'in' places. Neumarkt in the Old Town has some lively music bars, including *Shooter's* at No 5, and open-air tables on the square. Live music or DJs can be heard most nights (except in summer) at the *Albani Bar (Steinberggasse 16)*; entry costs Sfr10 to Sfr30. *Paddy O'Brien's (Merkurstrasse 25)* is an Irish pub with free live music some nights. At Archstrasse 8 there's *Scarlett*, a disco open Wednesday to Sunday (cover Sfr8 or Sfr13), and a couple of bars, such as the inexpensive Biergarten, open nightly.

Getting There & Away

There are several trains an hour to Zürich airport (Sfr7.20, 15 minutes) and Zürich itself (Sfr10.60). Many trains also run to Schaffhausen and Lake Constance. By road the N1 (E60) motorway goes from Zürich, skirts Winterthur and continues to St Gallen and Austria. Main roads also go to Constance and Schaffhausen.

Getting Around

All buses go to/from the bus station on Bahnhofplatz. Single bus journeys in the town cost Sfr2.10, though it's Sfr3.60 to Oberwinterthur (get a 24-hour pass for Sfr7.20 instead). Rent bicycles from the train station or (slightly cheaper) from Dynamoo on Rudolfstrasse. There are cheap parking garages around the station.

Basel & Aargau

In the densely populated northern area, affluent towns (and most of the country's nuclear power stations!) fill the landscape rather than the scenic vistas found elsewhere. To enjoy the countryside you can nip over to Germany and the Black Forest, easily accessible from Basel.

The relative dearth of scenic attractions does not mean that the region is not worth a visit. On the contrary – there are some fine old town centres and some particularly diverting museums and art galleries.

The region comprises the cantons of Basel (split into two half-cantons, City and District, in 1833) and Aargau. Unlike in other tourist regions, there is no centralised regional tourist office. The Basel city tourist office has some information on Basel District, and there's an Aargau Tourismus office (☎ 062-746 20 40, fax 746 20 41) in Zofingen, but for the nitty-gritty you'd be best to contact local tourist offices direct.

Highlights

- Discover the museums and nightlife of Basel, a town where three countries meet.
- See Basel's famous Fasnacht, a festival starting at 4 am.
- Take a side trip to the Black Forest – the *real* cuckoo-clock region.
- Rejuvenate in Baden – a health spa dating from Roman times.

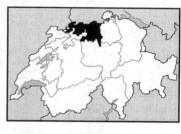

Basel-city   Aargau   Basel-District

Basel

☎ 061 • pop 177,000 • elevation 273m

Basel (Bâle in French, sometimes Basle in English) is Switzerland's second largest city. It is a major centre for commerce, particularly the chemical and pharmaceutical industry, yet retains an attractive Old Town and offers many interesting museums. Influences from neighbouring France and Germany and a large student population make Basel a vibrant and creative city. It is also the home of the liveliest carnival in Switzerland. Don't miss it if you're in the country on the Monday after Ash Wednesday.

Basel had its origins as a Roman settlement founded in 44 BC, and was successively occupied by the Alemanni, Franks and Burgundians until it became part of the Germanic Empire in 1032. By this time the Bishop of Basel had already been granted secular authority over the town by the Emperor Henry II. The town hosted the Council of Basel (1431–48), which attempted (unsuccessfully) to avoid a schism in the Catholic church. In 1460, under the patronage of Pope Pius II, the University of Basel (the oldest in Switzerland) was opened. Basel joined the Swiss Confederation in 1501 and 28 years later adopted the Reformation. The famous Renaissance humanist, Erasmus of Rotterdam (1466–1536), was associated with the city. Basel reached the peak of its influence in the 18th century.

BASEL & AARGAU

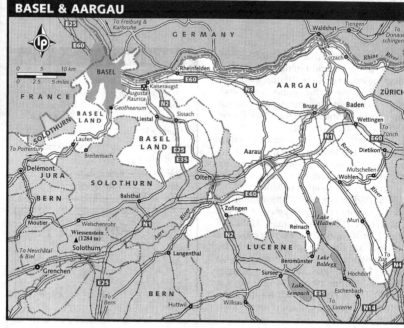

Orientation

Basel's strategic position on the Rhine River at the dual border with France and Germany has been instrumental in its development as a commercial and cultural centre. On the north bank of the Rhine is Kleinbasel (Little Basel), surrounded by German territory. The pedestrian-only Old Town and most of the sights are on the south bank in Grossbasel (Greater Basel). Historically, the 'Klein' tag was partially a denigrating term as it was a working-class locality. The relief bust of *Lälle Keenig*, or 'Tongue King' (at the crossroads at the southern end of the Mittlere Brücke) sticking his tongue out at the northern section, just about sums up the old attitude.

Grossbasel has the SBB Bahnhof, the train station for travel within Switzerland. Tram Nos 1 and 8 go from here to the Old Town centre. In Kleinbasel is the Badischer Bahnhof (BBF), the station for travel to Germany.

Information

Tourist Offices The main tourist office (☎ 268 68 68, fax 268 68 70, ✉ office@ baseltourismus.ch) and a train information counter are by the Mittlere Brücke (bridge) at Schifflände 5. Opening hours are 8.30 am to 6 pm Monday to Friday, and 10 am to 4 pm Saturday. Less than 2km south is the main SBB Bahnhof which has bike rental (7 am to 9 pm daily), money exchange (6 am to 9 pm daily) and another tourist office (☎ 271 36 84), open 8.30 am to 6 pm Monday to Friday and 8.30 am to noon Saturday. Between 1 June and 30 September the tourist office is open 8.30 am to 7 pm weekdays, 8.30 am to 12.30 pm and 1.30 to 6 pm Saturday and 10 am to 2 pm Sunday.

Post & Communications The main post office (4001 Basel 1, Freie Strasse) is in the centre, though by the SBB train station there's a large post office (4002 Basel 2,

Post Passage 9) with a daily emergency counter (surcharge payable).

Email & Internet Access DataComm, Steinvorstadt 79, charges just Sfr3/5 for 30/60 minutes. It's open 9 am to 10 pm or midnight daily (2 to 10 pm on Sunday).

Travel Agencies The SSR office (☎ 284 90 60, Steinenberg 19), is open 10 am to 6 pm Monday to Friday and 10 am to 2 pm Saturday. The American Express travel representative is Reise Müller (☎ 281 33 80), Steinenvorstadt 33.

Bookshop The best place for English-language books, travel guides and maps is Bider & Tanner (☎ 206 99 99), Aeschenvorstadt 2. Late opening is till 9 pm on Thursday. Arcados (☎ 681 31 32), Rheingasse 69, is a gay bookshop with an information service, open 11 am to 4 pm Saturday year-round, 12.30 to 7 pm Tuesday to Friday from June to September, and noon to 7 pm Monday to Friday from October to May.

Medical & Emergency Services The Cantonal Hospital (☎ 265 25 25), Petersgraben 2, has a casualty department. Call ☎ 117 for the police and ☎ 144 for an ambulance.

Walking Tour

The tourist office hands out free do-it-yourself guides to walks through the Old Town, taking in cobbled streets, colourful fountains and 16th-century buildings. The **Fischmarkt** is the core of the Old Town, and is graced by a Gothic fountain. The **Spalentor** gate tower is 700 years old, a remnant from the time when the city was encircled by a protective wall. The **Rathaus** (town hall) was built in the 16th century and has been impressively restored. It looks very patrician with its vivid red facade, embellished with shields, painted figures and a golden spire. Peek into the frescoed courtyard; the statue here depicts Munatius Plancus, the founder of the town.

The **cathedral** *(Münster)* is an unmistakable landmark, with Gothic spires built in red sandstone. It was consecrated in 1019,

yet parts were added or replaced for a further 500 years. Though the exterior is Gothic, inside it is mostly Romanesque. Take in the view of the Rhine from the rear of the cathedral. Also noteworthy is its Romanesque St Gallus doorway, fringed by a scene showing the Judgement of the Dead. Erasmus died in Basel in 1536 and his red marble tomb can be found in the north aisle.

Be sure to take a look at the **Tinguely Fountain** on Theaterplatz. It's a typical display by the Swiss sculptor, Jean Tinguely, with madcap machinery playing water games with hoses – art with a juvenile heart. In the SBB train station main hall is another example of his work, a massive mobile incorporating steel girders, wheels, coloured lights and animal heads. He died shortly after finishing it, before it was even officially opened in late 1991.

Museums

Depending upon taste and inclination, you could spend days in Basel's 35 museums. Contemporary arts, history, ethnography, natural history, musical instruments, cinema and pharmaceuticals are just some of the fields explored. Ask for the museums booklet in English from the tourist office. Most museums are closed on Monday (but not all); a few are free, and many of the others (cantonal museums) are free on the first Sunday of the month. Consider buying the museum pass for Sfr23; it's valid for three days for most museums.

The **Museum of Fine Arts** (Kunstmuseum), St Albangraben 16, holds the largest art collection in Switzerland, and covers religious, Swiss and modern art. Important German artists represented include Konrad Witz and Holbein the Younger. The museum is open 10 am to 5 pm Tuesday to Sunday, and costs Sfr7 (students Sfr5), except on the first Sunday in the month when it's free. It has an excellent collection of Picasso's work. The artist was so gratified when the people of Basel paid a large sum for two of his paintings that he donated a further four from his own collection. More modern art is housed in the **Fondation Beyeler**, Baselstrasse 101, Riehen (take tram No 6). It's

BASEL (BÂLE)

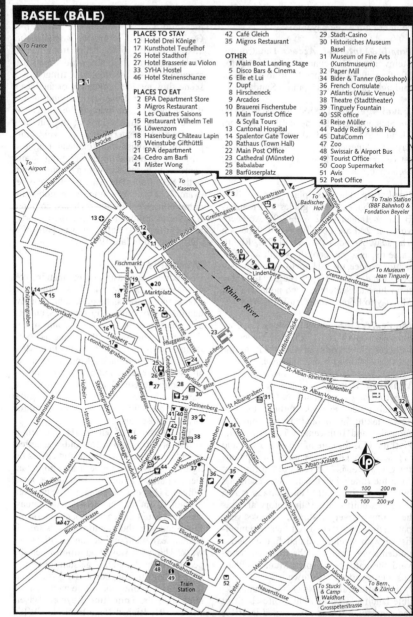

PLACES TO STAY
12 Hotel Drei Könige
17 Kunsthotel Teufelhof
26 Hotel Stadthof
27 Hotel Brasserie au Violon
33 SYHA Hostel
46 Hotel Steinenschanze

PLACES TO EAT
2 EPA Department Store
3 Migros Restaurant
4 Les Quatres Saisons
15 Restaurant Wilhelm Tell
16 Löwenzorn
18 Hasenburg Château Lapin
19 Weinstube Gifthüttli
21 EPA department
24 Cedro am Barfi
41 Mister Wong

42 Café Gleich
35 Migros Restaurant

OTHER
1 Main Boat Landing Stage
5 Disco Bars & Cinema
6 Elle et Lui
7 Dupf
8 Hirscheneck
9 Arcados
10 Brauerei Fischerstube
11 Main Tourist Office
13 Cantonal Hospital
14 Spalentor Gate Tower
20 Rathaus (Town Hall)
22 Main Post Office
23 Cathedral (Münster)
25 Babalabar
28 Barfüsserplatz

29 Stadt-Casino
30 Historisches Museum
   Basel
31 Museum of Fine Arts
   (Kunstmuseum)
32 Paper Mill
34 Bider & Tanner (Bookshop)
36 French Consulate
37 Atlantis (Music Venue)
38 Theatre (Stadttheater)
39 Tinguely Fountain
40 SSR office
43 Reise Müller
44 Paddy Reilly's Irish Pub
45 DataComm
47 Zoo
48 Swissair & Airport Bus
49 Tourist Office
50 Coop Supermarket
51 Avis
52 Post Office

open 10 am to 5 pm (8pm Wednesday) daily and is closed Tuesday. Entry costs Sfr8.

Museum Jean Tinguely is at Grenzacher-strasse (take bus No 31 or 36). Opened in 1996, it houses a large, impressive and sometimes humorous collection of the artist's work. Many of the pieces rattle, shake, rotate and squeak at the touch of a button. Powerful exhibits include *Mengele – Dance of Death*, partially constructed from the burnt ruins of a neighbour's farm-house, and *Klamauk*, a much modified trac-tor that formed part of the artist's funeral procession through Fribourg. It's open 11 am to 7 pm Wednesday to Sunday; entry costs Sfr5 (Sfr3 students and seniors).

The **Paper Mill** (Papiermühle), St Alban Tal 37, was once awarded the accolade of the best museum in Europe. You can make your own paper and watch the experts at work (open 2 to 5 pm Tuesday to Sunday; entry Sfr9, students Sfr6).

Zoo

Basel's zoo rivals Zürich's in importance. It's laid out in a large rectangular park near the SBB station, and has a varied collection from around the world. Some of the rare and highly prized species on display include Indian rhinos, pygmy hippos, golden lion tamarins and king penguins. Feeding times *(Fütterungen)*, displayed by the entrance, are fun to watch. The big cats devour bloody slabs of meat at 4 pm daily. It is open 8 am to 6.30 pm daily (5.30 pm win-ter, 6 pm March, April, September and Oc-tober). Entry costs Sfr12 for adults, Sfr10 for students and senior citizens, Sfr5 for children, and Sfr27 for families.

Markets

There's a daily fruit and vegetable market in Marktplatz. Barfüsserplatz is the venue for the flea market, every second and forth Wednesday in the month from January to mid-October, and the Christmas Market.

Organised Tours

Contact the main tourist office for details. Most tours are from mid-May to mid-October. Options include city tours by foot

The First Hippie

The first man ever to take an LSD 'trip' was Swiss. In 1943 Albert Hofmann was a chemist working for the Sandoz drug company in Basel. While conducting tests during a search for a migraine cure he synthesised lysergic acid diethylamide (LSD), and the chemical was accidentally absorbed through his finger-tips. Shortly afterwards the mind-bending sensations began, and he experienced a pow-erful series of psychedelic pictures and a dreamlike state.

Hofmann's next excursion with the drug, a deliberate experiment, produced the first 'bad trip', in which he thought a demon had in-vaded him and his neighbour was a witch. Heavy, man!

LSD was soon taken up by writers and artists, such as Aldous Huxley, who saw it as a creative and elevating force. It was later crucial in the evolution of the '60s flower generation, who believed it could be an instrument for world peace. From 1953 the CIA conducted extensive tests, lasting many years, to establish its usefulness as a truth drug. Tests on whether LSD had any clinical value were curtailed when the drug was outlawed in 1966.

Fifty years after his discovery, Mr Hofmann (then 87) defended the drug in an interview with the British newspaper, *The Independent*, saying medical tests should be carried out to establish its potential. He went on to express the hope that LSD may one day become part of our mainstream culture, with the same ac-ceptability as alcohol.

In the meantime, mine's a pint.

(Sfr10) or bus (Sfr20), or a half-day tour of Germany's Black Forest (Sfr55).

Special Events

Basel is a carnival town. The **Vogel Gryff** festival at the end of January celebrates the chasing away of winter from Kleinbasel. The three key figures: the griffin *(Vogel Gryff)*, the savage *(Wilde Mann)* and the lion *(Leu)*, dance to the beat of drums on a raft on the Rhine, facing the town. Later they dance in the streets of Kleinbasel.

On the Monday after Ash Wednesday, Basel commences a three-day celebration, the **Fasnacht** spring carnival. It kicks off at 4 am exactly with the **Morgestraich**, when the street lights are suddenly extinguished and the procession starts to wend its way through the central district. All the participants wear elaborate costumes and masks. Some carry large painted lanterns, others play flutes or drums. Bars and cafes stay open all night to ensure the celebrations don't flag. SBB puts on special night trains from other towns for this event. The main parades are on the Monday and Wednesday afternoons, when the large floats get wheeled out and fruit, flowers, confetti and candies are thrown into the crowd. On Tuesday afternoon is the children's parade. Speciality food for the carnival is *Zibelewaaire*, an onion flan.

On the Sunday evening before Morgestraich, in Liestel, there's **Chienbäse**, a dramatic and scorching-hot fire parade; take the train from Basel (Sfr4.80, 30 minutes).

Trade fairs play an important part in the Basel calendar, and have done so ever since the city was granted its licence to stage such events in 1471. Important ones are the **Autumn Fair** (Herbstmesse, starting the Saturday preceding 30 October and continuing for over two weeks), the **Swiss Industries Fair** (MUBA) held every spring, and **Art 30**, the contemporary art fair in June.

Places to Stay

Hotels are expensive and liable to be full during the numerous trade fairs and conventions (when prices rise). Be sure to book ahead. There are no trade fairs in July and August, which helps during these months. The tourist office in the SBB Bahnhof reserves rooms for Sfr10 commission. The same service is undertaken in the Schifflände office for Sfr5. Check the tourist office hotel list for cheaper, out-of-town places.

Places to Stay – Budget

Camping Six kilometres south of the SBB train station is *Camp Waldhort (☎ 711 64 29, Heideweg 16, Reinach)*. To get there, take tram No 11 to Landhof. It's open from March to October.

Hostel The SYHA *hostel (☎ 272 05 72, fax 272 08 33, St Alban Kirchrain 10)* is convenient for the centre of town, near tram No 3 (stop: St Alban Tor). Dorm beds are Sfr28.60, and singles/doubles cost from Sfr69.60/79.20. Reception is shut from 10 am to 2 pm, though the doors stay open.

Hotels Unfortunately, there aren't really any budget hotels. In the Old Town, *Hotel Stadthof (☎ 261 87 11, fax 261 25 84, Gerbergasse 84)* has standard singles/doubles for Sfr80/120, using hall shower and without breakfast. Reception is in the restaurant on the 1st floor.

In Kleinbasel, try *Badischer Hof (☎ 692 41 44, fax 692 34 29, Riehenring 109)*. This hotel/restaurant has rooms with TV for Sfr75/120, or Sfr80/130 with private shower; add Sfr5 per person for breakfast. Staff are friendly, and food in the inexpensive restaurant is pretty good (closed Sunday, plus Saturday in July and August).

Near the pedestrian zone is *Hotel Steinenschanze (☎ 272 53 53, fax 272 45 73, Steinengraben 69)*, which has uncluttered white singles/doubles from Sfr110/160 with private shower and toilet. The price for students under 26 is reduced to Sfr55 per person for the first three nights, except during trade fairs.

Perhaps the best deal is at *Hotel Brasserie au Violon (☎ 269 87 11, fax 269 87 12, ☻ auviolon@prolink.ch, Im Lohnhof 4)*, a former prison. Tiny doorways lead into reasonably sized rooms (two cells knocked through) with shower/WC. Most singles/doubles are Sfr90/120, though there are some rooms with a queen-sized bed for Sfr80 (single or double occupancy). Breakfast is Sfr10, and the restaurant is good (closed Sunday and Monday).

Places to Stay – Mid-Range

The most interesting hotel in Basel is the *Kunsthotel Teufelhof (☎ 261 10 10, fax 261 10 04, ☻ info@teufelhof.com, Leonhardsgraben 47)*. Each of the rooms was assigned to a different artist to create a piece of environmental art. All rooms will stay intact for about two years before being reassigned to a new artist. The shock of waking up in a piece of art is quite something. The rooms have private bath or shower/WC, and prices start at Sfr250/277 for singles/doubles. Some rooms are more elaborately kitted out than others, but all are a welcome respite from standard hotel fixtures. Prices are from Sfr175/265 in the Galeriehotel annex, where rooms are created by designers rather than artists. Its expensive 1st floor restaurant has an excellent reputation, and there is also a bar, Weinstube and theatre on site.

Places to Stay – Top End
If you can afford to really splash out on accommodation, make for the *Drei Könige* (☎ *261 52 52, fax 261 21 53, Blumenrain 8)*. It has welcomed luminaries through its portals since 1026 – royals such as Princess (later Queen) Victoria, and the likes of Napoleon, Voltaire and Dickens. You can join them, but only if you can afford the king's ransom of at least Sfr255/420 for a single/double. Breakfast buffet is Sfr32 extra. The three kings referred to in the hotel's name were Emperor Conrad II, his son, the future Henry III, and the last king of Burgundy, Rudolf III, who met at the inn in the year it was founded. As a result of their meeting the territory that became Switzerland was incorporated into the Germanic Empire. The present building dates from 1844, and the three kings on the facade are now the three wise men.

Places to Eat
Eating in Basel is generally a better deal than accommodation. The SBB train station has a *Migros* supermarket and across the road is a *Coop*. Both have a counter for hot snacks, and both are open 6 am (7.30 am on weekends) to 10 pm daily.

Self-Service The *EPA* department stores, at Gerbergasse 4 in the centre and Untere Rebgasse in Kleinbasel, have a cheap restaurant. *Migros* restaurants are on Untere Rebgasse and on Sternengasse. All these places are open normal shop hours, with late opening till 8 pm on Thursday.

Mister Wong (Steinenvorstadt 1a) offers adequate Asian food from Sfr10, and a salad bar. It is open to 11.30 pm, or later, daily.

Other Restaurants Steinenvorstadt has lots of restaurants, including *Café Gleich* at No 23, a popular place for affordable vegetarian food (closed weekends). *Cedro am Barfi*, a large restaurant at Streitgasse 20, has pizzas from Sfr12 and four-course lunches for Sfr16.

Restaurant Wilhelm Tell (Spalenvorstadt 38), by the Spalentor city gate, sticks to traditional Swiss food. Tasty meals start at Sfr14, with Röstis available evening only. For Italian and Tunisian food from Sfr16, call in at *Restaurant Salmen* next door. Both places are closed Sunday.

For Basel specialities in a typical ambience, try *Weinstube Gifthüttli* (☎ *261 16 56, Schneidergasse 11)*. Meals start at Sfr14.50, with more expensive choices available in the smarter section upstairs. Menus are written in incomprehensible Swiss-German dialect, with English and German translations. It's closed Sunday lunchtime. Opposite is the slightly more down-to-earth *Hasenburg Château Lapin*, with snacks and meals from Sfr6.80 to Sfr40. Drinkers mostly fill the tables in the evening (closed Sunday).

Löwenzorn (☎ *261 42 13, Gemsberg 2)*, is something of a local secret, serving typical Swiss fare. This 16th-century house offers a choice of four dining areas and a courtyard garden. Small dishes are reasonably cheap, and lunch menus with soup go from Sfr15, though most meals are in the range Sfr17 to Sfr44 (closed Sunday).

Stucki (☎ *361 82 22, Bruderholzallee 42)*, in the suburbs south of the SBB station, is rated as one of the top restaurants in all Switzerland (closed Sunday and Monday). You have to pay for the reputation, of course, with à la carte main courses costing Sfr40 to Sfr75 and menus above Sfr100, but its creative concoctions merit a taste. Duck (*le canard* in French) is a speciality at Sfr140 for two (closed Sunday and Monday). Duck (Sfr65) and poultry is also a favoured choice at **Les Quatre Saisons** (☎ 690 87 20) in the Hotel Europe, Clarastrasse 43. This popular gourmet French restaurant is closed Sunday.

Entertainment

Basel has a busy cultural scene, with many theatre groups and two symphony orchestras. *Basel Live*, free from the tourist office, comes out every two weeks and contains full listings.

For more basic evening entertainment, explore the beer halls, especially in Kleinbasel. **Brauerei Fischerstube** (Rheingasse 45) brews its own beer. There are four varieties, starting at Sfr4.70 per half litre. A good place that attracts an 'alternative' crowd is **Hirscheneck** (☎ 692 73 33, Lindenberg 23). Beer is Sfr5.20 for 0.5L and it serves food. There's live music downstairs (entry around Sfr10) starting at 10 pm most Tuesdays, Fridays and Saturdays (not in summer); if there's no band on Friday or Saturday, there's a year-round disco instead (entry from Sfr5). Also quite alternative, with events ranging from live music, DJs, theatre and discussions, is **Kaserne** (☎ 681 26 33, Klybeckstrasse 1b). Gay bars **Dupf** (Rebgasse 43) and **Elle et Lui** (Rebgasse 39), are open 5 pm and 4 pm daily, respectively. At Claraplatz there are stairs leading down to several disco bars and a cinema.

On the Grossbasel side, try the late-night bars in the **Stadt-Casino** complex on Barfüsserplatz, or there's **Paddy Reilly's Irish Pub** (Steinentorstrasse 45). **Atlantis** (☎ 228 96 98, Klosterbergstrasse 13), one of the best venues in town. It has live music most nights (rock, R & B, jazz etc), with entry around Sfr15. There's a free disco some weekends, and a new restaurant is opening up. Another good place is **Babalabar** (Gerbergasse 76). It has a disco section with different musical themes nightly, where entry costs Sfr5 during the week (closes 2 am) or Sfr10 on Friday and Saturday (closes 3 am). Entry is free before 11 pm and beer is Sfr5 for 0.30L.

Getting There & Away

Air EuroAirport serves Basel, Mulhouse and Freiburg. It's 5km to the north-west, in France, and has several flights daily to main European destinations. For information, call ☎ 325 31 11 (same code as Basel). The Swissair office at the SBB station also deals with Crossair (☎ 0848-85 20 00), which is the main user of the airport.

Train Basel is a major European rail hub. For most international trains you pass the border controls in the station, so allow extra time to make your connection. All trains to France go from the SNCF section of SBB Bahnhof. There are four to five trains a day to Paris (Sfr69) and connections to Brussels and Strasbourg. Trains to Germany stop at Badischer Bahnhof (BBF) on the north bank; local trains to the Black Forest stop only at BBF, though fast IC and EC services stop at SBB too. Main destinations via BBF are Frankfurt (Sfr77, plus around Sfr19 German rail supplement), Cologne, Hamburg and Amsterdam. Two to three trains an hour run to Freiburg (40 minutes). For German travel inquire directly at BBF, as you can sometimes get special deals that aren't available from SBB. Services within Switzerland go from SBB; there are two fast trains an hour to both Geneva (Sfr72; via Bern or Biel/Bienne) and Zürich (Sfr31).

Car & Motorcycle The E25/E60 motorway heads down from Strasbourg and passes by EuroAirport, and the E35/A5 hugs the German side of the Rhine.

Car Rental Both Hertz (☎ 205 92 22, Nauenstrasse 33) and Avis (☎ 206 95 45, Aeschengraben 31), in the Hilton Hotel, have offices near the SBB station and branches at the airport.

Boat An enjoyable, if expensive, way to travel north is to take a boat down the Rhine. The landing stage is between Johanniterbrücke and Dreirosenbrücke. Inquire at Scylla Tours (☎ 264 94 84, fax 264 94 80, ✉ info@scylla-tours.com), Blumenrain 2, next to the tourist office. See the Getting There & Away chapter for more on long-distance routes. Short excursions by Basler Personenschiffahrt (☎ 639 95 00, fax 639 95 06), depart from near the tourist office, several times a day in the summer. Its Web site is at www.bpg.ch.

Getting Around
Buses run every 20 to 30 minutes from 5 am to around 11.30 pm between the airport and the SBB station. It's the yellow bus that goes from outside the Swissair office (Sfr2.80, 15 minutes) at the station. Trains are equally frequent. The trip by taxi costs around Sfr35.

In the city, buses and trams run every six to 10 minutes. Tickets cost Sfr1.80 for up to and including four stops, or Sfr2.60 for the whole central zone. A day pass costs Sfr7.80, though if you stay in Basel your accommodation will give you a 'mobility ticket', valid for free public transport. Another great transport deal is the city bikes on offer for *free* daily loans at the white shed outside SBB Bahnhof, near the tram stops. They're available around June to October, and the office is open 8 am to 10 pm daily. Other locations for free bike loan are Theaterplatz, Schifflände and Claraplatz.

Parking garages are dotted around – there are several between the SBB station and the pedestrian zone. Expect to pay at least Sfr1.50 an hour. Small ferries cross the Rhine at various points in the centre (Sfr1.20; day passes not valid), a pleasant alternative to using the bridges.

If you need a taxi, look outside the train stations or ring ☎ 691 77 88 or ☎ 271 22 22.

Around Basel

AUGUSTA RAURICA
These Roman ruins by the Rhine are the largest in Switzerland, and an easy excursion from Basel. The Roman colony was founded in 43 BC and swelled to a population of 20,000 in the 2nd century. Restored remnants include an open-air theatre and several temples. The **Roman Museum** (Römermuseum) has an authentic Roman house amongst its exhibits (Sfr5, Basel museum pass valid; closed Monday morning). There's no charge to walk around the rest of the site.

The trip by local train from Basel to Kaiseraugst takes 15 minutes (Sfr4.80 each way); it's then a 10-minute walk to the site. In summer, taking the boat is another option from Basel.

GOETHEANUM
This architecturally distinctive place is the centre of the world Anthroposophical Society. There are regular performances of classical music or theatre (☎ 706 44 44), or you can take a tour of the site (☎ 706 42 69). It's in Dornach; from Basel, take tram No 10 or the train (Sfr3.60), then walk up the hill.

BLACK FOREST
The Black Forest (Schwarzwald), named for its dark canopy of evergreens, is an ideal excursion from any of the northern border towns between Basel and Schaffhausen. This hiking region is actually the home of the cuckoo clock, for so long associated with Switzerland itself. Hansel and Gretel of childhood fiction encountered their wicked witch here, but today's busloads of tourists would probably scare off any would-be witches.

Orientation & Information
The Black Forest lies east of the Rhine between Basel and Karlsruhe (Germany). It's roughly triangular in shape, about 160km long and about 50km wide where it abuts the Swiss border. Freiburg is the unofficial capital of the southern Black Forest, although many other small towns in the area have excellent tourist information offices – all can give information about accommodation and restaurants. Freiburg's tourist office (☎ 0761-388 1880, fax 370 03) is at Rotteckring 14.

Currency exchange is available in Germany at banks, train stations and post offices, but commission is charged so you'd do best to change money before you leave Switzerland. Some shops and restaurants will accept Swiss francs directly.

The country telephone code for Germany is ☎ 49.

Things to See
Though taking advantage of the countryside will be the main focus, there's still

BLACK FOREST REGION

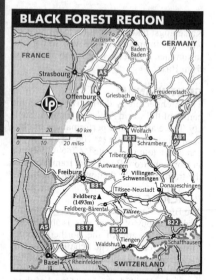

lots of history and culture to explore in the region.

Freiburg's main tourist sight is the **cathedral** (Münster), a classic example of high and late-Gothic architecture. Its red pinnacles loom over Münsterplatz. Of particular interest are the stone and wood carvings, stained-glass windows, the west porch and the pierced spire. The pedestrian area of the town is great for walking tours, and the many resident students make this place both relaxed and lively.

The area between Freudenstadt and Freiburg is cuckoo clock country, and a few popular stops are **Triberg** (where two rival outfits each claim to have the world's biggest cuckoo clock), **Schramberg** and **Furtwangen**. Prices for cuckoo clocks in the Black Forest region of Germany are generally lower than in Switzerland. The history and traditional lifestyle of the region are well documented in the **Deutsches Uhrenmuseum** (German Clock Museum) in Furtwagen and the **Schwarzwald Museum** (Black Forest Museum) in Triberg. Triberg also has a famous **Wasserfall** (waterfall), which hurtles down 163m over seven stages (admission charge).

The Danube

The Danube (Donau) rises in the Black Forest and flows all the way to the Black Sea. It's ideal for hiking, biking and motoring tours. Donaueschingen is recognised as being the source of the river, and this town is the start of the cycle track (Donauradweg) that runs most of the way along the river right into and through Austria. The two tributary rivers that rise even deeper in the Black Forest, the Brigach and the Breg, are also worth investigating.

Activities

There are 7000km of marked **hiking** trails to explore. Three long-distance routes running north from the Swiss border are: the 280km Westweg from Basel, the 230km Mittelweg from Waldshut-Tiengen, and the 240km Ostweg from Schaffhausen. In the southern Black Forest, the Feldberg area provides great hikes; consider using Todtmoos or Bonndorf as a base. The 10km gorge, the Wutachschlucht, near Bonndorf, is justifiably famous. If you haven't time to explore the Black Forest thoroughly, take the Schauinslandbahn, on the outskirts of Freiburg up to the 1284m Schauinsland peak (DM20 return; about Sfr16). It's a good starting point for one-day and half-day hikes.

If you fancy switching countries and currencies to get yet another skiing fix, there's some winter downhill **skiing** around Feldberg (DM36 for a day pass; about Sfr29), but cross-country skiing is more widespread.

Getting There & Away

Trains run hourly between Basel and Karlsruhe, calling at Freiburg en route. There is also a scenic railway between Freiburg and Constance. By road, the A5 skirts the western side of the forest (linking Basel and Frankfurt) and on the eastern side is the A81.

Getting Around

Trains run north and east from Freiburg. The prettiest stretch (called the Höllental route) is from Freiburg to the Titisee lake. The Germans rave about this but it's nothing compared to most Swiss train journeys. Where the train fails to go, the bus system usually provides the way, albeit sometimes infrequently. Ask at transport information centres about special bus and railpasses for the region.

The main tourist road, the Schwarzwald-Hochstrasse (B500), runs from Baden-Baden to Freudenstadt and Triberg to Waldshut. Cycling is a good way to get about, despite the hills (look for rental in Baden-Baden and Freiburg train stations).

Aargau Canton

This industrial and residential canton is rather lacking in tourist attractions, though some towns retain well-preserved old centres. That includes the cantonal capital, **Aarau**, which was formerly the seat of the mighty Habsburg family. Mid-way between Aarau and Baden are the ruins of the Habsburg Castle, offering excellent views from its tower.

BADEN
☎ 056 • pop 16,500 • elevation 388m
Baden has a dual reputation, as an electro-mechanical engineering centre and as a leading spa town.

Orientation & Information
Baden is split into two localities about 15 minutes' walk apart: the Altstadt (Old Town centre) to the south and the spa centre to the north, with the train station positioned conveniently between the two. By the station is the main post office (5400 Baden 1) and the postbus departure point. A few metres farther on, at Bahnhofstrasse No 50, is the tourist office (☎ 222 53 18, fax 22 53 20, @tourismus@baden-schweiz.ch), open 8.30 am to noon and 2 to 6 pm Monday to Friday and 10 am to noon Saturday. Ask about free guided walks on Monday afternoon.

Things to See & Do
Baden's status as a health spa is thanks to the presence of 19 hot **sulphur springs**, with the highest mineral content of any Swiss spa. Their curative properties have been known for 2000 years and are believed to be effective in the treatment of rheumatism, respiratory and cardiovascular complaints, and even some neurological disorders. Alternatively, the springs may be of interest if you simply like wallowing in a very hot bath. Pools in all the major hotels are open to everyone. Depending on the place, entry costs between Sfr8 and Sfr15, or much more if you want special treatments such as mudpacks or a massage. The only pool large enough for swimming is the Thermalbad in the Hotel Verenahof.

The Old Town centre has some interesting features, including a **covered bridge** (Holzbrücke) and step-gabled houses. Ascend the stairs near the city tower (Stadtturm) for a bird's-eye view of the town. The **Bailiff's Castle** (Landvogteischloss) is on the east side of the Limmat River. Inside is a historical museum (Sfr5; closed Monday). Between the Altstadt and the station is the **Swiss Children's Museum** (Schweizer Kindermuseum), Ölrainstrasse 29, featuring all sorts of games, ancient and modern, that can be viewed and played. It is only open 2 to 5 pm on Wednesday and Saturday and 10 am to 5 pm Sunday; entry costs Sfr7 for adults, Sfr5 for students and Sfr3 for children. West of the spa centre is **Stiftung Langmatt**, Römerstrasse 30, a stately home with a good collection of French Impressionist art (Sfr10, students Sfr5). From 1 April to 31 October, it's open 2 to 5 pm daily except Monday (11 am to 5 pm on weekends). Baden also has a casino and a theatre.

Places to Stay
Campingplatz Aue (☎ 221 63 00) is a 15-minute walk from the station: cross the Limmat River at Hochbrücke, just beyond the Altstadt, then take the first right into Kanalstrasse. It overlooks the river and is open from 1 April to 31 October.

The SYHA *hostel (☎ 221 67 36, fax 221 76 60)* is nearby at Kanalstrasse 7. It is closed from Christmas to mid-March, costs Sfr24.30, and the reception is closed from 9.30 am to 5 pm.

Hotel Hirschen (☎ 222 69 66, Badstrasse 22), on the opposite side of the

Limmat River from the spa, is the cheapest hotel. Singles/doubles using hall showers are Sfr46/92 but they are unrenovated. If you can afford it, stay at *Atrium-Hotel Blume* (☎ 222 55 69, fax 222 42 98, Kurplatz 4) in the spa centre. It's a cheery place featuring an excellent Romanesque inner courtyard with a fountain and plenty of foliage. Singles/doubles with private shower/WC start at Sfr126/195, or Sfr79/148 using hall facilities. Breakfast is buffet-style and the hotel has its own small thermal pool.

Places to Eat
Below ground level in the station are market stalls and takeaway shops, as well as an *EPA* department store with a cheap self-service restaurant. Nearby, opposite the post office, is a *Migros* supermarket and restaurant. The Manor department store on Schlossbergplatz has a *Manora* restaurant. All these places have late opening till 8 pm on Wednesday; Migros is also open till 8 pm on Friday.

In the Old Town, try *Chen Lay* (Untere Halde 2), for Chinese food; it has two-course lunches from Sfr13.50 (closed Monday).

Rebstock, up the road at No 21, is more traditional and more expensive (closed Sunday and Monday). Also close by is *Krone* (Kronengasse 2), with inexpensive Swiss and Yugoslavian food, and a riverside terrace (closed Wednesday).

Getting There & Away
Baden is just 17 minutes away from Zürich by train (Sfr8.60). It is also within Zürich's S-Bahn network (lines S6 and S12, 30 minutes). By road, it is simple to get to Zürich (N1/E60 motorway) and the German Black Forest town of Waldshut (highway 5).

ZOFINGEN
☎ 062 • pop 10,000 • elevation 440m
Zofingen has an attractive old centre with historic fountains, remnants of ancient fortifications and gabled houses with overhanging roofs. It's worth a stop-off but not a big detour (it's on the rail route between Basel and Lucerne). It has a tourist office (☎ 745 00 05, fax 745 00 02), Marktgasse 10 (closed weekends), and a SYHA *hostel* (☎ 752 23 03, fax 752 23 16, General Guisan Strasse 10) that's closed mid-December to 1 March.

Fribourg, Neuchâtel & Jura

This region includes the cantons of Fribourg (population 227,900), Neuchâtel (population 165,200) and Jura (population 68,900), as well as the north-west tip of the canton of Bern.

The canton of Fribourg is tacked on to a tourist region that is otherwise dominated by the long chain of the Jura Mountains. It is this canton that provides many of the highlights: the historic town of Murten, the delightful cheese-making centre of Gruyères, and Fribourg itself. On the other hand, don't neglect a visit to the watch-making towns, merrily ticking away in the Jura Mountains. The most important of these are Neuchâtel and La Chaux-de-Fonds in the canton of Neuchâtel.

The Neuchâtel canton produces both red and white wine, and a well-known rosé (oeil-de-perdrix). The first vineyard in Neuchâtel was planted by monks in the 10th century, under the auspices of providing communion wine. Locally-produced brandies include Marc, Prune and Kirsch.

Most towns in the canton of Jura have a street named after the 23 June. It was on this day in 1974 that a popular vote supported its creation as a separate canton. Previously it had been part of the canton of Bern, despite tensions and grievances dating back to the 19th century. The Federal Constitution was accordingly amended and, on 1 January 1979, the new canton came into being. It is ironic, therefore, that the Jura region should still be lumped within the same tourist region as part of its former ruler.

Neuchâtel and Murten are sites for Expo – see the boxed text 'Expo.02 – Switzerland Welcomes the World' in the Facts for the Visitor chapter.

Orientation & Information

This region is within French-speaking Switzerland, except for the eastward edge of Fribourg canton where German is

Highlights

- Explore the picturesque town centres of Fribourg, Murten & Gruyères.
- Join a cheesey tour in Gruyères.
- Watch the clocks and automata in museums in Neuchâtel, La Chaux-de-Fonds and Le Locle.
- Dine at the 'Restaurants de nuit' in Neuchâtel canton.
- Enjoy cross-country skiing and horse-riding in the Jura Mountains.

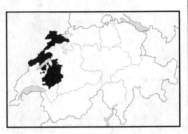

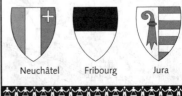

Neuchâtel   Fribourg   Jura

spoken. The area north and west of Lac de Neuchâtel includes the relatively gentle slopes of the Jura Mountains, a range which extends all the way along the French border almost to Geneva. In contrast, the Fribourg area south-east of the lake is mostly in the Mittelland plain. Following are the main regional tourist offices, though there are also several sub-regional offices serving specific areas. Each office can send useful information, but some brochures are only in French or German.

Info Pays de Fribourg (☎ 026-915 92 92, fax 915 92 99, ✆ info.tourisme@pays-de-fribourg.ch) Restoroute de la Gruyère, CH-1644, Avry-devant-Pont

Tourisme neuchâtelois (☎ 032-889 68 90, fax 889 62 96, ✆ tourisme .neuchatelois@ne.ch) Hôtel des Postes, CP 1374, CH-2001 Neuchâtel

Jura Tourisme (☎ 032-952 19 52, fax 952 19 55, ✆ crs@jura.ch) Rue de la Gruère 1, CH-2350 Saignelégier

Office du tourisme du Jura bernois (☎ 032-493 64 66, fax 493 61 56, ✆ information@jurabernois-tourisme.ch) Ave de la Liberté 26, Case postale 759, CH-2740 Moutier

Getting Around

Arc Jurassien is a day card (Sfr25) covering selected buses and trains in the Neuchâtel, Jura and Jura bernois regions. A 'Plus' version (Sfr39 or Sfr44) extends the area of validity. *Onde Verte* is a zonal pass for Neuchâtel canton, valid for one week; there are also passes available for one month/year. One zone (such as Neuchâtel town) costs Sfr26 or it's Sfr70 for the whole canton. In Fribourg canton, the Fri-Pass is a day pass for Sfr26, valid on GFM buses and trains (available in summer only).

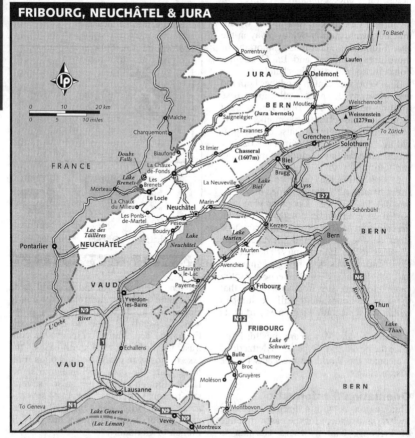

There are no motorways in the Jura region, but other main roads make getting around by car easy, even in winter.

Fribourg Canton

In the 15th and 16th centuries Fribourg was protected from Bern's expansionist policies by a treaty of association signed in 1403. This alliance held firm despite Fribourg remaining Catholic in the face of the Reformation. The town even managed to extend its own territory during this period, and gobbled up several regions to the south and west, such as Gruyères and Broye.

FRIBOURG

☎ 026 • pop 36,500 • elevation 630m
Built on the hilly banks of a river bend and with a skyline dominated by a cathedral, Fribourg (Freiburg in German) is a little reminiscent of Bern. This is not too surprising as it was founded in 1157 by Duke Berchtold IV of Zähringen, father of the bear hunter who founded Bern, Berchtold V. It became a free imperial city in 1478 at the end of the Burgundy Wars. Three years later it joined the Swiss Confederation, the first French-speaking town to do so. Fribourg's prosperity in the Middle Ages was based on manufacturing; affluent artisans were drawn to the city and many of their Gothic houses still survive in the medieval town centre. Other main attractions are its churches and art galleries. The entrepreneur Georges Python was the founder of the Catholic university in 1889.

Orientation

Fribourg is a bilingual cantonal capital. The Sarine River (Saane in German) marks the linguistic divide: inhabitants on the west bank mostly speak French, and those on the east bank, German. Street names may differ, depending upon the language used; Rue de Morat and Murtengasse, for example, are two versions of the same address. Both street names usually appear on street signs.

Much of the Old Town is on the west bank of the river, with the main focal point being the Cathedral of St Nicholas. The train station (Gare CFF) is conveniently central. Leading from it is the shopping street, Ave de la Gare; this becomes Rue de Romont (pedestrian-only) and opens out into the hub of the town, Place Georges-Python.

Information

The tourist information office (☎ 321 31 75, fax 322 35 27, ✉ Office.Tourisme@ fribourg.ch) is by the station at Ave de la Gare 1. The opening hours are 9 am to 12.30 pm and 1.30 to 6 pm Monday to Friday and 9 am to 12.30 pm Saturday (plus 1.30 to 4 pm from May to September). It helps find rooms without charging. The train station has money-exchange facilities from 6 am to 8.30 pm daily, plus storage lockers (Sfr3) and bike rental.

The main post office (1700 Fribourg 1) is close to the station on Ave de Tivoli.

Internet access is at Café des Grand Places (see under Entertainment) or at Scottish Pub (☎ 466 82 02), west of the centre at Route Jura 47.

SSR Voyages (☎ 322 61 61), the budget travel agency, Rue de Lausanne 35, is open 9.30 am to 6 pm weekdays, and 9 am to noon Saturday.

Things to See

A walking tour of the Old Town centre features several historic **fountains**, mostly constructed in the 16th century. They depict figures as varied as St George (outside the town hall), Samson (Place de Notre-Dame) and Christ with the Samaritan woman (Rue de la Samaritane). These are copies; the originals are in the Museum of Art and History. There are a number of good spots for **panoramic views** of the town, particularly Route des Alpes, Chemin de Loret on the south of the river, and the two bridges, Pont de Zaehringen and Pont du Milieu. The latter yields the classic view of the town that appears on many tourist posters. Consider taking a guided tour of the centre by mini train (Sfr8.50, Sfr5 for children), departing from Place Georges-Python daily except Monday in summer.

Town Hall The 16th-century town hall *(hôtel de ville)* features a clock tower and a fine double staircase. In front of the building is the **Morat Linden Tree**, which has an interesting story behind it. In 1476 the Swiss defeated Charles the Bold at Murten (Morat). The messenger who conveyed the good news to the people of Fribourg died of exhaustion immediately after uttering his announcement. As even the Swiss hadn't sorted out proper compensation for death or injury at work in those days, by way of scant recompense they planted the linden twig decorating his hat. The present tree is said to

be a descendent of this twig. The messenger's journey from Murten is retraced in a popular race on the first Sunday in October.

Cathedral of St Nicholas Construction of this Gothic cathedral, on Rue des Chanoines, was started in 1283. Around the main portal is a representation of heaven and hell and the Last Judgement. Inside, notice the distinctive organ that took six years to build in the 19th century. The stained glass windows (by Joseph Mehoffer) are bright and lively, except those in the **Chapel of the Holy Sepulchre** near the entrance.

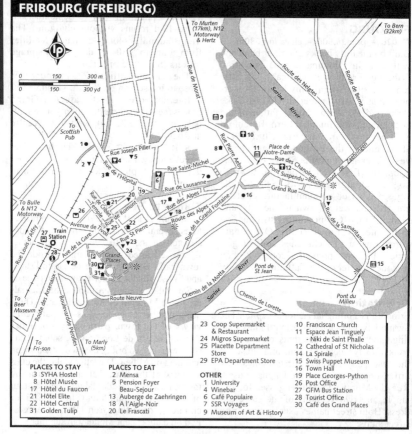

FRIBOURG (FREIBURG)

PLACES TO STAY	PLACES TO EAT		23 Coop Supermarket & Restaurant	10 Franciscan Church
3 SYHA Hostel	2 Mensa		24 Migros Supermarket	11 Espace Jean Tinguely - Niki de Saint Phalle
8 Hôtel Musée	5 Pension Foyer Beau-Sejour		25 Placette Department Store	12 Cathedral of St Nicholas
17 Hôtel du Faucon	13 Auberge de Zaehringen		29 EPA Department Store	14 La Spirale
21 Hôtel Elite	18 A l'Aigle-Noir			15 Swiss Puppet Museum
22 Hôtel Central	20 Le Frascati		OTHER	16 Town Hall
31 Golden Tulip			1 University	19 Place Georges-Python
			4 Winebar	26 Post Office
			6 Café Populaire	27 GFM Bus Station
			7 SSR Voyages	28 Tourist Office
			9 Museum of Art & History	30 Café des Grand Places

These blue and purple tones, put together by Alfred Manessier in 1977, create a suitably sombre mood in which to view the sculptural group, *The Entombment* (1433). The 74m **tower**, completed in 1490, has a great view, but it's only open from mid-June to early October (Sfr3, students Sfr2). Hours are 10 am to 5 or 5.15 pm daily, except lunchtimes and Sunday morning.

Franciscan Church The Église des Cordeliers on Rue de Morat dates from the 13th century, but was much modified 500 years later. On the right upon entering is an impressive wooden triptych which was carved and gilded around 1513. Yet what really grabs the attention is the large triptych above the high altar. It was painted in 1480 by two different anonymous artists, who signed their work by drawing carnations. The triptych depicts a crucifixion and other religious scenes.

Museum of Art & History The Musée d'Art et d'Histoire, Rue de Morat, has an excellent collection of late-Gothic sculpture and painting. It is housed in the Renaissance Hôtel Ratzé, with annexes in the former slaughterhouse and armoury. The underground corridors and rooms are atmospherically lit. Particularly effective is the cavernous chamber where religious statues are juxtaposed with mobile sculptures. The latter eerily combine animal skulls with rusted-metal machine components, and were constructed by Jean Tinguely (1925–91), who was born in Fribourg. Tinguely is also responsible for the mobile fountain in Grand-Places, but it's not as impressive as his similar effort in Basel.

Also look out for the wooden relief panels that were carved in around 1600. These show biblical scenes in fantastic detail, especially the *Flight in Egypt* panel. The museum is open 10 am to 5 pm Tuesday to Sunday and 8 to 10 pm on Thursday evening. Entry is free (Sfr8 during temporary exhibitions).

Other Museums & Galleries New in 1998, the fairly small **Espace Jean Tinguely – Niki de Saint Phalle** features the work of both artists, but especially the latter. Unfortunately,

de Saint Phalle's best creations can only be viewed via a TV film. It's open 10 am to 5 pm Wednesday to Sunday and 8 to 10 pm on Thursday evening (Sfr5). The **Swiss Puppet Museum** (Musée Suisse de la Marionnette) is at Derrière-les Jardins 2, and entry costs Sfr5 (students Sfr4, children Sfr3). It's open 2 to 5 pm on weekends only. There is also a **Beer Museum** in the large brewery at Passage du Cardinal, just south of the station. Appointments must be made on ☎ 429 22 11.

Places to Stay

Camping The nearest camp site is *La Follaz* (☎ 436 24 95), 5km south of town in the village of Marly, overlooking a river. It is open from early April to the end of September. *Camping Schiffenen* (☎ 493 19 17) is north of Fribourg by Schiffenensee, at Düdingen. This lakeside camp site is open year-round, but it's more expensive.

Hostel The SYHA *hostel* (☎ 323 19 16, fax 323 19 40, Rue de l'Hôpital 2) is in a hospital wing. Beds in the mostly six-bed dorms cost Sfr25.45, or it's Sfr31.45 for double occupancy of a dorm. Curfew is at 10 pm (keys available) and there's a kitchen. The hostel is closed from 9 am to 6 pm and from early November to late February.

Hotels *Hôtel du Faucon* (☎ 347 16 70, fax 347 16 75, Rue de Lausanne 76) is on a central pedestrian street and has a cheap restaurant. Small, functional rooms are Sfr55/100 for singles/doubles with private shower or Sfr45/80 without; triples are Sfr120. Knock off Sfr5/10 for stays exceeding three nights, and 10% if you're a student.

The rooms are nicer and larger in the *Hôtel Musée* (☎/fax 322 32 09, Rue Pierre-Aeby 11); reception is closed Sunday, unless you've reserved ahead. It has rooms using a hall shower for Sfr45/90; rooms with private shower/WC and TV are Sfr55/100. *Hôtel Central* (☎ 347 22 88, fax 347 22 89, Rue St Pierre 3) has good-value rooms for Sfr60/90, all with private shower/WC and TV. These are often snapped up, so telephone ahead. Reception and the restaurant close at 6 pm on Sunday.

Hôtel Elite (☎ 322 38 36, fax 347 16 75, Rue du Criblet 7), near Place Georges-Python, offers better-appointed rooms and two bars. Rooms with private shower/WC and TV start at Sfr90/130, with discounts possible on weekends. *Golden Tulip* (☎ 351 91 91, fax 351 91 92, @ info@fribourg.goldentulip.nl) is the soaring block at Grand-Places 14. Charges start at Sfr175/220 (Sfr110/130 on weekends) for large, smart rooms with four-star facilities; it has a reasonably-priced restaurant and free parking.

Places to Eat

There are plenty of good food choices in town. See Entertainment for other suggestions.

Self-Service You can eat for around Sfr10 in the *EPA* department store opposite the station (stand-up tables only) or at the *Coop (Rue St Pierre)*. The *Migros* supermarket next door has no restaurant. All are open till 9 pm on Thursday. The best deal is at the university *Mensa*, which has meals with soup from just Sfr6.20. It's open 11 am to 1.30 pm and 5.30 to 7.30 pm Monday to Friday. *Pension Foyer Beau-Sejour (Rue Joseph Piller 4)* is open similar hours for lunch; it's less hectic and nearly as cheap. The *Placette* department store (late opening on Thursday), Rue de Romont, has a *Manora* restaurant on the 5th floor, with good help-yourself buffets. The train station has fast food and an *Aperto* supermarket, open 6 am to 10 pm daily.

Other Restaurants The restaurant in the *Hotel Musée* (see Places to Stay) has excellent Chinese food. Stick to the barer cafe side for a four-course meal, a real steal for Sfr16; dishes on the other side are above Sfr25 (closed Sunday).

Hôtel Central (see Places to Stay) is also good, and has great prices. Most meals, including Italian and Swiss food, are Sfr7.50 to Sfr17. For pizzas from Sfr12, try out *Le Frascati (Rue de Romont)* – it's one of the few places open on Sunday.

The *Buffet de la Gare* (☎ 322 28 16) on the 1st floor of the train station has quality food with prices to match (closed on Sunday and mid-July to late August); downstairs is more affordable (open daily). *A l'Aigle-Noir* (☎ 322 49 77, Rue des Alpes 10) has good French dishes from Sfr35 (closed Sunday and Monday).

The best restaurant in Fribourg is said to be the *Auberge de Zaehringen* (☎ 322 42 36, Rue de Zaehringen 13), which is closed Sunday evening and Monday. Its Brasserie has meals from Sfr25, art on the walls, and three-course lunches for Sfr19.50; the Galerie has gourmet menus and is closed from 1 July to mid-August.

Entertainment

Winebar (Rue de l'Hôpital 39) is a young, sociable venue with special events on weekends and a techno bar upstairs. Entry is free and drinks are cheap. If you want to mix with Fribourg's students, head for *Café Populaire (Rue Saint-Michel 9)*, open daily. *Café des Grand Places (Grand-Places 12)* has a cafe on the ground floor with a world-wide menu (eg, Mexican, Indian). It's open daily, but closed till 6 pm on weekends. Upstairs is a bar with themed music nights (eg, salsa on Thursday and Sunday); entry is Sfr5 and it's closed Monday and Tuesday.

Fri-son (☎ 424 36 25, Route de la Fonderie 13), south of the station, spins rap, reggae, soul, techno and house music. *La Spirale* (☎ 322 66 39, Place du Petit St Jean 39) welcomes jazz and blues musicians. Entry for either place costs around Sfr15.

Getting There & Away

Fribourg is on the north/south N12 (E27) which connects Lake Geneva to Bern and beyond. Trains run hourly to Neuchâtel (Sfr19 via Murten; takes one hour), and even more frequently to Geneva (Sfr41, around 90 minutes) and Bern (Sfr11.80, 30 minutes). GFM Buses (green with an orange stripe; Swiss Pass valid) depart from the rear of the train station and go to nearby destinations such as Avenches (Sfr8) and Bulle (Sfr13.60). A side trip to consider by GFM bus is to the scenic Lake

Schwarz (Sfr13.60 one way, Sfr21.80 return, one hour).

A local car rental firm is Garage Lehmann (☎ 424 26 26), Ave Beauregard 16.

Getting Around
Walking is fine in the centre, although those hills can get a bit wearing. Bus tickets are Sfr1.50 to Sfr2, or it costs Sfr5 for a day pass (Sfr10 for three days). All the city bus lines stop by the station and Place Georges-Python. There is parking at Grand-Places, or underground at Place Georges-Python.

ESTAVAYER-LE-LAC
☎ 026 • pop 4100 • elevation 455m
Frogs are the unique attraction of this lakeside resort. They're all 130 years old and inside glass cases in the museum. Much of the medieval town centre looks like it has been preserved under glass too – another Swiss town that seems to have avoided the ravages of time.

Orientation & Information
The small train station has bike rental but no lockers (staff will hold luggage on request). It's 400m from the old centre; you can orientate yourself using the map outside. The tourist office (☎ 663 12 37, fax 663 42 07, ✉ office.tourisme@estavayer-le-lac.ch) is in a travel agent, Inter Voyages SA, by the UBS Bank on Place du Midi. It's open 9 am to noon and 2 to 6 pm Monday to Friday, and in July and August, it's also open 10 to noon and 3 to 5 pm Saturday and Sunday.

Things to See & Do
Francois Perrier, an eccentric 19th-century military man, spent much of his leisure time killing frogs, preserving their skins, and filling them with sand, then arranged them in parodies of human situations, complete with props. The **Regional Museum** displays 108 of his stuffed frogs engaged in courting, studying, playing games and much more. The result is halfway between the cute and the bizarre. Young kids are fascinated by it. Other exhibits include weapons and kitchen utensils, and a surprisingly extensive collection of railway lanterns and signs. Also notice the novel three-faces-in-one portraits on the right wall just before you go downstairs. It is open 9 to 11 am and 2 to 5 pm from 1 March to 31 October (closed Monday, except in July and August). The rest of the year it's only open 2 to 5 pm Saturday and Sunday. Entry costs Sfr4 for adults, Sfr3 for senior citizens and students, and Sfr2 for children.

When you tire of amphibians you can be aquatic yourself in the pleasure boat harbour, or try water-skiing (get towed around the lake by a special cable-way; Sfr10 for two circuits), windsurfing and sailing.

The old Gothic centre is well worth a wander. The 13th-century **castle** is well preserved and is now the home of the cantonal police. Also step into the **St Laurent Church** for a look at the fresh stained-glass and the heavily barred altar.

Places to Stay & Eat
Camp at *Nouvelle Plage* (☎/fax 663 16 93), by the lake to the right of the harbour. It's open from around April to September and costs Sfr6.40 per person and from Sfr7 per tent.

My Lady's Manor (☎ 663 23 16, fax 663 19 93, ✉ phyl.pritchett@bluewin.ch, Route de la Gare), between the station and the centre, is an excellent deal. It's a genuine stately home, with ornamental furnishings, converted in piecemeal fashion to hotel rooms (Sfr45 per person, using hall showers). There's extensive gardens and off-street parking (closed November to February).

Hôtel Fleur-de-Lys (☎ 663 42 63, fax 663 48 78, Route de la Gare 12), near the tourist office, is above a bar and has good rooms, some with a view, balcony and TV. Singles/doubles are Sfr70/120 with shower/WC, or singles using hall shower are Sfr50.

For comfortable rooms by the lake (from Sfr77 per person), try *Hôtel du Lac* (☎ 663 52 20, fax 663 53 43, Place du Port 1). It also has a restaurant.

Tea Room Carmen (Rue de l'Hôtel de Ville 5) is where you can consume very cheap snacks and Italian food. It closes on Monday and at 7.30 pm (11 pm in summer) from Tuesday to Saturday and 6 pm on Sunday. *Restaurant Centenaire* (Rue du Four) has pizzas from Sfr11 and a small terrace (closed Tuesday).

Also good is the **Gerbe d'Or** *(Rue du Camus)*, opposite the Denner supermarket. The cafe has lunches with soup for Sfr15.50 and a range of other meals; a more expensive restaurant awaits upstairs. Both parts are closed Monday evening and Sunday.

Getting There & Away
Estavayer-le-Lac is on the direct road and rail route between Fribourg and Yverdon, or it's a short detour off the northbound highway 1 from Lausanne. Estavayer is also a stop for boat services on Lac de Neuchâtel; it's 1½ hours to Neuchâtel and 1¼ hours to Yverdon, with around three departures a day from late May to late September, except on Monday. Inquire at the tourist office or telephone LNM (☎ 032-725 40 12) in Neuchâtel for more information.

MURTEN
☎ 026 • pop 5300 • elevation 450m
In May 1476, Charles the Bold (the Duke of Burgundy), still smarting from his recent defeat by the Swiss Confederates at Grandson, set off from Lausanne to lay siege on Murten. Two weeks after his arrival in the town the Swiss army arrived in force and trapped the Burgundians on the shore of the lake. The Duke fled with his life, but 8000 of his men were butchered or drowned.

Picturesque Murten retains a strong sense of history and has much of its medieval fortifications still intact. The lake provides added attractions.

Orientation & Information
French speakers call this place Morat, while German speakers call it Murten. You can take your pick as it's right on the linguistic divide, though most of the inhabitants speak German. It is on the eastern shore of Lake Murten (Lac de Morat, Murtensee) and Bern is 28km to the east. The train station is 300m outside the city walls and has money-exchange daily to midnight and bike rental. There's a map outside so you can orientate yourself. The post office (3280) is opposite.

The tourist office (☎ 670 51 12, fax 67⬛ 49 83, ✉ murtentourismus@bluewin.ch) i⬛ in the centre at Französische Kirchgasse ⬛ near the Bern Tower. In winter (approxi⬛ mately October to March) it's open 10 an⬛ to noon and 2 to 5 pm Monday to Friday. I⬛ summer it's open to at least 6 pm, plus 1⬛ am to 2 pm Saturday. It has a useful book⬛ let giving information on activities, excur⬛ sions, and biking and hiking tours. Mos⬛ hotels and restaurants close for part of th⬛ winter; the tourist office compiles a list.

Things to See & Do
Spend an hour or so roaming around th⬛ cobbled streets of the walled centre, admir⬛ ing the arcaded houses displaying window⬛ boxes and shutters. Dwellings in the centr⬛ were rebuilt in stone after being destroyed in a fire in 1416. There's a free guided tou⬛ on Friday in July and August (inquire at th⬛ tourist office). The **castle** dates from th⬛ 13th century and offers a view of the lak⬛ from the courtyard. At the north-east end o⬛ Hauptgasse is the distinctive **Bern Tower** also 13th century. The best view of th⬛ centre is from the city walls themselves. Ascend at the tower behind the Germa⬛ church on Deutsche Kirchgasse and wal⬛ clockwise to get the best view of the tower⬛ and rows of brown-tiled roofs. You coul⬛ also stroll around Stadtgraben, a path circ⬛ ling the outside of the walls, where yo⬛ might see locals toiling in their garden al⬛ lotments beside the ancient fortifications.

Outside the walls near the castle is th⬛ **Historical Museum**, housed in the old wate⬛ mill. In 1829 the dredging of the Broye⬛ canal and the drawing of the marshes cause⬛ a lowering of the lakes at the foot of th⬛ Jura. This uncovered evidence of ancien⬛ dwellings dating from 4000 BC, and thes⬛ archaeological finds were just lying ther⬛ for any wanderer to pick up. Fortunately many found their way to this museum. I⬛ addition to these relics, and the cannon⬛ from the battle of Murten, there are variou⬛ oddities. There's a huge bullet that killed a⬛ elephant, dated and decorated leather fir⬛ buckets – a compulsory household utensi⬛ after the 1416 fire – and some surprisingly suggestive pewter council flagons (with an arm caressing the spout). Opening hours are 10 am to noon and 2 to 5 pm Tuesday to Sunday from 1 May to 1 October. In winter it's closed mornings (and weekdays in January and February). Admission costs Sfr4 for adults, Sfr3 for seniors, Sfr2 for students, and Sfr1 for children.

Lake Murten provides numerous recreational possibilities, and the harbour is by the walled centre. Circular tours of the lake depart from late May to late September (tickets on the boat). Contact the tourist office, the harbour authorities (☎ 670 26 03) or the train station (☎ 670 26 46) for details. Fishing permits can be obtained from the Préfecture (☎ 670 22 57) in the castle. There is a beach (and a swimming pool) near the Historical Museum. For the sailing school and boat hire, contact Pierre Tschachtli (☎ 670 48 17). There's also a watersport school (☎ 415 22 22) and La Bise Noire (☎ 670 23 17), a windsurfing school.

At the beginning of March, Murten celebrates its **carnival**, comprising three days of fun and parades. On the first Sunday in October, there's the Murten-Fribourg race; up to 8000 participants retrace the 17km route of the messenger who relayed news of the Battle of Murten. Participants are not expected to re-enact the journey too faithfully – the man died upon arrival!

Places to Stay
Opposite Murten station, *Hotel-Restaurant Bahnhof (☎ 670 22 56)* has plenty of parking. Standard singles/doubles using hall shower are Sfr60/100; doubles for Sfr120 have private facilities. Book ahead.

The other hotels are in Murten's old centre, where the best budget choice is the small and welcoming *Hotel Ringmauer (☎ 670 11 01, fax 672 20 83, Deutsche Kirchgasse 2)*. Rooms are Sfr60/105 with hall showers. *Hotel Krone (☎ 670 52 52, fax 670 36 10, Rathausgasse 5)* has rooms from Sfr105/150 with private shower/WC and TV. Next door is the *Hotel Murtenhof (☎ 672 90 30, fax 672 90 39)*, offering the same standard and prices, but with the advantage of private parking. Most rooms have interesting

decor with patches of old brickwork showing through the modern plaster (intentionally!). Both places have more expensive rooms overlooking the lake.

Places to Eat
There's a *Coop* supermarket with a restaurant on Bahnhofstrasse near the castle. It has a terrace, menus from around Sfr9 and is open until 7 pm Monday to Thursday, until 8 pm Friday, and to 4 pm Saturday. Other than here, or *Weisses Kreuz (Rathausgasse 31)* for expensive fish specialities, it's probably best to stick to the following hotels.

Hotel Krone is the best place to eat, if all the gastronomic plaques outside are to be believed; there's a quality restaurant on the 1st floor and a fairly cheap downstairs section (closed Tuesday). *Hotel Murtenhof* has a good salad buffet (Sfr7.50 for a smallish plate) and views of the lake. There's a range of meals (including vegetarian) and prices (from Sfr12), and it's closed Monday. *Hotel Ringmauer* has hot food from about Sfr16 (closed Sunday evening and Monday).

Getting There & Away
There are hourly trains to/from Fribourg (Sfr10, 30 minutes). For Bern (Sfr11.80, 35 minutes) and Neuchâtel (Sfr10.80, 30 minutes), change at Kerzers. Avenches (Sfr3) is just two stops and eight minutes away on the hourly train to Payerne, which is also on the route to Lausanne (Sfr25).

Murten is on highway 1, which runs from Lausanne in the south and links with the motorway to Bern. Neuchâtel and Biel can be reached by boat on the 'three lake tour' in the summer; contact the harbour authorities or the tourist office for details (see also the Around Biel section in the Swiss Mittelland chapter).

Getting Around
Walking is the best way to get around. If you're driving, parking is limited within the town walls (maximum 90 minutes from 8 am to 6 pm daily: Sfr1.80 per hour), but there's a parking garage by the Coop.

FRIBOURG, NEUCHÂTEL & JURA

AROUND MURTEN
Avenches
This village is 8km south of Murten along highway 1 (E4) and within canton Vaud. It was built on the site of the old capital of the Helvetii, a Celtic tribe who were the first inhabitants of the region. Later it became a flourishing Roman town and reached the peak of its influence in the 1st and 2nd centuries. At this time its population was around 10 times greater than its present total of 2000. The town's defences – a high wall and ring of fortified observation towers – were not sufficient to prevent it being destroyed in 259 by the Germanic Alemanni tribe.

Little remains of its former glory except a large amphitheatre (seating 12,000), a Roman Museum and the occasional turret. The Roman Museum, **Musée romain d'Avenches**, Ave Jomini, is open 10 am to noon and 1 pm to 5 pm Tuesday to Sunday. From October to March, it's open from 2 to 5 pm and is closed mornings. Entry costs Sfr2 (children Sfr1).

Ask the tourist office (☎ 675 11 59, @ otavenches@bluewin.ch), in the town centre at Place de l'Église 3, for directions to outlying ruins. It's open 8 am to noon and 1.30 pm to 5.30 pm Monday to Friday, and from April to September, it's also open 9 am to noon Saturday. Avenches also has a new equestrian centre, the largest in Switzerland.

There's an SYHA *hostel (☎ 675 26 66, Rue du Lavoir 5)* with dorm beds for Sfr23; the hostel closes from mid-October to mid-April. It's situated about a 15-minute walk from Avenches train station; take Ave General Guisan and walk to the far south-west corner of the old centre (or take the bus to 'Restaurant Croix Blanc').

Payerne
If you're driving along the Lausanne-Murten highway 1, it's worth stopping for a brief look at the former abbey in Payerne, a small town in Vaud, 10km south of Avenches. The 11th-century Romanesque abbey church, just a couple of minutes from the train station, has been extensively and impressively restored. It's open daily, and the entry price of Sfr3/2 for adults/students and seniors includes a small museum. If there's an exhibition in the adjoining chapterhouse, admission jumps to Sfr12/10.

GRUYÈRES
☎ 026 • pop 1500 • elevation 830m
This picturesque town attracts busloads of tourists with its fine 15th- to 17th-century houses and commanding castle. Visitors can catch the odd scent of cheese in the air, too.

Orientation & Information
Gruyères is on the western edge of the Pre-Alps in the canton of Fribourg. The small train station will hold baggage behind the counter, but opening hours are limited. The main village is a 10-minute walk up the hill. Buses and cars must be left in the free car park at the entrance to the village.

The tourist office (☎ 921 10 30, fax 921 38 50) is at the start of the main street. It's open 8.30 am to noon and 1.30 to 5 pm Monday to Friday; from around July to mid-September there's no lunch-break and it also opens 9 am to 5 pm Saturday and Sunday. There are no banks; change money at the train station as the tourist office offers terrible rates. There are no street names in this tiny place.

Things to See
If you can avoid the tour buses, Gruyères is a great place to linger and enjoy the harmonious setting and relaxed atmosphere. The main street is extremely photogenic. The impact is immediate upon entering the village. You see the road dipping down to a central fountain, flanked on either side by quaint old buildings with hanging signs, and all dominated in the distance by the rising turrets of the castle and mountain peaks beyond.

Castle Château de Gruyères offers an expansive view from its 13th-century ramparts. The dungeon is also 13th century, but much of the rest of the castle dates from after the fire in 1493. It was once the home of the Counts of Gruyères who held sway over the whole Sarine Valley from the 11th to the 16th century. Inside there are various items on display, such as ecclesiastical

Evening sun on Montreux, Lake Geneva Region

'X' marks the spot . . .

The imposing St Peter's Cathedral, Geneva

Main street of the big cheese, Gruyères, Fribourg

Ballooning at Château d'Oex, Lake Geneva Region

Torch-ed bearers, Lausanne

The famous Edelweiss

A SMART car . . . the only Swiss made car

vestments (booty from the battle of Murten), tapestries and period furniture. Look out for representations of the crane (*grue* in French), the heraldic emblem of the Counts of Gruyères. There are also temporary and permanent displays of 'art fantastique', said to be the most important collection of art with fantstical themes in Europe. It provides a bizarre and dreamlike counterpoint to the rest of the castle. Allow about 1½ hours in total. It's open daily: 9 am to 7 pm from June to September; 9.30 am to noon and 1.30 pm to 4 pm from November to February; and 9 am to noon and 1 to 5 pm at other times of the year. Admission costs Sfr5 or Sfr2 for students and children.

Museum HR Geiger Further art in the sci-fi/fantasy genre can be seen courtesy of HR Geiger, creator of the monster in the *Alien* films. This museum covers his work (paintings, sculptures, furniture, etc) from the 1960s to the present, and includes sketches that relate to his movie work. The top floor exhibits pieces from his personal art collection. Entry costs Sfr8 (students/ seniors Sfr6) and it's open 1 to 5 pm Tuesday to Sunday, or 10 am to 6.30 pm daily in summer. It's a new museum so hours may change; a bar and a train ride are planned.

Cheese-Making Gruyère is one of the best known of Swiss cheeses, and it's one of the main cheeses used in fondue. It takes nearly 12L of full cream milk to make 1kg of Gruyère, and there are 12 different stages in the three-month production process.

Two local dairies allow you to see cheese-making in action and buy the finished product. The most convenient is in Pringy (☎ 921 14 10), opposite Gruyères train station, where the cheese is made into 'wheels' weighing 35kg (free entry). It is open 8 am to 7 pm daily, but the best time to go is when the cheese is actually in production, from 9 to 11.30 am and 1 to 3.30 pm (shorter hours on Sunday, and not Monday afternoon).

The most active phase is when the cheese is pumped from the vat to the moulds, about 1½ hours after the start. This modern dairy gets through over 13,000L of milk per day.

There's a slide show and commentary in English that's informative but rather over-stresses the 'harmony with nature' aspect (this has more to do with 'bull' than 'cow', despite the many references to the latter).

There's another dairy in a 17th-century chalet in Moléson, 5km south-west of Gruyères. It is open 9.30 am to 10 pm every day from mid-May to mid-October, but again you should try and visit during cheese production hours (Sfr3, seniors Sfr2). This one uses old-fashioned production methods. The Moléson tourist office (☎ 921 24 34) can tell you more.

Wax Museum The small Musée de Cire is in Moléson, and recreates influential figures from Swiss history such as the creator of the Red Cross, Henri Dunant. It is open daily except Tuesday and entry is free.

Activities
The Gruyère region offers winter cross-country skiing, plus a few easy and medium downhill runs, particularly at Charmey and Moléson. The 2002m Moléson peak also boasts an impressive panorama of the taller peaks further south. Signposted walking trails can be found everywhere, including on Moléson and neighbouring Vudalla (1668m).

Places to Stay & Eat
There are only four small hotels in the centre of Gruyères so it's a good idea to book ahead. Don't even think of staying overnight in one of these hotels if you're on a tight budget, though you could camp at *Haute Gruyère* (☎ 921 22 60), 5km south of Gruyères at Enney.

The cheapest place in Gruyères village is *Hôtel de Ville* (☎ 921 24 24, fax 921 36 28, ✉ hoteldeville-gruyeres@ swissonline.ch), in the main street, where all rooms have private shower/WC and TV; singles/doubles cost Sfr80/120 and triples/quads Sfr150/180. Also in the main street, *Hostellerie St Georges* (☎ 921 83 00, fax 921 83 39) costs Sfr80/120 from November to March, and Sfr160/250 from April to October. *Hostellerie des Chevaliers* (☎ 921 19 33, fax 921 25 52, ✉ hotel_chevaliers@bluewin.ch), by

The Making of Chocolate

Cocoa plantations had already been important in Central America for over 1000 years before Hernando Cortez first transported cocoa back to Europe in 1528. Europeans initially consumed chocolate only in liquid form, often with wine, beer or pepper added. Eating chocolate in solid form did not become popular until the 19th century, when tea and coffee replaced drinking chocolate as the beverage of choice. But still ingredients were added to the chocolate that we would consider strange today, such as barley, rice, oatmeal and even meat extracts.

Swiss chocolate built its reputation in the 19th century, thanks to pioneering spirits such as François-Louis Cailler (1796–1852), Philippe Suchard (1797–1884), Henri Nestlé (1814–90), Jean Tobler (1830–1905), Daniel Peter (1836–1919) and Rodolphe Lindt (1855–1909). Cailler established the first Swiss chocolate factory in 1819, near Vevey, after he learned the chocolate trade in Italy. Daniel Peter was the first person to add milk to chocolate (1875). Lindt invented the production method called conching, a rotary aeration process that gives chocolate its smooth, melt-in-the-mouth quality.

The cocoa bean is actually very bitter and needs a sweetener – even dark chocolate is two-fifths sugar. The growing areas are equatorial countries, particularly Brazil, the Ivory Coast, Ghana and Nigeria. Harvest times are May and October to November. The beans, after being extracted from the cocoa fruit, are left to ferment for two to six days. They're then dried and shipped to the chocolate manufacturing countries. The USA is the biggest chocolate manufacturer in the world. Switzerland is only the 10th biggest, but the Swiss by far consume more chocolate than anybody else – 11.3kg per person per year, 43% more than their nearest rivals, the Norwegians.

At the factory, the cocoa beans are cleaned, roasted (to develop the aroma) and crushed. The husks are extracted and used in the chemical industry. Different types of beans are blended according to the recipe and ground into a fine paste. Part of the cocoa paste is then processed to extract cocoa butter, a yellowish fat comprising about 50% of the original bean. The powder that is left after extracting the cocoa butter is used for various purposes, including making instant chocolate drinks. The cocoa butter itself is used to make white chocolate, or is re-combined with the remaining cocoa paste to make plain or milk chocolate.

The cocoa paste, cocoa butter, sugar and milk (if milk chocolate) is kneaded, rolled and conched until it is a completely smooth, homogeneous liquid. After tempering (a heating and cooling process) it is finally ready to be shaped into chocolate sweets or bars. Like centuries ago, the use of additives and fillings is common, even though the ingredients have changed. Common fillings nowadays are Praline (crushed and caramelised almonds and hazelnuts, said to have been discovered after a kitchen accident in 1671), nougat, truffles and marzipan. Adding meat extracts, as they did with the 'Royal Prussian Patented Chocolate Product' in late 19th century Berlin, is no longer done. Perhaps a niche market exists for some meat-oriented entrepreneur?

---

the car park, is the biggest and classiest hotel and has a quality restaurant. Rooms start at Sfr100/140.

In Moléson, *Hotel-Restaurant Plan Francey* (☎ 921 10 42, fax 921 30 38) has singles/doubles for Sfr44/78 and dormitory beds for Sfr27.

Inevitably, cheesy creations figure strongly when contemplating a bite to eat. As well as looking at the hotel restaurants, try *Auberge de la Halle* which has its filling *Soupe de Chalet* (mushrooms, pasta,

cheese, etc) for Sfr17.50. *Café-Restaurant des Remparts*, on the other side of the main road, is reasonably priced (for Gruyères) and offers a range of meals, such as fondue for Sfr20 (open daily). There will be a restaurant in the Pringy cheese dairy once extensions are completed in 2000.

Getting There & Away

From Fribourg, Gruyères can be reached by taking the hourly bus (Sfr13.60, 30 minutes) to Bulle (see the following section) and the hourly train (Sfr3, 10 minutes) from there. Coming from the south, change trains at Montbovon. Infrequent buses connect Gruyères station, Gruyères village and Moléson.

The main road route is the north-south N12 (E27) motorway from Vevey to Fribourg and Bern, which passes by Bulle. There are also good roads heading south and east through the mountains from Gruyères and Broc.

BULLE
☎ 026 • pop 9700 • elevation 770m
Five kilometres north-west of Gruyères is Bulle, with a 13th-century castle (now administrative offices). Behind the castle is the regional museum, **Musée Gruérien**, with a reasonable collection including paintings, furniture, costumes, room interiors and religious artefacts. It is open 10 am to noon and 2 to 5 pm Tuesday to Saturday, and Sunday and holidays in the afternoon only. Entry costs Sfr5 (students Sfr4).

Between the train station and the castle is a tourist office (☎ 912 80 22). At the same junction is *Café Fribourgeois*, with Swiss food, good two-course lunches for Sfr14, and an antique orchestral machine that's activated on request. *Hôtel du Tonnelier* (☎ 912 77 45, fax 912 39 86, Grand-Rue 31), has singles/doubles with themed decor and shower/WC for Sfr60/90, and some singles without shower for Sfr45. It also has two restaurants and a cellar bar. A *Coop* supermarket and restaurant is at Grand-Rue 35.

Bulle is the main transport hub for the Gruyère region, accessible by train and bus.

BROC
☎ 026 • pop 2000
Broc, a few kilometres north of Gruyères, is known mainly for the **Nestlé-Caillers Chocolate factory** (☎ 921 51 51). You can see a 20-minute film about chocolate-making with an English commentary (free), help yourself to some free samples and buy the products. Visits are permitted on weekdays from late April to late October, but you must phone ahead.

Around the back is **Electrobroc** (☎ 352 52 52), a power station and energy information

centre. Free two-hour tours are conducted at 10 am and 2 pm on Saturday between March and December.

Broc can be reached from Bulle by a small train: for the above sights, get off after the village at Broc Fabrique (Sfr3).

Neuchâtel Canton

The first inhabitants of this region were lake dwellers who settled as early as 3000 BC. The 2nd Iron Age in Europe is referred to as 'La Tène Period', after the settlement on the eastern end of Lake Neuchâtel where a store of weapons and utensils were discovered. Modern industries include watchmaking, precision engineering, and printing and publishing. The observatory in Neuchâtel town gives the official time-check for all Switzerland.

NEUCHÂTEL
☎ 032 • pop 32,000 • elevation 430m
Neuchâtel is the capital of its canton. It's a relaxing town on the north-west shore of the largest lake that's totally within Switzerland, Lake Neuchâtel.

The descendants of Ulrich II became known as the Counts of Neuchâtel from the early 12th century. The territory was elevated to a principality at the beginning of the 17th century, with Henry II of Orléans-Longueville as its head. The title of Prince ultimately devolved to Frederick-William III of Prussia, who allowed Neuchâtel to join the Swiss Confederation in 1815. Yet, curiously and incompatibly, the canton remained a principality under Prussia until 1848, when a bloodless revolution won it the status of a republic.

The French spoken in Neuchâtel is said to be the purest in Switzerland.

Orientation & Information
The train station (Gare CFF) changes money from 5.45 am (6.30 am on Sunday) to 9 pm daily and rents out bikes. It also has lockers (Sfr2 and Sfr5), luggage storage, restaurants and a train information office (open weekdays and Saturday morning).

From the station, take bus No 6 (or walk for 10 minutes) to get to the hub of the town, Place Pury, on the edge of the central pedestrian zone. The tourist office (☎ 889 68 90, fax 889 62 96, @ tourisme.neuchatelois@ ne.ch) is nearby in the main post office, Place du Port, by the harbour. It's open 9 am to noon and 1.30 to 5.30 pm on weekdays and 9 am to noon Saturday. In July and August, it's open 9 am to 7 pm Monday to Saturday and 4 to 7 pm Sunday. Pick up a copy of its walking tour of the town centre. The office covers the whole canton and has several cycling and hiking maps (some are free), and gives out a 'Passeport inter-musées', good for entry-fee reductions.

The main post office (Poste Principal, 2001) is open 7.30 am to 6.30 pm weekdays and 8 to 11 am Saturday. There's another post office just opposite the train station (2002 Neuchâtel 2), which has an out-of-hours counter open daily (Sfr1 surcharge).

Do laundry at Salon Lavoir Lavmatic, Rue des Moulins 27 (closes 8 pm). Bar au 21, Faubourg du Lac 43, has one computer terminal for Internet access (Sfr5/8 for 30/60 minutes).

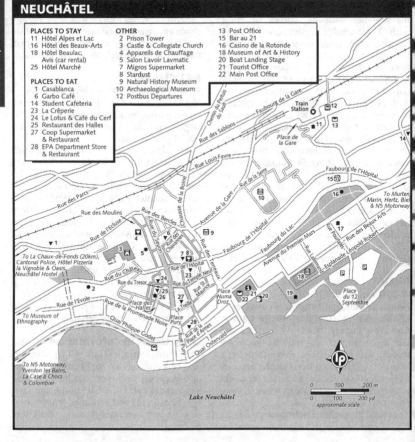

NEUCHÂTEL

PLACES TO STAY
11 Hôtel Alpes et Lac
16 Hôtel des Beaux-Arts
18 Hôtel Beaulac;
     Avis (car rental)
25 Hôtel Marché

PLACES TO EAT
 1 Casablanca
 6 Garbo Café
14 Student Cafeteria
23 La Crêperie
24 Le Lotus & Café du Cerf
25 Restaurant des Halles
27 Coop Supermarket
     & Restaurant
28 EPA Department Store
     & Restaurant

OTHER
 2 Prison Tower
 3 Castle & Collegiate Church
 4 Appareils de Chauffage
 5 Salon Lavoir Lavmatic
 7 Migros Supermarket
 8 Stardust
 9 Natural History Museum
10 Archaeological Museum
12 Postbus Departures

13 Post Office
15 Bar au 21
16 Casino de la Rotonde
18 Museum of Art & History
20 Boat Landing Stage
21 Tourist Office
22 Main Post Office

Things to See & Do

The centrepiece of the Old Town is the **castle** (with free guided tours in summer) and the adjoining **Collegiate Church**. The castle dates from the 12th century and now houses cantonal offices. Walk along the ramparts for a view over the town. The church combines Gothic and Romanesque elements. Its most striking feature is a cenotaph of 15 statues dating from 1372. This depicts medieval knights and ladies (most of whom have been identified) standing in suitably pious postures. Nearby, the **Prison Tower** (entry Sfr0.50) offers a good view of the area and has interesting models showing the town as it was in the 15th and 18th centuries. It's closed from October to March. While roaming around the centre, look out for the six historic fountains which were built around the turn of the 16th century. They were all the work of Laurent Perroud. In particular, the fountain at the north end of Rue du Trésor is attractively situated.

Museums Don't miss the **Museum of Art and History** (Musée d'Art et d'Histoire), Esplanade Léopold Robert 2, which is especially noted for three 18th-century clockwork figures. They were built between 1764 and 1774 by Jaquet Droz who was formerly a watchmaker based in La Chaux-de-Fonds. The technical achievement in constructing these automata was incredible for the time, and they were performed before admiring crowds in the fairs and royal courts of Europe.

The most elaborate is the Writer, who can be programmed to dip his pen in an inkpot and write up to 40 characters. This is achieved via 120 internal revolving discs; the adjustment of these is so fine – to within 0.1mm – that if the room gets too hot the expansion of the metal can cause him to make spelling mistakes! The Musician can play up to five tunes; it's a real organ she plays, not a disguised musical box, and she moves her eyes and appears to breathe as her fingers strike the keys. The Draughtsman is technically the simplest, but he still has a repertoire of six drawings.

The clockwork figures were purchased for the museum in 1909 for Sfr75,000, and it is so protective of them that they are only activated on the first Sunday of each month. On other days you can see them at rest and watch a film (in English) explaining their history and functions. Elsewhere in the museum are clocks, coins, decorative arts, and works by Swiss painters. Entry is Sfr7 (Sfr4 for students and children), except on Thursday when it's free. The museum is open 10 am to 5 pm Tuesday to Sunday.

Also interesting is the **Museum of Ethnography** (Musée d'ethnographie), Rue St Nicolas 4, which concentrates mainly on exhibits from Africa, Bhutan and Oceania (Sfr7 or Sfr4 for students and children). It's on the westward continuation of Rue du Château and is closed on Monday. The **Natural History Museum** (Musée d'histoire naturelle) is at Rue des Terreaux 14 (Sfr6, students and seniors Sfr3, children free, free for everyone on Wednesday). It's open 10 am to 5 pm Tuesday to Sunday. The **Archaeological Museum** (Musée cantonal d'archéologie), Ave du Peyrou 7 (free), is open 2 to 5 pm daily except Monday.

Lake Neuchâtel

Cruises on the lake are well worth considering in the summer, and the neighbouring lakes of Biel and Murten are also accessible via a canal. Boat trips can be a relaxing day out with meals on board or simply a means to continue onward travel. For more information, contact the boat company LNM (☎ 725 40 12) at the harbour. (See also the Around Biel section in the Swiss Mittelland chapter). A one-day pass for travel on the lake costs Sfr42, or Sfr29 with a Half-Fare Card. It costs Sfr7 to transport bikes.

Special Events

Neuchâtel hosts the **Grape Harvest Festival** (Fête des Vendanges) on the last weekend in September. It includes parades and costumes, and a fair amount of drunken revelry. At the end of June, there's **Festi-Jazz** by the lakeside.

Places to Stay

Camping There are camp sites a few kilometres away on either side of Neuchâtel. *La Tène Plage (☎ 753 73 40)* in Marin is open from April to September and costs Sfr6.30 per adult, from Sfr6 for a tent and Sfr2.20 for parking. It's by the lake, a short walk from Marin Epagnier train station. *Paradis Plage (☎ 841 24 46)*, by the lake in Colombier, has loads of facilities but it's more expensive (open March to October). Bus No 5 goes to Colombier from Place Pury in Neuchâtel. By car, you can take either the N5 or Quai Philippe-Godet.

Hostel *Oasis Neuchâtel (☎ 731 31 90, fax 730 37 09, Rue du Suchiez 35)* is over 2km from the town centre; take bus No 1 to Vauseyon, then walk three minutes towards Centre sportiv Le Chanet. This small, friendly independent hostel offers vegetarian meals and kitchen facilities; check-in is from 5 to 9 pm. Beds are Sfr23 in dorms, Sfr28 in doubles, or Sfr20 (own sleeping bag needed) in a garden tepee. It's usually open from Easter to 31 October.

Hotels Cheaper than the hotels is B&B accommodation in private houses. They're out of town, but some are convenient for bus routes; inquire at the tourist office. *Hôtel-Pizzeria le Vignoble (☎ 731 12 40, fax 725 72 70, Châtelard 3)* has fairly basic singles with hall shower for Sfr40, and singles/doubles with private shower for Sfr45/90. Take bus No 1 to Vignoble. *Hôtel-Restaurant du Poisson (☎ 753 30 31, fax 753 06 25, Ave Bachelin 7, Marin)*, on the same bus route in the opposite direction, is another budget possibility. Rooms are Sfr50/100 with shower or Sfr45/90 without.

Hôtel Marché (☎ 724 58 00, fax 721 47 42, Place des Halles 4) is ideally central, with rooms overlooking the square (you may find these noisy if you're a light sleeper). Rooms vary in size, each has a TV, but showers are in the hall. Prices are Sfr70/100, and an extra bed in the room costs Sfr35. It's closed Sunday until 2 pm and Monday.

Hôtel des Beaux-Arts (☎ 724 01 51, fax 724 08 30, Rue Pourtalès 3) is friendly and reasonably central. Rooms with private shower/WC are Sfr122/170, and there are few rooms using hall shower for Sfr78/125. Prices for singles are negotiable – yo should be able to get lower rates than these. The inexpensive restaurant is open daily.

Hôtel Alpes et Lac (☎ 723 19 19, fax 72 19 20, ✉ hotel@alpesetlac.ch), opposite th train station, has refurbished rooms with bathroom and TV from Sfr98/148, o Sfr110/160 with lake view.

Hôtel Beaulac (☎ 723 11 11, fax 725 6 35, Esplanade Léopold Robert 2) is a four star place overlooking the harbour. Larg rooms from Sfr160/220 have all the expecte amenities. There are two restaurants on site

Places to Eat

Local specialities include tripe, and *tomm Neuchâteloise chaude*, a baked chees starter. Fish from the lake, especially trou *(truite)*, is another treat.

Self-Service By Place Pury is an *EPA* de partment store with a cheap restaurant Nearby is a *Coop (Rue de la Treille 4* supermarket and restaurant with simila prices. There is also a *Migros* supermarke on Rue de l'Hôpital, with a snack counter All these places have late opening till 8 pm on Thursday. Weekday lunches for aroun Sfr9 are available in the *student cafeteria* a Cité Universitaire *(Ave de Clos-Brochet)*.

Other Restaurants *La Crêperie (Rue de l'Hôpital 7)* is popular with mainly youngis locals. If you don't like thin pancakes you' think this place is a load of crêpe, becaus that's all it serves. The price is betwee Sfr2.70 and Sfr9.70, depending on the fill ing, of which there's a wide choice rangin from the exotic to the mundane. A coupl would make a light meal (open daily).

Le Lotus (☎ 724 27 44, 1st floor, Rue d l'Ancien 4) serves excellent oriental foo (mainly Thai) for around Sfr30. At groun level is the *Café du Cerf* where two o three-course meals (lunch and dinner) ar Sfr19 and Sfr24. In the evening it's mainly used as a drinking venue, attracting young crowd with its beer on draught *(bie ression*, Sfr4.70 for 0.5L) and in bottles from around the world (about Sfr6 for 0.3L). Both parts are closed on Sunday.

The gourmet's choice is *Restaurant des Halles (☎ 724 31 41)* in the historic 16th-century building with a turret on Place des Halles. The cooking is mainly French in style with main courses starting at Sfr32 and multi-course menus at Sfr75 or more. It's on the 1st floor and is closed on Sunday and Monday. Downstairs, the Brasserie serves good-sized tasty pizzas costing Sfr13.50 to Sfr18.50 (open daily).

Restaurants de Nuit Neuchâtel canton is unique in allowing restaurants to stay open all night, and there are usually plenty of people eager to take advantage of this fact. The emphasis is often more on drinking than eating; usually there's a large bar and loud music, with the restaurant section in a side room. These places are typically open from 9 pm to 6 am, and can actually stay open later than nightclubs that don't serve food. *Garbo Café (Rue des Chavannes 7)* is in the Old Town (closed Monday). It has burgers and pizza from Sfr7; note that the beer is cheaper in the restaurant side (Sfr4 before midnight, Sfr5 after). There's an entry fee on weekends only (Sfr20 including a drink). *Casablanca (Rue de l'Ecluse 56)* is a little less central (closed Tuesday).

Entertainment

A bar-restaurant favoured by students is *Appareils de Chauffage (Rue des Moulins 37)*, also known as Chauffage Compris. There's free live music on Thursdays (not in summer) and decent lunch menus from Sfr13.50. It's open daily. *Stardust (Rue de l'Hôpital 4)* is a bar and disco open from about 9 pm nightly (cover charge at weekends). *La Case à Chocs (☎ 721 20 56, Quai Philippe Godet 16)*, in a former brewery, is an 'alternative' venue where there is live music most weekends (Sfr5 to Sfr15), and occasional cinema and art shows.

Casino de la Rotonde (Faubourg du Lac) has a range of attractions, including a cabaret with cavorting girls (from 10 pm nightly except Sunday), restaurant (with cheap pizzas), disco, Salsa bar and rooftop bar (open from 4 pm).

Getting There & Away

There are hourly fast trains to Geneva (Sfr42, 70 minutes), Bern via Kerzers (Sfr17.20, 35 minutes), Basel (Sfr37, 98 minutes), Biel (Sfr10, 20 minutes), and many other destinations. Around two an hour run to Yverdon (Sfr11.80, 20 minutes). Neuchâtel is also the hub for buses and trains into the Neuchâtel Jura. Postbuses leave from outside the station. The bus to Le Locle (Sfr16.40, one hour) via La Chaux du Milieu departs every two hours.

Avis car rental (☎ 723 11 67) is at the Hôtel Beaulac, Esplanade Léopold Robert 2, and Hertz (☎ 730 32 32) is less central at Rue Pierre-à-Mazel 25.

Boat Boat services on the lake are most frequent from the end of May to late September, though a few boats also sail in winter. There are several departures a day (except Monday) to Estavayer-le-Lac (Sfr14.60, 1½ hours) and Yverdon (Sfr23, three hours), and daily boats to Murten (Sfr15.40, 1½ hours).

Getting Around

Local buses cost Sfr1.60 to Sfr2.60, depending upon the length of the journey (colour-coding on dispensers tell you what you need). A 24-hour ticket costs Sfr6. All local buses hit the main transport hub, Place Pury. Street parking in blue zones (usually 90-minute limit) is free in town.

AROUND NEUCHÂTEL

Vineyards clothe the hills on the northern shore of Lac de Neuchâtel. Families have been making wines here for many generations, and most producers are still small-scale concerns. The tourist office has a list of cellars where the local product can be sampled. Red wines come from the Pinot Noir grape and white wines from the Chasselas. The white wine, by the way, must be poured from a height of at least 15cm above the glass for the best results. A bit of a problem if you're just swigging it from the bottle.

Marin is 6km north-east of Neuchâtel; here you'll find **Papiliorama**, a hot and humid tropical garden within a large dome. Inside are over 1000 butterflies of all sizes and hues, and a hatchery where, if you're lucky, you'll see chrysalises breaking out of their cocoons. There are also numerous colourful and exotic birds flying around, plus tropical plants, fish, tortoises and an insectarium. Next door is **Nocturama**, a dome for night creatures from Latin America. A combined ticket costs Sfr11 (Sfr9 students, Sfr5 for children) and they're open 9 am (10 am for Nocturama) to 6 pm daily, reducing to 10 am to 5 pm daily in winter.

The domes are near the Marin Centre, a huge shopping complex with a *Migros* supermarket and restaurant. Take bus No 1 from Place Pury and get off after Marin village at Bellevue, or take the local train to Marin Epagnier. If driving, go north-east along Ave du Premier Mars. Nearby in Marin is a new **Park & Museum of Archaeology** (Parc et Musée d'archéologie; free); Neuchâtel tourist office can tell you more.

In Peseux, south-west of Neuchâtel by bus No 1, there's a demonstration of **chocolate-making** (free). Telephone ahead on ☎ 032-731 31 55.

The best view of the Alps and the lakes can be achieved from **Chaumont** (1087m). It's just 20 minutes by car (heading north-east) from the centre of Neuchâtel, or take bus No 7 to La Coudre (direction: Hauterive), then a short funicular ride (Sfr4.60 up or Sfr9.20 return).

LA CHAUX-DE-FONDS

☎ 032 • pop 37,700 • elevation 1000m

This is the largest town in the region and the highest in Switzerland. It's an important centre for watch and clock-making and the impressive horology museum is the main reason for a visit. The architect Le Corbusier was born in the town in 1887 and various examples of his innovative work can be seen.

Orientation & Information

The tourist office (☎ 919 68 95, fax 919 62 97, @ tourisme.montagnes@ne.ch) is at Espacité 1, in the ground floor of the tall tower (with a viewing terrace), a seven-minute walk from the train station. Opening hours are 9 am to 12.15 pm and 1.30 to 5.30 pm weekdays, and 9 am to 12.15 pm and 1.30 to 6 pm Saturday. In July and August weekday hours extend to 9 am to 6.30 pm.

Things to See

It was the technical expertise of Huguenot refugees, settlers in Geneva at the end of the 16th century, that started Switzerland on the way to its current annual production of more than 100 million watches. The craft soon spread throughout the Jura, which quickly established itself as the centre of the industry.

The International Museum of Horology (Musée International d'Horlogerie), Rue des Musées 29, tells you everything you need to know about time-keeping. Many signs are in English. It displays a variety of clocks and watches from the earliest constructed to the latest; some are extremely elaborate and beautiful. The various sections explain and illustrate all aspects of watch-making, including construction, engraving and enamelling. There's plenty to amuse kids, eg, a machine that tests reaction times. In the car park is a 15-tonne carillon that chimes every 15 minutes. Allow one to two hours to get around. Admission costs Sfr8 (Sfr7 for seniors, Sfr4 for children and students, Sfr18 for families) and it's open 10 am to noon and 2 to 5 pm Tuesday to Sunday (no lunch-break in summer). It's free on Sunday mornings.

Next door to the Horology museum is the **Museum of Fine Arts** (Musée des Beaux-Arts). It has an interesting contemporary art section plus many works by Swiss painters. Local boys Léopold Robert, Le Corbusier and Edouard Kaiser are well represented. It's open from 10 am to noon and 2 to 5 pm, Tuesday to Sunday, and costs Sfr6 for adults, Sfr4 for children, seniors and students, and Sfr14 for families (free on Sunday mornings). The **Museum of Natural History** (Musée d'histoire naturelle) is above the main post office; it's free and closed on Monday.

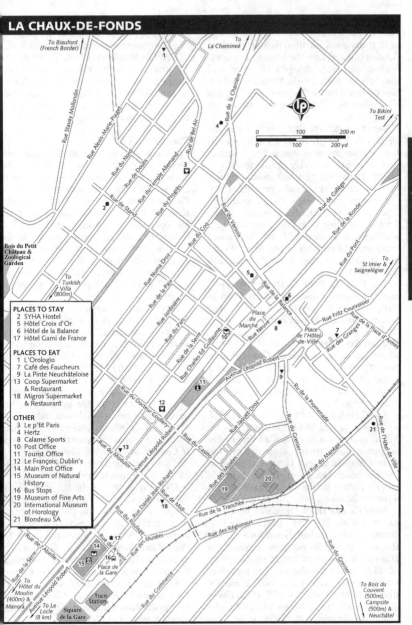

LA CHAUX-DE-FONDS

To Biauford
(French Border)

To
La Cheminée

To Bikini
Test

0   100   200 m
0   100   200 yd

To
St Imier &
Saignelégier

Bois du Petit
Château &
Zoological
Garden

To
Turkish
Villa
(800m)

Place
du
Marché

Place
de l'Hôtel
de-Ville

PLACES TO STAY
2 SYHA Hostel
5 Hôtel Croix d'Or
6 Hôtel de la Balance
17 Hôtel Garni de France

PLACES TO EAT
1 L'Orologio
7 Café des Faucheurs
9 La Pinte Neuchâteloise
13 Coop Supermarket
   & Restaurant
18 Migros Supermarket
   & Restaurant

OTHER
3 Le p'tit Paris
4 Hertz
8 Calame Sports
10 Post Office
11 Tourist Office
12 Le François; Dublin's
14 Main Post Office
15 Museum of Natural
   History
16 Bus Stops
19 Museum of Fine Arts
20 International Museum
   of Horology
21 Blondeau SA

To
Hôtel du
Moulin
(400m) &
Manora

To Le
Locle
(8 km)

Square
de la Gare

Train
Station

Place de
la Gare

To Bois du
Couvent
(500m),
Campsite
(500m) &
Neuchâtel

Various buildings that relate to Le Corbusier's early life or work are described in an itinerary available from the tourist office. Around town, follow the running eye symbol (yes – an eye with legs!). The interior of the Turkish Villa (Villa Schwob), which was designed by Le Corbusier in 1917, can be viewed by telephoning in advance on ☎ 912 31 47.

Blondeau SA (☎ 968 39 43), Rue de l'Hôtel de Ville 26-28, is a small cowbell foundry. Visitors may watch the artisans at work (free), but you must telephone ahead. Each bell cast is handmade from Parisian burnt sand, and every third day the molten metal (80% copper and 20% zinc) is poured into the prepared casts. This is the most interesting stage to see, and happens around 8.30 am. The metal takes only 10 minutes to one hour to cool and is then removed from the cast and smoothed.

The **Bois du Petit Château** contains a zoological garden and a vivarium. Entry is free; walk to the north-west end of Rue Docteur Coullery or take bus No 4.

Places to Stay

There's camping at **Bois du Couvent** (mobile ☎ 079-240 5039) on the edge of a wood 2km behind the main station, off Boulevard de la Liberté. It's open from May to September.

The SYHA **hostel** (☎ 968 43 15, fax 968 25 18, Rue de Doubs 34) has dorm beds for Sfr24, doubles for Sfr62 and a kitchen. Reception is closed from 9.30 am to 5 pm, but there's daytime access. The hostel closes in November and December. To avoid the 15-minute walk from the station, take bus No 4 (or No 22 after 7 pm).

Hôtel Croix d'Or (☎/fax 968 43 53, Rue de la Balance 15) has simple singles/doubles sharing one hall shower for Sfr32/64. Breakfast is Sfr7.50 per person. Nearby is **Hôtel de la Balance** (☎ 968 26 12, fax 968 05 66, ✉ info@hoteldelabalance.ch), providing smallish rooms with shower cubicle and TV from Sfr49/69; breakfast is Sfr7. **Hôtel Garni de France** (☎ 913 11 16, fax 913 18 49, Rue Daniel-Jean-Richard 46), by the station, has

rooms ranging from simple (Sfr45/76) to comfortable (Sfr88/146), but it has something of a sleazy reputation. Breakfast costs Sfr8.

Hôtel du Moulin (☎ 926 42 26, fax 926 5 18, Rue de la Sere 130) has comfortable nicely decorated rooms with TV and shower for Sfr80/100. Some cheaper rooms are available using the hall showers. The hotel has a car park and even a 10-pin bowling alley.

Places to Eat

There's a **Migros** supermarket and self-service restaurant on the 3rd floor in the glass-roofed Métropole shopping centre 200m to the right of the station. Nearby is a **Coop** (Rue de la Serre 37). It's not self-service, but it's nearly as cheap as those tha are (open to 7 pm weekdays and 5 pm Saturday). In a big shopping complex to the south-west of town is **Manora** (Blvd de Eplatures 20), with good buffet-style food for around Sfr11 (open daily). Take bus No 2 (or No 44 after 7 pm) and get off a Eplatures.

An excellent choice is **Café de Faucheurs** (Rue des Granges 5). It's unobtrusive, small, and frequented by locals. There's no written menu, so ask the serve about the few dishes on offer. You can ea very well for Sfr10 to Sfr15. The service i friendly but can be slow; no problem – set tle down and have a couple of drinks. Prices, especially for the open wines, are unbelievably low (closed weekends).

Croix d'Or, already recommended unde Places to Stay, has an Italian restaurant calle **Il Caminetto**. There are filets de perch fo Sfr18.80 and good pizzas for Sfr10.80 to Sfr14.50. It's open to midnight daily.

L'Orologio (☎ 968 19 00, Rue Alexis Marie-Piaget 1) offers a choice of cuisine ranging from affordable (fondue or pizz from Sfr16) to gourmet (multi-course menus from Sfr49). It's closed Sunday. **Le Pinte Neuchâteloise** (Rue du Grenier 8) i more central and under the same ownership For grilled meats (from Sfr29) cooked ove a wood fire in a converted farmhouse, try **La Cheminée** (Rue de la Charrière 91) next to the Pâquerette stop of bus No 2. It' closed Sunday and Monday.

Le Corbusier – Man of Concrete

Le Corbusier was born Charles Edouard Jeanneret on 6 October 1887 at Rue de la Serre 38. His adopted name is derived from that of his maternal grandfather (Lecorbesier). In 1917 he moved to Paris where his career began in earnest. Le Corbusier was one of the key innovators behind the development of the International Style of Architecture which achieved dominance in the 20th century, and especially since the 1950s.

Characteristic features of this style are the use of modern engineering techniques and modern materials (particularly reinforced concrete and steel) to create functional buildings with pure, straight lines. Aesthetic considerations weren't overlooked, although today's boring office complexes and blocks of flats are clear descendants of this genre. Some of Le Corbusier's own creations, however, explore spatial relations in a much more dynamic way.

The modern vision of functional design inspired by Le Corbusier encompasses not only buildings, but whole planned towns, too. Chandigarh, a state capital in India, was planned by Le Corbusier, and he structured it to be a unified entity, like a living organism. He died in 1965 in France.

Entertainment

Le p'tit Paris (☎ 968 65 33, Rue du Progrès 4) serves good, mid-priced food and has a cellar called **La Cave**, where there's live music (usually jazz) most Fridays and Saturdays. Entry is free or up to Sfr15 and beers are not expensive.

Bikini Test (☎ 968 06 66, Joux Perret 3) is a venue that has live music (entry around Sfr20) and occasional dance and alternative films. It's on the edge of town to the north-east: take bus No 2 or 22.

Le François (Ave Léopold Robert 32A) is an unofficial 'restaurant de nuit'; next door is a busy Irish pub, **Dublin's**.

Getting There & Away

Trains run to Neuchâtel every hour (Sfr10, 50 minutes). Local trains run to Basel via Saignelégier and Delémont, but this is a slow journey: travelling via Biel is quicker. Postbuses connect the smaller places; schedules are available from the tourist office. To Neuchâtel by car, a direct road and tunnel (highway 20) means you can get there in 20 minutes. A slower route is via Vue des Alpes (1283m), giving an expansive view of the Alps. From here, detour a couple of kilometres to the Tête de Ran Hotel, then climb a steep path for 15 minutes. The panorama at this belvedere (1422m) is even better.

There is a postbus service running northwards to the French border at Biaufond, with onward buses to Charquemont. The road is in good condition, if rather winding.

Hertz (☎ 968 52 28) has a car rental office at Rue de la Charrière 15.

Getting Around

Buses become less frequent at around 7 pm when some routes combine to form a new route under a new number. Rides cost Sfr2 for adults and 'juniors' (age 16 to 25) or Sfr1.20 for 'enfants' (age six to 15). A six-strip ticket costs Sfr10 (Sfr6.50 for enfants and juniors) and a day pass is Sfr5 (Sfr4 for enfants). There's a major bus hub just to the right of the train station.

NEUCHÂTEL MONTAGNES

Less rugged than the Alps, these mountains make fewer demands on hikers (1500km of maintained and marked footpaths, some accessible in winter) and cyclists (1760km of bike paths). In winter, there is some downhill skiing (30 ski lifts), but of greater importance is cross-country skiing. In all there are 400km of cross-country trails; some of these are groomed regularly and a few are even lit. For equipment rental, try Calame Sports (☎ 032-968 24 40), Neuve 3, La Chaux-de-Fonds. Ice skating on frozen lakes is also popular, particularly on Lake Taillères.

In addition to watch-making, agriculture and milk production are important to the local economy. A network of postbuses connects the smaller towns and villages in the region, although departures can be infrequent.

Le Locle

Le Locle is an important watch-making centre. It was in the late 18th century that Daniel Jean-Richard introduced this skill to the Neuchâtel Jura, practising his craft in Le Locle. The town's **Museum of Horology** is located in 18th-century Château des Monts. There are some grand period rooms as well as numerous timepieces that span the centuries from the earliest devices to the latest technological innovations. Experience an aural earthquake as dozens of clocks simultaneously chime the hour. An unusual automation in the Maurice Sandoz room depicts an old woman with a stooped gait supporting herself on two walking sticks. The museum is open 10 am to 5 pm Tuesday to Sunday from May to October, or 2 to 5 pm from November to April. Admission costs Sfr7 for adults, Sfr6 for seniors, Sfr4 for students, and Sfr17 for families.

About 2km from the town are the **Col-des-Roches Underground Mills**. These mills exploit the underwater flow of the Bied River on its way to join the Doubs River. It was Jonas Sandoz who started the work of widening existing fissures in the rock and creating waterfalls and wells. By the end of the 17th century the underground complex included a thresher, two flour mills, an oil mill and a saw mill. The building on the surface dates from 1844. The mills were gradually allowed to fall into disuse and for much of the 20th century were used as a slaughterhouse. Renovations to turn the mills into a tourist attraction started in 1973. There's an exhibition in the entrance hall and large pieces of machinery in the underground caves. The site is open 10 am to noon and 1.30 to 5.30 pm every day from 1 May to 31 October (no lunch break in summer); entry costs Sfr7 for adults, Sfr6 for seniors, Sfr4 for students aged up to 25, and Sfr16 for families.

For more information, contact Le Locle tourist office (☎ 032-931 43 30, fax 931 45 06), Daniel Jean-Richard 31.

Getting There & Away From La Chaux-de-Fonds, Le Locle is only seven minutes and 8km (Sfr3) by the hourly train that originates at Neuchâtel; the bus is the same price. Trains also run into France to Morteau and beyond. The Col-des-Roches Underground Mills can be reached by postbus on the more-or-less hourly Le Locle-La Brévine service (Sfr8 each way). For postbus information, ring ☎ 032-931 32 31.

Doubs Basins

The Doubs Basins is the area on the French border where the River Doubs broadens into Lake Brenets (Lac de Chaillexon on the French side of the border). Along part of its length, the shapes of the limestone cliffs are reputed to resemble famous historical figures such as Louis-Philippe (hardly flattering – gives a new significance to the description 'craggy features'). There's also the **Doubs Falls** (Saut du Doubs) which hurtle down from a height of 27m. Contact the boat operator, NLB (☎ 032-932 14 14), for short cruises of the lake in summer. Boats sail between the village of Les Brenets and the waterfall; to walk between these two points takes an hour. The **Chemin des Planètes** between Le Locle and Doubs Falls is a path modelled on scaled-down distances between the planets in the solar system.

Les Brenets is 5km from Le Locle. Trains run frequently and cost Sfr3 each way.

Jura Canton

FRANCHES MONTAGNES

This is the part of the Jura mountain chain that is within the canton of Jura. It is usually overlooked by foreign visitors, which means that relatively inexpensive accommodation can be found. It's an area of pastures and woodlands where there are 1500km of hiking trails and 200km of prepared cross-country ski trails. Horse-riding is another popular activity; the horses in the area are known for their gentleness and calm disposition. There are equestrian centres in around 30 towns and villages offering all-in weeks, weekends, or simple hourly rides. Che

Cindy (☎ 032-951 16 85, 🅔 chezcindy@ yahoo.fr), La Theurre 1, a few kilometres east of Saignelégier, charges Sfr25 per hour, or the weekend rate including rides, meals and accommodation on Saturday night is Sfr190 for adults (in a double room) and Sfr120 for kids (in a dorm).

The main town in the region is **Saignelégier,** where the annual national horse show, Marché-Concours, is held on the second weekend in August. You can get more information from Jura Tourisme (see the introduction to this chapter). It's open 9 am to noon and 2 to 6 pm Monday to Friday, and 10 am to 3 pm Saturday and Sunday.

A convenient hotel is *Café du Soleil (☎ 032-951 16 88, fax 951 22 95, 🅔 cafe-du-soleil@bluewin.ch, Marché-Concours 14)*, with dorms for Sfr22, and singles/doubles for Sfr64/112 with shower/ WC, and Sfr53/96 without.

Getting There & Away

Saignelégier is on the rail line between La Chaux-de-Fonds (Sfr12.60, takes 40 minutes) and Basel (Sfr27, 95 minutes with change at Glovelier). By car, there are two famous viewpoints you can visit on the way to this part of the Jura. The

GEOFF STRINGER

An example of Jura architecture

norther-most one is at **Weissenstein** (make for the Kurhaus Weissenstein at 1284m), 10km from Solothurn. The road continues to Moutier where it branches to either Delémont or Tavannes. The more southern of the two routes starts at La Neuveville, on the shore of Lake Biel. A minor road winds up from here to St Imier (33km). This road is usually impassable in winter and spring and ascends the **Chasseral** (1607m) peak. Stop off at the Hôtel du Chasseral, where there is a viewing table, then walk 30 minutes to the telecommunications tower for a 360° panorama. From either Weissenstein or Chasseral you can see the broad expanse of the Alps spread out before you.

Geneva

☎ 022 • pop 175,000 • elevation 375m

Geneva (Genève in French, Genf in German) is Switzerland's third-largest city, comfortably encamped on the shores of Lake Geneva (Lac Léman). But Geneva belongs not so much to French-speaking Switzerland as to the whole world. Whether the issue is world climactic changes or peace in the Balkans, the mediators rush to the neutral territory of Geneva to seek common ground. It is truly an international city. More than one in three residents are non-Swiss and 250 international organisations are based here. Among the most important are the European headquarters of the United Nations, the International Red Cross and the World Health Organisation.

For the administrators, secondment to Geneva must seem more like a holiday than hard work. The city enjoys a fine location. Strolls around the lake on a sunny day are hugely enjoyable, as are boat excursions. The cuisine is excellent and varied, and the same applies to the cultural diversions. Geneva is a city in pristine condition: it is clean, efficient and safe. Some say it is too successful in these respects, and complain the city is sterile. Some people wouldn't recognise a good thing if it waved a dozen flags and shouted in their ear.

History

Geneva was occupied successively by Romans and Burgundians and became a powerful bishopric from the 5th century. It was partially subservient to the Imperial Emperor, but that did not prevent the House of Savoy from making repeated attempts to gain control of the city, which was becoming increasingly affluent through its fairs and markets.

Under pressure from the Swiss Confederation, the Duke of Savoy agreed in 1530 to leave Geneva alone. A couple of years later the Reformation was introduced to the city by Guillaume Farel, who was followed and superseded by John Calvin. Calvin's teachings were so effective in Geneva that it

HIGHLIGHTS

- See the Jet d'Eau – the world's tallest fountain.
- Examine the extensive museum collections.
- Explore CERN, a leading physics research centre with the world's biggest machine.
- Sample the varied international cuisine.
- Get on the trail of the thriving alternative arts scene.

Geneva

became known as the 'Protestant Rome'; there ensued a time of austerity in which fun became frowned upon. Corrupting habits like dancing and wearing jewels were actually forbidden (yet interestingly, around the same time the taking of interest on a loan was legalised). Such a repressive environment might be expected to deter visitors, but over the ensuing centuries, Geneva earned a reputation as an intellectual centre and attracted many free thinkers, such as Rousseau and Voltaire, and those following in their footsteps.

In the meantime Geneva had to put up with another incursion from Savoy. Led by the duke, Charles Emmanuel, an attempt was made to take the city on the night of 11 December 1602. An advance guard scaled the city walls with the intention of opening the gates and letting in the main force. The Savoyards were spotted by a sentry just in time, and the whole force was routed with the loss of only 18 Genevese lives. An event from this victory is commemorated in the annual Escalade festival (see Special Events section later in this chapter).

After this success in 1602, Geneva had no further trouble with Savoy, but in 1798 the French annexed the city and held it for nearly 16 years. During this period it was the capital of the French Léman Department. Geneva was freed on 1 June 1814 and within a year it was admitted to the Swiss Confederation.

Orientation

Geneva and the small enclave of Swiss territory around the south-west lip of Lake Geneva constitute both a separate canton and a distinct tourist region. The canton is home to 400,000 people. The centre of the city hugs the shore of the lake and is split through the middle by the westward progress of the Rhône. Conveniently in the centre of town on the northern side of the river is the main train station, Gare de Cornavin. To the south of the river lies the old part of town *(vieille ville)*, with the pedestrian-only Grand-Rue at its core. Most of the museums skirt the old section. East of the Old Town is Gare des Eaux-Vives, the French Railways station for trains running south-east into France.

The two parts of the city are often known as *rive droite* (right bank, ie, north of the Rhône) and *rive gauche* (left bank, ie, the south). Geneva's most visible landmark in summer is the 140m Jet d'Eau, a giant fountain spouting water into the lake from a pier on the southern shore.

International organisations are mostly north of the station, and the main shopping area is around Rue du Rhône, on the south bank.

The Thursday following the first Sunday in September is a public holiday in Geneva.

Information

Tourist Offices The main tourist office (☎ 909 70 00, fax 909 70 11, ✉ info@geneve-tourisme.ch), 18 Rue de Mont-Blanc, is usually open 9 am to 6 pm Monday to Saturday. From mid-June to 1 September hours lengthen to 8 am to 6 pm on weekdays and 8 am to 5 pm on Saturday and Sunday. Pick up the free weekly *Geneva Agenda* booklet, covering art events, exhibitions, nightclubs, sights and restaurants. The *info-jeunes* brochure has lots of useful budget information. A tourist office counter (see the Geneva Station Area map) is also in the railway station, open the same hours as the main office except that summer hours are 9 am to 8 pm weekdays and 9 am to 6 pm weekends. Next door are information offices for trains (closed Sunday) and city public transport (open daily).

Detailed information on the city is dispensed at Arcade d'Information de la Ville de Genève (☎ 311 99 70, fax 311 80 52, ✉ geneve-tourisme.ch), on Pont de la Machine. It is open 10 am (noon on Monday) to 6 pm weekdays and 10 am to 5 pm Saturday.

The Centre d'Accueil et de Reseignements (CAR; ☎ 731 46 47; see the Geneva Station Area map) has tourist and accommodation information, geared mostly to youths and backpackers. It is based in a blue bus at the station end of Rue du Mont-Blanc and is open 9 am to 11 pm daily from mid-June to 31 August. Assistance and information for young people is at Centre d'Information pour Jeunes (☎ 311 44 22), 13 Rue Verdaine, from 10 am (2 pm on weekends) to 10 pm daily.

The above places should be able to give you the Vélo-Cité map – it's excellent, and free! Another tourist information counter is in the arrivals hall of the airport.

Dialogai (☎ 906 40 40, ✉ dialogai@hivnet.ch), 11-13 Rue de la Navigation, provides information, publishes a guide to the gay scene in the region, and runs a bar on the premises that's open 5 pm Wednesday to Sunday.

Money The exchange office in Gare de Cornavin is open 6.45 am to 9.30 pm daily

GENEVA

GENEVA (GENÈVE)

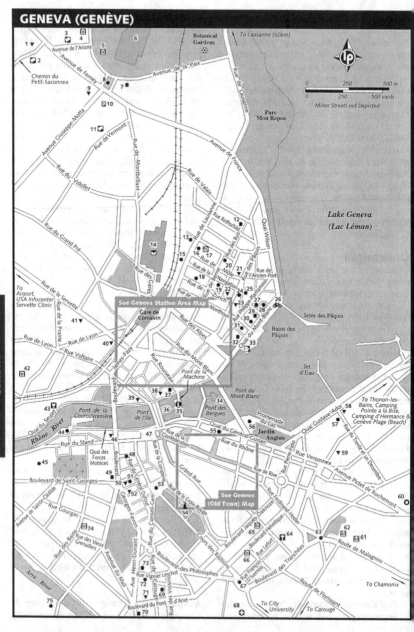

GENEVA

GENEVA (GENÈVE)

PLACES TO STAY
7 Centre Masaryk
12 SYHA Hostel
27 Hotel de la Cloche
29 Noga Hilton & Le Cygne Restaurant
32 Hotel Beau Rivage & Le Chat Botté Restaurant
37 Hotel Ambassador
49 Hotel Beau-Site
69 Hotel le Prince
70 Hotel Carmen
73 Forget Me Not

PLACES TO EAT
1 Les Continents
9 OMPI Building
21 Migros Supermarket & Restaurant
22 Le Blason
23 Auberge de Savièse
38 Sugar Hut
39 Le Neptune
40 La Trattoria
41 Kong Restaurant
46 Le Béarn
50 Victoria
52 Cave Valaisanne et Chalet Suisse
58 L'Amiral

59 Dent de Lion
71 Café Universal

OTHER
2 New Zealand Consulate
3 Canadian Consulate
4 International Red Cross & Red Crescent Museum
5 Musée Ariana
6 Palais des Nations
8 Place des Nations
10 Varembé Parking Garage
11 UK Consulate
13 Horizon Motos (Motorcycles)
14 Post Office
15 Europcar
16 Avis
17 Telephone Discount
18 Budget; Bureau de Change Michel
19 Dialogai
20 Hertz
24 Sixt
25 Edelweiss Manotel
26 Free Bicycle Rental
28 Swiss Cottage
30 Casino
31 American Library
33 Swiss Boat Departures
34 Île Rousseau

35 Arcade d'Information de la Ville de Genève
36 Tour d'Île
42 Voltaire Museum
43 l'Interdit & Le Loft
44 l'Usine
45 Artamis (arts venues)
47 Place Bell Air
48 Place de la Synagogue
51 Victoria Hall
53 Place Neuve
54 Promenade des Bastions & Reformation Monument
55 Place du Lac
56 CGN Ticket Booth & Boat Departures
57 Salon Lavoir (Laundrette)
60 Gare des Eaux-Vives
61 Horology Museum
62 Museum of Natural History
63 Place Emile Guyénot
64 Russian Church
65 Museum of Art & History
66 Petit Palais
67 Place Edouard Claparède
68 Cantonal Hospital
72 SSR Travel Agency
74 Museum of Modern & Contemporary Art
75 Centre Sportif des Vernets

GENEVA

(8 pm in winter). The best rates seen while researching this edition were at the Bureau de Change Michel, 32 Rue de Zürich, open 9 am to 6.30 pm weekdays and 9 am to 1 pm Saturday (Sfr1 commission on travellers cheques) and at the office at 9 Rue de Chatepoulet (cash only), open 9 am to 7 pm weekdays, and 9 am to 6 pm Saturday. In the airport, banks are open daily and charge Sfr5 commission to change cash (so change commission-free in the adjoining train station); they make no charge to redeem travellers cheques.

Post & Communications The main post office (1211 Genève 1) is at 18 Rue du Mont-Blanc. It is open 7.30 am to 6 pm Monday to Friday, and 8 to 11 am Saturday. The large post office (1211 Genève 2) behind the station has emergency counters (Sfr1 surcharge) open till late daily (closed Sunday morning).

Email & Internet Access There are many places where you can surf; some of the cheaper places are:

Club Vidéo ROM
(☎ 731 47 48), 19 Rue des Alpes; Sfr5 per hour; open 11 am (3 pm Sunday) to past midnight daily
Telephone Discount
(☎ 731 24 00), 23 Rue de Prieuré; Sfr2.50/5/10 for 15/30/60 minutes; also cheap international phone calls. It's open till 11 pm (closed lunchtimes and Sunday morning)
Placette Department Store
4th Floor, Rue de Cornavin; Sfr10 per hour using prepaid card

Travel Agencies American Express (☎ 731 76 00; see the Geneva Station Area map) is at 7 Rue du Mont-Blanc, open 8.30 am to 5.30 pm Monday to Friday (6 pm in summer) and 9 am to noon Saturday. The

26 Countries in One

Switzerland has been viewed as being a single country since the Rütli meadow oath in 1291. Yet up to 1848 the cantons were more-or-less independent states with separate armies, currencies and customs duties between each border. Even now they have their own constitution, government, police force, laws, courts and schools. Some cantons even describe themselves as a republic to emphasise their independence (eg, Jura, Neuchâtel and Geneva). There are variations between cantons in income tax levels, the fees charged for obtaining Swiss citizenship, and in many other fields (eg, in the matter of organ donation for transplant, consent is presumed in some cantons but must be explicitly given in others).

Four categories of control have been identified in the sharing of power between country and canton. In the first category, the federal government has absolute authority: customs, currency, post and telecommunications, railways and navigation. In the second, the cantons are in charge: police, social services, housing and religion. In the third, the legislative powers belong to the Confederation, but the cantons are responsible for implementation: weights and measures, road traffic, military affairs, unemployment, social insurance, and civil and criminal courts. In the fourth category, powers are shared: taxation, road construction, hunting and fishing, health insurance, education and training.

Although many Swiss are determined to hold onto regional autonomy, increasing numbers are questioning the efficiency of allowing small-scale cantons to run parallel services to their neighbours. Diversity can have other problems too: some Zürich residents resent the fact that wealthy commuters from low-tax Zug work in Zürich and enjoy services that they pay nothing towards.

JENNY JONES

Representatives from cantons Uri, Schwyz and Unterwalden take the Oath, 1291

The move to combine some cantons is now under way. Signatures are being collected in Geneva and Vaud to force a referendum on a possible merger between those two cantons, and the six small cantons of Central Switzerland have started tentative talks about forming a single region. The Swiss statistics office has identified that based on common history, geography and interests, Switzerland can be divided into as few as seven regions. Significantly, the new constitution drafted in 1998 states that cantonal regions can now be altered without requiring a federal referendum. After more than 700 years, it seems that some form of closer integration is now inevitable.

student and budget travel agency SSR (☎ 329 97 33 or 36), 3 Rue Vignier, is open 9.15 am to 6 pm Monday to Friday. Many other travel agencies and airline offices are concentrated along Rue Chantepoulet and Rue du Mont-Blanc.

Libraries The Bibliothèque de la Cité, in the Old Town at 5 Place de Trois-Perdrix, has English-language newspapers on the 4th floor (closed Sunday and Monday). The American Library (☎ 732 80 97), 3 Rue de Monthoux, is a place to browse among stacks of English-language books (closed

Monday). It also gives out the free *Guide to English-speaking Geneva*, an excellent guide geared towards residents.

Bookshops Elm Book Shop (☎ 736 09 45), 5 Rue Versonnex, sells English-language books, as do the rest of the places mentioned here. Good shops for second-hand books from around Sfr3 are Librairie des Amateurs, 15 Grand-Rue (see the Geneva Old Town map), and Book Worm (☎ 731 87 65), 5 Rue Sismondi. Book Worm is closed Monday and open Sunday, and has a tiny restaurant with great Sunday lunches. Artou

☎ 818 02 40), 8 Rue de Rive, is a good place for travel books, and sells air tickets.

Radio Stations The English-language WRG (88.4 MHz FM) has news on the hour. Radio 74 (88.8 MHz FM) broadcasts news from the BBC.

Laundry Lavseul (☎ 735 90 51), 29 Rue de Monthoux, is self-service and open 7 am to midnight daily. There is another self-service laundry at Rue du Trente.

Medical Services Ring ☎ 111 (premium rate) for information on medical services on call. The Cantonal Hospital (☎ 372 33 11), 24 Rue Micheli du Crest, has an emergency department.

Permanence Médico Chirurgicale (☎ 731 21 20), 21 Rue de Chantepoulet, is a private clinic, open 24 hours a day. Dental treatment is at the Servette Clinic (☎ 733 98 00), 60 Ave Wendt, 8 am to 7 pm weekdays, and every second weekend to 6 pm.

Emergency The national emergency numbers apply: ☎ 117 for police, ☎ 118 for the fire brigade, ☎ 144 for an ambulance and ☎ 140 for the car breakdown service. There's a rape hotline on ☎ 345 20 20.

Dangers & Annoyances On sunny days youngsters smoke dope in the Jardin Anglais and along the pier of the Jet d'Eau (some may consider this an opportunity rather than an annoyance). Hard drug users tend to congregate around here too. They don't usually cause problems, but it might be wise to exercise caution around this area at night.

Walking Tour
Recorded commentary from the tourist office details 26 points of interest in the Old Town (Sfr10, plus Sfr50 deposit; duration around 2½ hours). There are also guided walks in summer (see Activities below).

A good starting point for a scenic walk is the Île Rousseau. It is noted for a statue in honour of the celebrated free thinker, who formulated his seminal thoughts on democracy while, in his own words, a 'citizen of Geneva'.

Turn right and walk along the southern side of the Rhône until you reach the 13th century **Tour d'Île**, once part of the medieval city fortifications. Walk south down the narrow, cobbled Rue de la Cité until it becomes Grand-Rue. Here, at No 40, is Rousseau's birthplace. Grand-Rue terminates at **Place du Bourg-de-Four**, the oldest square in Geneva. It was once a Roman forum, evolved into a medieval marketplace, and now has a fountain and touristy shops.

Take Rue de la Fontaine to reach the lakeside. Anti-clockwise round the shore is the **Jet d'Eau**. Calling this a fountain is something of an understatement. The water shoots up with incredible force (200km/h, 1360 horsepower) to create a 140m plume. At any one time, seven tonnes of water is in the air, and much of it, depending on the whims of the wind, falls on spectators who venture out on the pier. It's activated from the beginning of March until early October, except during gusty weather.

Carouge, formerly a separate town and now known for its boutiques, bohemian atmosphere and 18th century architecture, is worth a stroll. Get there by bus No 12 or 13.

St Peter's Cathedral
The centre of town is dominated by the imposing, partially Romanesque, partially Gothic, Cathédrale de St Pierre. John Calvin preached here from 1536 to 1564; his seat outlasted him and can be seen in the north aisle. The body of the church still matches the austerity of Calvin's teaching in its lack of ostentation. This is in contrast to the small side chapel, first on the right after entering, with its ornate walls, windows and hanging light. Back in the main church, notice the aisle ceilings and the stained glass windows. There is a good view from the tower, which is open until 5.30 pm or later daily (entry Sfr3).

The cathedral rests upon a significant if unspectacular archaeological site (entry Sfr5, students Sfr3, closed Monday), with some fine 4th century mosaics amid the crumbling foundations.

GENEVA

Parks & Gardens

South of Grand-Rue, the **Promenade des Bastions** is a pleasant park which contains a massive monument to the Reformation. The giant figures of Bèze, Calvin, Farel and Knox are flanked by smaller statues of other important figures and by carved depictions of events instrumental in the spread of the movement. It was created in 1917. The scale is deceptively large; Calvin and his chums stand 4.5m tall, and it is over 100m long.

On the lakefront near the Old Town, the **Jardin Anglais** features a large clock composed of flowers. Colourful flower gardens and the occasional statue line the promenade on the northern shore of the lake, and lead to two relaxing parks. One of these, the **Botanical**

JENNY JONES

Gold Coin displaying coat of arms

Gardens (Jardin Botanique), features exotic plants, llamas and an aviary. It's open 8 am to 7.30 pm daily (9.30 am to 5 pm in winter); entry is free.

Museums & Galleries

Geneva is not a bad place to get stuck on a rainy day as there are more than 30 museums, many of which are free. Most are closed Monday. An exception is the ceramics museum, **Musée Ariana**, sited in an attractive building on Ave de la Paix, which is open Wednesday to Monday (free). Details of this and other museums are in the tourist office's free booklet; collections encompass contemporary art, motor cars, ethnography and much else.

Museum of Art & History The Musée d'Art et d'Histoire, 2 Rue Charles Galland is one of the most

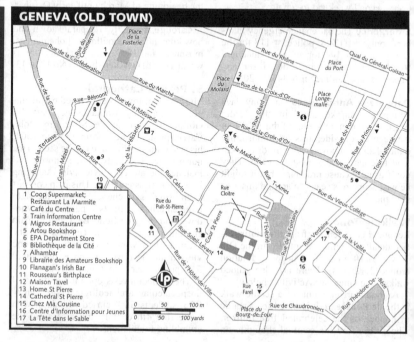

GENEVA (OLD TOWN)

1 Coop Supermarket;
   Restaurant La Marmite
2 Café du Centre
3 Train Information Centre
4 Migros Restaurant
5 Artou Bookshop
6 EPA Department Store
7 Bibliothèque de la Cité
8 Alhambar
9 Librairie des Amateurs Bookshop
10 Flanagan's Irish Bar
11 Rousseau's Birthplace
12 Maison Tavel
13 Home St Pierre
14 Cathedral St Pierre
15 Chez Ma Cousine
16 Centre d'Information pour Jeunes
17 La Tête dans le Sable

important museums. The vast and varied collection comprises some 500,000 items, including paintings, sculpture, room interiors, weapons and archaeology.

A highly prized exhibit is *La Pêche Miraculeuse* by Konrad Witz. It was painted as an altarpiece for the cathedral and shows fishermen distracted from tending their catch, looking on in awe and astonishment as Christ walks on the water. What is remarkable about the composition is that Witz transposed the scene onto Lake Geneva, and in the background you can see Genevan houses, Mont Blanc and the foothills of Mt Salève.

Elsewhere there is a room of paintings by Ferdinand Hodler, particularly showing Alpine scenes, and several important works by Quentin de la Tour. The museum is open 10 am to 5 pm Tuesday to Sunday; entry is free.

International Red Cross & Red Crescent Museum The Musée International de la Croix-Rouge et du Croissant-Rouge, 17 Ave de la Paix, is a compelling multimedia trawl through atrocities perpetuated by humanity in recent history. The message is supposed to be one of hope (as proclaimed by the banner above the reception counter, 'Each person has a shared responsibility to humanity'), but the horrors etch deeper in the mind than the palliative.

The achievements of the Red Cross (and the Moslem adjunct, the Red Crescent) are well documented; but people keep fighting, as the films, photos, sculptures and soundtracks vividly illustrate. The scale of the problem is brought home by the *seven million* index cards compiled by the Red Cross during WWI to keep track of prisoners. Allow around 1½ hours to see the 11 areas of the museum, arranged in chronological order. Admission costs Sfr10 (Sfr5 for students and senior citizens, free for children under 12) and it is open 10 am to 5 pm Wednesday to Monday. Buses 8 and F from Place de Cornavin drop you outside.

The Creation of the Red Cross

In the days of the Habsburgs, the vast Austrian Empire included northern Italy. During the campaign for the independence and unification of Italy, the Austrian forces under Emperor Franz Josef I were defeated in a major engagement against French and Sardinian troops led by Napoleon III.

The two forces met at Solferino in Lombardy, northern Italy, on 24 June 1859. Fighting was intense and fierce – there were 40,000 casualties in a single day. Henry Dunant (1828–1910), a businessman and philanthropist from Geneva, visited the scene of the battle three days later. He was appalled to find wounded soldiers still lying on the battlefield, dying from wounds that would not have been fatal had treatment been available.

He was so moved by their plight that he financed the publication of *A Memory of Solferino* in 1862. Inside, he made the proposal that there should be formulated 'some international principle, sanctioned by a Convention inviolate in character, which, once agreed upon and ratified, might constitute the basis for societies for the relief of the wounded'. The following year a committee was set up with the intention of pursuing this aim, with Dunant as the secretary and Henri Dufour as the first president. In 1864 the Geneva Convention was adopted and the International Red Cross became fully established as a humanitarian organisation.

The flag of the Red Cross was a red cross on a white background. But as the organisation became more established worldwide, the association of the cross with Christianity proved to be problematical. Muslims found that the image of the cross 'offends the sensibilities'. Thus, during the Russo-Turkish War of 1875–78, the Turks were given permission to replace the cross with a red crescent, and the Red Crescent Movement was born.

In 1901, Henri Dunant was co-winner of the first Nobel Peace Prize.

Petit Palais This compact gallery at 2 Terrace Saint Victor is expertly presented. The art sometimes encompasses the room decor in which the paintings and sculptures are displayed, creating a powerful effect. The gallery covers modern art, including impressionist, surrealist and abstract works, and among the famous names represented are Picasso, Chagall, Renoir, Cézanne and Monet. The section on the Paris School is particularly good. This privately owned gallery is pricey for its size: Sfr10 for adults and Sfr5 for senior citizens and students (up to 25 years). It is open 10 am to 6 pm weekdays, and 10 am to 5 pm weekends.

While you're in the area, wander down Rue Lefort to look at the **Russian church**, with gold domes that shimmer from afar on a sunny day. The small interior is a clutter of religious images.

Museum of Natural History The Musée d'Histoire Naturelle, 1 Route de Malagnou, has dioramas, minerals and anthropological displays. Living species are exhibits in the aquarium and vivarium sections, but the dinosaurs, shown in their natural environment, are not alive. It's open 9.30 am to 5 pm Tuesday to Sunday; entry is free.

Horology Museum The Musée de l'Horlogerie et de l'Emaillerie, 15 Route de Malagnou, hints at the importance of clocks and watches to the Genevan economy, and shows expert work in enamel on timepieces and other objects. It's open 10 am to 5 pm Wednesday to Monday; free entry.

Maison Tavel The oldest private house in the Old Town is Maison Tavel, 6 Rue du Puits St-Pierre. It is notable for a very detailed relief map of Geneva as it was in 1850. It covers 35 sq metres and took the architect, August Magnin, 18 years to construct. The museum also gives a good account of Geneva's life and times from the 14th to the 19th centuries (detailed English notes available). It's open 10 am to 5 pm Tuesday to Sunday; entry is free here also.

Voltaire Museum Voltaire's residency in Geneva is celebrated in the Voltaire Museum at 25 Rue des Délices (open 2 to 5 pm Monday to Friday; admission free).

United Nations

The Palais des Nations was once the headquarters of the defunct League of Nations. It is now the European home of the offspring of that organisation, the United Nations (UN), and the focal point for a resident population of 3000 international civil servants. The hour-long tour of the interior is only moderately interesting, and costs Sfr8.50 (students Sfr6.50). Paying for the tour allows entry to the extensive gardens, where there's a towering grey monument coated with heat-resistant titanium, donated by the USSR to commemorate the conquest of space.

It's open on weekdays from November to March and daily from April to October. Guided tours are conducted from 10 am to noon and 2 to 4 pm (9 am to 6 pm in July and August). You need to show your passport to get in.

CERN

CERN, near Meyrin, is a laboratory for research into particle physics funded by 19 nations. It accelerates electrons and positrons down a 27km circular tube (the world's biggest machine) and the resulting collisions create new forms of matter – it achieved world headlines in 1996 by creating anti-matter for the first time. The Microcosm multimedia exhibition explains it all (free; English text), and is open 2 to 5 pm Monday, and 9 am to 5 pm Tuesday to Saturday. Take bus No 15 from the train station. Three-hour guided tours of the site are free; Saturday is the day for the general public (reserve well ahead on ☎ 767 84 84, fax 767 87 10, ✆ visits-service@cern.ch).

Mountain Views

Lake Geneva is often clouded over in winter, but if you gain some height you can attain good views of peaks poking above the cloud layer. Genevese often make for viewpoints in the Jura mountains to enjoy the winter sun, which make equally good

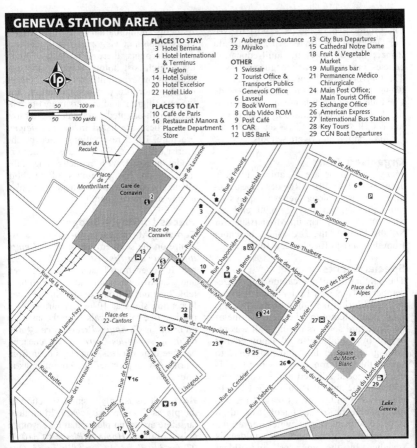

GENEVA STATION AREA

PLACES TO STAY
3 Hotel Bernina
4 Hotel International & Terminus
5 L'Aiglon
14 Hotel Suisse
20 Hotel Excelsior
22 Hotel Lido

PLACES TO EAT
10 Café de Paris
16 Restaurant Manora & Placette Department Store

17 Auberge de Coutance
23 Miyako

OTHER
1 Swissair
2 Tourist Office & Transports Publics Genevois Office
6 Lavseul
7 Book Worm
8 Club Vidéo ROM
9 Post Café
11 CAR
12 UBS Bank

13 City Bus Departures
15 Cathedral Notre Dame
18 Fruit & Vegetable Market
19 Mulligans bar
21 Permanence Médico Chirurgicale
24 Main Post Office; Main Tourist Office
25 Exchange Office
26 American Express
27 International Bus Station
28 Key Tours
29 CGN Boat Departures

summer excursions. Another possibility is Mont Salève (1100m) to the south-east. Take bus No 8 to Veyrier and walk across the border into France to reach the cable car (Sfr15.10 return, or Sfr19 including Geneva travel pass). It operates daily from May to September, Tuesday to Sunday during April and October, and only weekends and holidays during winter (closed 1 November to 25 December).

Activities

There are several sports centres in the city. Centre Sportif des Vernets (☎ 418 40 00), 4

Rue Hans Wilsdorf, has a swimming pool (Sfr5; students Sfr2) and ice skating rink (same price) and is open 9 am daily except Monday. Swim in the lake at Genève Plage (Sfr7, children Sfr3.50, including entry to a large pool with waterslide) on the southern shore, or more centrally at the Bains on Jetée des Pâquis (Sfr2, children Sfr1) on the northern shore.

Conducted walking tours depart from the Mont Blanc tourist office. The Old Town walk (two hours; Sfr12, students and seniors Sfr8) departs at 10 am, Monday to Friday in summer, Saturday year-round.

Courses
The Migros École Club (☎ 319 61 61; see the Geneva Old Town map), 5 Rue du Prince, has all sorts of adult-education courses, including French language classes. The Université de Genève (☎ 705 71 11, ℮ elcfete@uni2a.uni2a.unige.ch), 3 Rue de Candolle, has French language classes lasting three weeks from mid-July to early October. Call ☎ 715 32 13 (℮ agep@fsp.ch) for information on private schools.

Organised Tours
Many excursions are organised by Key Tours (☎ 731 41 40), 7 Rue des Alpes, ranging from trips along Geneva's quays by minitrain (summer only; Sfr6.90, children Sfr4.90) to a day trip up Mont Blanc for Sfr208. Pick up the *Excursions* brochure from the tourist office or Key Tours.

Special Events
The celebration of l'Escalade on 11 December is Geneva's best known festival. In 1602, during the Duke of Savoy's unsuccessful attempt to take Geneva, one of the Savoyard soldiers on the wall was repelled by a housewife who poured her boiling soup over him and proceeded to smash the cauldron over his head. This event has been adapted and is commemorated in the annual Escalade festival. In many Genevan homes, as part of the traditional celebrations, a chocolate cauldron is filled with marzipan which represents the vegetables of the soup. The cauldron is smashed by the youngest and oldest person present, then it and its contents are quickly consumed with un-Calvinistic eagerness. As well as the ritual of the soup pot, there are torch-lit processions in historic costumes and a huge bonfire in the cathedral square.

Spanning two weekends in the beginning of August, the Fêtes de Genève is a time of jollity, parades, open-air concerts and fireworks. During the Bol d'Or, on a Saturday in mid-June, Lake Geneva is alive with the bobbing white sails of some 600 sailing boats. The race to the far end of the lake and back takes over five hours.

Places to Stay
As befits an international city that receives many important visitors on unlimited expense accounts, there is no lack of high-class, high-cost hotels. Happily, the city also has an excellent selection of places offering dormitory accommodation, and various religious and university institutions have youth-oriented singles/doubles at low rates. These are listed in the *info-jeunes* brochure. Hotel reservations made by the tourist office cost Sfr5, or use the accommodation boards with free telephone in the train station. Ask the tourist office about 'Welcome to Geneva' vouchers if you plan to stay over a weekend.

Places to Stay – Budget
Camping About 7km north-east of the city centre on the southern lakeshore is *Camping Pointe a la Bise (☎ 752 12 96)*, Vesenaz. It's open from Easter to late October, and costs Sfr6 per adult and from Sfr6 for a tent. Take bus E from Rond-Point de Rive. Reception shuts at 10 pm. A farther 7km north, a five-minute walk from the last stop on bus E, is *Camping d'Hermance (☎ 341 05 05, Chemin des Glerrets)*. It's cheaper, has free beach access, and stays open from April to 30 September. Reception shuts at midnight.

Hostels This is only a small selection of the places listed in *info-jeunes*. In particular, there are seven places that take women only – of these, *Home St Pierre (☎ 310 37 07, fax 310 17 27, 4 Cour St Pierre)*, by the cathedral, is a favourite among young female travellers.

North of the Rhône The SYHA *hostel (☎ 732 62 60, 28-30 Rue Rothschild)* is big, modern and busy, with helpful and knowledgeable staff. Large dorms are Sfr24 year-round, doubles cost Sfr60 with shower and there are a few family rooms. Dinners (Sfr11.50), a TV room, laundry and kitchen facilities (Sfr1) are all available. The hostel is closed from 10 am to 4 pm (to 2 pm in summer) and there is a flexible midnight curfew. If you tire of eating at the hostel, try the cheap university cafe next door on the other side of Rue des Buis (closed weekends).

Centre Masaryk (☎ *733 07 72, 11 Ave de la Paix*) has dorms for Sfr30 with an 11 pm curfew. Reception is open 8 am to 8 pm. Singles/doubles/triples cost Sfr45/80/105 and you can get a key for late access. Take bus No 5 or 8 from Gare de Cornavin.

South of the Rhône *Cité Universitaire* (☎ *839 22 22, fax 839 22 23, 46 Ave Miremont*) has hundreds of beds. Take bus No 3 from Cornavin to the terminus at Champel, south of the city centre. Dorm beds in July and August cost Sfr17 (they're restricted to groups the rest of the year). Rooms are usually subject to a three-night minimum stay: singles/doubles cost Sfr45/61 or Sfr38/55 for students. A double studio with kitchen, toilet and shower costs Sfr68. Prices exclude breakfast (Sfr6). Reception is open 8 am to noon (9 to 11 am on Sunday) and 2 pm (6 pm on weekends) to 10 pm.

Forget Me Not (☎ *320 93 55, fax 781 46 45, Rue Vignier 8*) has simple, student-style rooms with sink for Sfr45/80. Dorms are Sfr25 and there's no breakfast.

Budget Hotels Choice in this category is limited, and at busy times you may be forced to move up or down-market.

North of the Rhône *Hôtel de la Cloche* (☎ *732 94 81, fax 738 16 12, 6 Rue de la Cloche*), is small, old-fashioned, friendly and liable to be full unless you call ahead. Big singles/doubles using hall shower are Sfr50/80; doubles with private shower are Sfr90 or Sfr110. Breakfast costs Sfr5.

L'Aiglon (☎ *732 97 60, fax 732 87 71, 16 Rue Sismondi*) has varying, sizeable doubles for Sfr90 with shower or Sfr110 with shower/WC and TV. Breakfast is Sfr10, reception is in the restaurant, and it's in a colourful, slightly seedy street.

Hôtel Lido (☎ *731 55 30, fax 731 65 01; see the Geneva Station Area map, 8 Rue de Chantepoulet*) has decent-sized rooms, compared to the Geneva average, and genial staff. Singles/doubles with private shower, toilet, TV and radio cost up to Sfr100/170 –

you'll pay less in winter, at weekends and for longer stays (negotiate prices).

South of the Rhône *Hôtel Beau-Site* (☎ *328 10 08, fax 329 23 64, 3 Place du Cirque*) gives one of the best deals in Geneva, with its kitchen facilities, free tea and coffee, and good-sized, old-fashioned rooms with high ceilings and creaky wood floors. Singles/doubles/triples are Sfr57/79/105 using the hall shower, Sfr68/88/105 with private shower, or Sfr80/108/120 with shower and toilet.

About 800m south is *Hôtel Carmen* (☎ *329 11 11, fax 781 59 33, @ hotelcarmen .gasser@bluewin.ch, 5 Rue Dancer*), providing big rooms with TV for Sfr75/90 with shower or Sfr52/70 without. Breakfast is Sfr7 and reception is open 24 hours.

Hôtel le Prince (☎ *807 05 00, fax 807 05 29, 16 Rue des Voisins*) has comfortable if smallish rooms with shower/WC, TV and telephone. Singles/doubles are Sfr85/105 with shower/WC, Sfr75/95 with shower only, or Sfr60/80 using hall shower.

Places to Stay – Mid-Range

There's not much to choose between the following tourist-class hotels which are within easy reach of the train station.

The three-star *Hôtel International & Terminus* (☎ *732 80 95, fax 732 18 43, @ internatinal-terminus@swissonline.ch*) is at 20 Rue des Alpes (see the Geneva Station map). Singles/doubles with shower/WC cost from Sfr80/90 up to Sfr150/220, depending on how busy they are. There's an inexpensive restaurant on site.

Hôtel Bernina (☎ *908 49 50, fax 908 49 51, 22 Place de Cornavin*) has renovated rooms with TV and telephone and charges Sfr105/150 with shower and Sfr80/105 without. *Hôtel Suisse* (☎ *732 66 30, fax 732 62 39, @ reservation@hotel-suisse, 10 Place de Cornavin*), is slightly nicer, with a swirling staircase and better appointed rooms, but it's also more expensive, starting at Sfr135/175.

Hôtel Excelsior (☎ *732 09 45, fax 738 43 69, 32 Rue Rousseau*), has fairly dull but perfectly adequate singles/doubles with the expected facilities from Sfr115/180.

GENEVA

Places to Stay – Top End

Dozens of four and five-star hotels will allow you to spend a fortune on accommodation if you wish. The lobbies of some of these places are so plush that you feel practically naked if you're not wearing formal dress. One such place is the *Hôtel Beau-Rivage* (☎ 716 66 66, fax 716 60 60, @ info@beau-rivage.ch, 13 Quai du Mont Blanc), an atmospheric 19th century hotel dripping with the opulence of the era. More modern but similarly lavish is the *Noga Hilton* (☎ 908 90 81, fax 908 90 90, 19 Quai du Mont Blanc). It's slightly cheaper (singles/doubles from Sfr350/450) and has its own swimming pool (free for guests). Both places have top-notch restaurants (see following Places to Eat section).

At the more affordable end of the scale and conveniently located is *Hotel Ambassador* (☎ 731 72 00, fax 738 90 80, @ ambahotel@iprolink.ch, 21 Rive Droite). Prices start at Sfr155/230; the rooms are well fitted-out but not exactly overflowing with space. Breakfast is Sfr16 extra and parking costs Sfr16 for 24 hours.

Places to Eat

Geneva is the cuisine capital of Switzerland. There is a staggering choice in styles and regional specialities. All price ranges are catered for but, as with hotels, getting what you want is easier if you have more money to spend. Eating is generally cheaper around Gare de Cornavin, or south of the Old Town in the vicinity of the university.

Fondue and raclette are widely available. Also popular is locally caught perch, which typically costs well over Sfr20 unless you can find it as a plat du jour.

Self-Service There is a small fruit and vegetable market, open daily except Sunday, on Rue de Coutance. *Aperto*, a supermarket in the train station, is open 6 am to 10 pm daily. The *Migros* in the airport is open 8 am to 8 pm daily. The *Migros* supermarket on Rue des Pâquis has a cheap self-service restaurant. For budget eating in the Old Town, make for the restaurant in the *EPA* department store *(Rue de la Croix*

d'Or), where meals are Sfr8 to Sfr14, or the *Coop* supermarket and *La Marmite* restaurant in the shopping centre at Place de la Fusterie. All these places have extended opening till 8 pm on Thursday, and are closed Sunday. The *Migros Restaurant (5 Rue du Prince)* in the Old Town has later opening; to 9 pm Monday to Thursday and to 7 pm Friday.

Restaurant Manora (4 Rue de Cornavin; see the Geneva Station Area Map) is a buffet-style restaurant with tasty daily dishes from Sfr10 and extensive salad and dessert bars. Always popular, it is open 7 am to 9.30 pm daily (9 am to 9 pm on Sunday).

Budget & Mid-Range Restaurants

Geneva has a variety of reasonably priced restaurants.

North of the Rhône La Trattoria *(1 Rue de la Servette)*, near the station, has excellent if pricey Italian food from Sfr15 (closed Sunday). Along the road at No 31 is *Kong Restaurant*, providing tasty Chinese dishes for about Sfr20. Visit at lunch on a weekday, when there are meals for Sfr12 including rice and starter, and Sfr17.50 secures an all-you-can-eat buffet (not Monday). It closes at 10 pm.

Le Blason (23 Rue des Pâquis) looks a typical bar/restaurant by day, with meals from about Sfr15, yet it also courts late-night clubbers by opening 4 am to 2 am daily (4 am to 8 am on weekends) – prices rise slightly for the insomniacs. *Auberge de Savièse* (☎ 732 83 30), nearby at No 20, is more touristy but has lunchtime plats du jour from Sfr13 and Swiss specialities such as fondue from Sfr19.90. It's closed till 5.30 pm on weekends.

Auberge de Coutance (☎ 732 79 19, 25 Rue de Coutance) is recommended for exquisite specialities from Sfr27.50, including duck delicacies. It's an atmospheric below-ground restaurant serving till 1 am (closed Sunday).

Café de Paris (☎ 732 84 50; see the Geneva Station Area map, 26 Rue du Mont-Blanc) serves up one dish only – succulent entrecôte steak with a special herb and butter sauce, chips and salad (Sfr36). It's well established and very busy, and the harassed table servers can be a bit abrupt at times (open 11 am to 11 pm daily).

Take advantage of the international flavour of Geneva to vary your diet. Explore the streets north of Rue des Alpes for cheapish Mexican, Chinese and Oriental food.

Sugar Hut (16 Rue des Etuves) has good Thai meals from about Sfr19, and it's closed until 6 pm on weekends. *Miyako (☎ 738 01 20, 11 Rue de Chantepoulet)*, is expensive but the quality is excellent. This Japanese restaurant has three-course business lunches for Sfr30 to Sfr36, and a full evening meal will cost around Sfr50 or more (closed Sunday).

If you're in UN district, note that many of the public buildings there have inexpensive cafes; the one in the *OMPI Building (Place des Nations)* has a good view.

South of the Rhône *Dent de Lion (14 Rue des Eaux-Vives)* is a small vegetarian place, open 9 am to 2.30 pm and 6.30 to 10 pm Monday to Friday. Meals start from Sfr15 and three-course lunches are Sfr25.

Chez Ma Cousine (6 Place du Bourg-de-Four), in the Old Town, is no wider than a corner shop and is often packed. It specialises in one dish; half-chicken, potatoes and salad for Sfr12.90. It's open 6 am to midnight Monday to Friday.

Nearby, *La Tête dans le Sable (☎ 310 25 50, 9 Rue Verdaine)* is a trendy place with several small rooms. Meals are anything from Sfr16 to Sfr55 and there's a good salad buffet.

Café du Centre (☎ 311 85 86; see the Geneva Old Town map, 5 Place du Molard) has outside seating in a pleasant square near the Old Town. Office staff relax here after work over a coffee or a beer. But it's not cheap; the lunchtime plat du jour costs Sfr17.50 and other meals are Sfr25 or more (open 7 am to 1 am daily).

The large and popular *Cave Valaisanne et Chalet Suisse (☎ 328 12 36, 23 Blvd Georges-Favon)* is an excellent place to try many varieties of fondue (starting at Sfr21.80); sometimes that atmosphere is so

thick with bubbling cheese that people on a diet can dine on the scent alone. It's open 8 am to 1 am daily. Close by is *Victoria (Place du Cirque)*, a stylish mid-priced brasserie owned by two gourmet chefs. It's open daily.

Café Universal (☎ 781 18 81, 26 Blvd du Pont d'Arve), is atmospheric, French and smoky. The mirrors and camp chandeliers attract theatrical patrons. Plats du jour are Sfr15 to Sfr17, and dinners are mostly above Sfr20. It's closed Sunday and Monday in summer. *L'Amiral (☎ 735 18 08, 24 Quai Gustave-Ador)* is a good place for fish dishes from Sfr25. The 'menu du touriste' is fillet of perch with salad and dessert for Sfr32 (open daily).

Restaurants – Top End Reserve ahead for all these places. *Le Béarn (☎ 321 00 28, 4 Quai de la Poste)* is one of the best restaurants in Geneva. It serves sumptuous fish specialities and creative cuisine (dishes around Sfr50, menus from Sfr90). The restaurant is closed weekends (except Saturday evening in winter) and from mid-July to late August. Of near comparable quality is *Le Cygne (☎ 908 90 81)* in the Noga Hilton hotel, 19 Quai du Mont-Blanc. The cooking is French-style; main course are in the Sfr40 to Sfr70 price range and there are over 400 different wines on the wine list. It is open daily.

Also very highly rated are *Le Chat Botté (☎ 716 66 66)* in Hôtel Beau-Rivage (open daily), 13 Quai du Mont-Blanc, *Les Continents (919 39 39)* in Hôtel Intercontinental, 7-9 Chemin du Petit Saconnex (closed weekends), and *Le Neptune (☎ 909 00 00)*, Hôtel du Rhône, 1 Quai Turrettini. Le Neptune has fish specialities (closed weekends).

Entertainment

Different genres of music are covered in various festivals through the year. Geneva is the home of the Orchestra of the Swiss Romande; it and other orchestras often perform at the *Victoria Hall (14 Rue du Général Dufour)*. English-speaking theatre thrives in Geneva on an amateur level. Contact *Theatre in English (☎ 341 51 90)* for

GENEVA

information and tickets. In cinemas, films usually retain their original soundtrack; look for VO (version original) to make sure. *Ciné Lac* is an outdoor cinema near Genève Plage, open in the summer.

A popular place to hang out in the evening is the Jetée des Pâquis, where there are snacks, drinks, and (usually) free live music.

Geneva has a flourishing alternative arts scene. A well-established venue is *l'Usine* (☎ 781 34 90, 4 Place de Volontaires), a converted old factory. It is now a centre for cinema, cabaret, theatre, concerts and homeless art objects. Most of it is closed Monday. Its Web site is at www.usine.ch. It has a good restaurant (inexpensive food) and a bar (0.3L of beer is Sfr2.50), though these are closed Sunday and Monday. Nearby, between Rue du Strand and Boulevard de Saint-Georges, is a spread-out collection of alternative arts venues known as *Artamis*. Also ask locally about in-vogue (and often short-lived) squats that put on various events.

Au Chat Noir (☎ 343 49 98, 13 Rue Vautier, Carouge) is a jazz and rock club with interesting decor and live music. Also good for drinks, food and live music is *Alhambar* (☎ 312 13 13; see the Geneva Old Town map, 10 Rue de la Rôtisserie), on the 1st floor at the back of the Alhambra cinema. It's open Tuesday to Sunday; its Web site is at www.alhambar.ch.

A good British/Irish meeting place is *Mulligans* (14 Rue Grenus) where Guinness costs Sfr8 a pint (0.56L). *Post Café* (7 Rue de Berne) has British sports on TV and limited, inexpensive food. Both places are open daily, but closed Sunday till 5 pm. A similar if larger place in the Old Town is *Flanagan's Irish Bar* (Rue du Cheval-Blanc), which is open from 4 pm and has live music in the cellar bar at weekends.

Geneva has plenty of plush nightclubs but they are expensive. One of the most popular discos is *l'Inderdit* (☎ 738 90 91, Quai du Seujet 18), open from about 10 pm to 5 am nightly. Next door is *Le Loft* (☎ 738 28 28), a bar-restaurant with a cabaret-style dinner show and dancing afterwards. It has a mixed gay/straight clientele and opens 7 am to 2 am weekdays and 5 am to 2 am weekends.

The *Casino* (19 Quai du Mont-Blanc) is open from noon daily. Go there to play Boule (the tame Swiss version of roulette) and slot machines. Folklore shows are not to everybody's taste, but *Edelweiss Manotel* (☎ 731 36 58, 2 Place de la Navigation) believes it has a 'genuine Alpine village in downtown Geneva'. Students of kitsch may want to see for themselves; the nightly show is free with dinner (fondue from Sfr23, other meals from Sfr30). *Swiss Cottage* (☎ 732 40 00, 6 Rue Barton) offers a similar deal.

Shopping

Geneva is well known as a place to buy watches, jewellery and enamel work. There are several less expensive places on Rue du Mont-Blanc with a good selection of Swiss knives. Various shops, such as the one opposite the Jardin Anglais, sell folklorish things. Some souvenir shops stay open till 11 pm. A flea market occupies Plaine de Plainpalais every Wednesday and Saturday.

Getting There & Away

Air Geneva airport is an important transport hub and has frequent connections to every major European city and many cities worldwide – see the Getting There & Away chapter for more information. EasyJet (☎ 848-88 82 22) has flights to London-Luton or London-Gatwick starting at Sfr69.

There's a Swissair office by the station on Rue de Lausanne, open 8.30 am to 6.30 pm Monday to Friday. Swissair is the booking agent for Crossair, which flies daily at least six times to Lugano, twice to Basel and a dozen times to Zürich. Internal flights are expensive; the full Geneva-Zürich one-way fare is Sfr223, though ask about special deals.

Bus International buses depart from the Gare Routière (☎ 732 02 30; see the Geneva Station Area map) on Place Dorcière off Rue des Alpes. There are four buses a week to London (Sfr150) and three a week to Barcelona (Sfr100) – advance reservations are advisable. There are three (one on Sunday and holidays) buses per day to Chamonix (Sfr41 one way, Sfr70 normal return, Sfr98 day return).

Train Fast TGV trains depart around five times a day to Paris-Lyon (Sfr78), and the journey takes 3½ hours. Reservations are essential and usually cost Sfr20 (Sfr5 for some Saturday trains). There are also regular international trains to Hamburg (Sfr273, plus reservation fee), Milan (Sfr81) and Barcelona (Sfr100) – ask about special reduced fares. There are train information offices in the station and at Place Longemalle.

There are more-or-less hourly connections to most Swiss towns. Zürich takes three hours (Sfr77), as does Interlaken West (Sfr65), both via Bern. Gare des Eaux-Vives is the station for Annecy and Chamonix. To get there from Gare de Cornavin, take bus No 8 or 1 to Rond-Point de Rive and then tram No 12.

Car & Motorcycle An autoroute bypass skirts Geneva, with major routes intersecting south-west of the city; the N1 from Lausanne joins with the E62 to Lyon (130km) and the E25 heading south-east towards Chamonix. Toll-free main roads follow the course of these motorways.

Rental Sixt (☎ 732 90 90), 1 Place de la Navigation, has the best day-by-day rates (from Sfr88 per day, unlimited kilometres). Its weekend deals (Sfr133) are for 72 hours.

Horizon Motos (☎ 732 29 90), 51 Rue de Lausanne, rents motorcycles (including helmets) ranging from 125cc to 1100cc; weekend rates (2½ days, unlimited kilometres) are Sfr87 to Sfr525. Monthly rates are very reasonable: a 650cc machine would cost Sfr1750 with unlimited mileage.

See the Getting Around chapter for rates for the multinationals. Each has an airport branch; their city branches are:

Avis (☎ 731 90 00) 44 Rue de Lausanne
Budget (☎ 900 24 00) 36 Rue de Zürich
Europcar (☎ 732 52 52) 37 Rue de Lausanne
Hertz (☎ 731 12 00) 60 Rue de Berne

Boat Compagnie Générale de Navigation (CGN; ☎ 312 52 23) by the Jardin Anglais operates a steamer service to all towns and major villages bordering Lake Geneva, including those in France. Most boats only operate between May and September, such as those to Lausanne-Ouchy (3½ hours, Sfr31) and Montreux (4½ hours, Sfr36). Both Eurail and Swiss railpasses are valid on CGN boats.

A CGN one-day pass costs Sfr50 (Sfr67 in 1st class). Another option is the Swiss Boat Pass (see the Getting Around chapter).

Getting Around

To/From the Airport Cointrin airport is 5km from the city centre. There are 200 trains a day from here to Gare de Cornavin (Sfr5; takes six minutes). Alternatively, take bus No 10 to Gare de Cornavin for Sfr2.20 (every 10 minutes). A metered taxi would cost Sfr25 to Sfr35.

Bus The city is efficiently serviced by buses, trolley buses and trams. There are ticket dispensers at stops. A ticket for multiple rides within one hour costs Sfr2.20, or a ticket valid for three stops within 30 minutes is Sfr1.50. A day pass costs Sfr5 for the city or Sfr8.50 for the whole canton. Pre-paid cards ('Carte@bus' cards) are available from the Transports Publics Genevois offices (open daily) in Gare de Cornavin and Rond-Point de Rive, and elsewhere. For Sfr20/30/50 you get travel credit to the value of Sfr21/32/55; the ticket machine debits your card when you select your ticket. Night buses (*Noctambus*) run at weekends only (Sfr3).

Car & Motorcycle See the previous Getting There & Away section for information about rentals.

Most streets in or near the centre have restricted parking 8 am to 7 pm Monday to Saturday (meters with 90-minute maximum stay; Sfr1.50 or Sfr2 per hour), and hotels rarely have private parking. Parking garages are clearly signposted. Those at Jardin Anglais and Varembé (near the United Nations) charge Sfr1 per hour or Sfr0.50 after

6 pm. Some others, like the one under Gare de Cornavin, are more expensive.

Taxi The cost for taxis is Sfr6.30 plus Sfr2.70 per kilometre within the city and Sfr3.50 outside. However, as fares aren't regulated some operators charge higher prices. Get a taxi by the station or ring ☎ 331 41 33.

Bicycle There's a SBB/CFF bike rental office at Gare de Cornavin, open daily. But from 2 May to 31 October you can borrow city bikes daily *free of charge* from Genev' Roule (☎/fax 740 13 43), sponsored by the Red Cross. Locations are: 17 Place de Montbrillant, Bains des Pâquis, Place du Rhône and Plaine de Plainpalais. Some ID and Sfr50 deposit is required.

Boat CGN (see the previous Getting There & Away section) offers excursions on the lake in summer, such as a 55-minute cruise with commentary (Sfr11; hourly from 11.05 am to 5.05 pm). There are also full-day, half-day and evening cruises, with the option of meals. Ticket offices and departures are on Quai du Mont-Blanc and by Jardin Anglais. Smaller companies along the quayside, such as Swiss Boat (☎ 732 47 47), operate similar excursions, but no travel passes are valid. Small boats *(mouettes)* cross between Geneva's two shores (city travel passes valid).

Lake Geneva Region

The tourist area known as the Lake Geneva Region consists of the canton of Vaud (pronounced Voh; Waadt in German). Long-standing rivalry between Vaud and neighbouring Geneva was probably behind the attempt in the early 1990s to exorcise the name 'Geneva' and market the region under the cantonal name. Unfortunately the strategy was unsuccessful as the name 'Vaud' meant little to most visitors, so the area is once again known as the Lake Geneva Region, or Région du Léman in French.

The canton of Vaud covers the area south of the cantons of Neuchâtel and Fribourg; in fact, not to overstress the point, it's the region around Lake Geneva (Lac Léman in French, though sometimes also known, much to Vaud's chagrin, as Lac de Genève). It is the towns on the shores of Lake Geneva that provide the most compelling reasons to visit the canton.

Vaud is well-known for its wines. A tour of wine-growers' cellars *(caveaux des vignerons)* is easy if you have your own transport. The communities bordering the lake to the west and the east produce wines with their own distinctive flavours, and these are discussed in the vineyard guide from the tourist office. A different tourist office booklet details the opening times of the cellars.

Highlights

- Ponder over the unique *l'Art Brut* collection, in Lausanne.
- Tour Vaud's vineyards.
- Visit Château de Chillon near Montreux.
- Indulge in Alpine sports, including hot air ballooning in Château d'Oex.
- Rock along to music festivals – Jazz in Montreux and Rock in Nyon.
- Enjoy the beauty of music boxes and automata in Sainte Croix.

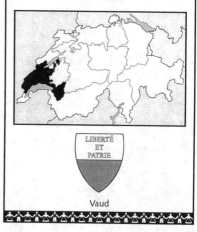

LIBERTÉ ET PATRIE

Vaud

History

In 1229 Vaud became a vassal territory of Savoy. In 1536 Bern declared war on Savoy and successfully took over the region. As Bern had an existing treaty of fellowship signed with Lausanne, the people of Vaud naturally thought this might result in them gaining more autonomy. But Bern thought differently; it installed a bailiff in the bishop's castle in Lausanne and proceeded to siphon off the city's wealth.

The situation was endured until January 1798 when Frédéric César de la Harpe, leader of the Liberal Party, declared Lausanne and Vaud independent under the title of the Lemanic Republic. Not surprisingly, Bern did not wholly go along with this assertion but the matter was settled in 1803 by Napoleon in his Act of Mediation, in which Vaud became an independent canton within the Swiss Confederation, and Lausanne was installed as the capital.

Orientation & Information

Vaud is almost exclusively French-speaking, and encompasses the three main geographical regions of Switzerland: the Jura Mountains in the west, the relatively flat plain of the Mittelland, and a section of the Alps in the south-east.

The regional tourist office (☎ 021-613 26 26, fax 613 26 00, ✆ info@lake-geneva-region.ch) is at 60 Ave d'Ouchy, CH-1006, Ouchy, Lausanne. Opening times are 8 am to 5.30 pm Monday to Friday. It provides regional brochures, a guide to vineyards in Vaud, and cantonal maps showing hiking routes accompanied by a brief desciption (in French) and cycling routes (all are free).

For information on Avenches and Payerne see Around Murten in the Fribourg, Neuchâtel & Jura chapter.

Getting Around

The Lake Geneva Region (Région du Léman) Pass gives free travel on three days in seven, with a 50% reduction on the other four days. It is valid for travel throughout the canton on buses and trains, and gives 50% off CGN boat services and 25% off some cable cars (eg, up to the Diablerets Glacier). It costs Sfr179/135 in 1st/2nd class, or Sfr143/108 for holders of a Swiss rail pass.

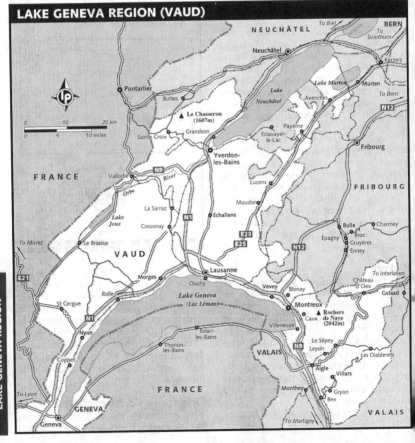

LAKE GENEVA REGION (VAUD)

_ausanne

☏ 021 • pop 125,000 • elevation 495m

his hilly city (loh-**san**) is Switzerland's fth-largest, and enjoys a thriving arts cene. Highlights include a Gothic cathdral, lake views and water sports. Don't iss l'Art Brut, one of Europe's most unsual art collections.

The Romans used to have a military amp called Lousonna, on the shores of the ke at Vidy. This was an important stop on e route from Italy to Gaul, via the Great Bernard Pass. With the invasion of the lemanni, the inhabitants abandoned this ttlement and joined the people who had ttled on the site of the present old city. he commercial and religious importance f Lausanne began to develop hand-inand, helped by its first bishop, St Marius, ho was previously based in Aventicum d came to live in the city in the 6th cenary. The Reformation arrived in 1529, anks to the preaching of Guillaume Farel, cohort of Calvin. But the conversion asn't underlined until the invading forces om Bern took over the city in 1536 and roceeded to ransack the Catholic urches.

Lausanne flourished in the following nturies despite its period of subservience Bern, and welcomed important literary gures such as Voltaire, Dickens, Byron d TS Eliot (who wrote _The Waste Land_ re). The city retains a fair measure of stas; it is the location of the Federal Tribunal, e highest court in the country, and has en the headquarters of the International lympic Committee since 1915.

rientation

e Old Town with its winding streets pped by the cathedral is above and north the train station. Place St François is the ain hub for local transport, and leading off is Rue de Bourg, the main shopping street. st west and downhill of Place St François Flon, an area of formerly derelict wareuses which has partially been taken over art galleries and trendy shops. The city

has grown to include the former fishing village of Ouchy, now a picturesque harbour sporting a cluster of hotels.

Information

Tourist Offices Lausanne Tourisme (☏ 613 73 21, fax 616 86 47, ☻ information@ lausannne-tourisme.ch) has two branches. The one in the train station is open 9 am to 7 pm daily. The office at 4 Place de la Navigation, by the harbour in Ouchy, is open 8 am to 6 pm daily (9 pm from April to September). Commission is charged for hotel reservations. Ask about the useful Lausanne Card, which is valid for two days. It costs Sfr15 and gives free public transport, 20-30% discounts on museums, and various reductions or benefits at shops and restaurants.

The tourist office for the Canton de Vaud is also in Ouchy: see the Orientation & Information section earlier in this chapter.

Train Station The main station (Gare CFF) has luggage lockers (Sfr3 and Sfr5), and a train information office open 8 am to 7 pm Monday to Friday and 8 am to 5 pm Saturday. Money-exchange counters are open 6.20 am to 7.30 pm daily, and bicycle rental is from 6.40 am to 7.40 pm daily.

Post & Communications The large post office (1002) at 15 Place St François is open 7.30 am to 6.30 pm Monday to Friday and 8 to 11 am Saturday. The main post office (Poste Principale 1001), by the station at 43 Ave de la Gare, has an emergency counter open daily.

Email & Internet Access In Comm (☏ 351 11 91, ☻ info@incomm.ch), 32 Rue du Petit-Chêne, is a communications centre (open shop hours) that offers internet access for Sfr7 (20 minutes) or Sfr15 (one hour).

Travel Agencies SSR (☏ 617 56 27), the student and budget travel agency, is at 20 Blvd de Grancy, open 9.15 am to 6 pm Monday to Friday and 9 am to noon Saturday. American Express (☏ 310 19 00), is at 14 Ave Mon Repos. Swissair (☏ 343 22 22) has an office at 26 Rue de Bourg.

LAUSANNE

PLACES TO STAY
13 Hotel Regina
17 Pension Bon-Séjour
31 Elite
34 Hotel Continental
38 Hôtel Excelsior
40 Hôtel Le Chalet
47 Le Château d'Ouchy
49 Hôtel du Port
51 Hôtel d'Angleterre

PLACES TO EAT
8 Migros Supermarket & Restaurant
9 Coop Supermarket & Restaurant
12 Placette Department Store
16 Café de l'Everche
18 Caroline Café
20 La Factoria
21 Restaurant Au Couscous
22 La Grappe d'Or
26 Manora
27 Ma-Jong
30 Paradiso
36 Calèche
42 Mövenpick Radisson Hotel
46 Boccalino
50 Crêperie Ouchy

OTHER
1 Palais de Beaulieu
2 Musée de l'Art Brut
3 Au Château bar/restaurant
4 Castle St Marie
5 Cathédrale
6 Palais de Rumine & Musée cantonal des Beaux-Arts
7 Place de la Riponne
10 MAD
11 l'Atelier Volant
14 D! Disco
15 Town Hall
19 Le Bleu Lézard bar/restaurant
23 St François Church
24 Post Office
25 Place St François
28 Flon Metro station
29 In Comm internet
32 Avis
33 Main Post Office
35 Gare Metro station
37 Tourist Information
39 Musée de l'Elysée
41 Regional Tourist Office
43 CGN Head Office
44 Ouchy Metro station
45 Main Tourist Office
48 CGN Boat Departure Point
52 Olympic Museum

To Neuchâtel (75km) & N1 Motorway
To Morges
To Ada-Logements
Avenue de Tivoli
Avenue de Morges
Avenue d'Echallens
Rue de Genève
Avenue de Beaulieu
Avenue des Bergères
Avenue A Vinet
Rue du Tunnel
Rue Dr César Roux
To Place de l'Ours, Hospital, Murten & Bern
Rue des Terreaux
Rue Neuve
Rue St Laurent
Rue de Genève
Rue des Côtes-de-Montbenon
Avenue Jules Gonin
Port Chaudéron
Rue du Grand Pont
Rue du Grand Chêne
Avenue Marc-Dufour
Avenue Louis-Ruchonnet
Rue du Petit Chêne
Place de la Gare
Avenue Sainte-Luce
Avenue de la Gare
Avenue Mont d'Or
Avenue W Fraisse
Boulevard de Grancy
Avenue Dapples
Botanical Gardens
To SYHA Jeunotel
Avenue de la Harpe
Rue St François
Rue Centrale
Rue de Bourg
Rue Enning
Rue Caroline
Rue Cheneau de Bourg
Rue St Martin
Rue Louis Curtat
Place de la Palud
Avenue Mon Repos
Avenue de Rhodanie
Chemin de Bellerive
To Camping de Vidy & Geneva (62km)
Avenue d'Ouchy
Avenue de l'Elysée
Chemin de Beau-Rivage
Place du Port
Port d'Ouchy
Lake Geneva (Lac Léman)
Quay d'Ouchy
To Montreux (31km)

Train Station

0   150   300 m
0   150   300 yd

Bookshops The Librairie Payot, 4 Place Pépinet, (☎ 341 33 31), is the biggest bookshop in French-speaking Switzerland, and has English books.

Medical Services The Vaudois University Hospital (☎ 314 11 11), Rue du Bugnon 46, provides emergency treatment.

Cathedral

The Cathedral, which has recently been renovated, is considered one of the finest medieval Gothic churches in Switzerland. It was built in the 12th and 13th centuries, and was consecrated by Pope Gregory X in 1275, in the presence of Rudolph of Habsburg, Emperor of the Holy Roman Empire. Its most striking decoration is the acclaimed rose window from the 13th century in the south transept. Also worthy of study are the main portals with their tiers of adorning statues, and the 16th century stalls in the north aisle (ask the tower cashier to turn on the lights). The cathedral is open daily until 7 pm (5 pm in winter) – but don't try to visit during Sunday morning services. Ascend the tower for a view worthy of a deity (Sfr2); it's open 8.30 to 11 am and 1.30 to 5.30 pm Monday to Saturday, and 2 to 4 pm Sunday. Also inquire about the free organ recitals in summer on Fridays.

The tradition of the nightwatch is still maintained in Lausanne; the hour is called from the cathedral tower between 10 pm and 2 am every night.

Old Town

Place St François has a **church** (Église St François), that was once part of a 13th century monastery. From the north-east corner, Rue St François becomes Rue du Pont and leads into Place de la Palud, which has a **Fountain of Justice**. This square is taken over by a market every Wednesday and Saturday morning. The 17th century building with the clock tower and the protruding winged dragons is the **town hall** (hôtel de ville), which sometimes has exhibitions in the foyer. The covered stairway leading up from the fountain climbs to the cathedral. About 200m north of the cathedral is the Château St Marie. This 15th century castle was once the residence of the bishops of Lausanne, and is now the seat of government of the Vaud canton. There's little to see except the view from the terrace.

Musée de l'Art Brut

This fantastic collection at 11 Ave de Bergières, put together by French artist Jean Dubuffet, was opened in Lausanne in 1976. 'Brut' means raw, crude, or rough, and that's exactly what you get.

None of the artists featured were properly trained or part of any artistic circle. On the contrary, many couldn't even take their place in normal society. Some were criminally insane, others simply eccentric; most spent at least some time in a mental institution. Some were so impaired that drawing was just about the only thing they could do. Philipp Schöpke, for example, was discharged from the army 'unable to even lace his shoes' (according to the military doctor) and went on to draw figures with the raw impact of primitive tribal icons. Often the people exhibiting started creating art only late in their lives, perhaps led to it following a crisis, after which they would draw or paint obsessively.

The work they produce breaks all the rules. It is vivid, startling, or just plain strange. There are sculptures made out of broken plates and discarded rags, faces made out of shells. Some insisted their drawings originated directly from the spirit world. One woman who believed she was a medium drew on long scrolls of paper in near darkness. As she unrolled fresh areas of paper she rolled up the sections she had completed, and therefore never had any idea what her work looked like in its entirety. A wooden wall shown upstairs was taken from an asylum; it's from a bare cell where Clément Fraisse was incarcerated for two years. The carved designs were done using a broken spoon, and after that was confiscated, the handle of his chamber pot.

Edmund Monseil found it hard to communicate with other people, especially women, and he spent most of WWII hiding from the Germans in an attic. His drawings are cramped, claustrophobic creations on small bits of paper, filled with glaring eyes surrounding the central figure or figures.

A potted biography of each artist (in English) is on display. This gives a valuable context, but remember that art often transcends personal circumstances, so don't limit yourself to spotting the obvious correlations between the artist's life and the themes or symbols in their work.

The gallery is open 11 am to 1 pm and 2 to 6 pm Tuesday to Sunday. The collection is not huge, but if you see and read everything you could easily be there for three to four hours. Entry costs Sfr6 for adults, Sfr4 for students, and it's free for children. It's near the Jomini stop on the route of bus Nos 2 and 3.

Palais de Rumine

This grand building overlooking the Place de la Riponne holds several museums. The main one is the **Fine Arts Museum** (Musée cantonal des Beaux-Arts), with many works by Swiss and foreign artists. Only a fraction of the works in the collection may be displayed, however, depending upon the frequent temporary exhibitions. It's open 11 am until 5 pm Friday to Sunday, until 6 pm Tuesday and Wednesday, until 8 pm Thursday, and closed Monday.

The other museum collections in the building cover natural history, anatomy, zoology, mineralogy, archaeology and history. They're open the same hours as the Fine Arts Museum, except they close at 6 pm on Thursday. Combined entry to all the museums is Sfr6 (students/seniors Sfr4, children free), or it's Sfr4 for any one museum, not including the Fine Arts Museum. All the museums are free on the first Sunday of the month.

Olympic Museum

Given that Lausanne is the base for the International Olympic Committee, it is perhaps inevitable that there's a museum devoted to the games. The Olympic Museum (Musée Olympique) is sited in a lavish new building in the Parc Olympique, 1 Quai d'Ouchy, atop a tiered landscaped garden

(good views). It tells the Olympic story using videos, archive film (including a 3-D show), touch-screen computers and memorabilia from the games. Medals from the summer and winter Olympics are displayed – those from the winter games are more varied in design. It's open 10 am to 6 pm Tuesday to Sunday (8 pm Thursday); in summer it's open till 7 pm daily. Entry is a hefty Sfr14 (students and seniors Sfr9, families Sfr34). Handheld audio commentary (in English) costs Sfr3.

Other Things to See & Do

Other museums in the city cover topics a diverse as photography (Musée de l'Elysée), pipes and tobacco, archive film and contemporary art. Tourist office literature details opening times and entry fees.

Lac Léman provides plenty of sporting opportunities. Contact the sailing school (école de voile) at Ouchy (☎ 635 58 87) or Vidy (☎ 617 90 00) for courses on wind surfing, water-skiing and sailing, and equipment rental for these activities. CGN (see the Getting There & Away section) provide a range of special boat cruises. The lakeside at Ouchy is a great place for a stroll at sunset. Lausanne's **Botanical Gardens** (free, open daily) are south-west of the station at Ave de Cour 14 (closed winter), and there are large areas of woodland to the north and east of the city.

Places to Stay – Budget

Camping Year-round camping is possible at *Camping de Vidy* (☎ 624 20 31, Chemin du Camping), just to the west of the Vidy sports complex. It has a lakeside location, stacks of facilities, and costs Sfr7.1 per adult and Sfr7 to Sfr11 for a tent. Bungalows are also available. To get there, take bus No 2 from Place St François. Get off Bois de Vaux and walk under the Autoroute towards the lake.

Hostel The SYHA *Jeunotel* (☎ 626 02 2 fax 626 02 26, 36 Chemin du Bois-de-Vaux is intended as a cross between a youth hotel and a hotel. West of the city centre, it offers no-frills accommodation in dorm

Sfr24 or Sfr28), singles/doubles (Sfr75/90 with shower/WC and TV or Sfr51/74 without), and triples/quads (Sfr84/112 without). The self-service restaurant serves cheap meals from Monday to Friday. Studio apartments are also available, on a monthly basis Sfr785/995 for one/two people), except in summer. Reception is open 24 hours. By bus, get off at the same stop as for Camping le Vidy.

Hotels & Pensions *Ada-Logements* (☎ 25 71 34, 60 Ave de Tivoli), is student oriented but takes tourists if there's space phone ahead). Singles/doubles are Sfr50/70. *Pension Bon-Séjour* (☎ 323 59 72, 10 Rue Caroline), in a residential block, is more central. Rooms cost Sfr40/66, some with shower; phone ahead.

Hôtel Excelsior (☎ 616 84 51, fax 616 84 58, 5 Chemin du Closelet) is an ageing place with good-sized rooms, some with TV. Prices are Sfr98/140 with shower, Sfr60/100 without. Much cosier is the small *Hôtel Le Chalet* (☎ 616 52 06, 49 Ave d'Ouchy), with a homey ambience and singles/doubles/triples for Sfr62/88/99. Young people may get a discount. There are hall showers, a garden, and breakfast is Sfr9.

Hôtel du Port (☎ 616 49 30, 5 Place du Port), formerly a good budget choice in Ouchy, will re-open in summer 2001 after upgrading facilities.

Places to Stay – Mid-Range
Hôtel d'Angleterre (☎ 617 41 45, fax 616 40 75, 9 Place du Port) on the Quai d'Ouchy in Ouchy, is due to re-open in summer 2000 after extensive renovation and modernisation. Byron wrote the *Prisoner of Chillon* here in 1816.

Hôtel Regina (☎ 320 24 41, fax 390 25 29, ✉ hotel-regina@gve.ch, 18 Grand St-Jean) is a convenient, comfortable hotel in the pedestrian zone. Rooms with shower/WC and TV are Sfr110/140 to Sfr170/225, depending on the season and size. *Elite* (☎ 320 23 61, fax 320 39 63, ✉ elite@worldcom.ch, 1 Ave Ste Luce) is similar in terms of quality and prices. But this family-run hotel has its own grounds, a

quieter location and easier parking, yet it's still conveniently central.

Places to Stay – Top End
The *Hotel Continental* (☎ 320 15 51, fax 323 76 79, ✉ hotelcontinental@bluewin.ch, 2 Place de la Gare) has stylish rooms right opposite the station. Prices start at Sfr152/249; breakfast-buffet, if required, costs Sfr18.

Enjoy the luxurious setting of *Le Château d'Ouchy* (☎ 616 74 51, 617 51 37, 2 Place du Port), a castle right near the port of Ouchy, dating from the 12th century. Rooms are lavishly furnished in Louis XIII style, and all have TV, toilet and bath or shower. Prices start at Sfr170/270 and rooms differ markedly in size. The hotel also has a good-quality restaurant and private parking.

Places to Eat
Self-Service There is a *Migros* restaurant at Rue Neuve, open weekdays to 7 pm and Saturday to 5 pm. A better bet is probably the buffet-style *Manora* (17 Place St François) open 8 am (9 am Sunday) to 10.30 pm daily. Main dishes are around Sfr11, and there's an excellent choice at the salad buffet (Sfr4.20 to Sfr8.90 per plate). Round the back is *Ma-Jong* (Escaliers du Grand-Pont 3), a near-equivalent serving Asian food for Sfr14 (closed Sunday).

Another excellent option is *Caroline Café* (4 Rue Caroline), in the Coop Centre. This is a food hall with a range of cheap meals – Swiss, Italian, Oriental, etc. It's open until at least 11.30 pm (closed Sunday). Inexpensive self-service restaurants are also in two department stores on Rue St Laurent: *Coop* and *Placette*.

Other Restaurants *Café de l'Everche* (4 Rue Louis Curtat), by the cathedral, has a lunch and evening two-course menu for Sfr15. It is a small place, with a pleasant garden around the back (closed Sunday lunch).

Restaurant Au Couscous (☎ 321 38 40, 2 Rue Enning), on the 1st floor, has a wide menu including Tunisian, Lebanese, vegetarian and macrobiotic food. Meals are Sfr16 to Sfr30 and it's open to midnight or 1 am daily.

La Factoria (2 Ave du Tribunal-Fédéral) is a youngish, quite trendy place with inexpensive meals and tapas (open daily). There's a disco downstairs.

Calèche (☎ 323 01 31), in the Hotel Alpha, Petit-Chêne 34, is a little lacking in atmosphere but has reasonable food. Plats du jour are from Sfr15.50 and a three-course menu is Sfr25 (all available lunch and evening). Fondues and grills are Sfr20 to Sfr37 (open daily). Just up the road is *Paradiso*, with Italian food from Sfr12 and a rooftop terrace that is open in summer (closed Sunday).

La Grappe d'Or (☎ 323 07 60, Rue Cheneau de Bourg 3) is excellent if very expensive. The cooking is mainly French, but sometimes with additional oriental flavours. Expect to pay upwards of Sfr30 for a starter and between Sfr50 and Sfr70 for a main course. Advance reservations are usually necessary (closed Saturday noon and Sunday).

In Ouchy, there are many restaurants around the port, most with good fish specialities. Slightly cheaper options are *Crêperie Ouchy (7 Place du Port)*, with crêpes from Sfr4.50, and *Boccalino*, an Italian place on Place de la Navigation with weekday lunches for Sfr14 and a huge choice of pizzas. Both places are open daily.

Along the road is the *Mövenpick Radisson Hotel (☎ 612 76 12)* which has several busy eating areas on the ground floor (open daily). Meals start around Sfr20, though the Pêcherie section is a little more expensive and refined.

Entertainment

Concerts, operas and ballets are staged at the *Palais de Beaulieu (☎ 643 21 11, 10 Ave des Bergières)*. Lausanne has its own chamber orchestra, and a famous ballet troupe directed by Maurice Béjart, called the Rudra Béjart Ballet. Reservations for these and other performances can be made at the Ouchy tourist office. The theatre scene flourishes at several venues in town – the tourist office has events listings. Every year at the beginning of July is the Festival Cité, a week-long celebration of music, dance and theatre.

There are plenty of options for a lively night out. *D!* is a large disco at Rue d Grand Pont (entry free or around Sfr10 closed Wednesday). *Le Bleu Lézard (1(Rue Enning)* has inexpensive food on th ground floor, and a cellar bar with free liv music or DJs most nights. *Au Château (. Place du Tunnel)* is a bar and restaurant tha brews its own beer (open from 5 pm).

MAD (☎ 312 11 22, 23 Rue de Genève is an interesting venue with DJs, cinem and variety performances. There's a disc from 11 pm on Friday and Saturday (Sfr2C or Sfr25 after midnight), and the cellar ba has free entry Tuesday to Thursday. Its We! site is www.mad.ch.

The nearby *l'Atelier Volant (☎ 311 5 80, Rue Côtes-de-Montbenon 12)* has the atre and cabaret.

Getting There & Away

Train Lausanne is on the direct TGV rou! to/from Paris (Sfr78, four or five departure a day). Advance reservations are compul sory, and cost Sfr15. Vallorbe (where yo can also pick up the Paris-bound TGV) serviced by hourly regional trains.

There are three trains an hour to/fron Geneva (Sfr20; 40 to 50 minutes), and on or two an hour to Bern. To Interlaken cos! Sfr54 via Bern or Sfr58 via the scenic MO! route (see Montreux's Getting There Away section). Fast trains run hourly t Yverdon-les-Bains (Sfr12.60, 25 minutes

Car & Motorcycle There are motorway linking Lausanne to Geneva and Yverdc (N1), Martigny (N9/E62), and Bern (N then N12).

Car Rental Companies include: Avi (☎ 340 72 00), 50 Ave de la Gare; Herr (☎ 12 53 11), 17 Place du Tunnel; and E(ropcar (☎ 323 91 52), 2 Ave Ruchonnet.

Boat Boats depart from Ouchy. Contact th head office of CGN (☎ 614 04 44), 17 Ave c Rhodanie, for information. The summer sea son is from the end of May to late Septembe when there are many departures a day an boats take in all resorts around the lak ncluding the French side. Bicycles can be taken on board the larger boats, but there are no car ferries. Lausanne has direct crossings to Evian-les-Bains in France, with departures every hour during the day (Sfr14, 35 minutes). If you want to do a lot of boat cruising buy a day pass for Sfr50 (Sfr67 in 1st class). The boat fare to Montreux is Sfr19.

Winter Services At least nine ferries a day cross over to Evian-les-Bains. A boat goes around the coast of the Swiss Riviera (stopping at Vevey, Montreux and the Château de Chillon) all the way to St Gingolph on the French border, before turning around again. It departs daily in autumn and spring, and on Sunday only from November to March.

Getting Around

Buses and trolley buses service most destinations, but there are also metro lines from Ouchy up to the main station (every seven minutes or so to midnight) and an almost non-stop service (to 8 pm) between the station and the Flon area. Another metro line goes from Flon to the western suburbs. Short trips on city transport of up to three stops cost Sfr1.30. Unlimited journeys for one hour cost Sfr2.20 or Sfr1.30 for children. Travel passes for 24 hours cost Sfr6.50 (half-price for children).

Parking garages can get expensive; the largest is at Place de la Riponne. Street parking in blue zones (1½ hours maximum) and red zones (15 hours) is free, but you need to display a time indicator (see the Getting Around chapter).

AROUND LAUSANNE

The shoreline west of Lausanne is called La Côte. **Morges** is a wine-growing centre with its own castle, built in 1286 by Louis of Savoy. Inside is a military museum containing weapons, uniforms, and 8000 toy soldiers (Sfr7, students Sfr5, children free). It's open daily from February to mid-December. The town hosts a tulip festival from April to May. **Rolle** also has a castle built by the Savoy dynasty in the 13th century. Like the one at Morges, it is right by the lake, but you can't visit it.

The town of **Nyon** is of Roman origin. It has several museums and (surprise, surprise) a castle that was home to the dukes of Savoy. The tourist office (☎ 022-361 62 61, fax 361 53 96, ✆ tourism@nyon.ch) can tell you more. The quintuple-towered château was started in the 12th century and extensively modified in the 16th century. Its elevated perspective allows a fine view from the terrace, though the castle and its Historical Museum are closed for renovations till about 2004.

Nyon's **Paléo Festival** is a well-known international rock festival lasting about six days in late July. There's a great atmosphere in the massive (free) camp site that springs up by the five music stages. The event attracts more than 200,000 people each year; tickets cost about Sfr45 per day at the venue, or they're cheaper in advance. Get details from ☎ 022-361 0101 (www.paleo.ch).

Coppet is halfway between Nyon and Geneva. It too has a castle, which can be visited by guided tour between April and October (Sfr10, or Sfr8 for students and seniors; closed mornings except in July and August). The interior contains furniture in the Louis XVI and Directoire styles. It became the home of Madame de Staël after she was exiled from Paris by Napoleon. She soon presided over a court that was visited by some of the literary elite of the day – Edward Gibbon and Byron among them.

Getting There & Away

All the towns mentioned are on the rail route between Lausanne and Geneva, although only the local trains stop at Coppet and Rolle. All of them can be reached by boat on Lake Geneva steamers run by CGN (☎ 0848-811 848). Fares from Lausanne are: Morges Sfr11, Rolle Sfr18, and Nyon Sfr24.

Swiss Riviera

The Swiss Riviera rivals its French counterpart in its ability to attract rich and famous residents. The name describes the stretch of Lake Geneva roughly between Lausanne and Villeneuve. A mild climate allows sub-tropical flora to flourish along the lake promenade.

The main resorts of the Riviera, Vevey and Montreux, work closely together. Either tourist office can supply the leaflet *On the Trail of Hemingway*, a walking tour that picks out locations associated with famous past visitors. The museum pass (Passeport Musées) is excellent value (Sfr15, valid for two months), giving free entry to all museums mentioned below, including the Château de Chillon. There are several free **swimming spots** on the lake, with the best ones situated around Vevey. Sailing, water-skiing, windsurfing, rowing and boat rental are all available.

The Montreux-Vevey Holiday Card, given to overnight guests, provides excellent benefits, such as free swimming pool entry, water-skiing and mini golf, a free 24-hour pass for bus No 1, and various reductions (including Sfr5 off the museum pass).

VEVEY
☎ 021 • pop 15,400 • elevation 385m
Like neighbouring Montreux, Vevey exudes a swanky ambience. The town has welcomed numerous celebrities in the past. A famous recent resident was Charlie Chaplin, who spent 25 years here until his death in 1977, and is buried in the Corsier cemetery.

Orientation & Information
The hub of the town is Grande Place (with lots of parking spaces), 250m ahead and to the left from the train station. The tourist office (☎ 922 20 20, fax 922 20 24, ✉ tourism@vevey.ch) is on this large square in the La Grenette building. Opening times are 8.30 am to noon and 1.30 to 6 pm Monday to Friday and 8 am to noon Saturday. The main post office (1800 Vevey 1) is 100m to the right of the station.

Internet surfing costs Sfr13 per hour at Cyberworld, 4 Rue du Torrent (open daily from noon).

Things to See & Do
Vevey has a 15th century church, **St Martin's**, up the hill behind the station. The old

streets east of Grande Place and the lakeside promenades are worth exploring – a tourist office brochure details points of interest. Apart from that, the main entertainment comes from several museums, all of which are closed on Monday.

The **Swiss Museum of Games** (Musée Suisse du Jeu) is certainly the most fun. The games are arranged according to various themes – educational, strategic, simulation, skill and chance, and there are many that you can play (explanations are in French). Admission costs Sfr6 (seniors and students Sfr3, children free) and it's open 2 to 6 pm. The museum is in the Château de la Tour de Peilz (where there's also a tower and a beach). Take trolley bus No 1 and get off at Place du Temple.

The head office of the huge Nestlé food company is in Vevey. It is responsible for the **Food Museum** (Musée de l'Alimentation), Rue du Léman, open 10 am to noon and 2 to 5 pm (no lunch break in summer). It takes a didactic look at food and nutrition in historical, scientific and sociological terms. Ask for the English text. The interactive computer games are enjoyable. Entry costs Sfr6, or Sfr4 for students, senior citizens and children.

The **Jenisch Museum**, Ave de la Gare 2, exhibits Swiss art from the 19th and 20th centuries and has a special section on Oskar Kokoschka, the Viennese expressionist. Admission is Sfr10 (Sfr8 seniors, Sfr5 students) and it's closed mornings in winter. The **Swiss Camera Museum**, 6 Ruelle des Anciens Fossés, near Grande Place, concentrates on the instruments rather than the images they produce. Admission costs Sfr5 for adults, Sfr4 for students and seniors, and it's free for children (closed winter mornings). Other museums in Vevey cover wine-growing and the history of the town.

Vevey, the capital of the Lavaux wine-growing region, is where the growers congregate for a huge summer festival. Unfortunately it's once every 25 years, and the last was in 1999. There's a folklore market every Saturday morning from mid-July to the end of August.

Places to Stay

Camp by the lake at *La Pichette* (☎ *921 09 97*), west of the centre towards St Saphorin. The site is open from 1 April to 30 September.

Yoba Riviera Lodge (☎ *944 57 11, fax 944 57 13*, ✉ *rivieralodge@bluewin.ch, Place du Marché*) has a great central location. Beds are Sfr35 in double rooms or Sfr25 (Sfr20 without sheets) in dorms. Breakfast is Sfr7, or use the kitchen. Reception is open 8 am to noon and 4 to 8 pm (phone ahead for later arrivals).

Pension Famille Bürgle (☎ *921 40 23, 16 Rue Louis Meyer*) offers large rooms and hall showers in an ageing building. The price is Sfr40 per person and it's open year-round. It's often full in summer with long-term guests, so check for vacancies by telephone (reservations not accepted).

Just off Grande Place in the Old Town is *Des Négociants* (☎ *922 70 11, fax 921 34 24*, ✉ *hotelnegociants@vevey.ch, 27 Rue du Conseil*), providing rooms from Sfr95/130 with private facilities. *Hotel De Famille* (☎ *921 39 31, fax 921 43 47, 20 Rue des Communaux*) by the station to the left (east), has an indoor swimming pool, sauna, and free private parking. Renovated singles/doubles with shower/WC and TV start at Sfr120/200.

Places to Eat

The train station has an *Aperto* supermarket, open 6 am to 9.30 pm daily. Opposite the post office is the Saint Antoine Centre Commercial, containing a supermarket, *McDonald's*, and a *Manora* buffet restaurant, open until 6.30 pm weekdays (8 pm Thursday) and 5 pm on Saturday. It has the usual salad and dessert bars, and main meals for Sfr9 to Sfr17.

A *Migros* supermarket and restaurant has entrances on both Ave Paul Cérésole and Rue de Lausanne. Cheap self-service food is also available at the *EPA* department store at Place Ste Claire. Both are open the same hours as Manora.

Two new cafe-restaurants are *National* and *Vertigo*, opposite each other on Rue du Torrent. They're popular amongst youngish people for both eating and drinking, and prices are reasonable.

For traditional local fare, explore the centre of town east of Grande Place. *Le Mazot* (*7 Rue du Conseil*), is a typical rustic place, with home cooking from about Sfr20.

Café-Restaurant du Raisin (☎ *921 10 28, Grande Place*), has a cafe on the ground floor (open daily) where meals start at Sfr16. In its plush gourmet restaurant upstairs (closed Sunday and Monday), main dishes cost from Sfr35 and multi-course menus from Sfr55.

Getting There & Away

Two or more trains an hour travel around the lake: Vevey is 15 minutes from Lausanne (Sfr6.20) and five minutes from Montreux (Sfr3). Trolley bus No 1 runs from Vevey to Montreux (Sfr2.60) and Villeneuve (Sfr3.30).

By boat, the fare is Sfr8.80 to Lausanne or Sfr5 to Montreux. Boats depart from the Débarcadère by Grande Place (also see Getting There & Away for Lausanne).

AROUND VEVEY

A steam train chugs along the 3km track from Blonay to Chamby, where a train museum houses some steam engines and machinery. Entry and the return trip costs Sfr12 (children Sfr6), but it only operates from early May to late October, on Saturday afternoon and Sunday. Spots near Vevey for good views and/or walks are Les Pléiades (1397m; accessible by train), Chexbres (a stop on the summer 'wine train' that runs to Puidoux), and Mont Pèlerin (1080m; accessible by funicular, and with a panoramic tower, Plein Ciel). En route to Les Pléiades is Lally, where *Les Sapins* (☎ *943 13 95, fax 943 71 19*) is a good choice for accommodation (Sfr50 per person) and food.

MONTREUX

☎ 021 • pop 19,700 • elevation 385m

Centrepiece of the Swiss Riviera, Montreux offers marvellous lakeside walks and access to the ever-popular Château de Chillon (pronounced Sheeyoh). The town's reputation grew in the 19th century as many

LAKE GENEVA REGION

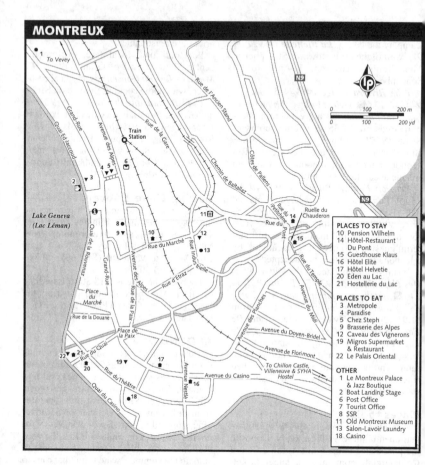

MONTREUX

To Vevey

Lake Geneva (Lac Léman)

Train Station

PLACES TO STAY
10 Pension Wilhelm
14 Hôtel-Restaurant Du Pont
15 Guesthouse Klaus
16 Hôtel Elite
17 Hôtel Helvetie
20 Eden au Lac
21 Hostellerie du Lac

PLACES TO EAT
3 Metropole
4 Paradise
5 Chez Steph
9 Brasserie des Alpes
12 Caveau des Vignerons
19 Migros Supermarket & Restaurant
22 Le Palais Oriental

OTHER
1 Le Montreux Palace & Jazz Boutique
2 Boat Landing Stage
6 Post Office
7 Tourist Office
8 SSR
11 Old Montreux Museum
13 Salon-Lavoir Laundry
18 Casino

artists, writers and musicians discovered the beauties of the area. Lord Byron, Peter Shelley and Mary Shelley (who wrote *Frankenstein* by the lake) were among the first of the literary influx – themselves following in the earlier footsteps of Jean Jacques Rousseau.

Montreux retains a strong musical tradition. It has hosted a major jazz festival annually since 1967 and a classical music festival since WWII. Montreux was also the site of a famous event in rock history. On 4 December 1971 the Casino Theatre in Montreux caught fire during a gig by Frank Zappa. The fire raged all night, casting a great pall of smoke over the placid waters of Lake Geneva. The burning building was watched by the band, Deep Purple, from across the lake, and inspired their classic track *Smoke on the Water*.

Orientation & Information

The train station (with bike rental, money-exchange counters, and luggage lockers) and the main post office (1820 Montreux 1) are on Ave des Alpes. The quickest way from here to the tourist office (☎ 962 84 84, fax 962 78 95, @ tourism@montreux.ch), in the Pavillon on the lake shore, is to take the lift down from round the back of Chez Steph (see Places to Eat). The office is open 9 am to noon and 1.30 to 6 pm Monday to Friday, and 9 am to noon Saturday. Hours are extended in summer, when the place is open daily. Staff make hotel bookings – ask well in advance if your visit coincides with one of the festivals.

The budget travel agency, SSR (☎ 961 23 00), is at 25 Ave des Alpes. The Salon-Lavoir self-service laundry, Rue Industrielle 30, costs only Sfr2.60 to wash and Sfr0.20 per 8½ minutes in the dryers. It's open 7 am to 6 pm Monday to Friday, to 5 pm Saturday.

Expensive (Sfr20 per hour) Internet access is at Le Montreux Palace, 100 Grand-Rue. It's open from noon (closed Monday).

Things to See & Do
Château de Chillon Chillon Castle (off the Montreux map) receives more visitors than any other historical building in Switzerland. Occupying a stunning position right on Lake Geneva, the fortress caught the public imagination when Lord Byron wrote about the fate of François de Bonivard, who was chained to the fifth pillar in the dungeons for four years in the 16th century. Byron is credited with scratching his own name on the third pillar, though it could equally well be the work of a more recent vandal.

Bonivard's crime was to preach about the Reformation, despite the vehement opposition of the Duke of Savoy who was then resident in the castle. Eschewing intellectual debate, the duke imprisoned Bonivard in his dungeon. Bonivard was only freed when Bernese troops, themselves followers of the Reformation, took over the region in 1536.

The castle dates from the 11th century, though it has undergone much modification and enlargement since then. Allow about two hours to view the tower, courtyards, dungeons and numerous rooms containing weapons, utensils, frescoes and furniture. Notice particularly the designs on the carved wooden chests and the ceiling in the **Great Hall**. Four models in the museum show how the castle has been altered over the years.

Entry costs Sfr7 for adults, Sfr5.50 for students and seniors, and Sfr3 for children. It is open 9 am to 7 pm daily from April to September, 9.30 am to 6 pm March to October, and 10 am to 5 pm during November to February. Last entry is one hour before closure. The castle is a pleasant 45-minute walk along the lakefront from Montreux (15 minutes from the youth hostel), or it's also accessible by local train (get off at Veytaux-Chillon) or trolley bus No 1 (Sfr2.60; get off at Veytaux).

In Montreux Old Town at 40 Rue de la Gare is a small museum, appropriately called the **Museum of Old Montreux** (Musée du Vieux Montreux). It recounts the history of the town and locality (Sfr6, students Sfr4) and opens daily from 1 April to 31 October.

Montreux's **casino** (☎ 962 83 83), on Rue du Théâtre, has gambling and a small cinema, plus several bars and nightclubs, including the Western Saloon where there's sometimes live country music.

Organised Tours
The MOB Railways counter in the tourist office books various excursions such as trips to Mont Blanc and Gruyères, and tours of local vineyards.

Special Events
Montreux's major festivals are in the summer. The best known is the **Montreux Jazz Festival**, lasting for two weeks in early July. The program is announced in late April, after which tickets are available from the ticket corner (☎ 0848-800 800) in branches of the UBS Bank throughout Switzerland, or from the Montreux Jazz Boutique (☎ 961 11 66), 100 Grand-Rue, which is near all the main venues. The festival reservations number is ☎ 963 82 82, or visit its Web site at www.montreuxjazz.com for info and tickets. There are many free concerts every day, but count on around Sfr40 to Sfr100 for one of the big evening gigs. The music is not only jazz; performers in 1999 included REM, Blondie, Alanis Morisette, BB King, James Taylor and Van Morrison.

The week-long **Golden Rose Television Festival** (Rose d'Or) is at the end of April, and hordes of the industry's professionals hit town.

The **Montreux-Vevey Music Festival** is an extravaganza of classical music lasting from late August to the end of September. Tickets for performances can cost anything from Sfr25 to Sfr140. Find out more from its Web site, www.montreux-festival.com, or Festival de Musique (☎ 966 80 25, fax 963 25 06), 5 Rue de Théâtre, Case postale 162, CH-1820, Montreux.

Places to Stay

Camping The nearest camping is at the presumptuously named *Les Horizons Bleus* (☎ 960 15 47) at Villeneuve. It's by the lake and the harbour, and is open from 1 April to 30 September. Take trolley bus No 1 from Montreux (Sfr2.60).

Hostel The SYHA *hostel* (☎ 963 49 34, fax 963 27 29, 8 Passage de l'Auberge, Territet), is a 30-minute walk along the lake clockwise from the tourist office (or take the local train or bus No 1). It's near the waterfront, under the train line, and open year-round. It has newish facilities, but the trains are noisy. Dorms are Sfr29 and doubles (bunk beds) are Sfr76. Check-in is from 4 pm (5 pm in winter), and it's closed in December and January.

Hotels & Pensions Most hotels drop their prices outside the summer season, and some close for a couple of months in winter.

Guesthouse Klaus (☎/fax 963 78 91, 1 Ruelle du Chauderon), offers a few bargain rooms in an elderly private house. Prices are Sfr30 to Sfr45 per person, without breakfast; call ahead. Nearby, next to a waterfall, is *Hôtel-Restaurant du Pont* (☎/fax 963 22 49, 12 Rue du Pont). Variable, homey singles/doubles cost Sfr60/120 with private shower/WC and TV. Reception usually closes at 3 pm on Monday.

Pension Wilhelm (☎ 963 14 31, fax 963 32 85, 13 Rue de Marché) charges Sfr55/100 for rooms without shower in an old-fashioned, family-run hotel. Doubles with own shower are Sfr110. *Hôtel Elite* (☎ 966 03 03, fax 966 03 10, @ hotel.elite@vtx.ch, 25 Ave du Casino) has renovated, new-looking rooms

with shower/WC and TV for around Sfr70/120.

Hostellerie du Lac (☎ 963 32 71, fax 963 18 35, 12 Rue du Quai), is the only affordable choice right by the lake. Rooms vary in style and facilities – some have lakeside balconies, all have TV and radio. Doubles start at Sfr85 with hall shower or Sfr130 with shower and WC. Subtract about Sfr15 for single occupancy (closed December and January).

Hôtel Helvetie (☎ 966 77 77, fax 966 77 00, @ helvetie@montreux.ch, 32 Ave du Casino), is a great place to stay. The large rooms, high ceilings and wide corridors give a wonderful feeling of space, as does the huge lobby area. There's also a rooftop terrace and chunky period radiators. All rooms have bath or shower, toilet, TV, mini-bar and telephone; prices start at Sfr130/180. There's also parking (Sfr12 for 24 hours) and a mid-price restaurant.

Eden au Lac (☎ 963 55 51, fax 636 18 13, @ edenmontreux@cdmgroup.ch, 11 Rue du Théâtre), occupies a fine site by the lake. The restaurant and lobby areas are very grand, which is partially reflected in the rooms; these start at Sfr160/200.

Places to Eat

The *Migros* supermarket at 49 Ave du Casino has a self-service restaurant, with late opening on Friday. *Chez Steph* (37 Ave des Alpes) is also self-service with meals for Sfr12 to Sfr20. The best thing about this place is the sunny terrace overlooking the lake. It's open 7 am to 10 pm daily (7 pm in winter), and gives a 10% discount to students.

Down the stairs (or lift) is another self-service place, *Paradise* (58 Grand-Rue), which is best for its extensive salad buffet (Sfr2.60 per 100 grams). It's open daily. Across the street is *Metropole*, with idyllic terrace and garden seating overlooking the lake. Meals, including pizzas, start about Sfr14 (open daily).

Brasserie des Alpes (23 Ave des Alpes) has a lunchtime menu du jour (Sfr15), and tasty pizza and pasta from Sfr14. It's a typical French cafe environment (closed Sunday).

Caveau des Vignerons (30 Rue Industrielle), in the old part of town, is the place

o go for fondue (from Sfr20). It also serves
illets of perch (Sfr25.50) and raclette, and
s closed for Saturday lunch and Sunday.

Le Palais Oriental (14 Quai du Casino),
s decked out in ceramic tiles and has a ter-
ace and a plush, Arabic interior. Iranian and
vegetarian food is around Sfr25 to Sfr40,
but the ambience and lakeside location make
up for the expense (closed Monday). Next
door, *Hostellerie du Lac* (see Places to Stay)
has a mid-price restaurant that is especially
good for fish specialities (open daily).

One of Switzerland's top gourmet restaurants is *Pont de Brent (☎ 964 52 30)*, north-
west of Montreux in the nearby village of
Brent, accessible by train. It has a terrace
and is closed on Sunday and Monday.

Getting There & Away
Hourly trains depart to/from Geneva and
take 70 minutes to cover the lakeside route
(Sfr29). From Lausanne, there are three
trains an hour (Sfr9.40) which take 19 to 35
minutes. Interlaken can be reached via a
scenic rail route serviced by MOB trains,
with changeovers at Zweisimmen and Spiez.
Railpasses are valid on the hourly service,
though there is a Sfr6 supplement for
'Panorama Express' trains only (about four
per day between Montreux and Zweisimmen). The track winds its way up the hill for
an excellent view over Lake Geneva. For
boat services, see Getting There & Away in
the Geneva and Lausanne sections.

AROUND MONTREUX
Rochers de Naye There is a magnificent
panorama of the lake and the Alps from this
viewing point at 2042m. Two restaurants at
the top allow you to enjoy the view in comfort, or you can stroll around a flattish, horseshoe-shaped ridge and visit the small Alpine
garden (Sfr2). It's a winding, scenic, 55-
minute train journey from Montreux. Trains
are run by MOB, the Half-Fare Card is valid,
and the Swiss Pass is free only up to Caux,
thereafter getting a discount of 25% (you pay
Sfr35.40). Inter-Rail gets 50% off for those
aged under 25 but Eurail is about as useful as
a clown costume at a funeral. Discounts
apply to the *full* return fare of Sfr61, which

actually is never charged. The normal return
deal from Montreux is Sfr50, and there are
sometimes further reductions, eg, the winter
return fare of Sfr32 includes a ski pass. Cars
can get as far as Caux, and the return fare
from there is Sfr40. The walk up from Montreux takes about 3½ hours.

North-West Vaud

This part of the canton of Vaud is dominated by the Jura mountain chain and Lac
de Neuchâtel.

YVERDON-LES-BAINS
☎ 024 • pop 24,000 • elevation 437m
Yverdon (**ee**-verdoh) has been a health
centre since Roman times. It's an enjoyable
lakeside resort and Vaud's second-largest
town after Lausanne. Yverdon is also a
venue for Expo.01 (see the boxed text in the
Facts for the Visitor chapter).

Orientation & Information
Yverdon is on the southern shore of Lake
Neuchâtel (Lac de Neuchâtel). The train
station exchanges money and rents bikes,
5.30 am (5.45 am Sunday) to 8.40 pm daily.
Next door is the post office (1400 Yverdon
1). The tourist office (☎ 423 62 90, fax 426
11 22, ❷ tourisme.info@yverdon-les-
bains.ch) is on Place Pestalozzi, at the start
of the pedestrian-only zone of the Old
Town. It is open 8.30 am to noon and 1.30
to 6 pm Monday to Friday (closes 5.30 pm
in winter; no lunch break in summer). It's
also open 9 am to noon on Saturday from
June to September.

Le Garage (☎ 426 04 95), Rue de la
Plaine 52, is a games arcade with one computer for Internet access.

Things to See & Do
The centre of town is clustered round the
13th century **castle**, built by Peter II of
Savoy. Inside is the **Musée du Château** containing local prehistoric artefacts, arms,
clothing, and a Ptolemaic Egyptian mummy.
The Guard's Tower is devoted to the cham-
pion of primary education, Heinrich

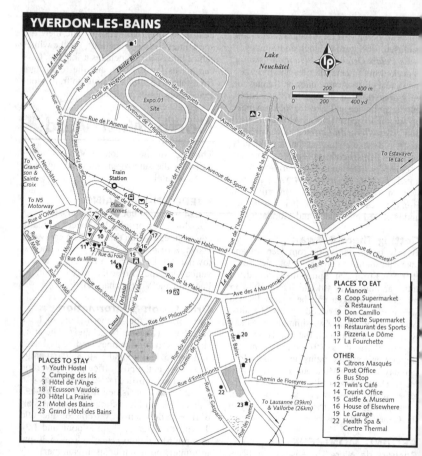

YVERDON-LES-BAINS

PLACES TO STAY
1   Youth Hostel
2   Camping des Iris
3   Hôtel de l'Ange
18 l'Ecusson Vaudois
20 Hôtel La Prairie
21 Motel des Bains
23 Grand Hôtel des Bains

PLACES TO EAT
7   Manora
8   Coop Supermarket
    & Restaurant
9   Don Camillo
10 Placette Supermarket
11 Restaurant des Sports
13 Pizzeria Le Dôme
17 La Fourchette

OTHER
4   Citrons Masqués
5   Post Office
6   Bus Stop
12 Twin's Café
14 Tourist Office
15 Castle & Museum
16 House of Elsewhere
19 Le Garage
22 Health Spa &
    Centre Thermal

Pestalozzi (1746-1827), whose educational institution was actually based in the castle for 20 years from 1805. It is open 10 am to noon Tuesday to Sunday from June to September and 2 to 5 pm year round. Admission costs Sfr6 (students/seniors Sfr5).

Opposite the castle at Place Pestalozzi 14 is the **Maison d'Ailleurs** (House of Elsewhere). This science fiction museum has temporary exhibitions, as well as permanent features: a mock-up of a spaceship, film stills, a room devoted to artist HR Giger (of *Alien* fame) and a library of books and magazines. It is open 2 to 6 pm Tuesday to

Sunday and entry costs Sfr6, or Sfr5 for students, children and senior citizens – ask about the combination ticket with the castle.

The lake offers the opportunity for various boat rides (see following under Getting There & Away) and the usual water sports, including windsurfing, water-skiing and sailing. There are 5km of sandy beaches by the town to stroll along.

Health Spa The water from the 14,000-year-old mineral springs starts off 500m below ground. By the time it hits the surface it has picked up all sorts of salubrious properties from the layers of rock, and is particularly good for sufferers of rheumatism and respiratory ailments. It has even spawned a bottled mineral water under the name of *Arkina* which is claimed to be effective in combating obesity.

The **Centre Thermal** (☎ 426 11 04, fax 423 02 32, @ info@thermes-yverdon.ch), the health complex to the east of the centre off Ave des Bains, offers a range of treatments. Even if you feel fine you can enjoy bathing in indoor and outdoor pools (temperature 28° to 34°C, entry Sfr13), take a sauna (Sfr30) or have a massage (Sfr55). It is open 8 am to 10 pm Monday to Friday, and 9 am to 8 pm weekends and holidays.

Places to Stay

Camping des Iris (☎ 425 10 89) is by the lake to the north-east of the station (well signposted). It is open from 1 April to late September and costs Sfr5.80 per person, Sfr5 per tent and Sfr2.50 for a car.

The SYHA **hostel** (☎ 425 12 33, fax 426 00 96, Rue du Parc 14) is a 12-minute walk from the station, near the lake. Dorms cost Sfr20.50, reception is closed from 9 am to 5 pm and the hostel is closed from 1 November to 31 March.

Yverdon has surprisingly few hotels. Less than 15 minutes' walk east of the Old Town is *Hôtel de l'Ange* (☎ 425 25 85, fax 426 31 20, Rue de Clendy 25), providing good-value rooms for Sfr65/100 with shower/WC and TV, or Sfr38/66 without. The restaurant is open daily. The only central place is *l'Ecusson Vaudois* (☎ 425 40 15, fax 425 44 85, Rue de la Plaine 29), with a ground floor cafe. Fresh, newly renovated rooms are Sfr63/100 using hall showers or Sfr82/120 with private shower/WC. It's within the restricted parking zone.

The top-quality hotels are on Ave des Bains, near the Centre Thermal, and all have a restaurant. *Motel des Bains* (☎ 426 92 81, fax 426 14 94) at No 21 starts at Sfr110/150, and *Hôtel La Prairie* (☎ 425 19 19, fax 425 00 79), No 9, at Sfr124/178. *Grand Hôtel des Bains* (☎ 425 70 21, fax 425 21 90), No 22, charges from Sfr175/230 (Sfr230/250 in high season) and

gives its guests free use of bicycles and free entry to the thermal pools.

Places to Eat

The Bel-Air shopping centre has a *Coop Restaurant* and a large supermarket. A *Placette Supermarket* is on Rue du Lac. *Manora (Rue de l'Ancienne Poste)*, the buffet-style restaurant chain, is open until 7 pm daily (8 pm Friday, 9 pm Sunday).

Don Camillo (Rue du Pré 10) has good pizzas (thin base, thick toppings) from Sfr13. Round the corner, *Pizzeria Le Dôme (Rue du Milieu 39)* has varied daily specials and a pavement terrace that catches the evening sun. Both places are closed Sunday.

La Fourchette (Rue du Casino 8) is a French restaurant with tasty meals for Sfr15 to Sfr35. It's also closed Sunday. The place for those with a discerning palate is *Restaurant des Sports (☎ 425 27 63, Rue du Milieu 47)* where main courses are around Sfr30, though it also has a simple ground floor cafe where meals start at Sfr14 (closed on Sunday evening and Monday).

Entertainment

There are several lively bars on Rue du Lac, and *Twin's Café (Rue du Milieu 43)* has free live music upstairs on Thursday night. *Citrons Masqués (☎ 426 56 98, Rue des Pecheurs 4)* is a three-storey venue with a bar/restaurant, exhibition room (free) and concert/DJ/events hall (entry around Sfr10).

Getting There & Away

Yverdon has direct trains to Lausanne (Sfr12.60, 25 minutes), Neuchâtel (Sfr11.80, 20 minutes) and Estavayer-le-Lac (Sfr6.20, 15 minutes). The train to Vallorbe (Sfr18) is awkward (via Cossonay) and takes two hours. By road is much easier as the N9 goes directly there. BGV buses depart infrequently (more often on school days) from in front of the train station (Sfr16.40, 40 minutes) and the Swiss Pass is valid.

Several times a day in summer (except Monday), boats sail to Neuchâtel (Sfr23, three hours). Stops en route include Grandson and Estavayer-le-Lac. You can even get as far as Solothurn by boat, by way of the Zihl canal to Lake Biel then on the Aare River. Call the boat company in Neuchâtel (☎ 032-725 40 12) for more information.

Getting Around

All local buses (Sfr1.50 per trip) leave from in front of the train station, bordering a large car park. There are parking meters on some streets (two-hour day-time maximum).

GRANDSON

The present **castle** at Grandson dates from the 13th century. Early in 1476 it was taken by Charles the Bold and his Burgundian troops, but they didn't hold it for long. On 2 March the same year the Swiss Confederates returned and easily defeated the Duke's forces. The vengeful Swiss strung up some of his men from the apple trees in the castle orchard. The rest scattered in disarray and left behind much artillery and treasure.

The castle has two museums. The **Historical Museum** tells the story of 1476 and other battles with dioramas and displays of weapons. The **Automobile Museum** has as its prize exhibit a white Rolls Royce formerly owned by Greta Garbo. It is open 9 am to 6 pm daily from April to October; hours shorten slightly in February/March; but wither to 1 to 5 pm Saturday and 9 am to 5 pm Sunday from November to January. Admission costs Sfr8 (senior citizens and students Sfr6). There is a tourist office in the castle (☎ 024-445 29 26).

Getting There & Away

Only the slow trains between Yverdon and Neuchâtel stop at Grandson (one every one to two hours). From Yverdon it costs Sfr2.40 and takes a few minutes. Bus departures from outside Yverdon station are more frequent. Better still, get there by enjoying the 5km stroll around the lake.

SAINTE CROIX

☎ 024 • pop 4500 • elevation 1066m

This town has been famous for its music boxes since the mid-19th century. The art of making these expensive items is well documented in the **CIMA Museum** (Centre International de la Méchanique d'Art), Rue de l'Industrie 2.

Music boxes contain a rotating spiked cylinder that bends and releases metal prongs, causing them to vibrate and hum melodiously. Some of the larger, more elaborate boxes also incorporate mini drums, bells, and accordions.

The best exhibits in the CIMA museum are the musical automata, such as the acrobats, a tiny Mozart, and Pierrot the writer. These and many other ingenious machines are activated by the guide on the 75-minute tour in French (English notes available). There are some good examples of early radios and phonographs, which the town started producing once music boxes became largely superseded by the new technology. Music boxes are still made, however, as the ground floor shop demonstrates.

The museum is open 1.30 to 6 pm Tuesday to Sunday, and entry costs Sfr9 for adults, Sfr8 for seniors, Sfr7 for students, Sfr6 for children and Sfr23 for families. The tourist office (☎ 454 27 02, fax 454 32 12) is in the same building. In nearby l'Auberson is the **Musée Baud**, Grand-Rue, displaying mainly older music boxes. It's open every afternoon from 1 July to 15 September (Sfr7, students Sfr6, children Sfr4), but only Saturday afternoon and Sunday for the rest of the year.

The highest point in the area is **Le Chasseron** (1607m). The summit provides a marvellous 360° panorama of the Alps, Lake Neuchâtel and the Jura. There is a car park which is a 45-minute walk from the top. Starting from Sainte Croix it takes less than two hours to walk to the summit.

Downhill skiing in the winter is centred on Le Chasseron and the adjoining summits. A one-day pass covering seven lifts costs Sfr27 (Sfr20 for children). The local ski school (☎ 454 10 61) can give group lessons (Sfr18 per person for two hours) or individual tuition. There are also 100km of cross-country trails.

Places to Stay & Eat

Sainte Croix has an SYHA *hostel* (☎ 454 17 10, fax 454 45 22, Rue Centrale 16), behind the Coop supermarket on Rue Nueve. It has a kitchen, charges Sfr25, and is closed from late October to just before Easter. The town only has a few hotels. The *Hôtel-Restaurant les Fleurettes* (☎ 454 22 94, fax 454 24 00, Chemin des Fleurettes), off Rue Nueve, has nicely furnished singles/doubles for Sfr45/90 with shower/WC, Sfr35/70 without. Check-in is from 4 pm, and the restaurant is reasonably priced and open daily.

Rue Nueve is the main shopping street and has several restaurants. *Buffet de la Gare*, by the station, is a plain place with cheap and simple food (closed Monday evening).

Getting There & Away
The only way to get there by train is on the hourly narrow-gauge line from Yverdon (Sfr9.40, 35 minutes). There is a fine view of the Alps and Lake Neuchâtel from the hill just outside Sainte Croix. Hourly postbuses run north from Sainte Croix to Buttes, which is connected by rail and bus to the northern Jura. A major road links Sainte Croix to Yverdon and Pontarlier in France.

VALLORBE
☎ 021 • pop 3200 • elevation 750m
This small industrial town has only recently developed its tourist attractions – the caves of the Orbe (since 1974), the Iron Museum (1980), Pré-Giroud Fort (1988), and the Railway Museum (1990). Unfortunately for Vallorbe, tourists have yet to arrive in droves.

Orientation & Information
Vallorbe is a couple of kilometres from the French border and English is not widely spoken. The train station (money-exchange counters, bike rental, Sfr2 lockers) is a seven-minute walk from the central street, Grand-Rue. A map outside shows the way. The tourist office (☎ 843 25 83, fax 843 22 62, ❷ contact@vallorbetourisme.ch) is just beyond Grand-Rue, in the Musée du Fer et du Chemin de Fer. It's open 9.30 am to noon and 1.30 to 6 pm daily from April to October, and open the same hours Monday to Friday from 1 November to 31 March. Ask about special sightseeing deals provided by the Passeport and the Clover Card.

Military Fort
An underground fort was constructed at Pré-Giroud in 1937 to guard the strategic Jourgne Pass and the route along the Vallée de Joux. Seemingly an unremarkable mountain chalet from the outside, below ground it can accommodate 130 men. There are dormitories, canteens, a kitchen, a telephone exchange, even an infirmary with an operating room. As it turned out, the fortress was never used in direct conflict and it was eventually allowed to fall into disuse.

The commune of Vallorbe purchased the fort from the federal authorities for the princely sum of one franc. Plastic dummies have now replaced flesh and blood personnel, but it still provides a fascinating hint of the myriad military installations that remain hidden away in the Swiss countryside. Despite the nominal purchase price it costs Sfr9 (Sfr8 students, Sfr5 children) to get in and join a 75-minute guided tour (notes in English). It is open noon to 5.30 pm on weekends and holidays from 1 May and 31 October (daily in July and August). Parking is available nearby. It takes over 60 minutes to walk there from Vallorbe or 40 minutes from Le Day train station, the next station in the direction of Lausanne. There is no bus service, though the driver on the Yverdon-Vallorbe bus can divert here if there's sufficient demand.

Caves
Less than 3km south-west of Vallorbe are stalactite and stalagmite caves, caused by the underground course of the Orbe River on its way to Lake Brenet. To get there, follow the signs for 'Source Grottos' (free parking outside). The one-hour guided tour of the caves costs Sfr12 (children Sfr6). In the entrance hall are displays of rare rocks and minerals. The caves are open from Palm Sunday to All Saint's Day (November 1st). It's shut Monday until the end of May, otherwise it's open 9.30 am to 4.30 pm daily (5.30 pm in summer).

A further 2km towards the Joux Valley is **Mont d'Orzeires**, where there is a reservation with grazing North American buffaloes (ie, bison) which has free entry. Some of these beasts graduate to the dinner plate in the reservation's restaurant (☎ 843 17 35) during spring and autumn.

Iron & Railway Museum

The Musée du Fer et du Chemin de Fer shows that iron has been important in Vallorbe since the 13th century. The main attraction is the traditional forge where a blacksmith can be seen diligently working away. Power for the furnace is derived from four large paddlewheels turning outside in the Orbe River. The railway section includes models, memorabilia, and a slide show. The museum is open the same hours as the tourist office, which doubles as the ticket office, and entry costs Sfr9 (Sfr8 students, Sfr5 children).

Activities

Mont d'Or (across the French border) and the Joux Valley provide opportunities for summer hiking and winter downhill and cross-country skiing. Sailing and windsurfing are just two of the water sports that are popular on Lake Joux. Contact the Vallorbe tourist office about local trout fishing.

Places to Stay

There's a TCS *camp site* (☎ 843 23 09), five minutes from the station by the Orbe River and alongside an open-air swimming pool. It is open during summer.

Auberge pour Tous (☎ 843 13 49, fax 843 13 89, ✉ auberge.pour.tous@ smile.ch, Rue du Simplon 11), is an independent hostel, seven minutes walk from both the train station and the tourist office. Dorms cost Sfr21.60 or Sfr23.60, singles/doubles are Sfr23/46, and there's an excellent apartment with shower/WC and TV for Sfr80. Reception is usually open all day and the hostel is open all year.

There is currently only one other local hotel, though the tourist office can supply a booklet of cheap private rooms. *Hôtel des Jurats* (☎ 843 19 91, Rue des Eterpaz), 1.5km east of the centre, has singles/doubles from Sfr56/102 with private shower/WC.

Places to Eat

There's more choice when eating out. Fish is a speciality of Vallorbe restaurants, especially local trout, or perch from the Joux Valley.

The main street, Grand-Rue, has three supermarkets and several places to eat. *Le Rio (Grand-Rue 27)*, has a smoky bar area with a restaurant beyond (closed Sunday). Lunch or dinner for Sfr14.90 includes starter or dessert. Opposite, at No 20, is *Le France* with good pizzas from Sfr12 and perch for Sfr21 (open daily).

Towards the train station is *Mont d'Or*, with decent prices and a friendly chef – there's pizza from Sfr11 and trout for Sfr17. It's closed Saturday night and Sunday.

Getting There & Away

The high-speed TGV service from Paris to Lausanne stops at Vallorbe. Border checks are on the train. One regional train an hour goes to Lausanne; it takes 45 minutes and costs Sfr15.40. By road, the quickest route is the eastwards N9 followed by the southwards N1, but it would be more fun to take the smaller roads across the Jura.

Trains also run along the western shore of Lake Joux and the Orbe River as far as Le Brassus. Roads go either side of the lake, with the quickest route along the eastern shore. A direct BGV bus goes north-east to Yverdon several times a day (Sfr15.80, 40 minutes).

Vaud Alps

Only the south-east corner of Vaud extends into the Alps, but it still boasts several interesting resorts and year-round skiing. A regional ski pass for the Vaud Alps (Alpes Vaudoises) costs Sfr49 for one day and Sfr263 for seven days, with reductions for children under age 16. You can also ski at Vaud resorts using the Gstaad Super Ski Region (see the Gstaad section in the Bernese Oberland chapter).

Hiking is a popular pastime in the summer, and all the resorts mentioned offer possibilities for circular hikes lasting from two to five hours. For further information, contact one of the tourist offices.

For holiday chalets, write to the local tourist office well in advance, listing requirements. Upon arrival, ask the tourist office about discounts that apply with the local Guest Card.

Aigle, a transport junction for Alpine resorts, has a wine museum in its 12th century château. It's open 1 April to 31 October (closed Monday except in July and August), and admission is Sfr7. Express trains on the Lausanne-Brig route stop at Aigle.

CHÂTEAU D'OEX
☎ 026 • pop 2900 • elevation 970m
This attractive family resort (shato-day) has quaint chalets and limited night life. There's an excellent blue (easy) ski run that goes all the way from Tête du Grin to Gerignoz, though there's also a good range of more difficult slopes. The ski school (☎ 924 68 48) charges Sfr22 for a half-day lesson. A one-day ski pass for the resort (50km of runs) costs Sfr33.

A speciality of Château d'Oex is **hot air ballooning**; for (expensive) passenger flights call ☎ 924 25 20. In late January the resort hosts the International Hot Air Ballooning Week, with daily special events or competitions. The group take-off is truly spectacular. **River-rafting** is another possibility. There's also a **museum** highlighting traditional crafts and dwellings of the local Enhaut district. It's closed Monday, Wednesday and for most of October (Sfr5). **Le Chalet** (☎ 924 66 77) is a touristy centre where there's cheese-making (daily except Monday), a model railway (Sfr2), a cheese and crafts shop, and a restaurant specialising in fondues.

The tourist office (☎ 924 25 35, fax 924 30 70, ✆ chateau-doex@bluewin.ch) is in the centre, below the hilltop clock tower.

Places to Stay & Eat
Accommodation prices are reasonable, even in high season. Camp year-round by the Sarine River at *Au Berceau* (☎ 924 62 34). The SYHA *hostel* (☎ 924 64 04, fax 924 58 43) is a 10-minute walk downhill

(signposted) from the train station. Beds cost Sfr24 and there's daytime access; it's closed from late October to late December.

Buffet de la Gare (☎ 924 77 17, fax 924 79 52), by the station, has singles/doubles for Sfr43/75 using hall showers. The restaurant is open daily and has reasonable meals from about Sfr15.

Near the cable car base station is *Beau Séjour* (☎ 924 74 23, fax 924 58 06), which charges from Sfr70/120 with shower or Sfr45/80 without. More expensive rooms have a TV and a view, and there's a restaurant round the back with a terrace.

A large *Coop* supermarket and restaurant is below the train station, with late opening on Friday. On the main street, near the tourist office, is *Le Relais*, serving decent pizza from Sfr12 (closed Tuesday evening and Wednesday).

Getting There & Away
The resort is on the scenic Montreux-Spiez rail route serviced by MOB trains. Departures are at least hourly and railpasses are valid. From Montreux it takes one hour and costs Sfr17.20 (plus Sfr6 reservation on Panoramic Express trains only). National roads run to Château d'Oex from Bulle, Aigle and Gstaad.

LEYSIN
☎ 024 • pop 2600 • elevation 1350 m
Leysin started life as a tuberculosis centre but it's now a well established skiing area with 60km of marked runs. A one-day local ski pass costs Sfr34. Many other sports are on offer, including the chance to try a Via Ferrata – a vertical 'footpath' negotiated via cables and rungs. Inquire at the Ecole Suisse d'Alpinisme Leysin (☎ 494 18 46, fax 494 33 75, ✆ eal@leysin.net), or the tourist office (☎ 494 22 44, fax 494 16 16, ✆ tourism@leysin.ch), based in the New Sporting Centre (open daily). Take in the scenery (views of the Rhône Valley and the Dents de Midi) from the revolving restaurant at the top of **Mt Berneuse** (2048m). The cable car costs Sfr13.50 one way, Sfr18 return, or the hike back to the village takes about 70 minutes.

LAKE GENEVA REGION

Places to Stay & Eat

There's year-round camping at *Semiramis* (☎ 494 39 39), at the lower end of the village.

The *Hiking Sheep Guesthouse* (☎/fax 494 35 35, ✉ hikingsheep@leysin.net) has justifiably received many enthusiastic traveller reports for its 'home away from home' ambience and friendly staff. It's two minutes walk from the Grand Hotel station. There's a kitchen and good communal facilities, and free guided hikes. Beds per person are Sfr26 in dorms or Sfr36 in doubles, without breakfast. Reception is closed from noon to 5 pm, and after 10 pm.

Les Orchidées (☎ 494 14 21, fax 494 18 10) is a family hotel by Vermont station, with Alp views and private parking. Singles/doubles cost from Sfr55/104 with shower.

The *New Sporting Centre* has a cheap restaurant, or visit *Le Leysin*, where cheese is made on the premises (menus around Sfr30). *L'Horizon* (closed Sunday evening and Monday) and *Prafandaz* (closed Tuesday) are both reasonably priced, and a scenic 20 minute walk above Leysin.

Getting There & Away

This spread-out resort is reached from Aigle by an hourly cog-wheel train (Sfr9.40 each way, 30 minutes) on which railpasses are valid. Leysin tourist office is a 10-minute walk down from the Vermont stop (free buses in winter). The road route (16km) is indirect: take highway 11 from Aigle (the road to Château d'Oex) then take a minor road at Le Sépey that doubles back to Leysin.

LES DIABLERETS

☎ 024 • elevation 1150m

This village is dominated by the mountain of the same name (3210m). The **glacier** at 3000m allows skiing virtually year-round, as well as offering fabulous views. There are two different cable cars running up to the glacier from the valley floor, and both are linked to the village by bus: starting from either Reusch or Col du Pillon you get to Cabane des Diablerets, where a further cable car whisks you almost to the summit at Scex Rouge. To ski from here all the way back down to Reusch is an exhilarating 2000m descent over 14km.

A one-day summer ski pass costs Sfr49, which although expensive, compares favourably to a simple return fare to the glacier of Sfr45. For winter skiing, use the regional pass or get the Diablerets-Villars pass costing Sfr42 for one day (reduced prices for students and families), which is not valid for the glacier. To explore the glacier by snow bus costs Sfr9. Les Diablerets hosts the **International Alpine Film Festival** at the end of September.

The tourist office (☎ 492 33 58, fax 492 23 48, ✉ diablerets@ bluewin.ch), to the right of the train station, can supply more information; it's open daily.

Places to Stay & Eat

There's year-round camping at *La Murée* (☎ 021-634 52 84) in the adjoining village of Vers l'Eglise.

Les Lilas (☎ 492 31 34, fax 492 31 57) just left of the station, has doubles for Sfr140 with shower/WC and TV, singles/doubles without for Sfr50/100, and a restaurant. To the rear is *Prairie* (☎ 492 33 41), a lovely rustic chalet with a few singles/doubles for only Sfr22/44; phone ahead.

Auberge de la Poste (☎ 492 31 24, fax 492 12 68, ✉ auberge_tfp@bluewin.ch), is also quaint, and charges Sfr44/88 using hall shower and without breakfast. The restaurant is reasonably priced (closed Sunday evening and Monday out of season).

La Potinière, by the tennis courts, has a two-course lunch menu for Sfr15.

Getting There & Away

By rail, Les Diablerets is also reached from Aigle: take the hourly train that goes via Le Sépey (Sfr10, 50 minutes). Alternatively, there's the postbus from Gstaad (Sfr11, 50 minutes) which departs every couple of hours. A good road runs from either direction.

VILLARS

☎ 024 • pop 1400 • elevation 1350 m

Villars shares the same local ski pass as Les Diablerets, yielding 96km of runs. It's a not-too-lively family resort, and the ski school (☎ 495 22 10) is particularly good for kids. This shares the same office as the tourist office (☎ 495 32 32, fax 495 27 94, *℮* information@villars.ch), near the post office and train station, which is open daily in season. The views across the Rhône Valley are inspiring, encompassing the Dents de Midi, Mont Blanc and the Trient Glacier. On the slopes, experts have few possibilities as most runs are geared towards beginners and intermediates. Ski lifts are not too crowded and the highest skiing is Chamossaire at 2113m.

Places to Stay & Eat

Hôtel St Louis (☎ 495 82 71) has beds (Sfr35) for groups and individuals in the west of the resort. The cheapest central accommodation is at *Hôtel Suisse* (☎ 495 24 25), with compact, wood-walled rooms for Sfr50 per person (doubles with own shower, singles using hall shower). It has a typical cafe-restaurant where meals start at Sfr13 (open daily). *Alpe Fleurie* (☎ 495 34 64, fax 496 30 77), by the post office, has rooms with shower/WC and TV for Sfr110/180. Next door, *Hôtel du Golf* (☎ 495 24 77, fax 495 39 78) pro-vides large, well-equipped rooms from Sfr195/260, and good hotel facilities. *La Chaumiere*, by the tourist office, is a tea room open to 6.30 pm daily except Thursday, serving pizzas (from Sfr11), crêpes (from Sfr5) and Swiss food.

The nearby town of Gryon offers further budget alternatives.

GRYON

This quiet, untouristed village at 1130m has several cheap places to stay – check with the tourist office (☎ 498 14 22, fax 498 26 22, *℮* gryon@swissonline.ch). The *Swiss Alp Retreat* (☎ 498 33 21, fax 498 35 31, *℮* chaletmartin@yahoo.com), based in the Chalet Martin, is five minutes' walk from Gryon train station (go past the post office and the Coop and look for the place on your left). The Swiss/Australian owners in this popular backpackers' place rent ski gear from only Sfr20 per day, organise excursions, and offer Internet access. Beds per person cost Sfr22/19 for the 1st/subsequent night in dorms, Sfr33/30 in doubles with private shower/WC, or Sfr28/25 in doubles without. There's a kitchen (no breakfast) and check-in is from 9 am to 9 pm. Telephone ahead. The train from Gryon to Villars is free with the ski pass.

Getting There & Away

From Bex to Villars, take the small, red hourly train (Sfr7.40 each way, 45 minutes; railpasses valid). Gryon is reached after 30 minutes. An hourly bus runs between Villars and Aigle (Sfr7.40, 30 minutes). The road from Villars to Les Diablerets is only open in the summer; there is a bus service that runs this route.

BEX

The town of Bex (pronounced Bay), on the Lausanne-Sion rail route, has the only operational salt mine in Switzerland, producing 150 tons of salt every year. It can be visited daily from 1 April to 15 October by guided tour (Sfr15), except during wet weather; call ☎ 024-463 24 62. The mines are north-east of town and are not easily accessible by public transport.

Valais

The dramatic Alpine scenery of Valais (Wallis in German) once made it one of the most inaccessible regions of Switzerland. The 10 highest mountains in the country – all of them over 4000m – are within this canton. Nowadays the mountains and valleys have been opened up by an efficient network of roads, railways and cable cars. It is an area of great natural beauty and, naturally enough, each impressive panorama has spawned its own resort.

The ski resorts in Valais are world-renowned. Zermatt is one of the oldest, and thrives on stupendous views of the Matterhorn. Verbier has a shorter history but is equally famous and gives access to a vast area of exciting and varied skiing. Less-known resorts such as Leukerbad offer perfectly satisfying skiing yet are much cheaper for ski-lift passes.

In all there are 47 listed ski centres. If that is not enough, just across the border in France is the magnificent Mont Blanc massif, famed for its skiing and scenery, and you can also ski in Italy from Zermatt.

In the summer, the mountains yield their treasures to hikers and mountaineers rather than skiers, but many resorts offer a whole host of additional sports, including angling, swimming, mountaineering, tennis and golf.

The extreme mountain terrain has meant that the Swiss have been forced to establish and maintain an incredibly extensive network of pipes and canals, to supply water for homes and irrigation in this remote canton. It has been estimated that this network, if laid end-to-end, could wrap completely around the equator, although the likelihood of anybody actually wanting to do this is very small. Some of these pipes feed the hydro-electric power installations, including the Grande Dixence Dam – a fantastic engineering feat and a good excursion from Sion. Much of the irrigation system is now very sophisticated, but in some parts the old *bisses* (*Suonen* in German dialect), narrow wooden aqueducts, are still in place.

Highlights

- View the highest mountains in Switzerland, including the Matterhorn.
- Holiday in scenic resorts with varied summer and winter sports.
- Experience traditional Alpine culture and unique cow fights.
- Visit the home of the traveller-rescuing St Bernard dogs.
- Sample the produce in the centre of Swiss wine production.

Valais

History

Sion's pre-eminence in Valaisan history started after the Bishop of Valais left Martigny in 580 in order to settle in Sion. After 999 the Bishop of Sion received the patronage of the Emperor Rudolph III of Burgundy; Sion became an Imperial city and the bishop was able to rule the territory of Valais from Martigny to the Furka Pass. A consistent thorn in the sides of successive bishops was the Dukes of Savoy, and in 1475 an army of Savoyards besieged the city. Sion was freed at the

VALAIS

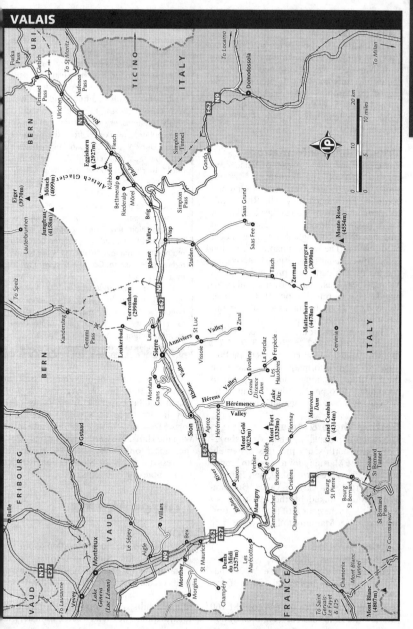

battle of the Planta with the help of the Swiss Confederation.

The invasion of the French in 1798 saw Valais become the Department of the Simplon. Napoleon was determined to control routes into Italy and he instigated the building of the Simplon Pass road which was opened in 1805. With the exit of Napoleon, Valais was able to join the Swiss Confederation in 1815.

Orientation & Information
The canton and tourist region of Valais covers an area of approximately 5220km, stretching from Lake Geneva to Ticino and bordering France and Italy. The Rhône Valley, particularly from Sion to Sierre, is known for its hot, dry climate. The French/German language divide cuts right through the middle of the canton. The western part of the canton is the Lower Valais (Bas Valais, Unterwallis) and the eastern part the Upper Valais (Haut Valais, Oberwallis), also known as Valais romand. The Germanisation of the Upper Valais dates from the migration of communities from the north in the 6th century.

The regional tourist office, Valais Tourisme (☎ 027-327 35 70, fax 327 35 71, @ info@valaistourism.ch) is at Rue de Pré-Fleuri 6, Sion. Information is available on the 1st floor; opening hours are 8 am to noon and 2 to 6 pm Monday to Friday. Its Web site is at www.valaistourism.ch.

Getting There & Away
The chains of mountains strung across the region make north-south progress extremely difficult. See Martigny for routes into France and Italy from western Valais, and Brig for transport routes in eastern Valais. Brig and Martigny are linked by the east-west N9 which follows the course of the Rhône, turning north from Martigny to Lake Geneva.

Getting Around
The Regionalpass Oberwallis is valid for seven days, and gives three free days on bus and train routes in Upper Valais, 50% off during other days, and 25% off cable cars. It is issued from June to October and costs Sfr160 (Sfr128 with Half-Fare Card; children Sfr80).

Valais Wine

Valais is Switzerland's main region for wine production, accounting for 37% of the total land area devoted to this industry. Two-thirds of the wine produced is white wine. Fendant is the name reserved exclusively for Valais white wine. It is dry and fruity, and goes well with cheese dishes, fish and Valais dried meats. Johannisberg is another well-known Valais white, and comes from the Sylvaner grape. Drink it to accompany fish, shellfish and asparagus. Like Fendant, it is ideal in fondue. Other whites you may come across are Muscat (good with fish) and Ermitage (good with cheese and poached fish). Amigne and Malvoise are dessert wines.

The principal red wine is Dôle, a product of the Pinot Noir and Gamay grapes. It is full-bodied and fruity, and is considered best with red meats, game and cheese; as is the robust red wine, Humagne. Goron is best with white meat and pork.

There are numerous vineyards and wine-growing villages bordering the Rhône between Martigny and Leuk. The regional or local tourist offices can give information about driving itineraries through this area.

There are summer-only bus passes for *Sion + Région* and *Martigny + Région*, which together cover all Lower Valais. Each is valid for three days within seven, and costs Sfr44, or Sfr35 for children and those with the Half-Fare Card. The Martigny Pass includes Mont Blanc Express/St Bernard Express trains and the Sion version includes some cable-car discounts.

Lower Valais

SION
☎ 027 • pop 26,200 • elevation 490m

From afar, Sion (Sitten in German) looks fantastic within its cusp of Valaisan peaks. It sits on the mostly flat ribbon of the Rhône Valley, yet rising from the town are two rounded hills, each topped by a medieval fortification. They lend a sense of history to

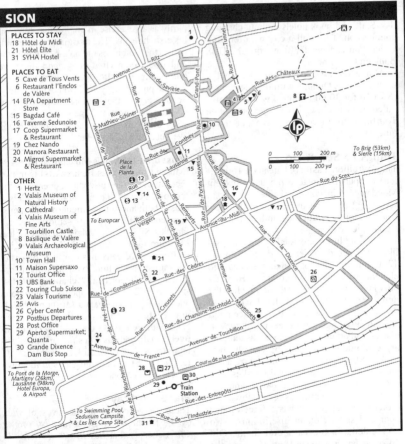

SION

PLACES TO STAY
18 Hôtel du Midi
21 Hôtel Élite
31 SYHA Hostel

PLACES TO EAT
5 Cave de Tous Vents
6 Restaurant l'Enclos
   de Valère
14 EPA Department
   Store
15 Bagdad Café
16 Taverne Sedunoise
17 Coop Supermarket
   & Restaurant
19 Chez Nando
20 Manora Restaurant
24 Migros Supermarket
   & Restaurant

OTHER
1 Hertz
2 Valais Museum of
  Natural History
3 Cathedral
4 Valais Museum of
  Fine Arts
7 Tourbillon Castle
8 Basilique de Valère
9 Valais Archaeological
  Museum
10 Town Hall
11 Maison Supersaxo
12 Tourist Office
13 UBS Bank
22 Touring Club Suisse
23 Valais Tourisme
25 Avis
26 Cyber Center
27 Postbus Departures
28 Post Office
29 Aperto Supermarket;
   Quanta
30 Grande Dixence
   Dam Bus Stop

To Brig (53km)
& Sierre (15km)

To Europcar

To Pont de la Morge,
Martigny (26km),
Lausanne (98km),
Hotel Europa,
& Airport

To Swimming Pool,
Sedunum Campsite
& Les Îles Camp Site

the town, which is accentuated by the cobbled streets and warren of side alleys in the centre. Thanks to its status as the cantonal capital, it is the location of several provincial museums.

The bishops of Sion, while enjoying the powers of temporal princes, had the habit of dispensing justice with an unecclesiastical ruthlessness and indulging in all sorts of worldly intrigues. The most famous Cardinal-Bishop was Mathieu Schiner who dispatched troops in the early 16th century to aid the papal throne. The political power of the bishops gradually waned

until it was removed completely under the 1848 constitution.

Orientation & Information

French-speaking Sion lies predominantly on the north bank of the Rhône River. The train station is conveniently central and has bike rental and money-exchange counters open daily. The post office (1950, Sion 1) is nearby. The tourist office (☎ 322 85 86, fax 322 18 82, ✉ info@siontourism.ch), Place de la Planta, is open 8.30 am to noon and 2 to 5.30 pm Monday to Friday, and 9 am to noon Saturday. In summer, hours are 8.30 am to 6 pm weekdays and 10 am to 4 pm Saturday. Staff will book hotels without charging commission. They sell a city map for Sfr3, which you can get for free from the UBS Bank on the corner.

Above the Aperto supermarket in the train station is Quanta, with Internet access (Sfr6/10 for 30/60 minutes) within a noisy video-games hall. Cyber Center on Ave de Tourbillon is more expensive but much quieter.

Things to See & Do

The **Tourbillon Castle** (Château de Tourbillon) is open 10 am to 6 pm daily (except Monday and in winter). Little remains to see except the exterior walls, but the view from the top is worth the climb and there's a good picnic area.

The other hill is crowned by the fortress-like **Basilique de Valère**. It dates from the 12th century and has faded frescoes and elaborately carved wooden stalls. Bursting out of the interior back wall, looking like the hull of a ship, is the oldest playable organ in the world, constructed in the 15th century. Next to the church is a museum dealing with history and ethnography, as well as temporary exhibitions. Entry to the church costs Sfr3, or Sfr6 including the museum (reduced rates for students, seniors and families).

On the way up to the castle and the church, spare five minutes for the town hall (hôtel de ville), which has a fine wooden door and some Roman inscriptions. Also take a look in the **cathedral** in the Old Town. It has a wooden triptych above the high altar and a Romanesque belfry dating from the 11th century.

Between Rue de Conthey and Rue de Lausanne is a tiny covered shopping arcade, and leading from this is the **Maison Supersaxo**, built in 1505 by Georges Supersaxo (1450–1529). The father of 23 children, he was a contemporary of the powerful bishop, Mathieu Schiner, a worldly cleric who courted European leaders to an unprecedented degree during his period in power. Between them they plotted the downfall of an earlier bishop, Josse de Silenen, and forced him into exile. But they later fell out, and

Supersaxo built this ostentatious dwelling partly as an exercise in one-upmanship over his erstwhile ally. The most impressive remnant is the Gothic rosette on the ceiling in the 2nd floor room (free entry, and there are notes in English). It's open 8 am to noon and 2 to 6 pm Monday to Friday. Ultimately, Schiner proved the dominant force, as he instigated the arrest of Supersaxo in Rome in 1512. Supersaxo was jailed for two years and eventually exiled to Vevey.

Museums The **Valais Museum of Fine Arts** (Musée Cantonal des Beaux-Arts) is in two sections of the old episcopal residences at the foot of the castle. It concentrates on Valaisan artists, both ancient and modern, and admission costs Sfr5 (students/seniors Sfr2.50, families Sfr10). The **Valais Archaeological Museum** (Musée Cantonal d'Archéologie), on Rue des Châteaux, has wordy displays but no English translations, which limits its appeal to the linguistically challenged (Sfr4, students Sfr2). Both are open 10 am to noon and 2 to 6 pm. The **Valais Museum of Natural History** (Musée Cantonal d'Histoire Naturelle), Ave de la Gare 42, is comparatively small, and has cases full of stuffed animals (open 2 to 6 pm; Sfr3, students Sfr1.50, families Sfr6). All the museums in the town are closed on Monday.

Places to Stay

There are two camp sites 4km west of Sion, by the Rhône River. *Sedunum* (☎ 346 42 68) is cheaper, but *Les Îles* (☎ 346 43 47) has more facilities and is open for most of winter. Take the Condémines postbus from the station.

The SYHA *hostel* (☎ 323 74 70, fax 323 74 38, Rue de l'Industrie 2) is behind the station (exit left and turn left under the tracks). It's in a modern building with a lift, TV room, kitchen (Sfr2 fee) and easy-going management. Beds in four-bed dorms are Sfr26.80 and double rooms are Sfr67.60. Reception is closed 10 am to 5 pm (9 am to 6 pm in winter) and the hostel is closed from late October to late January, except over Christmas/New Year. Get a key to avoid the curfew.

If you have your own transport it is easily viable to stay in Pont de la Morge, 2km west of Sion, where singles/doubles are Sfr40/80 at *Auberge des Collines* (☎ 346 20 80), or Sfr35/68 without breakfast at *Relais du Simplon* (☎ 346 20 30, fax 346 69 24). Both places are close to each other on the main road, Rue de Savoie. Postbuses to Aven and Ardon leaving from Sion station stop at the Pont de la Morge post office.

Sion itself has no truly budget hotels, but you get decent facilities for your money. Close parking can be difficult at *Hôtel du Midi* (☎ 323 13 31, fax 323 61 73, Place du Midi 29), which has a pricey restaurant and corridors painted an unsettling pink/orange colour. Singles/doubles start at Sfr50/90 with private shower and TV, or Sfr65/110 also with toilet.

Hôtel Élite (☎ 322 03 27, fax 322 23 61, Avenue du Midi 6) was extensively renovated in 1996. Singles/doubles with own shower/toilet and TV are Sfr70/120. There's a restaurant, a lift, and parking around the back.

The most central four-star place, *Europa* (☎ 322 24 23, fax 322 25 35, Rue de l'Envoi 19), is a little out of the way in the west of Sion. Rooms have all amenities and start at only Sfr100/170. It has a bar, sauna and restaurants on site, and there is good disabled access.

Places to Eat

There is a huge *Migros* shopping complex five minutes' walk from the station at Avenue de France. The self-service restaurant on the ground floor is closed Monday morning. An *EPA* department store with a restaurant is opposite the tourist office on Rue de Lausanne, and a *Coop*, also with a restaurant, is on Avenue du Midi. All three have meals for around Sfr10 and late opening till 7.30 pm on Friday. Attached to the Placette department store is a buffet-style *Manora Restaurant* (Avenue du Midi), open until 7 pm weekdays, 6 pm Saturday and 4 pm Sunday.

Pizzerias include *Chez Nando (Rue des Remparts)*. For more authentic eating, explore the small bistros and brasseries in the central pedestrian district. *Taverne*

Sedunoise (Rue de Rhône 25) is typical and inexpensive, with meals from Sfr14 (closed Saturday evening and Sunday). *Bagdad Café (Rue de Lausanne 3)* has attentive service and affordable daily specials (closed Sunday and Monday).

A good mid-price choice is *Restaurant l'Enclos de Valère* (☎ 323 32 30, Rue des Château 18), a small and quiet French restaurant with meat and fish dishes above Sfr30 and multi-course menus from Sfr69 (closed Sunday and Monday in winter, and all of January). Valais wines start at Sfr28 a bottle and the lunch plate is Sfr15. On a sunny day take to the outside tables in the attractive garden. Almost next door at No 16 is the *Cave de Tous Vents*, an atmospheric cellar offering fondue from Sfr38 for two. It's open nightly from 5 pm to midnight (closed July and August).

Getting There & Away

The airport (☎ 322 24 80) is 2km west of the train station; bus No 1 goes there (Sfr2.40), or you can take a taxi for around Sfr15. There are year-round flights to Zürich (50 minutes) and winter flights to London and Amsterdam.

Sion is a major postbus centre, with numerous routes leaving from outside the train station; for information, call ☎ 327 34 34 or ask in the train station. All trains on the express route between Lausanne (Sfr30, 70 minutes) and Brig (Sfr17, 40 minutes) stop at Sion. The N9 motorway passes through the south of Sion, with exits on both the western and eastern sides of the city. There's free parking by the swimming pool, five minutes' walk west of the youth hostel.

Europcar (☎ 323 86 86) is at Garage Delta, Rue de Lausanne 148. Hertz (☎ 322 37 42) is at Garage du Nord, Ave Ritz 33, and Avis (322 20 77) is at the garage at Ave de Tourbillon 23-25.

AROUND SION
Grande Dixence Dam

This dam is hugely impressive because of its sheer size. Almost six million cubic metres of concrete went into building it, and it's twice the volume and twice the height

268 Lower Valais – Martigny

(284m) of the Great Pyramid of Egypt. It retains 400 cubic metres of water and produces annually 1600kWh of hydroelectricity. To appreciate the beauty of the surroundings you need to gain some height, and footpaths and a cable car (from Le Chargeur to the lake, Sfr8 return) allow you to do this. It's at the end of the Hérémence Valley and is circled by high peaks. *Hôtel-Restaurant le Ritz* (☎ 027-281 13 22, fax 281 37 54), by the car park, is open in summer and offers cheap rooms and dorms.

Getting There & Away The road from Sion to the dam is closed in winter and spring. A private bus service runs between the two places two to five times a day from late June to mid-October. The journey takes an hour and costs Sfr27.20 return. Take the Theytaz bus from directly outside the train station in Sion (Swiss Pass valid).

Hérens Valley

This is the other valley south from Sion. It promotes itself as the 'true' Valais, where villagers in traditional costumes carry out their traditional lifestyle. Exactly how much of this is tourism-inspired tradition is difficult to gauge. What isn't open to doubt are the many hiking possibilities and the copious wildlife – look out for the black woodpecker, the largest in Europe, which has a red marking on its head. The main resorts are south of Evolène. Buses run from Sion several times a day year-round to La Forclaz (change in Les Haudères), and beyond to Ferpècle in summer only.

MARTIGNY

☎ 027 • pop 14,300 • elevation 476m
Martigny is the oldest town in Valais. It was seized by the Roman Empire in 15 BC, and in the reign of Emperor Claudius was given the snappy name of Forum Claudii Vallensium.

Orientation & Information

French-speaking Martigny is an important junction at the 'L' bend of the Rhône River. The hub of the town is Place Centrale, where you will find the tourist office (☎ 721 22 20,

fax 721 22 24, 📧 info@martignytourism.ch), open 9 am to noon and 1.30 to 6 pm Monday to Friday, and 9 am to noon Saturday. In summer it's also open 2 to 6 pm on Saturday, and in July and August from 10 am to noon and 4 to 6 pm on Sunday. The train station (with bike rental and money exchange) is 1km to the north-east of Place Centrale, and most of the Roman remains are to the south. The Cinema-Casino on Avenue de la Gare has an Internet cafe.

Things to See & Do

After visiting the tourist office, exit by the interior door leading directly to the stairway of the town hall. There's an impressive stained glass window over three floors (55 sq metres) created by Edmond Bille. Nearby is the 17th century church of **Our Lady of the Fields** (Notre Dame des Champs), with a rococo altar and a belfry combining Romanesque and Gothic elements. Also take a look at the chapel of **Our Lady of Compassion Church** (Notre Dame de Compassion), by the Dranse River, noted especially for its *ex-voto* paintings. Above the chapel is the 13th century **Bâtiaz Castle** (Château de la Bâtiaz), thrusting up from the hill. It is open July to October only, but you can climb up at any time for a good view of the valley. In this direction are two vineyards within a 50-minute walk (follow signs for Chemin du Vignoble).

Pick up the leaflet from the tourist office which shows a **walking tour** (*Promenade archéologique*) of the main Roman ruins. The **Roman Amphitheatre** can seat 6000 people and is the site for the annual Combats de Reines (see Special Events later in this chapter).

The main cultural attraction in the town is the **Fondation Pierre Gianadda**, on Rue du Forum. Not only does it have a Gallo-Roman Museum (the best exhibit is a bronze three-horned bull's head – a Gallic divinity), but it also has a busy program of classical music concerts, and an art exhibition periodically reviewing major artists. In the garden are more archaeological excavations, interestingly juxtaposed with modern

MARTIGNY

To St Maurice & Lausanne

To Geneva (136km) & Lausanne (71km) (by N9 Motorway)

Train Station

Place de Rome

Parc du Manoir

Place Centrale

Rue Hôtel-de-Ville

Martigny-Bourg Station

To City Garni

To Cha

0 150 300 m
0 150 300 yd

PLACES TO STAY
4 Hôtel Relais Grand Quai
14 TCS Camp Site
15 Hôtel du Stand
18 Auberge Poste
19 Hôtel du Forum; Le Gourmet Restaurant

8 Migr... & Restaurant
11 Lion d'Or
12 Café-Restaurant Les Touristes
13 Lord's Sandwich

OTHER
1 Bâtiaz Castle
2 Our Lady of Compassion Chapel
5 Cinema-Casino
6 Post Office
9 Tourist Office
10 Our Lady of the Fields Church
16 Fondation Pierre Gianadda
17 Roman Amphitheatre

art sculptures (by Miró, Moore, Arp, Segal etc) on the green lawns.

The **automobile museum**, within the Fondation, houses an impressive collection of historic cars, spanning the spectrum from a 1897 Benz (maximum speed 25kmh) to a 1929 Mercedes (maximum speed 200kmh). A few of the early Swiss cars (like the 1910 and 1911 Turicum) have a horn by the steering wheel, connected by a metal tube to a serpent's head on the front mudguard. When you blow the horn the serpent emits a goose-like honk – who said the Swiss haven't got a sense of humour!

The Fondation is open 9 am to 7 pm daily (10 am to 6 pm from late October to early May, and with a lunch break in winter). Entry costs Sfr12 for adults, Sfr9 for seniors, Sfr5 for children (to 10 years) and students, and Sfr25 for families. Ask for the English notes at the ticket desk.

Within 10km of Martigny are three picturesque gorges: Trient, Durnand, and Triège, all accessible by train.

Special Events

Martigny hosts the 10-day **Valais Regional Fair** (Foire du Valais) starting at the end of

Cow Fights

A peculiarity of Valais is the *Combats de Reines* (Kuhkämpfe in German), cow fights which are organised in villages to determine which beast is most suited to lead the herd up to the summer pastures. The cows that take part in these combats are from the Hérens breed, renowned for their fighting instincts. The cows charge, lock horns and then try to push each other back. The events have outgrown the traditional *raison d'être*. Breeding is big business; a winner, acclaimed to be the 'queen' of the herd, can be worth Sfr20,000, and much more in terms of prestige. Techniques such as genetic selection and embryo freezing are used to get the most effective contenders to the field of combat. Once selected, they are fed oats concentrate (believed to act as a stimulant), and sometimes even wine.

Contests take place on selected Sundays from late March to late May and from August to late September, and are usually accompanied by much celebration and consumption of Valaisan wine. The combatants rarely get hurt, and tourists concerned about animal welfare probably wouldn't find the spectacle distasteful (unlike with Spanish bullfighting). There is a grand final in Aproz in May on Ascension Day and the last meeting of the season is held at Martigny's Foire du Valais in early October. Aproz is only a 10-minute postbus ride from Sion.

September. The fair concludes with **Combats de Reines** contests (see the boxed text, 'Cow Fights'). Tickets to view the proceedings in the amphitheatre are around Sfr16 for seats and Sfr10 to stand.

In December, the **Bacon Fair** (Foire du Lard), takes place, an annual event dating back to the Middle Ages.

Places to Stay

The TCS *camp site* (☎ 722 45 44, Rue de Levant 68) is reasonably convenient for the centre. It's open year-round and reception is open 7 am to 10 pm daily. Charges are Sfr6.40 per adult and from Sfr7.50 for a tent. Beds in dorms cost Sfr20 without breakfast.

Basic rooms using hall shower cost Sfr45/80 at *Auberge Poste* (☎ 722 25 17, Ave du Grand St Bernard 81). Opposite at No 74 is the more plush *Hôtel du Forum* (☎ 722 18 41, fax 722 79 25) with rooms from Sfr95/130 with private shower/toilet and TV. *City Garni* (☎ 723 36 00, fax 723 36 01, Place St-Michel 7), another five minutes' walk south-west (not far from Martigny-Croix station), has singles/doubles with shower for Sfr50/100. More central is *Hôtel du Stand* (☎ 722 15 06, fax 722 15 06, Ave du Grand St Bernard 41), with maze-like corridors and modern rooms with shower/toilet for Sfr65/94.

A five-minute walk from the station by the tracks is *Hôtel Relais Grand Quai* (☎ 722 20 50, fax 723 21 66, Rue du Simplon 33) offering plenty of parking and decent-sized rooms with bathroom and TV for Sfr70/100 or less.

Places to Eat

There is a large *Migros* supermarket with groceries and general goods at Rue du Manoir. The restaurant has meals for around Sfr10 and a comprehensive salad buffet (late opening till 8 pm on Friday).

Hôtel Relais Grand Quai (see Places to Stay section earlier) has quite a smart restaurant but low prices. There's a lunch special for Sfr15 including soup and dessert, and snacks and meals for Sfr7 to Sfr30 (closed weekends).

Café-Restaurant Les Touristes (Place Plaisance) is not particularly touristy, despite its name, and is better than its fading exterior suggests. Good Italian and Swiss food starts at Sfr13 (closed Sunday and Monday). Slightly cheaper places for Italian food are *Au Grotto* (Rue du Rhône 3), which has pavement seating, and *Lion d'Or* (Ave du Grand St Bernard 1), which is closed Sunday and Monday. For sandwiches and other fast food, try *Lord's Sandwich* (Place Plaisance). There's also pleasant dining along the tree-lined pavement opposite the tourist office.

Restaurant Léman (Rue du Léman 19), has a garden and Swiss food from Sfr12; there's also a section with mid-price French cuisine (closed Monday evening and Sunday). The best restaurant in Martigny is *Le Gourmet* at the Hôtel du Forum (see Places to Stay section earlier). It offers seasonal specialities from Sfr50 and three different set menus (closed Sunday evening and Monday).

Getting There & Away
Martigny is on the main rail route running from Lausanne (Sfr23, one hour) to Brig (Sfr25, 55 minutès). Buses go from Martigny via Orsières and the Great St Bernard Tunnel to Aosta in Italy (Sfr30, at least two departures a day).

The following trains are private lines; the Swiss Pass and Eurail are valid, and Inter-Rail gets 50% off. The Mont-Blanc Express usually goes hourly to Chamonix in France (see the Mont Blanc section for more details). The fare is Sfr30 (Sfr49 day return) and the journey takes one to two hours; you usually have to change trains at the border. Martigny is also the departure point for the St Bernard Express, which goes to Le Châble (Sfr9.40; bus connection for Verbier) and Orsières.

AROUND MARTIGNY
Les Marécottes
To the west of Martigny, this small chalet village has a zoo exhibiting Alpine species in their natural habitat (Sfr7.50, open May to October). From Martigny, take the Chamonix train (Sfr7.40; see Mont Blanc section).

St Maurice
This small town is named after the Roman Christian who, along with many of his followers, was massacred in 302 for refusing to worship the gods of Rome. Points of interest are the 11th century abbey church, and the castle, which has a military museum (closed Monday). Trains from Martigny run every 30 minutes (Sfr5.60, 10 minutes).

Champéry
Running south-west from Monthey is the Illiez Valley, terminating in the ski resort of Champéry. It's a chalet-style village and shares the vast Portes du Soleil ski region with several other Swiss and French ski resorts. Runs near Champéry are predominantly intermediate although experts have plenty of opportunity for off-piste skiing. Prices in the village are reasonable. The resort is beneath the Dents du Midi, and an excellent view of this mountain range can be achieved from **Croix de Culet** (1963m), a viewpoint a short walk from the top of the Planachaux cable car. Another good, inexpensive, and relatively uncrowded resort for skiing the Portes du Soleil is nearby **Morgins**. The Champéry tourist office (☎ 024-479 20 20, fax 479 20 21, ◙ champery-ch@ portesdusoleil.com) can tell you more.

From Aigle (20 minutes along the track from Martigny to Lausanne), a train runs via Monthey every hour to Champéry (Sfr11.80, one hour).

Orsières
Winding its way south of Martigny is highway 21 (E27), leading to the Great St Bernard Pass and beyond into Italy. The town of Orsières is as far as you can get by rail. From here you can walk (1¼ hours), take the bus or drive to **Champex** and its attractive lake. A cable car ascends above the lake to **La Breya** (2374m). The view from here includes the Grand Combin (4314m) to the south-east. The cable car closes between seasons (Sfr8/12 one way/return).

Bourg St Pierre
South of Orsières is Bourg St Pierre, where Napoleon stayed during one of his incursions over the Alps. Beyond the town, the 9km Great (Grand) St Bernard tunnel, opened in 1964, allows year-round access to Italy. The old road over the **Great St Bernard Pass** is closed in winter and leads to an historic **Hospice**. The resident monks have been rescuing travellers stranded in the snows since the 11th century, aided in the task by the famous St Bernard dogs (nowadays Alsatians are used). It is estimated that over the years, more than 2000 people have been saved by the clerics and their canines.

The first mention of the St Bernard dogs was in 1708. A century later, one of the best-known of the breed, Barry I, toiled for 12 years in the snow drifts. After his death he was rewarded with a visit to the taxidermist, and now stands in the Natural History Museum in Bern.

A more recent Barry (one of a long line) is in the vestibule of the hospice. Some living specimens can be seen in the kennels. The hospice museum (Sfr6, children Sfr4) tells the history of the rescue work and has church relics and ornaments. It is open from June to October, which coincides with the period that the twice-daily bus runs from Martigny (Sfr16.20, one hour). Buses are more frequent from Orsières. Buses go as far as the hospice, or you can walk the famous path from Bourg St Pierre in under two hours.

The *hospice* (☎ 027-787 12 36) provides dorm beds (Sfr27) and rooms (Sfr34 per person); add Sfr16 for half-board.

MONT BLANC
☎ 33 (France), 04 (Chamonix)
• pop 97,000 • elevation 1037m

If there aren't enough mountains in Switzerland to sate your appetite for skiing and scenery, a trip to Mont Blanc makes an excellent and easily arranged excursion. At 4807m Mont Blanc is the highest mountain in the Alps, and with the valley floor some 3800m below the peak, the views are nothing short of spectacular. Unfortunately, by its sheer massiveness the mountain does tend to attract cloudy weather, so choose your day to visit carefully. The two easiest departure points from Switzerland are Geneva and Martigny.

Orientation & Information
Mont Blanc is on the border with France and Italy. On the French side is the resort of Chamonix, one of the oldest in the Alps, which still retains much of its Victorian architecture. The tourist office (☎ 50 53 00 24, fax 50 53 58 90, ✉ info@chamonix.com) at Place du Triangle de l'Amitié, opposite Place de l'Église, is open daily and has extensive information. In winter it sells a confusing variety of ski passes covering different areas.

The Office de Haute Montagne (☎ 50 53 22 08), 2nd floor, 109 Place de l'Église, also dispenses information for walkers, hikers and mountain climbers.

Across the Italian border is the resort of Courmayeur. For information contact the tourist office (☎ 0165-84 20 60, fax 84 20 72). Its Web site is at www.courmayeur.com. The two resorts are connected by the Mont Blanc Tunnel (see the following Getting There & Away section). The country telephone code for France is ☎ 33 and for Italy is ☎ 39.

Things to See & Do
Chamonix Chamonix has exciting if fragmented skiing. One day passes start from 134FF, though a general Cham' Ski pass costs 241FF. One day's ski/shoes rental will cost around 100FF. The **Vallée Blanche**, a 20km glacier hanging from the shoulder of Mont Blanc, is the most famous area and the world's longest ski run. You reach this via the Aiguille du Midi cable railway, and the trip up provides heart-pumping views (200FF return). There is also the **Mer de Glace Glacier** which can be reached by a cog-wheel railway or by foot from the village. **Le Brévent** peak on the west side of the valley furnishes more hiking opportunities, fine views of Mont Blanc and some fairly gentle skiing. Chamonix's mix of Victorian and more modern buildings makes the village an appealing place in which to stroll. For more information about Chamonix, refer to Lonely Planet's *France*.

Courmayeur The Italian side of the mountain offers a good range of intermediate runs and an excellent ski school. Most of the runs face Mont Blanc (Monte Bianco in Italian) so the views are great. It is also possible to ascend Mont Blanc itself (with a guide) and ski down the other side to Chamonix on the Mer de Glace Glacier, but seek advice before you consider this. The village is atmospheric and reasonably lively, with lots of old buildings to enjoy. For more information about Courmayeur, refer to Lonely Planet's *Italy*.

Circuit of Mont Blanc

It's one of the best known walks in the Alps but only a third of it is in Switzerland. This is an international walk, a three country excursion all the way around the highest mountain in Western Europe. The walk covers 215km, reaches a maximum altitude of more than 2500m and typically takes 10 to 14 days. The circuit passes through beautiful Alpine scenery and offers stunning views of the mountains along the Mont Blanc range, and undeniably its international nature adds to the pleasure.

The walk can start and finish in any of the three countries. In France the most convenient starting point is Les Houches, in the Chamonix Valley a few kilometres west of Chamonix itself. It's on a railway line and at 1800m it is also the lowest point on the whole circuit. In Italy the select Alpine resort of Courmayer, close to the southern end of the Mont Blanc tunnel, is the best place to start. In Switzerland there are a number of good places to commence, including the lakeside mountain resort of Champex and the Col de la Forclaz pass, conveniently reached by buses from the town of Martigny.

The circuit is a comfortable walk with *gîtes* (hostel-like bunkrooms) in many villages, mountain refuges in a number of the more remote locations and, for comfort loving walkers, a variety of hotels and guest houses. Unfortunately many places close down in the late autumn for a short break before the winter skiing season. The weather may be fine for walking but at those times you will need to carry camping equipment. There are no border formalities along the route; in fact it can be difficult to know you have crossed a border, but until the euro comes fully into use you will need a variety of currencies.

From the Col de la Forclaz starting point the route makes a steep climb to Col de la Balme, marking the border between Switzerland and France. Here the route enters the Chamonix Valley and follows the southern side of the valley, looking across the pricey French mountain resort of Chamonix to the pristine summit of Mont Blanc and its surrounding peaks. West of Chamonix the walk descends to the valley floor at Les Houches then immediately climbs up the other side to round the western end of the Mont Blanc massif and cross the Col de la Seigne into Italy. Passing through some of the most remote country on the route the walk descends along the Veny Valley to Courmayeur, then climbs up the Ferret Valley to the Grand Col Ferret where it re-enters Switzerland. In Switzerland, the walk passes through a series of delightful small villages along the Swiss portion of the Ferret Valley, before climbing to Champex and through the high Alpine pastures known as the Bovine back to the starting point.

Tony Wheeler

Getting There & Away

The narrow-gauge train line from Saint Gervais-Le Fayet (20km west of Chamonix) to Martigny (42km north of Chamonix) stops at 11 towns in the Chamonix Valley, including Chamonix itself. There are nine to 12 return trips a day. You usually have to change trains on the Swiss border at Châtelard. Le Fayet serves as a rail head for long-haul trains to destinations all over France, and this is the easiest route to Geneva, about two hours away.

Chamonix bus station is next to the train station. SAT Autocar (☎ 50 53 01 15) has buses to Annecy (95.30FF), Grenoble (157FF), Geneva (188FF, 1½ to two hours) and Turin (145FF, three hours).

The road from Chamonix to Martigny follows closely the route of the narrow-gauge railway for much of the distance. From Geneva, the E25 motorway runs all the way to Le Fayet, then an ordinary main road takes over for the last 17km to Chamonix.

There are normally two ways to get from Martigny to Courmayeur: either via Chamonix and through the Mont Blanc Tunnel, or via the E21a and the Great St Bernard Pass (closed in winter) to Aosta, and the E21b from there. This latter route can be duplicated by a combination of train and bus (the bus section over the pass only runs in summer). The Mont Blanc Tunnel was closed in 1999 following a devastating fire, and it won't re-open till at least 2001. The latest price for cars was 145/180FF one-way/return.

VERBIER
☎ 027 • pop 2100 • elevation 1500m
Verbier is a trendy, sophisticated resort that receives hordes of weekend visitors from Geneva, 170km away, yet its history as a tourist centre is extremely short. In 1945 Verbier had just 27 permanent residents, and the first proper ski lift opened as late as 1947. Nowadays it has one of the largest cable cars in Switzerland, Le Jumbo, which flies up Mont Fort holding 150 passengers.

Orientation & Information
Verbier is scenically situated on a south-west facing ledge above Le Châble, the terminus of the railway. The resort proper is up the hill from Verbier village. The hub of Verbier is Place Centrale, where you will find the tourist office (☎ 775 38 88, fax 775 38 80, @ verbiertourism@verbier.ch). It's open 8.30 or 9 am to noon daily and 2 to 6.30 pm weekdays or 4 to 6.30 pm Saturday. Hours lengthen in high season. Just off the square is the post office and postbus terminus. Verbier is mostly shut from late October to early December and in May, and that includes the cable cars. The resort has a free bus service in season. Families, children and senior citizens get substantial discounts on lift prices for skiing and hiking. Harold's Burger on Place Centrale has Internet access.

Skiing
The full ski pass gives access to one of the finest ski areas in the world, comprising 400km of runs and 100 ski lifts. It costs Sfr56 for one day, Sfr318 for a week and Sfr1148 for the season. Cheaper passes for specific areas are also available. Improved lifts mean that long queues are no longer part of the Verbier experience.

The skiing is exciting and varied, and there are many opportunities for experts to flaunt their off-piste skills, particularly at Attelas and Mont Fort. Experienced skiers can take on the Four Valleys circuit – 80km of black and red runs which can just about be completed in one day. Mont Fort at 3330m is high enough to allow summer skiing on its glacier (Sfr38 per day, from around early June to early August). The less demanding intermediate runs between Les Attelas and the village get pretty crowded, yet the Savoleyres area on the other side of the resort is less busy and just as good. Most of the resort runs are too difficult for beginners to handle though there are three ski and snowboarding schools (group lessons Sfr38).

Maison du Sport (☎ 775 33 63 @ info@verbier-sportcenter.ch), behind the post office, offers ski-mountaineering, heli-skiing and other interesting (and expensive) options. A five-day trek along the Haute Route to Zermatt reaches a maximum altitude of 3800m and costs Sfr900 per person.

Hiking
The tourist office gives out a map with brief descriptions (in French) and times of various hiking trails around the resort. From Les Ruinettes, it takes two hours to ascend to the ridge at Creblet, and down into the crater to the lake, Lac des Vaux. To get up to Mont Fort and enjoy the magnificent view (including Mont Blanc), non-skiers need to take a bus or walk from Les Ruinettes to the Jumbo cable car. Allow around an hour for the full ascent. Mont Gelé gives a better view of the valley below Verbier.

For non-skiers, day passes on the lift cost between Sfr19 and Sfr36 depending upon the area of validity.

Other Activities
Two popular sports are hang-gliding and paragliding. Solo flights or those with an instructor in tandem are possible. Either the Parapente school (☎ 771 68 18) or Ma (☎ 771 55 55), based in Hotel Rosa Blanche offer 30-minute tandem flights for Sfr150. Verbier hosts a paragliding competition

every August. There's an 18-hole **golf course** with fine views. Get information from the tourist office or the golf club (☎ 771 71 88).

Bruson

This pleasant, unspoilt village is on the other side of the valley, a 40-minute walk uphill from Le Châble, or take the bus from the train station (Sfr3). Bruson is included in the general ski pass and has steep, uncrowded skiing, but is worth visiting in its own right. It's full of picturesque wooden chalets, and many traditional storage barns are raised on stilts, with circular stones to keep the rats out.

Special Events

In late July the resort hosts the **Verbier Festival & Academy**, an important classical music and spoken word event (☎ 711 82 82). Check out the Web site at www.verbierfestival.com. Sports events include the **Xtreme Freeride Contest**, featuring daring snowboarders.

Places to Stay

The cheapest option in Verbier is a few private rooms – check with the tourist office. Holiday chalets are also reasonable (book well in advance). Otherwise, prices are high, even in low season.

For budget accommodation you must stay down in the valley at Le Châble. It has a winter *camp site* (☎ 776 20 51) for caravans only, and a few small, cheap hotels. The best deal is *La Ruinette* (☎/fax 776 13 52), along from the tourist office, charging Sfr45/90 for singles/doubles with shower and sometimes toilet and balcony. The inexpensive cafe/restaurant is closed Sunday. For other choices, ask at the tourist office (☎ 776 16 82, fax 776 15 41), just up from the station and next to the bank.

In Verbier, *Hôtel Rosa Blanche* (☎ 771 55, fax 771 70 55, Rue de la Barmettaz), not far from Place Centrale, is pre-booked in winter, but has the best prices in summer: singles/doubles for Sfr58/110 with shower/WC, Sfr45/90 without. *Mont-Gelé* (☎ 771 30 53, fax 771 13 16), by the base of the Les Ruinettes cable car, charges from

Sfr95/145. *Ermitage* (☎ 771 64 77, fax 771 52 64, Place Centrale), starts at Sfr125/180, and has TVs and parking.

Many places offer half-board as standard, like *De La Poste* (☎ 771 66 81, fax 771 34 01, Rue de Médran), which has its own indoor swimming pool and garden terrace. Per person prices range from Sfr89 (hall shower) to Sfr170 (own shower/WC and balcony). One of the top places to stay is *Rosalp* (☎ 771 63 23, fax 771 10 59, ☻ rosalp@ verbier.ch), a little farther along Rue de Médran, with large, well-equipped rooms starting at Sfr285/410 (Sfr195/270 in summer) for B&B.

Places to Eat

Cheap eating is also fairly problematic in Verbier, unless you're happy resorting to fast food from *Harold's*, a burger and pizza place on Place Centrale. There are some supermarkets – the *Denner (Rue de Verbier)* is convenient (and it's the cheapest for alcohol!). Just downhill is *Hacienda Café (Rue de Verbier)*, which offers pizzas from Sfr12, Mexican food and other dishes from Sfr17 and good lunch menus from Sfr14. It has happy hour from 5 to 6.30 pm, and live music on weekends in high season (open daily). Nearby, next to Migros, is *Traiteur Tandoori*, with Indian assiettes du jour, lunch and evening, from Sfr12 (open daily).

Fer a Cheval, near the Medran lift, has pizzas from Sfr14 and is one of the liveliest places for après-ski. *Channe Valaisanne*, off Place Centrale, has lunch/dinner from around Sfr15/25, including fondue. *Le Sonalon*, on the lower Savoleyres slopes, is similarly priced and has a fast-growing local reputation.

La Pinte in the Hotel Rosalp (see Places to Stay section earlier) offers stylish dishes for around Sfr25 to Sfr40 (open daily). The same hotel also has the *Restaurant Pierroz*, one of the top restaurants in Switzerland. Creative cuisine and seasonal specialities may tempt you to extend your mortgage; expect to pay around Sfr35 for a starter and Sfr45 to Sfr60 for a main course (closed between seasons).

Entertainment

Nightlife is lively, if pricey. *Pub Mont-Ford*, near the base of the Attelas cable car, is a busy and bawdy après-ski bar, particularly popular with English speakers. *Farinet (Place Centrale)* has free bands for après-ski. *Farm Club*, on Rue de Verbier and near Place Centrale, is a rather aloof and expensive nightclub, open from 11 pm (closed in summer). *Tara*, by the pharmacy off Place Centrale, attracts a younger set.

Getting There & Away

From mid-December to mid-April a direct bus goes from Martigny, taking 45 minutes (Sfr14.40); there are three a day on Saturday, and one on Friday evening.

Trains from Martigny run hourly year-round, take 30 minutes and terminate at Le Châble (Sfr9.40). Verbier bus departures are coordinated with train arrivals (Sfr5, 20 minutes). In season, a cable car also ascends from Le Châble (Sfr7/10 one way/return). The road from Martigny to Verbier (27km) is good and there are car parks at the entrance to the resort, at the ski lifts and near Place Centrale.

MAUVOISIN DAM

This dam at the end of the Bagnes Valley reaches a height of 237m and walls in a reservoir of 180 million cubic metres. Postbuses depart from Le Châble. Only a few continue as far as Fionnay and thereafter to Mauvoisin, and this section of the journey is completely closed down from early October to mid-June. From Les Ruinettes above Verbier you can walk along the valley to Fionnay in five hours.

SIERRE

☎ 027 • pop 15,000 • elevation 540m

Sierre (Siders in German) is one of the sunniest towns in Switzerland and lies on the French/German language divide, though French is favoured. The tourist office (☎ 455 85 35, fax 455 86 35, @ sierre-salgesch.ch) is in the train station and is open 8 am to 7 pm Monday to Friday and 8 am to noon Saturday. In high season hours are 8 am to 7 pm daily.

Things to See & Do

There are several châteaux and historic houses in and around the town. The tourist office's Promenade des Châteaux shows walking routes, though most buildings are private and can only be viewed from outside. Sierre is surrounded by vineyards and appropriately enough has a **wine museum** (Weinmuseum) in the Château de Villa (sometimes called Manor Villa), north-west of the centre at the end of Ave du Marché. It is open each afternoon except Monday from March to October, and only on Friday, Saturday and Sunday in the winter. Sfr5 gets entry to both parts of the museum – the other part is in the suburb of Salgesch (Salquenen in French).

Places to Stay & Eat

Ask the tourist office about 'third night free' accommodation deals. East of the centre is an area of protected woodland which contains several camp sites, including the TCS site, *Bois de Finges* (☎ 455 02 84), open from late April to early October. *La Poste* (☎ 455 10 03, fax 455 86 35), ahead and right of the train station, has old-fashioned rooms from Sfr65/110 with private shower and doubles without from Sfr80. There are cheaper places out of the centre, such as *Auberge des Collines* (☎ 455 12 48, fax 455 42 60) to the south, near the river and sport facilities (Sfr45/75 without shower). *Terminus* (☎ 455 11 40, fax 455 23 14), one block in front of the station, has three-star rooms with shower/WC and TV from Sfr95/140, and a restaurant with a terrace.

A *Migros* supermarket and restaurant is five minutes to the left of the station on Ave General Guisan, with late opening till 8 pm on Friday. A *Manora* buffet-style restaurant is in the Centre Commercial to the west of the centre, open shopping hours; take bus No 1 from the station.

Getting There & Away

Around two trains an hour stop at Sierre on the main Lausanne-Brig route. The town is the leaping off point for Crans Montana; take the red SMC bus from outside the station (Sfr10.80). There's a funicular that oes up to Montana, which may one day be xtended to reach the ski slopes.

ANNIVIERS VALLEY
☎ 027

his valley runs south from Sierre. The in-abitants are known for their nomadic abits, which are gradually dying out. Trad-tionally, they spend the winter in mountain illages then migrate in the summer to work n the vineyards around Sierre.

In the valley there is an enjoyable and cenic 6km **planetary walk** at 2200m to 500m, starting at Tignousa (above St Luc) nd ending at the Weisshorn Hotel (☎ 475 11 6). Along the way are models of the planets n the solar system on a scale of one to 100 illion. Information boards alongside give a ass of statistics. Near the start of the walk the François-Xavier Bagnoud Observa-ry, where telescopes can be used day and ight – inquire at the St Luc tourist office ☎ 475 14 12, fax 475 22 37, @ saint-luc@ sinfo.ch).

The funicular from St Luc to Tignousa fr8.50/12 one way/return) stops running etween seasons. From Weisshorn Hotel, alk back to Tignousa, or down to the val-y to pick up a bus. Around six buses a day epart from Sierre and go as far as Zinal, a ountaineering centre at the end of the alley; contact the Zinal tourist office ☎ 475 13 70) or check out its Web site at ww.zinal.ch.

RANS MONTANA
027 • pop 7000 • elevation 1500m

his French-speaking twin resort claims to e the sunniest ski area in the country. It's shionable and affluent and boasts the ost famous golf course in the Alps.

rientation & Information
rans to the west and Montana to the east to-ther create a large built-up sprawl amid lf a dozen lakes. Crans tourist office (☎ 485 00, fax 485 08 10, @ information@ ans-montana.ch) is on the main street, e Centrale, by the modern church. This ad joins to Route du Rawyl and thence to e de la Gare, Montana's main street.

Montana's tourist office (☎ 485 04 04) is on this road, backing on to the post office. Local buses are free within this urban area all year. Each tourist office covers both re-sorts, and they are open daily in high season and weekdays and Saturday morning in low season. Free hotel reservations can be made on ☎ 485 04 44.

Skiing
The skiing is good for all abilities, with the majority of runs being at intermediate level. The Plaine-Morte Glacier (3000m) allows reasonably testing skiing even in the sum-mer. In all, the skiing area offers 160km of slopes, 41 lifts and 50km of cross-country tracks. Ski passes cost Sfr47 (Sfr28 chil-dren) for one day, or Sfr56 (Sfr34) to in-clude the glacier.

Other Activities
As ever in the Alps, excellent views and **hiking** are encountered if you take the cable cars up into the mountains. In the summer there is **golf**, at nine-hole (Sfr40) or 18-hole (Sfr80) courses; contact the Golf Club (☎ 485 97 97). The resort hosts the Euro-pean Masters golf tournament in early September.

There's a strong following for **bridge** games and players meet every afternoon from 3 pm in the Aïda-Castel Hotel.

Places to Stay & Eat
The *camp site (☎ 481 28 51, fax 481 05 51)* by Lake Moubra, open from mid-June to 30 September, also has dorms for Sfr21 per person.

Pension Centrale (☎/fax 481 37 67, Rue Centrale), back from the street near Route du Rawyl, is the best budget deal. It has neat, compact singles/doubles for Sfr60/120 with a big bathroom and TV, or Sfr40/80 without. There's parking and a cafe/bar. *Du Télé-phérique (☎ 481 33 67)*, at the Cry d'Er cable car in Crans, charges Sfr130 for doubles with shower/WC and Sfr50 for singles without. The restaurant closes at 6 pm in summer. *Hôtel Régina (☎ 481 35 22, fax 480 18 65, @ hotelregina@swissonline.ch)*, on Ave de la Gare, has cheerful singles/doubles priced from Sfr82/138 with shower and toilet or Sfr62/118 without.

Supermarkets include the **Coop** in Montana centre, open daily. Eating can be a fairly expensive proposition, unless you stick to the many pizzerias. **Le Raccard** *(Route du Rawyl)* in Crans, has a range of affordable dishes, and good lunch menus including coffee. In Montana, **Olympic**, and the next door **Le Vieux Moulin** *(Allée Katherine Mansfield)*, are both OK for a variety of meals and menus, including pizzas, and have streetside tables. **Hotel Primavera** *(☎ 481 42 14, Ave de la Gare)* has several eating areas offering a range of meals from Sfr14 to Sfr20, in a casual to fairly formal environment. Rooms cost from Sfr93/170 in this three-star hotel.

Getting There & Away
From Sierre the bus takes around 35 minutes and departs hourly (Sfr10.80). There are two different roads winding up the vineyard-covered hillside to the resort, so you can make it a circular trip either by bus or car. There's also a funicular from Sierre (Swiss Pass valid), and a direct bus from Sion to Crans.

Upper Valais

LEUKERBAD
☎ 027 • pop 1700 • elevation 1411m
Leukerbad (Loèche-les-Bains in French) is the largest thermal centre in Europe. The Romans had a settlement here, and in the 19th century the town was a popular stopover for travellers negotiating the Gemmi Pass to/from the Bernese Oberland.

Orientation & Information
Leukerbad, 16km north of Leuk, is an attractive resort amid a semicircle of adjacent peaks. German is the main language. The tourist office (☎ 472 71 71, or ☎ 472 71 77 for commission-free hotel reservations, fax 472 71 51, ✉ info@leukerbad.ch) is in the centre. Opening hours are 9 am to noon and 1.30 to 6 pm Monday to Friday (5 pm Saturday); in high season it is also open 9 to

11.30 am Sunday. There's a hotel board wit free phone inside, and a useful Guest Car In the same complex is the town hall, po office, a parking garage and the bus static with daily money-exchange facilities. Ca must not be used in the centre at night.

Things to See & Do
There are 10 different places to take to th waters, but the biggest and the best is th Burgerbad (☎ 470 11 38), open daily. It ha many different pools, inside and outside, i cluding whirlpools and water massage jet The temperature ranges from 28° to 44°C Entry costs Sfr20 for adults, Sfr15 for st dents and Sfr10 for children. There are r ductions with the Guest Card and fo multiple entry tickets. The complex also ha a sauna and fitness studio which cost extr Another centre is Alpentherme (☎ 472 7 72), where a two-hour treatment in th Roman-Irish bath costs Sfr53 (reservatio required). The tourist office can give detai of training and regeneration programs ar medical treatments.

The main **skiing** area is the Torrenthor (2998m), yielding mostly runs of mediun difficulty, but there are a few easy ones ar a demanding run that descends 1400n One-day ski passes cost Sfr41 (studen Sfr34, children Sfr20), or Sfr54 (Sfr4 Sfr28) combined with entry to a spa. Acti ities in the Sportarena (☎ 470 10 37) i clude ice skating (Sfr10 for half a day curling and tennis.

A cable car ascends the sheer side of th northern ridge of mountains to the Gemr Pass (2350m). It's a good area for hikin The cable car costs Sfr20 return, or Sfr each way. It takes two hours to walk up. summer pass for the cable cars, baths ar other facilities costs Sfr35 (students Sfr2 children Sfr18) for one day.

In mid-July Leukerbad hosts a clow festival.

Places to Stay
Camping Sportarena (☎ 470 10 37) is ope from May to October. The site has a T room and a washing machine and it cos Sfr8.20 per adult, Sfr5 for a tent or car.

Dormitory accommodation costs Sfr38 er person (Sfr52 for half-board) at *Tourist-nlager Bergfreude (☎ 470 17 61, fax 470 0 36, Teretschenstrasse)*, not far from the iemmi cable car. *Weisses Rössli (☎ 470 33 7, fax 470 33 80)*, an attractive place off)orfplatz, has singles/doubles using hall howers for Sfr55/110 and large doubles vith own bath for Sfr130. A few doors own is the smaller, slightly cramped *'hamois (☎ 472 76 00, fax 472 76 11)*, with ooms for Sfr50/100 – most are singles. *Iotel Derby (☎ 472 24 72, fax 472 24 88, ,ichtenstrasse)*, on the road towards the iemmi cable car, has rustic-style rooms for fr75/150 with shower/WC and TV or fr60/120 without (cheaper in summer).

The four-star *Badehotel Regina 'herme (☎ 472 25 25, fax 472 25 26, 🖳 reginatherme@rhone.ch)*, on Kliben-trasse on the north side of the resort, has s own thermal pools. Rooms at half-oard start at Sfr130/260.

'laces to Eat

,eukerbad has few budget places to eat, ex-ept for *Primo (Kunibergstrasse)*, uphill rom Hotel Derby. It's a supermarket with a elf-service restaurant, and meals cost from fr8 (open shop hours).

Opposite the tourist office is *Heilquelle*, vith vegetarian meals between Sfr10 and fr20; it also has Valais dishes above Sfr15, nd a garden pizzeria section (open daily). cross the road is *Römerhof*, with live music n season and affordable set menus. Down the lleyway is a large *Migros* supermarket.

Walliser Kanne, across from Weisses lössli, serves cheese specialities from Sfr15, nd is usually closed Monday. It also has a izzeria and a Chinese restaurant. *Hotel)erby* (see Places to Stay section earlier) has good restaurant where main courses cost fr12 to Sfr38. The lunch menu for Sfr16 in-ludes a salad buffet.

ietting There & Away

,euk is on the main rail route from Lau-anne to Brig. An hourly blue postbus goes rom outside Leuk train station to Leuker-ad, usually at seven minutes past the hour;

last departure is 8.07 pm (Sfr10 each way, 30 minutes). The scenic road winds a bit but is in good condition.

BRIG
☎ 027 • pop 11,000 • elevation 688m

Brig is at the crossroads for various major transport routes, meaning an overnight stay may be necessary at some point. Stockalper Castle is well worth a visit.

Orientation & Information

Brig is the main town in the Upper Valais. The centre is south of the Rhône River and east of its tributary, the Saltina River. The train station has a money-exchange office (with credit card cash advances), open daily. The tourist office (☎ 921 60 30, fax 921 60 31, 🖳 info@brig-tourismus.ch) is on the 1st floor of the station, open 8.30 am to noon and 1.30 to 6 pm Monday to Friday, and 8.30 am to noon Saturday or (in sum-mer) 9 am to 4 pm. It makes free hotel reservations, or use the hotel board with free phone outside. Postbuses leave from outside the train station. Directly ahead is Bahnhofstrasse, leading to the core of the town. There's Internet access at the train station, though Datacomm on Rhonesand-strasse has lower rates.

Stockalper Castle

Made out of granite and volcanic rock, Stockalperschloss on Alte Simplonstrasse was formerly Switzerland's largest private residence, and is instantly recognisable by its three onion domes. The central courtyard is particularly attractive. There are hourly guided tours of the interior in summer, last-ing 50 minutes (in English if there's the de-mand). The museum section is interesting, provided you can get the guide to translate the German signs. It is open from 1 May to 31 October and the tour costs Sfr5, or Sfr2 for children.

The main fascination of the castle derives from the man who built it, Kaspar Jodok von Stockalper (1609–91), self-dubbed the Great Stockalper. He made a vast amount of money from salt and other products by con-trolling trade with Italy over the Simplon

Pass. Probably a greater fortune was made from dealing in mercenaries, especially to France. His success allowed him to mix with royalty and helped to build up the reputation and prosperity of Brig itself. He built most of the centre of the town and at one stage owned half of the Upper Valais. In those days a humble maid had to work 10 years to buy a single cow. With only part of his fortune Stockalper could have bought cows stretching from the Furka Pass (the eastern border of Valais) all the way to Geneva.

Small wonder the people of Brig found him and his ostentatious wealth unbearable, and he was overthrown. Much of his wealth was confiscated, and he was eventually forced to flee in fear across the border to Italy. It was six years before he was able to return, to die unmourned shortly afterwards.

Places to Stay

Restaurant Matza (☎ 923 15 95, Alte Simplonstrasse 18) has a few simple rooms using hall shower for Sfr35/70; add Sfr10 per person if you want breakfast (closed Sunday, unless pre-booked). *Café la Poste* (☎ 924 45 54, fax 924 45 53, Furkastrasse 23) has renovated rooms with private shower cubicle for Sfr50/100. To get there, turn right from the station and left on Furkastrasse.

Over the Saltina River from the Old Town is *Good Night Inn* (☎ 921 21 00, fax 921 21 99, @ GNI@brig-wallis.ch, Center Saltina), a large hotel with a restaurant and free parking. Modern singles/doubles with bathroom, telephone and TV are Sfr79/99. Nearby is *Hotel-Restaurant Central* (☎ 923 50 20, fax 923 50 61, Gliserallee 50) with old-style, almost grand rooms with the same facilities for about Sfr75/100 (negotiable in slack times). A little farther out, on the bus route to Visp, is *Gliserallee* (☎ 923 09 26, Gliserallee 130), a restaurant with a few singles/doubles for Sfr50/90 with shower or Sfr40/80 without.

Places to Eat

There is a *Migros* supermarket and self-service restaurant opposite and to the left of the station. The restaurant is open 7.30 am to 6.30 pm Monday to Friday and until 4 pm on Saturday, but the supermarket section is closed until 1.30 pm Monday.

Matza (see Places to Stay section earlier) has pizzas from Sfr12.50 and Valais dishes. The menu with starter costs Sfr14, or Sfr1 for students (closed Sunday). *Channe Molino Ristorante* (Furkastrasse 5), is little more expensive for Italian food, but this place has a pleasant rear garden patio (open daily).

Restaurant zum Eidgenossen (Schulhausstrasse 2), off Bahnhofstrasse, has Valais meat plates (air-dried cold meat cut into thin slices) for Sfr20 and Sfr21, fondue for Sfr18 and a daily special with soup for Sfr16. The ground floor is a small bar; the dining area upstairs specialises in steaks. *Hotel du Pont* (Marktplatz 1) has several eating areas, ranging from casual to fairly formal. Grills, fish and house specialities are upwards of Sfr23, though small meals start at Sfr12.

Getting There & Away

Hourly buses leave Brig for Saas Fee (Sfr17.40) and call at Visp en route.

Brig is an important junction for rail users. It is a stop on the Glacier Express line from Zermatt to St Moritz, and it connects the route to Locarno through Italy with the service to Interlaken via Spiez. BVZ trains to Zermatt depart hourly (Sfr63 return, valid for one month) from the track outside the main station entrance.

The Spiez-Locarno rail route is of interest to drivers as it includes vehicle-carrying trains. The Brig-Spiez section passes through the Lötschberg Tunnel and is particularly crucial as there is no corresponding road route. To transport a car or camper van through the tunnel section (Goppenstein to Kandersteg) costs Sfr2 (motorcycles Sfr16, bicycles Sfr8) including occupants. Trains run every 30 minutes from 6.10 am to 11.10 pm (plus a last train at midnight) and the journey takes 1 minutes.

There is a cycling track along the north bank of the Rhône, and bikes can be rented from Brig or Visp train station.

The Simplon Tunnel & Pass From Brig to Locarno via the 20km Simplon Tunnel takes 2½ hours and costs Sfr50. Take your passport as you change trains at Domodossola in Italy.

Vehicles can't use the tunnel; the only option is taking the Simplon Pass (open in winter) at 2005m. This road is steep, winding and time-consuming but does provide excellent views as it passes through the Gondo Gorge, and on one stretch the Aletsch Glacier is visible. It was Napoleon Bonaparte who was responsible for building the first proper road through here; it was the strategic importance of this pass that he had on his mind when he set 30,000 men to work upgrading the original track after the battle of Marengo (1800).

BRIGERBAD

Brigerbad is a paradise of open-air thermal swimming baths. Some pools are curative and others are ideal for just swimming and frolicking, particularly the one with underwater jet propulsion. There are five pools in the open air with a water temperature of 26° to 37°C. Entry costs Sfr10 (children Sfr6) for the whole day and it's open 9.30 am to 6 pm daily from late May to late September. There's also a unique grotto pool (Sfr8).

Campingplatz Brigerbad (☎ 946 46 88) is part of the thermal complex, so campers get reduced admission to the pools. It's open from mid-May to mid-October and costs Sfr7.40 per person plus Sfr10 per site. Facilities include a restaurant, shop and washing machines.

Getting There & Away

Postbuses go from both Brig (Sfr3.60; 6km, 20 minutes) and Visp (4km, 10 minutes) every 90 minutes.

VISP

☎ 027 • pop 6500 • elevation 650m
Visp stands at the entrance to the valley leading to Zermatt and Saas Fee, but has few tourist attractions in its own right.

Orientation & Information

The tourist office (☎ 948 33 33, fax 948 33 35, ✉ visp@rhone.ch) is eight minutes'

walk from the train station (which has money-exchange facilities daily), in the La Poste Kulturzentrum. To get there, walk down Bahnhofstrasse and turn left at Kaufplatz. It's open 9 am to 6.30 pm Monday to Friday and (in July and August) from 9 am to 4 pm Saturday. The postbus station and post office are ahead and to the right of the train station (400m).

Things to See & Do

The pedestrian-only old centre is fairly attractive with its cobbled streets and shuttered windows. You could also make for the cinema on Napoleonstrasse, or the swimming pool near the Mühleye camp site, open June to September. Alternatively, there's the 2½-hour hike up the hill to the wine-growing village of Visperterminen (the highest in Europe at 1336m); an hourly bus does the same trip in 25 minutes. The La Poste Kulturzentrum (☎ 948 33 11) stages several productions per week, including concerts (mostly classical), cabaret, opera and theatre.

Places to Stay & Eat

Mühleye (☎ 496 20 84) is one of several camp sites. It's west of the Vispa River, open May to October.

There's a cluster of mid-price hotels near the station, or some cheap choices that are less conveniently situated (ask the tourist office). A decent compromise is *Hotel Adler* (☎ 946 34 62, fax 946 49 86, Brückenweg), by the bus station. It's on the 6th floor of a tower block and has rooms from Sfr50/90 with private shower, toilet and TV. Add Sfr10 per person for breakfast. *Hotel Touring* (☎ 948 05 00, fax 948 05 05) has three stars and is right next to the station; singles/doubles with bathroom start from Sfr75/140.

By the bus station are *Migros* and *Coop* supermarkets, both with a restaurant, and *Restaurant-Bar Commerce* (Kantonsstrasse), with good pizzas from Sfr13.50 and a garden (closed Sunday). *Barock Café* (Bahnhofstrasse 4) is a popular youngish venue. It has Asian food from Sfr20, a lunch menu (Sfr15) and chubby angels on the wall (closed Sunday).

Getting There & Away

See the previous Brig section for more details. Frequent buses and trains traverse the 10km to/from Brig (Sfr3.60). Services to/from Zermatt and Saas Fee stop at Visp, but when leaving those resorts you may need to continue to Brig for the quickest onward connection. If you take the Zermatt train, parking is free in Visp at the 'park & ride' car park between the station and the post office.

ZERMATT

☎ 027 • pop 5340 • elevation 1605m

This skiing and mountaineering resort bathes in the reflected glory of one of the most famous peaks in the Alps, the Matterhorn. On Friday 13 July 1865, a party of seven led by Edward Whymper set out on the first successful ascent of this mountain. The climb up took 32 hours and was completed without problems. But on the way down, one of the team slipped and sent himself and three others crashing to their deaths in a 1200m fall down the North Wall. Only Whymper and two Swiss guides survived to tell the tale.

Mountaineers still flock here, and some never leave; their names end up inscribed in stone in the town cemetery. Skiers come here to enjoy virtually year-round skiing. The more sedentary come simply to enjoy the awe-inspiring views.

Zermatt doubled in size during the skiing boom of the 1960s and 1970s, but not without its problems along the way – in February 1963 it suffered a wave of typhoid infections and it was a month before the source of the problem was discovered in the water supply. Things have long since settled down. For the rich and stylish, Zermatt is a place to see and be seen. The water is perfectly safe, although the elite seem content instead to drink alcohol at 'peak' prices in the plusher clubs.

Orientation & Information

The massive Matterhorn stands sentinel at the head of the valley. Zermatt (1605m) is car-free except for electric taxis and buses, and street names are rarely used. The tourist office (☎ 967 01 81, fax 967 01 85, ✉ zermatt@wallis.ch), on the right of the train station, has detailed information in

English. It is open 8.30 am to noon and 1.30 to 6.00 pm Monday to Friday, and 8.30 am to noon Saturday. During the high season it is open 8.30 am to 6 pm weekdays, 8.30 am to 7 pm Saturday, and 9.30 am to noon and 4 to 7 pm Sunday. Inside and in the station are accommodation boards with a free telephone. Next door is Zermatt Tours, a travel agency which changes money without commission (daily in season, otherwise closed Sunday), though there are several banks.

The Alpin Center (☎ 966 24 60, fax 966 24 69, ✉ alpincenter@zermatt.ch) on Bahnhofstrasse contains the ski and snowboard school and the mountain guides office (*Bergführerbüro*). It is open 8.30 am to noon and 4 to 7 pm from 1 July to 30 September, and only 5 to 7 pm from late December to mid-May. For climbing the Matterhorn they recommend previous experience, one week's preparation, and the small matter of a Sfr670 guide fee, Sfr40 reservation fee and Sfr144 for accommodation. Also ask here about Haute Route ski-touring and heli-skiing or check out the Web site at www.zermatt.ch/alpincenter/e

The more expensive hotels often charge up to 40% less in low season, though many places close between seasons. Some souvenir shops in the resort are open daily. The post office (post code 3920) is on the main street. Internet access is at Pöstli Pub, or it's cheaper at Mountain Hostel (Sfr6/10 for 30/60 minutes).

Telephone ☎ 967 20 00 for emergency helicopter rescue, and ☎ 117 for avalanche information in winter.

Things to See & Do

There are excellent views from any of the cable cars and gondolas. The cog-wheel railway to **Gornergrat** (3100m) is a particular highlight. This mountain railway is the most popular in the country and every year around three million people take the trip. It takes 25 to 43 minutes and there are two to three departures an hour. The fare is Sfr38 to go up and Sfr63 return; Inter-Rail and the Half-Fare Card holders get 50% off and the Swiss Pass, 25% off, but a Eurailpass is as much use as a snorkel to a skier.

Along the way you're rewarded with magical views of the Matterhorn (sit on the right-hand side) and the surrounding peaks. The view from the midway station of Riffelalp to the north is a fine composition of swathes of trees (yellow and green in the autumn) and the mountains ringing the valley. From Gornergrat you get a different perspective of the Matterhorn (but not really superior to the view from parts of the village, in my opinion) and a marvellous panorama of the peaks around Monte Rosa. It takes around five hours to walk up from Zermatt to Gornergrat.

The village itself is well worth exploring. Glance inside the **Parish church**, where there are good altar pieces and an unusual ceiling mural. **Hinter Dorf**, off the main street, is the oldest part of the village. It's crammed with traditional, tumble-down wooden Valais homes, a world away from the flashy boutiques by the church that sell glass ornaments, figurines and expensive knick-knacks. Notice the stone discs on the stilts of the storage barns in Hinter Dorf; they're intended to keep out rodents.

A walk in the **cemetery** is a sobering experience for would-be mountaineers, as

ZERMATT

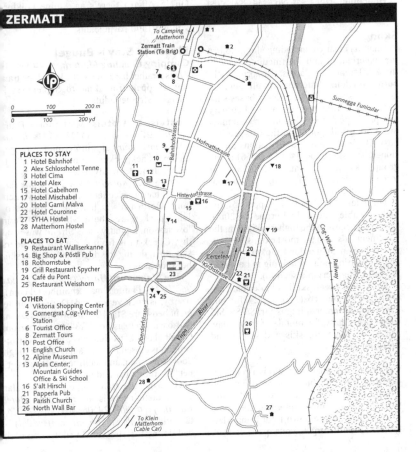

PLACES TO STAY
1 Hotel Bahnhof
2 Alex Schlosshotel Tenne
3 Hotel Cima
7 Hotel Alex
15 Hotel Gabelhorn
17 Hotel Mischabel
20 Hotel Garni Malva
22 Hotel Couronne
27 SYHA Hostel
28 Matterhorn Hostel

PLACES TO EAT
9 Restaurant Walliserkanne
14 Big Shop & Pöstli Pub
18 Rothornstube
19 Grill Restaurant Spycher
24 Café du Pont
25 Restaurant Weisshorn

OTHER
4 Viktoria Shopping Center
5 Gornergrat Cog-Wheel Station
6 Tourist Office
8 Zermatt Tours
10 Post Office
11 English Church
12 Alpine Museum
13 Alpin Center; Mountain Guides Office & Ski School
16 S'alt Hirschi
21 Papperla Pub
23 Parish Church
26 North Wall Bar

numerous monuments tell of deaths on Monte Rosa and the Matterhorn. The **Alpine Museum** has exhibits on mountain ascents, local fauna, the development of Zermatt and famous visitors. It's open 10 am to noon and 4 to 6 pm daily in summer and 4.30 to 6.30 pm Sunday to Friday in winter. Entry costs Sfr5 (children Sfr1). Around the back is the **English church**, where there are more mountaineering epitaphs. A pair from Cambridge University in England were lost in the mountains in August 1959. Their bodies were only found 30 years later.

Helicopter rides (☎ 967 34 87) cost Sfr170 per person for a 20-minute flight.

Skiing

Zermatt has many demanding slopes to test the experienced and intermediate skier in three different skiing areas; Rothorn, Stockhorn and Klein Matterhorn. In all there are 245km of ski runs, and free ski buses simplify transferring between areas. February to April is peak time, but in early summer the snow is still good and the lifts are less busy. Beginners have fewer options on the slopes. The ski school (☎ 966 24 66) offers group ski lessons at Sfr130/180 for three/five days, or Sfr45 for a two-hour snowboarding lesson.

The Klein Matterhorn is topped by the highest cable station in Europe (3820m), providing access to the highest skiing on the Continent. It's also the most extensive summer skiing in Switzerland (36km of runs), and the starting point for skiing in Italy (see the following Cervinia section).

A day pass for all ski lifts in Zermatt, excluding Cervinia, costs Sfr62/324 for one day/week. Summer skiing is Sfr58/258. Ski shops open daily for rental – for one day, prices are Sfr28 for skis and stocks and Sfr15 for boots.

Cervinia This Italian ski resort is a good day trip from Zermatt, but be sure to note the closing times of cable cars to avoid being stuck there overnight. Intermediate skiers can handle the route down from Klein Matterhorn (don't forget your passport). A

one-day pass to ski Klein Matterhorn and Cervinia costs Sfr62. Passes covering a Zermatt/Cervinia lifts cost Sfr196 for a minimum three days. Cervinia offers good, long runs for beginners and intermediates, and reasonable prices for food and drink. It's just a pity that visually the resort is a bit of an eyesore, with too many concrete-block constructions looking like building site leftovers. Non-skiers can't get down to Cervinia purely by cable car, and glacier crevasses make attempts to hike down hazardous.

Special Events

On 15 August there's an Alpine Folklore parade (the Folkloreumzug) and music involving 1400 participants.

Places to Stay – Budget

Camping *Camping Matterhorn* (☎ 967 39 21) is a rather bare site to the left of the train station, open from June to September. It charges Sfr9 per adult.

Hostels & Hotels Matterhorn Tours (☎ 966 27 37, fax 966 27 35, ✉ info@ matterhorn-tours.ch), in Zermatt, arranges cheap 'backpacker' rooms and apartments. Inquire in advance.

The SYHA *hostel* (☎ 967 23 20, fax 967 53 06) has an excellent view of the Matterhorn. Dorm beds at half-board (dinner or lunch packet) are a hefty Sfr46, or Sfr36 in low season. Laundry costs Sfr8 to wash and dry. Check-in is from 4 pm but the doors stay open during the day. The hostel is shut between seasons.

The *Matterhorn Hostel* (☎ 968 19 19, fax 968 10 15), ✉ info@matterhornhostel.com), nearby, is open year-round. Dorms (four to eight beds) are Sfr24/29 in low/high season, and basic doubles are Sfr34/36 per person. Optional breakfast/dinner is Sfr6/12. The reception is closed from 11 am to 4 pm though doors stay open, and facilities include Internet, TV room, bar and garden.

Opposite the train station and popular with mountaineers is the renovated *Hotel Bahnhof* (☎ 967 24 06, fax 967 72 16, ✉ hotel_bahnhof@hotmail.com) with 12-bed dorms for Sfr30 and a shower on each floor. Compact, wood-panelled singles/doubles are Sfr64/94 with shower or Sfr54/84 without. Prices are without breakfast but there's a kitchen. The hotel is closed from around mid-October to mid-December.

Hotel Gabelhorn (☎ 967 22 35) is a fine budget choice in the Hinter Dorf area of the village. It's a friendly little place (only 20 beds) with smallish but comfortable rooms for Sfr50/88, plus Sfr1 to use the hall showers in the morning. Doubles with shower are Sfr98.

Nearby, *Hotel Mischabel* (☎ 967 11 31, fax 967 65 07, ✉ mischabel.zermatt@reconline.ch) is a wooden chalet with balconies and a garden. There are singles with shower/WC for Sfr67, and singles/doubles/triples at Sfr57 per person using hall shower.

Places to Stay – Mid-Range
Hotel Garni Malva (☎ 966 39 39, fax 966 39 35) overlooking the east side of the river, has rustic-style rooms, all with a balcony. Singles/doubles are Sfr85/170 with bathroom and TV or Sfr75/150 without. *Hotel Cima* (☎ 967 23 37, fax 967 55 39) in front of the station and halfway to the river, is slightly smaller and has rooms from Sfr80/150 with shower and Sfr55/110 without.

Hotel Couronne (☎ 966 23 00, fax 966 23 02, ✉ couronne.zermatt@reconline.ch) has an excellent location overlooking the river. Renovated rooms with bathroom and TV cost from Sfr110/200. There's a 1st floor terrace and a sauna.

Places to Stay – Top End
Zermatt offers a wide choice of four-star hotels. *Alex Schlosshotel Tenne* (☎ 967 18 01, fax 967 18 03, ✉ tenne.zermatt@reconline.ch) near the train station, is architecturally interesting and combines art nouveau and rustic motifs. *Hotel Alex* (☎ 966 70 70, fax 966 70 90, ✉ hotel.alex.zermatt@spectraweb.ch), owned by the same family, is behind the tourist office. It also has creative touches in the decor department, and there's an indoor swimming pool, whirlpool and sauna (free for guests of both hotels), and many other facilities including a terrace

garden. The bar and disco (free entry) gets busy with people of all ages. Both hotels start at around Sfr200 per person with very appetising multi-course dinners included as standard.

Places to Eat
Get supplies from the *Coop* in the Viktoria Shopping Center opposite the train station. Close to the church is *Big Shop*, an eat-in or takeaway place, with simple food for under Sfr14 (open 7 am to 7 pm daily).

Beyond the church on the main street, the *Café du Pont* is a rustic place, exuding a red glow from the lampshades. Raclette snacks are Sfr7.50 and other meals start at Sfr12. The Valais dried meat plate is Sfr23. The next door *Restaurant Weisshorn* is similar, except that the choice is more varied; fondue is Sfr21 and Rösti is Sfr15. Also recommended is *Restaurant Walliserkanne*, by the post office, which has pizzas, fondue, meat dishes and Valais specialities for Sfr14 to Sfr27. Below ground level is *Il Ristorante*, open in the evening for mid-price Italian food in a suitably Romanesque setting. All four restaurants are open daily in season.

Grill Restaurant Spycher, on the east side of the river by the Hotel Aristella, has interesting and varied dishes from Sfr32 to Sfr50, and English menus. Flambés are a speciality. It's in a small chalet and has an extensive wine list (open daily in season from 6.30 pm). Another quality place is *Rothornstube* in the Perren Hotel on the east side of the river. It has main dishes from Sfr20 and menus where you can select the number of courses (two/three/four courses for Sfr25/32/38). It's open daily, but closed at lunchtime in winter.

Entertainment
North Wall Bar, near the SYHA hostel, is about the cheapest and best bar in the village, and popular with resort workers. It has ski videos, music, good pizzas from Sfr10 and beer at Sfr4.50 for half a litre. The bar is closed between seasons, otherwise it's open 6.30 pm to midnight daily.

Down the hill, the more expensive *Papperla Pub* is busier for après-ski, aided by live music daily, and has pizzas from Sfr12. *S'alt Hirschi*, in the old part of the village, is a good place for a beer (Sfr5 for 0.50L) in a less hectic environment. It has limited food in winter (open from 3 pm daily) but not in summer (open from 9 pm; closed Monday and Tuesday). There are many other bars and clubs where you drink, dance and unwind. Just follow your eyes and ears.

Getting There & Away
Train Hourly trains depart from Brig, calling at Visp en route. The steep and scenic journey takes 80 minutes and costs Sfr34 one-way, or Sfr63 return. It is a private railway; the Swiss Pass is valid, Inter-Rail earns 50% off for those under 26 but there is no discount for Eurailpass holders. The only way out is to backtrack, but if you're going to Saas Fee you can divert there from Stalden Saas.

Zermatt is the start of the famous Glacier Express to Graubünden, one of the most spectacular train rides in the world. It takes nearly eight hours to reach St Moritz, and costs Sfr138 in 2nd class and Sfr229 in 1st class. In summer, reservations are compulsory whether needed or not (Sfr9 fee, even if you have a railpass). This fee isn't payable on normal trains following the same route, and it doesn't apply on the Glacier Express if you're only going to/from Brig or Visp.

Car As Zermatt is car-free, you need to park cars at Täsch (Sfr4.50 to Sfr11 per day) and take the train from there (Sfr7.40). There is a road from Täsch, but it's private and tourists are never granted permits to use it. See the Visp section earlier in this chapter for another parking option.

SAAS FEE
☎ 027 • pop 1670 • elevation 1800m
The self-styled 'Pearl of the Alps' is in the valley adjoining its more famous neighbour, Zermatt. It may not have the Matterhorn, but there are plenty of other towering peaks to overwhelm the senses, and after a hard day's hiking or skiing there are various nightspots to help you unwind. But at night you have to rein yourself in even as you're letting yourself go. A slightly bizarre notice in the Hotel Walliserhof warns:

Please do not disturb the fairly-like (sic) charm of Saas Fee. Night's rest after 10 pm. Any disturbance of the night's rest is strictly prohibited in the entire village, including on public squares and streets. Our guardians are instructed to denounce marplots and to fine them with Sfr200.

Orientation & Information
Saas Fee is spread out in a long line. The village centre and ski lifts are to the left (south-west) of the bus station. The village extends at least as far to the right-hand side as well; in this direction there are a few hotels and many holiday chalets.

The tourist office (☎ 958 18 58, fax 958 18 60, ✉ to@saas-fee.ch) is opposite the bus station. Opening hours are 8.30 am to noon and 2 to 6.30 pm Monday to Friday, 8 am to 7 pm Saturday, and 9 am to noon and 3 to 6 pm Sunday. In low season, hours shorten but it's still open daily. The office makes hotel reservations (free if on the spot; Sfr10 commission if you phone in advance), or you can use the free phone outside. The tourist office's price list has a functional map. As in other ski resorts, many places shut between seasons. The local Guest Card earns various discounts.

The bus station houses a post office (post code 3906), and Sfr2 luggage lockers. Hotel Dom (☎ 957 23 00) has Internet access, but non-guests pay more (Sfr10/18 for 30/60 minutes).

Things to See & Do
Saas Fee is on a ledge above Saas Grund (1560m), and is surrounded by an impressive panorama of 13 peaks exceeding 4000m. **Skiing** is the primary activity and winter is the most important season. Electric taxis aren't numerous so you might want to stay near the ski lifts. About 100km of ski runs favour beginners and experts though intermediates also have sufficient choices. Snowboarding is also good, but off-piste skiing is hazardous due to the many glaciers. A general lift pass costs Sfr58 (Sfr35 children) for

one day and Sfr300 (Sfr180 children) for one week. Ski rental places are open daily (standard prices). The village has two natural ice rinks.

The tourist office has a map of summer **hiking** trails in the region which cover a total of 280km. Even in winter, 20km of marked footpaths remain open. The Saas Valley seven-day Wanderpass covers transport and other attractions and costs Sfr149/299 for individuals/families (summer only).

The highest underground funicular (metro) in the world operates all year to **Mittelallalin** at 3500m, ascending 500m in 2½ minutes. It gives access to the Feegletscher, a centre for summer skiing with 20km of runs above 2700m. Under the top station is the Ice Pavilion, 10m below the surface of the ice. It expounds on glacier-related topics, employing dummies, ice sculptures, and child-oriented displays. Entry costs Sfr7 (children Sfr3.50). Above ground there's a revolving restaurant or a cheaper self-service restaurant with a stationary terrace. Either way, the food is over-priced but the views are fabulous. From Saas Fee to Mittelallalin by cable car then funicular costs Sfr46 each way or Sfr58 return (children half-price).

Back down in the village there is the **Saaser Museum**, which tells the history of the resort and gives details about local folklore and building interiors (entry Sfr4). It's open weekday afternoons in winter and daily except Monday in summer. There's also a sports centre near the bus station with swimming, tennis, a gymnasium and a sauna. There's a mountaineering office (☎ 957 32 10) as well as a couple of ski/snowboarding schools. Ski-mountaineering is possible along the famous Haute Route all the way to Chamonix.

Places to Stay

Camping There are three year-round camp sites down in Saas Grund, a 10-minute bus ride away; the cheapest is *Bergheimat* (☎ 957 20 66).

Hotels The *Albana*, five minutes to the north-east of the tourist office, is an excellent deal. Two to five-bed rooms (singles must share, dorm-style) cost Sfr33 to Sfr48 per person, and each has a shower/WC and balcony as well as great breakfast buffets. Half-pension costs Sfr12 extra. It's advisable to book in advance in winter, and it's closed in off-season. Reception is in the *Hotel Mascotte* (☎ 957 27 24, fax 957 12 16) which has rooms for Sfr55 per person with private shower/WC. Also ask here about *Chalet Alba*, costing Sfr20 per person. All three places are side-by-side.

About 12 minutes north-east of the tourist office, on the ski bus route, is *Alp Hitta* (☎ 957 10 50). The apartments for one to seven people, each with a TV, telephone and small kitchen, are available all year. At Sfr39 per person (Sfr28 without breakfast) it's a bargain.

In the south of the village, convenient for the ski lifts, is *Garni Feehof* (☎ 957 23 08, fax 957 23 09), with good-value wood-walled singles/doubles for Sfr55/110 with shower or Sfr48/96 without. There's a sun terrace and TV room and several apartments with kitchens. It's open year-round and reception is in the front office; arrive or telephone before 6.30 pm.

Opposite is *Hotel Imseng* (☎ 958 12 58, fax 958 12 55), with dorms with triple-level bunks for Sfr20/25 in summer/winter. Add Sfr5 if you need sheets. Singles/doubles using hall shower are Sfr75/120 (Sfr50/100 in summer), and breakfast is Sfr15. Reception opens from 8.30 am to noon and 2 to 7 pm.

Close to the tourist office, try the friendly, family-run *Hotel Bergheimat* (☎ 957 20 30, fax 957 30 82, **@** info@ bergheimat.ch). Wood-panelled rooms with balcony start at Sfr69 per person with shower/WC or Sfr64 without. Reception closes at 6 pm in low season.

The chalet-style *Alpenblick* (☎ 957 16 45, fax 957 16 65), left of the bus station and next to the swimming pool, has hotel rooms or apartments with shower/WC and TV for about Sfr80 per person. This place overlooks a fantastic garden, with a huge rock covered in various implements and carved tree trunks.

Hotel Allalin (☎ 957 18 15, fax 957 31 15, **@** hotel.allalin@saas-fee.ch), five minutes north-east of the tourist office, is an affordable four-star place, with a free sauna and whirlpool. Half-board rooms are Sfr178/326, or Sfr151/272 in summer.

Walliserhof (☎ 958 19 00, fax 958 19 05, ✉ ferienart.walliserhof@saas-fee.ch) in the centre, has comfortable rooms finished in pine and floral fabric, with large balconies. As in many other hotels, rooms facing south are more expensive. Half-board starts at Sfr287/482 (Sfr210/352 in summer) for rooms with all the expected amenities, and dinners are gourmet standard.

Places to Eat

The cheapest eating is at the various Metzgerei (butcher shops) where you can get hot takeaways, such as *Dorf Metzg*, near the tourist office, which has roast chicken, chips and sausages. There are supermarkets on the main street.

Eat pizza from Sfr13 at *Boccalino* near the ski lifts. It's open daily and has a sun terrace. *Restaurant Vieux Chalet*, downhill near the tourist office, is good for cheese specialities, ranging from raclette snacks to many types of fondues (Sfr22 and up). It's a small cosy place, with extra seating upstairs (closed Monday). *Restaurant Alp Hitta* (see earlier Places to Stay section) has a rustic atmosphere, complete with background Alpine music. Raclette is Sfr6, fondue is Sfr20, and other Walliser meals start at Sfr14. It is open daily, except from mid-April to mid-June and mid-October to mid-December when it closes down.

Also rustic, with farm implements hanging from the walls, is *La Ferme*, on the main street near the tourist office (open daily). It has a satisfying two-course lunch menu for Sfr22, simple veggie meals from Sfr12.50 and other main courses for Sfr20 to Sfr40. On the same road towards the ski lifts is *Gletschergarten*, with a wide selection of meals ranging from Sfr15 to Sfr45, and a garden and terrace (open daily).

Fletschhorn (☎ 957 21 31) is one of the top 20 restaurants in Switzerland. It's in a quiet location beyond the northern part of the village, about a 10-minute walk from Alp Hitta (or get them to pick you up in their electric car). It's relatively affordable, though multi-course menus cost above Sfr130, and it closes between seasons.

Getting There & Away

Up until 1951, the only transportation available to Saas Fee from Saas Grund was by foot or mule-train. Things are a little easier now, although you still can't get there by train. Hourly buses depart from Brig via Visp, take one hour and cost Sfr17.40, or Sfr33 for a day return. You can transfer to/from Zermatt at Stalden Saas. Reserve two hours ahead for all buses leaving Saas Fee.

Like Zermatt, Saas Fee is car-free. Park at the entrance to the village, where the first 24 hours costs Sfr13. Get a Sfr4 per day reduction thereafter with the Guest Card by validating it at the tourist office.

ALETSCH GLACIER
☎ 027

This vast river of ice is an inspiring sight. It's the longest glacier in the Alps, stretching from the Jungfrau (4158m) in the Bernese Oberland to a plateau above the Rhône River. Its southern expanse is fringed by the Aletschwald, one of the highest pine forests in Europe (2000m).

Orientation & Information

There are two resorts on the southern rim, separated from the forest by a ridge of hills. The westernmost is Riederalp (1925m), which has a tourist office (☎ 928 60 50, fax 928 60 51, ✉ info@riederalp.ch). An easy walk to the east is the largest resort, Bettmeralp (1939m), also with a tourist office (☎ 928 60 60, fax 928 60 61, ✉ info@bettmeralp.ch). Further east is tiny Kühboden (2212m). All these places are car-free. Ask for the Guest Card (Gästekarte) giving useful discounts.

Things to See & Do

Summer hiking is excellent in the Aletsch forest along numerous marked trails. Either tourist office can give details of guided walks around and across the glacier. Riederalp also has an Alpine dairy and an Alpine museum. Kühboden gives access to the

Glaciers

With fears of global warming, glaciers are increasingly under scrutiny. Of the world's supply of fresh water, 80% is stored in ice and snow, and 97% of this is in Antarctica and Greenland. But glaciers are important in the rest of the world, too. Without glacier meltwater, many areas at the foot of high mountain ranges, such as Valais, would be desert or steppes. Within Switzerland, the most extensive and highest glacial regions are in Valais and the Bernese Alps. Most glaciers are receding, some at an alarming rate; unless global warming is reversed it is estimated that the Les Diablerets Glacier will disappear by 2025. Already, summer skiing is no longer possible in the Engadine Valley as the glacial slopes have shrunk so much.

There's much more to glaciers than lumps of ice. They start off as snow, which over the course of years gets compressed to firn (sometimes called névé). About 10m depth of fresh snow makes 1m depth of firn, which eventually evolves into ice. Surprisingly, it takes longer to become ice in 'cold' glaciers (ie, those below 0°C, such as the one at Titlis) than in 'temperate' glaciers (like the Obere Glacier in Grindelwald). Glaciers are filled with air bubbles, created during the transformation of snow to ice, and the gas content of these bubbles may be modified by water-flows in a temperate glacier.

The ice at the bottom of glaciers (in the ablation zone) may be centuries old, and makes it possible to measure past environmental pollution. The eruption of Krakatau in 1883 can be measured in glacial ice, and there are traces of the 1977 Sahara dust storms in Alpine glaciers. The peak of nuclear testing and fallout, 1963, is a benchmark year in dating glacial ice.

Ice avalanches from glaciers account for an average of nearly two deaths per year in Switzerland. The worst recent disaster was at Allalin on 30 August 1965, when 88 people died. Glaciers are always moving. You may think that the movement is so slow as to be insignificant, but owing to the movement of the Titlis Glacier, the masts of the ski lifts there have to be repositioned three to four times a year. In the course of the summer huge crevasses are opened up in the ice which have to be filled in before skiing starts again in the winter. But they can still be hazardous – never leave the marked trails when skiing on glaciers.

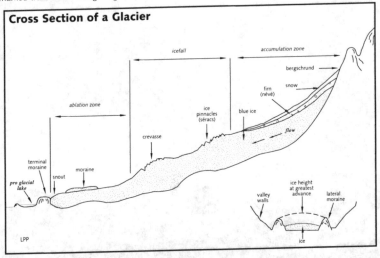

Cross Section of a Glacier

icefall

accumulation zone

bergschrund

ablation zone

firn (névé)

snow

ice pinnacles (séracs)

blue ice

flow

crevasse

terminal moraine

snout

moraine

pro glacial lake

ice height at greatest advance

valley walls

lateral moraine

ice

LPP

Eggishorn (2927m), providing possibly the best view of the glacier. In the Aletsch region there are 83km of ski runs and 32 lifts. The skiing is mostly intermediate or easy. There are several versions of ski passes costing between Sfr35 and Sfr52 per day.

Places to Stay & Eat

In Riederalp, the *Naturfreundehaus* (☎ 927 11 65) has dorms without breakfast for Sfr23 (there's a kitchen), and it closes between seasons. The *Hotel-Restaurant Bergdohl* (☎ 927 13 37, fax 927 40 61), by the Blausee chairlift, has wood-panelled rooms from Sfr55/110 with shower/WC, or Sfr45/90 without (for B&B). In winter, half-pension starts at Sfr105/210 or Sfr95/180.

In Bettmeralp, try *Garni Sporting* (☎ 927 22 52, fax 927 37 18) not far from the Bettmerhorn lift, with singles/doubles with shower/WC from Sfr55/110 (Sfr70/140 in winter), or the nearby and comfortable *Alpfrieden* (☎ 927 22 32, fax 927 10 11) starting at Sfr85/150 (Sfr125/230 in winter).

Both Riederalp and Bettmeralp have a supermarket. Also look for the bakeries *(Bäckerei)* and Metzgerei for cheap snacks. Eat pizzas in *Postillon* in Bettmeralp or a *Boccalino* in the Hotel Alpenrose in Riederalp. The Alpenrose also has *Walliser Kanne*, a more expensive restaurant with cheese specialities.

Getting There & Away

The base stations for these resorts are on the rail route between Brig and Andermatt. Cable-car departures are linked to train arrivals. Mörel up to Riederalp costs Sfr8 each way, the same as from Betten up to Bettmeralp. From Fiesch all the way up to Eggishorn via Kühboden costs Sfr30.80. Some versions of the ski pass include these cable cars.

Ticino

Situated south of the Alps and enjoying a Mediterranean climate, Ticino (Tessin in German) gives more than just a taste of Italy. Indeed, it once belonged to Italy. Como and Milan contested control for many years until the Dukes of Milan gained the ascendancy. Swiss encroachment on the area began in 1478 when the canton of Uri annexed the Valle Leventina (Leventina Valley), on the southern side of the St Gotthard Pass.

The Swiss Confederation gradually expanded southwards until by 1513 it had control of the whole area. Except for Bellinzona, which was under the authority of Uri, Schwyz and Unterwalden, Ticino became the joint property of the then member cantons. But the Confederation did little to develop its new acquisition and the region languished. Ticino remained politically tied (and subservient) to the Confederates until 1798 when France imposed its Helvetic Republic. Ticino then became a free canton, and despite the years as a subject territory, opted to officially join the Confederation in 1803, this time on equal terms.

Although Swiss order and efficiency pervades the canton's Mediterranean flavour, the native people are darker skinned than their compatriots in other regions, and the cuisine, architecture and vegetation reflect that found farther south. Italian is the official language in this Catholic canton. Many people also speak French and German but you will find English less widely spoken than in the rest of Switzerland. The region offers mountain hikes and dramatic mountain valleys in the north; water sports and relaxed, leisurely towns in the south.

Orientation & Information

Ticino is the fourth largest Swiss canton. Winters are mild but the best time to visit is spring to autumn, when the flowers bloom, the lakes come alive, and the piazzas become places to watch the world drift by. Average

HIGHLIGHTS

- Savour the taste of Italy, Swiss-style.
- Relax in a Mediterranean climate.
- Enjoy free summer music festivals.
- Visit museums and piazzas and experience stunning hill-top views in Locarno and Lugano.
- Take a boat tour on Lake Lugano.

Ticino

afternoon temperatures for Lugano are around 28°C in July and August, 17°C in April and September, and 7°C in December and January. Locarno gets more than 2300 hours of sunshine per year, with an average yearly temperature of 15.5°C.

Public holidays taken in Ticino, in addition to the normal Swiss national holidays, are:

Epiphany 6 January
St Joseph's Day 19 March
Labour Day 1 May
Corpus Christi variable date
Sts Peter and Paul Day 29 June
Assumption 15 August
All Saints' Day 1 November
Immaculate Conception 8 December

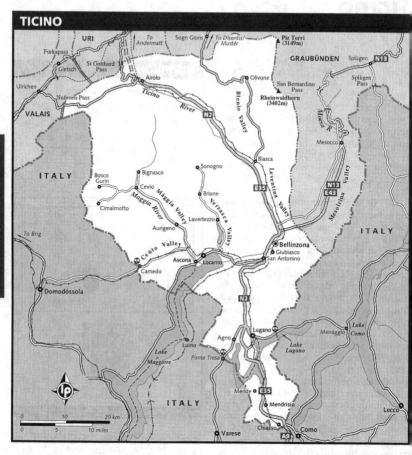

TICINO

The regional tourist office is Ente ticinese per il turismo (☎ 825 70 56, fax 825 36 14, 825 36 14, ✉ ett@ www.tourism-ticino.ch), Villa Turrita, Via Lugano 12, Casella postale 1441, CH-6501 Bellinzona. Opening hours are 8 am to noon and 2 to 6 pm Monday to Friday. The office can provide hotel, museum and restaurant information, as well as detailed brochures covering walking, cycling and architecture.

Local tourist offices sell a fishing permit that covers the whole canton: Sfr40 for two days or Sfr100 for 15. Fishing is allowed year-round on lakes Lugano and Maggiore, but only from April to September on other lakes and rivers.

The whole canton shares the same telephone code: ☎ 091.

Getting Around

The Lugano Region pass gives free travel on Lago di Lugano, and on regional public transport in and around Lugano (including the funiculars up Monte Brè and San Salvatore). It also gives 50% off a number of other routes, including transport on land and water around Locarno. The price is Sfr92 (Sfr82 with Swiss railpasses) for seven days,

Ticinese Cuisine

Pizza and pasta are everywhere throughout Switzerland, but there are various dishes that you rarely see outside Ticino or authentic Italian restaurants. *Risotto con funghi* is liquidy rice with saffron and mushrooms. It is often served with *osso bucco*, a circular slab of veal or (less expensively) pork, with the bone marrow in the centre. *Polenta* is an accompaniment to all sorts of dishes, particularly *brasato* (braised beef). It's made from maize and looks like yellow mashed potato. *Cazzöla* is a selection of meats with cabbage and potatoes. *Cicitt* are small sausages. *Mazza casalinga* is a selection of delicatessen cuts. Finish off with *zabaione*, an egg and Marsala dessert.

A *trattoria* is a simple, generally family-run *ristorante* (restaurant), and the term *locanda* denotes a trattoria with accommodation. *Birreria* is an establishment where the function of the food is mostly to provide respite from the main activity of beer drinking. *Osteria* is the wine-led equivalent.

For authentic eating in rural areas, search out a country inn, called a *grotto* or a *cavetto*. Wherever you eat, consider washing down your meal with a Ticinese Merlot. Around 88% of local wine produced is Merlot, a red characterised by its full-bodied taste. 'VITI' on the label is a seal of very high quality.

or Sfr70 (Sfr62) for three free days and reductions on the other four. It is available in 2nd-class only and is issued from around Easter to October. Reduced prices for children are available, but get a Family Card instead (see the Getting Around chapter).

In the past there used to be an equivalent pass for the Locarno/Ascona Region; ask locally if it has been resurrected. In the meantime there's the Ticino Card, giving reductions or free travel on a few bus and cable car routes around Locarno and the Valle Mággia. It is valid for three days between mid-June and mid-October, and costs Sfr35 for adults and Sfr75 for families.

For stays of one month or more, inquire about *Arcobaleno* zonal passes for Ticino.

Bellinzona

☎ 091 • pop 17,100 • elevation 230m
The capital of Ticino is a city of castles. It is set in a valley of lush mountains, and stands at the southern side of two important Alpine passes, San Bernardino and St Gotthard.

Orientation & Information
The train station has a money-exchange counter (open 6 am to 8.30 pm daily), bike rental, and an Aperto supermarket (open to 9 pm daily). Walk left for five minutes to reach the main post office (Posta 1, 6500), Viale Stazione 18. The tourist office (☎ 825 21 31, fax 825 38 17, ✉ bellinzona.turismo@ bluewin.ch) is in the same building, open 8.30 am to 6.30 pm Monday to Friday, and 9 am to 12.30 pm Saturday. It sells maps, including a local hiking map (Sfr7) showing routes and durations. The cobbled streets south of the post office, up to and including Piazza Indipendenza, are banned to private vehicles from 8 pm to 7 am, and for certain periods during the day.

Castles
The three medieval castles which dominate the town are testimony to Bellinzona's historical importance, based on its key location at the crossroads of the major routes through the Alps. All the castles are well preserved and offer marvellous views of the town and surrounding mountains.

The most central and largest castle is **Castelgrande**; walk up, or take the lift from Piazza del Sole. It dates from around the 6th century, and is open daily for visits to the grounds (free). Its museum covers archaeology and history and is open 10 am to 6 pm Tuesday to Sunday (Sfr4, students/seniors Sfr2). **Castello di Montebello**, slightly above the town, has a small museum that proffers further archaeological and historical displays (same hours and prices as Castelgrande). Quite a trek up the hill is the smaller **Castello di Sasso Corbaro**. It hosts temporary

TICINO

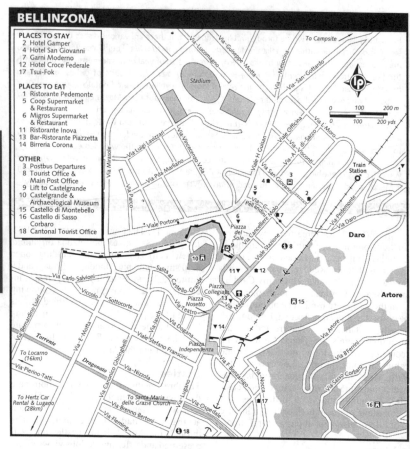

BELLINZONA

PLACES TO STAY
2 Hotel Gamper
4 Hotel San Giovanni
7 Garni Moderno
12 Hotel Croce Federale
17 Tsui-Fok

PLACES TO EAT
1 Ristorante Pedemonte
5 Coop Supermarket & Restaurant
6 Migros Supermarket & Restaurant
11 Ristorante Inova
13 Bar-Ristorante Piazzetta
14 Birreria Corona

OTHER
3 Postbus Departures
8 Tourist Office & Main Post Office
9 Lift to Castelgrande
10 Castelgrande & Archaeological Museum
15 Castello di Montebello
16 Castello di Sasso Corbaro
18 Cantonal Tourist Office

---

exhibitions (Sfr5, students/seniors Sfr2) but has no grounds to explore. No buses go up but you may be able to beg a lift back down again from the car park. The castles are often respectively referred to as that of Uri, Schwyz and Unterwalden, after the bailiffs of the cantons who ruled the town from the 16th century.

Church

The **Chiesa di Santa Maria delle Grazie**, Via Lugano, features a 15th century fresco of the crucifixion, comparable to the more famous version of the scene in the Santa Maria Church in Lugano. The artist who painted the impressive fresco is unknown. The church recently suffered extensive fire damage, but renovations should be completed in 2000.

Special Events

Every Saturday morning there's a **market** that sprawls across the main street at Piazza Collegiata. There are stalls selling flowers, fruit and vegetables, clothes and crafts, plus there's usually a couple of buskers (street musicians) to liven things up. It's very much a social occasion, with locals standing around chatting rather than indulging in any frenzied buying. This relaxed approach to life becomes rather more animated during the **Rabadan Carnival**, which stretches over several days and starts on a Thursday, 7½ weeks before Easter Sunday.

Bellinzona has the happy habit of hosting open-air music festivals. **Piazza Blues** runs for three days in late June (1st night free; following two nights Sfr20 each). **Music Open Air** in the south-west suburb of Monte Carasso is three days of free rock/funk/pop in mid-July. A few days later is the **Kingdom Festival**, with more open-air rock and pop, but this time costing at least Sfr30 per day.

Places to Stay

The *camp site* (☎ 829 11 18, *Bosco di Molinazzo*), costs Sfr6 per person, Sfr3 for a car, Sfr16 for a camper van and from Sfr5.50 for a tent. It is open from about Easter to mid-October, and is by the river in the northern suburb of Molinazzo.

Bellinzona hasn't got a very wide choice of hotels, so book ahead if you can. *Tsui-Fok (☎/fax 825 13 32, Via Nocca 20)*, offers oldish rooms with hall showers. Singles/doubles are Sfr45/70; add Sfr5 per person for breakfast. Reception and the restaurant are closed till 6.30 pm on Monday and between 2.30 to 6.30 pm on other days. Nearer the station is *Garni Moderno (☎/fax 825 13 76, Viale Stazione 17b)*, part of Caffè della Posta (closed Sunday). It has new-looking rooms for Sfr55/90, and doubles with a small bathroom for Sfr120. *Hotel San Giovanni (☎/fax 825 19 19, Via San Giovanni 7)* is nearly as good, and they are gradually renovating. Singles/doubles are Sfr60/90, and doubles with a shower cubicle are Sfr100. Its cafe is closed Sunday afternoon.

Ideally situated in the centre is *Hotel Croce Federale (☎ 825 16 67, Viale Stazione 12)*, with singles/doubles/triples for Sfr95/140/160. All rooms have shower/WC and TV, and the hotel has a pizzeria. Top-of-the-range in Bellinzona are three-star hotels. The best deal is at *Hotel Gamper (☎ 825 37 92, fax 826 46 89 Viale Stazione 29)*, opposite the station. This modern high-rise with a lift has rooms with balcony, bathroom, telephone and TV for around Sfr130/180.

Places to Eat

The *Migros (Piazza del Sole)* and the *Coop (Via H Guisan)* supermarkets both have restaurants. A supermarket and the buffet-style *Ristorante Inova* are downstairs in the Innovazione department store on Viale Stazione. You can eat for around Sfr10 in all these of restaurants, and they have late opening until 9 pm on Thursday.

Many restaurants are closed on Sunday, so that might be a good day to consider going on a diet. As you might expect, there are plenty of pizzerias around town. The one in Hotel Croce Federale is good; prices start at Sfr10 and there are outside tables. *Birreria Corona (Via Camminata 5)* has a cafe-type front section and a smarter restaurant at the rear, with the same menu. There are pizzas (from Sfr10), and other meals from Sfr12 to Sfr33 (closed Sunday). *Bar-Ristorante Piazzetta (Piazza Collegiata 1)* also has several sections, and features mediterranean cooking from around Sfr17 (closed Sunday).

If you don't fancy making Sunday a day of rest for your stomach, look in at *Ristorante Pedemonte (☎ 825 33 33, Via Pedemonte 12)*. It's popular with locals but not many tourists find it as it's on the inaccessible side of the station. You really get personal service in this small place where there's no written menu; instead, the server describes what's cooking for the night. Choices are limited, but invariably tasty. Expect to pay around Sfr15 for a starter or salad and Sfr30 for a main course (lunches are cheaper). It's closed on Monday. Quality food can also be savoured at the restaurant in the *Castelgrande (☎ 826 23 53)*, or there are cheaper dishes from Sfr15 in the grotto or on the terrace; all parts are closed on Mondays.

Getting There & Away

Bellinzona is on the train route connecting Locarno (Sfr6.80) and Lugano (Sfr10.80). The journey takes around 30 minutes in either direction, with two trains an hour. It is also on the Zürich-Milan route. Postbuses head north-east to Chur (Sfr50); you need to reserve your seat the day before (no fee), at the train station or on ☎ 825 77 55. There is

TICINO

a good cycling track along the Ticino River to Lago Maggiore and Locarno.

Postbuses depart from Via C Molo, one block away from the train station.

Car Rental Hertz (☎ 826 10 33) is at Via F Zorzi 40 and Europcar (☎ 820 60 40) is at Via San Gottardo 71, north of the town centre. Avis has no local office.

Lugano

☎ 091 • pop 29,000 • elevation 270m
Switzerland's southernmost tourist town offers an excellent combination of sunny days, watery pursuits and hillside hikes. It's the largest city in Ticino and the fourth most important financial centre in Switzerland.

Before the Swiss arrived on the scene in 1512, Lugano was successively under the jurisdiction of the Bishop of Como and the Duke of Milan. In the days of France's Helvetic Republic it was the citizens of Lugano who started the move for Ticino to officially join the Swiss Confederation, proclaiming themselves 'Liberi e Svizzeri' (Free and Swiss).

Orientation
Lugano is on the shores of Lake Lugano. The train station is above and to the west of the Old Town. Take the stairs or the funicular (Sfr0.90, Swiss Pass valid) down to the centre which is dominated by piazzas. The most important one, the Piazza della Riforma, contains the Neo-Classical Municipio building. Paradiso, a suburb to the south, is the departure point for the funicular up to Mt San Salvatore. The other mountain that looms over the town, Mt Brè, is to the east. The airport is 3km west of the train station.

Information
Tourist Office The tourist office (☎ 913 32 32, fax 922 76 53, ✆ infor@ lugano-tourism.ch), Riva Giocondo Albertolli, is on the lake side of the Municipio building. Opening hours are 9 am to 6.30 pm Monday to Friday, 9 am to 12.30 pm and 1.30 to 5 pm Saturday, and 10 am to 2 pm

Sunday. In winter, opening hours reduce to 9 am to 12.30 pm and 1.30 to 5.30 pm weekdays only. Ask about the Guest Card if you're staying at least three days in the region, and pick up the *Regione Lago di Lugano Official Guide* which is in four languages.

Train Station The train information office is open 8.20 am to 6.30 pm weekdays (5 pm Saturday), and also has a counter for hotel reservations. There's also a free hotel telephone round the corner. The counter for Swissair check-in (for Zürich airport only) also deals with bike rental, and is staffed 7 am to 6.30 pm daily. The money-exchange office is open to 7.45 pm daily. The Aperto supermarket is open 6 am to 10 pm daily.

Post & Communications The main post office (Posta 1, 6900) is in the centre of the Old Town at Via Della Posta 7. Opening hours are 7.30 to 6.15 pm Monday to Friday, and 8 am to 11 am Saturday. Services are available during additional hours subject to a surcharge.

Internet access is at City Disc, Via P Peri, with late opening till 9 pm on Thursday. Charges are Sfr4/8/10 for 20/40/60 minutes.

Medical & Emergency Services Call the police on ☎ 117, and dial ☎ 111 for a doctor or dentist. The hospital, Ospedale Civico (☎ 805 61 11), is at Via Tesserete.

Old Town
Winding alleyways, pedestrian-only piazzas and colourful parks make Lugano an ideal town for walking around. At 9.30 am on Monday from April to October, the tourist office conducts a free guided walk of the centre; make a reservation the day before. Spend some time in the **Parco Civico**, east of the Casino. Magnolias and camellias flower in March, and a month later rhododendrons and azaleas burst forth.

The **St Mary of the Angels Church** (Santa Maria degli Angioli), Piazza Luini, has a pair of frescoes by Bernardino Luini dating from 1529; the most powerful depicts the Crucifixion. Below the train station is the **St Lawrence Cathedral** (Cattedrale San

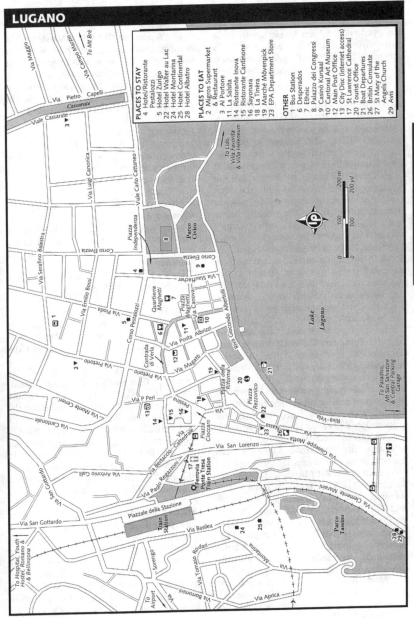

LUGANO

PLACES TO STAY
4 Hotel/Ristorante Pestalozzi
5 Hotel Zurigo
22 Hotel Walter au Lac
24 Hotel Montarina
25 Hotel Continental
28 Hotel Albatro

PLACES TO EAT
2 Migros Supermarket & Restaurant
3 Al Portone
11 La Salsita
14 Ristorante Inova
15 Ristorante Cantinone
16 Sayonara
18 La Tinèra
19 Marché Mövenpick
23 EPA Department Store

OTHER
1 Bus Station
6 Desperados
7 Ethnic
8 Palazzo dei Congressi
9 Casinò Kursaal
10 Cantonal Art Museum
12 Main Post Office
13 City Disc (Internet access)
17 St Lawrence Cathedral
20 Tourist Office
21 Boat Departures
26 British Consulate
27 St Mary of the Angels Church
29 Avis

Lorenzo), noted for its Renaissance facade (1517), particularly the three fine doorways that overlook the lake. Inside are frescoes dating from a similar era, and choir stalls with mini statues protruding from each armrest. The tabernacle at the end of the aisle is 16th century.

Museums & Galleries The **Thyssen-Bornemisza Gallery**, Villa Favorita, Castagnola, is a famous private art collection. In 1992 the Old Masters of the collection were transferred to Spain, but what's left behind is pretty impressive. It constitutes 150 works by American and European artists from the 19th and 20th century, covering all major styles from abstract to photorealism. The wealthy Baron von Thyssen-Bornemisza (the family amassed its fortune from steel) can only get richer, as the gallery charges as much as Sfr10 (Sfr6 for students) for admission, or more if there's a special exhibition. Opening hours are 10 am to 5 pm Friday to Sunday between early April and 31 October. Take the boat from Piazza Rezzonico or bus No 1 from Lugano.

Five minutes' walk east is the **Museum of Extra-European Cultures** (Museo delle Culture Extraeuropee), in the Villa Heleneum on Via Cortivo. It lacks signs in English, but the statues, fertility symbols, masks and photographs are extremely evocative of ancient tribal lifestyles without needing words. Entry costs Sfr5 (Sfr3 for students), and it's open 10 am to 5 pm Tuesday to Sunday from March to October. If you walk back from Gandria (see the Lake Lugano section) you pass by this museum.

The **Cantonal Art Museum** (Museo cantonale d'Arte), Via Canova 10, has a worthwhile modern art collection from the 19th and 20th centuries. Ticinese artists are well represented. It costs Sfr7 (students Sfr5) to get in, or Sfr10 (Sfr7) if there's a special exhibition. Opening times are 10 am to 5 pm Wednesday to Sunday, and 2 pm to 5 pm Tuesday. Additional contemporary art is at the **Modern Art Museum** (Museo d'Arte Moderna), Riva Antonio Caccia 5, towards Paradiso (Sfr10; closed Monday). You can

walk or take bus Nos 1 or 9 from Piazza Rezzonico.

The **Alpenrose Chocolate Museum**, Via Rompada, Casalano, gives a rundown of the history of chocolate and its manufacturing process (Sfr3). Visitors can view production in the factory from an elevated walkway. It is open 9 am to 8 pm daily (5 pm on weekends). Get there by the Ferrovia Ponte Tresa.

Activities
The Lido, just east of the Cassarate River, offers a swimming pool and sandy beaches for Sfr7 a day, and it's open 9 or 9.30 am to at least 6 pm daily from 1 May to mid-September.

Places where you can water-ski, sail and windsurf are listed in the official guide; prices are given. Club Nautico-Lugano (☎ 649 61 39), charges Sfr10 per hour for windsurfing and Sfr2.20 per minute for water-skiing.

Pedalos near the boat landing stage can be hired for about Sfr16 per hour.

Courses
The Migros scuola club (☎ 922 76 21), Via Pretorio 15, for languages and other courses, is in the same building as the supermarket.

Special Events
Primavera Concertistica is a series of classical music concerts held during April and May. They are performed in the Palazzo dei Congressi, in the Parco Civico. Tickets cost Sfr40 (Sfr20 for students/seniors) to Sfr100. Inquire at the tourist office. Free open-air **music festivals** are the Estival Jazz in early July and the Blues to Bop Festival at the end of August. In late July there is a spectacular fireworks display over Lago di Lugano.

Places to Stay – Budget
Camping There are five camp sites by the arm of the lake that loops up near Agno airport. All are open from approximately Easter to the end of October. The Ferrovia Ponte Tresa train from in front of the main station gets you to the vicinity. *Eurocampo* (☎ 605 21 14) is the largest site, and costs Sfr8.70 per adult and Sfr6 per tent. *La Piodella*

(☎ 994 77 88) is slightly more expensive but has good facilities and is open virtually year-round. It's south-west of Lugano in Muzzano, reached by postbus.

Hostel The relaxed SYHA *hostel (☎ 966 27 28, fax 968 23 63, Via Cantonale 13)* is a hard 20 minutes' walk uphill from the train station (signposted), or take bus No 5 to Crocifisso (Sfr1.20). Dorm beds are Sfr23 and doubles are Sfr56 or (with kitchen) Sfr70. Add Sfr7 for breakfast and subtract Sfr3 per night if you're staying four nights or more. It's a refreshing family-run place, with classical music wafting through the reception and breakfast area, CNN (the American news channel) on the TV, and its own extensive grounds, including an outdoor swimming pool. Reception is shut from 12.30 to 3 pm but the dorms stay open throughout the day. The hostel closes from 31 October to mid-March.

Hotels Around the back of the train station is *Hotel Montarina (☎ 966 72 72, fax 966 00 17, ✆ asbest@tinet.ch, Via Montarina 1)*, in two buildings with a garden, kitchen and free use of a swimming pool. Beds in large dorms are Sfr20, plus Sfr4 if you don't have sheets. Singles/doubles are Sfr50/80 and triples/quads are Sfr105/140, all with a sink in the room. Singles/doubles with own shower/WC are Sfr65/120. Buffet breakfast is available for Sfr12. Reception is open 8 am to around 9 or 10 pm and the hotel is closed from 31 October until about two weeks before Easter.

En route to the youth hostel is *Ristorante Bar Romano (☎/fax 966 22 17, Via San Gottardo 103)*, with simple but pleasant rooms for only Sfr38/76. Reservations are advised, especially for Sunday when the bar is closed. *Pensione FJM Home Union (☎ 966 27 56, fax 967 64 40, Via Vergiò 3, Breganzona)*, to the west (take bus No 4), has some tourist rooms for only Sfr25/50; call ahead.

In Paradiso, try *Hotel Dischma (☎ 994 21 31, fax 994 15 03, ✆ dischma@swissonline.ch, Vicolo Geretta 6)*, set back from the road. It has a jolly hostess, a bar, and rooms with shower/WC and (usually)

balcony. Singles/doubles are Sfr65/110 and four-course dinners are Sfr18.

Hotel Ristorante Pestalozzi (☎ 921 46 46, fax 922 20 45, Piazza Indipendenza 9) has singles/doubles/triples for Sfr92/144/206 with own shower/WC or Sfr60/100/140 without. The top (fourth) floor has newer rooms in a modern, minimalist style; rooms on other floors combine old, solid brown furniture with modern features. There's a lift.

Places to Stay – Mid-Range & Top End

Hotel Zurigo (☎ 923 43 43, fax 923 92 68, Corso Pestalozzi 13), is conveniently central and has plenty of parking. Newly renovated singles/doubles/triples are Sfr95/140/160 with private shower/WC, and singles using hall shower are Sfr60. All rooms have TV and the hotel is closed in December and January.

In Paradiso is *Victoria au Lac (☎ 994 20 31, fax 994 20 32, ✆ victoria@albacom.ch, Via General Guisan 3)*. The lobby evokes the British Raj in India, though the rooms have standard decor. Sizeable singles/doubles are Sfr120/180 and have bathroom and TV. They may close for part of winter.

Hôtel Walter au Lac (☎ 922 74 25, fax 923 42 33, ✆ hotel@walteraulac.ch, Piazza Rezzonico 7) is centrally situated near Piazza Riforma (closed February) and offers good lake views in all rooms. Attractive singles/doubles with TV and bathroom are Sfr110/170. Near the station is *Hotel Continental (☎ 966 11 12, fax 966 12 13, ✆ info@continentalpark.ch, Via Basilea 28)*, with large if plainish rooms from Sfr95/160, with the same amenities. It closes in winter and manages Beauregard, a cheaper annexe (Sfr80/150), as well as Montarina (mentioned above). Along the road, *Hotel Albatro (☎ 921 09 21, fax 921 09 27, Via Clemente Maraini 8)*, is a new hotel with garage parking, an outside pool, and air-con rooms for Sfr145/180.

Lugano has a dozen four-star hotels. Of these, the *Holiday Inn (☎ 986 38 38, fax 986 38 39, Via Geretta 15)*, near the Paradiso funicular, is good value, with large, renovated, standardised rooms for Sfr190/280. The indoor and roof-top swimming pools, fitness room and sauna are all free for guests.

Places to Eat

Self-Service There is a large *Migros* supermarket, snackbar and restaurant on Via Pretorio, with the usual meals and salad/dessert buffets. An *EPA* self-service restaurant in the department store is similar and can be found on Via Nassa at Piazzetta San Carlo. It has late opening till 9 pm on Thursday.

Up the stairs from Cioccaro Piazza is *Ristorante Inova*, a buffet-style place where the food is cooked in front of you. An excellent deal is the pizza or pasta for around Sfr10 where you can select the ingredients for the sauce from the counter. Salad plates are Sfr4.20 to Sfr9.90, and it's open daily to 10 pm. *Marché Mövenpick (Via Giacomo Luvini)* has a similar set up and marginally higher prices.

Cheap to Mid-Price Restaurants Any number of restaurants around town offer pizza and pasta; many have outside tables. *Ristorante Cantinone (Piazza Cioccaro)* has a large selection of good-sized pizzas from Sfr11.50 and is open 9 am to midnight daily.

Also good and cheap for Italian and vegetarian food is *Hotel Restaurant Pestalozzi* (see Places to Stay), open 6 am to 11 pm daily (kitchen till 9.30 pm). It's an alcohol-free restaurant with a wide choice of daily specials from Sfr9.50 to Sfr18, sometimes including soup.

Across Piazza Cioccaro from Ristorante Cantinone is the large *Sayonara*. It has the usual pizza/pasta, as well as local dishes such as polenta from Sfr11.50 to Sfr35 (open daily). *La Tinèra (Via dei Gorini)*, off Piazza della Riforma, has a typical Ticinese ambience and meals for Sfr11 to Sfr27. Local wines start at Sfr1.70 per decilitre. It's not unusual to have to queue before you can be seated (closed on Sunday).

La Salsita (Via Vegezzi 4) is a popular Mexican restaurant, with candle lighting at night. A youngish crowd comes for meals from Sfr20 (closed Monday).

In Paradiso, by the funicular station, is *Hotel Schmid*. It has a restaurant with a terrace, pizzas from Sfr9.50 and a dish of the day for Sfr16. Close by is *Ristorante Bar Paradiso (Via San Salvatore)*, which is similarly priced and also good (closed Sunday).

Gourmet Restaurants Eating in Lugano can be a superb if wallet-withering experience. *Al Portone (☎ 923 55 11, Viale Cassarate 3)* is the best in town. It has up-market Italian cuisine and closes Sunday and Monday. Another gourmet place is *Santabbondio (☎ 993 23 88, Via Fomelino 10, Sorengo)* near Agno airport (closed Saturday lunch, Sunday evening, and Monday).

Entertainment

For drinks, pittas and paninis amid tropical decor, try *Ethnic* in the pedestrian-only Quartiere Maghetti (closed Saturday lunch and Sunday). *Desperados (Via al Forte 4 – entrance off Vicolo Orfanotrofio)* is a late-night disco bar (closed Monday). The *Casinò Kursaal (Via Stauffacher)* has dancing, drinking, gambling and a cinema.

Getting There & Away

Agno airport has Crossair flights nonstop to/from Basel, Bern, Geneva and Zürich, with departures several times a day. There are also direct connections to Florence and Venice. Crossair can be contacted on ☎ 610 12 12.

Lugano is on the same road and rail route as Bellinzona. To St Moritz, two postbuses run daily in summer; in winter there's only one, and only on Friday, Saturday and Sunday (daily over New Year). The cost is Sfr63 (plus a Sfr10 supplement, not covered by Swiss travel passes) and it takes four hours. You need to reserve your seat the day before at the bus station, the train information office in the train station, or by phoning ☎ 807 85 20. All postbuses leave from the main bus depot at Via Serafino Balestra, but you can pick up the St Moritz bus and many others outside the train station 15 minutes later.

For further train and boat information see the Bellinzona and Lake Lugano sections.

Car Rental Offices include: Hertz (☎ 923 46 75), Via San Gottardo 13, Europcar

TICINO

(☎ 971 01 01), Via Monte Boglia 24, and Avis (☎ 913 41 51) Via Clemente Maraini 8; they all have an airport office. Sud (☎ 994 17 19), Clemente Maraini 14, is a local operator.

Getting Around

Getting to the airport involves taking the small train (the Ferrovia Ponte Tresa runs every 20 to 30 minutes) in front of the train station, getting off at Agno, and walking for 10 minutes. The same train goes to the chocolate museum and Caslano; the Swiss Pass is valid, city travel passes aren't. A taxi from the town centre to the airport costs up to Sfr30.

Pick up a bus map from the tourist office; bus Nos 1 and 6 go to Paradiso. A single trip costs Sfr1.20 to Sfr1.90 (ticket dispensers indicate the appropriate rate) or it's only Sfr5 for a one-day pass. Weekly passes are available from transport offices, including the Lugano Region pass (see Getting Around at the beginning of the chapter).

There are various parking garages in town, all identified in the tourist office's *Official Guide* – charges are Sfr1 to Sfr2 per hour. Alternatively, park for free at the Cornaredo sports stadium in the north and take bus No 3 into town.

Call ☎ 971 21 21 or ☎ 971 91 91 for a taxi.

AROUND LUGANO

The tourist office has free written guides detailing walks of up to three hours' duration heading south along the lake, or north towards Locarno. Touring the lake itself by boat is an unmissable pleasure on a sunny day (see the following section). Also unmissable – quite literally – are the two peaks soaring over the town, **Monte San Salvatore** and **Monte Brè**. Lugano has dubbed itself the 'Rio de Janeiro of the Old Continent' for the resemblance that Monte San Salvatore (912m) bears to Rio's Sugarloaf Mountain. The funicular from Paradiso up Monte San Salvatore operates from mid-March to mid-November only and costs Sfr12 to go up or Sfr18 return. From the top you get an excellent perspective of the meandering contours of the lake. The walk

down takes a little over an hour back to Paradiso or Melide.

Monte Brè (925m) offers a clearer view of the curve of the bay round Lugano. To ascend the peak, you can take the funicular from Cassarate which costs Sfr13 to go up or Sfr19 return; it runs year-round though it's often closed for maintenance in January. A cheaper way to get up Monte Brè is to drive, or take bus No 12 from the main post office to Brè village, and walk about 15 minutes from there.

Lake Lugano

There are many points of interest around the lake, easily visited on a day tour if you don't fancy a longer excursion. Boats are operated by the Società Navigazione del Lago di Lugano (☎ 971 52 23, ✉ lake.lugano@bluewin.ch). Examples of return fares from Lugano are Gandria (Sfr16.60), Melide (Sfr16.60) and Morcote (Sfr23.80). If you want to visit several places, buy a pass: one day costs Sfr32, three days costs Sfr48 and one week costs Sfr58. There are reduced fares for children, but they go free if you have a Family Card.

The departure point from Lugano is by the Piazza della Riforma. Boats sail year-round, but the service is more frequent and extensive from late March to late October. During this time some boats go as far as Ponte Tresa, so you could go one way by boat and return to Lugano on the Ponte Tresa train. The Swiss Pass is valid and the Half-Fare Card gets reductions.

One-way postbus fares are Sfr4.40 to Melide and Sfr6.80 to Morcote.

GANDRIA

Gandria is an attractive village where the houses tumble down the hill right to the water's edge. Piers and boathouses, with small craft dangling from pulleys, stand in lieu of garages as no cars can get near most of these houses; only alleys and stairways separate the compact dwellings. A popular round trip is to take the boat from Lugano and to walk back along the shore to

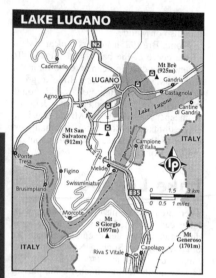

LAKE LUGANO

Castagnola (around 40 minutes), where you can visit Villa Heleneum and/or Villa Favorita, or simply continue back to Lugano by foot or bus No 1.

From Gandria, take the path by the church. A few minutes after leaving the village you reach a small cove where the main road can be seen winding its own course above. The bare rock here reveals striking patterns in its curved fault lines.

There are a couple of hotels in Gandria. Next to the boat landing stage awaits *Miralago* (☎ *971 43 61, fax 971 41 13)*, open from 1 April to 31 October. Accommodation costs Sfr78 for compact doubles with sink, available as singles in low season for Sfr50. The restaurant (open daily) offers spaghetti for around Sfr16, and meat dishes ranging from simple cutlets to giant fillets.

Across the lake from Gandria is the **Customs Museum**, at Cantine di Gandria, accessible by boat. It tells the story of the development of customs in the area, using documents, dummies, and confiscated exhibits. An interesting section reveals the ploys used by smugglers over the years. Common tricks include false-bottomed shoes, hollowed out books and modified fuel tanks.

The museum is open 1.30 to 5.30 pm daily, from 31 March to late October, and entry is free. As there are only minimal notes in English you can get around in 30 to 40 minutes.

CAMPIONE D'ITALIA

This really is part of Italy – a forgotten anomaly surrounded by Switzerland. It's not immediately obvious you're in another country: there are no border formalities (but take your passport anyway), many cars in the village have Swiss number plates and they still use Swiss francs and Swiss telephones. Not everything is the same, though – the post boxes are red, not yellow as in Switzerland, and the police officers and police cars bear Italian livery.

Another difference is in the gambling laws: there are none of those Swiss restrictions so the casino does brisk business especially, ironically, with Swiss visitors. The casino might lose its appeal though, when the liberalisation of the Swiss gambling regulations comes into effect (no fixed date yet). It is open 3.15 pm to around 2 am daily and smart dress is required; you pay Sfr15 entry to get Sfr10 gambling chips. There are also slot machines open from 1.15 pm (no dress code, no entry charge). In the evening there is a special bus service from Piazza Rezzonico in Lugano to the casino (Sfr6.20 each way; travel passes not valid).

The tourist office (☎ 649 50 51), Via Volta 3, and the post office are opposite each other. From the boat landing stage, go slightly to the right and about 50m up the hill.

If you want to eat lunch in Italy, there's the ***Bar-Pizzeria Rally Club*** right next to the boat landing stage, with pizza starting at Sfr10 and other reasonably-priced snacks and meals (closed Wednesday in low season). They want Swiss money but you know you're not in Switzerland when you go to the 'gents' and find a squat-over-the-hole lavatory instead of the usual pristine Swiss porcelain with electronic sensors. Those seeking more elegance and higher quality (and prices) can saunter across the road to ***Ristorante Taverna***, also closed Wednesday.

MONTE GENEROSO

The panorama provided by this summit (1701m) includes the lakes, the Alps, and even the Apennines on a clear day. It can be reached by taking the boat (except in winter), train or car to Capolago, and then the funicular (Sfr33 up or Sfr46 return; reductions for children and with the Lugano Region pass). The funicular closes in November, and doesn't run Monday or Tuesday in winter unless they're public holidays.

CERESIO

☎ 091

This is the area south of Lugano, a peninsula created by the looping shoreline of Lake Lugano. There are walking trails dissecting the interior and small villages dotting the lakeside. The tourist office in Melide (☎ 649 63 83, fax 649 56 13, **ⓔ** ceresio@ ticino-info.ch), by the train station, covers the whole region. Opening hours are 8.30 am to noon and 1.30 to 6 pm Monday to Friday.

There is a SYHA *hostel* (☎ 995 11 51, fax 995 10 70) in Casaro, Fignio, open from 1 March to late October. Dorm beds cost Sfr25, and there are cooking facilities. It's near the postbus stop, and a couple of daily boats call at Fignio except in winter. The postbus from Lugano to Morcote goes via either Melide or Fignio, and departs approximately hourly. Year-round boats also connect Morcote and Melide to Lugano.

Some of the roads in Ceresio afford excellent views, particularly the upper road from Melide to Lugano, passing through Carona at 602m. Carona (hourly postbus from Lugano) is also a suitable starting point for a number of hikes.

Melide

Melide is on the bulge of the shore from which the N2 motorway slices across the lake. The main attraction of this village is Swissminiatur (☎ 640 10 60, **ⓔ** info@ swissminiatur.ch), where you'll find 1:25 scale models of more than 110 national attractions. Children and adults can spend a great couple of hours wandering around the faithfully reproduced replicas. The models

are so good that it can help you decide if you want to go on to see the real thing, and there are many boats, cable cars and trains whizzing about the place to complete the picture.

The park is open 9 am to 6 pm daily from mid-March to the end of October. If the weather is fine it may also open in the afternoons from November to mid-December. Admission costs Sfr11 for adults and Sfr7 for children, and the program for Sfr2 is essential as there are no other signs. Take advantage of the cheap self-service restaurant inside, or the EPA supermarket by the car park. Boats stop in Melide at Swissminiatur (five minutes' walk away) or Paese (10 minutes' walk).

Places to Stay & Eat *Brandner Garni* (☎ 649 86 02, *Via Pocobelli 19*), in the centre, has a fading Mediterranean look and singles/doubles for Sfr45/85 using hall showers; phone ahead as the new owner may change the set-up. *Al Boccalino* (☎ 649 77 67, fax 649 73 98, *Via Borromini 27*) is set back from the lake. It provides comfortable rooms from Sfr55/90 with bathroom and TV or Sfr45/80 without. There's a typical Ticinese restaurant, which is closed on Thursday in winter, and has meals from Sfr10.

Giardino (☎ 649 79 97, *Lungolago G Motta*), near the Paese boat stop, is an Italian restaurant with many varieties of pizza from Sfr10 (open daily). It has a few rooms using hall shower for Sfr45/90. Opposite is *Hotel Del Lago* (☎ 649 70 41, fax 649 89 15, **ⓔ** hoteldellago@ticino.com) at No 9, offering mid-price rooms and meals.

Morcote

This photogenic fishing village clusters at the foot of Monte Abostora. It is graced with well-preserved arcaded houses and quaint alleyways. Narrow stairways lead up to the church of **Santa Maria del Sasso**, a 15-minute climb. The views are excellent, and the church itself has frescoes (16th century), busts of bishops, and carved faces on the organ. Nearby, the cemetery shows the Italian practice of displaying images of the

TICINO

TICINO

faces of the deceased amid the gravestones and bouquets.

Parco Scherrer, 400m left (west) from the boat stop, offers an eclectic collection of architectural styles from around the world, including copies of famous buildings and generic types (eg, Temple of Nefertiti, Siamese tea-house). It's all set in subtropical parkland, open 10 am to 5 pm daily between 15 March and 31 October (6 pm in July and August). Admission costs Sfr7 (students/seniors Sfr5, children Sfr1).

At the boat landing stage is a tourist office (☎/fax 996 11 20), open 1 to 5 pm daily, plus Saturday morning. Across the road is a covered arcade where shops offer souvenirs and unusual odds and ends. The walk along the shore to Melide takes around 50 minutes.

Places to Stay & Eat Morcote lacks a budget hotel. ***Ristorante Battello con Alloggio*** *(☎ 996 1260)*, in the covered arcade, has three rooms with TV but using hall showers. Prices are Sfr50/80/100 for one/two/three people, and breakfast is Sfr10 (closed December and January). ***Oasi*** *(☎ 996 14 97)*, 200m towards Melide, is open mid-March to early October. Singles/doubles are Sfr60/120 with a shower cubicle or Sfr50/100 without. Both places have Ticinese dishes starting at Sfr13. A little beyond Oasi is a ***Coop*** supermarket (early closing on Wednesday).

Della Posta *(☎ 996 11 27, fax 996 17 79)*, right by the post office, has rooms with private shower/WC and TV from about Sfr95/120 (open March to October). It is also a reasonable place to eat, with pizza and pasta starting at Sfr13 and meat and fish dishes around Sfr30, served either at the sunny 1st-floor terrace, the ground floor part, or the lakeside section. There are also plenty of other restaurants queuing for your custom along the quayside.

MENDRISIO
South of Lake Lugano is Mendrisiotto and Lower Ceresio. It is a fine area for walking tours around the rolling valleys and unspoilt villages. Mendrisio is the district capital (population 6500) and has a tourist office

(☎ 646 57 61, fax 646 33 48, @ etm@ tinet.ch). It has several interesting old churches and buildings, and is especially worth a visit for the Maundy Thursday Procession or the Wine Harvest in September.

MERIDE
The Fossil Museum (Museo dei Fossili) in Meride, to the north-west of Mendrisio, displays vestiges of the first creatures to inhabit the region – reptiles and fish dating back 200 million years. The museum is open 8 am to 6 pm daily (free entry). Near the town is a circular nature trail, complete with periodic information panels.

Locarno

☎ 091 • pop 15,000 • elevation 205m
Locarno lies at the northern end of Lake Maggiore and is Switzerland's lowest town. Tourist literature trumpets that it enjoys the country's sunniest climate (around 2300 hours per year) though several other towns, especially in Valais, make the same claim. Locarno achieved prominence when it hosted the 1925 Peace Conference which intended to bring stability to Europe in the aftermath of WWI.

Orientation & Information
The train station has money-exchange counters (open 9 am to 6 pm daily), bike rental (5.30 am to 6.45 pm daily; returns until 9 pm), and a transport information office. A few minutes to the west is the core of the town, Piazza Grande. The tourist office (☎ 751 03 33, fax 751 90 70, @ locarno@ticino.com) is here at Largo Zorzi, through the same entrance as the Casinò Theatro. It has brochures on many parts of Switzerland, gives detailed information on the Lake Maggiore region, makes free hotel reservations and offers various guided tours such as to Milan (Sfr62) and Ticino's northern valleys. Opening hours are 9 am to 6 pm Monday to Friday. The tourist office is also open 10 am to 4 pm Saturday and 10 am to 2 pm Sunday from mid-March to mid-October.

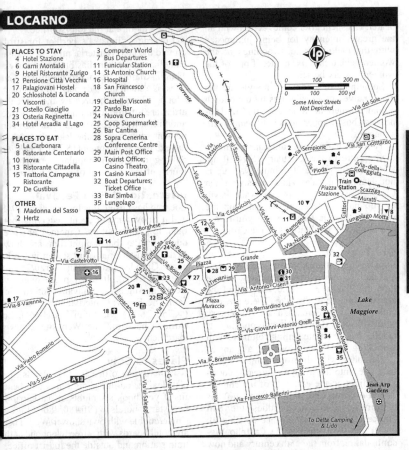

LOCARNO

PLACES TO STAY
4 Hotel Stazione
6 Garni Montaldi
9 Hotel Ristorante Zurigo
12 Pensione Città Vecchia
17 Palagiovani Hostel
20 Schlosshotel & Locanda Visconti
21 Ostello Giaciglio
23 Osteria Reginetta
34 Hotel Arcadia al Lago

PLACES TO EAT
5 La Carbonara
8 Ristorante Centenario
10 Inova
13 Ristorante Cittadella
15 Trattoria Campagna Ristorante
27 De Gustibus

OTHER
1 Madonna del Sasso
2 Hertz

3 Computer World
7 Bus Departures
11 Funicular Station
14 St Antonio Church
16 Hospital
18 San Francesco Church
19 Castello Visconti
22 Pardo Bar
24 Nuova Church
25 Coop Supermarket
26 Bar Cantina
28 Sopra Cenerina Conference Centre
29 Main Post Office
30 Tourist Office; Casino Theatro
31 Casinò Kursaal
32 Boat Departures; Ticket Office
33 Bar Simba
35 Lungolago

Piazza Grande also has the main post office (Posta 1, 6600), a shopping arcade and cafes with outside tables. North and west of the piazza is the old part of town *(città vecchia),* where the often pedestrian-only streets are small and sometimes confusing. The hospital *(ospedale;* ☎ 756 71 11) on Via Castelrotto has a casualty department.

Internet access is available at Computer World, Via S Gottardo 1 (Sfr3 plus Sfr0.20 per minute), which is open shop hours, or at Pardo Bar, Via della Motta 3 (Sfr4 for 20 minutes), open 8.30 am to 1 am daily.

Madonna del Sasso

This sanctuary overlooks the town and lake from a prominent position on the hillside. It was built after the Virgin Mary appeared in a vision to a monk, Bartolomeo d'Ivrea, in 1480. There's a small museum (limited opening times; Sfr2.50, children and students Sfr1.50), a church (chiesa; open daily) and several very distinctive statue groups on the stairway.

The best-known painting in the church is *La Fuga in Egitto* (Flight to Egypt; 1522) by Bramantino. Also don't miss *Il Transporto al Sepolcro* by Antonio Ciseri (1821-91), with the haunting, mournful face of the central bearer. His silent grief comes across with all the greater intensity for being juxtaposed with the melodramatic swoonings of the women behind him (no matter if one of the women is Mary herself).

Something of a contrast in style are the many naive votive paintings by the church entrance, where the Madonna and Child appear as ghostly apparitions in life-and-death situations.

There is a frequent funicular from the town centre to the sanctuary (Sfr4.10 up, Sfr6 return), but the 20-minute walk up is not demanding (take Via al Sasso off Via Cappuccini). At least take the walk down, as you pass some ancient shrines on the way. On the Via Crucis route you're accompanied by the Stations of the Cross.

Old Town
Explore the Italianate piazzas and arcades, and admire the Lombardic houses. At one time the Piazza Grande curved around the actual shoreline of the lake. There are several interesting churches. The 17th century **Nuova Church** (Chiesa Nuova) on Via Cittadella, has an ornate ceiling complete with frolicking angels, and outside a giant St Christopher with disproportionately tiny feet. Peer into the decaying, arcaded courtyard adjoining the east side of the church. The **St Antonio Church** (Sant' Antonio) has paintings by Orelli, as does the **San Francesco Church** (San Francesco Chiesa).

Off Via Fr Rustica is the **Castello Visconti**, dating from the 15th century and now housing a museum with Roman and Bronze Age exhibits, and modern art (Sfr5, students Sfr3; open 10 am to noon and 2 to 5 pm Tuesday to Sunday). Locarno was believed to be a glass manufacturing town in Roman times, which accounts for the strong showing of glass artefacts in the museum.

Activities
From the sanctuary, a cable car flies up to **Cardada**, and thereafter a chair lift soars to **Cimetta** at 1672m. From either stop there are fine views and several walking trails, and the transport up runs year round.

Paragliding is possible up here, as is winter skiing – inquire at the tourist office.

Locarno's climate is perfect for strolls around the lake. Wisteria, mimosa, azaleas, camellias and magnolias bloom as early as March. **Giardini Jean Arp** (Jean Arp Gardens) is a small lakeside park off Lungolago Motta, where sculptures by the surrealist artist are scattered among the palm trees and tulips. It is free to swim in various convenient spots around the lake, though you have to pay Sfr6 (students Sfr4) at the Lido. Sailing is another popular activity; the tourist office has a list of hiring outlets.

International Film Festival
Locarno has hosted this festival since 1948 and it's now a major event, receiving more than 150,000 visitors. Cinemas are used during the day, but at night films are shown in the open-air on a giant screen in the Piazza Grande (admission Sfr20/25 for one/two films). It takes place over two weeks in August. Get advance information from the Festival Internazionale de Film (☎ 756 21 21), Via Luini 3, CH-6600 Locarno. Check out the Web site at www.pardo.ch.

Places to Stay
Ask the tourist office for the 'Hotels Special' leaflet, outlining discounts and benefits if you book six nights at participating two-star hotels (Sfr480/780 for single/double with own shower/WC). There are hotel boards with a free telephone at the train station and outside the tourist office.

Places to Stay – Budget
Camping *Delta Camping* (☎ 751 60 81) is very expensive at Sfr20 (Sfr30 in high season) minimum per site plus Sfr10 (Sfr17 per person. But it is a five-star site with copious facilities, and it's open from March to October.

Hostels The new SYHA *Palagiovani Hostel* (☎ 756 15 00, fax 756 15 01, Via Varenna 18), is about 500m west of Piazza Grande. There's a range of rooms and prices, starting at Sfr31 for dorms and

Sfr57/66 for singles/doubles. In low season prices reduce about 10% (30% for singles) and it's open year round. There's a garden, restaurant (three-course lunch/dinner for Sfr11.50) and bike rental for Sfr15 per day. Reception closes from 10 am to 3 pm.

There are also two non-SYHA hostels in the Old Town. *Pensione Città Vecchia* (☎/fax 751 45 54, ✉ cittavecchia@datacomm.ch, Via Toretta 13), is the best. Beds in varying-sized dorms (from three beds) are Sfr24, plus Sfr4.50 each if you require sheets or breakfast. Both are provided with the few singles/doubles at Sfr35 per person (hall showers). Check-in is from 1 to 9 pm and keys are available. It is open from 1 March to sometime in November; reserve ahead (by telephone is OK) at peak times.

Ostello Giaciglio (☎ 751 30 64, fax 752 38 37, Via B Rusca 7), is expensive at Sfr30 without breakfast in sometimes cramped dorms, but at least it has a kitchen and is open year-round. Inquire at Garni Sempione opposite for reception.

Hotels Opposite the station is *Garni Montaldi* (☎ 743 02 22, fax 743 54 06, Piazza Stazione). Modern singles/doubles with telephone and cable TV cost from Sfr60/120 with shower, Sfr98/180 with shower/WC, or Sfr55/100 without. It's particularly good value in the low season when they often give the best rooms for the lowest price (open year-round). Reception is also here for *Hotel Stazione*, an older building to the rear, which is closed from 1 November to 31 March. It has singles/doubles with shower for Sfr47/88.

Osteria Reginetta (☎/fax 752 35 53, ✉ reginetta.locarno@bluewin.ch, Via della Motta 8) has singles/doubles/triples for Sfr42 per person, or Sfr49 including breakfast. Rooms are cheerful and reasonably spacious, and there's a shower/WC on each floor (closed in winter).

Places to Stay – Mid-Range & Top End

Schlosshotel (☎ 751 23 61, fax 751 73 23, ✉ schlosshotel@ticino.com, Via B Rusca) in the Old Town, is a place with character

and a slightly regal air, in its own grounds with private parking. All rooms are different but have shower/WC and TV as standard. Prices start around Sfr96/156 and it's open from late March to early November.

Hotel Ristorante Zurigo (☎ 743 16 17, fax 743 43 15, Viale Verbano 9) offers comfortable accommodation by the lake. Gold-coloured metal bedsteads, tastefully arranged pictures and patterned tiled floors give the rooms some style. Prices start at Sfr91/126 for a single/double in winter, rising to Sfr150/188 in summer. All rooms have TV and private shower/WC, but rooms with a lake view are more expensive.

Hotel Arcadia al Lago (☎ 756 18 18, fax 756 18 28, ✉ treff-arcadia@swissonline.ch, Via Orelli 5) is a four-star family hotel overlooking the lake, open 1 March to mid-November. It has modern spacious rooms, all with large balcony, TV, private bathroom, mini bar, and telephone. Prices start at Sfr160/270 for single/double occupancy and there are larger apartments suitable for families. The hotel has a roof terrace and an outdoor swimming pool.

Places to Eat

Lake Maggiore yields many different varieties of fish, particularly perch (persico) and whitefish (corigone).

There is a *Coop* supermarket on Piazza Grande, with late opening till 9 pm on Thursday. Opposite is a Migros Hobby Centro, with the *De Gustibus* snack bar, open 9 am to 9 pm Monday to Saturday. It serves pizza slices (Sfr4), chips and other snacks. A branch of *Inova* awaits on Piazza Stazione, by the train station. See the Lugano entry for more on this buffet-style restaurant, which is open until 10 pm daily.

The place to go for fish specialities is *Ristorante Cittadella* (☎ 751 58 85, Via Cittadella 18) – its plush upstairs section serves little else. Main dishes are around Sfr35 to Sfr50, although downstairs you can also tuck into pizzas from Sfr12 (closed Sunday in summer). There are plenty of other places where you can eat cheaply and well on pizza and pasta, such as *La Carbonara* near the station, *Trattoria Campagna Ristorante*

TICINO

(Via Castelrotto) close to St Antonio Church, and *Lungolago* (see under Entertainment).

The *Locanda Visconti* restaurant of the Schlosshotel is atmospheric, with lunches and pasta for around Sfr15, and other main courses starting at around Sfr25 (closed Sunday). *Hotel Ristorante Zurigo* has a lakeside terrace and good food from Sfr16.50, with a couple of vegetarian choices. (See Places to Stay for both the above locations.)

For a gastronomic feast, where the food is served on sparkling silver salvers, go to *Ristorante Centenario* (☎ 743 82 22, Lungolago 17). It's one of the best restaurants in Ticino, but the prices might make you flavour its French cuisine with the salt of your own tears. The three-course menu costs Sfr52, multi-course evening menus are Sfr80 to Sfr130, and à-la-carte dishes are around Sfr40 to Sfr55. The restaurant is closed on Sunday and Monday.

Entertainment

Lungolago, on Lungolago Motta, is a popular evening drinking venue for youngish locals (beer Sfr3.50), and has pizzas from only Sfr10.50 and outside tables (open daily). *Bar Simba* nearby is similar, but with more posing youths and a disco feel. *Bar Cantina (Piazza Grande)* has a large selection of different wines stacked up on the shelves and cheap, simple meals at lunchtime. Early evening on Friday and Saturday (till 9 pm) live music of a dance-along accordion-based variety is played. It attracts a range of ages but particularly an older set, and somehow veers between the authentic and the excruciating. Wine costs from Sfr2.10 a glass.

The *Casinò Kursaal* by the tourist office offers a choice of theatre, cinema, gambling (Boule and slot machines) and drinking. Classical concerts are held at the Castello Visconti and the Sopra Cenerina conference centre on Piazza Grande, but especially in the atmospheric environment of the San Francesco church. The tourist office sells tickets for most venues.

Getting There & Away

There are trains every one to two hours from Brig, passing through Italy en route

(Swiss Pass valid). The cost is Sfr50 and it takes 2½ hours. It involves changing trains at Domodóssola across the border, so bring your passport.

Postbuses to the surrounding valleys leave from outside the train station, and boats (see the Lake Maggiore section following) from near Piazza Grande.

The St Gotthard pass provides the road link (N2) to central Switzerland. Hertz (☎ 743 50 50) is at Via Sempione 12.

Getting Around

At Piazza Grande there are street parking spaces (Sfr1, maximum 30 minutes) and an underground garage (Sfr24 for 24 hours). Local buses, including to Ascona, are run by Fart (that's the company name, not the means of propulsion). Single trips cost Sfr2.40 or more, or it's Sfr6.60 for a regional day pass. The Swiss Pass is valid.

AROUND LOCARNO
Lake Maggiore

Only the north-east corner of Lake Maggiore is in Switzerland; the rest slices into the Lombardy region of Italy. Navigazione Lago Maggiore (NLM; ☎ 751 18 65) operates boats across the whole lake. Limited day passes cost Sfr11, but the Sfr20 version (Sfr16 for people over 60) is valid for all the Swiss basin, and is also available for seven days (Sfr50). The Sfr33 pass (Sfr72 for seven days) covers the Italian section too. Boats sail from one week before Easter until the penultimate Sunday in October, though there are special services during March to Italy, eg, to the Wednesday market in Luino (Sfr23 return from Locarno) and the Sunday market in Cannobio (Sfr21 return).

In addition to the steamers, hydrofoils (reservations compulsory, Sfr3 each way) also go to the Italian resorts. Services extend as far as Arona (Sfr33 day return) in the south, where there's an antiques market on the third Sunday of each month. The only car ferry across the lake is in Italy, from Intra to Laveno. The Swiss Pass is not valid on any boats. NLM produces a free brochure in English describing all the Swiss and Italian lakeside resorts.

South-west of Ascona are the **Isles of Brissago**, famous for the botanical gardens (Sfr6, closed in winter) where subtropical flora thrive. By boat, Ascona to the isles is fr11 return. **Ronco**, beautifully situated opposite the isles, is a great drive from Locarno. The trip by Fart bus (No 21) takes 20 minutes. This region is best known for cigar manufacturing. Ask the local tourist office (☎ 793 11 70) about free tours of the cigar factory in nearby Brissago.

Ascona

Ascona is Locarno's smaller twin on the opposite side of the delta of the Maggiore River. The village is known as a centre for arts, and the backstreets are filled with art galleries and craft shops. The beginning of the century saw the arrival of 'back to nature' utopians and anarchists, and the aspirations of this movement is the subject of the **Casa Anatta Museum** on Monte Verità take the small 'Buxi' bus from the post office, Sfr1). It's open every afternoon except Monday from April to October (Sfr6, students/seniors Sfr4).

Museo comunale d'arte moderna in the Palazzo Pancaldi, Via Borgo 34, includes paintings by artists connected with the town, among them Paul Klee, Hans Arp, Ben Nicholson and Alexej Jawlensky. The museum is open 10 am to noon and 3 to 6 pm Tuesday to Saturday, 4 to 6 pm Sunday, and entry costs Sfr5.

For 55 years Ascona has hosted **Settimane Musicali**, an international classical music festival lasting from the end of August to mid-October. It also has **New Orleans Jazz** at the end of June where musicians play from several open-air stages (free during the day, Sfr8 general entry per night).

The Ascona tourist office (☎ 791 00 90, fax 792 10 08, @ ascona@etim.ch), Casa Serodine, is by the church tower near the waterfront. Usual opening hours are 9 am to 6 pm weekdays and to 4 pm Saturday, though they vary with demand.

Places to Stay & Eat The waterfront is one long parade of mid-price hotels and restaurants with outside tables. *Al Porto* (☎ 785 85 85, fax 785 85 86, @ info@alporto-hotel.ch), on Piazza Giuseppe Motta, is typical of these, with singles/doubles from Sfr102/206, some with lake view and balcony. Rooms have bathroom, TV and telephone, and are located in four different buildings. The restaurant is closed on Wednesday in winter and has outside tables and meals for Sfr16.50 to Sfr50, encompassing pasta, meat, fish and vegetarian choices.

There are few budget options. Via Borgo, connecting the post office to the lake, has a couple of pizzerias, while **Verbano Ristorante** (☎ 791 12 74, Via Borgo 19), has affordable meals and some singles/doubles using hall shower for Sfr45/90. *Garni Silvia* (☎ 35 13 14, Via Circonvallazione 7) has large, fresh rooms with hall showers, though they're slightly more expensive (closed January and February). Down the road towards the post office is a *Coop* supermarket.

Getting There & Away Take bus No 31 from Locarno's train station or Piazza Grande; it stops at Ascona post office with departures every 15 minutes (Sfr2.40). Boat services on Lake Maggiore stop at Ascona.

Northern Valleys

The two valleys north of Locarno are dead-ends, but they make enjoyable day trips and allow you to explore areas relatively untainted by tourism. Take refreshment in rustic *grotti* (country inns). Both the Mággia and Verzasca valleys can be visited on a weekly tour (Sfr39) from April to October; reserve at the Locarno tourist office.

All these northern valleys proffer scenic delights, although the minor road winding over the San Bernardino is perhaps the most spectacular (closed from November to May). The motorway is open year-round.

Maggia Valley

Valle Mággia follows the Maggia River, passing small villages, until at Cevio it splits, the first of many divisions into smaller valleys. Take the left branch then a right into the valley that terminates at **Bosco Gurin**. This village was settled by folk from the Valais in the 12th century, and it is the only place in Ticino where German is the principal language spoken. Fart bus No 10 runs hourly from Locarno to Cevio (takes 50 minutes), but the postbus is less frequent for the 50-minute trip on to Bosco Gurin. The total same day return fare is Sfr30; if you stay overnight the fare leaps to Sfr44.40.

Baracca Backpacker (☎ 207 15 54, Aurigeno) has a three-bed dorm and a seven-bed dorm, plus a kitchen, garden and other amenities. The charge is Sfr22 (own sleeping bag needed) and it's open from 1 April to 31 October. Get off bus No 10 at Ronchini and follow the signs.

Verzasca Valley
Val Verzasca is wilder and less developed than Valle Mággia. It's the site for the thrilling 'Golden-Eye' bungy-jump; if you want to give it a try contact Trekking Team (☎ 01-950 33 88). Its Web site is at www.trekking.ch.

Lavertezzo is a good place to take a dip in the river. **Brione**, where the valley forks, has a castle and a 14th century church. The right-hand fork goes to **Sonogno**, noted for its simple, stone-built houses. Postbuses run

from Locarno only every two hours or so the journey takes 70 minutes and cost Sfr32 return.

Cento Valley
Centovalli (literally 'a hundred valleys') heading west, is the route to Domodóssola in Italy. At **Rè**, on the Italian side, there is procession of pilgrims on 30 April each year, a tradition that originated after a painting of the Madonna was reported to star bleeding upon being struck by a ball.

Leventina Valley
From Bellinzona, the Valle Leventina is the rail and road route to Andermatt and Zürich. There is the choice of taking the motorway (N2/E35) or a smaller parallel road. En route, the town of **Biasca** has a 12th century Romanesque church with a tall belfry and some fading frescoes. At Biasca, the valley splits: Val Blenio is the route to Disentis, or the Vorderrhein.

Mesolcina Valley
North-east of Bellinzona is the Valle Mesolcina, leading to the San Bernardino Pass and the Hinterrhein. Again, there is a choice of taking a motorway (N13/E43) or smaller road (highway 13).

Graubünden

nce upon a time, tourists in Switzerland
ere a summer phenomenon. Then in 1864,
ohannes Badrutt, the owner of the En-
adiner Kulm Hotel in St Moritz, offered
ur English summer guests free accommo-
ation if they returned for the winter. He
old them they were missing the best time of
ne year. Although dubious, the English
ere unable to refuse a free offer. They re-
urned, enjoyed themselves, and winter
ourism was born.

Today Graubünden (Grisons, Grigioni,
rishun) has some of the most developed
nd best known winter sports centres in the
vorld, including Arosa, Davos, Klosters,
lims and, of course, St Moritz. Tourism is a
najor earner for the canton; around 50% of
ne population is directly or indirectly em-
loyed in the sector, and it accounts for 20%
f overnight stays in Switzerland as a whole.

Away from the international resorts,
iraubünden is a relatively unspoiled region
f rural villages, Alpine lakes and mountain
istas. In addition to tourism, the generation
f hydro-electric power is important to the
ocal economy.

In medieval times the region was known
s Rhaetia, and was loosely bound together
y an association of three leagues. The mod-
rn name for the canton was derived from
ne *Grauer Bund*, or Grey League. Conquest
f the area by an outsider was virtually im-
ossible because of the mountainous terrain
221 separate communities were scattered
vithin 150 distinct valleys. Graubünden
oined the Swiss Confederation in 1803.

Orientation & Information

iraubünden is the largest Swiss canton,
overing an area of 7106 sq km, ranging in
ltitude from 270m (Misox) to 4049m (Piz
ernina). There are two major rivers in this
anton; the Rhine and the Inn. The Alps
over most of the terrain, accounting for the
ict that it is also the most sparsely popu-
ited canton, with a mere 26 inhabitants per
quare kilometre. The Septimber Pass,

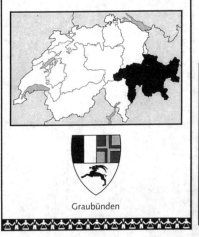

Graubünden

Julier Pass and Maloja Pass are transit
routes through the Alps that have been important since Roman times.

Chur is the cantonal capital, and has the
tourist office headquarters, Graubünden
Ferien (☎ 254 24 24, fax 254 24 00,
🝔 contact@graubuenden.ch), 2nd floor,
Alexanderstrasse 24, with information on
the whole canton. The office is in the building marked 'Publicitas', near the train station, and information is dispensed from 8
am to 6 pm weekdays (personal callers

GRAUBÜNDEN

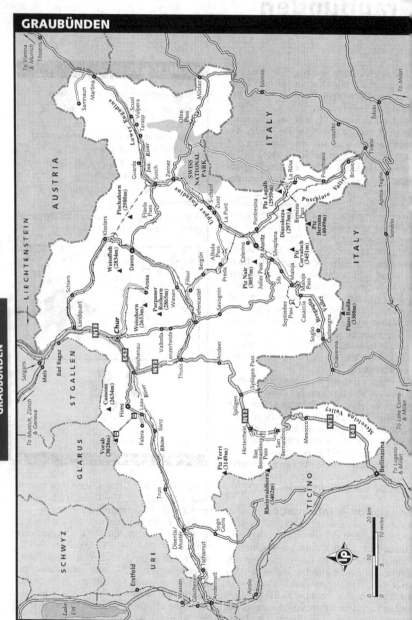

GRAUBÜNDEN

welcome) and from 8 am to 5 pm weekends (telephone inquiries only). Another Graubünden tourist office open the same hours is in the Heidiland motorway service station on the N13 autobahn, north of Chur in the Marienfeld/Fläsch area.

Holiday apartments abound in Graubünden and are often better value than hotels and pensions. A minimum stay of one week (Saturday to Saturday) is normal and they generally need to be booked well in advance. Tourist offices compile lists of these, and can inform you about an even cheaper option – private rooms.

Language
The extent to which the mountains have dominated and isolated the region can be heard in the language. In the north (around Chur and Davos) the people speak German, in the south, Italian, and in between (St Moritz, Lower Engadine, Vorderrhein Valley) mostly Romansch. Yet even between neighbouring valleys there can be significant linguistic differences. Take the word 'cup' as an example. In German it's *Tasse*, Italian it's *tazza* and Romansch it's *cuppina*. None of these words for cup are used in the Hinterrhein Valley (where they say *scariola)*, the Albula Valley *(cuppegn)* or the Müstair Valley *(cupina)*.

The use of Romansch is gradually in decline and linguists fear it may disappear altogether, despite efforts to preserve it. Already, German speakers account for 65% of the Graubünden population, with Romansch down to 17%.

When to Go
Most of the Alpine resorts mentioned in this chapter virtually close down in May and November and for one or two weeks either side. It's a good time to go if you hate crowds and just want to do a lot of walking, but bear in mind that most if not all of the cable cars will be shut down. Tourist offices will be able to provide exact running times. There will always be a fair selection of restaurants and hotels still open, and the restaurants you find are likely to be pretty good, as they're the ones that can attract the

local trade. Hotels may be prepared to negotiate on rates.

Peak season is approximately Christmas to the end of February, and July and August.

Activities
Museums and galleries are not the main reason to visit Graubünden. Instead, it is the majestic scenery and outdoor activities that attract visitors. There are 10,500km of walking trails, 1500km of ski slopes and 870km of cross-country ski trails. There's a famous 5km toboggan run on the Albula Pass from Preda to Bergün (with one-way toboggan rental).

Graubünden has more than 600 lakes, and those offering the greatest choice of water sports are the lakes at Lenzerheide-Valbella, St Moritz, Sils/Maloja and Silvaplana. All these lakes have sailing schools. Expect to pay about Sfr40/80 an hour for sailing boat rental/lessons. Three days (nine hours) tuition at a windsurfing school is around Sfr240 (including equipment), or one hour's board and wet suit rental is about Sfr20. Motorboats are forbidden on all of Graubünden's lakes and rivers.

Getting Around
Public Transport Graubünden has a regional transport pass issued between 1 May and 31 October and valid for 15 days. It is good for a 50% discount on main transport routes throughout the region (extending to Bellinzona, Andermatt and Samnaun) for the duration of the pass, and for free travel in five days on selected lines, encompassing Tirano (in Italy), St Moritz, Scuol, Davos, Arosa, Disentis/Mustér and Chur. The price is Sfr140 in 2nd class (Sfr120 with Swiss railpasses) and Sfr215 (Sfr180) in 1st class. The version giving three free days in seven costs Sfr105 (Sfr85) in 2nd class and Sfr170 (Sfr140) in 1st class. Buy them from stations of the Rhätische Railway or Graubünden post offices.

The Regionalpass Plus is a superior version. Though prices are around 25% to 30% higher it's definitely better value, as 36

GRAUBÜNDEN

cable cars are included (free on three or five days, 50% off on the other days). You also get postbus routes free on three or five days, instead of only at 50% off.

Car & Motorcycle Motorways barely invade Graubünden's territory, but the roads are excellent given the difficulties of the terrain. There are three main passes from northern Graubünden to the southern valleys of Bregaglia and Engadine; from west to east they are: Julier (open year-round), Albula (summer only) and Flüela (year-round, but may close in bad weather). These approximately correspond to three exit points into Italy: Maloja, Bernina and Fuorn/Ofen (all open year-round). The Oberalp Pass, the route west to Andermatt, is closed in winter but, as at Albula, there is the option of taking the car-carrying train instead. It is advisable to carry snow chains in winter.

Chur

☎ 081 • pop 33,500 • elevation 585m
Chur (pronounced *khoor*, which has a rasping, throat-clearing sound) is the canton's capital and largest town, yet has a very compact centre. It has been continuously inhabited since 3000 BC. The city was virtually destroyed by fire in 1464, and German-speaking artisans poured in to carry out the rebuilding. They transformed the linguistic landscape too, for the city had previously been Romansch-speaking.

Orientation & Information
The train station has luggage lockers, bike rental and money-exchange counters (7 am to 8 pm daily). The main post office (Hauptpost, 7001) is by the train station. Five minutes' walk away is Postplatz, where there's another post office (7002) and, 120m down the road, the tourist office (☎ 252 18 18, fax 252 90 76, @ info@churtourismus.ch), Grabenstrasse 5. It's open 1.30 to 6 pm Monday, 8.30 am to noon and 1.30 to 6 pm Tuesday to Friday, and 9 am to noon Saturday. Pick up a free copy of the two walking

tours of the mostly pedestrian-only Old Town, which lies immediately to the south. The office makes hotel reservations (no commission) and has free small maps, or better ones for Sfr3.

Many shops in the centre stay open to 9 pm on Friday nights. SSR (☎ 252 97 76), the budget travel agency, is at Untere Gasse. Nearby on Grabenstrasse is Malteser's Wäsch-Egga, a self-service laundry with English instructions, open 9 am (noon on Sunday) to midnight daily. It costs from Sfr6 to wash and Sfr3 to dry. Rampa (☎ 284 89 28), Tittwiesenstrasse 60, is a computer shop with Internet access, but it's inconveniently situated north of the station.

Things to See & Do
Chur has an attractive Old Town with 16th century buildings, fountains and alleyways. Follow the faded green and red footprints on the pavement that correspond to the tourist office walking tours. Arcas (on the green walking route) is a photogenic square with a church spire rising in the background.

Augusto Giacometti designed three of the windows in the 1491 **Church of St Martin**. By the church is the **Rätisches Museum**, Hofstrasse 1, displaying a standard provincial collection relating to local history, furniture, crafts and costumes, although the odd Egyptian sarcophagus is an unexpected addition (German signs only). It is open 10 am to noon and 2 to 5 pm Tuesday to Sunday, and admission costs Sfr5 (students Sfr2.50).

In the impressive **Cathedral**, built from 1150, are a number of interesting features, including the carved heads on the choir stalls. The particularly fine **high altar**, made by Jakob Russ from 1486–92, is the largest Gothic triptych in Switzerland. It's just a pity that it's so dark and distant that you can't appreciate it properly. (There are two tiers of alarms to keep you away.) The crypt contains valuable religious reliquaries from the Middle Ages. It can be viewed 10 am to noon and 2 to 4 pm Monday to Saturday, but you need to get the key from the 1st floor of Hofstrasse 2.

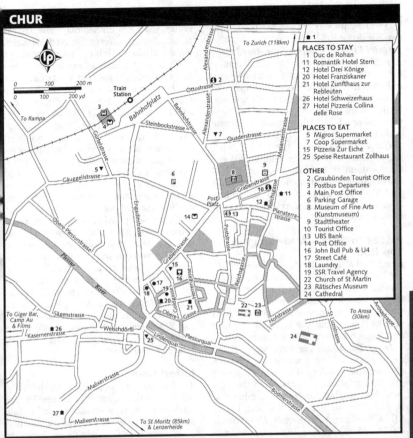

CHUR

PLACES TO STAY
1 Duc de Rohan
11 Romantik Hotel Stern
12 Hotel Drei Könige
20 Hotel Franziskaner
21 Hotel Zunfthaus zur Rebleuten
26 Hotel Schweizerhaus
27 Hotel Pizzeria Collina delle Rose

PLACES TO EAT
5 Migros Supermarket
5 Coop Supermarket
15 Pizzeria Zur Eiche
25 Speise Restaurant Zollhaus

OTHER
2 Graubünden Tourist Office
3 Postbus Departures
4 Main Post Office
6 Parking Garage
8 Museum of Fine Arts (Kunstmuseum)
9 Stadttheater
10 Tourist Office
13 UBS Bank
14 Post Office
16 John Bull Pub & U4
17 Street Café
18 Laundry
19 SSR Travel Agency
22 Church of St Martin
23 Rätisches Museum
24 Cathedral

The **Museum of Fine Arts** (Kunstmuseum) on Postplatz contains modern art, including a generous gathering of work by the three Giacomettis: Alberto, Augusto and Giovanni. Note also the sci-fi designs by local artist, HR Giger. If you think the style bears some resemblance to the monster in the film *Alien*, you're right – that beastie with its metallic grin was his brainchild. If you like his stuff, check out his bar (see the following Entertainment section). Entry to the museum costs around Sfr6 to Sfr10 depending on special exhibitions (reductions for students and seniors). It's open the same

hours as the Rätisches Museum, except for late opening (8 pm) on Thursday.

To enjoy indoor or outdoor swimming, tennis and ice skating, look to the **Obere Au Sportzentrum** (☎ 254 42 88), to the northwest of town (take bus No 2).

Places to Stay – Budget

Camp Au (☎ 284 22 83), by the sports centre, costs Sfr7.20 per person and from Sfr6.20 for a tent. It is open year-round.

Hotel Schweizerhaus (☎ 252 10 96, fax 252 27 31, Kasernenstrasse 10) is a recently renovated bar and restaurant. It has dorms for Sfr30, and singles/doubles for Sfr55/110 with shower and Sfr40/80 without. Breakfast is Sfr5.

Hotel Pizzeria Collina delle Rose (☎/fax 252 23 88, Malixerstrasse 32), five minutes' walk uphill from town and also known as Rosenhügel, has rooms with shower and TV from Sfr70/130, or Sfr45/90 without. Its restaurant (closed Monday) serves good pizzas from Sfr12.50, and there's ample parking.

Hotel Franziskaner (☎ 252 12 61, Kupfergasse 18), in the Old Town, has singles/doubles for Sfr60/100 using hall shower, doubles with shower and toilet for Sfr120, and an inexpensive restaurant. Prices may change once extensive renovations are completed.

Places to Stay – Mid-Range & Top End

Hotel Drei Könige (☎ 252 17 25, fax 252 17 26, Reichsgasse 18) has lots of art on the corridors and in the rooms, and an atmospheric bar/cafe. Singles/doubles with TV start from Sfr85/130 with shower/WC or Sfr65/100 without. Garage parking is available and it also stages occasional folk and jazz concerts.

Hotel Zunfthaus zur Rebleuten (☎ 252 13 57, fax 257 13 58, Kupfergasse 1), is in a 500-year-old building. The rooms are simpler than might be expected from the frescoed frontage, but they're reasonable value at Sfr85/165 with shower/WC and TV, or Sfr40/80 without. *Romantik Hotel Stern (☎ 252 35 55, fax 252 19 15, Reichsgasse 11)* – with a name like that it also inspires certain expectations – is infused throughout with the fresh scent of Arve pine. All rooms have shower/WC and TV and start at Sfr105/195. Parking is free in the courtyard.

Duc de Rohan (☎ 252 10 22, fax 252 45 37, ✉ ducderohan@gr-net.ch, Masanserstrasse 44) is showing its age, but has a swimming pool and sauna among its facilities. Rooms with shower/WC and TV start at Sfr80/140.

Places to Eat

There is a *Coop* supermarket and self-service restaurant on Alexanderstrasse, open to 6.30 pm Monday to Thursday, 9 pm on Friday and 5 pm on Saturday. The *Migros* on Gürtelstrasse offers a similar deal (except without alcohol) and is open the same hours.

There are a couple of pizzerias side-by-side on Grabenstrasse. Prices start at Sfr11 and both have outside seating. *Trattoria da Gabriele* is closed Sunday. *Pizzeria Zur Eiche* is open daily and also serves Röstis.

Speise Restaurant Zollhaus (Malixerstrasse 1) has two parts (open daily). Bierschwemme is the downstairs bar and serves meals and lunch specials for around Sfr12. Upstairs is the calmer and more cultured Bündnerstube, where there's a larger range of meals and prices (from Sfr12.50), including a section for Chinese food.

For well-prepared regional food in rustic surroundings, go to *Hotel Stern* (see Places to Stay). Main dishes are around Sfr18 to Sfr40, or you can splash out on the seven-course Bündner menu at Sfr152 for two. Lunchtime eating is cheaper, with three menus (one vegetarian) from Sfr17 including soup (open daily). Also good is the atmospheric restaurant in *Hotel Zunfthaus zur Rebleuten* (see Places to Stay), with a range of prices starting at around Sfr16.50 (closed Tuesday until 5 pm).

Entertainment

The *Stadttheater* is opposite the tourist office, which sells tickets for most events. Theatre productions are very occasionally in English, and a variety of musical events are staged.

A lively area for nightlife is Goldgasse and Untere Gasse. There are several bars with loud taped music and dancing, including *U4*. Part of the same building is *John Bull*, which has an entrance on Grabenstrasse; a young crowd turns out to play table football and video games. *Street Café (Grabenstrasse)* has a vivid and arty interior. These bars in the city centre close at midnight, though if you walk just a few minutes to Welschdörfli, there are a couple of dancing bars that open later.

Farther west, by the Agip stop (bus No 1 or the Flims postbus), are a couple more discos, *P1* and *Planet Sound* (entry fee on weekends). Also here is the silver and black

Giger Bar (*Comercialstrasse 23*), tucked behind the Migros Hobby Center. The place is owned by the artist HR Giger and is a must for anyone interested in sci-fi themes. The decor makes it look like something out of a space movie. You half expect those skeletal chairs that curve above your head to ingest you at any moment. Photography is not allowed. Beers (0.3L) cost Sfr3.50 and it's open 8 am to midnight daily except Sunday.

Getting There & Away
There are rail connections to Davos, Klosters and Arosa, and fast trains to Sargans (the station for Liechtenstein, only 22 minutes away) and Zürich (85 minutes, Sfr38). Chur can be visited on the Glacier Express route (see Getting There & Away in the St Moritz section). Postbuses leave from the new terminus above the train station, including the express service to Bellinzona (advance reservations essential on ☎ 256 31 66). Graubünden's one motorway, the N13 (E43), goes north from Chur to Zürich and Lake Constance.

Car Rental Avis (☎ 252 39 73) is at Kalchbühlstrasse 12, and Hertz (☎ 252 32 22) is at Kasernenstrasse 88.

Getting Around
Bahnhofplatz is the hub for all local buses, which cost Sfr2.20 per journey. At around 8 pm routes combine and services are less frequent, though there's the option of taking postbuses instead.

The old centre is mostly pedestrian-only. For parking, look for signs for several parking garages on the edge of the old quarter (eg, on Gäuggelistrasse).

Around Chur

Chur is within easy reach of several ski areas.

LENZERHEIDE & VALBELLA
☎ 081 • elevations 1470m & 1540m
These linked resorts are beautifully situated on either side of Heidsee lake, with surrounding woodland and soaring peaks.

Relatively few foreign visitors make it here, but it's a great place for relaxation and sports. It offers a quiet nightlife, and skiing mainly geared towards beginners and intermediates. A one-day ski pass costs Sfr52 for adults, Sfr42 for youths and seniors or Sfr31 for children, all with off-peak reductions.

The Parpaner Rothorn (2865m) is the highest point that can be reached by cable car, and has several walking trails radiating from the summit. Contact the Lenzerheide tourist office (☎ 385 11 20, fax 385 11 21, @ Lenzerheide@spin.ch) for more information. Its Web site is at www.lenzerheide.ch. There is a SYHA *hostel* (☎ 384 12 08, fax 384 45 58, Voa Sartons 41), but it's 30 minutes' walk from the Valbella bus stop and closed in the off season.

Getting There & Away
Either resort is easily reached by hourly bus from Chur (Sfr9.40, 40 minutes). They're on highway 3, the route from Chur to St Moritz that goes over the Julier Pass.

FLIMS
☎ 081 • pop 2380 • elevation 1100m
This well-established ski resort is favoured more by the Swiss than by foreign visitors.

Orientation & Information
Flims has two sections, about 1km apart. Except where noted, all the places mentioned are on the main road connecting the two. Flims Dorf is larger, more residential, and slightly closer to the ski lifts. Flims Waldhaus is flanked by woodland and has most of the hotels. It also has the tourist office (☎ 920 92 02, fax 920 92 01, @ contact@alpenarena.ch), open 9 am to noon and 1 to 6 pm Monday to Friday, and 9 am to noon Saturday; in high season also Saturday afternoon and Sunday morning. Postbuses stop at the tourist office, and at the post office (7017) in Flims Dorf.

Activities
Skiing The 'White Arena' skiing area covers Flims, Laax and Falera (225km of runs). Skiing is mostly intermediate or easy

GRAUBÜNDEN

and extends as high as 3000m. A one-day ski pass includes ski buses and costs Sfr54 (Sfr5 supplement on weekends and holidays, reduction in low season). There are 60km of cross-country skiing trails.

Hiking In summer, the hiking network covers 200km, including to the Rhine Gorge (dubbed the Swiss Grand Canyon). At the summit of the Cassons there is a circular walking route, the *Naturlehrpfad*, that yields delights of flora, fauna and geology. It takes around 2½ hours to complete the circuit; take the chair lift then cable car from Flims to Cassonsgrat (Sfr32 one way or return). Even in winter there are 60km of footpaths.

River Rafting The mighty Rhine River (Rhein in German) has two sources, both in Graubünden: the Vorderrhein and the Hinterrhein. River-rafting is fast and furious on the 17km stretch of the Vorderrhein between Ilanz and Reichenau. In summer, Swissraft (☎ 911 52 50, fax 911 30 90) in Flims Waldhaus offers half/full-day rafting for Sfr99/143. The price includes transfers to/from Flims – useful as there's no direct transport. Its Web site is at www .swissraft.ch.

Other Activities Swissraft also offers canyoning, mountain biking, hot-air balloon trips and passenger paragliding flights. The nearest lake for summer swimming and boat hire is Caumasee. For fishing in the Rhine and Caumasee, get a permit from the tourist office.

Places to Stay

There's a Guest Card for staying in the resort. Hotel boards with free telephone are outside the tourist office and the Dorf post office. Camp at *Prau* (☎ 911 15 75), five minutes' walk from the tourist office towards Laax. It is open year-round.

The cheapest beds are at *Backpacker Hotel Gutveina* (☎/fax 911 29 03, *gutveina@spin.ch, Via Gutveina*), just off the main road between Waldhaus and Dorf. It's an oldish, unrenovated house with a relaxed atmosphere, kitchen, TV room kitted

out with aeroplane seats, and garden. Dorms are Sfr29 without sheets, and singles/ doubles are Sfr40/70. Breakfast is Sfr6, check-in is from 5 pm (6 pm in summer) and there's a daytime lock-out.

An excellent and inexpensive choice is *Guardaval* (☎ 911 11 19, fax 911 11 79) in Waldhaus. The rooms are a good size, many with a balcony, and staff are solicitous. Parking is ample. Singles/doubles start at Sfr65/110 with private shower or singles using a hall shower are Sfr45; add about Sfr10/20 in winter.

Hotel Vorab (☎ 911 18 61, fax 911 42 29 *flimsvorab@bluewin.ch*) is a convenient three-star hotel opposite Dorf post office. Rooms with shower/WC, TV and sometimes balcony start at Sfr108/176 (Sfr75/140 in summer).

Places to Eat

There are supermarkets in both Dorf and Waldhaus. The *Hotel Albana*, by the Cassons chair lift, has an inexpensive but comfortable restaurant on the 1st floor, with a sun terrace. The Tagesteller (with starter) costs Sfr17.50 and pizzas start at Sfr12.50. Pizza/pasta is slightly pricier at *Pomodoro* in Waldhaus.

Between Dorf and Waldhaus is *Grischuna*, serving a three-course daily menu for Sfr20 and regional specialities for Sfr22 to Sfr40 (closed Monday in summer). It has rooms as well but they are rather cramped for the price.

Hotel Vorab (see Places to Stay) has two restaurants, providing a range of vegetarian, Italian and mid-price meals.

Getting There & Away

Flims is not on a train route (the nearest stations are Reichenau and Ilanz). Postbuses run to Flims and the other villages in the White Arena area hourly from Chur (Sfr11.80 to Flims Waldhaus, 40 minutes).

AROSA

☎ 081 • pop 2600 • elevation 1800m

Arosa is a relaxing resort at 1800m, spread out in the Schanfigg Valley amid lakes and woodland.

Orientation & Information

Arosa has two parts: Ausserarosa (Outer Arosa) is the main resort and Innerarosa is the older section of the village. Ausserarosa is grouped around the shores of Obersee at the train terminus. The train station has money-exchange counters, luggage storage and bike rental.

From Oberseeplatz, take Poststrasse, heading uphill in the direction of Inner-arosa. Within five minutes you'll reach the tourist office (☎ 378 70 20, fax 378 70 21, 🖃 arosa@arosa.ch), open in summer 8 am to noon and 2 to 6 pm Monday to Friday, 9 am to 1 pm (and also 2 to 4 pm July to mid-August) Saturday. Winter hours are 9 am to 6 pm Monday to Friday, 9 am to 5.30 pm Saturday, and 4 to 6.30 pm Sunday. Buses in the resort are free; they stop at 7 pm, after which in winter you can take the 'night express' (Sfr3) until 2 am. Car drivers should note that there is a traffic ban from midnight to 6 am.

The main post office (7050) is at Oberseeplatz.

Activities

Arosa has over 70km of **skiing** for mixed abilities based on three main mountains. In particular, beginners have a good choice of runs, and the ski school can be contacted on ☎ 377 11 50. The highest skiing point is the Weisshorn at 2653m. Ski passes cost Sfr50 for one day and Sfr256 for one week (senior/youth reductions). In addition to cross-country skiing, Arosa features several ice skating rinks (natural and artificial), curling and tobogganing (from Tschuggen down to the village). Hot-air balloon flights (☎ 391 37 14) cost from Sfr340 per person.

In the summer, there is a free bathing beach at **Untersee**. The larger **Obersee** is used for rowing boats and pedalos (Sfr12 to Sfr17 per hour). Permits for trout fishing in both lakes can be obtained from the tourist office.

Arosa has 200km of maintained **hiking** trails, with good options even in winter. The walk up to Weisshorn from the village takes about 3½ hours and the panorama attained is extensive and elevating (viewing table).

The cable car costs Sfr24 or Sfr30 return (no reduction with Eurail or Inter-Rail), but you could consider buying the seven-day general hiking pass for Sfr60. Reserve in advance at the tourist office for the guided nature observation walk (Sfr10).

Other activities include horse riding, tennis and golf (nine-hole course).

Places to Stay – Budget

The *camp site* (☎ 377 17 45) is in a quiet location on the edge of the village, down from the tourist office. It is open year-round and costs Sfr8.30 per adult, Sfr4.50 for a tent and Sfr2.50 for a car.

For the SYHA *hostel* (☎/fax 377 13 97, Seewaldstrasse) from the tourist office, head uphill then take the first left. Like many hotels, it is closed from mid-April to mid-June and from mid-October to mid-December. Dorms cost Sfr26 (B&B) in summer and Sfr38 (half-board) in winter. Half-board prices for double rooms are Sfr96 (twin or bunk beds). The reception is closed from 10 am to 5 pm but there's daytime access. Get a key for late entry.

Hotels & Pensions Many hotels and pensions have a surcharge for short stays (one or two nights), particularly in winter. *Bellaval* (☎ 378 84 84, fax 378 84 48), next to and run by the Weisshorn cable car, has dorms; inquire about bargain deals in combination with a ski or hiking pass. *Suveran* (☎ 377 19 69, fax 377 19 75) is a small wooden chalet on the edge of the woods, above the Catholic church. Simple but good-value rooms using hall showers are Sfr44/78 in summer and Sfr55/100 in winter; add Sfr10 for short stays.

Pension Daheim (☎ 377 50 79), just off the main road and towards Innerarosa, is small scale, old fashioned and homey. Rooms with half-board are only Sfr58/116 in summer, Sfr68/136 in winter. There's a bathroom on each floor. *Lindemann's Garni* (☎ 377 50 79, fax 377 34 39, Oberseeplatz), above Denner, is convenient and affordable, charging Sfr95/170 for singles/doubles with shower or Sfr90/160 without. Summer prices start at Sfr55/90.

GRAUBÜNDEN

Hotel Touring (☎ *377 31 21, fax 377 24 86),* near the tourist office, has average rooms with shower/WC, some with TV and communal balcony, and good dinners (Sfr20 extra). Prices are Sfr58 per person in the summer and Sfr98 in the winter.

Places to Stay – Mid-Range & Top End

Hotel Alpensonne (☎ *377 15 47 fax 377 34 70,* @ *alpensonne@swissonline.ch)* is up the hill not far from the Brüggli lifts. The rooms are reasonably spacious, with private shower/WC and TV, and the south-facing ones have a big balcony with a fine view. Prices for half-board start at Sfr98/186 in summer and Sfr160/290 in winter. *Hotel Obersee* (☎ *377 12 16, fax 377 45 66)* has comparable rooms and a good location by Obersee, anticlockwise from the train station. Its B&B prices start at Sfr85/140 in summer, Sfr123/188 in winter. Dinner is Sfr35. *Posthotel* (☎ *377 01 21, fax 377 40 43),* is a well-equipped four-star place right by the train station, with its own parking. Rooms with half-board start at Sfr110/220 in summer and Sfr170/340 in winter.

Places to Eat

There's a *Denner* supermarket near the train station and a *Coop* by the tourist office. Between the tourist office and Oberseeplatz is the *Café-Restaurant Oasis,* where you can get simple but tasty meals from Sfr10. It closes at 7 pm and all day Tuesday, except in the winter season when it's open to 11 pm daily.

Opposite is the alcohol-free *Orelli's Restaurant,* offering good vegetarian dishes for around Sfr15 and a salad buffet for Sfr7.50 to Sfr11.50 per plate. It has a wide selection of other meals (including children's menus) between Sfr12 and Sfr25, and it's open 7.30 am to 9 pm daily. Rooms with shower and TV are also available. A little up the hill is *Quellenhof,* where there's a decent restaurant with meals for a range of prices (closed Sunday evening and Monday in the off season).

By the Obersee, anticlockwise from Oberseeplatz, is the *Hotel Carmenna,*

which has a pizzeria open in winter only from 5 pm (pizzas from Sfr12.50), and another inexpensive restaurant with a sun terrace open during the day, including in summer. There's also a fondue Stübli.

Also worth considering is the restaurant at *Alpensonne* (see Places to Stay), where meals cost about Sfr15 to Sfr45. There's a four-course evening menu for around Sfr40. *Hotel Anita* (☎ *377 11 09),* near the Catholic church, has a quality restaurant that's closed in summer.

Entertainment

The tourist office has lists of daily events. The village church is the site for occasional concerts. The *Casino* by the tourist office has gambling and games, as well as a restaurant, cinema and nightclub. *Hotel Carmenna* (see Places to Eat) has live piano music in the bar in the evening during the season.

Getting There & Away

The only way to get here is from Chur; take the narrow-gauge train from in front of the train station (Sfr11.80 each way). Departures are hourly and the trip takes an hour. It's a winding, very scenic journey with views of mountains, pine trees, streams and bridges (sit on the right). The road follows the same route. Snow chains are recommended in winter.

Davos

☎ 081 • pop 13,300 • elevation 1560m
Originally known as a health resort, Davos is simply one of the best skiing areas in the world. It includes the legendary Parsenn-Weissfluh area, where ski runs descend up to 2000m.

Orientation & Information

Davos, too large to have a ski village atmosphere, is a 4km-long conurbation stretched beside the train line and the Landwasser River. It comprises two contiguous areas each with its own train station: Davos Platz and Davos Dorf. Both stations have

Crans-Montana area

Mountain village of Zermatt

The hills are alive in the Valais region

Mountaineers flock to Zermatt, and some never leave.

Winter stash, Zermatt

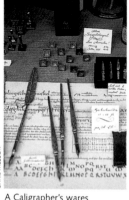

A Caligrapher's wares

St Moritz Lake

Life in St Moritz

Souvenir cow bells

The breathtaking view of the Gorner Glacier from Gornergrat railway (3100m), Valais

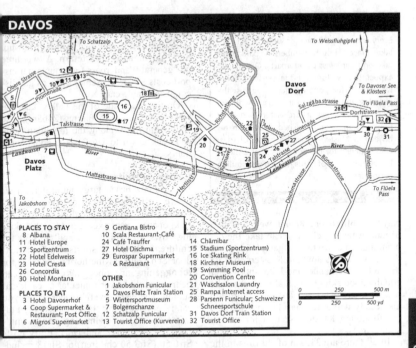

DAVOS

PLACES TO STAY
8 Albana
11 Hotel Europe
17 Sportzentrum
22 Hotel Edelweiss
23 Hotel Cresta
26 Concordia
30 Hotel Montana

PLACES TO EAT
3 Hotel Davoserhof
4 Coop Supermarket &
   Restaurant; Post Office
6 Migros Supermarket

9 Gentiana Bistro
10 Scala Restaurant-Café
24 Café Trauffer
27 Hotel Dischma
29 Eurospar Supermarket
   & Restaurant

OTHER
1 Jakobshorn Funicular
2 Davos Platz Train Station
5 Wintersportmuseum
7 Bolgenschanze
12 Schatzalp Funicular
13 Tourist Office (Kurverein)

14 Chämibar
15 Stadium (Sportzentrum)
16 Ice Skating Rink
18 Kirchner Museum
19 Swimming Pool
20 Convention Centre
21 Waschsalon Laundry
25 Rampa internet access
28 Parsenn Funicular; Schweizer
   Schneesportschule
31 Davos Dorf Train Station
32 Tourist Office

0   250   500 m
0   250   500 yd

GRAUBÜNDEN

money-exchange counters and lockers but only Davos Dorf has bike rental (in summer).

Davos Platz, to the south-west, is the centre of most of the activity. The main street is Promenade, with one-way traffic from Dorf to Platz. Talstrasse, a parallel street, is one-way in the opposite direction. The main tourist office or Kurverein (☎ 415 21 21, fax 415 21 00, @ davos@davos.ch) is at Promenade 67, open 8.30 am to 6 pm Monday to Friday, and 8.30 am to 12.30 pm Saturday. In high season it's open until 4 or 5 pm Saturday and (not in summer) 10 am to noon Sunday. Another tourist office (open similar hours, except with a weekday lunch break) is opposite the Dorf train station, next to a post office (7260). The main tourist office makes room reservations without commission. The main post office (7270) is at Postplatz in Davos Platz.

The Visitor's Card allows free travel on local buses and trains, as does the general ski pass (and the Swiss Pass). A self-service Waschsalon (laundry) is at Promenade 102, open 8 am to 6.30 pm Monday to Friday. Rampa (☎ 420 11 11), Promenade 123, is a computer shop with Internet access (Sfr5/12 for 20/60 minutes).

Museums

Although Davos is mostly a place for outdoor pursuits, there are several small museums with limited opening hours in and around the town, such as the **Wintersportsmuseum** at Promenadestrasse 43 (Sfr5). The most significant is the **Kirchner Museum** at Ernst-Ludwig-Kirchner-Platz, displaying the world's largest collection of work by the expressionist painter, who died in Davos in 1917 (Sfr7; closed Monday).

Skiing

Davos offers huge variety for experienced and intermediate skiers and snowboarders. The Weissfluh ski area goes as high as 2844m, and from here you can ski all the

Royal Race

Every January in Davos an unusual ski race takes place – British members of parliament take on their Swiss counterparts. One would expect that victory for the ski-bred Swiss would be a foregone conclusion against the piste-less British, and so it is, usually. But in 1995 Britain scored a rare victory, aided by Prince Charles who swished over from his holiday in Klosters to lend a hand. Charles, who qualified for the British team as a member of the House of Lords, turned in a sterling performance.

way to Kublis, over 2000m lower and 12km distant. Alternatively, you can take the demanding run down to Wolfgang (1629m) or the scenic slopes down to Klosters. Across the valley, Brämabüel and Jakobshorn offer equally good skiing for all abilities, and the nearby areas of Pischa and Rinerhorn are also easily within reach of Davos. See also the following Klosters section for further skiing areas.

In all there are 315km of ski runs in the Davos/Klosters region, which are covered by the general REGA pass costing Sfr116 (Sfr70 children) for a minimum two days. Six days cost Sfr268 (Sfr161), and there are discounts in low season and for senior citizens. One-day passes for specific areas cost between Sfr26 (Sfr22) and Sfr54 (Sfr32).

Though the resort is not a great place for beginners, there are several ski and snowboard schools, such as the Schweizer Schneesportschule (☎ 416 24 54), Promenade 157. Its Web site's at www.ssd.ch. There are 75km of cross-country trails open from December to April.

Hiking

The mountains provide extensive hiking options (450km of paths), including to Klosters. The views of the Alps are excellent from Weissfluh, and you can walk to the top in about 3½ hours in summer. The easy way is to take the Parsenn funicular from near Dorf station up to Weissfluhjoch, and the cable car from there up to Weissfluhgipfel. The combined fare is Sfr23 up, Sfr21 down, and Sfr28 return. A two/three day general Wanderpass for mountain transport costs Sfr41/52. Senior citizens get discounts on cable cars.

On the other side of the valley, take the bus and cable car to Pischa (2465m). The walk from there, along the mountain ridge and back down to Dorf, takes about three hours.

Other Activities

Davos Platz has a large natural ice rink where **ice hockey** games are staged in the winter. It is complemented by an artificial rink, open all year except in May. Ice skating costs Sfr5 for adults and Sfr3.50 for children. There's a sports stadium next door. Schatzalp or Rinerhorn is the place for **tobogganing**, and toboggans (*Schlitten*) can be hired at the lower funicular or cable-car station. There are several places where you can take **paragliding** 'taxi' flights or get tuition. The indoor **swimming pool** is midway between Platz and Dorf. Entry costs Sfr6.50 (Sfr3.50 children) or Sfr13 including the sauna. North of Dorf is **Davoser See**, where there are swimming (free beach) and water sports. Horse and mule trekking is another Davos attraction.

Special Events

Davos hosts an International Music Festival from late July to mid-August, featuring a variety of classical works. Get information and tickets from the main tourist office. In December there's a Nordic skiing World Cup event.

Places to Stay – Budget

Camping Camp at *Färich* (☎ 416 10 43), close to Davos Dorf on the road to the Flüela Pass. It is open from mid-May to 30 September.

Hostel The SYHA *hostel* (☎ 416 14 84, fax 416 50 55) is nicely situated by woods on the far side of Davoser See (take bus No 6 or 11 from Dorf to Hochgebirgsklinik, then it's a five-minute walk). Dorms cost Sfr23 and reception is shut from 9.30 am to 5 pm. The hostel is closed between seasons. Other places with dormitory accommodation are shown in the hotels booklet available from the tourist office.

Hotels & Pensions Except for a few Garni places, all hotels offer half-board as well as B&B. The *Sportzentrum (☎ 415 36 36, fax 415 36 37, Talstrasse 41)* has colourful, functional four-bed dorms for Sfr58 and singles/doubles from Sfr73/126 (less Sfr13 per person in summer and Sfr10 if you don't want dinner). *Hotel Montana (☎ 416 34 44, Bahnhofstrasse 2)* by Dorf station is a bargain, offering B&B singles/doubles with bathroom and TV for Sfr60/100 in winter and Sfr45/70 in summer. Check-in is from 5 pm and advance reservations are via Reisebüro Christoffel (☎ 413 34 08, fax 413 70 92, Promenade 41).

Albana (☎ 413 58 41, fax 413 78 86, ✆ hotel.albana.davos@spin.ch, Talstrasse 18) has oldish rooms with bathroom for about Sfr90/160 in winter and Sfr65/110 in summer. This B&B place has a pizzeria on site.

Hotel Edelweiss (☎ 416 10 33, fax 416 11 30, ✆ edelweiss-davos@gr-net.ch, Rossweidstrasse 9) is a welcoming place with a range of rooms, including triples and quads with bunk beds. Singles/doubles start at Sfr127/174 with shower/WC and Sfr92/164 without (Sfr97/128 and Sfr69/118 in summer). These are half-board rates, and there's private parking.

Places to Stay – Mid-Range & Top End

Concordia (☎ 416 32 22, fax 416 50 48, ✆ concordia@gr-net.ch, Promenade 124) has good prices for a three-star place. Rooms at half-board start at Sfr135/230 and have shower/WC, TV and telephone, though in summer they only take groups. There's parking and a bar on site.

Hotel Cresta (☎ 416 46 66, fax 416 46 85, Talstrasse 57) has a sauna, solarium, swimming pool and other facilities. Half-board prices start at Sfr180/320 in winter and Sfr115/190 in summer.

There are more than a dozen four-star hotels with stacks of facilities. *Hotel Europe (☎ 413 59 21, fax 413 13 93, ✆ europe@bluewin.ch, Promenade 63, Davos Platz)* has an indoor swimming pool that's free for guests. Rooms (B&B) start at Sfr225/360 in winter and Sfr138/246 in summer.

Places to Eat & Drink

There is a *Eurospar* supermarket with a self-service restaurant close to Davos Dorf station. Near Platz station is a new *Coop* supermarket and restaurant. Both are licensed and have meals for Sfr10 to Sfr15. They have late opening till 8 pm on Friday, and the Coop restaurant is also open till 5.30 pm Sunday.

Within Davos Platz station is *Buffet Loki*, open to 9 pm daily, where meals start at Sfr13. Just up the hill is the Rätia Centre on Postplatz, with a *Migros* supermarket and a cafe. *Café Trauffer (Promenade 118)* has a sun terrace, bar, and simple meals starting around Sfr11 (closed Monday in the off season).

Hotel Dischma (Promenade 128) has a choice of affordable places to eat; try the Röstizzeria (open from 6 pm) for pizzas and Röstis or the Dorfbeiz for a range of meals. The downstairs Chäshütte has cheese dishes, as well as dancing and live music (open from 7.30 pm; closed Monday).

By the Hotel Europe on Promenade is *Scala Restaurant-Café*, with outside seating. The decor inside includes huge plants, modern art and a giant portrait of Gorbachev on one wall. There's a range of meals and prices, starting at Sfr10.50. The three-course lunch menu is Sfr17.50 (open daily). Upstairs is a Chinese restaurant where main courses are around Sfr30 (open daily from 6 pm). *Gentiana Bistro (Promenade 53)* is a specialist in snail dishes *(Schnecken;* Sfr12.80 to Sfr25.80) and meat and cheese fondues (from Sfr23.80). It closes Wednesday in summer.

The best place to eat is in *Hotel Davoserhof (☎ 415 66 66, Postplatz)*, near Platz station. It specialises in Swiss food, with main dishes around Sfr35 to Sfr70. The business lunch costs Sfr49 and evening menus are

GRAUBÜNDEN

around Sfr100. Another top-notch place is the restaurant in **Hubli's Landhaus** (☎ *416 21 21, Kantonsstrasse)*, between Davos Dorf and Klosters at Davos Laret (closed Monday and winter lunchtimes). Lunch/dinner starts at about Sfr20/35.

Entertainment
Bolgenschanze *(Skistrasse 1)* is a hotel favoured by young snowboarders. It has a restaurant, and in winter there are discos and live music (entry fee on weekends). Another good drinking place is **Chämibar** *(Promenade)*, which serves limited food. **Hotel Davoserhof** *(Postplatz)* has a bar where there is a nightly DJ.

Getting There & Away
Davos is on the Rhätische Bahn rail route between Landquart and Filisur, with trains running hourly. To Chur you usually change at Landquart (Sfr26, two hours), which is also the junction for trains north and to Zürich. Change at Filisur for St Moritz; the total journey takes 1½ hours and costs Sfr27. En route you might be tempted to alight at Wiesen station, where there's a precipitous gorge and hiking paths.

To the Lower Engadine, postbuses run from Davos, and trains go via the new Vereina narrow-gauge rail tunnel that starts near Klosters.

Highway 28 leads to Klosters and Landquart; snow chains are most likely to be needed in winter on the stretch between Davos and Klosters.

KLOSTERS
☎ 081 • pop 3800 • elevation 1194m
Favourite resort of Britain's Prince Charles, Klosters provides the atmosphere of a traditional skiing village that is lacking in neighbouring Davos. Expect fewer diversions in the evening.

Orientation & Information
Like Davos, Klosters is split into two. Klosters Platz is the most important part, and is compactly grouped around the train station. Exit right and turn right for the tourist office, or Kurverein (☎ 410 20 20,

fax 410 20 10, ✉ info@klosters.ch), open Monday to Saturday and in winter high season also Sunday morning – exact hours vary with demand. Staff make commission-free hotel reservations. The post office (7250) is opposite the station.

Two kilometres to the left of the station is the smaller enclave of Klosters Dorf, with several hotels, a tourist office and the Madrisa cable car. Klosters buses are free with a Guest Card or ski pass.

Activities
The same skiing passes are available as mentioned in the Davos section. Above the village at 2300m is the Gotschnagrat, accessible from the cable car by the train station. It gives access to the fearful Gotschnawang, one of the hardest runs in the world. One of Prince Charles' companions died in an avalanche here in 1988, and they now only open it if conditions are perfect. On the other side of the valley, the Madrisa region has runs favouring beginners and intermediates; a day pass only for this region costs Sfr43 (Sfr25 children). Fifty kilometres of cross-country skiing trails run east from the village, for which a pass costs Sfr5/12 per day/week. Book at the tourist office for skiing tuition.

The village also boasts swimming pools, tennis courts and a sports centre with an artificial ice rink. The tourist office has a leaflet giving times and descriptions (in English) of nearby hikes.

Places to Stay
The tourist office can supply lists of private rooms (from Sfr20 per person) and the numerous holiday apartments. See Places to Eat for further accommodation suggestions.

The SYHA hostel, **Soldanella** *(☎ 422 13 16, fax 422 52 09, Talstrasse 73)*, is a 12-minute, mostly uphill trek from the station (head right, turn left at the junction and look for the signs). Dorm beds cost Sfr25.50 and singles/doubles/triples are Sfr36.50 per person. Dinners (Sfr11.50) are sociable, help-yourself affairs. There's a games room and English novels but too few showers for comfort. Reception is shut from 9.30 am to 5 pm ut the doors remain open, and there's no urfew. The hostel is closed between seasons.

Malein (☎ *422 10 88, Landstrasse 120*), midway between Platz and Dorf, is slightly nconvenient and slightly run down, but it's keenly priced. Singles/doubles are fr50/100 and doubles with private shower are Sfr114 (Sfr40/80 and Sfr94 in summer). Phone ahead.

Jost (☎ *422 33 44, fax 422 41 61, Landstrasse*), adjacent to the Dorf tourist office, s a chalet with mismatched furnishings and some balconies. Singles/doubles with shower/WC cost from Sfr65/94 in summer and Sfr87/128 in winter. The cheapish restaurant is open daily.

Bündnerhof (☎ *422 14 50, fax 422 40 04, ✉ bhof@bluewin.ch, Doggilochstrasse 2*), across the river from the Platz tourist office, gives more comfort and is family oriented. Winter/summer prices are around Sfr110/100 per person for half-board.

Hotel Alpina (☎ *410 24 24, fax 410 24 25, ✉ hotel@alpina-klosters.ch, Bahnhofstrasse 1*), opposite the station, has good rooms from Sfr204/358 (Sfr128/216 in summer). Prices are higher in the guesthouse section but the bathrooms are a treat in these rooms – they're fitted with jacuzzis and other luxuries. Use of the swimming pool, sauna and fitness room are included. Apartments (with kitchen, without breakfast) are also available, and garage parking is Sfr15 per night.

Places to Eat

Fifty metres to the right from the train station is a *Coop* supermarket and restaurant. Meals are around Sfr11 (open till 6.30 pm daily in winter, closed Sunday in summer).

To the right of the station on Bahnhofstrasse is *à Porta*, with a garden terrace. Pizza starts at Sfr13.50, and it also has pasta, grills and a salad buffet. The three-course lunch and evening menu is Sfr19.50 (open daily in season). Nearby at No 12 is *Chesa Grischuna*, which has piano music at 5 pm for the après-ski crowd. There are some cheapish meals (from Sfr15), including vegetarian choices, on the daytime 'Kleine Karte',

though evening dining runs to Sfr30 or more for varied main dishes.

Gasthaus Casanna (☎ *422 12 29, fax 422 47 56, Landstrasse 171*) has a range of Swiss and other meals from Sfr10, served in the bar section or the plusher adjoining room. It also has standard bedrooms for Sfr60 per person using hall shower. Telephone ahead in off season as the restaurant (and reception) is closed weekends. Along the road towards Dorf is *Sonne* (☎ *422 13 49, fax 422 19 48, Landstrasse 155*) which usually has tempting smells issuing from the wood-panelled restaurant (closed Monday and Tuesday). The midday Tagesteller is Sfr15; regional main courses are otherwise mostly Sfr25 to Sfr45, though there are cheaper light meals. Rooms cost Sfr60 per person.

The best restaurant is the *Walserstube* in the Hotel Walserhof (☎ *410 29 29, Landstrasse 141*). It serves superb seasonal specialities and regional dishes for around Sfr50 – good value considering the quality. It's run by the Bollingers: Mr is in charge of the kitchen and Mrs circulates amongst the guests. Reserve ahead, especially for weekends (open daily, but closed in the off season).

Getting There & Away

See Getting There & Away for Davos, as Klosters is on the same rail route between Landquart and Filisur. Klosters to Davos Platz takes 30 minutes and costs Sfr8.60.

Engadine Valley

This valley gets its name from the Inn River (En in Romansch) that meanders along its length. It is divided into two sections, the Upper Engadine (Oberengadin) from Maloja to Zernez, and the Lower Engadine (Unterengadin), stretching from Zernez to Martina, by the Austrian border. The scenery is tremendous, but the mountains don't have the same vertical impact as they do in some other parts of the Alps as the valley floor is so high, averaging around 1500m. The valley is traditionally Romansch-speaking,

GRAUBÜNDEN

GEOFF STRINGER

An example of Engadine architecture

although almost everyone also speaks German, and tourist-industry personnel usually speak English too. Turn to the Language Guide at the back of the book for translations of key words.

The Engadine is an excellent valley for exploration by car, bus or train, in part because the contrast between the sophisticated international resorts and the unpretentious rural villages is so marked. In the latter category, many houses display the traditional *sgraffito* design that runs like a floral trim around the edges of building exteriors. These designs, often incorporating arabesques, scrolls and rosettes, are made by scratching off a plaster covering to reveal a different colour underneath. This method of decoration is characteristic of the Engadine.

There is a low, middle and high season in both summer and winter. Hotel prices peak in the winter season; the change can be quite significant for middle-range to top-end hotels or very minimal in budget places. Prices quoted here are for the peak season (usually winter), though for St Moritz summer prices are also given as a comparison. Ferien Region Engadin (☎ 081-842 65 73, fax 842 65 25) books hotels, holiday apartments and package deals throughout the Engadine.

Chalandamarz, a spring and youth festival, is celebrated in the Engadine on 1 March. The **Schlitteda**, an ancient custom involving a procession of colourful horse-drawn sledges, can be seen in St Moritz, Pontresina and Silvaplana in January.

Skiing

The regional ski pass for the Upper Engadine covers 350km of downhill runs serviced by 55 cable cars and funiculars. I includes skiing in St Moritz and the surrounding resorts such as Sils, Silvaplana Celerina, Pontresina, Diavolezza and Zuoz Most of the skiing is too daunting for beginners, but there are many options for intermediates. The general pass costs Sfr5; for one day and Sfr304 for one week; children and youths aged under 20 years get reductions. Passes for specific areas are available but the general pass gives huge variety for little extra cost. It even include train and postbus transport between the different areas and entry for the indoor swimming pools in St Moritz and Pontresina. Rental for skis, boots and sticks is Sfr43 for one day. There's free car parking at all valley stations except at Chantarella.

The region also boasts 160km of cross-country trails (equipment rental Sfr20). The famous **Engadine Ski Marathon** takes place on the second Sunday in March. It starts a Maloja, crosses over the frozen lakes at Sils and Silvaplana, passes by the south-east side of St Moritz lake and finishes between Zuoz and S-chanf, a distance of some 42km. It's a great spectacle, with around 12,000 professional and amateur skiers taking part. The elite take about one hour 20 minutes to complete the course, but the 'fun' contestants make it last most of the day. If you don't want to join the crowds at the beginning or end of the race, a good place to watch is the approach to Pontresina. There's a tricky bit as they leave the woods where many amateurs are sent tumbling (to sympathetic laughter from spectators), and then a downhill section where they can regain their composure.

Alternatively, Stazersee (Lej da Staz) allows a clear view of the skiers. It's a pleasant 35-minute walk from St Moritz (clockwise round its lake).

Getting Around

See St Moritz for getting to/from the Engadine. From St Moritz, Rhätische Bahn trains go as far as Scuol every hour (Sfr26, takes

1½ hours). Stops en route include Zuoz (Sfr8.60, 45 minutes), Zernez (Sfr16.40, one hour) and Guarda (Sfr22, 1¼ hours). In the other direction you can take the postbus every 30 to 60 minutes from St Moritz that goes as far as Maloja (Sfr9.40, 35 minutes) with stops at Silvaplana (Sfr3.60, 15 minutes) and Sils (Sfr6.20, 20 minutes). These buses start at Pontresina and go via Celerina before reaching St Moritz Dorf (Schulhausplatz and the Bahnhof) and St Moritz Bad.

The *Ferienkarte* postbus pass covers the Lower Engadine and the Müstair Valley, giving seven days' free travel within two weeks. It costs Sfr65 (Sfr50 with Half-Fare Card; Family Card accepted for children's travel), or Sfr45 if you take three days travel in seven. A similar pass covering the Upper Engadine and Bregaglia Valley costs Sfr60, or Sfr35 for three days in seven. In summer, hikers can get a head start with a six-day cable car/train pass for Sfr96, or a six-trip ticket for Sfr69. Mountain transport details and hiking tips are listed in the pocket-sized *Engadin ferien Bergbahnen* brochure.

MALOJA
☎ 081 • pop 300 • elevation 1809m
Maloja, a one-street settlement, has Silser See (Lej da Segl) to the north. Immediately to the south is the Maloja Pass, which doesn't rise above the village yet falls away sharply on the far side into the Bregaglia Valley. The local dialect is a mix of Italian and Romansch. The tourist office (☎ 824 31 88, fax 8245 36 37, ✉ maloja@bluewin.ch) is open 8.30 am to noon and 2 to 6 pm Monday to Friday, and (in the high season) 9 to 11 am Saturday. It can give advice about all-day hikes over nearby passes, such as the historic Septimer Pass to the north or the Muretto Pass south to Italy, and also organises excursions: hiking on the three-pass tour with a guide and returning by bus costs Sfr55.

The artist Giovanni Segantini lived in the village from 1894 until his death in 1899, and his studio (*Atelier*) can be viewed (3 to 5 pm except Monday from early July to mid-October and early February to mid-April; Sfr2). Paintings are also on display in the Belvedere Tower (accessible in the

summer; free), around which is a protected area of glacial pot-holes and flowers.

Places to Stay & Eat
Camp by the lake at **Plan Curtinac** (☎ 824 31 81), open from 1 June to mid-September. The SYHA *hostel* (☎ 824 32 58, fax 824 35 71) is between the post office and the tourist office, in two buildings on either side of the garage. It has a kitchen, dorms and doubles, and is closed between seasons. Reception is only open 8 to 9 am, 5 to 6 pm, and 8 to 9 pm, though the doors are open through the day. Formerly for groups only, it plans to start taking individuals, so phone ahead to check.

The elderly Frau Ratti (☎ 824 31 28) has one single, two doubles and one quad (bunk beds) at Sfr30.50 per person, without breakfast but with use of a kitchen. Her house is the whitish one, back from the road, across the forecourt from the tourist office.

Opposite the youth hostel is **Sporthotel** (☎ 824 31 26, fax 824 34 90), with decent singles/doubles from Sfr75/150 with private shower/WC or Sfr58/116 without, reducing in low season. It has a restaurant and bar with a range of food, including vegetarian options, starting at about Sfr10. Nearby is **Restaurant Chesa Alpina**, with a nice garden round the back. Local and regional dishes are Sfr12 to Sfr40 and it's closed Monday. There is a supermarket opposite the post office (closed Wednesday afternoon).

Another possibility is **Hotel-Restaurant Longhin** (☎ 824 31 31, fax 824 36 77, ✉ hotel.longhin@bluewin.ch), at the Engadine end of the village. It has variable, simple rooms with shower and toilet for Sfr80/140. The restaurant is closed Wednesday.

SILS
☎ 081 • pop 600 • elevation 1800m
Peaceful Sils (Segl in Romansch) has two parts: Baselgia by the lake, and Maria at the foot of the mountains, where most of the amenities are located (including all the places mentioned below). Postbuses stop at both parts, though through car traffic is restricted (park in the garage). A cable car ascends to Furtschellas (Sfr12 up, Sfr10

GRAUBÜNDEN

down, Sfr18 return; children half-price) at 2312m, where there is a network of hiking trails and ski slopes. Water sports are also major attractions.

The philosopher Friedrich Nietzsche spent his summers in Sils from 1881 to 1888. **Nietzsche Haus** (Sfr4, students and seniors Sfr2, children free) is open 3 to 6 pm daily, except Monday, in summer and winter. He wrote several important works here, such as *Also Sprach Zarathustra*. You won't learn much about the man's life unless you can read German, but the many photos are interesting; it's amusing to see how his moustache grew in stature during the course of his life, from a skimpy floss fringing his upper lip in his student days to a bloated hedgehog bristling under his nose at the time of his death.

The tourist office (☎ 838 50 50, fax 838 50 59, ✉ info@sils.ch) is nearby. Its opening hours are 8.30 am to 6 pm Monday to Friday, and in the high season 9 to noon and 4 to 6 pm Saturday and (winter only) 4 to 6 pm Sunday.

Places to Stay & Eat

Baukantine Kuhn (☎ 826 52 62, fax 826 59 30) provides dorm beds from Sfr15 to Sfr30 per person and has a kitchen. It is by the river, on the south bank about halfway towards Silvaplaner See.

Close to the tourist office is *Pension Schulze* (☎ 826 52 13), which doubles as a cafe and bakery. Ageing singles/doubles are Sfr70/140 with private shower or Sfr60/120 without. Just down the road is *Restorant Survial*, serving pasta from Sfr12, daily specials for Sfr16, and grills and fish from Sfr24. It's open 11.30 am to 9.30 pm daily in season. A *Volg* supermarket is at the other end of Maria village.

By the post office is *Seraina*, which has an affordable restaurant with a terrace, and *Maria* (☎ 826 53 17, fax 826 50 64), which smells of pine and offers rooms with private shower/WC from Sfr125/240 (half-pension).

SILVAPLANA
☎ 081 • pop 850 • elevation 1815m
On a bay jutting between the two lakes, Silvaplana (Silvaplauna in Romansch) is a centre for water sports, especially windsurfing. The tourist office (☎ 838 60 00, fax 838 60 09, ✉ silvaplana@bluewin.ch), in the centre at Via Maistra, can give details. Across the causeway is **Surlej**, providing access to skiing slopes and marvellous views from Piz Corvatsch (3451m). The cable car costs Sfr23 up, Sfr16 down and Sfr33 return.

There are various hotels in the village (inquire at the tourist office), but nowhere is particularly cheap.

ST MORITZ
☎ 081 • pop 5600 • elevation 1856m
St Moritz is where the jet set come to play and pose. It's one of the world's best known holiday spots for the wealthy, and has been for a century or more. The not-so-rich who want to linger on the fringes of the elite can stay around the lake in St Moritz Bad. Here you can eat and sleep without taking out a mortgage – there's even a SYHA hostel (gleaming and expensive, but a hostel nonetheless).

Visitors can enjoy a huge variety of winter and summer sports. There is diverse downhill skiing, and probably the best cross-country skiing in the Alps. The toboggan Cresta Run is one of the resort's big draws (see the following Celerina section). If you can't afford to partake in the activities, at least people-watching is fun and free. Health treatments are also part of the St Moritz package. The curative properties of its waters have been known for 3000 years.

Orientation & Information
St Moritz (San Murezzan in Romansch) exudes health and wealth from the slopes overlooking the lake that shares its name (St Moritzersee in German, Lej da San Murezzan in Romansch). The train station near the lakeside rents bikes in summer and changes money from 6.50 am to 8.10 pm daily. It also has a hotel board with a free telephone. Up the hill on Via Serlas is the post office (7500) and five minutes farther on is the tourist office or Kurverein (☎ 837 33 33, fax 837 33 77, ✉ information@stmoritz.ch) at Via Maistra 12. It's open 9 am to noon and 2 to 6 pm Monday to Friday, and Saturday

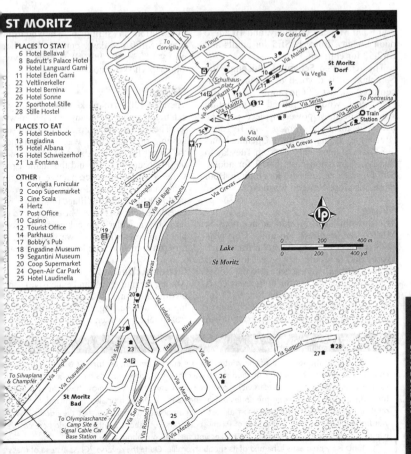

ST MORITZ

PLACES TO STAY
6 Hotel Bellaval
8 Badrutt's Palace Hotel
9 Hotel Languard Garni
11 Hotel Eden Garni
22 Veltlinerkeller
23 Hotel Bernina
26 Hotel Sonne
27 Sporthotel Stille
28 Stille Hostel

PLACES TO EAT
5 Hotel Steinbock
13 Engiadina
15 Hotel Albana
16 Hotel Schweizerhof
21 La Fontana

OTHER
1 Corviglia Funicular
2 Coop Supermarket
3 Cine Scala
4 Hertz
7 Post Office
10 Casino
12 Tourist Office
14 Parkhaus
17 Bobby's Pub
18 Engadine Museum
19 Segantini Museum
20 Coop Supermarket
24 Open-Air Car Park
25 Hotel Laudinella

morning. In high season, it's open 9 am to 6 pm Monday to Saturday and (winter only) 4 to 6 pm Sunday. St Moritz Bad is about 2km south-west from the main town, St Moritz Dorf. Local blue buses run between the two, as do postbuses.

Not much stays open during November, May and early June. In winter, St Moritz has plenty of sun and snow, but is colder than might be expected for its altitude. Some streets have parking meters (one- to four-hour maximum on weekdays; Sfr1 per hour), or there is one-hour free parking at Parkhaus on Schulhausplatz.

Bobby's Pub, Via dal Bagn, has Internet access. It's open 10 am to 1 am daily, and charges Sfr2 for 10 minutes.

Museums
The **Engadine Museum**, Via dal Bagn 39, gives a good introduction to the style of dwellings and simple interiors you may encounter if you explore the Engadine Valley, and some rather patrician interiors you probably won't encounter. The building itself is typical, featuring sgraffito designs on the facade. Traditional stoves and archaeological finds complete the collection. It is

open 9.30 am (10 am in winter) to noon and 2 to 5 pm Monday to Friday, and 10 am to noon Sunday. Entry is Sfr5 for adults and Sfr2.50 for children.

The renovated **Segantini Museum**, Via Somplaz 30, is devoted to the local 19th-century artist Giovanni Segantini (1858–99), who specialised in mountain scenes. The most powerful piece painting here is the three-part *Werden, Sein, Vergehen* (Becoming, Being, Passing). Opening hours are 10 am to noon and 3 to 6 pm Tuesday to Sunday. Admission costs Sfr10 for adults, Sfr7 for students, and Sfr3 for children. Both museums close between seasons.

Skiing

The downhill skiing area adjacent to St Moritz is centred around Corviglia (2486m), accessible by funicular from Dorf. From Bad a cable car goes to Signal (shorter queues), giving access to the slopes of Piz Nair. A ski pass for both areas costs up to Sfr55 (children/youths Sfr28/49) for one day. If you ski on Piz Corvatsch, above nearby Silvaplana, you can ski back down

to Bad via the demanding Hahnensee run. For tuition in skiing or snowboarding (about Sfr80 per day), contact the school on ☎ 833 80 90; Web site: www.stmoritz.ch/skischool.

Hiking

There are 120km of marked hiking paths you can tramp along, and many are open in winter. The tourist office has a map giving suggestions (in English) for walking throughout the Upper Engadine. Above St Moritz soars the Piz Nair (3057m), and the summit provides a marvellous perspective of Alpine peaks and the lakes and valley below. Walking to the top from the village in summer will take three hours or more. The easy way to get up is by funicular then cable car; the complete trip costs Sfr21 each way and Sfr32 return (no reduction with Inter-Rail or Eurail).

Other Activities

Among the numerous (and expensive) sports on offer are tennis, squash, horse riding, sailing and windsurfing. Golf is played on the frozen lake in winter, and in the summer a

St Mo-RITZY Guests

Despite being at the forefront of the winter sports scene in the 19th century, St Moritz hasn't become a mass-market holiday destination in the way that many other resorts have. The main reason for this is its enduring air of exclusivity – one feels the wealthy want to enjoy the facilities without the bother of having to barge the proles out of their path. Average mortals who meander into the rarefied atmosphere of St Moritz Dorf almost feel compelled to apologise that they don't own a wardrobe full of fur coats and a fleet of flashy sports cars. Just about anything you do here costs a pile of money; even window shopping makes you feel nervous about your budget.

St Moritz is by no means ashamed of its snobbish profile. Quite the reverse. 'Class instead of Mass' is its motto. St Moritz's director of tourism describes the typical guest as 'exclusive, chic, elegant, sporty'. Another of the resort's slogans is 'Top of the World'. One begins to wonder whether this refers more to the guest profile than to the physical location. Publicity handouts effuse about the local 'champagne climate' – again, they're probably not talking about the weather.

As if the parade of plush shops and fur coats was not enough to underline the message, various events take place that emphasise the champagne and caviar angle, including curling on Corviglia where the curling stones are shaped like champagne bottles. Recently, Pommery introduced a new champagne, 'Brut St Moritz', and 200,000 bottles were imported for the resort's new millennium celebrations. There's also an annual Gourmet Festival at the end of January (20 restaurants in or near St Moritz have a Gault Millau 'gourmet' rating), and here things can get a little over the top, with events such as Cigar Gourmet Nights designed to 'celebrate the art of cultivated smoking'! While the gourmets light up their big ones, the rest of us can merely watch and wonder.

the 18-hole course in nearby Samedan (☎ 861 04 66), where one day's green fees is Sfr90. For fishing in the Upper Engadine you need a permit (an outrageous Sfr73 for one day for foreigners; local residents pay Sfr25); get them from Fischzuchtanstalt Hauptfisch-ereiaufseher Anton Klucker (☎/fax 833 67 52). A tandem ride off Corviglia by paraglider costs Sfr220; call ☎ 833 24 16 in winter, or ☎ 087-880 14 04 year-round. For the cresta run, see Celerina below.

Buying a **health treatment** in the spa is another way to spend money. For informa-tion on treatments available in the Health Spa Centre, telephone ☎ 833 30 62.

Places to Stay – Budget
Hotel prices peak at around mid-December to mid-February. The summer high season, July and August, isn't quite so expensive. Many hotels have reduced seven-day deals.

Camping The *Olympiaschanze* camp site (☎ 833 40 90) is 1km south-west of St Moritz Bad; it is open from late May to late September and costs around Sfr8 per adult and Sfr6.30 per tent.

Hostel
The SYHA *Stille Hostel* (☎ 833 39 69, fax 833 39 69, Via Surpunt 60, St Moritz Bad), has good, modern facilities. Compulsory half-board per person is Sfr43 in four-bed dorms or Sfr55.50 in double rooms. Laun-dry costs Sfr4 per load and there's mountain bike rental for Sfr15 per day. Reception is closed from 9 am to 4 pm but the down-stairs doors stay open, and the hostel is open year-round. Buses from the station to Mal-oja stop at the Hotel Sonne (Sfr2.40), six minutes' walk from the hostel.

Hotels
The nearest thing to a budget hotel in Dorf is *Hotel Bellaval* (☎ 833 32 45, fax 833 04 06) right by the train station, though the staff aren't the most amenable folks. Singles/doubles using hall shower are Sfr67/130 in the summer or winter season. Doubles with own shower and toilet (Sfr170) are reasonably large, if slightly bare. Add Sfr10 per person if staying under

four nights. Half-pension costs Sfr20 per person. On Tuesday, when the restaurant is shut, reception is closed from 11 am to 5 pm.

The *Sporthotel Stille* (☎ 833 69 48, fax 833 07 08, ✉ hotel.stille@bluewin.ch), next door to the hostel, attracts a young and sporty crowd; in winter it has its own bar and occasional disco. Modern but basic singles/doubles are Sfr65/110 for B&B in the summer, and doubles are Sfr166 for half-pension in the winter. All rooms are doubles, with a bathroom per pair of rooms. It's open year-round, but in summer there's no reception from 11.30 am to 4.30 pm. Also in Bad, but north of the Inn River, is *Hotel Bernina* (☎ 833 60 22, fax 833 19 40, ✉ botel-bernina-stmoritz@bluewin.ch, Via dal Bagn). It's only good value in the sum-mer when rooms start at Sfr75/150 with pri-vate shower or Sfr60/130 without. Prices almost double in winter and these average rooms simply don't merit the increase, though dinner becomes included.

Places to Stay – Mid-Range
In Bad is the *Hotel Sonne* (☎ 833 03 63, fax 833 60 90, ✉ hotelsonne@swissonline.ch, Via Sela 11), which has singles/ doubles/triples with shower/WC, TV, tele-phone and balcony starting at Sfr95/160/ 210 in summer or Sfr105/180/225 in winter, plus a few cheaper rooms with hall facilities. Rooms are in the main building or two nearby annexes. There's free private parking and free use of the public swimming pool. *Veltlinerkeller* (☎ 833 40 09, fax 833 37 41, Via dal Bagn 11), has a lift and characteris-tic, pine-scented rooms with shower/WC and TV; prices start at Sfr95/160 in winter and Sfr105/180 in summer.

Staying in the centre of St Moritz Dorf involves splashing out on at least a three-star hotel. Two good family hotels are close together on Via Veglia, around the back of the tourist office; in summer, prices at *Hotel Eden Garni* (☎ 833 61 61, fax 833 91 91, ✉ eden-stmoritz@bluewin.ch) start at Sfr97/188 and *Hotel Languard Garni* (☎ 833 31 37, fax 833 45 46, ✉ languard@ bluewin.ch) at Sfr100/180. There's little to choose between them in the standard of rooms. Eden has a nice central atrium although Languard's prices rise less in winter (around 25% instead of 35%).

Places to Stay – Top End
The place to see and be seen is the renowned **Badrutt's Palace Hotel** (☎ 837 10 00, fax 837 29 99, 🖂 palace@palace-st-moritz.ch, Via Serlas). Of course, you have to pay for the privilege – rooms with half-board cost at least Sfr290/490 in summer and a heart-stopping Sfr460/810 in winter. The public areas reek of class and taste (men must wear a jacket and tie after 7 pm), but some cheaper rooms aren't as lavish as you might expect.

Places to Eat
The cheapest restaurants are between Dorf and Bad. There is a **Coop** supermarket in Via dal Bagn, with late opening till 8 pm on Friday. Next door there's **La Fontana**, a rustic-type bar/restaurant with candle lighting, and mostly Italian meals from Sfr12. It is open 9 am (11 am Sunday) until midnight daily.

Veltlinerkeller (see Places to Stay) is nearby, and features Engadine sgraffito outside and beheaded animals inside. If the hunting trophies don't put you off your food, tuck into a wide choice of pasta, grills, omelettes, fish or schnitzels for Sfr12 to Sfr40 (closed Sunday in the off season). The popular **Hotel Sonne** (see Places to Stay) has pasta, salads and grills. Tasty pizzas, cooked in a traditional wood-burning oven, are Sfr12 to Sfr16. It is open 7 am to midnight daily, and has a bar area.

Eating in Dorf is not necessarily an asset-stripping experience if you stick to lunchtime specials, which many good-quality restaurants offer. **Hotel Albana** (Via Maistra 6), has winter lunches with soup for Sfr17, or for Sfr20 with an additional starter. The four-course evening menu costs from Sfr45, and main courses top Sfr38 (open daily). The restaurant of the **Hotel Schweizerhof** (Via dal Bagn 54) has a lunch menu with starter for Sfr16.

The restaurant of the **Hotel Steinbock** (Via Serlas 12), near the post office, is good value and popular with locals. Pasta and

'Tellerservice' meals start at Sfr17 but you could pay much more, and it's open daily during the season. **Engiadina** (Plazza da Scuola 2, Schulhausplatz) is famous for fondue, and that's the best thing to eat here (from Sfr26.50 per person – Sfr32 with champagne!). It's closed on Sunday.

Try an expensive taste of the high life at the top of the Corviglia funicular by sampling the truffles, caviar and desserts at **La Marmite** (☎ 833 63 55). Queue or reserve ahead in season, when it's open daily. On the floor above there's a reasonably cheap self-service restaurant, with a terrace. The best valley restaurant is **Jöhri's Talvo** (☎ 833 44 55, Via Gunels 15), beyond Bad in nearby Champfèr. It's closed Monday in low season.

Entertainment
Nightlife is lively and varied, but unless you have plenty of money, forget it! Around 20 bars and clubs have dancing and/or music. Perhaps the most elegant place is the **King's Club** in Badrutt's Palace Hotel, open from 10 pm nightly and with a hefty entrance fee. The Stübli in the **Hotel Schweizerhof** has free live music nightly – from 10 pm except Monday in summer, from 5 pm in winter. It gets very busy for après-ski. **Bobby's Pub** attracts a younger set. **Cine Scala**, on Via Maistra by the Schiefer Turm (the Leaning Tower), shows films in the original language; seats cost Sfr13 or Sfr16.

Concerts, theatre and other events are staged by St Moritz Cultur (☎ 832 21 31), based in the Laudinella Hotel in St Moritz Bad.

Getting There & Away
Bus To Lugano, two postbuses run daily in summer; in winter there's only one, and only on Friday, Saturday and Sunday (daily over New Year). The cost is Sfr63 (plus a Sfr10 supplement, not covered by Swiss travel passes) and the seat must be reserved the day before; ☎ 837 67 64. To get to Austria, see the Scuol section later in this chapter.

Train Nine daily trains travel south to Tirano in Italy with connections to Milan.

The famous Glacier Express links St Moritz to Zermatt (Sfr138) via the 2033m Oberalp Pass. The majestic, scenic route takes 7½ hours to cover the 290km and crosses 291 bridges. Novelty drink glasses in the dining car have sloping bases to compensate for the hills – but you must remember to keep turning them around! Reservations (Sfr9, not covered by railpasses) are compulsory on these trains, but only in the summer and only for the stage between Disentis and Brig. Reservations are not required for normal trains following the same route.

Car & Motorcycle The roads around St Moritz are good, if winding. See the Getting Around section in the chapter introduction for details of which passes are open in winter.

Car Rental Hertz (☎ 833 27 84) is at the Kulm Garage, Via Maistra and Europcar (☎ 837 36 34) is at Via Somplaz 33, near the Segantini Museum.

CELERINA
☎ 081 • pop 1550 • elevation 1730m
This resort (Schlarigna in Romansch) by the Inn River is 30 minutes' walk from St Moritz and shares the same ski slopes. In the winter it is known for its famous Olympic **bob run** and **cresta run**. The 1.6km-long bobsleigh run is the oldest in the world and the only one made from natural ice. It starts by St Moritz lake and one 'taxi-ride' trip costs Sfr220 (☎ 830 02 00). The cresta run (a toboggan course enticingly known as the skeleton run) was created by British tourists in 1885; it's over 1km and starts near the Schiefer Turm in St Moritz. Booking a course of five rides costs Sfr450 (☎ 833 46 09). The finish for both runs is the western end of Celerina. Check out the Web sites: www.olympia-bobrun.ch and www.cresta-run.com.

The tourist office (☎ 830 00 11, fax 830 00 19, ✉ info@celerina.ch) is in the village centre at the corner of Via Maistra and Via la la Staziun. It is open 8.30 am to noon and 2 to 6 pm Monday to Friday, and (in season) 10 am to noon and 3 to 5 pm Saturday.

Places to Stay & Eat
Celerina has many holiday apartments, a few private rooms, and a couple of places with dorms, including *Restaurant Alte Brauerei* (☎ 832 18 74, fax 832 18 77, Via Maistra), in the direction of the cresta run.

Opposite is *Veltlinerkeller* (☎ 832 28 68), with a restaurant and six simple rooms (hall showers) for Sfr60/110. Two doors away is *Demont Garni* (☎ 833 65 44, fax 833 80 82) with smallish but pleasant singles/doubles with TV for Sfr80/140 with shower/WC or Sfr70/120 without.

To the north-east is *Hotel Trais Fluors* (☎ 833 88 85, fax 832 10 01, Via Samedan), with red window shutters and varying rooms and small apartments. Singles/doubles start at Sfr51/102 with hall showers; doubles with shower are Sfr120. Nearby is the comfortable *Arturo* (☎ 833 66 85, fax 833 88 60, Via Maistra). Rooms are Sfr85/170 and have private shower/WC, TV and telephone; the restaurant has a good selection of mid-price food and wine (open daily). Opposite, the *CCC Café* provides cheaper meals.

There are two supermarkets, a *Coop* beyond Arturo and a *Volg* opposite the tourist office.

Getting There & Away
Celerina is easily reached from St Moritz by train (Sfr2.40), which takes you to the village centre, or postbus (Sfr3), which leaves you by the cresta run or in the centre.

ZUOZ
☎ 081 • pop 1300 • elevation 1750m
Zuoz has some undemanding skiing (day pass Sfr40, or Sfr20 for children), but a greater attraction are the beautiful Engadine houses sporting traditional sgraffito designs. The main square looks suitably immune to contamination by modern life, and features a fountain bearing the coat of arms of the influential Planta family. The bear's paw motif reappears in the church, which also has windows in the chancel designed by Augusto Giacometti. The small prison tower next door contains some torture implements – don't annoy the staff of the

GRAUBÜNDEN

tourist office (☎ 854 15 10, fax 854 33 34, ℮ zuoz@compunet.ch), because they look after the key. Office opening hours are 9 am to noon and 3 to 5 or 6 pm Monday to Friday, and (high season) 9 to 11 am Saturday. There is a post office at the train station.

Places to Stay & Eat

Private rooms include **Chesa Walther** *(☎ 854 13 64)* opposite the tourist office (Sfr35 per person without breakfast; kitchen use costs Sfr5 per day). The restaurant downstairs offers a range of meals (Sfr10 to Sfr40; open daily). Near the main square, **Ferienlager Sonder** *(☎ 854 14 39)* has dorms (four- to 10-bed rooms) for just Sfr15 without breakfast. Daytime check-in is possible (phone ahead). Next door, **Pension Albanas** has singles/doubles for Sfr60/100 using hall showers, and a simple restaurant. Check in at the adjacent **Hotel Klarer** *(☎ 854 13 21, fax 854 12 14)*, where comfortable rooms with shower/WC and TV start at Sfr105/162. Opposite is **Crusch Alva**, with excellent, fairly pricey food.

Supermarkets are by the train station and the tourist office. **Restorant Dorta**, on the far side of the train station, offers a traditional Engadine experience, with regional food (from Sfr19) in a rustic, converted barn (closed Monday). About 300m farther, by the river, is **Sur En Restorant**, providing cheapish self-service fare. It's open 8 am to 7 pm daily and has a sun terrace.

ZERNEZ

☎ 081 • pop 1000 • elevation 1474m

Zernez is another attractive Engadine village, but its main claim to fame is as the headquarters of the Swiss National Park.

Orientation & Information

By the Zernez entrance to the park is the National Park House (☎ 856 13 78, fax 856 17 40), open daily from around June to October, when the park itself is open. It can give details of hiking paths, route descriptions, the best locations to see particular animals, and other information. Its Web site is at www.nationalpark.ch. A similar lowdown can be picked up at the Zernez tourist office (☎ 856 13 00, fax 856 11 55, ℮ info@zernez.ch), on the main street leading from Zernez train station (six minutes' walk). Look for the *infuormaziun* sign; opening hours are 8 or 8.30 am to noon and 2 to 6.30 pm (5 pm in winter) Monday to Friday, and in summer 8.30 am to noon and 2 to 4 pm Saturday. There's no charge to enter the park and parking is free. S-chanf (pronounced Sh-kanf), to the south-west of the park, also has a tourist office (☎/fax 854 22 55) in the Raiffeisen bank (closed Wednesday afternoon).

Swiss National Park

The park comprises 169 sq km of woodland and mountains where flora and fauna flourish in a stringently protected natural environment. Ibexes, chamois and marmots are left to roam at will. You can roam the park too, but not at will, as deviating from the paths is not permitted. Numerous other regulations prohibit camping, littering, lighting fires, cycling, picking flowers, bringing dogs into the park, or disturbing the animals in any way. Less relevant to tourists, you also may not allow cattle to graze. Fines of up to Sfr500 may be imposed for violations.

A three-hour walk south from Zernez is the scenic Cluozza Valley, where there's cheap accommodation (see below). Another three-hour walk goes from S-chanf to

The red deer lives in forests and Alpine meadows throughout Switzerland.

Trupchun. This is especially popular in October when you can get close to large deer. The Naturlehrpfad circuit near Il Fuorn gives an opportunity to see bearded vultures, which have been released into the wild since 1991.

It is likely that the area of the national park will be expanded from 2000.

Places to Stay & Eat

Camping *Cul* (☎ 856 14 62) is around the back of Zernez station and open from 1 May to late October. *Hotel Bär-Post* (☎ 851 55 00, fax 851 55 99, **ℯ** baer-post@ bluewin.ch), in the centre, has dormitory beds for Sfr18 without breakfast (add Sfr5 per stay if you need sheets), a kitchen, sauna and parking spaces. Singles/doubles with shower/WC, TV and breakfast start at Sfr75/120 and its restaurant has food for Sfr12 to Sfr35.

Near the station on the main street is *Filli* (☎ 856 10 72, fax 856 14 30, **ℯ** fillibaeck@bluewin.ch) with newly built rooms with shower/WC and TV from Sfr55/100. The restaurant has a good choice of cheap meals from Sfr10, including pizza/pasta and schnitzels. *Adler* (☎ 856 12 13, fax 856 19 59), towards the park, costs up to Sfr75 per person with shower or Sfr45 without.

Spöl (☎ 856 12 79, fax 856 19 48, **ℯ** hotel.spoel@engadin.net) in the centre of the village, has fresh, attractive rooms with private facilities including TV from Sfr95/140. It has a decent restaurant with outside tables. There is a *Coop* opposite the tourist office, with no half-day closing.

Il Fuorn (☎ 856 12 26, fax 856 18 01), in the middle of the national park by the main road, has rooms for Sfr95/160 with shower/toilet or Sfr55/110 without. It also has dorms (Sfr17 without breakfast). Also in the park is *Chamanna Cluozza* (☎ 856 12 35), sometimes called the Blockhaus. It can only be reached by foot, and has dorm beds for Sfr25 and doubles/quads for Sfr35 per person. Add Sfr10 for breakfast and Sfr18 for dinner. Both places are open from around June to October.

Getting There & Away

From Zernez, the train fare is Sfr7.40 to S-chanf, Sfr8 to Zuoz (25 minutes) and Sfr11.80 to Scuol (30 minutes).

The main road through the park, highway 28, goes from Zernez, over the Ofen Pass (2149m; Pass dal Fuorn in Romansch), and into Italy. This route is covered by postbus; there are six to nine departures a day between Zernez and Müstair. The park can also be entered on foot from close to S-chanf and Scuol.

MÜSTAIR

The village of Müstair, at the far side of the park by the Italian border, has the convent of St John the Baptist, founded in the 8th century. Inside there is a unique series of wall paintings from the Carolingian period (around 800 AD), and a statue of Charlemagne from the 12th century. The wall paintings comprise 90 fresco panels, and their historical importance have accorded the church the status of a Unesco world heritage site. For more information contact ☎ 858 55 66, or check out its Web site at www.muestair.ch.

GUARDA
☎ 081 • pop 180 • elevation 1653m
This is one of the best preserved villages in the Engadine, with tiny cobbled streets, fountains and many houses bearing sgraffito engravings. It easily merits an hour or so exploring its confines. The village is above the valley floor and has expansive views (Guarda means 'look' in Romansch – that's good advice). Guarda is 30 minutes' walk from the train station by the steep footpath, or you can take the postbus (Sfr2.40), which runs every two hours in the day time. The train station is 15 minutes from either Zernez or Scuol-Tarasp. Contact the small tourist office (☎ 862 23 42) for information on limited accommodation.

SCUOL
☎ 081 • pop 2060 • elevation 1250m
The approach along the valley towards Scuol is very scenic, and you pass Schloss Tarasp rising impressively on a ridge to the

GRAUBÜNDEN

south. Scuol is close to the smaller resorts of Vulpera and Tarasp, which are on the south side of the Inn River.

Orientation & Information

Spread-out Scuol is the main resort in the Lower Engadine. The train station is over 1km west of the village centre. Take the small local bus (Sfr2 for a day pass in summer; free ski bus in winter) or walk down the hill for 10 minutes to reach the tourist office (☎ 864 94 94). It is open 8 am to noon and 2 to 6.30 pm Monday to Friday, 10 am to noon and 2 to 6 pm Saturday, and 4 to 6 pm Sunday. In low season, hours reduce to 8 am to noon and 2 to 6 pm weekdays only. The post office (7550) is next door. Lower Scuol is another five to 10 minutes' walk east and downhill.

Things to See & Do

Lower Scuol has some incredibly quaint Engadine dwellings and cobbled squares. It's well worth a wander (or the local bus does a scenic circuit of town). There's a museum (Sfr3, children Sfr1) devoted to the Lower Engadine which is open only limited hours during the season – check with the tourist office. **Schloss Tarasp** (☎ 864 93 68) was built in 1040 and was controlled by the Austrians until 1803. It can be visited by guided tour (Sfr7, children Sfr3).

There is **skiing** above Scuol up to 2800m, a total of 80km of runs, the longest being 12km. A one-day pass costs Sfr46 for adults, Sfr37 for youths/seniors, and Sfr23 for children. Swissraft (☎ 911 52 50) offers a choice of **white-water rafting** trips from Sfr50. Its Web site is at www.swissraft.ch.

Scuol is a **health spa**, and there are around 25 mineral springs in the vicinity. The Bogn bathing and health centre charges Sfr23 for 2½ hours in the pools, sauna and steam bath. Its Roman-Irish Bath is a regimen of hot and cold baths also lasting 2½ hours (Sfr54). The Schneebade Pass (Sfr65 for one day) covers skiing, bathing and other facilities.

Places to Stay & Eat

There is camping at *Gurlaina* (☎ 864 15 01), by the southern banks of the Inn. It's

open for the summer and winter seasons and costs Sfr7.50 per adult and from Sfr8.50 for a tent.

Contact the tourist office about the many holiday apartments. *Hotel Garni Grusaida* (☎ 864 14 74, fax 864 18 77) is on the east side of Scuol and has singles/doubles for Sfr58/116, or Sfr65/130 with private shower/WC. *Café Collina* (☎ 864 03 93, fax 864 86 93), opposite the tourist office, costs from Sfr65/130 for pleasant, non-standardised rooms with TV, shower and toilet. The restaurant serves pizza and pasta from Sfr13 (closed Sunday).

Hotel Quellenhof (☎ 864 12 15, fax 864 02 34) has a similar standard of accommodation, albeit a bit more expensive. The food is better value if you go for the lunch and evening three-course daily menu for around Sfr18 (closed Sunday).

Hotel Engiadina (☎ 864 14 21, fax 864 12 45), a typical Engadine building in picturesque Lower Scuol, has renovated rooms with private shower/WC and TV for around Sfr100/160, and a mid-price restaurant that's closed Sunday evening and Monday.

There is a *Coop* supermarket on the main street, with no half-day closing. *Schü-San* is a Chinese takeaway in the Bogn bathing centre, with meals from Sfr9 (open daily).

Getting There & Away

The train from St Moritz terminates at Scuol-Tarasp station. Postbuses from the station continue year round to Martina, Samnaun (a duty-free area in Switzerland), and Austria (as far as Landeck). From early June to late October, several buses a day run between Susch and Davos (Sfr20, 45 minutes). Susch is on the rail route towards Zernez, and near the new Vereina rail tunnel to Klosters.

Bernina Pass Road

This road runs from Celerina in a south-easterly direction to Tirano in Italy. It links the Bernina and the Poschiavo Valleys by way of the Bernina Pass at 2323m. There are some great hiking trails in the surrounding mountains, and these are identified and described in the *Summer Panorama Map* available for Sfr2.50 from the tourist office in Pontresina. This map also details winter skiing in the valley. The ski lifts are covered by the Upper Engadine ski pass (see the Engadine Valley section).

Getting There & Away
Trains run every one to two hours from St Moritz to Tirano, stopping at all stations en route. There's no through postbus service, even though the pass is open for traffic year-round.

PONTRESINA
☎ 081 • pop 1750 • elevation 1800m
Pontresina is at the mouth of the Bernina Valley, close enough to the Engadine for the Engadine Ski Marathon to loop down to the village en route to Zernez. Interesting features in the village are the pentagonal Moorish tower, and the Sta Maria chapel with frescoes dating from the 13th and 15th centuries. There's also an Alpine museum (Sfr5, closed Sunday).

Orientation & Information
The train station is to the west of the village and changes money. Cross over the two rivers, Rosegg and Bernina, for the centre and the tourist office (☎ 838 83 00, fax 838 83 10, ✉ pontresina@compunet.ch). It's open 8.30 am to noon and 2 to 6 pm Monday to Friday, and 8.30 am to noon Saturday and (in the high season) 4 to 6 pm Saturday and Sunday.

Skiing
Like most of the resorts in the vicinity, Pontresina has plenty of sports facilities to offer the visitor. There's not very much skiing from Pontresina's own mountain, Alp Languard (2261m), but it's feasible to use the resort as a base for exploring the slopes farther down the valley, at Piz Lagalb and Diavolezza. A one-day ski pass to cover these areas costs Sfr47 (children/youths Sfr24/33).

Hiking
In the summer, hiking trails wind away from Alp Languard in all directions; the chair lift

to the summit runs from the end of May to mid-October and costs Sfr14 each way and Sfr20 return (children half-price). It takes 2½ hours to walk to Muottas Muragli (2453m), overlooking the junction of the Bernina and Engadine Valleys. This is the best spot for a view of the course of the Inn River.

Mountaineering
Pontresina is well known as a mountaineering centre. Located in the same building as the tourist office, its mountaineering school (☎ 838 83 33, fax 838 83 80, ✉ ski-bergsteigerschule@bluewin.ch) is the largest in Switzerland and has a program of tours virtually year-round, either on skis or on foot. Prices for the week including half-pension are typically around Sfr950, and one-day excursions are also available from Sfr80. For details, write to the Schweizer Bergsteigerschule, CH-7504, Pontresina.

Places to Stay & Eat
There is camping at *Plauns* (☎ 842 62 85), about 2km to the south, open for the summer and winter seasons.

The SYHA *hostel* (☎ 842 72 23, fax 842 70 31) is right next to the train station, and is closed between seasons. Reception is shut from 9.30 am to 4 pm (check-in up to 9 pm) but there's daytime access to the building. Six-bed dorms cost Sfr31.50 and two-bed rooms are Sfr110. Taking dinner (Sfr11.50) is compulsory in the main season, but this is no hardship as the food is good (three courses, and there's plenty of it). The hostel runs the self-service *Restaurant Tolais* from the same premises, providing cheap meals; it's open until 8.30 pm daily (closed Monday and Tuesday in low season).

Between the tourist office and the post office is *Pension Valtellina* (☎ 842 64 06, Via Maistra), where old-fashioned singles/doubles with hall shower cost Sfr54/108. There are many places to eat along Via Maistra, but the only inexpensive option is searching for daily specials, or compiling a snack at the *Coop* supermarket near the post office (no half-day closing). *Bahnhof* (☎ 838 80 00, fax 838 80 09), by the station, has meals from about Sfr15 and cosy rooms for Sfr75 per person. The **Sportpavillon** has an inexpensive pizzeria, open till 11 pm daily.

Hotel Müller (☎ *842 63 41, fax 842 68 38,* @ *info@hotel-mueller.ch, Via Maistra*) offers a range of comfortable rooms from Sfr115/210 with shower/WC and TV, and has lower 'senior' rates. **Steinbock**, south of the post office, is a good choice for mid-price food (open daily).

Getting There & Away
Hourly trains from St Moritz take 11 minutes and cost Sfr4.40. Postbuses leave from the centre of Pontresina by the post office, and run about every 30 minutes to St Moritz, via Celerina.

CHÜNETTA
This is a well-known belvedere above the Morteratsch train station and below the Morteratsch Glacier. It can be reached in only about a 30-minute walk from the station and the views are more than worth the effort.

DIAVOLEZZA
Diavolezza (2973m) offers inspiring views of the Bernina Massif, but no longer has summer skiing. Take the train to Bernina Diavolezza and then the cable car (Sfr19 up, Sfr14 down or Sfr26 return). Alternatively, get off the train at the previous stop, Bernina Suot, and take the trail up, which gets steep after a gentle start (takes 2¾ hours).

PIZ LAGALB
This peak (2898m) is on the opposite side of the valley and gives comparable views of a landscape of mountains, glaciers and lakes. Take the cable car from the Bernina Lagalb station which costs Sfr16 up, Sfr11 down and Sfr21 return (children half-price). The walk down from the peak to the next station along, Ospizio Bernina, takes 1½ hours.

ALP GRÜM
This viewing point at 2019m provides a tremendous view over the Poschiavo Valley to the south, with the lake shimmering below and the mountains above. The *Hotel Ristorante Belvedere* provides refreshment.

From here you can walk down to Caviglia in one hour or back to Ospizio Bernina in 1½ hours.

Getting There & Away
The train from St Moritz takes one hour and costs Sfr23.60 return. The closest you can get by car is Ospizio Bernina; walk or take the train from there.

Bregaglia Valley

From the Maloja Pass (1815m), the road spirals downwards to the Bregaglia Valley (Bergell in German), cutting a course running south-west into Italy. The road then splits; one arm leads north and back into Switzerland via the Splügen Pass, and the other goes south to Lago di Como and on to Milan. The postbus from St Moritz to Lugano branches off from the Milan road to circle the western shore of the lake.

As the valley proceeds in a south-westerly direction, the villages betray an increasing Italian influence. **Stampa** was the home of the artist Alberto Giacometti (1901–66), and is now the location of the tourist office (☎ 081-822 15 55, fax 822 16 14) for the Bregaglia.

SOGLIO
☎ 081 • pop 220 • elevation 1095m

This tiny, idyllic village is close to the Italian border and has no tourist office. It commands excellent views over the valley, and faces the smooth-sided Pizzo Badile (3308m). Soglio rests on a south-facing ledge, reached from the valley floor by a narrow, winding road.

The village is a warren of small lanes and alleys overlooked by picturesque stone houses, and there is a church with an Italianate bell tower and a 'to die for' view from the cemetery. Soglio is the starting point for several **hiking** trails, most notably the historic **Panorama Hochweg**, which easily lives up to its name. It takes around four hours to reach Casaccia, 11km distant and down in the valley. Stampa, also on the valley floor, takes 1½ hours.

Places to Stay & Eat

Mürias (☎ 822 15 00), near the bus stop, is a tiny place that doubles as a kiosk; singles/doubles with shower are Sfr60/110. *Stüa Grande* (☎ 822 19 88, fax 822 19 88), by the church, has variable-sized rooms and charges from Sfr63/68 per person without/with shower. The restaurant has meals from Sfr15 to Sfr40 and a nice terrace with a view; it's closed on Monday and Tuesday in winter, and for the whole of January.

The best place to stay in Soglio is *Palazzo Salis* (☎ 822 12 08, fax 822 16 00), 50m up from the post office. This place really is like a palace, with paintings and portraits on the walls, suits of armour, hunting trophies and fine old furniture. There are several lobbies, an open fire and an extensive, secluded garden. The rooms are grand, too, with porcelain stoves and stucco or wooden ceilings. Doubles are Sfr200 with shower/WC and singles/doubles with hall shower are Sfr75/150 without. They're well worth the money for the atmosphere. It's open early March to late November, and has a restaurant where pasta is Sfr14 to Sfr24 and fish/grills start at Sfr30.

Getting There & Away

Buses from St Moritz to Castasegna run along the Bregaglia Valley. Alight at the post office at Pomontogno and take the bus to Soglio from there (Sfr3 each way; six to 10 departures per day).

GRAUBÜNDEN

North-East Switzerland

The north-east of Switzerland is often over-looked by visitors. That's a pity, because although it doesn't have the scenic grandeur of the southern areas, the rolling green hills are equally enticing. The region is overloaded with castles (most of them private) and attractive town centres. Stein am Rhein has probably the prettiest main square in all Switzerland. Lake Constance (Bodensee) is another big draw, providing summer recreation possibilities and access to attractions in neighbouring Germany and Austria.

History

Glarus was one of the earliest converts to the Swiss Confederation, joining in 1352. Schaffhausen joined in 1501 after the Swabian War, and Appenzell in 1513 during the Swiss attempts to subjugate Milan. During this period of expansionist policies by the Confederation, Thurgau became a sovereign territory and St Gallen an 'allied canton' (with inferior rights). Both became full cantons in Napoleon's 1803 reorganisation of the Helvetic Republic.

The north-east could easily have become larger than it is; in 1510 the German town of Constance would have been admitted, had not the Confederates shied away from altering the urban/rural balance, and in 1918 the Austrian state of Vorarlberg wanted to join the Confederation, a request turned down by the great powers in 1919.

Orientation & Information

The north-east tourist region includes the cantons of Schaffhausen, Thurgau, St Gallen, Appenzell and Glarus. It also takes in the Principality of Liechtenstein which is dealt with in the following chapter.

Most of the land is fairly flat, making it suitable for dairy and arable farming. The Appenzell region is famous for the production of the cheese of the same name. Textiles are also important, particularly in St Gallen, where embroidered lace has an international

Highlights

- Explore the picturesque town centres in St Gallen, Appenzell and Stein am Rhein.
- Visit St Gallen's cathedral and abbey library – a world heritage site.
- Learn about cheese-making in Stein.
- Cruise along the River Rhine.
- Enjoy water sports on Lake Constance.
- Witness open-air parliament in Appenzell in April.

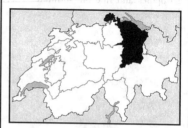

Appenzell Innerrhoden

Glarus

Appenzell Ausserrhoden

Schaffhausen

St Gallen

Thurgau

reputation. The metal and machine industries also make a significant contribution to the local economy.

The north-east is also noted for its high concentration of small and medium-size breweries. Liquid assets to look out for include Falkenbier (brewed in Schaffhausen),

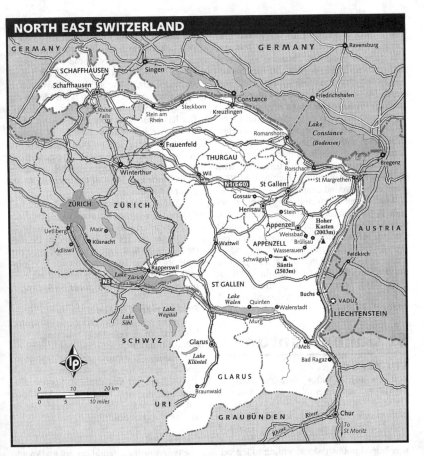

NORTH EAST SWITZERLAND

GERMANY

GERMANY

Ravensburg

SCHAFFHAUSEN

Singen

Schaffhausen

Friedrichshafen

Constance

Rhine
Falls

Steckborn

Stein am
Rhein

Kreuzlingen

Lake
Constance
(Bodensee)

Romanshorn

Frauenfeld

THURGAU

Bregenz

Winterthur

Wil

Rorschach

St Margrethen

N1(E60)

St Gallen

Gossau

ZÜRICH

ZÜRICH

Herisau

Stein

Uetliberg

Maur

Appenzell

Hoher
Kasten
(2003m)

Küsnacht

Weissbad

Brülisau

AUSTRIA

Adliswil

Wattwil

APPENZELL

Wasserauen

Feldkirch

Schwägalp

Säntis
(2503m)

Rapperswil

Lake Zürich

ST GALLEN

N3

Lake
Walen

Buchs

Quinten

Walenstadt

VADUZ

Lake
Sihl

Lake
Wägital

Murg

LIECHTENSTEIN

SCHWYZ

Glarus

Mels

Lake
Klüntal

Bad Ragaz

GLARUS

0   10   20 km
0   5   10 miles

Braunwald

URI

GRAUBÜNDEN

River

Chur

Rhine

To
St Moritz

Löwengarten Bier (Rorschach) and Locher
Bräu (Appenzell).

The region's best-known mountain is
Säntis (2503m), although there are some
higher peaks in the southern part. Aside
from Lake Constance, which it shares with
Germany and Austria, the largest lake in the
north-east is Lake Walen *(Walensee)*. The
Rhine Falls, near Schaffhausen, are a noisy,
often dramatic spectacle.

The local people in rural parts have a reputation for being traditional, parochial folk.
This is reflected in the fact that they still conduct the ancient practice of an open-air

parliament *(Landsgemeinde)*. This annual
meeting, where citizens vote by show of
hands on local matters, is well worth viewing. In Appenzell Innerrhoden the vote is on
the last Sunday in April in Appenzell village.
Appenzell Ausserrhoden abandoned the
Landsgemeinde system only a few years ago.

Information for the north-east is covered
by the St Gallen tourist office; contact details are as listed in the following St Gallen
Canton section, except for the email address
(e info@ostschweiz-i-ch). There are also
various regional offices, such as Thurgau
(e tgtourismus@bluewin.ch).

Getting Around

The canton of Thurgau has a regional one-day pass, the Thurgauer Tageskarte. It covers a 1111km network of rail, bus and boat travel, and costs Sfr27.50, or Sfr17.50 for children (six to 16 years) and those with the Half-Fare Card. This is bound to save you money, particularly if you're planning a lengthy boat trip on the Rhine River or Lake Constance. Towns bordering Thurgau, like St Gallen, Winterthur and Schaffhausen are covered, as is the route to Engen in Germany. The pass is issued year-round. Parents travelling with children should acquire a Family Card (see the Getting Around chapter).

The Appenzellerland Toggenburg regional pass covers routes in and around Säntis, Ebenalp, Appenzell, Stein, plus St Gallen, Romanshorn, Rorschach and less well-known places further east, extending as far as Hohenems in Austria. The price is Sfr78 (Sfr63 for Swiss railpass-holders) for three days' free travel in seven, or Sfr98 (Sfr79) for five in 15. It's issued from 1 May to 31 October.

St Gallen Canton

ST GALLEN

☎ 071 • pop 70,300 • elevation 670m

In 612 AD, an itinerant Irish monk called Gallus fell into a briar. An irritating mishap, most people would think, but Gallus interpreted this clumsy act as a sign from God and decided to stay put and build a hermitage. He was helped in this task, according to legend, by a bear. From this inauspicious beginning, the town of St Gallen evolved and developed into an important medieval cultural centre, reaching the peak of its influence in the 10th century. The Reformation was brought to St Gallen in 1529 by Joachim von Watt, known as Vadian. His statue stands in Marktgasse.

Orientation & Information

St Gallen is the seventh largest city in Switzerland. The train station has the usual facilities, including train information, lockers, money-exchange counters and bike rental. The main post office (Hauptpost,

9001) is opposite the train station, and is also the departure point for postbuses. The transport hub for city buses is also by the station.

Two minutes away is the tourist office (☎ 227 37 37, fax 227 37 67, **@** info@stgallen-i.ch), Bahnhofplatz 1a, which is open 9 am to noon and 1 to 6 pm Monday to Friday, and 9 am to noon on Saturday. The office has a free hotel booking service. Pick up its *Tourist Information* booklet in English, which has a map and coupons for discounts. A few minutes to the east is the pedestrian-only Old Town, dominated by the twin spires of the cathedral. Most of the main sights are clustered in this area.

The budget travel agency, SSR (☎ 223 43 47) is at Frongartenstrasse 15, open from Monday afternoon to Saturday morning.

Internet access at the Media Lounge (☎ 244 30 90, **@** welcome@medialounge.ch), Katerinengasse 10, costs Sfr1 for five minutes (minimum Sfr2). It's open 9 am to 9 pm weekdays, 10 am to 5 pm Saturday.

Pedestrian Centre

St Gallen has a distinctive old-city centre. It's full of interesting buildings with colourful murals, carved balconies and relief statues. The most striking feature of the centre are the oriel windows; some of the best are on Gallusplatz, Spisergasse, Schmiedgasse and Kugelgasse. Also look out for the busy market on Marktplatz on Wednesday and Saturday.

Cathedral

The twin-tower cathedral cannot and should not be missed. It's the final incarnation of Gallus' original hermit's cell and the subsequent monastery. Work was begun in 1755 and the 68m towers were erected in 1766. Completed in 1768, it's immensely impressive and impressively immense. The ceiling frescoes are by Josef Wannenmacher; unfortunately, in poor light the darkness of the colours masks the detail of the paintings. The stucco embellishments are the work of the Gigi brothers. Also look out for the pulpit, arches, statue groups and woodcarvings around the confessionals. It's open daily except during services.

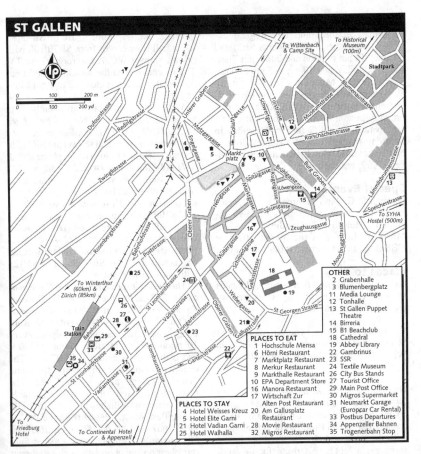

ST GALLEN

0   100   200 m
0   100   200 yd

To Wittenbach
& Camp Site

To Historical
Museum
(100m)

Stadtpark

To Winterthur
(60km) &
Zürich (85km)

Train
Station

To
Friedburg
Hotel

To Continental Hotel
& Appenzell

To SYHA
Hostel (500m)

PLACES TO EAT
1 Hochschule Mensa
6 Hörni Restaurant
7 Marktplatz Restaurant
8 Merkur Restaurant
9 Markthalle Restaurant
10 EPA Department Store
16 Manora Restaurant
17 Wirtschaft Zur
   Alten Post Restaurant
20 Am Gallusplatz
   Restaurant
28 Movie Restaurant
32 Migros Restaurant

PLACES TO STAY
4 Hotel Weisses Kreuz
5 Hotel Elite Garni
21 Hotel Vadian Garni
25 Hotel Walhalla

OTHER
2 Grabenhalle
3 Blumenbergplatz
11 Media Lounge
12 Tonhalle
13 St Gallen Puppet
   Theatre
14 Birreria
15 B1 Beachclub
18 Cathedral
19 Abbey Library
22 Gambrinus
23 SSR
24 Textile Museum
26 City Bus Stands
27 Tourist Office
29 Main Post Office
30 Migros Supermarket
31 Neumarkt Garage
   (Europcar Car Rental)
33 Postbus Departures
34 Appenzeller Bahnen
35 Trogenerbahn Stop

Abbey Library

Adjoining the cathedral is the Stiftsbibliothek, containing some beautifully etched manuscripts from the Middle Ages and a splendidly opulent rococo interior. The graceful lines of the wooden balustrades in the main hall show rare artistry. In total, the library contains 140,000 volumes. There's even an Egyptian mummy dating from 700 BC. Entry costs Sfr7 or Sfr5 for students and children. Opening times are: 9 am to noon and 1.30 to 5 pm Monday to Saturday and 10.30 am to noon and 1.30 to 4 pm Sunday from April to October; and 9 am to noon and 1.30 to 4 pm Monday to Saturday from December to March. It's closed for most of November.

Museums

St Gallen has several museums vying for attention in the Stadtpark, off Museumstrasse to the east of the Old Town. The most significant is probably the **Historical Museum** (Historisches Museum). Of particular note are the models and maps of the town, illustrating the successive versions of the monastery-turned-abbey. Elsewhere in the museum there are some excellent tiled stoves and panelled state rooms, as well as portraits, uniforms, ceramics and ethnological exhibits. Entry costs Sfr6 (students Sfr2) and it's open 10 am to noon and 2 to 5 pm Tuesday to Saturday, and 10 am to 5 pm Sunday.

The **Textile Museum** (Textilmuseum), Vadianstrasse 2, displays an extensive collection of intricately-worked lace and embroidery, spanning three centuries. It's open 10 am to noon and 2 to 5 pm Monday to Saturday (except closed Saturday from 1 November to 31 March) and costs Sfr5 (students Sfr2, children free).

Special Events
Openair St Gallen is a three-day rock festival in late June; performers in 1999 included Metallica, Blondie and Van Morrison. Inquire at the tourist office or UBS Bank ticket corner (☎ 0848-800 800).

Places to Stay
Exhibitions and conferences can make beds scarce and prices high; busy times are usually April and October.

Camping The nearest camping is north of St Gallen at *Leebrücke* (☎ 298 49 69) in Wittenbach, accessible by postbus. It's open April to October.

Hostel The SYHA *hostel* (☎ 245 47 77, fax 245 49 83, Jüchstrasse 25) is a signposted, 15-minute walk east of the Old Town (pedestrians should follow the hostel signs with the adult and child – the other hostel signs are a less direct route for drivers). However, it's easier to take the orange Trogenerbahn from outside the station to 'Schülerhaus' (Sfr2.40) and walk a few minutes up the hill until you see the hostel on the left. Beds are Sfr24 in a dorm or Sfr33 in a double room. Reception is closed from 9.30 am to 5 pm but there's usually daytime access to communal areas. Get a key to avoid the curfew. The hostel closes from mid-December to early March, though it may be open for groups.

Hotels & Pensions *Hotel Weisses Kreuz* (☎/fax 223 28 43, Engelgasse 9) is the best

value, though some walls are thin. It has varying singles/doubles from Sfr45/80 using hall showers, or from Sfr70/100 with private shower/WC. A few rooms have TV. The reception is in the metallic blue-lit bar downstairs, which is closed 2 to 5 pm Monday to Friday.

West of the centre, but conveniently close to the Vonwil stop of bus No 7, is *Friedburg* (☎ 277 10 93, fax 277 10 45, Burgstrasse 72). Simple rooms using hall shower are Sfr48/96, and the restaurant is open daily; phone ahead.

Hotel Elite Garni (☎ 222 12 36, fax 222 21 77, Metzgergasse 9-11) is central, has a lift, and offers a choice of rooms. Singles/doubles are Sfr90/140 with shower/ WC or Sfr70/100 with shower only, while singles using hall shower are Sfr60. *Hotel Vadian Garni* (☎ 223 60 80, fax 222 47 48, Gallusstrasse 36) has attractive modern-looking rooms with TV, from Sfr65/95, or Sfr84/128 with own shower and WC.

The best mid-price deal is the *Continental* (☎ 272 06 06, fax 272 06 07, Teufener Strasse 95). It's a little bit out of the way, but bus No 5 stops out the front (stop: Ruhbergstrasse) and goes to Bahnhofplatz every 10 minutes. Comfortable rooms with TV and bath or shower start at Sfr97/185. The cheaper rooms face the main street and there is garage parking for Sfr12. The restaurant (closed Sunday) is reasonable value, with Swiss dishes for Sfr13 to Sfr38.

The Best Western *Hotel Walhalla* (☎ 222 29 22, fax 222 29 66, ✉ hotelwalhalla@ bluewin.ch) is a conveniently situated four-star place on Bahnhofplatz, with restaurants and a bar. Standard, renovated rooms with all facilities start at Sfr170/260.

Places to Eat
Eating can be pretty good in St Gallen across the range. At the basic level, look out for various fast-food stalls selling St Gallen sausage and bread for around Sfr5. The university *Hochschule Mensa*, west of the train tracks at Dufourstrasse (take bus No 5), offers cheap weekday lunches.

A large *Migros* supermarket and restaurant is near the tourist office on St Leonhardstrasse. Self-service food is also available in the restaurant of the EPA department store at Bohl 6. A *Manora* restaurant is in the Manor department store on Marktgasse. All are open until 6.30 pm weekdays (9 pm on Thursday) and 5 pm on Saturday.

On and around Marktplatz are several options, including a *McDonald's* and a branch of *Merkur* (for reliable, inexpensive food). Next door to EPA is *Markthalle*, with affordable meals either in the bar or the smarter brasserie (closed Sunday). Close by are two restaurants straddling Marktplatz and Neugasse, *Hörni* and *Marktplatz*. Both are similar, open daily, and offer food for a range of prices. Hörni has a wide selection of beers, and courts the weekend clubbers by staying open from 8.45 am Friday through to 4 am Sunday – without a break! Marktplatz restaurant has an upstairs section, where prices are slightly higher.

Near the tourist office is *Movie Restaurant* (*St Leonhardstrasse 32*), which has movie memorabilia and menus written on cinefilm canisters. It's busy, and youngish, and has meals for above Sfr19. During lunch times, except on Sunday, a similar price will include a starter and soft drink.

A good mid-price place is *Wirtschaft Zur Alten Post* (☎ 222 66 01, Gallusstrasse 4). The food is typically Swiss, with meat and fish dishes mostly above Sfr25. Lunch menus, including vegetarian options, start at Sfr17. Small and cosy, this restaurant fills quickly, so reserve ahead. It's closed on Sunday and Monday.

Top-of-the-range in prices and quality is *Am Gallusplatz* (☎ 223 33 30, Gallusstrasse 24). You can construct your own multi-course feast from a number of options (from Sfr65 for three courses), or go with one of the set menus. Main dishes are about Sfr40, or Sfr25 at lunch. The style is French and it's closed Saturday lunchtime and all day Monday.

Entertainment
The *Grabenhalle* (☎ 222 82 11, Blumenbergplatz) is a major venue for rock and jazz concerts, and other arts events. *Gambrinus* (☎ 222 47 71, Wassergasse 5) is a bar/restaurant with live jazz nightly. The

cover charge is around Sfr25 (usually on Wednesday and Saturday) or free. It also has reasonable, inexpensive food (closed Sunday and Monday).

There are plenty of enjoyable bars and discos in the pedestrian centre. Several are on Brühlgasse, including *B1 Beachclub* at No 28 (open Thursday to Saturday nights, entry Sfr8) and *Birreria* at No 45, a crowded bar that claims to stock 700 different beers (open daily).

There are several theatres in the city, including the *Puppet Theatre (Lämmlisbrunnenstrasse 34)*. Classical concerts are often performed at the *Tonhalle (Museumstrasse 25)*. The tourist office has details, and sells tickets for some events.

Getting There & Away
St Gallen is the transport hub for the northeast. It's just a short train or bus ride to/from Lake Constance. There are also regular trains to Bregenz in Austria (Sfr16), Constance (Sfr16.40), Chur (Sfr34) and Zürich (Sfr29; takes 70 minutes, via Winterthur).

By car, the main link is the N1/E60 motorway, which runs from Zürich and Winterthur to the Austrian border. It passes close to the centre of town, just slightly to the north.

For car hire, go to Avis (☎ 277 35 77), Zürcherstrasse 246, Hertz (☎ 278 84 74), down the road at No 63, or Europcar (☎ 222 11 14), at the Neumarkt garage, Vadianstrasse.

Getting Around
Journeys on the bus cost Sfr2, though you could also pay Sfr20 for 12 tickets, Sfr7 for a day pass, or Sfr30 for one week. Buy tickets from dispensers; there's a fine of Sfr50 if you're caught without one. Individual bus tickets are not valid on the Trogenerbahn, where the fare depends upon distance, but the general day passes and the 12-strip tickets *are* valid (as far as Rank).

There are many parking garages in town, including by the tourist office. To park all day in a blue zone, buy an 'Erweiterte Blaue Zone' ticket for Sfr6 from the tourist office or a police station. Otherwise, blue zones are free and subject to a 90-minute limit (no limit from 7 pm to 7 am and at weekends).

RAPPERSWIL

☎ 055 • pop 7200 • elevation 405m

This small town on the north bank of Lake Zürich is in the canton of St Gallen. The tourist office (☎ 220 57 57, fax 220 57 50, ☻ touristinfo@rapperswil-jona.ch) is three minutes from the train station, by the lake at Fischermarktplatz, and is open 10 am to 5 pm daily (1 to 5 pm in winter). The town has a castle which dates from the 13th century and provides a good view from its terrace.

Rappersweil has a connection with the Knie circus, a travelling show that visits many Swiss towns from March to November. A small **Circus Museum** details the history of the Knie family and has videos of past shows (Sfr4, children Sfr2). Enter via the tourist office. There's also **Knies Kinderzoo** (children's zoo), situated behind the station (signposted). There are animal rides, performing sea lions and other attractions such as a pirate's ship. Entry costs Sfr8 for adults and Sfr4 for children, and it is open mid-March to 31 October.

Places to Stay & Eat

The SYHA *hostel* (☎ 210 99 27, fax 210 99 28, Hessenhofweg 10), is close to the lake in the suburb of Jona. Dorms cost Sfr28, singles/doubles are Sfr48/76, and it is closed from around 2 November to 29 January. In the sports complex near the children's zoo is the *Familien Herberge Lido* (☎ 210 33 98). Dorm beds are only Sfr17 (plus Sfr4 for sheets) without breakfast, but phone ahead as it's likely to close in a few years. Check-in is from 5 pm.

Jakob (Hauptplatz 11) is pricey but still one of the cheaper hotels. Singles/doubles are Sfr80/140, with shower/WC and new fittings in grey and white. The bar/cafe has good, inexpensive food (mostly Italian). *Du Lac*, on Fischmarktplatz, has a few rooms (from Sfr69/100 with shower) and a couple of restaurants. Reserve rooms for both places via the tourist office.

Bahnhof Buffet in the train station has cheap self-service Swiss and Italian dishes, and mid-price Chinese food (open daily). Opposite the station is a large *Migros* complex, with a supermarket and a cafe area with limited hot meals and snacks. It's open until 6.30 pm weekdays (8 pm Wednesday and Friday) and 5 pm Saturday and Sunday.

Getting There & Away

Rapperswil is 50 minutes by train from St Gallen (Sfr23). From Zürich (Sfr14.20), the S5 takes 30 minutes; S7 takes 40 minutes but it's a more scenic lakeside trip. Zürich's cantonal tickets are valid. Rapperswil can also be reached by boat from Zürich (Swiss Pass valid).

WALENSEE

This lake at 419m is flanked by the impressively steep Churfirsten mountains to the north. Wedged between the crags and the water on this side is **Quinten**, a tiny place with just a couple of guesthouses. There's no road there – you have to walk from Walenstadt (one hour) or take a boat. Boats go year-round from Murg on the south shore, though other boat tours of the lake are in the summer only. Contact Schiffsbetrieb Walensee (☎ 081-738 12 08) for details. The main rail route from Zürich to Sargans passes along the southern shore of the lake.

Appenzellerland

If you ever hear a joke in Switzerland, the inhabitants of Appenzellerland are likely to be its target. They are known for their parochialism and are considered (unfairly, of course) to be several stages lower on the evolutionary ladder than the rest of humanity. Politically, Appenzellerland is divided into two half-cantons, Innerrhoden and Ausserrhoden. Appenzell itself is in Innerrhoden.

Women were finally allowed to vote for the first time in Innerrhoden cantonal affairs in 1991, and then only after the supreme court ruled their exclusion by the men unconstitutional. The men of Ausserrhoden, reluctantly but without coercion, allowed the women to have their say the year before.

Such resistance to change has its advantages for the tourist in that Appenzellerland has a quaint air of being unaffected by modern life. It is a region of farms, verdant hills and villages with characteristic gabled houses. Several mountains enliven the hiking possibilities.

Activities

Hiking Pick up the hiking map (Sfr1) from one of the local tourist offices, which gives a summary of routes and average walking times. All the peaks in the region can be ascended by foot if you don't want to take the cable car. There's a **geologischer Wanderweg** (geological path) linking Hoher Kasten, Stauberen, Saxerlücke, Fälensee lake and Brülisau. There are 14 information boards along the several alternative routes, detailing geological features. Start at the highest point by taking the train to Weissbad, the bus to Brülisau, and the cable car to Hoher Kasten (Sfr18 up, Sfr13 down, Sfr23 return). See the Säntis section for more walking suggestions.

Skiing Skiing is not a major activity, but it's still possible. The main area for downhill is the **Kronberg** (1663m), with just 10km of runs, which is reached by cable car from Jakobsbad. There are also some slopes on Ebenalp and above Appenzell. A one day pass for either area costs Sfr30, or a three-day lift pass for both costs Sfr70 (children Sfr50); they're available from the Appenzell tourist office. There are also some ski schools and cross-country skiing trails.

APPENZELL

☎ 071 • pop 5000 • elevation 785m

The smell of the countryside – cows and their waste products – permeates the air in pastoral Appenzell. The village is a delight to wander around (albeit crowded with tourists on summer weekends), with traditional old houses, painted facades and lush surrounding pastures.

Orientation & Information

The train station (with money-exchange and bike rental) is 400m from the centre of town.

The tourist office (☎ 788 96 41, fax 788 96 49, @ ferien@appenzellerland.ai.ch) is in the centre on Hauptgasse, a mostly pedestrian-only street. It has information on all of Appenzellerland and is open 8 am to noon and 2 to 5 pm Monday to Friday (6 pm in summer), and 9 am to noon and 2 to 4 pm Saturday (5 pm in summer). Call ☎ 0800-801 887 (toll-free) for hotel reservations.

Things to See & Do

Hauptgasse is an attractive main street, with wrought-iron hanging signs, and souvenir shops (open daily including Sunday) selling locally-made wares, such as embroidery and decorated confectionery. Take a look inside the village **church** on Hauptgasse and admire the gold and silver figures flanking the baroque altar. The **Appenzell Museum**, in the same building as the tourist office, has folklorish exhibits (Sfr5, Sfr3 students; closed winter Mondays); ask for the extensive English notes. Over the river lies the **Alpenbitter Distillery** (☎ 787 17 17). It offers free tours for groups from Monday to Saturday, which you may be able to join if you telephone ahead. Otherwise, there are open tours at 10 am on Wednesday from April to November.

The streets are bedecked with flags and flowers on the last Sunday in April. This is when the locals vote on cantonal issues by a show of hands in the open-air parliament, the Landsgemeinde. It takes place, not surprisingly, in Landsgemeindeplatz. People wear traditional dress for the occasion and many of the men carry swords or daggers as proof of citizenship.

Places to Stay & Eat

There is year-round camping at *Eischen* (☎ 787 50 30). *Gasthaus Hof* (☎ 787 22 10, fax 787 58 83), off Landsgemeindeplatz, has dorms for Sfr28, doubles with shower/WC for Sfr130, and a few singles/doubles without for Sfr65/110). There's private parking, and a restaurant with a wide range of cheapish Swiss food.

Hotel Taube (☎ 787 11 49, fax 787 56 33), a rustic chalet by the corner of

Swiss Cheese

Switzerland has 1200 village cheese dairies producing around 130,000 tonnes of cheese per annum. The most popular variety is Emmental (55,000 tonnes), followed by Gruyère (23,000 tonnes). It all starts with fresh milk, which is heated and stirred. At the correct temperature rennet is added: this curdles the milk. After further heating, stirring and slicing (eg, with a cheese harp), the resultant cheese grains are extracted from the watery mass (in traditional dairies, by lifting it out with a cheesecloth). The cheese is pressed into circular moulds to form 'wheels'. The size of the cheese wheel depends on the type of cheese – they're as heavy as 60 to 130kg in the case of Emmental. When cooled, these are immersed in a saline bath, within which the cheese discharges water, absorbs salt, and forms its rind.

The cheese is then stored in a cool cellar – though Emmental cheese also has several weeks in a warm, moist fermenting cellar (this causes gas pockets of carbonic acid to form, which creates Emmental's distinctive holes). Months will pass before the cheese attains its full flavour and is allowed to reach the plate and the palate. Semi-hard cheese (eg, Appenzeller) matures the quickest. Hard cheeses, with a lower water content, take the longest – up to three years in the case of Sbrinz cheese.

Postplatz, has singles/doubles for Sfr70/140 with shower/WC, or Sfr60/120 without. Its restaurant has good food, including vegetarian dishes, for about Sfr18.

By the station is *Big Ben Pub & Pizzeria*, where pizzas start at Sfr11 (closed Tuesday). *Gasthaus Traube*, just off Hauptgasse, has small meals from Sfr11, but most dishes top Sfr18 (closed Monday). A *Coop* supermarket is nearby.

Restaurant Sonne (Landsgemeindeplatz), has daily specials from Sfr15 (closed Wednesday in winter), and cheaper 'senior' meals. *Hotel Säntis* (☎ 788 11 11, fax 788 11 10, ✆ romantikhotelsaentis@bluewin.ch, Landsgemeindeplatz), provides more expensive options for both eating and sleeping; rooms start at Sfr110/180.

Getting There & Away

The red, narrow-gauge Appenzell train leaves from the front and to the right of the main St Gallen station (Swiss Pass and Eurail valid; Inter-Rail gets half-price). It meanders along, criss-crossing the course of the road, and takes around 40 minutes. There are two routes so you can go back a different way. Departures from St Gallen are approximately every half hour, via Gais (Sfr10) or Herisau (Sfr12.60).

STEIN

Appenzell culture and crafts are highlighted in this small village. The **Appenzell Showcase Cheese Dairy** (Appenzeller Schaukäserie) provides the opportunity to see the famous cheese undergo a 10-stage progress from pure milk to a ripened cheese wheel. A viewing gallery allows you to watch every move made by the white-clad workers as they rush around manipulating gleaming metal vats and presses. (There's no sneaking a quiet fag behind the churns for these people.)

It's free and open 9 am to 7 pm daily (6 pm from 1 November to the end of February), but it's more interesting to go when the various processes are instigated, from 9 to 11 am and (sometimes) 1 to 3 pm. A brochure in English explains the different stages and contains cheese recipes on the reverse. There's a restaurant on site.

Next door is the **Folklore Museum** (Volkskunde Museum). In addition to the periodic weaving demonstrations, displays include furniture, cowbells, decorated harnesses and traditional pipes. The best exhibit is the collection of simple, childlike, yet evocative pictures of village life, usually showing herders leading lines of cattle. Cows in the foreground are often the same size as those in the distance – the newfangled notion of artistic perspective obviously hadn't reached Appenzellerland at the time (19th century!).

It takes only an hour or so to get round, and costs Sfr7 (Sfr6 students, Sfr3.50 children). It's open 10 am to noon and 1.30 to

5 pm from Tuesday to Saturday, 10 am to 6 pm on Sunday, and 1.30 to 5 pm on Monday from April to October. It's open 10 am to 5 pm Sunday only during the rest of the year.

Getting There & Away
The St Gallen bus (direction: Herisau) passes through woodland and rolling countryside, takes 15 minutes, and drops you right opposite the cheese dairy. The fare is Sfr5 and departures are every one to two hours.

SÄNTIS
Although a mere tiddler in Swiss terms, the Säntis mountain (2503m) is the highest peak in the vicinity, and accordingly offers a marvellous panorama (from the restaurant or terrace) that encompasses Lake Constance, Lake Zürich, the Alps and the Vorarlberg Mountains. To get there, take the train to Urnäsch (on the Appenzell to Herisau line) and transfer to the bus (approximately hourly) to Schwägalp (total fare Sfr13). From Schwägalp (where there's a demonstration cheese dairy, open daily), a cable car ascends to the summit every 30 minutes. It runs 7.30 am to 6.30 pm in summer, 8.30 am to 5 pm in winter. The fare is Sfr21.40 up, Sfr18.50 down, and Sfr30 return.

From Säntis, you can walk along the ridge to the neighbouring peak of **Ebenalp** (1640m) in about 3½ hours. At Wildkirchli on Ebenalp there are prehistoric caves showing traces of Stone Age habitation. The descent to Seealpsee lake on foot takes 1½ hours. Alternatively, a cable car runs between the summit and Wasserauen approximately every 30 minutes (Sfr17 up, Sfr13 down, Sfr22 return). Wasserauen and Appenzell are connected by rail (Sfr3.60).

Schaffhausen Canton

SCHAFFHAUSEN
☎ 052 • pop 34,300 • elevation 404m
The capital of the canton that bears its name, Schaffhausen joined the Swiss Confederation in 1501. It is known as a centre

for heavy industry, communications and arms. During WWII, in 1944 and 1945, it was 'accidentally' bombed by the USA (see the boxed text). Thankfully its medieval town centre survived the shelling, and today merits a leisurely exploration.

Orientation & Information
Schaffhausen is an enclave of Swiss territory surrounded by Germany on the north bank of the Rhine. The train station is adjacent to the Old Town, and has lockers, bike rental, and daily money-exchange counters (to 7 pm, or 5 pm Sunday). There are also information offices for both Swiss and German trains.

The tourist office (☎ 625 51 41, fax 625 51 43, @ tourist@swissworld.com) is in the heart of the Old Town at Fronwagturm. It is open 9 am to 5 pm Monday to Friday, and 10 am to noon Saturday. In summer, weekend hours are 10 am to 4 pm Saturday, 10 am to 1 pm Sunday. Postbuses depart from the rear of the station and local buses from the front. The main post office (8201) is also opposite the station.

Things to See & Do
The attractive Old Town centre is bursting with oriel windows, painted facades and ornamental fountains. The best streets are Vordergasse and Vorstadt, which intersect at Fronwagplatz. From May to October the tourist office organises a guided walking tour of the centre most afternoons (Sfr10, children Sfr5).

Vordergasse has the most distinctive house in the centre, the 16th-century **Haus zum Ritter**, decorated in scenes from mythology and Roman history. These drawings are a relatively recent copy of work done by Tobias Stimmer in 1570. Fragments of the originals can be seen in the **Allerheiligen Museum**, by the cathedral in Klosterplatz. The rest of the collection ranges from ancient bones to modern art. Entry is free and it's open 10 am to noon and 2 to 5 pm Tuesday to Sunday.

Get an overview of the town from the **Munot**, a fortification atop a vine-covered hill. The summit can be attained within 15 minutes from the centre. Aside from the

The Second World War

How Switzerland managed to avoid getting sucked into the 1939-45 war is a question without an easy answer. Swiss pilots shot down with equal diligence Allied and German planes that violated its air space, yet Swiss neutrality involved covert help to both sides too. So Switzerland would have survived whichever side won – somehow the Swiss managed the trick of backing both horses in a two horse race.

The country's civil defence was not so developed in those days, and it would have been relatively easy for Hitler to sweep in and take the northern cities, if not the Alpine regions. Indeed, in July 1940 General Guisan realised that the borders could not be held against attack, and re-deployed the army from frontier posts to entrenched positions in the Alps. A possible invasion would have been eased by the high level of support in Switzerland for Nazi Germany (not least from the president of the Federal Council), boosted by the common border and language. Nazi party members numbered 4000 in Basel alone.

When Paris fell in 1940 the Nazis discovered a secret agreement for the exchange of military information between Switzerland and France. This could easily have been used by Hitler as a pretext for invasion. But a neutral Switzerland had its uses to the Nazis, not least in providing a safe haven for the art treasures and assets pilfered from conquered lands (see the boxed text on banks in the Facts about Switzerland chapter).

To keep Germany at bay, Switzerland also used negotiation and bluff. In a famous (and probably aprocryphal) conversation between a member of the German military and General Guisan, the German asked what would happen if the Nazis sent down a force to take Switzerland. Guisan told him that he could have more than 500,000 men mobilised to defend the country within a few hours. 'And what would happen if we sent down a force double that size?' probed the German. Guisan replied simply, 'Then each man would have to shoot twice.'

Diplomatic relations were kept open with both the Allies and the Nazis, allowing Switzerland to be a conduit through which the belligerents could communicate, and the country undertook tasks like exchanges of prisoners of war. Exactly how far Switzerland had to go to pacify Hitler is not in the public domain, but it is accepted that some arms (tank parts etc) produced by the town of Schaffhausen ended up in Germany. Whether this was by intent or 'accident' is also not clear.

Strange and secretive things happen in wartime. Perhaps it is a coincidence that American bombers, on a mission to southern Germany on 1 April 1944, 'mistakenly' identified Schaffhausen as a German target and unloaded their bombs. The town suffered about 100 casualties, with most bombs falling around the train station and in the nearby woods. The Americans' excuse to the outraged Swiss for this error was that there were navigational difficulties induced by bad weather. Swiss outrage was merely inflamed by this explanation, as weather conditions on the day in question were extremely clear.

The Americans later qualified their version of events by saying that the divisional leader had been shot down earlier, and the winds they encountered were much stronger than expected. The USA paid full compensation to Switzerland, and created guidelines that no target would be bombed within 50 miles of the Swiss frontier, unless positively identified. Curious, therefore, that on 22 February 1945 Schaffhausen again suffered 'accidental' bombing, this time leaving 16 dead.

impressive view, this 16th-century keep boasts a couple of old canons. It's free and open daily: 8 am to 8 pm in summer and 9 am to 5 pm from October to April.

The Rhine Falls (see the following Rhine Falls section) is an easy excursion from the town. Another essential excursion while in the area is a trip along the river. The 45km from Schaffhausen to Constance is considered one of the Rhine's most beautiful stretches, passing by meadows, castles and ancient villages. (See the Stein am Rhein and Lake Constance sections following for more details.)

Places to Stay

Camp by the river at *Rheinwiesen* (☎ *659 33 00*), a couple of kilometres east of the town in Langwiesen, and accessible by postbus. It's open from 1 May to mid-September.

The SYHA *hostel* (☎ *625 88 00, fax 624 59 54, Randenstrasse 65*) is 15 minutes' walk west of the train station, or take bus No 3 to Breite. Dorms cost Sfr23, there's a kitchen, and the reception is closed from 9 am to 5.30 pm. The hostel closes from 1 November to the end of February.

There's not much budget accommodation in the town centre. *Gasthaus zum Engel* (☎ *659 39 04, Adlergasse 11*) has just eight beds; singles/doubles are Sfr50/90 with hall showers. It's 10 minutes' walk from Schaffhausen train station, across the river in Feuerthalen. Phone ahead as reception hours are irregular. *Lowen* (☎ *643 22 08, Im Hösli 2*) has rooms for Sfr60/100, or Sfr70/120 with private shower. It's 3km north of town in Herblingen, reached by city bus No 5.

Park Villa (☎ *625 27 37, fax 624 12 53, Parkstrasse 18*), south of the station by the west side of the tracks, costs from Sfr148/179 for comfortable rooms with shower/WC, or Sfr98/130 without. Some rooms in this friendly, atmospheric place have luxurious antique furnishings, and there's plenty of parking.

The only four-star hotel is the convenient *Hotel Bahnhof* (☎ *624 19 24, fax 624 74 79,* ✉ *mail@hotelbahnhof.ch, Bahnhofstrasse 46*). Rooms are quiet and large, with all amenities, and cost from Sfr140/210.

Places to Eat

You can eat for less than Sfr12 at either the *Migros* supermarket and restaurant at Vorstadt 39, the *EPA* department store and restaurant at Vordergasse 69, or *Manora* in the Manor department store near Fronwagplatz. The food is self-service and good value, and all three places have late opening till 8 pm on Thursday and Friday. There's also *China Town Take Away* (*Vorstadt 36*), with Chinese food from Sfr9.50. You can eat in for the same price (open daily till 11 pm).

Several cafes have outside seating on and around Fronwagplatz, which is ideal on a sunny day. *Restaurant Falken* (*Vorstadt 7*) offers Italian and Swiss food from about Sfr13 (open daily). Next-door, *Zur Flamme* (*Vorstadt 9*) has good vegetarian food from about Sfr15 (closed Monday evening and Sunday). The best pizzas (from Sfr13) are at *Pizzeria Romana* (*Unterstadt 18*), which is closed Wednesday.

For a taste treat, go to *Rheinhotel Fischerzunft* (☎ *625 32 81, Rheinquai 8*). It is acclaimed as one of the top restaurants in Switzerland, a justification for spending around Sfr70 per main dish. It combines Oriental and French styles, particularly incorporating fish, and it's closed Tuesday. Rooms (also expensive) are available too.

Getting There & Away

There are hourly trains to Zürich (Sfr16.40; 40 minutes). Basel can be reached by either Swiss (Sfr45, via Zürich) or German (Sfr20.20) trains. Travel to Constance by German train (via Singen) costs Sfr12.20.

Steamers travel to/from Constance several times a day in summer, and the trip averages four hours; they depart from Freier Platz. The Untersee und Rhein boat company (☎ *25 42 82,* ✉ *info@urh.ch*) is at Freier Platz 7. Schaffhausen has excellent road connections radiating out in all directions.

THE RHINE FALLS (RHEINFALL)

This is the largest waterfall in Europe, and makes a tremendous racket as the Rhine crashes down a 23m drop. The average flow of water is 600 cubic metres per second in summer and 250 cubic metres in winter. The highest ever recorded was 1250 cubic metres per second in the summer of 1965. Impassable to shipping, the falls contributed greatly to the past expansion of Schaffhausen, 3km up-river, as boats were forced to unload cargo there.

From the north bank of the river the falls are less steep and less violent. You need to cross the bridge to the south side to get a true impression of the power of the water flow. The viewpoint from the Schloss Laufen is best. A stairway leads right down to the edge, where the water leaps and boils and sprays the edge of the platform. You need to pay Sfr1 to the Schloss souvenir shop (open daily) to gain access to the staircase, though when the shop shuts in the evening you can walk down for nothing. In the summer, you can take short boat trips from Schloss Laufen for about Sfr6.50.

Places to Stay & Eat
Within the Schloss is an ageing SYHA *hostel* (☎ 052-659 61 52, fax 659 60 39) where the doors are locked from 10 am to 5 pm and there's a midnight curfew. Dorms cost Sfr22 and the hostel is closed from mid-November to mid-March. Kitchen facilities are available for a Sfr2 daily charge.

Stock up or eat in the *Migros* supermarket/restaurant in Neuhausen (no half-day closing). *Schloss Laufen* (☎ 052-659 67 67) has two restaurants, where lunches start at Sfr11, but evening meals are Sfr18 or more unless you stick to vegetarian food. It's closed Monday and Tuesday in the off season, and throughout January and February.

Getting There & Away
From Schaffhausen, the falls are a 40-minute stroll westward along the river. Alternatively, take bus No 1, 6 or 9 to Neuhausen and get off one stop after the Migros in the centre; then follow the brown signs leading to the north bank of the river (five minutes). Reaching Schloss Laufen via a pedestrian bridge takes another 10 minutes.

STEIN AM RHEIN
☎ 052 • pop 2940 • elevation 407m
Delightful Stein am Rhein has a captivating medieval centre. Unused film in your camera stands no chance – the Rathausplatz will claim it in seconds. Inevitably, such beauty has its down side. Stein receives 31,300 overnight visitors annually – quite manageable for its small population. However, over *one million* people per year visit on day trips. The tour buses rolling through are in danger of choking the place to death. If possible, try to visit outside the summer crush.

Orientation & Information
Stein reclines on both sides of the Rhine River. The train station is on the south side, and has money-exchange, bike rental and left luggage facilities. Take Bahnhofstrasse and turn right then left to cross the river for the Old Town (an eight-minute walk). Leading off the pivotal Rathausplatz is Oberstadt (both are pedestrian-only), where awaits the tiny tourist office (☎ 741 28 35, fax 741 51 46) at No 10. Its opening hours are 9 to 11 am and 2 to 5 pm Monday to Friday and (June to September) Saturday morning. A small post office is on Brodlaubegass; another is located by the train station.

Things to See & Do
The first thing to do is admire the splendid facades of the buildings all around the **Rathausplatz**. It is the most photogenic square in Switzerland. Many of the murals depict the animal or object after which the house is named, such as the Sun, Red Ox or White Eagle. A particularly good pairing of pictorial scenes is at Nos 1 and 2. The former was painted by Thomas Schmid from 1520–25; it is the oldest fresco in the Rathausplatz. No 2 displays the most recent work, painted by Alois Carigiet in 1956. Opposite, the impressive Rathaus has some historical exhibits on the 2nd floor – telephone ahead to view (☎ 741 54 25). No 17 contains a small museum of phonographs (Sfr3 entry; open daily, March to October).

Museum Lindwurm, Unterstadt 18, is a four-storey preserved residence that evokes the bourgeois and agricultural lifestyle of the 19th century (Sfr5, students Sfr3). It's open 10 am to 5 pm daily except Tuesday from March to October.

The streets around the square are worth exploring, too. There are several gate towers dating from the 14th century, including one at the end of Understadt. **Kloster St Georgen** is a former Benedictine monastery dating from the 12th century. It houses a museum of local history and art, open 10 am to 5 pm March to October (closed Monday; Sfr3, children and students Sfr1.50).

On the hill above the town, **Burg Hohenklingen** offers a commanding view of the

Appenzell's traditional charm, North East Switzerland

MARTIN MOOS

Laughing cow has a bad day!

MARTIN MOOS

The Rhein waterfall (Rheinfall), North East Switzerland

MARTIN MOOS

CHRIS MELLOR

Historic town Stein am Rhein

Resturant sign, Appenzell, North East Switzerland

MARTIN MOOS

Border control

The Three Sisters mark the Austrian border

Liechtenstien's royal castle commands a stunning hill top view.

The picturesque village of Ruggell surrounded by Swiss peaks

Church in Ruggell

own and river, and a restaurant (closed
Monday and the months of January and
February).

Places to Stay

Stein camp site, *Grenzstein* (☎ 741 51 44),
is about 2km from the village by the Rhine.
It is open year round and costs Sfr7 per
adult and from Sfr5 for a tent. Good facilities on site include washing machines,
camp shop and restaurant.

The SYHA *hostel* (☎ 741 12 55, fax 741
51 40, Hemishoferstrasse 87) is 1.5km out
of the centre. Hemishoferstrasse is the continuation of Understadt to the west, and the
hostel is two minutes from the beach. It's
closed from 1 November to the end of February and beds cost Sfr23. Reception is
closed 9 am to 5.30 pm.

Gästehaus Garni Bleichehof (☎ 741 22
57) charges Sfr50/80 using hall showers but
it's not really viable unless you have your
own transport or don't mind walking over
2km (head towards Burg Hohenklingen
then follow the brown signs – there's no
street name).

Staying in the centre is a budget-busting
proposition. *Mühlethal Gasthaus* (☎ 741
27 25, Öhningerstrasse), 200m east of the
tourist office, is the cheapest, with smallish
singles/doubles with shower/WC for
Sfr70/100. *Hotel Adler* (☎ 742 61 61, fax
741 44 40, Rathausplatz 2) has comfortable
rooms for Sfr120/160 with own
shower/WC, TV and telephone. Garage
parking costs Sfr12 and it has a quality
restaurant (closed Tuesday). It is also the reception and breakfast site for the *Motel
Roseberg*, on the south side of the river.
Rooms here are slightly smaller, prices start
at Sfr95/100 and there's ample free parking.

Places to Eat

As if to deliberately counterbalance the
splendour of the Old Town centre, the *Migros* supermarket and restaurant is housed
in a dreary concrete block with all the flair
of a bomb shelter; it defaces Grossi Schanz,
a few minutes north of the Obertor gate
tower. It's open 8.30 am to 6.30 pm Monday to Friday and 8 am to 4 pm Saturday.

Restaurant Jumbo (Öhningerstrasse 10)
is a Chinese place with a two-course weekday buffet for Sfr15. Evening meals are expensive here, as they are at most of the other
restaurants. Fish dishes are a speciality at a
number of places in the centre, including at
Salmenstübli (Understadt 15). Most prices
are in the range of Sfr20 to Sfr35, though
there are cheaper lunches and vegetarian
meals (closed Monday).

For top quality, look to *Sonne* (☎ 741 21
28, Rathausplatz 13). It's the oldest restaurant in town (the building dates from 1463)
and is closed on Tuesday and Wednesday. It
serves fish dishes and seasonal specialities
for around Sfr40 to Sfr50, and open (decanted) wines.

Getting There & Away

Travel to Zürich (S-Bahn S29) costs Sfr22.
Stein am Rhein is also on the hourly train
route linking Schaffhausen (Sfr6.80) and
Rorschach (Sfr19). The easiest way to St
Gallen (Sfr24) is via this route, changing at
Romanshorn. Regular buses to Singen in
Germany (Sfr5) depart from the train station.

A boat trip along this stretch of the Rhine
is a real pleasure (see Getting Around in the
Lake Constance section). The same sights
can be perused by car on highway 13, which
runs along the south bank of the river. Although the other towns and villages en route
aren't as perfectly preserved as Stein am
Rhein, many feature attractive church
spires, half-timbered houses and hilltop castles. Places to look out for, and perhaps
linger awhile, are Ermatingen, Mannenbach
and Steckborn to the east, and Diessenhofen
to the west.

Lake Constance

Lake Constance (or Bodensee in German) is
a giant bulge in the sinewy course of the
Rhine and offers a choice of water sports, relaxation or cultural pursuits. Constance (German: Konstanz) the town achieved historical
significance in 1414 when the Council of
Constance was convened to try to heal huge
rifts in the Catholic Church. The consequent

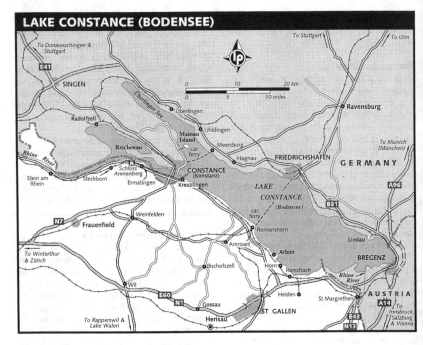

LAKE CONSTANCE (BODENSEE)

burning at the stake of the religious reformer, Jan Hus, as a heretic, and the scattering of his ashes over the lake, failed to halt the impetus towards the Reformation.

Lake Constance is a summer area, though on the German side of the lake, the pre-Lent, late-winter Fasnacht celebrations can be lively, helped along by Constance's large student population.

Orientation

Lake Constance is shared by Switzerland, Germany and Austria and is 395m above sea level. Constance (Konstanz) is the largest town on the lake and sits on the end of the peninsula between the two western arms, the Überlinger See and the Unter See. Constance proper is in Germany, although the adjoining town of Kreuzlingen is Swiss and really all part of the same conurbation. Border controls between the two are very low key. Romanshorn and Rorschach are the other two main towns on the Swiss side.

In addition to Constance, the German stretch of the lake features two other main tourist centres, Meersburg and the island of Lindau. The only town of note in the Austrian part of the lake is Bregenz.

Information

Local tourist offices often have information that covers the whole lake, though there's also a general office: Internationales Bodensee-Tourismus (☎ 07531-90 94 0, fax 90 94 94, ✉ info@bodensee-tourismus.de), Insel Mainau, D-78465 Konstanz. Resorts in all three countries are covered in this section, and prices listed are given in the local currency. One Swiss Franc is worth around DM1.2 (Deutschmarks) and 8.5AS (Austrian Schillings).

Both currencies will soon be superseded by the euro, which is worth about Sfr1.62. In Germany and Austria, post offices provide the most cost-effective money-exchange facilities, though as you'll pay ommission, try to change money in witzerland. Most shops and restaurants vill accept neighbouring currencies, but erhaps at an unfavourable rate. The telephone country code for Germany is ☎ 49 and for Austria it is ☎ 43.

Things to See & Do

Although there is some sightseeing to be done, the main point of being here is to enjoy the lake and the many water sports on offer. In Switzerland, there are sailing schools at Kreuzlingen (☎ 071-688 80 20) and Romanshorn (☎ 071-463 51 21). Other schools are mentioned below. You can swim at swimming pools, private beaches (entry fee) or free public beaches. The international **Bodensee Festival** takes place from early May to early June. Most of the events (concerts, cabaret, theatre etc) are on the German side of the lake. Get information from the Bodensee-Festival GmbH (☎ 07541-92 32 0, fax 33 32 3), Olgastrasse 21, D-88045 Friedrichshafen.

Places to Stay & Eat

Accommodation and food are cheaper in Germany and Austria than in Switzerland, so it could make sense to use one of those two countries as a base for exploring the whole lake. Most places round the lake are smaller-scale establishments, so book ahead in season. Contact tourist offices well in advance for lists of holiday apartments.

Other places to stay include pensions, inexpensive private homes (usually a three-day minimum stay is required), many camp sites (generally closed from November to March) and hostels. Hostel prices in Germany are lower for people under 27 (so-called juniors). There is no junior/senior distinction in Bregenz or the Swiss hostels. All hostels mentioned under the following towns are HI-affiliated.

Places to eat with a lakeside view are invariably more expensive. Be sure to sample some of the Bodensee's aquatic inhabitants on your dinner plate, such as trout (Forelle) or whitefish (Felchen).

Getting There & Away

Direct trains run hourly from Schaffhausen to Kreuzlingen and the journey takes one hour. Excursions to the lake are easy from St Gallen: direct trains go to Romanshorn and Rorschach, and a direct bus goes to Arbon and Rorschach Hafen (Sfr7.40). Constance has train connections every one to two hours to Zürich and Donaueschingen (DM22.40). Trains from Munich go to Lindau (2½ hours). Trains from Switzerland to Bregenz go via St Margrethen. Bregenz is on the main express rail route through Austria, with regular direct trains to Innsbruck, Salzburg and Vienna.

Access to the lake by road is good on all sides. From Zürich, the N1 (E60) motorway runs north-east via Winterthur and St Gallen, to the Austrian border near Rorschach. The N7 branches off just after Winterthur and leads to Kreuzlingen.

Getting Around

Train & Bus Although trains link Bregenz, Lindau, Friedrichshafen and Constance, buses often provide the easiest land connections between these places. Meersburg isn't even on the railway line, and can be reached by bus from Friedrichshafen or by car ferry from Constance (see the following Boat section).

On the Swiss side, buses serve many locations, but for travelling around the lake shore you'll need to take the train. This route, formerly in the hands of the SBB, recently transferred to the privately-run Mittelthurgaubahn (Mthb). The company's performance is being watched carefully; if it's successful, it will retain the route permanently and it may herald further parcelling off of SBB routes into private hands. Single rail fares from Rorschach Hafen are: Horn Sfr2.40, Arbon Sfr3, Romanshorn Sfr5.60, and Kreuzlingen Sfr11.80.

Car The B31 hugs the northern shore of the lake but it can get busy. Likewise on the southern shore, where highway 13 shadows the course of the railway line around the lake, linking all the Swiss resorts mentioned in this section.

Cycling A 270km bike track encloses the lake and is well signposted. The Cyclists' Touring Club in Britain (see the Getting There & Away chapter) produces useful notes to accompany a circular tour.

In Constance, a couple of places rent bikes for only DM17 per day (cheaper by the week), such as Pro Velo (☎ 07531-2 93 29), Konzilstrasse 3. Bregenz train station also rents bikes (AS150 per day), as do the larger stations on the German side, and the Swiss stations at Rorschach Hafen, Arbon, Romanshorn and Kreuzlingen.

Boat The most enjoyable way to get around is by boat. Ferries (dubbed the *Weissen Flotte* – white fleet) follow a number of routes, travelling across, along, or around the lake from early March to late October, with the more frequent services starting in late May. The Swiss Pass and the Thurgauer Tageskarte (see Getting Around in the chapter introduction) are valid only for the Swiss side of the lake (with the exception of the Romanshorn-Friedrichshafen ferry with the Thurgau day pass). The Inter-Rail pass no longer gets any reduction; Eurail gets 50% off the Rorschach-Lindau and Romanshorn-Friedrichshafen ferries, and 35% off the Romanshorn-Rorschach service.

For boat information, contact the operators based in Switzerland (☎ 071-463 34 35, ✉ info@sbsag.ch), Austria (☎ 05574-428 68, ✉ ge.bodenseeschiffahrt@pv.qebb.at) or Germany (☎ 07531-28 13 98, ✉ info@bsb-online).

A Bodensee Pass (Sfr41 for 15 days, Sfr99 for a year) entitles the holder to purchase half-price tickets within the validity period on boats, trains and buses. The seven day version (Sfr47) includes one day of completely free travel, or Bodensee passholders can purchase day passes for free travel separately (Sfr12 for one day, Sfr36 for a set of three passes). They can also get a special boat-only version of the Family Card (for free travel for kids), free of charge.

Bregenz to Constance by boat (via the German shore, DM20.80) takes three hours 30 minutes, with up to seven departures per day. Boats also cruise along the Rhine from Kreuzlingen and Constance all the way Schaffhausen, via the island of Reichen and Stein am Rhine. The total journey tak three hours 40 minutes heading downstrea to Schaffhausen and 4½ hours going th other way (Sfr27.50 single/return with th Thurgauer Tageskarte).

Between Meersburg and Constan there's a car ferry that sails year-roun every 15 minutes in the day, every 30 mi utes in the evening and hourly all throug the night. The fare is DM2.20 per perso plus DM1.50/3 per bicycle/motorcycle an from DM9.50 per car. In Meersburg, boa depart only a few minutes' walk from th centre, but in Constance, you need to g to/from Staad (bus No 1 from the Bahnhof Another car ferry sails year-round betwee Romanshorn and Friedrichshafen. Depar ures are hourly from at least 8.30 am to 5.3 pm, with extra early/late services mo days. The fare is Sfr8 per person pl Sfr6/18 per bicycle/motorcycle and fro Sfr24 per car, and the journey takes 40 mi utes. The boat landing stage in Romansho is directly outside the train station.

CONSTANCE (KONSTANZ)
☎ 07531 • pop 77,000

In Constance, the tourist office (☎ 13 30 3 fax 13 30 60, ✉ info@touristinformatio stadt.konstanz.de), Bahnhofplatz 13, is to th right as you leave the train station. It's ope Monday to Friday in winter, daily in summe The SBB counter in the Schweizer Bahnho section of the station changes money withou charging commission.

The town's most visible feature is th Gothic spire of the **cathedral** (Münster added only in 1856 to a church that wa started in 1052. The views from the top a excellent. Follow the walking tour of th historic centre prescribed in the tourist o fice leaflet, lingering in the **Stadtgarten**. I north-west Constance there's a footbridg to **Mainau Island**, a tropical garden that wa established by the royal house of Swede (entrance DM18, or DM5 in winter). Com bination tickets are available that includ **Sea Life** and the connecting boat. Newl opened in 1999, Sea Life costs DM1

(DM11/14 for kids/students) on its own, and has aquariums and high-tech marine displays. Constance has a public beach at **Strandbad Horn**, open May to September.

Places to Stay & Eat
The DJH **hostel** (☎ *3 22 60, fax 3 11 63, Zur Allmannshöhe 18)* is open from March to October and costs DM21.50/26.50 for juniors/seniors. Take bus No 4 from the station. There's an accommodation board outside the tourist office.

Central places include **Pension Graf** (☎ *128 68 90, Wiesenstrasse 2)*, with simple singles/doubles from DM53/92, or **Barbarossa** (☎ *2 20 21, fax 2 76 30, Obermarkt 8-12)* with a range of rooms from DM50/90.

Seekuh *(Konzilstrasse 1)* is a student-type bar that dishes up great food and company. Salads, pasta and pizza are around DM11 and it's open every evening until about 1 am. Also try **Cleopatra** *(Bahnhofstrasse 8)* for Egyptian food, or the university **Mensa** for cheap lunches. **Graf Zeppelin** (☎ *2 37 80)*, on Untere Laube by Stephansplatz, has more class and atmosphere. Fish dishes are around DM25 (open daily).

KREUZLINGEN
☎ 071 • pop 16,200 • elevation 404m
Kreuzlingen has a tourist information counter in the TCS travel agent (☎ 672 38 40, fax 672 17 36, ✉ info@kreuzlingen-tourismus.ch), Hauptstrasse 39. Head left from the main train station. Opening hours are 8.30 am to noon and 1.45 to 6 pm Monday to Friday, and 8.30 am to noon Saturday.

There's not very much to see in the town, except perhaps the 17th-century **St Ulric's Church** on Hauptstrasse. Most of the attractions are on the German side of the border. The main crossing points are at Hauptstrasse and Konstanzerstrasse. There's a smaller crossing by the east side of the rail-tracks that is usually unattended in the evening. Using this route you can walk to the centre of Constance from Kreuzlingen youth hostel in 20 minutes, rather than messing around taking two trains.

A possible excursion when the weather is poor is to nearby **Frauenfeld**, where the

cantonal museums of Thurgau are located: the Historisches Museum in the Schloss, the Naturmuseum in the Luzernerhaus, and the Kunstmuseum (Fine Arts Museum) which is located on the outskirts of town. Frauenfeld is 40 minutes by train (Sfr15.40 one way; change at Weinfelden). About 10km west of Kreuzlingen is the Napoleon Museum in Schloss Arenenberg.

Places to Stay
Fischerhaus camp site (☎ *688 49 03)* is by the lake, 1.5km from the tourist office. The SYHA **hostel** (☎ *688 26 63, fax 688 47 61, Promenadenstrasse 7)* is 10 minutes' walk from Kreuzlingen Hafen station (turn left, then left again over the tracks). It features communal showers and good buffet breakfasts in a stately old building situated in parkland. Dorm beds cost Sfr22.80 and it is open from 1 March to 31 November.

For hotels, you could just as easily stay in Constance, or there's a couple of places opposite the train station: **St Gallerhof** (☎ *672 60 20)* costs Sfr55/110 for rooms with shower/WC, or the friendlier **Bahnhof-Post** (☎ *672 79 72 fax 672 49 82)* has singles/doubles with shower/WC and TV for Sfr90/115, and singles for Sfr50 without.

Places to Eat
In Kreuzlingen there's a huge **Coop** supermarket, down the side street opposite the tourist office. The restaurant (but not the supermarket) is open Sunday, until 5 pm. Ultra-cheap is the self-service restaurant in the **EPA** department store, on the corner of Hauptstrasse and Parkstrasse. About 200m along the street is **Park Kafi** *(Hauptstrasse 82)*, with meals for Sfr13 to Sfr18, including vegetarian dishes (open daily). **Restaurant Seeburg** (☎ *688 47 75)*, by the youth hostel, offers quality cuisine in a cultured setting. Main dishes start at Sfr18 (closed Tuesday and Wednesday).

ROMANSHORN
☎ 071 • pop 8000 • elevation 399m
About 20km south-east of Kreuzlingen, this industrial town is of minimal sightseeing interest, but is a convenient base thanks to

the direct ferry service to Friedrichshafen (see the Lake Constance Getting Around section above for details). The tourist office (☎ 463 32 32, fax 461 19 80) is in the train station, open daily in summer, Monday to Saturday in winter.

Places to Stay & Eat

Camping is at *Strandbad Amriswil* (☎ 463 47 73), west of Romanshorn at Uttwil. The SYHA *hostel* (☎ 463 17 17, fax 461 19 90, Gottfried Keller Strasse 6) is five minutes from the station. Dorm beds are Sfr20 and it is open from 1 March to 31 October.

Hotel Garni (☎ 461 10 80, fax 461 10 69, Bahnhofstrasse 56), 1km from the station, has ample parking. New-looking rooms with shower/WC are Sfr60/110; next door is a large *Migros* supermarket and restaurant.

Bodan (☎ 463 15 02, fax 463 15 01), opposite and to the right of the station, has singles/doubles for Sfr60/120 with shower/WC and Sfr45/90 without. Its restaurant is open daily and specialises in schnitzels (from Sfr14/18 small/big). There are several other places to eat close by.

ARBON

☎ 071 • pop 8500 • elevation 398m

The tourist office (☎ 447 85 15, fax 447 85 10), 200m to the left of the station at Bahnhofstrasse 40, is in a travel agency. Walk 10 minutes in the same direction for the historic centre of town. With its castle and old churches it certainly merits a stroll. The castle was built in the 16th century and is home to an historical museum (Sfr2) that is open 2 to 5 pm daily from May to September. It's open Sundays only in spring/autumn. There are also a number of eye-catching, half-timbered houses in the vicinity.

Places to Stay & Eat

Camp at *Strandbadcamping Buchhorn* (☎ 446 65 45). *Hotel Krone* (☎ 446 10 87, Bahnhofstrasse 20) has rooms for just Sfr36/70, or Sfr50/88 with private shower. The restaurant offers cheap meals from Sfr9, but it and reception are closed at weekends. *Pension Garni Sonnenhof* (☎/fax 446 15 10, Rebenstrasse 18), in a

residential street, has kitsch garden statues and rooms from Sfr45/80. *Hotel Restaurant Park* (☎ 446 11 19, fax 446 22 26, Parkstrasse 7), behind Hotel Krone, charges Sfr85/140 for rooms with shower, toilet and TV.

By the station is a *Migros* restaurant and supermarket, with a lake terrace and late opening till 8 pm on Friday. *Gasthof Frohsinn* (Romanshornerstrasse 15) brews its own palatable beer; eat from Sfr15 in the downstairs bar (where there's live music some Monday evenings) or in the plusher and pricier upstairs restaurant. Those on a spending spree can wander into *Gasthaus Römerhof* (☎ 447 30 30, Hauptstrasse), in a distinctive old building attached to the ancient town fortifications. Main courses are above Sfr30 and it is closed on Monday.

RORSCHACH

☎ 071 • pop 9500 • elevation 398m

The main points of interest are around the Rorschach Hafen train station; the main Rorschach station, which is on the St Gallen-Bregenz route, is a couple of kilometres to the east of the centre. The Hafen station is also the departure point for the hourly cogwheel train which climbs a scenic route to the health resort of **Heiden**. The tourist office (☎ 841 70 34, fax 841 70 36, ✉ info@tourist-rorschach.ch) is opposite the Hafen station and near the post office. It's open 9.30 am to noon and 2 to 5.30 pm weekdays except Monday morning. It's closed mornings in winter, open Saturday morning in summer.

From the Hafen station walk left (east) down Hauptstrasse to see some fine oriel windows, particularly at Nos 33, 31 and the town hall, No 29. You could also check the murals and vaulted ceilings in the Mariaberg teacher training college on Seminarstrasse.

By the station and by the lake is the **Automobil, Motorrad und Automaten Museum**, with a fairly absorbing collection of ancient cars, motorcycles, vending machines and juke boxes. It's open daily from March to November (all day on Sunday and in July and August, afternoons only at other times). Entry costs Sfr7, or Sfr4 for children.

Horn is a pleasant 50-minute amble clockwise from Rorschach. It has a few hotels and restaurants, plus the Shipper's Shop (☎ 841 56 68), Seestrasse 64, with a sailing school, boat and yacht charter and all sorts of water sports gear for sale.

Other water sports schools in and around Rorschach include Delfino Segelschule (☎ 845 40 20) and Windsurf und Snowboard-Center Staad (☎ 855 33 22).

Places to Stay & Eat
Rorschach's SYHA *hostel (☎ 841 54 11)* is for groups only. The cheapest hotel in the centre of Rorschach is *Hotel Löwen (☎ 841 38 87, Hauptstrasse 92)* with fair-sized singles/doubles for Sfr40/80. Each has a shower cubicle in the room. Downstairs there's a British-style pub with snacks and live music nightly. A couple of doors along the road at No 88 is *Hotel Rössli (☎ 844 68 68 fax 841 00 47)*, with nicely proportioned rooms from Sfr79/135 with own shower, toilet and TV.

Rorschach has a better than average, licensed *Coop* restaurant, around the back of the post office on Poststrasse, with menus from Sfr10 and a salad buffet. It has late opening to 9 pm on Friday and is also open to 7 pm on Sunday (unlike the supermarket section). Opposite the tourist office is *Pizzeria Roma*, with 33 types of pizza from Sfr10 to Sfr19.50, plus pasta and fish dishes. *Kornhausstube*, next to the tourist office, is typically Swiss, with meals from Sfr14 (closed Monday).

BREGENZ
☎ 05574 • pop 27,100 • elevation 398m
Bregenz is the provincial capital of Vorarlberg, Austria's smallest state. The tourist office (☎ 43 39 10, @ tourismus@ bregenz.vol.at), Bahnhofstrasse 14, is open 9 am to noon and 1 to 5 pm Monday to Friday and 9 am to noon Saturday, except in July and August when hours are extended. The post office is on Seestrasse (Postamt 6900).

The Old Town is worth a stroll. Its centre-piece and the town emblem is the bulbous baroque **St Martin's Tower** built in 1599. Follow the walking route described in the tourist office leaflet. The **Pfänder Mountain** (1064m) offers an impressive panorama over the lake and beyond. Walk up or take the cable car (AS70 one way, AS125 return). The **Bregenz Festival** takes place from late July to late August. Operas and classical works are performed from a vast waterborne stage on the edge of the lake, but you need to book months in advance from the Kartenbüro (☎ 40 76), Postfach 311, A-6901. Check out its web site at www.bregenzerfestspiele.com. Finally, like Constance, Bregenz has a casino that attracts many gamblers from Switzerland.

Places to Stay & Eat
Seecamping (☎ 718 95, Bodangasse 7) is 3km west of Bregenz train station. The HI *hostel (☎ 428 67, fax 428 674, Belruptstrasse 16A)* is open 1 April to 30 September. Dorm beds cost AS126 excluding sheets and there's a place to leave bags during the day.

Private rooms are the best bargain (ask the tourist office), though the central *Hotel Krone (☎ 421 17, fax 459 43, Leutbühl 3)* has good-value doubles (AS500, or AS720 with private shower). *Pension Gunz (☎ 436 57, Anton Schneider Strasse 38)* has simple singles/doubles for AS360/680 with private shower, and it's closed Tuesday. *Pension Sonne (☎/fax 425 72, Kaiserstrasse 8)* is family-run and charges AS440/800 with private shower/WC, AS350/640 without.

The GWL shopping centre has a *Spar* supermarket with cheap self-service restaurant. Chinese food is a bargain throughout Austria, so call in at *China-Restaurant Da-Li (Anton Schneider Strasse 34)*, where weekday two-course lunches are AS65. *Brauhaus (Anton Schneider Strasse 1)* has a range of Austrian and vegetarian dishes from AS75 (open daily).

LINDAU
☎ 08382 • pop 25,000
Lindau is just inside Bavaria, near the Austrian border. Tourist information (☎ 260 030, fax 260 026) is directly opposite the station and open weekdays (plus Saturday mornings in summer).

NORTH-EAST SWITZERLAND

This island village spills over onto the adjoining north shore. Take a walking tour along **Maximilianstrasse**, **Ludwigstrasse**, and the **harbour** with its Bavarian Lion monument and lighthouse. Also note the muralled **Altes Rathaus** at Reichsplatz. Windsurf-Schule Kreitmeir (☎ 233 30) offers classes and rentals at Strandbad Eichwald.

Places to Stay & Eat
Park Camping Lindau am See (☎ 722 36) is 3km south-east of Lindau. The DJH *hostel* (☎ 967 10, fax 967 150, Herbergsweg 11) charges DM27, but only juniors and families may stay.

On the island, the cheapest deals are *Gästehaus Limmer* (☎ 58 77, In der Grub 16) and *Gästehaus Lädine* (☎ 53 26, In der Grub 25). Both have basic rooms from around DM40/75.

For food, budget travellers should head to *Früchtehaus Hannes (In der Grub 36)*. It offers fruit, vegetables, meats, fish, pastas and ready-mixed salads, all sold by weight. There are tables inside and it's open to 6 pm weekdays and to 1 pm Saturday). *Goldenes Lamm Restaurant* (☎ 57 32), on Paradiesplatz, is quite touristy but reasonably priced.

FRIEDRICHSHAFEN
Graf Zeppelin was born in Constance but first built his overgrown cigar-shaped balloons in this town, an endeavour commemorated in the superb **Zeppelin Museum** (DM12, concessions DM6; closed Monday, except on public holidays), Seestrasse 22. Friedrichshafen's DJH *hostel* (☎ 07541-724 04, Lindauer Strasse 3) charges DM23/28 for juniors/seniors. Phone ahead as it's often full.

MEERSBURG
☎ 07532 • pop 5200
Meersburg is the prettiest town on the lake, with terraced streets and vineyard-patterned hills. The helpful tourist office (☎ 431 110, fax 431 120, @ info@meersburg.de) is up the steep hill at Kirchstrasse 4. It's open weekdays year round, and Saturday morning in summer.

Marktplatz offers great vistas and leads to **Steigstrasse**, lined with lovely half-timbered houses. The 11th-century **Altes Schloss** is the oldest structurally intact castle in Germany and houses ancient weaponry (open daily; DM9, students DM6). The adjacent **Neues Schloss** is classic baroque and contains an excellent staircase (open daily April to October; DM5, students DM2).

Überlingen, about 14km to the west, features the astonishing **Cathedral of St Nicholas**. This has a dozen side altars and a wooden four-storey central altar dating from the 17th century, bedecked in intricate carvings. Another impressive baroque church can be found at **Birnau**.

Meersburg is a good base for water sports, with schools for windsurfing (☎ 53 30), sailing (☎ 55 11), waterskiing (☎ 364) and scuba diving (☎ 92 77); the tourist office can supply details.

Places to Stay & Eat
Hagnau, 4km east of Meersburg, has three camp sites side-by-side, including *Camping Schloss Kirchberg* (☎ 07545-64 13). The DJH *hostel* (☎ 07551-42 04), Alte Nussdorfer Strasse 26, in Überlingen, costs DM23/28 for juniors/seniors.

In Meersburg centre, the cheapest place is the cosy *Hotel Zum Lieben Augustin* (☎ 65 11, Unterstadtstrasse 35), charging DM40/80. Uphill from town, *Haus Säntisblick* (☎ 92 77, Lassberg Strasse 1) has rooms for the same price, and a swimming pool. *Gasthof zum Bären* (☎ 432 20, fax 432 244, Marktplatz 11) is a good choice for both food and accommodation. Rooms with shower start at DM85/150.

Quality dining places include *Winzerstube zum Becher* (Höllgasse) and *Bistro 3 Stuben* (Kirchstrasse), though backpackers may prefer the prices at *Go-In*, a fast food joint at Unterstadtstrasse 8.

Liechtenstein

n some ways you could be forgiven for thinking Liechtenstein is part of Switzerland. The Swiss franc is the legal currency, all travel documents valid for Switzerland are also valid for Liechtenstein, and the only border regulations are on the Austrian side. Blink and you might miss it; the country measures just 25km from north to south, and 6km (on average) from east to west. Switzerland also represents Liechtenstein abroad and in foreign policy (subject to consultation).

But a closer look reveals that Liechtenstein is really quite distinct. The ties with Switzerland began only in 1923 with the signing of a customs and monetary union. Before that, it had a similar agreement with Austria-Hungary from 1852 to 1919. Unlike in Switzerland, there is no military service and no army. In fact, the country last went to war in 1866; soldiers guarded an Alpine pass, and never once made contact with the enemy. The armed might of Liechtenstein, numbering 80 men, was disbanded in 1868.

It also has its own reigning monarch. The present dynasty of rulers has controlled lands here since 1699, mostly by remote control from their estates in the former Czechoslovakia. Prince Franz Josef II was the first ruler to actually live in Liechtenstein, in the castle above Vaduz, the capital and seat of government. He died in 1989 after a reign of 51 years and was succeeded by his son, Prince Hans Adam II.

Although it shares the Swiss telephone and postal system, Liechtenstein issues its own postage stamps. It is a prosperous country and the people are proud of their independence.

Facts about Liechtenstein

Liechtenstein was colonised by the Rhaetians after 800 BC and conquered by the Romans in 15 BC. Christianity appeared

HIGHLIGHTS

- Climb up to the scenically-situated castle above Vaduz.
- Sample local wines and collect postage stamps.
- View the museum collections in Vaduz.
- Ski 'on the cheap' in Malbun.

Liechtenstein

in the region in the 4th century. The country's modern history began when Prince Johann Adam of Liechtenstein purchased the Lordship of Schellenberg (1699) and the County of Vaduz (1712) from the impoverished German nobles who had previously governed them. Although he already owned vast tracts of land in Austria, Hungary, Bohemia and Moravia, the purpose of this purchase was to qualify for a vote in the Diet of Princes. It became a principality on 23 January 1719 by decree of the Holy Roman Emperor, Charles VI.

Liechtenstein remained a principality under the Holy Roman Empire until 1806, when Napoleon took it into his Confederacy of the Rhine as part of his machinations against Prussia. Following Napoleon's fall and the Congress of Vienna in 1815, it joined the German Confederation, before achieving full sovereign independence when that fell apart in 1866. The modern constitution was drawn up in 1921. Even today the prince retains the power to dissolve parliament and must approve every act before it becomes law. As in Switzerland, the people can initiate or reject legislation by referendum.

Prince Hans Adam succeeded Franz Josef II in November 1989, although he had effectively been running the state since 1984. He has always tried to stamp his own authority on the government, going so far as dissolving parliament in 1989 when the politicians failed to give support to his plan to build a new museum for his art collection. The prince is also keen to ensure that the country doesn't blindly follow Switzerland's lead in international affairs, and campaigned actively for EEA (European

Economic Area) membership. In 2000 Prince Hans Adam campaigned for constitutional reforms that will actually limit his own powers in some ways. He is pushing for a referendum and has threatened to relocate himself (and his art collection) to Vienna if he doesn't get his way.

In December 1992, shortly after the Swiss 'No' to the same issue, 55% of Liechtensteiners voted in favour of EEA membership. The country was formally admitted to the EEA in 1995. Despite going separate ways over the EEA issue, the open border between Liechtenstein and Switzerland remains intact. Liechtenstein has no plans to seek full EU membership.

Despite its small size, Liechtenstein has two political regions, Upper and Lower, yielding a total of 25 parliamentary members. As in Switzerland, local communities (11 in number) have a fair degree of autonomy. There are three distinct geographical areas: the Rhine Valley in the west, the edge of the Tirolean Alps in the south-east, and the northern lowlands. The current population is 31,320, with a third of that total made up of foreign residents.

Liechtenstein is well known as a tax haven, and a significant proportion of national income is derived from this status. The government is understandably sensitive about bad press from acceptance of funds from dubious origins. Although the banks have agreed to tighter controls, there are no plans to do away with numbered bank accounts. In 1999, a damning report by the

Did you know... ?

- Income tax in Liechtenstein is only 1.2%.
- The wealth of the royal family is estimated to be worth UK£3.3billion.
- There are 80,000 companies registered in the principality.
- Deposits in Liechtenstein's banks add up to around £50 billion.
- Liechtenstein is the world's largest exporter of false teeth.

German Federal Intelligence Service claimed that money laundering was rife in Liechtenstein. The report alleged that bankers, politicians and the judiciary assisted each other with 'illegal financial transactions on behalf of international criminals'.

Wine production is important to the economy, as are exports of dentures. Liechtenstein is one of the richest countries per capita in the world, and unemployment is only an isolated phenomenon (at the end of 1998 it was at an unusually high level: 2% or 482 people!) Such is its economic strength, that it even employs guest workers from affluent Switzerland! Inflation is always low – 0% in 1998.

The abbreviation for the country is FL (standing for Fürstentum Liechtenstein), which is used on vehicle registration plates. About 80% of the population are Catholic. The official language is German, although most people also speak French and English. The Austrian greeting *Grüss Gott* is more common than the Swiss *Grüezi*. Women were given the vote only as recently as 1984 (the men claimed they didn't want it). In September 1990, Liechtenstein became a member of the United Nations.

Facts for the Visitor

See the Switzerland Facts for the Visitor chapter for practical details not covered here.

Tourist information abroad is distributed through Switzerland Tourism. Local offices in Liechtenstein are well organised and you can pick up the excellent and free *Tourist Guide*. This is updated annually and tells you everything you might want to know about the country. A hotel and pension list is given out that covers the whole country.

Prices in Liechtenstein are comparable to those in Switzerland, and it shares the same level of VAT (7.5%). Shops are usually open 8 am to noon and 1.30 to 6.30 pm Monday to Friday, and 8 am to 4 pm Saturday. Banks share the same weekday hours except they shut around 4.30 pm.

Liechtenstein does not celebrate Switzerland's National Day (1 August) – it has its own National Holiday on 15 August. It also has public holidays on all the main Catholic feast days, as well as on Labour day on 1 May. Although the stamps are different, postal rates are the same as for Switzerland.

Public telephones are maintained by Telecom FL, and unlike Swisscom boxes, they don't have an electronic phone book. But Telecom FL does have a shop (☎ 237 74 47) at Austrasse 77, about 1km south of Vaduz, where there's free internet access. Liechtenstein's telephone country code is 423. There are no regional telephone codes.

It would be slightly unfair – but not very far removed from the truth – to say that if Liechtenstein was not a separate country, few people would bother to visit. As it is, many people come here only for the stamps – a stamp in the passport and stamps on a postcard for the folks back home. But it's worth lingering to appreciate the prince's art collection, and to enjoy the scenery.

Getting There & Away

Liechtenstein has no airport (the nearest is in Zürich) and getting there by postbus is easiest. There are usually three buses an hour from the Swiss border towns of Buchs (Sfr2.40) and Sargans (Sfr3.60) which stop in Vaduz. By train, Zürich to Sargans takes an hour. Buses run every 30 minutes from the Austrian border town of Feldkirch; you sometimes have to change at Schaan to reach Vaduz (the Sfr3.60 ticket is valid for both buses). A few local Buchs-Feldkirch trains stop at Schaan (bus tickets are valid).

By road, route 16 from Switzerland passes through Liechtenstein via Schaan and ends at Feldkirch. The N13 follows the Rhine along the Swiss/Liechtenstein border; minor roads cross into Liechtenstein at each motorway exit.

Getting Around

Postbus travel within Liechtenstein is cheap and reliable; fares cost Sfr2.40 or Sfr3.60, with the higher rate for journeys exceeding 13km (such as Vaduz to Malbun). The only drawback is that some services finish early, for example, the last of the hourly buses from Vaduz to Malbun leaves at 6.20 pm (takes 35 minutes). Get a timetable from the Vaduz tourist office. A Postauto-Netz pass valid for one week/month costs only Sfr10/20.

For car hire, contact Avis (☎ 232 59 44), Winkel Garage, Im alten Riet 23, Schaan, or Budget (☎ 392 13 88), Reisebüro Linsi Tours, Landstrasse 221, Triesen. There are eight taxi companies in the country; in Schaan, ring ☎ 233 35 35 or ☎ 232 18 66.

For bicycle hire, go to the Swiss train station in Buchs or Sargans, or try Melliger AG (☎ 232 16 06), Kirchstrasse 10, Vaduz. Prices are Sfr20 per day, and bikes can be picked up the evening before rental begins. It is open to 6 pm Tuesday to Friday and to noon Saturday.

Vaduz

☎ 423 • pop 4975 • elevation 455m

Despite being the capital of Liechtenstein, Vaduz is little more than a village, but it still contains most of the points of interest in the country.

Orientation & Information

Vaduz is the geographical and political centre of the country. Two streets, Städtle and Äulestrasse, diverge and then rejoin, thereby enclosing the centre of town. Everything of importance is near this small area, including the bus station. Open-air car parking at Äulestrasse costs Sfr1 per hour (maximum three hours). Städtle is pedestrian only.

The Vaduz tourist office (☎ 232 14 43, fax 392 16 18, ✉ touristinfo@lie-net.li), Städtle 37, has a room-finding service for those who call in person and information on the whole country. It is open 8 am to noon and 1.30 to 5.30 pm Monday to Friday. The office is also open 9 am to noon and 1 to 4 pm on Saturday from May to October; and 10 am to noon and 1 to 4 pm on Sunday from July and August. Staff members are kept busy putting surprisingly dull souvenir stamps in visitors' passports (Sfr2).

The main post office, (FL-9490) Äulestrasse 38, is open 8 am to 6 pm Monday to Friday, and 8 to 11 am on Saturday. The post office has an adjoining philatelic section that is open 8.30 am to noon and 1.30 to 4.30 pm weekdays. The Library (Landesbibliothek), Gerberweg 5, has newspapers and Internet access (closed Sunday).

Things to See & Do

Although the **Vaduz Castle** (Schloss Vaduz) is not open to the public, the exterior graces many a photograph and it is worth climbing up the hill for a closer look. At the top, there's a good view of Vaduz and the mountains, and a network of marked walking trails along the ridge. The **National Museum** (Landesmuseum), Städtle 43, has historical and folklore exhibits, but it's closed for the foreseeable future.

The **State Art Collection** (Staatliche Kunstsammlung) at Städtle 37 is wholly devoted to temporary exhibitions that invariably contain something special. It includes parts of the incredibly rich art collection that the princes of Liechtenstein have acquired over the centuries. It is open 10 am to noon and 1.30 to 5.30 pm daily(5 pm November to March). Admission costs Sfr5 (students/seniors Sfr3). Opposite, the **Kunstmuseum Liechtenstein** is a lavish new art museum that should be completed by the end of 2000.

The **Postage Stamp Museum** (Briefmarkenmuseum), next to the tourist office, contains 300 frames of national stamps issued since 1912. Located in just one room, it is free and open daily, the same hours as the State Art Collection.

A **Ski Museum** awaits at Bangarten 10 (Sfr5; open weekday afternoons). Look out for processions and fireworks on 15 August, Liechtenstein's national holiday.

It is possible to sample the wines from the prince's own vineyard, but only for groups of 10 or more people, and advance reservations are essential. Contact the Hofkellerei (☎ 232 10 18), at Feldstrasse 4.

Places to Stay

Vaduz has minimal budget accommodation, but as Liechtenstein is so small you can pretty much base yourself anywhere – see Around Vaduz for other options.

Hotel Falknis (☎ 232 63 77, Landstrasse 92), is a 15-minute walk (or take the post-bus) from the centre of Vaduz north towards Schaan. Reasonable singles/doubles are Sfr50/100 with a shower on each floor.

Gasthof Au (☎ 232 11 17, fax 232 11 68, Austrasse 2), is south of the centre. Comfortable singles/doubles, some with balcony, are Sfr80/120 with shower, or Sfr60/95 without; triples are Sfr145. Eating is pleasant and fairly inexpensive in its garden restaurant (closed Monday). *Landhaus Prasch (☎ 232 46 63, fax 232 54 86, 🖂 prasch@supra.net)*, situated on Zoltstrasse, is nearby. This quaint place has an indoor swimming pool and sauna but is closed from November to April. Rooms with shower/WC start at about Sfr90/120 (cheaper in off-season).

Hotel Engel (☎ 236 17 17, fax 233 11 59, Städtle 13), has singles/doubles with private shower and TV starting at Sfr100/150, or Sfr140/175 if you want a bath and balcony.

Parkhotel Sonnenhof (☎ 232 11 92, fax 232 00 53, 🖂 real@sonnenhof.lol.li), on Grasiger Weg, to the north-east, is more luxurious and has an indoor swimming pool and sauna (free for guests). There are good views from its elevated perspective and the rooms are bright and cheerful. It's closed over Christmas/New Year. Prices start at Sfr220/320 and it has a guests-only restaurant.

Places to Eat

Restaurants are expensive in Vaduz, so look out for lunchtime specials. Just off Äulestrasse is a *supermarket*, open to 6.30 pm weekdays and 4 pm on Saturday. Next door is *Azzurro*, with smallish pizzas from

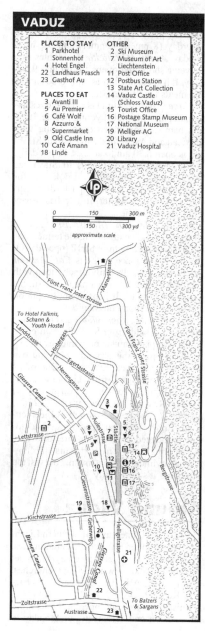

VADUZ

PLACES TO STAY	OTHER
1 Parkhotel Sonnenhof	2 Ski Museum
4 Hotel Engel	7 Museum of Art Liechtenstein
22 Landhaus Prasch	11 Post Office
23 Gasthof Au	12 Postbus Station
	13 State Art Collection
PLACES TO EAT	14 Vaduz Castle
3 Avanti III	(Schloss Vaduz)
5 Au Premier	15 Tourist Office
6 Café Wolf	16 Postage Stamp Museum
8 Azzurro & Supermarket	17 National Museum
9 Old Castle Inn	19 Melliger AG
10 Café Amann	20 Library
18 Linde	21 Vaduz Hospital

0   150   300 m
0   150   300 yd
approximate scale

Sfr10, plus sandwiches and salads. This stand-up place is open to 7 pm Monday to Saturday (8 pm in summer) and 5 pm on Sunday. *Avanti III (Städtle 5)* doubles as a souvenir shop, and opens till around 9 pm daily. It has outside tables and so-so snacks and meals for Sfr5 to Sfr14.

Linde (Kirchstrasse 2) is a bar and restaurant, popular with local young people. It offers bamboo-dominated decor along with Mexican and Asian food (Sfr15.50 to Sfr30) and is open 8.30 am to at least 11 pm daily.

Hotel Engel (see Places to Stay) has Swiss meals from Sfr17. Look out for *Schwingerhörnli*, a filling pasta dish usually available in winter. It also has pricey Chinese specialities.

Old Castle Inn (Äulestrasse 22), a British-style pub with an outside terrace, has main meals starting from Sfr17 (open daily). Another good place to try is *Café Amann (Äulestrasse 56)*. Its daily lunch menu with soup is Sfr16.50, and other meals and snacks cost Sfr6 to Sfr15. It is open until 7 pm on weekdays and noon on Saturday.

Café Wolf (1st floor, Städtle 29) has lunch menus with soup from Sfr22.80, and occasional live piano music on winter evenings. In the shop on the ground floor you can gorge on quality confectionery. One of its specialities is cognac-filled chocolate snail-shapes (Sfr12.80 for six). It's open daily.

Hotel Real has *Au Premier (☎ 232 22 22, Städtle 21)*, the best restaurant in Liechtenstein. Enjoy seasonal specialities and locally produced wine in an interior where the lighting comes from dozens of shimmering cylinders. Most main courses top Sfr40 and it's open daily.

Around Vaduz

The lowland (Unterland) of northern Liechtenstein is dotted with small communities. There's little to do except enjoy the quiet pace of life and view the village churches. Pottery-making is demonstrated at Schaedler Keramik (☎ 373 14 14) in **Nendeln**. Admission is free and opening hours are 8 am to noon and 1.15 to 6 pm Monday to Friday. The Rofenberg in **Eschen-Nendeln** was formerly a place of public execution and is now the site of the Holy Cross Chapel. **Schellenberg** has a Russian monument, commemorating the night in 1945 when a band of 500 heavily armed Russian soldiers crossed the border. They had been fighting for the German army, but they came to defect, not attack.

Triesenberg, on a terrace above Vaduz, commands an excellent view over the Rhine valley and has a pretty, onion-domed church. There's also a museum devoted to the Walser community which journeyed from Valais to settle here in the 13th century. It is open every afternoon except Monday (and Sunday from September to May) and admission costs Sfr2, or Sfr1 for students. The Walser dialect is still spoken here.

In the extreme south of the country is **Balzers**, which is dominated by the soaring sides of Burg Gutenberg. The interior of the castle is closed to the public, but there are plans in the long term to make it a museum.

Places to Stay

Liechtenstein has two camp sites, both open year-round. *Bendern (☎ 373 12 11)* is by the river in the north, while *Camping Mittagspitze (☎ 392 26 86)*, is south of Triesen, and has dormitory beds for Sfr12.

The SYHA *hostel (see the Liechtenstein map; ☎ 232 50 22, fax 232 58 56, Untere Rütigasse 6)*, is open from 1 March to 31 November, with dorm beds costing Sfr26.30 and doubles Sfr64.60. Reception is closed 10 am to 5 pm, when the doors are also locked, and there's a 10 pm curfew. It is 30 minutes' walk from Buchs or 10 minutes' walk from Schaan. Take the road to Vaduz and turn right at Marianumstrasse.

Check the tourist office hotel list for private rooms and other accommodation – there are some cheaper deals outside Vaduz. Schaan, for example, has *Hotel Post (☎ 232 17 18, fax 233 35 44, ✉ wwct@lie-net.li)*, situated by the bus station, providing singles/doubles from Sfr45/90 with shower, or Sfr38/76 without.

MALBUN

☎ 423 • pop 100 • elevation 1600m

Nestled amid the mountains in the south-east, tiny Malbun is Liechtenstein's ski resort. The skiing is inexpensive if not too extensive. The runs are for beginners and intermediates, with just a couple of stretches for experts. The resort has snowboard and skiing schools. A general ski pass for one day/one week costs Sfr35/156 for adults, Sfr29/129 for students to age 27 and seniors, and Sfr23/102 for children, all with reductions in the off season. One day's equipment rental costs Sfr43 including skis, shoes and poles, from the sports shop (☎ 263 37 55). The Sareis chairlift operates in summer too (Sfr7.50/11.70 one way/return).

Two kilometres from Malbun is the Väluna Valley, the main area for cross country skiing. The road from Vaduz terminates at Malbun. The tourist office (☎ 263 65 77, fax 263 73 44, ✉ malbuninfo@lie-net.li) is by the first bus stop and is open 9 am to noon, and 1.30 to 5 pm daily except Sunday (1 to 4 pm on Saturday). It's closed during the off season from mid-April to 31 May, and 1 November to mid-December.

Malbun has no bank, but the sports shop changes money. The ATM by the tourist office doesn't accept Visa cards.

Places to Stay & Eat

There are six hotels, each with a restaurant. By the bus stop is *Alpenhotel Malbun* (☎ 232 11 81, fax 232 16 24), with smallish, wooden rooms using hall shower for Sfr45 per person. In two nearby buildings are newer singles/doubles with shower/WC, TV and balcony for Sfr95/150. There's also a swimming pool, and decent rates for half-board. *Turna* (☎ 232 34 21, fax 263 51 73, ✉ lampert1@bluewin) by the Sareis ski lift, also has a swimming pool. Modern singles/doubles with TV start at Sfr70/110, or Sfr80/130 with private shower and toilet.

Add about Sfr10 to all the above prices in winter. Both hotels have inexpensive restaurants with outside terraces and meals from around Sfr12. There's also a supermarket open daily.

Appendix I – Alternative Place Names

The following abbreviations are used:
(E) = English
(F) = French
(G) = German
(I) = Italian
(R) = Romansch

Basel (E,G) – Basle (E), Bâle (F), Basilea (I)
Bern (E,G) –Berne (E,F), Berna (I)
Bernese Mittelland (E) – Berner Mittelland
  (G), Le Plateau Bernois (F)
Bernese Oberland (E) –
Berner Oberland (G)
Biel (G) – Bienne (F)
Brig (E,G) – Brigue (F)

Chur (E,G) – Coire (F)

Fribourg (E,F) – Freiburg (G), Friburgo (I)

Geneva (E) – Genève (F), Genf (G),
  Ginevra (I)
Graubünden (E,G) – Grisons (F), Grigioni
  (I), Grishun (R)

Lake Brienz (E) – Brienzersee (G)
Lake Constance (E) – Bodensee (G)
Lake Geneva (E) – Genfersee (G), Lac
  Léman or Lac du Genève (F)
Lake Geneva Region (E) –
  Genferseegebiet (G), Région du Léman (F)
Lake Lucerne (E) – Vierwaldstättersee (G)
Lake Maggiore (E) – Lago Mggiore (I)
Lake Thun (E) – Thunersee (G), Lac de
  Thoune (F)
Lake Zug (E) – Zugersee (G),
  Lac de Zoug (F)
Leuk (E,G) – Loeche (F)

Leukerbad (E,G) – Loeche-les-Bains (F)
Lower Valais (E) – Unterwallis (G), Bas
  Valais (F)
Lucerne (E,F) – Luzern (G), Lucerna (I)

Matterhorn (E,G) – Cervino (I)
Mont Blanc (F) – Monte Bianco (I)

Neuchâtel (E,F) – Neuenburg (G)

Rhine River (E) – Rhein (G)

Sarine River (E) – Saane (G)
Schaffhausen (E,G) – Schaffhouse (F),
  Sciafusa (I)
Sierre (E,F) – Siders (G)
Sion (E,F) – Sitten (G)
Solothurn (E,G) – Soleure (F), Soletta (I)
St Gallen (E,G) – St Gall (F), San Gallo (I)
St Moritz (E,G) – Saint Moritz (F), San
  Murezzan (R)
St Peter's Island (E) – St Peterinsel (G),
  Île de St Pierre (I)
Switzerland (E) – Suisse (F), Schweiz (G
  Svizzerra (I), Svizzra (R)

Ticino (E,I) – Tessin (G,F)

Upper Valais (E) – Oberwallis (G), Haut
  Valais (F)

Valais (E,F) – Wallis (G)
Vaud (E,F) – Waadt (G)
Visp (E,G) – Viége (F)

Winterthur (E) – Winterthour (G)

Zug (E,G) – Zoug (F)
Zürich (G) – Zurich (F), Zurigo (I)

Appendix II – Acronyms

The following abbreviations are used:
(F) = French
(G) = German
(I) = Italian

ACS (G)	Automobile-Club der Schweiz – Swiss Automobile Club
AHV (G)	Senior Citizens
ATMs	Automatic Teller Machines, also known as Bancomats or Bankomats
AVS (F)	Senior Citizens
BIJ (F)	Billet International de Jeunesse – Card for those under 26 giving discounts on international rail travel
CFF (F)	Chemins de Fer Fédéraux Suisse – Swiss Federal Railway
EC	EuroCity trains
EPA	Name of an inexpensive chain of department stores
FIYTO	Federation of International Youth Travel Organisation
FFS (I)	Ferrovie Federali Svizzere – Swiss Federal Railway
HI	Hostelling International
IC	InterCity trains
ICE	InterCity Express trains
IDP	International Driving Permit
ISIC	International Student Identity Card
RADAR	Royal Association for Disability & Rehabilitation
SAC	Swiss Alpine Club
SBB (G)	Schweizerische Bundesbahnen – Swiss Federal Railway
SBC	Swiss Bank Corporation – Société de Banques Suisses (F), Schweizerischer Bankverein (G), Società di Banca Svizzera (I)
SCCV (G)	Swiss Camping & Caravanning Federation
SSR-Reisen (G)	Swiss student travel agency
SSCV (G)	Swiss Ski School Federation
SYHA	Swiss Youth Hostel Association – Auberges de Jeunesse Suisses (F), Schweizer Jugendherbergen (G), Alberghi Svizzeri per la Gioventù (I)
TCS (G)	Touring Club der Schweiz – Swiss Touring Club
TGV (F)	Train à grande vitesse – very fast train
UBS	Union Bank of Switzerland – Union de Banques Suisse (F), Schweizerische Bankgesellschaft (G), Unione di Banche Svizzere (I)
Voyages-SSR (F)	Swiss student travel agency
WWOOF	Willing Workers on Organic Farms

Language

SWISS GERMAN

Though German-speaking Swiss have little trouble with standard High German, they use Swiss German, or *Schwyzertütsch*, in private conversation and in most unofficial situations. Contrary to the worldwide trend of erosion of dialects, its usage is actually increasing. Swiss German covers a wide variety of melodic dialects that can differ quite markedly from High German, often more closely resembling the German of hundreds of years ago than the modern version. It's as different to High German as Dutch is. Swiss German is an oral language, rarely written down, and indeed there is no standard written form (in fact, they can't even agree on how to spell 'Schwyzertütsch'). Newspapers and books almost invariably use High German and it is also used in news broadcasts, schools and the federal parliament. But people are more comfortable with their own Swiss German, and may even attempt a completely different language when speaking to foreigners rather than resort to High German.

Germans themselves often have trouble understanding Schwyzertütsch. To English-speakers' ears High German sounds like it's full of rasping 'ch' sounds, but even Germans think that Schwyzertütsch sounds like a lot of throat-clearing. A reason for this is that the Germanic 'k' becomes 'ch' in High German only at the middle and end of words, whereas in Swiss German it also applies at the beginning. Hence, the relatively manageable *Küchen-kästchen* (kitchen cupboard) in High German becomes almost unpronounceable *chuchichäschtli* in Swiss German.

To make matters even more complicated, regional dialects are strongly differentiated for such a small country, thanks to the isolating effect of mountain ranges (and the lack of a written 'standard'). In the south, such as in Upper Valais, an older form of dialect has been preserved. Eastern dialects have words in common with all other German vernaculars, whereas in western dialects, some Old Alemannic names have been retained. For example, meadow is *Wiese* in High German, *wise* in eastern dialects and *matte* in the west. The letters 'b', 'd 'and 'g' are voiceless in Swiss German, and hardened in eastern dialects into an unaspirated 'p', 't' and 'gg', hence the High German *bitte, danke* and *Gans* (please, thank you, goose) become *pitte, tankche* and *ggans*; 'st' is always pronounced as 'sht'. Visitors will probably note the frequent use of the suffix *-li* to indicate the diminutive, or as a term of endearment.

With no written form and so many dialects, it's impossible to provide a proper vocabulary for Swiss German. Commonly used greetings are *Grüezi* (Hello) and *Uf Wiederluege* (Goodbye); 'tram' is *Tram*, not *Strassenbahn*, and 'holiday' is *Ferien*, not *Urlaub*. Versions of French words are often used: 'thank you' is not *danke* but *merci* (though pronounced 'mur-see' rather than the correct French, 'mair-see'); 'bicycle' is *vélo*, not *Fahrrad*; 'ice cream' is *glace*, not *Sahneneis*. In pronunciation, double vowel sounds are common – 'good' sounds more like 'gu-et' than the High German *gut*.

For more information, read *Dialect and High German in German-Speaking Switzerland*, published by Pro Helvetia, the Arts Council of Switzerland.

HIGH GERMAN
Pronunciation

Unlike English or French, German does not have silent letters: you pronounce the **k** at the start of the word *Knie* (knee), the **p** at the start of *Psychologie* (psychology), and the **e** at the end of *ich habe* (I have).

Vowels

As in English, vowels can be pronounced long (as the 'o' in 'pope'), or short (as the 'o' in 'pop'). As a rule, German vowels are long before a single consonant and short before two or more, eg, the **o** is long in the word *Dom* (cathedral), but short in the word *doch* (after all).

a	short, as the 'u' in 'cut', or long, as in 'father'
au	as the 'ow' in 'vow'
ä	short, as in 'hat', or long, as in 'hare'
äu	as the 'oy' in 'boy'
e	short, as in 'bet', or long, as in 'obey'
ei	as the 'ai' in 'aisle'
eu	as the 'oy' in 'boy'
i	short, as in 'inn', or long, as in 'marine'
ie	as in 'siege'
o	short, as in 'pot', or long, as in 'note'
ö	as the 'er' in 'fern'
u	as in 'pull'
ü	similar to the 'u' in 'pull' but with stretched lips

Consonants

Most German consonants sound similar to their English counterparts. One important difference is that **b**, **d** and **g** sound like 'p', 't' and 'k', respectively, at the end of a word.

ch	throaty, as in Scottish *loch*
j	as the 'y' in 'yet'
ng	always one sound, as in 'strong'
qu	as 'kv'
r	trilled or guttural
s	as in 'see' or as the 'z' in 'zoo'
sch	as the 'sh' in 'shore'
st	usually pronounced 'sht'
sp	usually pronounced 'shp'
v	more like an English 'f'
w	as an English 'v'
z	as the 'ts' in 'tsar'

Greetings & Civilities

Hello (Good day).	*Guten Tag.*
Goodbye.	*Auf Wiedersehen.*
Please.	*Bitte.*
Thank you.	*Danke.*
That's fine/You're welcome.	*Bitte sehr.*
Sorry. (excuse me, forgive me)	*Entschuldigung.*
Yes.	*Ja.*
No.	*Nein.*
Just a minute.	*Ein Moment!*

Signs

Eingang/Einfahrt	Entrance
Ausgang/Ausfahrt	Exit
Auf/Offen/ Geöffnet	Open
Zu/Geschlossen	Closed
Rauchen Verboten	No Smoking
Polizei	Police
WC/Toiletten	Toilets
Damen	Women
Herren	Men
Bahnhof	Train Station
Hauptbahnhof	Main Train Station
Notausgang	Emergency Exit

Language Difficulties

Do you speak English?	*Sprechen Sie Englisch?*
Does anyone here speak English?	*Spricht hier jemand Englisch?*
I understand.	*Ich verstehe.*
I don't understand.	*Ich verstehe nicht.*
Please write that down.	*Können Sie es bitte aufschreiben?*

Getting Around

What time does ... leave?	*Wann fährt ... ab?*
What time does ... arrive?	*Wann kommt ... an?*
the boat	*das Boot*
the bus (city)	*der Bus*
the bus (intercity)	*der (Überland)bus*
the tram	*die Strassenbahn*
the train	*der Zug*
next	*nächste*
first	*erste*
last	*letzte*
I'd like ...	*Ich möchte ...*
a one-way ticket	*eine Einzelkarte*
a return ticket	*eine Rückfahr-karte*
1st class	*erste Klasse*
2nd class	*zweite Klasse*
Where is the ...?	*Wo ist die ...?*
bus stop	*Bushaltestelle/*
tram stop	*Strassenbahnhalte-stelle?*

I'm looking for ...	Ich suche ...
Can you show me (on the map)?	Können Sie mir (auf der Karte) zeigen?
Go straight ahead.	Gehen Sie geradeaus.
Turn left.	Biegen Sie links ab.
Turn right.	Biegen Sie rechts ab.
near/far	nahe/weit

Around Town

I'm looking for ...	Ich suche ...
a bank	eine Bank
the city centre	die Innenstadt
the ... embassy	die ... Botschaft
my hotel	mein Hotel
the market	den Markt
the police	die Polizei
the post office	das Postamt
a public toilet	eine öffentliche Toilette
the telephone centre	die Telefon-zentrale
the tourist office	das Verkehrsamt

bridge	Brücke
castle	Schloss
cathedral	Dom
church	Kirche
hospital	Krankenhaus
island	Insel
lake	See
main square	Hauptplatz
market	Markt
monastery	Kloster
mosque	Moschee
old city	Altstadt
palace	Palast
ruins	Ruinen
square	Platz
tower	Turm

How much is it ?	Wieviel kostet es?

Accommodation

Where is a cheap hotel?	Wo ist ein billiges Hotel?
What is the address?	Was ist die Adresse?
Could you write the address, please?	Könnten Sie bitte die Adresse aufschreiben?

Emergencies – German

Help!	Hilfe!
Call a doctor!	Rufen Sie einen Arzt!
Call the police!	Rufen Sie die Polizei!
Leave me in peace.	Lassen Sie mich in Ruhe.
Get lost!	Hau ab! (inf)
I'm lost.	Ich habe mich verirrt.
Thief!	Dieb!
I've been raped/ robbed!	Ich bin vergewaltigt/ bestohlen worden!

Do you have any rooms available?	Haben Sie noch freie Zimmer?
I'd like ...	Ich möchte ...
a single room	ein Einzelzimmer
a double room	ein Doppelzimmer
a room with a bathroom	ein Zimmer mit Bad
to share a dorm	einen Schlafsaal teilen
a bed	ein Bett

How much is it ...?	Wieviel kostet es ...?
per night	pro Nacht
per person	pro Person

May I see it?	Kann ich es sehen?
Where is the bathroom?	Wo ist das Bad?

Food

bakery	Bäckerei
delicatessen	Delikatessengeschäft
grocery	Lebensmittelgeschäft
restaurant	Restaurant/Gaststätte
breakfast	Frühstück
lunch	Mittagessen
dinner	Abendessen

I'd like the set menu, please.	Ich hätte gern das Tagesmenü bitte.
Is service included in the bill?	Ist die Bedienung inbegriffen?
I'm a vegetarian.	Ich bin Vegetarier/ Vegetarierin (m/f)

LANGUAGE

Time & Dates

What time is it?	*Wie spät ist es?*
today	*heute*
tomorrow	*morgen*
in the morning	*morgens*
in the afternoon	*nachmittags*
in the evening	*abends*
Monday	*Montag*
Tuesday	*Dienstag*
Wednesday	*Mittwoch*
Thursday	*Donnerstag*
Friday	*Freitag*
Saturday	*Samstag/Sonnabend*
Sunday	*Sonntag*
January	*Januar*
February	*Februar*
March	*März*
April	*April*
May	*Mai*
June	*Juni*
July	*Juli*
August	*August*
September	*September*
October	*Oktober*
November	*November*
December	*Dezember*

Numbers

0	*null*
1	*eins*
2	*zwei* (*zwo* on the telephone)
3	*drei*
4	*vier*
5	*fünf*
6	*sechs*
7	*sieben*
8	*acht*
9	*neun*
10	*zehn*
11	*elf*
12	*zwölf*
13	*dreizehn*
14	*vierzehn*
15	*fünfzehn*
16	*sechzehn*
17	*siebzehn*
18	*achtzehn*
19	*neunzehn*
20	*zwanzig*
21	*einundzwanzig*
22	*zweiundzwanzig*
23	*dreiundzwanzig*
30	*dreissig*
40	*vierzig*
50	*fünfzig*
60	*sechzig*
70	*siebzig*
80	*achtzig*
90	*neunzig*
100	*hundert*
1000	*tausend*

one million   *eine Million*

FRENCH
Swiss French

Neuchâtel is where the purest form of French is spoken, yet you won't find very much difference from standard French wherever you go. Of course there are some local expressions and regional accents. A female waitress is a *sommelière*, not a *serveuse*, and a postal box is a *case postale* not a *bôite postale*. Although the normal French numbers are understood, some locals use *septante* for 70, *huitante* for 80 and *nonante* for 90. Swiss Romande is a term used to refer to French-speaking Switzerland.

Pronunciation

Most letters in French are pronounced more or less the same as their English equivalents. A few which may cause confusion are:

j	as the 's' in 'leisure', eg *jour* (day)
c	before **e** and **i**, as the 's' in 'sit' before **a**, **o** and **u** it's pronounced as English 'k'. When undescored with a 'cedilla' (**ç**) it's always pronounced as the 's' in 'sit'.

French has a number of sounds that are difficult for Anglophones to produce. These include:

- The distinction between the 'u' sound (as in *tu*) and 'oo' sound (as in *tout*). For both sounds, the lips are rounded and projected forward, but for the 'u' the tongue is towards the front of the mouth, its tip against the lower front teeth, whereas for the 'oo' the tongue is towards the back of the mouth, its tip behind the gums of the lower front teeth.

The nasal vowels. With nasal vowels the breath escapes partly through the nose and partly through the mouth. In English, the 'ing' in 'sing' is similar to a nasal vowel; in French there are three, as in *bon vin blanc* (good white wine). These sounds occur where a syllable ends in a single **n** or **m**; the **n** or **m** is silent but indicates the nasalisation of the preceding vowel.

• The **r**. The standard **r** of Parisian French is produced by moving the bulk of the tongue backwards to constrict the air flow in the pharynx while the tip of the tongue rests behind the lower front teeth. It's similar to the noise made by some people before spitting, but with much less friction.

Greetings & Civilities

Hello.	*Bonjour.*
Goodbye.	*Au revoir.*
Please.	*S'il vous plaît.*
Thank you.	*Merci.*
That's fine/You're welcome.	*Très bien/Je vous en prie.*
Excuse me.	*Excusez-moi.*
Sorry. (excuse me, forgive me)	*Pardon.*
Yes.	*Oui.*
No.	*Non.*
Just a minute.	*Attendez une minute.*

Language Difficulties

Do you speak English?	*Parlez-vous anglais?*
Does anyone here speak English?	*Est-ce qu'il y a quelqu'un qui parle anglais?*
I understand.	*Je comprends.*
I don't understand.	*Je ne comprends pas.*
Please write that down.	*Est-ce-que vous pouvez l'écrire?*

Getting Around

What time does ... leave?	*À quelle heure part ...?*
What time does ... arrive?	*À quelle heure arrive ...?*

the boat	*le bateau*
the bus (city)	*l'(auto)bus*
the bus (intercity)	*l'(auto)car*
the tram	*le tramway*
the train	*le train*
next	*prochain*
first	*premier*
last	*dernier*

I'd like ...	*Je voudrais ...*
a one-way ticket	*un billet aller simple*
a return ticket	*un billet aller-retour*
1st class	*première classe*
2nd class	*deuxième classe*

Where is the ...?	*Où est ...?*
bus stop	*l'arrêt d'autobus*
tram stop	*l'arrêt de tramway*
train station	*la gare*

I want to go to ...	*Je veux aller à ...*
Can you show me (on the map)?	*Est-ce que vous pouvez me le montrer (sur la carte)?*
Go straight ahead.	*Continuez tout droit.*
Turn left.	*Tournez à gauche.*
Turn right.	*Tournez à droite.*
near/far	*proche/loin*

Around Town

I'm looking for ...	*Je cherche ...*
a bank	*une banque*
the city centre	*le centre-ville*
the ... embassy	*l'ambassade de ...*
my hotel	*mon hôtel*
the market	*le marché*
the police	*la police*
the post office	*le bureau de poste*
a public toilet	*des toilettes*
a public telephone	*une cabine téléphonique*
the tourist office	*l'office de tourisme*

bridge	*le pont*
castle, mansion	*le château*
cathedral	*la cathédrale*
church	*l'église*
hospital	*l'hôpital*
island	*l'île*
lake	*le lac*

Signs

Entrée	Entrance
Sortie	Exit
Ouvert/Fermé	Open/Closed
Chambres Libres	Rooms Available
Complet	Full/No Vacancies
Renseignements	Information
Interdit	Prohibited
(Commissariat de) Police	Police Station
Toilettes, WC	Toilets
Hommes	Men
Femmes	Women

main square	la place centrale
mosque	la mosquée
old city	la vieille ville
palace	le palais
quay/bank	le quai/la rive
ruins	les ruines
square	la place
tower	la tour

| How much is it ? | C'est combien? |

Accommodation

Where is a cheap hotel?	Où est un hôtel bon marché?
What is the address?	Quelle est l'adresse?
Could you write the address, please?	Est-ce vous pouvez écrire l'adresse, s'il vous plaît?
Do you have any rooms available?	Est-ce que vous avez des chambres libres?

I'd like ...	Je voudrais ...
a single room	une chambre pour une personne
a double room	une chambre double
a room with a bathroom	une chambre avec douche et W.C.
to stay in a dormitory	coucher dans un dortoir
a bed	un lit

How much is it ...?	Quel est le prix ...?
per night	par nuit
per person	par personne

| May I see it? | Je peux la voir? |
| Where is the bathroom/shower? | Où est la salle de bain/douche? |

Food

bakery	boulangerie
cake shop	pâtisserie
cheese shop	fromagerie
delicatessen	charcuterie
grocery	épicerie
restaurant	restaurant
breakfast	petit déjeuner
lunch	déjeuner
dinner	dîner

| I'd like the set menu, please. | Je prends le menu. |
| I'm a vegetarian. | Je suis végétarien/ végétarienne (m/f) |

Time & Dates

What time is it?	Quelle heure est-il?
today	aujourd'hui
tomorrow	demain
yesterday	hier
in the morning	le matin
in the afternoon	l'après-midi
in the evening	le soir

Monday	lundi
Tuesday	mardi
Wednesday	mercredi
Thursday	jeudi
Friday	vendredi
Saturday	samedi
Sunday	dimanche

January	janvier
February	février
March	mars
April	avril
May	mai
June	juin
July	juillet
August	août
September	septembre
October	octobre
November	novembre
December	décembre

Emergencies – French

Help!	Au secours!
Call a doctor!	Appelez un médecin!
Call the police!	Appelez la police!
Leave me alone!	Fichez-moi la paix!
I've been robbed.	On m'a volé.
I've been raped.	On m'a violée.
I'm lost.	Je me suis égaré/ égarée. (m/f)

Numbers

0	zéro
1	un
2	deux
3	trois
4	quatre
5	cinq
6	six
7	sept
8	huit
9	neuf
10	dix
11	onze
12	douze
13	treize
14	quatorze
15	quinze
16	seize
17	dix-sept
18	dix-huit
19	dix-neuf
20	vingt
21	vingt-et-un
22	vingt-deux
30	trente
40	quarante
50	cinquante
60	soixante
70	soixante-dix/septante
80	quatre-vingts/huitante
90	quatre-vingt-dix/nonante
100	cent
200	deux cents
1000	mille
one million	un million

ITALIAN
Swiss Italian

There are some differences between the Ticinese dialect and standard Italian, but they aren't very significant. You may come across some people saying *bun di* instead of *buon giorno* (good morning/day) or *buona noc* (pronounced 'nockh') instead of *buona notte* (goodnight).

Pronunciation
Vowels

a	as in 'art', *caro* (dear); sometimes short, *amico/a* (friend)
e	as in 'tell', *mettere* (to put)
i	as in 'inn', *inizio* (start)
o	as in 'dot', *donna* (woman); as in 'port', *dormire* (to sleep)
u	as the 'oo' in 'book', *puro* (pure)

Consonants

c	as 'k' before **a**, **o** and **u**; as the 'ch' in 'choose' before **e** and **i**
ch	as the 'k' in 'kit'
g	as the 'g' in 'get' before **a**, **o**, **u** and **h**; as the 'j' in 'jet' before **e** and **i**
gli	as the 'lli' in 'million'
gn	as the 'ny' in 'canyon'
h	always silent
r	a rolled 'rr' sound
sc	as the 'sh' in 'sheep' before **e** and **i**; as 'sk' before **a**, **o**, **u** and **h**
z	as the 'ts' in 'lights', except at the beginning of a word, when it's as the 'ds' in 'suds'

Note that when **ci**, **gi** and **sci** are followed by **a**, **o** or **u**, the 'i' is not pronounced unless the accent falls on the 'i'. Thus the name 'Giovanni' is pronounced 'joh-**vahn**-nee', not 'jee-oh-**vahn**-nee'.

Word Stress

A double consonant is pronounced as a longer, more forceful sound than a single consonant.

Stress generally falls on the second-last syllable, as in *spa-**ghet**-ti*. When a word has an accent, the stress falls on that syllable, as in *cit-**tà*** (city).

Greetings & Civilities

Hello.	*Buon giorno.* (polite)
	Ciao. (informal)
Goodbye.	*Arrivederci.* (polite)
	Ciao. (informal)
Please.	*Per favore/piacere.*
Thank you.	*Grazie.*
That's fine/	*Prego.*
You're welcome.	
Excuse me.	*Mi scusi.*
Sorry. (excuse me,	*Mi scusi/Mi perdoni.*
forgive me)	
Yes.	*Sì.*
No.	*No.*
Just a minute.	*Un momento.*

Language Difficulties

Do you speak English?	*Parla/Parli inglese?* (polite/informal)
Does anyone here speak English?	*C'è qualcuno che parla inglese?*
I understand.	*Capisco.*
I don't understand.	*Non capisco.*
Could you write that down, please?	*Può scriverlo per favore?*

Getting Around

What time does ... leave/arrive?	*A che ora parte/ arriva ...?*
the boat	*la barca*
the bus	*l'autobus*
the train	*il treno*
first	*il primo/a* (m/f)
next	*il prossimo/a* (m/f)
last	*l'ultimo* (m/f)
I'd like a ... ticket.	*Vorrei un biglietto ...*
one-way	*semplice* or *di solo andata*
return	*di andata e ritorno*
1st class	*prima classe*
2nd class	*seconda classe*
Where is ...?	*Dov'è la fermata ...?*
the bus stop	*dell'autobus*
the tram stop	*del tram*
I want to go to ...	*Voglio andare a ...*
Can you show me (on the map)?	*Me lo puo mostrare (sulla carta/pianta)?*

Signs

Ingresso/Entrata	**Entrance**
Uscita	**Exit**
Informazione	**Information**
Aperto	**Open**
Chiuso	**Closed**
Proibito/Vietato	**Prohibited**
Polizia/	**Police**
Carabinieri	
Questura	**Police Station**
Camere libere	**Rooms**
	Available
Completo	**Full/No Vacancies**
Gabinetti/Bagni	**Toilets**
Uomini	**Men**
Donne	**Women**

Go straight ahead.	*(Si va/Vai) sempre diritto.*
Turn left.	*Gira a sinistra.*
Turn right.	*Gira a destra.*
near/far	*vicino/lontano*

Around Town

I'm looking for ...	*Cerco/Sto cercando*
a bank	*un banco*
church	*la chiesa*
the city centre	*il centro (città)*
the ... embassy	*l'ambasciata di ...*
my hotel	*il mio albergo*
the market	*il mercato*
the museum	*il museo*
the post office	*la posta*
a public toilet	*un gabinetto/bagn pubblico*
the telephone centre	*il centro telefonico SIP*
the tourist office	*l'ufficio di turisme d'informazione*
bridge	*il ponte*
castle	*il castello*
cathedral	*il duomo/la cattedral*
church	*la chiesa*
island	*l'isola*
main square	*la piazza principale*
market	*il mercato*
mosque	*la moschea*
old city	*il centro storico*

palace	*il palazzo*
ruins	*le rovine*
square	*la piazza*
tower	*il torre*

| How much is it? | *Quanto costa?* |

Accommodation

Where is a cheap hotel?	*Dov'è un albergo che costa poco?*
What is the address?	*Cos'è l'indirizzo?*
Could you write the address, please?	*Può scrivere l'indirizzo per favore?*
Do you have any rooms available?	*Ha camere libere?/C'è una camera libera?*

I'd like ...	*Vorrei ...*
a single room	*una camera singola*
a room with a double bed	*una camera matrimoniale/per due*
a room with a bathroom	*una camera con bagno*
to share a dorm	*un letto in dormitorio*
a bed	*un letto*

How much is it ...?	*Quanto costa ...?*
per night	*per la notte*
per person	*per ciascuno*

| May I see it? | *Posso vederla?* |
| Where is the bathroom? | *Dov'è il bagno?* |

Food

bakery	*panetteria*
delicatessen	*gastronomia*
grocery	*negozio d'alimentari*
restaurant	*ristorante*
breakfast	*(prima) colazione*
lunch	*pranzo/colazione*
dinner	*cena*

| I'd like the set menu. | *Vorrei il menu turistico.* |
| Is service included in the bill? | *È compreso il servizio?* |

Emergencies – Italian

Help!	*Aiuto!*
Call ...!	*Chiami ...!/ Chiama ...! (polite/informal)*
a doctor	*un dottore/ un medico*
the police	*la polizia*
There's been an accident	*C'è stato un incidente!*
I'm lost.	*Mi sono perso/a.*
Go away!	*Lasciami in pace! Vai via!* (inf)

| I'm a vegetarian. | *Sono vegetariano/ vegetariana* (m/f) |
| I don't eat meat. | *Non mangio carne.* |

Time & Dates

What time is it?	*Che ora è?/ Che ore sono?*
today	*oggi*
tomorrow	*domani*
yesterday	*ieri*
in the morning	*di mattina*
in the afternoon	*di pomeriggio*
in the evening	*di sera*

Monday	*lunedì*
Tuesday	*martedì*
Wednesday	*mercoledì*
Thursday	*giovedì*
Friday	*venerdì*
Saturday	*sabato*
Sunday	*domenica*

January	*gennaio*
February	*febbraio*
March	*marzo*
April	*aprile*
May	*maggio*
June	*giugno*
July	*luglio*
August	*agosto*
September	*settembre*
October	*ottobre*
November	*novembre*
December	*dicembre*

Numbers

0	zero
1	uno
2	due
3	tre
4	quattro
5	cinque
6	sei
7	sette
8	otto
9	nove
10	dieci
11	undici
12	dodici
13	tredici
14	quattordici
15	quindici
16	sedici
17	diciassette
18	diciotto
19	diciannove
20	venti
21	ventuno
22	ventidue
30	trenta
40	quaranta
50	cinquanta
60	sessanta
70	settanta
80	ottanta
90	novanta
100	cento
1000	mille

one million   *un milione*

ROMANSCH

Romansch dialects tend to be restricted to their own particular mountain valley. Usage is gradually being undermined by the steady encroachment of German, and linguists fear that the language may eventually disappear altogether. There are so many dialects that not all the Romansch words listed in this book will be understood. See the Graubünden chapter for some examples of regional variations. The main street in villages is usually called *Via Maistra*.

Useful Words & Phrases

Please.	Anzi.
Thank you.	Grazia.
Hello.	Allegra.
Good morning.	Bun di.
Good evening.	Buna saira.
Good night.	Buna notg.
Goodbye.	Adieu/Abunansvair.
tourist office	societad da traffic
room	la chombra
bed	il letg
closed	serrà
left	sanester
right	dretg
woman	la dunna
man	l'um
cross-country skiing	il passlung
food	mangiar
bread	il paun
cheese	il chaschiel
fish	il pesch
ham	il schambun
drink	baiver
milk	il Latg
wine	il vin

Monday	Lündeschdi
Tuesday	il Mardi
Wednesday	Marculdi
Thursday	la Gievgia
Friday	Venderdi
Saturday	Sanda
Sunday	Dumengia

Numbers

1	in
2	dus
3	trais
4	quatter
5	tschinch
6	ses
7	set
8	och
9	nouv
10	diesch

Acknowledgments

Thanks

Many thanks to the travellers who used the 1st edition of this book and wrote to us with helpful hints, useful advice and interesting anecdotes. Your names follow:

Abe Brouwer, Adam Johnson, Alan Harrison, Alan, Nancy & Becky Howenstine, Alice B Peterson, Allan Bailey, Alyson France, Andrew Johnson, Anja Delen, Ann Sy, Barbara Meyer, Baylor Lancaster, Becky Edwards, Betty McGeever, Betty Mekeel, C Sassr, Caroline Henderson, Carrie Kuntz, Cassandra Carmichael, Celine Doody, Charles Arnade, Charles G Aschmann, Cheryl Burghardt, Chong Lee Ling, Chris Doggen, Chris Horan, Christina Norton, Colin Cha Fong, D Carlier, D Richard Owen, D Trevino, Dahlia Sharon, Dave & Karen Hinchen, David Baxter, David Bean, Delphine Lafarge, Don Maxwell, Douglas Shone, E J M Warren, Elizabeth Britton, Erik Van Zetten, G E Pasek, G Hennings, Gavin Mooney, Geoff Caflisch, Georg Steed, Gisela Bonnie, Gunn Iren Kjur, Heather Mcmahon, Heidi Bolt, Heidi Gibbeson, Heidi Sigmond, Helen Woo, Helga von Graevenitz, Herb & Lola Suttie, Herman Scholz, Ian Pye, James Saunders, Jan Wall, Jennifer Freeman, Jennifer Oats-Sargent, Jenny Boyd, Joe McSpedon, Joel Brueziere, John & Elisabeth Cox, John Dryden, John Rennie, John Smyth, K Lauber , Kate Duffell, Katie Zuzek, Kelly Mitchell, Kent Hunt, Koller, Josef & Terry, Krist Tack, Kristien Van Cromphaut, Leonard Dvorson, Les Planards, Leyla Alyanak, Lisa Burns, Ludo De Vleesschauwer, Marcus Pueller, Mark H Pollock, Martin Kunzli, Mathieu Baehni, Melbourne Boynton, Michael & Karen Hofman-Body, Michael Body, Michel Thuriaux, Moniba & Reto Leutwiler, Monique Telfer, Nerida Davis, Niçk Hall, Nicola Furey, Nicole Varol, Nisha Gambhir, Patrick Coleman, Paul Castain, Paul Connolly, Peter L B Mynors, Peti Polin, Philip Panell, R Vincent, Rachel Greig, Richard Carr, Robert Powell, Rod Touzel, Roger Nash, Rolf Herrmann, Rolf Manz, S & M Putallaz-Van Loo, Sally Paschoud, Sandra Telfer, Shelby Polakoff, Sidney Hill, Simon Hawkins, Simon Li, Stephan Hasselberg, Steve Murphy, Steven Flanders, Stewart Nicolson, Sue Tanck, Thng Hui Hong, Tim Hammond, Todd Reeder, Tracey Steele, Tracy Ebsworth, Van Mechelen, Vivian Wright, Warren Muir

LONELY PLANET

Phrasebooks

Lonely Planet phrasebooks are packed with essential words and phrases to help travellers communicate with the locals. With colour tabs for quick reference, an extensive vocabulary and use of script, these handy pocket-sized language guides cover day-to-day travel situations.

- handy pocket-sized books
- easy to understand Pronunciation chapter
- clear & comprehensive Grammar chapter
- romanisation alongside script to allow ease of pronunciation
- script throughout so users can point to phrases for every situation
- full of cultural information and tips for the traveller

'... vital for a real DIY spirit and attitude in language learning'
– *Backpacker*

'the phrasebooks have good cultural backgrounders and offer solid advice for challenging situations in remote locations'
– *San Francisco Examiner*

Arabic (Egyptian) ● Arabic (Moroccan) ● Australian *(Australian English, Aboriginal and Torres Strait languages)* ● Baltic States *(Estonian, Latvian, Lithuanian)* ● Bengali ● Brazilian ● British ● Burmese ● Cantonese ● Central Asia (Uyghur, Uzbek, Kyrghiz, Kazak, Pashto, Tadjik ● Central Europe *(Czech, French, German, Hungarian, Italian, Slovak)* ● Eastern Europe *(Bulgarian, Czech, Hungarian, Polish, Romanian, Slovak)* ● Ethiopian (Amharic) ● Fijian ● French ● German ● Greek ● Hebrew ● Hill Tribes ● Hindi & Urdu ● Indonesian ● Italian ● Japanese ● Korean ● Lao ● Latin American Spanish ● Malay ● Mandarin ● Mediterranean Europe *(Albanian, Croatian, Greek, Italian, Macedonian, Maltese, Serbian, Slovene)* ● Mongolian ● Nepali ● Pidgin ● Pilipino (Tagalog) ● Portugese ● Quechua ● Russian ● Scandinavian Europe *(Danish, Finnish, Icelandic, Norwegian, Swedish)* ● South-East Asia *(Burmese, Indonesian, Khmer, Lao, Malay, Tagalog Pilipino, Thai, Vietnamese)* ● South Pacific Languages ● Spanish (Castilian) *(also includes Catalan, Galician and Basque)* ● Sri Lanka ● Swahili ● Thai ● Tibetan ● Turkish ● Ukrainian ● USA *(US English, Vernacular, Native American languages, Hawaiian)* ● Vietnamese ● Western Europe *(Basque, Catalan, Dutch, French, German, Greek, Irish, Italian, Portuguese, Scottish Gaelic, Spanish (Castilian), Welsh)*

onely Planet Journeys

ourneys is a unique collection of travel writing – published by the company that
understands travel better than anyone else. It is a series for anyone who has ever
perienced – or dreamed of – the magical moment when they encountered a strange cul-
re or saw a place for the first time. They are tales to read while you're planning a trip,
hile you're on the road or while you're in an armchair in front of a fire.

These outstanding titles explore our planet through the eyes of a diverse group of inter-
tional writers. JOURNEYS books catch the spirit of a place, illuminate a culture, recount
crazy adventure or introduce a fascinating way of life. They always entertain, and always
rich the experience of travel.

ALI BLUES
aveling to an African Beat
eve Joris (translated by Sam Garrett)

ought, rebel uprisings, ethnic conflict: these are the predominant images of West
rica. But as Lieve Joris travels in Senegal, Mauritania and Mali, she meets survivors,
scinating individuals charting new ways of living between tradition and moderni-
With her remarkable gift for drawing out people's stories, Joris brilliantly captures
e rhythms of a world that refuses to give in.

HE GATES OF DAMASCUS
eve Joris (translated by Sam Garrett)

is best-selling book is a beautifully drawn portrait of day-to-day life in modern
ria. Through her intimate contact with local people, Lieve Joris draws us into the
scinating world that lies behind the gates of Damascus. Hala's husband is a politi-
l prisoner, jailed for his opposition to the Assad regime; through the author's
endship with Hala we see how Syrian politics impacts on the lives of ordinary
ople.

HE OLIVE GROVE
avels in Greece
atherine Kizilos

atherine Kizilos travels to fabled islands, troubled border zones and her family's
lage deep in the mountains. She vividly evokes breathtaking landscapes, generous
ople and passionate politics, capturing the complexities of a country she loves.

eautifully captures the real tensions of Greece' – *Sunday Times*

NGDOM OF THE FILM STARS
urney into Jordan
nnie Caulfield

ngdom of the Film Stars is a travel book and a love story. With honesty and
mour, Annie Caulfield writes of travelling in Jordan and falling in love with a
douin with film-star looks.

She offers fascinating insights into the country – from the tent life of traditional
omen to the hustle of downtown Amman – and unpicks tight-woven western
yths about the Arab world.

LONELY PLANET

Lonely Planet Travel Atlases

L onely Planet has long been famous for the number and quality of its guidebook maps. Now we've gone one step further and produced a handy companion series: Lonely Planet travel atlases – maps of a country produced in book form.

Unlike other maps, which look good but lead travellers astray, our travel atlases have been researched on the road by Lonely Planet's experienced team of writers. All details are carefully checked to ensure the atlas corresponds with the equivalent Lonely Planet guidebook.

- full-colour throughout
- maps researched and checked by Lonely Planet authors
- place names correspond with Lonely Planet guidebooks
- no confusing spelling differences
- legend and travelling information in English, French, German, Japanese and Spanish
- size: 230 x 160 mm

Available now: Chile & Easter Island • Egypt • India & Bangladesh • Israel & the Palestinian Territories • Jordan, Syria & Lebanon • Kenya • Laos • Portugal • South Africa, Lesotho & Swaziland • Thailand Turkey • Vietnam • Zimbabwe, Botswana & Namibia

Lonely Planet TV Series & Videos

L onely Planet travel guides have been brought to life on television screens around the world. Like our guides, the programs are based on the joy of independent travel and look honestly at some of the most exciting, picturesque and frustrating places in the world. Each show is presented by one of three travellers from Australia, England or the USA and combines an innovative mixture of video, Super-8 film, atmospheric soundscapes and original music.

Videos of each episode – containing additional footage not shown on television – are available from good book and video shops, but the availability of individual videos varies with regional screening schedules.

Video destinations include: Alaska • American Rockies • Argentina • Australia – The South-East • Baja California & the Copper Canyon • Brazil • Central Asia • Chile & Easter Island • Corsica, Sicily & Sardinia – The Mediterranean Islands • East Africa (Tanzania & Zanzibar) • Cuba • Ecuador & the Galapagos Islands • Ethiopia • Greenland & Iceland • Hungary & Romania • Indonesia • Israel & the Sinai Desert • Jamaica • Japan • La Ruta Maya • London • The Middle East (Syria, Jordan & Lebanon • Morocco • New York City • Northern Spain • North India • Outback Australia • Pacific Islands (Fiji, Solomon Islands & Vanuatu) • Pakistan • Peru • The Philippines • South Africa & Lesotho • South India • South West China • South West USA • Trekking in Uganda & Congo • Turkey • Vietnam • West Africa • Zimbabwe, Botswana & Namibia

The Lonely Planet TV series is produced by: Pilot Productions
The Old Studio
18 Middle Row
London W10 5AT, UK

LONELY PLANET

Lonely Planet Online

Whether you've just begun planning your next trip, or you're chasing down specific info on currency regulations or visa requirements, check out Lonely Planet Online for up-to-the-minute travel information.

As well as miniguides to more than 250 destinations, you'll find maps, photos, travel news, health and visa updates, travel advisories and discussion of the ecological and political issues you need to be aware of as you travel. You'll also find timely upgrades to popular guidebooks that you can print out and stick in the back of your book.

There's an online travellers' forum (The Thorn Tree) where you can share your experience of life on the road, meet travel companions and ask other travellers for their recommendations and advice.

There's also a complete and up-to-date list of all Lonely Planet travel products including travel guides, diving and snorkeling guides, phrasebooks, atlases, travel literature and videos, and a simple online ordering facility if you can't find the book you want elsewhere.

Lonely Planet Diving & Snorkeling Guides

Beautifully illustrated with full-colour photos throughout, Lonely Planet's Pisces books explore the world's best diving and snorkeling areas and prepare divers for what to expect when they get there, both topside and underwater.

Dive sites are described in detail with specifics on depths, visibility, level of difficulty, special conditions, underwater photography tips and common and unusual marine life present. You'll also find practical logistical information and coverage on topside activities and attractions, sections on diving health and safety, plus listings for diving services, live-aboards, dive resorts and tourist offices.

LONELY PLANET

Guides by Region

Lonely Planet is known worldwide for publishing practical, reliable and no-nonsense travel information in our guides and on our Web site. The Lonely Planet list covers just about every accessible part of the world. Currently there are thirteen series: travel guides, shoestring guides, walking guides, city guides, phrasebooks, audio packs, city maps, travel atlases, diving & snorkeling guides, restaurant guides, first-time travel guides, healthy travel and travel literature.

AFRICA Africa on a shoestring • Africa – the South • Arabic (Egyptian) phrasebook • Arabic (Moroccan) phrasebook • Cairo • Cape Town • Cape Town city map • Central Africa • East Africa • Egypt • Egypt travel atlas • Ethiopian (Amharic) phrasebook • The Gambia & Senegal • Healthy Travel Africa • Kenya • Kenya travel atlas • Malawi, Mozambique & Zambia • Morocco • North Africa • Read This First Africa • South Africa, Lesotho & Swaziland • South Africa, Lesotho & Swaziland travel atlas • Swahili phrasebook • Tanzania, Zanzibar & Pemba • Trekking in East Africa • Tunisia • West Africa • Zimbabwe, Botswana & Namibia • Zimbabwe, Botswana & Nambia Travel Atlas • World Food Morocco
Travel Literature: The Rainbird: A Central African Journey • Songs to an African Sunset: A Zimbabwean Story • Mali Blues: Traveling to an African Beat

AUSTRALIA & THE PACIFIC Auckland • Australia • Australian phrasebook • Bushwalking in Australia • Bushwalking in Papua New Guinea • Fiji • Fijian phrasebook • Healthy Travel Australia, NZ and the Pacific • Islands of Australia's Great Barrier Reef • Melbourne • Melbourne city map • Micronesia • New Caledonia • New South Wales & the ACT • New Zealand • Northern Territory • Outback Australia • Out To Eat – Melbourne • Out to Eat – Sydney • Papua New Guinea • Pidgin phrasebook • Queensland • Rarotonga & the Cook Islands • Samoa • Solomon Islands • South Australia • South Pacific • South Pacific Languages phrasebook • Sydney • Sydney city map • Sydney Condensed • Tahiti & French Polynesia • Tasmania • Tonga • Tramping in New Zealand • Vanuatu • Victoria • Western Australia
Travel Literature: Islands in the Clouds • Kiwi Tracks: A New Zealand Journey • Sean & David's Long Drive

CENTRAL AMERICA & THE CARIBBEAN Bahamas, Turks & Caicos • Bermuda • Central America on a shoestring • Costa Rica • Cuba • Dominican Republic & Haiti • Eastern Caribbean • Guatemala, Belize & Yucatán: La Ruta Maya • Jamaica • Mexico • Mexico City • Panama • Puerto Rico • Read This First Central & South America • World Food Mexico
Travel Literature: Green Dreams: Travels in Central America

EUROPE Amsterdam • Amsterdam city map • Andalucía • Austria • Baltic States phrasebook • Barcelona • Berlin • Berlin city map • Britain • British phrasebook • Brussels, Bruges & Antwerp • Budapest city map • Canary Islands • Central Europe • Central Europe phrasebook • Corfu & Ionians • Corsica • Crete • Crete Condensed • Croatia • Cyprus • Czech & Slovak Republics • Denmark • Dublin • Eastern Europe • Eastern Europe phrasebook • Edinburgh • Estonia, Latvia & Lithuania • Europe on a shoestring • Finland • Florence • France • French phrasebook • Germany • German phrasebook • Greece • Greek Islands • Greek phrasebook • Hungary • Iceland, Greenland & the Faroe Islands • Istanbul City Map • Ireland • Italian phrasebook • Italy • Krakow •Lisbon • London • London city map • London Condensed • Mediterranean Europe • Mediterranean Europe phrasebook • Munich • Norway • Paris • Paris city map • Paris Condensed • Poland • Portugal • Portugese phrasebook • Portugal travel atlas • Prague • Prague city map • Provence & the Côte d'Azur • Read This First Europe • Romania & Moldova • Rome • Russia, Ukraine & Belarus • Russian phrasebook • Scandinavian & Baltic Europe • Scandinavian Europe phrasebook • Scotland • Slovenia • Spain • Spanish phrasebook • St Petersburg • Switzerland • Trekking in Spain • Ukrainian phrasebook • Venice • Vienna • Walking in Britain • Walking in Ireland • Walking in Italy • Walking in Spain • Walking in Switzerland • Western Europe • Western Europe phrasebook • World Food Italy • World Food Spain
Travel Literature: The Olive Grove: Travels in Greece

INDIAN SUBCONTINENT Bangladesh • Bengali phrasebook • Bhutan • Delhi • Goa • Hindi & Urdu phrasebook • India • India & Bangladesh travel atlas • Indian Himalaya • Karakoram Highway • Kerala • Mumbai (Bombay) • Nepal • Nepali phrasebook • Pakistan • Rajasthan • Read This First: Asia & India • South India • Sri Lanka • Sri Lanka phrasebook • Trekking in the Indian Himalaya • Trekking in the Karakoram & Hindukush • Trekking in the Nepal Himalaya
Travel Literature: In Rajasthan • Shopping for Buddhas • The Age Of Kali

LONELY PLANET

Mail Order

Lonely Planet products are distributed worldwide. They are also available by mail order from Lonely Planet, so if you have difficulty finding a title please write to us. North and South American residents should write to 150 Linden St, Oakland, CA 94607, USA; European and African residents should write to 10a Spring Place, London NW5 3BH, UK; and residents of other countries to PO Box 617, Hawthorn, Victoria 3122, Australia.

ISLANDS OF THE INDIAN OCEAN Madagascar & Comoros • Maldives • Mauritius, Réunion & Seychelles

MIDDLE EAST & CENTRAL ASIA Arab Gulf States • Central Asia • Central Asia phrasebook • Dubai • Hebrew phrasebook • Iran • Israel & the Palestinian Territories • Israel & the Palestinian Territories travel atlas • Istanbul • Istanbul to Cairo • Jerusalem • Jerusalem City Map • Jordan & Syria • Jordan, Syria & Lebanon travel atlas • Lebanon • Middle East on a shoestring • Syria • Turkey • Turkey travel atlas • Turkish phrasebook • Yemen

Travel Literature: The Gates of Damascus • Kingdom of the Film Stars: Journey into Jordan • Black on Black: Iran Revisited

NORTH AMERICA Alaska • Backpacking in Alaska • Baja California • California & Nevada • California Condensed • Canada • Chicago • Chicago city map • Deep South • Florida • Hawaii • Honolulu • Las Vegas • Los Angeles • Miami • New England • New Orleans • New York City • New York city map • New York Condensed • New York, New Jersey & Pennsylvania • Oahu • Pacific Northwest USA • Puerto Rico • Rocky Mountain • San Francisco • San Francisco city map • Seattle • Southwest USA • Texas • USA • USA phrasebook • Vancouver • Washington, DC & the Capital Region • Washington DC city map

Travel Literature: Drive Thru America

NORTH-EAST ASIA Beijing • Cantonese phrasebook • China • Hong Kong • Hong Kong city map • Hong Kong, Macau & Guangzhou • Japan • Japanese phrasebook • Japanese audio pack • Korea • Korean phrasebook • Kyoto • Mandarin phrasebook • Mongolia • Mongolian phrasebook • North-East Asia on a shoestring • Seoul • South-West China • Taiwan • Tibet • Tibetan phrasebook • Tokyo

Travel Literature: Lost Japan • In Xanadu

SOUTH AMERICA Argentina, Uruguay & Paraguay • Bolivia • Brazil • Brazilian phrasebook • Buenos Aires • Chile & Easter Island • Chile & Easter Island travel atlas • Colombia • Ecuador & the Galapagos Islands • Healthy Travel Central & South America • Latin American Spanish phrasebook • Peru •Quechua phrasebook • Rio de Janeiro • Rio de Janeiro city map • South America on a shoestring • Trekking in the Patagonian Andes • Venezuela

Travel Literature: Full Circle: A South American Journey

SOUTH-EAST ASIA Bali & Lombok • Bangkok • Bangkok city map • Burmese phrasebook • Cambodia • Hanoi • Healthy Travel Asia & India • Hill Tribes phrasebook • Ho Chi Minh City • Indonesia • Indonesia's Eastern Islands • Indonesian phrasebook • Indonesian audio pack • Jakarta • Java • Laos • Lao phrasebook • Laos travel atlas • Malay phrasebook • Malaysia, Singapore & Brunei • Myanmar (Burma) • Philippines • Pilipino (Tagalog) phrasebook • Read This First Asia & India • Singapore • South-East Asia on a shoestring • South-East Asia phrasebook • Thailand • Thailand's Islands & Beaches • Thailand travel atlas • Thai phrasebook • Thai audio pack • Vietnam • Vietnamese phrasebook • Vietnam travel atlas • World Food Thailand • World Food Vietnam

ALSO AVAILABLE: Antarctica • The Arctic • Brief Encounters: Stories of Love, Sex & Travel • Chasing Rickshaws • Lonely Planet Unpacked • Not the Only Planet: Travel Stories from Science Fiction • Sacred India • Travel with Children • Traveller's Tales

FREE Lonely Planet Newsletters

We love hearing from you and think you'd like to hear from us.

Planet Talk

Our FREE quarterly printed newsletter is full of tips from travellers and anecdotes from Lonely Planet guidebook authors. Every issue is packed with up-to-date travel news and advice, and includes:

- a postcard from Lonely Planet co-founder Tony Wheeler
- a swag of mail from travellers
- a look at life on the road through the eyes of a Lonely Planet author
- topical health advice
- prizes for the best travel yarn
- news about forthcoming Lonely Planet events
- a complete list of Lonely Planet books and other titles

To join our mailing list, residents of the UK, Europe and Africa can email us at go@lonelyplanet.co.uk; residents of North and South America can email us at info@lonelyplanet.com; the rest of the world can email us at talk2us@lonelyplanet.com.au, or contact any Lonely Planet office.

Comet

Our FREE monthly email newsletter brings you all the latest travel news, features, interviews, competitions, destination ideas, travellers' tips & tales, Q&As, raging debates and related links. Find out what's new on the Lonely Planet Web site and which books are about to hit the shelves.

Subscribe from your desktop: www.lonelyplanet.com/comet

Index

Text

A

Aare Gorge 138
Aargau Canton 197-8
accommodation 56-70
activities 57-66, **59**
adventure sports 65-6
aerial sports 65
air travel 74-8, 86
  buying tickets 74-6
  departure taxes 76
  fly-rail baggage service 76
  to/from Africa 78
  to/from Asia 78
  to/from Australia and New
    Zealand 78
  to/from Canada 77-8
  to/from continental Europe 77
  to/from the UK 76-7
  to/from the USA 77
Aletsch Glacier 288-90
Alp Grüm 338
Alpine Folklore parade,
  Zermatt 284
Alpine Pass Tour 139-40
Altdorf 158-9
Andermatt 167-8
Anniviers Valley 277
Appenzell 347-8
Appenzellerland 346-9
Arbon 358
architecture 30
Arosa 318-24
arts 29-30
Ascona 309
Augusta Raurica 195
avalanches 60
Avenches 208

B

Baden 197-8
Balzers 366
banks 25
Basel 187-95, **190**
  entertainment 194
  getting around 195
  getting there & away 194-5
  museums 189-91

Bold indicates maps.

places to eat 193-4
places to stay 192-3
special events 191-2
tourist office 188
zoo 191
Basel & Aargau 187-98, **188**
Beckenried 156
Bellinzona 293-6, **294**
Bern 96-106, **99**
  bear pits 98
  entertainment 104-5
  getting around 105-6
  getting there & away 105
  museums 100-1
  Parliament 100
  places to eat 103-4
  places to stay 102-3
  shopping 105
  special events 102
  spectator sports 105
  tourist offices 97
Bernese Oberland 113-42, **114**
Bernina Pass Road 336-8
Bex 261
Biasca 310
bicycle travel 82-3, 93
  see also cycling
Biel (Bienne) 106-9, **107**
birds, see fauna
Black Forest 195-7, **196**
Blue Lake 140
boat travel 84, 94
  Bernese Oberland 131
  Lake Constance 356
  Lake Neuchâtel 213
books 44-6
Bourg St Pierre 271-2
Bregaglia Valley 338-9
Bregenz 359
Brienz 136-7
Brienzersee, see Lake Brienz
Brig 279-81
Brigerbad 281
Broc 211
Brunnen 157
Brunni 160
Bruson 275
Bulle 211
bungy jumping 65-6
  Jungfrau Region 121
  Mt Titlis 161

bus travel 78-9, 86
business hours 53-4

C

camping, see accommodation
Campione d'Italia 302
cantons 226, **17**
canyoning 66
car & motorcycle travel 81-2, 90
  Alpine passes 92
  camper van 82
  car purchase 93
  car rental 92
  motorcycle touring 82
  motorway tax 82
  paperwork & preparations 81
  road rules & signs 90
caves 257-8
  St Beatus 134-5
Celerina 333
Cento Valley 310
Central Switzerland 143-68, **144**
Ceresio 303-4
Chamonix 272
Champéry 271
Champex 271
Château d'Oex 259
Château de Chillon 251
cheese 348
  Appenzell 348
  Gruyères 209
children, travel with 52
chocolate 175-6, 210
  Nestlé-Caillers factory 211
Chünetta 338
Chur 314-7, **315**
climate 21-2
Constance 356-7
constitution 18
Cook, Thomas 123
Coppet 247
costs, see money
Courmayeur 272
courses 55, 101, 176, 232
cow fights 270
Crans Montana 277-8
crime 52-3
Croix de Culet 271
cultural considerations 30-1
currency, see money

cycling 63, 65
    see also bicycle travel

D
Dada, the birth of 173
Danube, The 196
Davos 320-4, **321**
Defence 19
Diavolezza 338
disabled travellers 51
documents 36-7
Doubs Basins 220
Doubs Falls 220
drinks 72
driving, see car & motorcycle
    travel

E
Ebenalp 349
ecology 22
economy 25-6
education 27-8
Einsiedeln 164-5
Einstein, Albert 101
Emmental Region 109-12
Engadine Valley 325-36
Engelberg 159-62, **160**
entertainment 72
environment 22
Estavayer-le-Lac 205-6
Expo 2001 54

F
fauna 22-3, 108, 334-5
fax services, see postal services
festivals, see also special events
    Bregenz Festival 359
    Fasnacht 148, 176, 192
    International Alpine Film
        Festival 260
    International Festival of
        Music 148
    International Film Festival
        306
    Montreux Jazz Festival
        250-2
    Montreux-Vevey Music
        Festival 252
    Openair St Gallen 344
    Paléo Festival, Nyon 247
    Verbier Festival &
        Academy 275
    Vogel Gryff 191
    World Snow Festival,
        Grindelwald 124

    Yehudi Menuhin Festival 141
Flag 163
Flims 317-8
flora 22-3, 108, 334-5
food 70-2
Franches Montagnes 220-1
Frauenfeld 357
Fraumünster Church 173
Freilichtmuseum Ballenberg 137
Fribourg 201-5, **202**
    getting around 205
    getting there & away
        204-5
    places to eat 204
    places to stay 203-4
    things to see 201-3
    tourist office 201
Fribourg Canton 201-11
Friedrichshafen 360

G
Gandria 301-2
gay travellers 51
Gemmi Pass 278
Geneva 222-38, **224**, **228**, **231**
    CERN 230
    entertainment 235-6
    getting around 237-8
    getting there & away
        236-7
    museums & galleries
        228-30
    parks & gardens 228
    places to eat 234-5
    places to stay 232-4
    shopping 236
    special events 232
    tourist office 223
    United Nations 230
geography 20-1
geological path,
    Appenzellerland 347
Gersau 156
Giessbach Falls 135-6
Gimmelwald 127-8
glaciers 289
    Aletsch Glacier 288-90
    Glacier Gorge 124
    ice palace 130
    Mer de Glace 272
    Upper Glacier 123-4
Goetheanum 195
golf
    Crans Montana 277
    Verbier 275
Gornergrat 282

government 24-5
Grande Dixence Dam 267-8
Grandson 256
Graubünden 311-39, **312**
Great St Bernard Pass 271-2
Gruyères 208-11
Gryon 261
Gstaad 141-2
Guarda 335

H
Habsburg family 15-6
hang-gliding 65
    Verbier 274-5
Harder Kulm 116
Harder Mann 116
health 47-50
Helvetic Republic 17
Hérens Valley 268
hiking 62, 63, 93
    Appenzellerland 347
    Black Forest region 196
    Crans Montana 277
    Davos 322
    Engelberg 162
    Graubünden 318
    Grindelwald 122-4
    Gstaad 141
    Joux Valley 258
    Mittelallalin 287
    Pontresina 337
    Saas Fee 287
    St Moritz 330
    Verbier 274
history 15-20
hitching 83, 93
Hodler, Ferdinand 111
holidays, see public holidays
horse-riding, Jura Canton
    220-1
hostels, see accommodation
hotels, see accommodation
hot air ballooning 65
    Château d'Oex 259

I
ice hockey, Davos 322
Interlaken 113-20, **117**
    entertainment 119-20
    getting around 120
    getting there & away 120
    places to eat 119
    places to stay 116-9
    shopping 120
    things to see & do 115-6
    tourist office 115

Internet access 44
Isles of Brissago 309

J

Jean Tinguely museum 191
Jung, Carl Gustav 28
Jungfrau 130-1
Jungfrau Region 120-31, **121**
Jura Canton 220-1

K

Kandersteg 140-1
Kleine Scheidegg 130
Klosters 324-7
Kreuzlingen 357

L

La Breya 271
La Chaux-de-Fonds 216-9, **217**
Lake Biel 108-9
Lake Brienz 131-7
Lake Constance 353-60, **354**
Lake Geneva Region 239-61, **240**
Lake Lucerne 152-9, **153**
Lake Lugano 301-4, **302**
Lake Maggiore 308-9
Lake Murten 207
Lake Neuchâtel 213
Lake Oeschinen 140
Lake Thun 131-7
Lake Uri 157-9
language 31-2, **32**
Lausanne 241-7, **242**
    entertainment 246
    getting around 247
    getting there & away 246-7
    Musée de l'Art Brut 243-4
    Olympic Museum 244
    Palais de Rumine 244
    places to eat 245-6
    places to stay 244-5
    tourist office 241
Lauterbrunnen 126-7
Le Brévent 272
Le Corbusier 219
Le Locle 220
Lenzerheide 317
lesbian travellers 51
Les Diablerets 260
Les Marécottes 271
Leukerbad 278-9
Leventina Valley 310

Liechtenstein 361-7, **362**
Lindau 359-60
Locarno 304-9, **305**
Lommiswil 112
LSD 191
Lucerne 145-52, **146**
    entertainment 150-1
    getting around 152
    getting there & away 151
    Kapellbrücke 147
    lion monument 147
    places to eat 150
    places to stay 148-50
    shopping 151
    special events 148
    things to see & do 147-8
    tourist offices 145
Lugano 296-301, **297**

M

Madonna del Sasso 305-6
Maggia Valley 309-10
Malbun 367
Maloja 327
Männlichen 129-30
Martigny 268-71, **269**
Maur 183-4
Mauvoisin Dam 276
Meersburg 360
Meiringen 137, **138**
Melide 303
Mendrisio 304
Meride 304
Military Fort, Vallorbe 257
money 38-42
    bargaining 41
    credit cards 39-40
    taxes 41-2
    euro 39
    tipping 41
Mont Blanc 272-4
Mont Fort 274
Monte Brè 301
Monte Generoso 303
Monte San Salvatore 301
Montreux 249-53, **250**
Morcote 303-4
Morges 247
Morgins 271
motorcycle travel, see car &
    motorcycle travel
Mt Pilatus 154
Mt Rigi 154-5
Mt Titlis 159-160
mountain transport 94
mountaineering 63

Pontresina 337
Zermatt 282
Mürren 128
Murten 206-7
Musée de l'Art Brut 243-4
music 29-30, see also festivals
Müstair 335

N

Nendeln 366
Neuchâtel 211-5, **212**
Neuchâtel Canton 211-20
Neuchâtel Montagnes 219-20
newspapers & magazines 46
Niesen 140
Nietzsche Haus 328
Nobel Prize winners 28-9
North-East Switzerland 340-60,
    341
Nyon 247

O

Olympic Museum 244
Orsières 271

P

paragliding 65, 274-5
Payerne 208
philosophy 28-9
photography & video 46
Piz Lagalb 338
planetary paths
    Anniviers Valley 277
    Doubs Basins, Neuchâtel 220
    Uetliberg 183
politics 24-5
Pontresina 337-8
population 26-7
postal services 42-4
public holidays 54-5

Q

Quinten 346

R

radio 46
rafting
    Château d'Oex 259
    Graubünden 318
    Les Diablerets 260
    Saane River 141
    Simme River 140
Rapperswil 346
Rè 310

Bold indicates maps.

recycling 22
Red Cross 229
Reichenbach Falls 137-8
Reichenbach Valley 138
religion 31
responsible tourism 35
restaurants de nuit, Neuchâtel 215
Rhine Falls 351-2
Rolle 247
Romanshorn 357-8
Ronco 309
Rorschach 358-9
Rothorn Bahn 136
Rütli meadow 19, 157, 226

S

Saas Fee 286-8
safety 52-3
Sainte Croix 256-7
St Gallen 342-6, **343**
St Gallen Canton 342-6
St Maurice 271
St Moritz 328-33, **329**
Säntis 349
Schaffhausen 349-51
Schaffhausen Canton 349-53
Schellenberg 366
Schilthorn 128-9
Schwyz 162-4
Schwyz Canton 162-8
science 28-9
Scuol 335-7
senior travellers 51-2
Sherlock Holmes Museum 138
shopping 73
Sierre 276-7
Sils 327-8
Silvaplana 328
Sion 264-7, **265**
skiing 58, 62
    Andermatt 167-8
    Appenzellerland 347
    Black Forest region 196
    Crans Montana 277
    Davos 321-2
    Engadine Valley 326
    Engelberg 160-1
    Graubünden 317-8
    Gstaad 141
    Joux Valley 258
    Jungfrau Region 121-2
    Jura Canton 220-1
    Leukerbad 278
    Malbun 367
    Pontresina 337
    Saas Fee 286-7
    St Moritz 330

Verbier 274
    Zermatt 284
Soglio 338-9
Solothurn 110-2
special events 54-5, *see also*
    festivals
spectator sports 72-3
Spiez 134
Stans 156
Stein 348-9
Stein am Rhein 352-3
Stockalper Castle 279-80
Stockhorn 140
Strandbad Horn 357
Swiss Mittelland 95-112, **96**
Swiss National Park 334-5
Swiss neutrality 16
Swiss Riviera 247-53

T

Taubenloch Gorge 109
telephone services 42-4
television 46
Tell, William 16, 158
tennis (Swiss Open) 141
theatre 29-30
theft, *see* crime
Thun 132-3, **132**
Thunersee, *see* Lake Thun
Ticinese cuisine 293
Ticino 291-310, **292**
tobogganing
    Davos 322
    Grindelwald 122
tourist offices 35-6
tours 84, 94
train travel 79-81, 87
    information & tickets 87
    luggage 89
    platforms & trains 89
    railpasses 80
travel passes 85
Triesenberg 366
Trümmelbach Falls 126

U

Uetliberg 183
Ulrich Zwingli 16
United Nations 230

V

Vaduz 364-6, **365**
Valais 262-90, **263**
Valbella 317
Vallée Blanche 272
Vallorbe 257-8

Vaud Alps 258-61
Verbier 274-6
Verzasca Valley 310
Vevey 248-9
Villars 260-1
violin-making school 136
visas 36
Visp 281-2

W

Walensee 346
walking 93, *see also* hiking
    Swiss Path 158
water sports 65
    Faulensee 135
    Joux Valley 258
wax museum, Gruyères 209
Weggis 155-6
Weissenstein 112, 221
Wengen 129
wild flowers, *see* flora
wine
    Morges 247
    Valais 264
Winterthur 184-6, **184**
women travellers 50-1
woodcarving school 136
work 55-6
WWII 350

Y

youth hostels,
    see accommodation
Yverdon-les-Bains 253-6, **254**

Z

Zähringen family 15
Zermatt 282-6, **283**
Zernez 334-5
Zofingen 198
Zug 166-7
Zuoz 333-4
Zürich 169-84, 170, **174**
    entertainment 180-1
    getting around 182-3
    getting there & away 181-2
    museums 173-6
    places to eat 179-80
    places to stay 177-8
    shopping 181
    special events 176
    spectator sports 181
    tourist office 170
    transport 182
    zoo 176
Zürich Canton 169-86

Boxed Text

Alpine Tunnels 87
Avalanche Warning 60
Banks & Bank Accounts 25
Birth of Dada, The 173
Circuit of Mont Blanc 273
Cow Fights 270
Creation of the Red Cross, The 229
Cycling in Switzerland 64
Defence 19
Did you know… ? 362
Doing Time in the Bern Patent
    Office 101
Emergencies – German 373
European Railpasses 80
Eurozone Finances 39
EXPO.01 – Switzerland
    Welcomes the World 54

Ferdinand Hodler 111
First Hippie, The 191
Glaciers 289
I Didn't Know They Were Swiss
    28
Internet Resources 44
Le Corbusier – Man of
    Concrete 219
Making of Chocolate, The 210
Mountain Myths & Legends 152
Mt Rigi & 19th-Century
    Tourism 155
Nein Merci 31
Royal Race 322
Rules for Life 53
St Mo-RITZY Guests 330
Second World War, The 350

Signs 372
Swiss Cheese 348
Swiss Flag, The 163
Swiss National Character, The
    27
Switzerland Goes Green 22
Thomas Cook: the First
    Conducted Tour of
    Switzerland 123
Ticinese Cuisine 293
Tourist Spending 41
Transports of Delight 88
26 Countries in One 226
Valais Wine 264
William Tell Tale, The 158
Zürich's Transport System 182

MAP LEGEND

CITY ROUTES

Freeway	Freeway
Highway	Primary Road
Road	Secondary Road
Street	Street
Lane	Lane
	On/Off Ramp

= = = =	Unsealed Road
→	One Way Street
	Pedestrian Street
⊓⊓⊓⊓⊓⊓	Stepped Street
)= = (	Tunnel
	Footbridge

REGIONAL ROUTES

	Tollway, Freeway
	Primary Road
	Secondary Road
	Minor Road

BOUNDARIES

—··—··—	International
—··—··—	State
— — —	Disputed
▬▬▬▬	Fortified Wall

HYDROGRAPHY

	River, Creek
—·—·—·	Canal
	Lake

	Dry Lake; Salt Lake
⊙ ⇝	Spring; Rapids
⑨ ⇥⇤	Waterfalls

TRANSPORT ROUTES & STATIONS

⊢–––O–	Train
⊢ + + + ⊢	Underground Train
–●– (M)	Metro
▬▬▬▬	Tramway
⊬–⊬–⊬–⊬–⊬	Cable Car, Chairlift

- - - -⊡	Ferry
- - - -	Walking Trail
· · · · · · ·	Walking Tour
	Path
	Pier or Jetty

AREA FEATURES

	Building
	Park, Gardens

	Market
	Sports Ground

	Forest
+ + + +	Cemetery

	Campus
	Plaza

POPULATION SYMBOLS

○ CAPITAL	National Capital
◉ CAPITAL	State Capital

● CITY	City
● Town	Town

● Village	Village
	Urban Area

MAP SYMBOLS

★	Place to Stay

▼	Place to Eat

●	Point of Interest

✈	Airport	⌂	Embassy, Consulate	🏞	National Park	🏊	Swimming Pool
⊖	Bank	⚓	Fountain	Ⓟ	Parking	🕎	Synagogue
▣	Bus Terminal	✚	Hospital	)(	Pass	☎	Telephone
▤	Cable Car, Funicular	⌨	Internet Cafe	★	Police Station	🎭	Theatre
▨	Castle, Château	✳	Lookout	▣	Post Office	❶	Tourist Information
⬛ ✝	Church	⚑	Monument	▣	Pub or Bar	🍷	Winery
▣	Cinema	🏛	Museum	❖	Shopping Centre	🦁	Zoo

Note: not all symbols displayed above appear in this book

LONELY PLANET OFFICES

Australia
PO Box 617, Hawthorn, Victoria 3122
☎ 03 9819 1877 fax 03 9819 6459
email: talk2us@lonelyplanet.com.au

USA
150 Linden St, Oakland, CA 94607
☎ 510 893 8555 TOLL FREE: 800 275 8555
fax 510 893 8572
email: info@lonelyplanet.com

UK
10a Spring Place, London NW5 3BH
☎ 020 7428 4800 fax 020 7428 4828
email: go@lonelyplanet.co.uk

France
1 rue du Dahomey, 75011 Paris
☎ 01 55 25 33 00 fax 01 55 25 33 01
email: bip@lonelyplanet.fr
www.lonelyplanet.fr

World Wide Web: www.lonelyplanet.com *or* AOL keyword: lp
Lonely Planet Images: lpi@lonelyplanet.com.au